Contents

To

Wolfram Krewitt (1962–2009)

whose passion for sustainable development will be greatly missed

Sustainable Development in Practice

Sustainable Development in Practice

Case Studies for Engineers and Scientists
Second Edition

Editors

ADISA AZAPAGIC and SLOBODAN PERDAN

School of Chemical Engineering and Analytical Science,
The University of Manchester

A John Wiley & Sons, Ltd., Publication

Library of Congress Cataloguing-in-Publication Data

Sustainable development in practice : case studies for engineers and scientists / editors, Adisa Azapagic and Slobodan Perdan. – 2nd ed.
    p. cm.
  Includes index.
  ISBN 978-0-470-71871-1 (cloth) – ISBN 978-0-470-71872-8 (pbk.)
  1. Engineering–Research. 2. Sustainable development. I. Azapagic, Adisa. II. Perdan, Slobodan.

  TA160.S87 2011
  620.0028'6–dc22

                                                                                          2010029203

A catalogue record for this book is available from the British Library.

This book is published in the following electronic formats: ePDF [9780470972854]; Wiley Online Library [9780470972847]

Set in 10/12pt. Times Roman by Thomson Digital, Noida, India.

First Impression   2011

About the Editors

Adisa Azapagic is Professor of Sustainable Chemical Engineering at The University of Manchester. Her research interests are in the areas of engineering for sustainable development, life cycle assessment, sustainable consumption and production and corporate sustainability. She has published widely in these areas, including the book on *Polymers, the Environment and Sustainable Development*, also published by Wiley. Adisa has held a number of international honorary appointments, such as: Erskine Fellow at University of Canterbury; UNESCO/ICSU/TWAS Fellow at ITAM, Mexico City; and Royal Academy of Engineering & Leverhulme Trust Scholar at University of Sydney.

Dr. Slobodan Perdan is Research Fellow at the University of Manchester. He is a philosopher by background with expertise and interests in the areas of sustainable development and moral philosophy. He has written on a variety of issues concerning sustainable development and has researched a wide range of subjects, including environmental philosophy, engineering ethics and corporate sustainability.

List of Contributors

Kevin Anderson School of Mechanical, Aerospace and Civil Engineering, The University of Manchester, Manchester M13 9PL, UK

Adisa Azapagic School of Chemical Engineering and Analytical Science, The University of Manchester, Manchester M13 9PL, UK

Alice Bows School of Earth, Atmospheric and Environmental Sciences and Sustainable Consumption Institute, The University of Manchester, Oxford Road, Manchester M13 9PL, UK

Zaid Chalabi London School of Hygiene & Tropical Medicine, Keppel Street, London WC1E 7HT, UK

Richard Darton Keble College, Oxford University, Oxford OX1 3PG, UK

Namy Espinoza-Orias School of Chemical Engineering and Analytical Science, The University of Manchester, Manchester M13 9PL, UK

Richard Fenner Centre for Sustainable Development, Department of Engineering, University of Cambridge, Trumpington Street, Cambridge CB2 1PZ, UK

Tony Fletcher London School of Hygiene & Tropical Medicine, Keppel Street, London WC1E 7HT, UK

Amparo Flores Centre for Sustainable Development, Department of Engineering, University of Cambridge, Trumpington Street, Cambridge CB2 1PZ, UK

Wolfram Krewitt German Aerospace Centre, Institute of Technical Thermodynamics, Pfaffenwaldring 38–40, 70569 Stuttgart, Germany

Hans Müller-Steinhagen German Aerospace Centre, Institute of Technical Thermodynamics, Head of Institute, Pfaffenwaldring 38–40, 70569 Stuttgart, Germany

Martin Pehnt Institut für Energie- und Umweltforschung, Heidelberg, Germany

Slobodan Perdan School of Chemical Engineering and Analytical Science, The University of Manchester, Manchester M13 9PL, UK

Heinz Stichnothe School of Chemical Engineering and Analytical Science, The University of Manchester, Manchester M13 9PL, UK and vTI, Institut für Agrartechnologie und Biosystemtechnik, Bundesallee 50, 38116 Barunschweig, Germany

Preface

This book is about sustainable development and its implications for science and engineering practice. It is aimed at engineering and science students and educators, as well as practising engineers and scientists.

Part 1 of the book explores the concept of sustainable development and its practical implications, gives an overview of the main approaches to measuring sustainability and introduces life cycle thinking, the approach applied throughout the book.

Recognising that practical interpretation of sustainable development depends on the context, Part 2 of the book is devoted to case studies. These are drawn from a range of sectors, including mining and minerals, energy, waste, food, health, sanitation, and transport. They explore scientific and technical aspects of different systems, but also consider relevant economic, environmental and social ramifications to position engineering and scientific practice in the context of sustainable development.

As demonstrated throughout the book, sustainable development poses significant challenges to science and engineering. However, we hope that the book also shows that meeting these challenges provides engineers and scientists with an opportunity to contribute to a better quality of life for everyone, now and in the future.

Adisa Azapagic and Slobodan Perdan
Manchester, April 2010

PART 1

1

The Concept of Sustainable Development and its Practical Implications

Slobodan Perdan

Sustainable development is an approach to development which focuses on integrating economic activity with environmental protection and social concerns. This chapter describes the emergence of the concept of sustainable development as a response to destructive social and environmental effects of the prevailing approach to economic growth and discusses its practical implications. The chapter argues that the transition to a more sustainable society requires new ways of meeting our needs which can reduce the level of material consumption and reduce environmental damage without affecting quality of life. This will require, above all, limiting the throughput of materials and energy in the economy and finding less wasteful ways of meeting needs through increasing efficiency, reusing materials and using sustainable technologies. However, as the chapter points out, meeting the objective of sustainable development requires not only reducing the scale of polluting activities and excessive levels of consumption, but also calls for well-planned actions to alleviate poverty and achieve greater equity and distribution of opportunities both within and between countries.

1.1 Introduction

Around the world we see signs of severe stress on our interdependent economic, environmental and social systems. Population is growing – it topped 6 billion in 2000, up from

Sustainable Development in Practice: Case Studies for Engineers and Scientists, Second Edition
Edited by Adisa Azapagic and Slobodan Perdan
© 2011 John Wiley & Sons, Ltd.

4.4 billion in 1980, and it is expected to reach 8 billion by 2025 (UNCSD, 2002). Excessive consumption and poverty continue to put enormous pressure on the environment. In many areas, the state of the environment is much more fragile and degraded than it was a few decades ago. Despite notable improvements in areas such as river and air quality in places like Europe and North America, generally there has been a steady decline in the environment, especially across large parts of the developing world (UNEP, 2002, 2007).

There are some alarming trends underway. Most recent global environmental assessments (UNEP, 2002, 2007, 2009; MA, 2005; Solomon *et al.*, 2007) put them into stark figures, characteristic examples of which include:

- Twenty per cent of Earth's land cover has been significantly degraded by human activity and 60% of the planet's ecosystems are now damaged or threatened (UNEP, 2009).
- Species are becoming extinct at rates which are a 100 times faster than the rate shown in the fossil record, because of land-use changes, habitat loss, overexploitation of resources, pollution and the spread of invasive alien species (MA, 2005; UNEP, 2007). Of the major vertebrate groups that have been comprehensively assessed, over 30% of amphibians, 23% of mammals and 12% of birds are threatened (UNEP, 2007).
- Concentrations of carbon dioxide, the main gas linked with global warming, currently stand at 386 parts per million, or more than 25% higher than in 150 years ago. Concentrations of other greenhouse gases, such as methane and halocarbons, have also risen (Solomon *et al.*, 2007).
- Global average temperatures have risen by about 0.74 °C since 1906, and the rise this century is projected to be between 1.8 and 4 °C; some scientists believe a 2 °C increase would be a threshold beyond which the threat of major and irreversible damage becomes more plausible (Solomon *et al.*, 2007; UNEP, 2007).
- Available freshwater resources are declining: some 80 countries, amounting to 40% of the world's population, are suffering serious water shortages; by 2025, 1.8 billion people will live in countries with absolute water scarcity (UNEP, 2007).
- Around half of the world's rivers are seriously depleted and polluted (UNEP, 2002).
- More than 2 million people worldwide are estimated to die prematurely every year from indoor and outdoor air pollution (UNEP, 2007).

Other noteworthy trends include:

- Around 1.4 billion people are living in extreme poverty (measured as $1.25 a day) (UN, 2009);
- The number of hungry people worldwide grew to 963 million, or about 14.6% of the world population of 6.6 billion, representing an increase of 142 million over the figure for 1990–1992 (FAO, 2009);
- More than 100 million primary school age children remain out of school (UN, 2009);
- Around 1.1 billion people still lack access to safe drinking water and an estimated 2.6 billion people today lack improved sanitation facilities (UNEP, 2007);
- Poverty claims the lives of 25 000 children each day (UNICEF, 2000).

These and a host of other trends suggest that our current development course is unsustainable. The high and increasing consumption of scarce resources, the resulting pollution compounded by population growth and the growing imbalance in development between different countries pose unacceptable risks to communities, nations and humanity as a whole. It has become clear that economic development that disregards environmental and social impacts can bring unintended and unwanted consequences, as evidenced by the threat of climate change, overuse of freshwater resources, loss of biological diversity and raising inequalities.

The concept of sustainable development has grown out of concerns about these adverse trends. In essence, it is an approach to development which focuses on integrating economic activity with environmental protection and social concerns.

1.2 Development of the Concept

The concept of sustainable development as we know it today emerged in the 1980s as a response to the destructive social and environmental effects of the prevailing approach to 'economic growth'.

The idea originated within the environmental movement. One of the earliest formulations of the concept of sustainable development can be found in the 1980's World Conservation Strategy jointly presented by the UN Environment Programme, the World Wildlife Fund and the International Union for Conservation of Nature and Natural Resources (IUCN/ UNEP/WWF, 1980). This early formulation emphasized that:

> For development to be sustainable, it must take account of social and ecological factors, as well as economic ones; of the living and non-living resource base; and of the long-term as well as the short-term advantages and disadvantages of alternative actions.

It called for three priorities to be built into development policies: the maintenance of ecological processes; the sustainable use of resources; and the maintenance of genetic diversity.

However, the concept of sustainable development gained a wider recognition only after the World Commission on Environment and Development (WCED) published its report 'Our common future' (also known as 'the Brundtland Report') in 1987. It was this report that gave the concept the prominence it has today.

The WCED report set the benchmark for all future discussions on sustainable development. The starting point for the commission's work was their acknowledgement that the future of humanity is threatened. 'Our common future' (WCED, 1987) opened by declaring:

> The Earth is one but the world is not. We all depend on one biosphere for sustaining our lives. Yet each community, each country, strives for survival and prosperity with little regard for its impacts on others. Some consume the Earth's resources at a rate that would leave little for future generations. Others, many more in number, consume far too little and live with the prospects of hunger, squalor, disease, and early death.

To confront the challenges of overconsumption on the one hand and grinding poverty on the other hand, the commission called for sustainable development, defined as 'development that meets the needs of the present without compromising the ability of future generations to meet their own needs'.

In order to reverse unsustainable trends the WCED recommended the following seven critical actions aimed at ensuring a good quality of life for people around the world (WCED, 1987):

- revive growth;
- change the quality of growth;
- meet essential needs and aspirations for jobs, food, energy, water and sanitation;
- ensure a sustainable level of population;
- conserve and enhance the resource base;
- reorient technology and manage risk; and
- include and combine environment and economics considerations in decision-making.

Since the Brundtland Report, a whole series of events and initiatives have brought us to the wide-ranging interpretation of sustainable development that we see today. One of the key events was, undoubtedly, the United Nations Conference on Environment and Development, more informally known as the Earth Summit, held in Rio de Janeiro in 1992. At the Earth Summit, representatives of nearly 180 countries endorsed the Rio Declaration on Environment and Development which set out 27 principles supporting sustainable development. The assembled leaders also signed the Framework Convention on Climate Change, the Convention on Biological Diversity, and the Forest Principles. They also agreed a global plan of action, Agenda 21, designed to deliver a more sustainable pattern of development, and recommended that all countries should produce national sustainable development strategies.

Ten years later, in September 2002, at the World Summit on Sustainable Development (WSSD) in Johannesburg, leaders and representatives of 183 countries reaffirmed sustainable development as a central element of the international agenda. The present governments agreed to a wide range of concrete commitments and targets for action to achieve sustainable development objectives, including (WSSD, 2002a):

- halve, by the year 2015, the proportion of people in poverty;
- encourage and promote the development of a 10-year framework of programmes to accelerate the shift towards sustainable consumption and production;
- diversify energy supply and substantially increase the global share of renewable energy sources in order to increase its contribution to total energy supply;
- improve access to reliable, affordable, economically viable, socially acceptable and environmentally sound energy services and resources;
- accelerate the development and dissemination of energy efficiency and energy conservation technologies, including the promotion of research and development;
- develop integrated water resources management and water efficiency plans by 2005; and
- achieve by 2010 a significant reduction in the current rate of loss of biological diversity.

The Johannesburg Summit moved the sustainability agenda further, and consolidated and broadened the understanding of sustainable development, particularly the important linkages between poverty, the environment and the use of natural resources.

These political events brought sustainable development firmly into the public arena and established it as a widely accepted goal for policy makers. As a result, we have seen a proliferation of sustainable development strategies and policies, innovative technological, scientific and educational initiatives, and new legislative regimes and institutions. The concept of sustainable development now influences governance, business and economic activity at different levels, and affects individual and society lifestyle choices.

In the last three decades, a continuing debate about what sustainability truly means has produced a plethora of definitions. A wide variety of groups – ranging from businesses to national governments to international organizations – have adopted the concept and given it their own particular interpretations.

The UK Government, for example, in its sustainable development strategy, defines sustainable development as 'the simple idea of ensuring a better quality of life for everyone, now and for generations to come' (DETR, 1999; DEFRA, 2005). The UK Government's sustainable development strategy aims to deliver a 'strong, healthy and just society within global limits' (DEFRA, 2005).

The strategy emphasizes that sustainable development means meeting the following four objectives at the same time, in the UK and the world as a whole:

- social progress which recognizes the needs of everyone;
- effective protection of the environment;
- prudent use of natural resources; and
- maintenance of high and stable levels of economic growth and employment.

Most countries in the developed world, and many developing countries, have now incorporated sustainability into their national planning, and defined sustainable development in their national contexts. According to national reports received from governments before the World Summit on Sustainable Development in 2002, about 85 countries have developed some kind of national sustainability strategy, although the nature and effectiveness of those strategies vary considerably from country to country (UNCSD, 2002).

The concept of sustainable development has also made inroads into the business community. In the last three decades, the understanding and acceptance of sustainable development within the business community have grown significantly. Most forward-looking companies and businesses are beginning to integrate sustainability into corporate strategies and practice. They recognize that the challenge of sustainable development for the business enterprise means adopting business strategies and activities that meet the needs of the enterprise and its stakeholders today while protecting, sustaining and enhancing the human and natural resources that will be needed in the future (IISD, 1992). This way of thinking is, for instance, behind the World Business Council for Sustainable Development (WBCSD), a wide coalition of more than 200 international companies (including some of the world's largest corporations) united by 'a shared commitment to sustainable development via the three pillars of economic growth, ecological balance and social progress' (WBCSD, 2010). Although not all of the WBCSD component corporations have exemplary environmental records, this coalition has been involved actively in the activities aimed at identifying and defining sustainable pathways for businesses.

Many professional organizations, including engineering and scientific associations, have incorporated sustainable development into their mission statements, statutes and codes. As an example, in their 'Melbourne communiqué' representatives of 20 chemical engineering organizations from around the world committed themselves to using their 'skills to strive to improve the quality of life, foster employment, advance economic and social development and protect the environment through sustainable development' (WCEC, 2001).

Finally, environmental organizations contributed significantly to the development of the concept of sustainable development. After all, sustainable development began life as one of their concepts. One of the most prominent and influential definitions comes from a 'Strategy for Sustainable Living' (UNEP/WWF/IUCN, 1991), another joint publication by the United Nations Environmental Programme (UNEP), International Union for the Conservation of Nature (IUCN), and World Wildlife Fund (WWF), in which sustainable development is defined as 'improving the quality of life while living within the carrying capacity of supporting ecosystems'. In a similar vein, in its 'Action for Global Sustainability', the Union of Concerned Scientists advocates that 'humanity must learn to live within the limits of natural systems while ensuring an adequate living standard for all people' (UCS, 2001).

These are just some of the many formulations which have over the years increased our understanding of what sustainable development means within many different contexts. The principle of sustainable development and many of its objectives have now been widely adopted, and the agenda has moved from the question of 'What does sustainable development mean?' on to the questions of 'How do we achieve sustainable development?' and 'How do we measure our progress towards achieving it?' (for more on measuring sustainability, see Chapter 2). Yet, in contrast to rapid progress on *developing* the *concepts* of sustainable development, progress on its *implementation* has been slow. Sustainable development, it is fair to say, remains largely theoretical for the majority of the world's population.

1.3 Sustainable Development: Implementation

Sustainable development presents a framework for change rather than a list of prescriptions to achieve it. There is, however, a growing consensus that the transition to a more sustainable society requires new ways of meeting our needs which can reduce the level of material consumption and reduce environmental damage without affecting quality of life. This will require, above all, limiting the throughput of materials and energy in the economy and finding less wasteful ways of meeting needs through increasing efficiency, reusing materials and using sustainable technologies.

Moving to a more sustainable path, however, does not only require a better management of the environment. Certain minimal socio-economic conditions must also be met to ensure the necessary consensus for short-term actions and long-term stability. 'Greening' industrial economies whilst ignoring the need for poverty alleviation and the redistribution of opportunity would not ensure long-term sustainability. True sustainability means ensuring a satisfying quality of life for everyone. Meeting this objective therefore, requires not only reducing the scale of polluting activities and reducing excessive levels of consumption, but also calls for well-planned actions to alleviate poverty and achieve greater equity and distribution of opportunities both within and between countries.

1.3.1 Sustainable Production and Consumption

According to the Johannesburg Plan of Implementation, adopted at the 2002 World Summit on Sustainable Development, 'fundamental changes in the way societies produce and consume are indispensable for achieving global sustainable development' (WSSD, 2002a).

There are some encouraging signs of a more sustainable production, such as energy efficiency improvements and lower consumption of raw materials per unit of production in industrialized societies. The European Union, for example, achieved significant economic growth in the 1990s without notable increases in its consumption of fossil fuels. This was mainly due to a shift in production and consumption from material- and energy-intensive sectors to services. However, these gains in efficiency have been offset by an increase in the volume of goods and services consumed and discarded. For instance, according to the Organization for Economic Cooperation and Development (OECD), the amount of waste generated in Europe between 1990 and 1995, increased by 10% and has continued to grow since. It is estimated that by 2020 Europe could be generating 45% more waste than it generated in 1995 (for more details on the issue of waste, see Chapter 10).

As more natural resources are being consumed and more pollution is generated, it is becoming clear that decoupling economic growth from adverse environmental impacts, such as emissions of greenhouse gases, waste production and use of hazardous materials, holds one of the keys to sustainable development.

While governments have an important role to play in this process by stimulating companies to act more sustainably through incentives, rewards and the threat of penalties, it is ultimately businesses that will deliver a supply of goods and services that are less damaging and more resource efficient (DEFRA, 2010).

Some producers have already responded to this challenge by using eco-design tools to rethink products and services: creating goods that perform as well or better than conventional products, using resources more productively, reducing pollution and improving profitability.

One of the prominent initiatives in this respect is the eco-efficiency approach, developed by the World Business Council for Sustainable Development (WBCSD).

Eco-efficiency calls for business to achieve more value from lower inputs of materials and energy and with reduced emissions. It applies throughout a business, to marketing and product development just as much as to manufacturing or distribution. The WBCSD has identified seven elements that business can use to improve their eco- efficiency and should be considered at each stage in the production process of all goods and services (WBCSD, 1996, 2000, 2001; de Simone and Popoff, 1997):

- reducing the material requirements (total mass consumed);
- reducing the energy intensity (energy consumed during every phase of production);
- reducing toxic dispersion (release of toxic substances to all media);
- enhancing material recyclability (reuse of materials or energy);
- maximizing sustainable use of renewable resources (avoiding depletion of finite resources);
- extending product durability (optimizing product life);
- increasing the service intensity (creating value added while reducing environmental impacts).

A central tenet of eco-efficiency is that it requires improvement in most, if not all, of the above elements over the medium to long term, while maintaining performance with respect to the others. These seven elements may be thought of as being concerned with three broad objectives (WBCSD, 2000).

- **Reducing the consumption of resources**: this includes minimizing the use of energy, materials, water and land, enhancing recyclability and product durability, and closing material loops.
- **Reducing the impact on nature**: this includes minimizing air emissions, water discharges, waste disposal and the dispersion of toxic substances, as well as fostering the sustainable use of renewable resources.
- **Increasing product or service value**: this means providing more benefits to customers through product functionality, flexibility and modularity, providing additional services and focusing on selling the functional needs that customers actually want. This raises the possibility of the customer receiving the same functional need with fewer materials and less resources. It also improves the prospects of closing material loops, because responsibility and ownership and, therefore, concern for efficient use remain with the service provider.

In short, eco-efficient companies and industries must deliver competitively priced goods and services that improve peoples' quality of life, while reducing ecological impacts and resource-use intensity to a level within the Earth's carrying capacity.

Increasing the resource productivity is an important measure in the move towards more sustainable economic activities. Yet, how much more efficient do companies and industries need to be to become more sustainable?

There have been some estimates that, globally, the goal should be to quadruple resource productivity throughout the economy so that wealth is doubled, and resource use is halved. This has been described as the need to achieve a 'Factor 4' increase in resource efficiency (von Weizsäcker *et al.*, 1997).

Often associated with 'Factor 4' is 'Factor 10', whose proponents argue that, in the long term, a 10-fold reduction in resource consumption in the industrialized countries is necessary if we are to approach sustainability (International Factor 10 Club, 1997; UNEP, 2000). The reasoning behind this is that, globally, consumption needs to be halved, but that the greatest reduction should be borne by those countries that are currently the most profligate in their use of resources. Thus, UNEP (2000) stated that 'a 10-fold reduction in resource consumption in the industrialized countries is a necessary long-term target if adequate resources are to be released for the needs of developing countries'.

Implementing sustainability strategies, such as Factor 4 and Factor 10, and increasing resource efficiency will require step changes in processes and products. This is unlikely to be achieved with incremental improvements. Shifting economic activity towards a more sustainable pattern will certainly require new ideas to encourage us to meet our needs in different, less harmful ways, and innovative approaches to the development and use of technologies, products and services.

Here, we turn our attention to the role of technology in this process.

1.3.2 Sustainable Technologies

Sustainable technologies enable humans to meet their needs with minimum impact on the environment. Many kinds of sustainable technologies already exist, ranging from direct solar and wind power to recycling. Some, such as wind and water power, were invented centuries ago. The others are much 'younger'; for example, the solar cell was invented in the

1950s. These technologies, however, have failed to become widespread largely for social and economic reasons, not technical ones. Many other technologies and practices that could reduce the environmental impacts of economic activities are also already available. For example, numerous technical means of improving the scope and rates of recycling of waste materials exist but are poorly used in many countries.

The latest technological advances offer even greater opportunities for a more sustainable production. Just as technological progress has been a major source of economic growth over the past two centuries, so today's technological transformations could play a pivotal role in achieving sustainable development. They offer the prospect of reconciling economic development and prosperity with environmental improvement, and create new possibilities for reducing environmental impacts, improving health, expanding knowledge, stimulating economic growth and ensuring a better quality of life. Leading these transformations are the accelerated developments in information and communications technology, biotechnology and just-emerging nanotechnology.

Innovations in information and communications technology nowadays enable us to process, store and rapidly distribute enormous amounts of information. By dramatically increasing access to information and communications, these new technologies are breaking barriers to knowledge and participation, offering tremendous possibilities for improving education and political participation. They also create new economic opportunities, thereby contributing to economic growth and employment creation.

Modern biotechnology – recombinant DNA technology – is transforming life sciences. Genetics is now the basis of life sciences, and much research in pharmaceuticals and plant breeding is now based on biotechnology. The power of genetics can now be used to engineer the attributes of plants and other organisms, creating the potential for huge advances, particularly in agriculture and medicine. Biotechnology can speed up plant breeding and drive the development of new crop varieties with greater drought and disease resistance, more nutritional value and less environmental stress. Pest-resistant genetically modified (GM) crops, for instance, could reduce the need to use pesticides that can harm soil quality and human health.

Designing new drugs and treatments based on genomics and related technologies offers potential for tackling the major health challenges facing poor countries and people. The cloning of Dolly the sheep has pushed scientific frontiers even further and will transform technology development for years to come. The mapping of the genes that comprise the human genome, together with the development of genetic screening, makes possible even the alteration of the human species itself!

To these two new technologies may soon be added a third, the just-emerging nanotechnology, which promises to revolutionize medicine, electronics and chemistry. Nanotechnology is evolving from scientific breakthroughs enabling engineering and science at the molecular level, and it is promising to create smaller and cheaper devices, using less material and consuming less energy. Although research into nanotechnology is still in its infancy, it has already created single-molecule transistors, an enzyme-powered biomolecular motor with nickel propellers, and a minute carrier able to cross from the blood to the brain to deliver chemicals to fight tumours. Future (still hypothetical) applications suggested include cheap, light materials strong enough to make space transport economical, nano-scale robots which will heal injured human tissue and remove obstructions in the circulatory system, and solar nanotechnologies which may in the future be able to provide energy to an ever-growing population.

These accelerated technological developments will undoubtedly further transform the way we live, work, communicate, produce and consume. Many products – vaccines for infectious diseases, drought-tolerant plant varieties for farmers in uncertain climates, clean energy sources for cooking and heating, Internet access for information and communications – contribute directly to sustainable development through improving people's health, nutrition, knowledge and living standards, reducing environmental pollution, and increasing people's ability to participate more actively in the social, economic and political life of their communities. They also deliver the necessary improvement in resource efficiency and contribute to economic growth through the productivity gains they generate.

However, just as technological advance in these instances opens new avenues for sustainable development, it also creates new risks. Every technological advance brings potential risks, some of which are not easy to predict. Nuclear power, once believed to be a limitless source of energy, came to be seen as a dangerous threat to health and the environment after the accidents at Three Mile Island in the United States and Chernobyl in Ukraine. Chlorofluorocarbons (CFCs), until recently widely used in refrigerators, aerosol cans and air conditioners, caused the depletion of the ozone layer and increased danger of skin cancer for people in the countries exposed to increased ultraviolet radiation. Reliance on fossil fuels as *the* energy source has led to increased atmospheric carbon dioxide levels and the prospect of global warming.

As in previous developments, today's technological advances raise concerns about their possible environmental, health and socio-economic impacts. There is, for instance, a growing public unease about some aspects of information and communications technology, such as the health risks associated with the use of mobile phones or the role of the Internet in facilitating drug trade and terrorist networks and the dissemination of child pornography. Some concerns are also raised about potential contribution of information technology to raising inequalities and widening the gap between the rich and the poor, both at national and global levels.

Cutting-edge biotechnological research has raised ethical concerns about the possibility of human cloning and the easy manufacture of devastating biological weapons. Serious questions have been asked about the potential risks posed by genetically modified organisms (GMOs) with some concerns that they could adversely affect other species, disrupt entire eco-systems and cause risks to human health. With genetically modified foods, the two main health concerns are that the introduction of novel genes could make a food toxic and that they could introduce new allergens into foods, causing reactions in some people. As to possible harms to the environment, the concern is that genetically modified organisms could reproduce and interbreed with natural organisms, thereby spreading to new environments and future generations in an unforeseeable and uncontrollable way. Doubt is also cast on the role of GM technology in providing the answer to food security, with the claim that technological solutions like GM crops overshadow the real social and environmental problems that cause hunger and malnutrition.

Most recently, some concerns about nanotechnology have been expressed as well. Echoing in some way the concerns about biotechnology, the problem areas include the environment ('What will the new nano-materials do when they are released?') and equity ('Who will benefit – just the rich, or the poor as well?').

It has been suggested that most effective response to technological risk is the adoption of a precautionary principle. The precautionary principle states that when an activity raises threats of harm to the environment or human health, precautionary measures should be taken even if some cause-and-effect relationships are not fully established scientifically (see Box 1.1 for more detail on the precautionary principle). Sometimes it seems to imply a generalized hostility to science and technology as such, but, more rationally, it means taking action before risks are conclusively established. It is, basically, a 'better-safe-than-sorry' principle.

Box 1.1   The precautionary principle

Although applied more broadly, the precautionary principle has been developed primarily in the context of environmental policy. It emerged in European environmental policies in the late 1970s and has since become enshrined in numerous international treaties and declarations. It was explicitly recognized during the UN Conference on Environment and Development (UNCED) in Rio de Janeiro 1992 and included in the so-called Rio Declaration. Since then, the precautionary principle has been implemented in various environmental instruments, and in particular in those related to global climate change, ozone-depleting substances and biodiversity conservation. It is, by the Treaty on European Union (1992), the basis for European environmental law and plays an increasing role in developing environmental health policies as well (Foster *et al.*, 2000).

Essentially, the precautionary principle specifies that scientific uncertainty is no excuse for inaction on an environmental or health problem.

Despite its seemingly widespread political support, the precautionary principle has engendered endless controversy and has been interpreted in different ways. In its strongest formulations, the principle can be interpreted as calling for absolute proof of safety before allowing new technologies to be adopted. For example, the World Charter for Nature (UN, 1982) states: 'where potential adverse effects are not fully understood, the activities should not proceed'. If interpreted literally, no new technology could meet this requirement (Foster *et al.*, 2000). Another strong formulation is set out in the Third Ministerial Declaration on the North Sea (1990), which requires governments to 'apply the precautionary principle, that is to take action to avoid potentially damaging impacts of [toxic] substances . . . even where there is no scientific evidence to prove a causal link between emissions and effects'. This formulation requires governments to take action without considering offsetting factors and without scientific evidence of harm.

A relatively soft formulation appears in the 1992 Rio Declaration on Environment and Development which opens the door to cost–benefit analysis and discretionary judgement. The Rio Declaration (UN, 1992) says that lack of 'full scientific certainty shall not be used as a reason for postponing cost-effective measures to prevent environmental degradation'.

Between these soft and strong formulations lie a wide range of other positions, which should not be surprising. The precautionary principle is still evolving, and its final character will be shaped by scientific and political processes. A range of formulations – from soft to strong – will continue to be used in different circumstances because different technologies and situations require different degrees of precaution.

However, development of science and technology is bound up with risks and, as the progress of science and technology accelerates, we have to get used to dealing with risk situations. These risks deserve our full attention, but cannot be the only consideration in shaping our choices of sustainable technologies. An approach to technology assessment that looked only at potential harms of technologies would be flawed. We need a full assessment to weigh the expected harms of a new technology against its expected benefits and compare these with the harms and benefits of existing and alternative technologies. To obtain a full picture of the risks and benefits, these assessments must be done on a life cycle basis, or from 'cradle to grave' (Azapagic, 2002). (The life cycle approach is discussed in more detail in Chapter 3.)

Furthermore, the full technology assessment must also take into consideration the context in which specific technological risks occur. The trade-offs of technological change vary from use to use, and from country to country. Different societies expect different benefits, face different risks and have widely varying capacities to handle those risks safely.

Take, for example, the controversy over GM foods. Opponents of the GM technology often ignore the harms of the status quo. European consumers who do not face food shortages or nutritional deficiencies see few benefits of genetically modified foods; they are more concerned about possible health effects. Undernourished farming communities in developing countries, however, are more likely to focus on the potential benefits of higher yields with greater nutritional value (UNDP, 2001). As Sakiko Fukuda-Parr, the lead author of a UN report that looked into potential benefits of new technologies for developing countries, put it:

> You and I don't really need the tomato with longer shelf life. On the other hand, a farmer in Mali facing crop failure every three years really needs better drought-resistant crops that biotechnology can offer.

So, the potential benefits that biotechnology has for the agriculture of developing countries is enormously different from the potential benefits for the agriculture in Europe or the OECD countries. Many developing countries might reap great benefits from genetically-modified foods, crops and other organisms (GMOs). For developing countries facing malnutrition, the unique potential of GM techniques for creating virus resistant, drought-tolerant and nutrient-enhanced crops, poses different choices. In their case, the risks of no change may outweigh any concerns over the potential health effects of GMOs.

Similarly, proponents of new technologies often fail to consider alternatives. Nuclear power, for example, should be weighed not just against fossil fuels but also against other – possibly preferable – alternatives such as solar power and hydrogen fuel cells. And many people argue that the use of genetically modified organisms should be weighed against alternatives such as organic farming, which in some situations could be a more suitable choice. 'The golden rice' controversy is an appropriate case to consider in this context.

The GM industry claims that a rice variety that is genetically modified to contain vitamin A ('the golden rice') could save thousands of children from blindness and millions of malnourished people from vitamin A deficiency (VAD). Yet, the golden rice could, if introduced on a large scale, exacerbate malnutrition and ultimately undermine food security because it encourages a diet based on one staple. For the short term, measures such as supplementation (i.e. pills) and food fortification are effective and cheaper. Promoting locally appropriate and ecologically sustainable agriculture and diet diversification programmes would address a wide variety of micronutrient deficiencies, not just VAD, and lead to a long-term solution.

The golden rice case highlights an important point when considering sustainable technologies: we must not fall into the trap of thinking that technological innovation is a universal remedy for our problems. To create a sustainable society, we must focus on strategies that address the root causes of our problems.

Treating the symptoms, regardless of how technologically advanced the treatment is, results only in short-term gains that may be offset by other factors. Consider, for example, the catalytic converter, a device used on cars to reduce the emissions on certain pollutants, notably carbon monoxide and hydrocarbons. Catalytic converters work well and are responsible for a dramatic decline in the pollution our cars produce. They are even responsible for a general 'cleansing' of the air in many urban centres. However, the number of motor vehicles in the world has increased from 630 million in 1990 to over 1 billion in 2000. Continuing expansion of the population and the ever-increasing number of vehicle-miles travelled per year (increasing in the USA alone by about 51 billion miles per year) could overwhelm the gains resulting from the use of catalytic converters (Chiras, 2003).

Certainly, there are many examples of how technologies can help us to move to a sustainable path (such as those considered in this book!). The authors of the Factor 4 concept, for instance, give 50 examples of technologies that could be called upon to deliver the necessary improvement in resource efficiency, including ultra fuel-efficient cars and low-energy homes (von Weizsäcker *et al.*, 1997).

Technological innovations can indeed offer new, less wasteful ways of meeting our needs through efficiency improvements, reuse, recycling and substitution of natural resources. Ultimately, however, sustainability will require social and institutional innovation just as much as technological innovation. It is a simple fact that, as we become more efficient at producing things, we will get wealthier. And as we get wealthier we are able to produce and consume more goods and services.

1.4 Economic Growth, Environmental Constraints and Social Concerns

World consumption has expanded at an unprecedented rate in the last century, with private and public consumption expenditures reaching $24 trillion in 1998, twice the level of 1975 and six times that of 1950 (WSSD, 2002b). Consumption in and of itself is not bad, of course – all living things must consume to maintain their biological existence. The real sustainability issue, however, is the extent of consumption and its environmental and social impacts. And, worryingly, global current consumption and production levels appear to be much higher than the Earth's sustainable carrying capacity (UNEP, 2009).

Carrying capacity is defined as the maximum number of individuals of a defined species that a given environment can support over the long term. The notion of limits is fundamental to the concept of carrying capacity.

Researchers and environmental organizations have promoted a range of new approaches to define these ecological limits and demonstrate the extent of our consumption. The ecological footprint is one of the most prominent of these approaches.

1.4.1 Ecological Footprint

The ecological footprint shows how much productive land and water is required to support a defined economy or population at a specified standard of living. Industrialized economies are considered to require far more land than they have, thus, through trade, impacting on resources in other countries. Also known as 'appropriated carrying capacity', this concept, too, incorporates the distributional aspects of sustainable production and consumption.

According to the latest ecological footprint studies (Venetoulis and Talberth, 2005; UNEP, 2009), humanity's footprint is 21.9 ha/person, while the Earth's biological capacity is, on average, only 15.7 ha/person, which means that humanity is currently exceeding the biosphere's ecological capacity by 39%. In other words, at present rates of consumption, we would need 1.39 Earths to ensure that future generations are at least as well off as we are now (Venetoulis and Talberth, 2005).

Owing to population increase, the biologically productive space available per person has decreased considerably in recent years. Leaving space untouched for other species – the authors of the Brundtland Report (WCED, 1987), for instance, invited the world community to set aside 12% of the biologically productive space for other species – makes the ecological deficit even larger.

National ecological footprints show that many countries are running ecological deficits, with their footprints larger than their own biological capacity. Others depend heavily on resources from elsewhere, which are under increasing pressure (Global Footprint Network, 2010).

Amongst the world's countries, rich nations such as United Arab Emirates, Kuwait and the USA exceed their biological capacities the most. On the other hand, some poor nations have the largest per capita ecological surpluses (positive ecological balances); for example, Mongolia, Nambia, Gabon, Mauritania and Papua New Guinea. On a continental basis, western Europe and North America had the greatest ecological footprints and ran negative ecological balances, while Africa, Latin America and other less consumptive regions had relatively smaller footprints and ran positive ecological balances (Venetoulis and Talberth, 2005).

In general, wealthier nations tend to run negative ecological balances, largely because of the high degree of correlation between affluence (expenditures) and fossil fuel consumption. As a rule, wealthier countries (despite technological advantages), were found to have larger footprints on a per capita basis as compared to their fellow global citizens that consume less. The ecological footprint of an average US citizen, for instance, is over five times more than is available per person world-wide and is 16 times more than the ecological footprint of an average person in Bangladesh (Redefining Progress, 2003).

Large 'ecological deficits' are common for industrialized regions and countries, and if everyone in the world were to live like an average person in high income countries, we would need some additional planets to support us all. The UK footprint, for instance, shows that, if everyone in the world consumed at the average UK rate, we would need three planets' worth of resources (WWF/SEI/CURE, 2006).

The ecological footprint is by no means a perfect measure. However, it is useful in many ways. First, by measuring a population's demands on the Earth's available biological capacity the ecological footprint enables us to understand better the environmental limits to human activity at the global scale. The ecological footprint studies cast light on rather worrying facts – we are overusing the Earth and depleting ecological assets at an increasing rate. They send us, therefore, a clear message: we have to be less profligate in our use of nonrenewable resources and thermodynamically irreversible processes if the planet is to be fit for us and for future generations to live on.

Second, the ecological footprints of nations reveal a huge disparity in access to environmental resources and an increasing gap between the developed and developing worlds. The patterns of consumption highlighted by the ecological footprint studies point to global inequality characterized by a growing 'lifestyle divide'. One side of the lifestyle divide is characterized by excesses of consumption by the minority one-fifth of the world population, which is responsible for close to 90% of total personal consumption; the other side is characterized by extreme poverty, where 1.4 billion live on less than US$1.25 per day (UN, 2009). This gap – partly a result of growing poverty and of affluence – is a serious threat to sustainable development.

Global inequality is evident in many aspects of consumption. Disparity in energy consumption, for instance, highlights global inequality clearly – people in developed countries use almost 10 times more energy per person than people in developing regions. It is not, of course, only energy consumption that is highly disproportional in global terms. It is estimated that the 15% of the world's population living in high-income countries account for 56% of the world's total consumption, while the poorest 40%, in low-income countries, account for only 11% of consumption (WSSD, 2002b).

Finally, by demonstrating disparity in the way global resources are used, the ecological footprint reminds us that sustainable consumption is inextricably linked with the question of *equity* with respect to access to available resources and opportunities.

1.5 Equity and Sustainable Development

The question of equity is at the heart of sustainable development. It focuses attention on redressing the enormous imbalances in political and economic power – between rich and poor countries and peoples, and amongst corporations, states, communities and generations.

The Brundtland Report strongly underlined that benefits and burdens from development and environmental policies should be distributed fairly among the members of society and between generations in order to promote social and economic equity. The report has repeatedly emphasized that a primary goal of sustainable development is greater equity, both within the current generation (intra-generational equity) and between generations (inter-generational equity).

1.5.1 Intragenerational Equity

One of the core principles of sustainable development is to achieve basic standards of material equity and social justice both within and between countries. Combating poverty and extending to all the opportunity to fulfil their aspirations for a better life are indispensable for achieving this aim.

The Brundtland Report pointed out that meeting essential needs requires not only economic growth for nations in which the majority are poor, but an assurance that those poor get their fair share of the resources required to sustain that growth (WCED, 1987). It also stated that 'the world in which poverty is endemic would always be prone to ecological catastrophes', pointing to significant links between poverty and the environment. Indeed, much environmental degradation in the developing world today arises from poor people seeking the basic essentials for human life: food, water, fuel and so on. Environmental degradation, on the other hand, has serious social and economic repercussions for the poor, including unsafe water and poor sanitation causing diseases and death of millions of people and children in developing countries, and health-threatening levels of pollution in the urban environment.

In addition, the poor tend to be the most vulnerable to the effects of environmental degradation. They tend to have much lower coping capacities and, therefore, they are particularly susceptible to the impact of disasters, drought, desertification and pollution. As the UN Intergovernmental Panel on Climate Change (IPCC) reports on the impacts of increased global temperatures point out, the poorest parts of the world will suffer most from climate change in the future. The impacts are expected to fall 'disproportionately on the poor' the reports claim, because most less-developed regions are vulnerable due to a 'larger share of their economies being in climate-sensitive areas', such as agriculture, and their low capacity to adapt to change (McCarthy *et al.*, 2001; Solomon *et al.*, 2007).

Unfortunately, the link between poverty and environment is often uncritically characterized as a 'vicious circle'. Population growth and inadequate resources are presumed to lead to the migration of the poor to ever more fragile lands or more hazardous living sites, forcing them to overuse environmental resources. In turn, the degradation of these resources further impoverishes them. Although this does sometimes happen, as a general model it is highly simplistic. Moreover, it often leads to policies that either protect the environment at the expense of the poor or reduce poverty at the expense of the environment.

The linkages between poverty and the environment are complex and require locally specific analysis to be understood – there is no simple causal link. In many areas, the non-poor, commercial companies and state agencies actually cause the majority of environmental damage through land clearing, agro-chemical use, water appropriation and pollution. Sometimes privileged groups force the poor onto marginal lands, where, unable to afford conservation and regeneration measures, their land-use practices further damage an already degraded environment. Indeed, unsustainable practices by the poor, such as slash-and-burn farming by displaced peasants, seriously damage tropical forests; but, as Norman Myers put it, 'blaming them for deforestation is like blaming soldiers for starting a war' (Myers, 2002).

There are also many examples in which very poor people take care of the environment and invest in improving it. Based on experience from around the world, 'win–win' options exist that can build better institutions and partnerships with poor people to create more robust livelihoods and healthier environments. These options simultaneously pursue two goals: reduced poverty and enhanced environmental protection.

Take, for example, the case of indoor pollution from cooking and heating. Around 1 billion people are affected by problems caused by the use of traditional biomass fuels for cooking and heating. They prepare food and heat their homes with fires that burn dung, wood, crop residues, charcoal or other combustible materials. While seemingly rather harmless, these cookstoves are major causes of massive environmental destruction. Many thousands of acres of forests and other ecosystems are degraded as people seek firewood and other biomass fuels. Besides the obvious harm to the ecosystem, deforestation and plant denudation are a major cause of soil erosion. Human health suffers too, as people are exposed to high levels of indoor pollution in poorly ventilated areas. Estimates suggest that indoor air pollution contributes to acute respiratory infections that kill some 4 million infants and children a year and decreases the overall health and life expectancy of millions more women and children (UNEP, 2007).

In the case of indoor pollution from cooking and heating, even a simple but well-thought change could create a win–win situation. Improving efficiency of traditional cookstoves to just 20%, for instance, can reduce the amount of firewood (ecological damage) and smoke (health impact) by half (McKinney and Schoch, 2003). Introducing a different and more appropriate technology, such as a solar cookstove or oven, will lead to an even better type of improvement. No biomass fuel is used, and no unhealthy smoke is produced. The solar cookstove is still relatively new and not yet widely used. Early efforts to introduce the new technologies were unsuccessful because many social factors, such as community needs and customs, were not considered. Simple considerations, such as including local artisans as stove makers, could often not only make new technologies more acceptable to the local population but also produce jobs for the community. Thus, simple actions such as improving cookstoves and including local artisans as stove makers will not only reduce harm to the environment and people's health, but also improve living standards. It is an example where developing appropriate technologies that are needed by the poor simultaneously tackles an environmental problem and improves the livelihoods of the poor. It is also a good example of how well-planned actions can break a vicious circle of poverty and environmental degradation.

It should also be noted that too often we deal with the consequences of poverty rather than the underlying causes.

In fact, the causes of poverty are often environmental in nature. For instance, environmental factors are responsible for almost a quarter of all disease in developing countries. The poor, particularly women and children, are most affected by environmental health problems. The most important hazard, particularly for urban populations in developing countries, is faecal contamination of water and food due to poor or nonexistent sewage systems and inadequate hygiene, compounded by unreliable and unsafe domestic water supply (see Chapter 12). There are other significant hazards. According to the World Health Organization (WHO), 90% of the global burden of malaria, which is estimated to kill 1 in 20 children under 5 years of age in sub-Saharan Africa, is attributable to environmental factors (WHO, 2009).

Tackling the causes of poverty, including environmental ones, is one of the world's major challenges in the twenty-first century. As already mentioned, the Johannesburg Summit on Sustainable Development agreed on the target to halve by the year 2015 the proportion of people living in extreme poverty.

But quite what this target might mean is obscured by the bewildering ambiguity with which the term 'poverty' is used, and by the many different indicators proposed to monitor poverty. There is no single definition of poverty. The term has been used to define the level of income obtained by households or individuals, lack of access to social services, as well as the inability to participate in society, economically, socially, culturally or politically (Maxwell, 1999). Different organizations, institutions and agencies use different concepts to describe poverty: income or consumption poverty, human underdevelopment, social exclusion, ill-being, lack of capability and functioning, vulnerability, livelihood unsustainability, lack of basic needs, relative deprivation and so on (Maxwell, 1999).

Different concepts imply different instruments to tackle poverty. Yet, defining poverty is only a start. Only by understanding causes can we begin to design, implement and evaluate programmes to alleviate poverty. In designing poverty programmes, it is advisable to respect the understanding of poverty articulated by poor people themselves. In some cases, this may mean implementing measures to increase income. But in others, the priority may be to reduce variability of income, or strengthen women's autonomy by improving the legal system, or improving the access to environmental resources and services.

Poverty is, indeed, a complex issue, and we cannot do it justice in this short chapter. Environmental issues are, of course, part of wider set of factors which contribute to making people poor. Breaking the 'vicious circle' of poverty and environmental degradation is, however, critical for sustainability. There are a number of practical actions that the international community can take in addressing this issue. These actions have been recognized and summarized by the UNDP and EU Poverty and Environment Initiative (UNDP-EU, 1999a, 1999b):

- strengthen participation of the poor in the preparation and implementation of national and local plans, policies and strategies;
- protect the current natural asset base of the poor through protecting the access they already have to critical resources (such as entitlements to land, water, trees, pastures, fishing grounds) – especially in cases where the poor are in a weak position to resist appropriation of these resources by other groups, and through protecting the environmental resources upon which the poor depend on their livelihoods;
- expand the natural asset base of the poor through transferring ownership of natural assets to the poor (such as the recognition of community forest law, the creation of community forest rights or rights to other resources) and promoting pro-poor land reform;
- co-manage and co-invest in environmental services and resource with the poor through promoting and strengthening community management of environmental resources, and assisting the poor to overcome the high initial costs for receiving better quality environmental services (such as water supply and sanitation, renewable energy and waste management);
- promote environmental infrastructure and technology that benefit the poor through a greater focus on tackling the environmental problems and hazards that impact most upon their health and livelihoods and through developing affordable and environmentally sound technologies that are needed by and can be used by the poor; and
- make resource transfers to the poor through reducing subsidies for environmental services that benefit the non-poor (such as energy and water) and increasing investments in areas in which the poor live and work.

Working up such programmes will be challenging. Yet, eradicating poverty and improving quality of life of the poor is an imperative of sustainable development. How we approach these issues will play a major role in determining whether we move toward or away from more sustainable paths.

1.5.2 Intergenerational Equity

As already mentioned, the idea of sustainable development implies not only our responsibility to assist the presently needy, but also refers to our obligations to consider the well-being of future generations. Indeed, the need to safeguard the interests of future generations has been an integral part of sustainable development from the very beginning of the concept.

One of the earliest UK Government documents on sustainable development states that we have 'the moral duty to look after our planet and to hand it on in good order to future generations' (UK Government, 1995).

This moral duty is based on the recognition of legitimate interests and rights of future generations to live in a physically secure and healthy environment, and, consequently, as the recognition of our moral responsibility to protect the natural environment to such an extent that the survival and well-being of future generations are not jeopardized (Perdan and Azapagic, 2000). In other words, we have a moral duty to ensure that future generations have as good a life as we have now, or better.

One interpretation of intergenerational equity is that the welfare of society as a whole may not be allowed to decline for the indefinite future. It is sometimes expressed as 'the constant capital rule': the value of the overall capital stock must not be allowed to decline for the indefinite future. This is known as the 'weak' sustainability model because it assumes that the forms of capital[1] are completely substitutable for each other. It does not matter what form the stock of capital takes as long as the total does not decline. While this position is consistent with intergenerational equity in demanding that equivalent or increased amounts of capital are passed to future generations, it allows the form of this capital to change. This opens the door to passing on to the next generation less of one kind of capital (e.g. natural capital) so long as there is more of another (e.g. built capital) to balance it.

However, one may argue that some ecological assets, such as the ozone layer or biological diversity, are not substitutable – they form 'critical' natural capital and the destruction of this capital could threaten the very survival of the human race. Moreover, while most manufactured and human capital can be replaced, the loss of natural capital is often irreversible (i.e. once natural capital assets are lost it may not be possible to recreate them). This view is often called 'strong' sustainability, and it demands that the equivalent stock of natural capital is preserved for future generations.

This discussion of 'weak' versus 'strong' sustainability is not just a theoretical concern; it also has important practical implications. For instance, some people think there should be no economic activities in protected areas because such areas usually contain irreplaceable natural or human capital and, as such, should be beyond reach for any human activity that will disturb them (IIED/WBCSD, 2002). Others may prefer tangible economic benefits even if they would mean diminishing natural capital such as biodiversity (for an example of such contrasting views, see Chapter 17).

The ongoing theoretical debates about 'weak' and 'strong' sustainability, however, should not obscure the main message: the goal of sustainable development is to sustain improvements of human well-being over time, and to ensure that what we do today will not deprive future generations of the means to meet their own needs.

Perhaps one way of understanding how to achieve this goal is to follow general principles of intergenerational equity. The following two principles may provide us with some guidance:

---

[1] The idea of 'capital' has five main forms: *built capital*, such as machinery, buildings and infrastructure; *human capital*, in the form of knowledge, skills, health and cultural endowment; *social capital*, the institutions and structures that allow individuals and groups to develop collaboratively; *natural capital*, which provides a continuing income of ecosystem benefits, such as biological diversity, mineral resources, and clean air and water; and *financial capital*, the value of which is simply representative of the other forms of capital.

1. the principle of not closing down options for future generations (for example, by making irreversible changes, including the elimination of species, or the using up of resources); and
2. the principle of maximizing future choices by making a considered judgement as to what are the most central, significant or important things to preserve and protect; for example, clean air, energy, biodiversity, cultural values.

While most people accept these principles, the difficulty comes in agreeing how to apply them. In practice, the principles of intergenerational equity become entangled with the issues of intragenerational equity. In some cases it may be possible to advance all the goals of sustainable development simultaneously: improve material well-being for this generation, spread that well-being more equitably, enhance the environment and pass on enhanced stocks of capital to future generations. In others, there may be a conflict between long-term sustainability objectives of preserving 'critical' natural capital, such as biodiversity, and immediate imperatives of providing basic needs of the poor, for instance through intensive agricultural development.

In many situations our decisions will have to involve trade-offs: between different objectives and dimensions, and sometimes between the current and future generations. However, if we apply the principles of sustainable development consistently, we stand a better chance of minimizing trade-offs amongst objectives of intra- and inter-generational equity, and finding the ways of integrating otherwise conflicting goals.

1.6 Conclusions

Sustainable development is an approach to environment and development issues which seeks to reconcile human needs and the capacity of the environment to cope with the consequences of economic systems. Despite its deceptively simple formulations, such as the Brundtland definition, sustainable development has multiple layers of meaning and some profound practical implications. In essence, it is a call to change our actions and to do things differently.

Sustainable development is a dynamic process that will continue to evolve and grow as lessons are learnt and ideas re-examined. Achieving its goals and objectives presents great challenges for all parts of society. Various means are available to facilitate putting sustainable development into practice. Some of these are well known; others are in experimental stages. In this introduction, we have argued that sustainable development depends both on reducing environmental destruction and on improving the quality of life of the world's poor, in ways that will not deprive future generations of means to meet their own needs.

A core principle of sustainable development is to improve human well-being and to sustain those improvements over time. This objective can be achieved by reducing excessive levels of production and consumption; that is, by limiting the material and energy throughput in the human economy, through a more efficient use of resources and by addressing the challenge of poverty eradication through concerted actions which tackle the causes of poverty and ensure that available resources are used to the benefit of all.

Sustainable development requires creativity and innovation at every level: social, economic, institutional and technical. There are many favourable trends underway and new and promising developments that give us hope. Important agreements have been reached to reduce global pollution, protect biodiversity and alleviate poverty. Many countries have begun to take steps to create economies that are better for the environment. Many businesses have introduced cleaner and more eco-efficient production processes that reduce pollution and other environmental impacts while delivering competitively priced goods and services. New technologies are also helping solve problems, as are individual actions. The public has become more aware that, as individuals, we each have a right, a role and a responsibility to contribute to sustainable development. Recycling rates are increasing and we, as consumers, are becoming ready to pay more for organic and other environmentally sound products. At the policy level, a greater attention has been paid to integrating the three conventionally separate domains of economic, environmental and social policy. A wide variety of activities ranging from consultation hearings as part of an environmental impact assessment, to co-management of natural resources are indicating that institutional processes are changing too, starting to recognize that increasing public participation in decision making is an important aspect of sustainable development.

These are encouraging signs, but there is still a lot more to do. In the final analysis, sustainability means securing a satisfying quality of life for everyone. We know what we have to do to achieve this goal – now it is time to do it.

References and Further Reading

Azapagic, A. (2002) Life cycle assessment: a tool for identification of more sustainable products and processes, in *Handbook of Green Chemistry and Technology* (eds J. Clarkand D. Macquarrie), Blackwell Science, Oxford, pp. 62–85.

Chiras, D.D. (2003) *Environmental Science: Creating A Sustainable Future*, 6th edn, Jones and Bartlett Publishers, Sudbury, MA.

De Simone, L. and Popoff, F. (1997) *Eco-efficiency: The Business Link to Sustainable Development*, MIT, Cambridge, MA.

DEFRA (2005) *Securing the Future – The UK Government Sustainable Development Strategy*, HMSO, London.

DEFRA (2010) The official UK Government website for sustainable development, Department for Environment, Food and Rural Affairs http://www.defra.gov.uk/sustainable/government/.

DETR (1999) A better quality of life: a strategy for sustainable development for the United Kingdom. Department of the Environment, Transport and the Regions: London, From http://www.sustainable-development.gov.uk/ (March 2003).

Third Ministerial Declaration on the North Sea (1990) Preamble. Final Declaration of the Third International Conference on Protection of the North Sea, March 7–8, 1990. *International Environmental Law*, **658**, 662–673.

Food and Agriculture Organization of the United Nations (FAO) (2009) The state of agricultural commodity markets 2009: high food prices and the food crisis – experiences and lessons learned. Rome.

Foster, K.R., Vecchia, P. and Repacholi, M.H. (2000) Science and the precautionary principle. *Science*, **288**, 979–981.

Global Footprint Network (2010) Footprint for nations. Available at http://www.footprintnetwork.org.

IIED/WBCSD (2002) Breaking new ground: mining, minerals and sustainable development. Final Report on the Mining, Minerals and Sustainable Development Project (MMSD). International Institute for Environment and Development and World Business Council for Sustainable Development. www.iied.org/mmsd (October 2002).

IISD (1992) Business strategy for sustainable development: leadership and accountability for the 90s. The International Institute for Sustainable Development, Deloitte & Touche and the World Business Council for Sustainable Development.

International Factor 10 Club (1997) Statement to governments and business leaders. Wuppertal Institute for Climate, Environment and Energy, Wuppertal.

McCarthy, J.J., Canziani, O.F., Leary, N.A. *et al.* (eds) (2001) *Climate Change 2001: Impacts, Adaptation and Vulnerability, IPCC Third Assessment Report*, Cambridge University Press, Cambridge.

Solomon, S., Qin, D., Manning, M. *et al.* (eds). (2007) *Climate Change 2007: The Physical Science Basis. Report of Working Group 1 to the Fourth Assessment Report of the Intergovernmental Panel on Climate Change*. Cambridge University Press, Cambridge.

Perdan, S. and Azapagic, A. (2000) Sustainable development and industry: ethical indicators. Environmental Protection Bulletin, Issue 066, May 2000, IChemE.

MA (Millennium Assessment) (2005) *Ecosystems and Human Well-Being: Current State and Trends*, vol. **1**, Island Press, Washington, Covelo, London.

Maxwell, S. (1999) The meaning and measurement of poverty. ODI Poverty Briefings 3, February 1999.

McKinney, M. and Schoch, R.M. (2003) *Environmental Science: Systems and Solutions*, 3rd edn, Jones and Bartlett Publishers, Sudbury, MA.

Myers, N. (2002) Biodiversity. Presentation to the Foreign and Commonwealth Office. March 2002, London.

Redefining Progress (2003) Ecological footprint. http://www.rprogress.org/programs/sustainability/ef/ (March 2003).

UCS (2001) Action for global sustainability. http://www.ucsusa.org/.

UK Government (1995) *This Common Inheritance. UK Annual Report 1995*. HMSO, London.

UN (1982) World Charter for Nature. UN GA Resolution 37/7.

UN (1992) Rio Declaration on Environment and Development. 13 June 1992 (UN Doc./CONF.151/5/Rev.1).

UN (2009) Rethinking Poverty – Report on the World Social Situation. Department of Economic and Social Affairs, New York.

UNCSD (2002) Implementing Agenda 21 – Report of the Secretary-General, Commission on Sustainable Development acting as the preparatory committee for the World Summit on Sustainable Development, Second session 28 January–8 February 2002. http://www.johannes-burgsummit.org/html/documents/no170793sgreport.pdf.

UNDP (2001) *Human Development Report 2001: Making New Technologies Work for Human Development, United Nations Development Programme*, Oxford University Press, Oxford.

UNDP-EU (1999a) Poverty & environment initiative: attacking poverty while improving the environment: practical recommendations. http://www.unpei.org/PDF/Attacking-Poverty-Rec-Eng.pdf.

UNDP-EU (1999b) Poverty & environment initiative, attacking poverty while improving the environment: towards win–win policy options. http://www.unpei.org/PDF/Attacking-Poverty-win-win-Eng.pdf.

UNEP (2000) *Global Environment Outlook 2000, United Nations Environment Programme*, Earthscan Publications, London.

UNEP (2002) *Global Environment Outlook 2002, United Nations Environment Programme*, Earthscan Publications, London.

UNEP (2007) *Global Environment Outlook 2007, United Nations Environment Programme*, Earthscan Publications, London.

UNEP (2009) *Year book 2009 – New Science and Developments in Our Changing World*, Earthprint.

UNEP/WWF/IUCN (1991) Caring for the Earth: a strategy for sustainable living. International Union for Conservation of Nature, Gland, www.iucn.org.

IUCN/UNEP/WWF (1980) World conservation strategy. International Union for Conservation of Nature and Natural Resources, Gland, www.iucn.org.

United Nations Children's Fund (UNICEF) (2000) The Progress of Nations 2000. New York.

Venetoulis, J. and Talberth, J. (2005) Ecological footprint of nations: 2005 update. Redefining Progress, Oakland, CA.

Von Weizsäcker, E., Lovins, A.B. and Lovins, L.H. (1997) *Factor Four: Doubling Wealth – Halving Resource Use*, Earthscan Publications, London, p. 244.

WBCSD (1996) Eco-efficiency principles from WBCSD. Eco-efficient leadership for improved economic and environmental performance. World Business Council for Sustainable Development, Geneva.

WBCSD (2000) Eco-efficiency: creating more value with less impact. http://www.wbcsd.org/Doc-Root/02w8IK14V8E3HMIiFYue/EEcreating.pdf (March 2003).

WBCSD (2001) The Business Case for Sustainable Development: Making a Difference toward the Johannesburg Summit 2002 and Beyond. World Business Council for Sustainable Development, Geneva.

WBCSD (2010) About the WBCSD. http://www.wbcsd.org.

WCEC (2001) Melbourne communiqué. 6th World Congress of Chemical Engineering, Melbourne, 24–28 September 2001.

WCED (1987) *Our Common Future*, World Commission on Environment and Development, Oxford, University Press, Oxford.

World Health Organization (WHO) (2009) World Malaria Report 2009. World Health Organization, Geneva.

WSSD (2002a) Key outcomes of the summit. http://www.johannesburgsummit.org (October, 2002).

WSSD (2002b) Facts about consumption and production patterns. http://www.johannesburgsummit.org/html/media_info/pressreleases_factsheets/wssd9_consumption.pdf.

WWF, SEI and CURE (2006) Counting consumption: CO_2 emissions, material flows and ecological footprint of the UK by region and devolved country. WWF-UK, Godalming.

2

Measuring Sustainable Development: An Overview

Slobodan Perdan and Adisa Azapagic

How to measure our progress towards achieving sustainable development has emerged as one of the key issues on the sustainability agenda. In recent years we have seen intensive efforts by a wide range of actors, such as international agencies, governments, nongovernmental organizations, communities and businesses to develop measurement systems and indicators that characterize progress towards sustainable development, or at least some of the dimensions of sustainability. This chapter gives an overview of some of the most prominent initiatives to measure sustainability at the international, national, local and corporate levels.

2.1 Introduction

Since its emergence in the 1980s, the idea of sustainable development has come a long way. There is no doubt that achieving sustainability has nowadays become a widely accepted societal goal in many countries. The European Commission, for instance, declared sustainable development as 'an overarching objective of the European Union set out in the Treaty, governing all the Union's policies and activities' (Council of the European Union, 2006). The UK Government, for its part, stated that 'sustainability is the future; sustainable development can guide our choices to get us there and create a place we want to live in' (Defra, 2010a).

Sustainable Development in Practice: Case Studies for Engineers and Scientists, Second Edition
Edited by Adisa Azapagic and Slobodan Perdan
© 2011 John Wiley & Sons, Ltd.

Other national governments and a wide range of actors, such as international and intergovernmental bodies, nongovernmental organizations (NGOs), communities and the private sector, have expressed the same or similar sentiments about the goal of sustainability.

Yet, how do we measure progress towards achieving this goal? While there is a broad consensus that managing activities and decision-making processes in order to move towards sustainable development requires new ways of assessing progress, there is no standardized or universally accepted methodology for measuring sustainability (Hardi *et al.*, 1997; Azapagic and Perdan, 2000).

For a long time the gross domestic product (GDP) has been regarded as an appropriate indicator of progress and widely used by policy makers, economists, international agencies and the media as the primary indicator of a nation's economic health and well-being.

However, while GDP is a good indicator of economic activity and, as such, a good measure of the success of an economy, it is largely inadequate as an indicator of sustainability (see Box 2.1). GDP has been called 'a brute measure of total economic activity' and been criticized for taking 'no account of increasing inequality, pollution or damage to people's health and the environment' (Friends of the Earth, 2010).

The view that GDP is a limited measure of progress is hardly new. Even one of the most prominent economists who helped to standardize the measurement of GDP, Simon Kuznets, was aware of GDP's shortcomings in measuring a nation's economic health and well-being. As early as 1934, he wrote that 'the welfare of a nation can scarcely be inferred from a measure of national income' (Talberth *et al.*, 2007).

Box 2.1   *Indicators*

The term 'indicator' comes from the Latin verb *indicare*, which means 'to disclose or point out, to announce or make publicly known, or to estimate or put a price on' (Adriaanse, 1993; Hammond *et al.*, 1995). Indicators have been widely used to measure progress in the fields such as economics, ecosystems, natural resources, quality of life, health and social issues and have proven to be useful tools for condensing large amounts of information into an easily understood format.

The major role of sustainability indicators is to indicate progress toward or away from some common goals of sustainable development in order to advise the public, decision makers and managers (Parris and Kates, 2003). Indicators are useful for decision makers particularly because they help (Hardi *et al.*, 1997):

To understand what sustainable development means in operational terms. In this sense, measurement and indicators are *explanatory tools*, translating the concepts of sustainable development into practical terms;

To make policy choices to move toward sustainable development. Measurement and indicators create linkages between everyday activities and sustainable development. Indicators provide a sense of direction for decision makers when they choose among policy alternatives: they are *planning tools*; and

To decide the degree to which efforts are successful in meeting sustainable development goals and objectives. In this sense, measurement and indicators are *performance assessment tools*.

In 1968, the late US Senator Robert Kennedy echoed these doubts about GDP, and his warning about its inadequacy has often been quoted in the GDP debate (Kennedy, 1968):

> ... the gross national product does not allow for the health of our children, the quality of their education, or the joy of their play. It does not include the beauty of our poetry or the strength of our marriages; the intelligence of our public debate or the integrity of our public officials. It measures neither our wit nor our courage; neither our wisdom nor our learning; neither our compassion nor our devotion to our country; it measures everything, in short, except that which makes life worthwhile.

There are indeed many reasons why GDP is not suited to measure sustainability. As its numerous critics point out, it merely represents a gross sum of products and services bought and sold, with no distinctions between transactions that enhance well-being and those that diminish it (Talberth *et al.*, 2007). GDP simply assumes that every monetary transaction adds to social well-being by definition, thus failing to distinguish between costs and benefits, productive economic activities from destructive ones, or sustainable consumption from unsustainable consumption.

In this way, expenditures triggered by crime, accidents, toxic waste contamination or corporate fraud, for instance, count the same as socially productive investments in education, healthcare, housing or sanitation. It is as if a business tried to assess its financial condition by simply adding up all business activity, lumping together income and expenses, assets and liabilities (Talberth *et al.*, 2007).

Because it fails to distinguish properly between welfare-enhancing and welfare-degrading expenditures, using GDP as an indicator of overall well-being often leads to perverse results. For instance, GDP increases with polluting activities and then again with clean-ups. Pollution is a double benefit to the economy, since GDP grows when we manufacture toxic chemicals and again when we are forced to clean them up. An oil spill will be reflected positively in GDP by creating a 'mini-economic boom', as the costs of clean up are very high (ESDI, 2010). Exploitation of forests and fossil fuels would show an increased GDP without taking into account environmental degradation and the resulting decrease in the real welfare of society in the longer term (Azapagic and Perdan, 2000). These and similar anomalies within GDP show that social and environmental aspects of progress, such as environmental pollution, resource depletion, health and poverty, can hardly be captured adequately by GDP.

As a result, in recent years we have seen a variety of attempts to use alternative economic indicators that would provide 'a more truthful picture of economic and social progress' (Redefining Progress, 2010).

Among these alternative economic indicators, the most conspicuous are the *Measure of Economic Welfare* (MEW), *Index of Sustainable Economic Welfare* (ISEW) and *Genuine Progress Indicator* (GPI). These alternative indicators of progress share a common feature: they all attempt to adapt conventional economic measures such as GDP or consumer expenditure to include social and environmental costs and benefits that normally lie outside the accounting framework.

The MEW was developed in the early 1970s by two US economists, William Nordhaus and James Tobin (Nordhaus and Tobin, 1972). This was in an attempt to adapt national accounts to provide a more accurate measure of changes in welfare over time. In their study 'Is growth obsolete?', they demonstrated that when a proper account is taken of factors which are not adequately measured by GDP, living standards could be shown to have grown by far less in the post-war period (Nordhaus and Tobin, 1972). MEW is often quoted as one of the first indicators which clearly showed the deficiencies of GDP as a measure of welfare and it has been a source of inspiration for others to develop alternative measures of progress.

The ISEW is a more recent attempt to adapt national accounts to include both benefits and costs of resource use which are not incorporated in the standard systems of national accounts. Developed initially by Daly and Cobb (1989), ISEW 'corrects' GDP over a range of issues, such as environmental damage, depletion of environmental assets and income inequality, to create an indicator which better measures how the economy delivers welfare for people. Adjusted in this way, the indicator gives a different picture of societal progress – apparent rises in living standards measured by conventional means are transformed into much smaller and less positive trends.

For instance, an ISEW study for the UK showed a striking difference between the growth from 1950 to 1996 expressed in terms of GDP and ISEW: in that period, the real GDP per head increased by 2.5 times, giving an average annual increase of 2 % (Jackson *et al.*, 1997). Applying the ISEW adjustments, however, shows that the trend is far more modest and includes periods of negative growth. Overall, the ISEW in 1996 was only 31 % higher than in 1950, which represents an annual average rate of growth of just 0.6 % (Jackson *et al.*, 1997).

According to the UK study, one of the major factors in the increasing divergence between GDP and ISEW measures in recent decades lies in their divergent treatment of the depletion of nonrenewable hydrocarbon reserves (essentially North Sea oil and gas). A further factor is the inclusion in the ISEW of the cumulative costs of global warming. Another important consideration is the welfare cost associated with growing income inequality. The UK ISEW, for example, makes an estimate of cumulative environmental damage and deducts the present value of future welfare losses associated with this based on an estimate of social aversion to such inequality.

The GPI, developed by the US-based lobby group 'Redefining Progress', is the most recent variant of the ISEW. The GPI starts with the same accounting framework as GDP, but then makes some crucial distinctions: it adjusts for factors such as income distribution, value of household, volunteer work, costs of crime and pollution and family breakdown. For instance, while GDP often counts pollution as a double gain (once when it is created and then again when it is cleaned up), the GPI, by contrast, subtracts the costs of air and water pollution as measured by actual damage to human health and the environment (Redefining Progress, 2010).

While methodologies are somewhat different, the MEW, ISEW and GPI (and other 'green' GDP accounting systems) all involve three basic steps (Stockhammer *et al.*, 1997; Neumayer, 2000). Calculations usually begin with estimates of personal consumption expenditures, which are weighted by an index of the inequality in the distribution of income to reflect the social costs of inequality. Additions are made to account for the nonmarket benefits associated with services from both household capital and public infrastructure, as well as volunteer time, housework, parenting and other socially productive time uses. Deductions are then made to account for purely defensive expenditures, such as pollution-related costs and/or the other costs that reflect the undesirable side effects of economic progress. Deductions for costs associated with degradation and depletion of natural capital incurred by the current and future generations are also made at this stage. In this way, 'green' GDP systems correct the deficiencies of GDP by incorporating aspects of the nonmonetized or nonmarket economy, separating welfare-enhancing benefits from welfare-detracting costs, correcting for the unequal distribution of income and distinguishing between sustainable and unsustainable forms of consumption (Talberth *et al.*, 2007).

Adjusted economic indicators, such as MEW, ISEW and GPI, are good examples of initiatives which attempt to align mainstream economic performance indicators with the objectives of sustainable development. By differentiating between economic activity that diminishes both natural and social capital and activity that enhances such capital, these alternative economic indicators are designed to measure sustainable economic welfare rather than economic activity alone. As such, they present a more nuanced perspective on development than the one offered by the conventional economic indicators. However, MEW, ISEW, GPI and other 'green' GDP accounting systems have not so far made significant inroads into the official decision-making process and, for the time being, GDP remains the world's most ubiquitous economic indicator of progress.

In addition to the adjusted economic indicators of progress described above, in recent years there have been a number of initiatives to develop noneconomic aggregate indices that characterize progress towards sustainable development, or at least some of the dimensions of sustainability. Some examples of these include the ecological footprint (Redefining Progress, 2010a), the Barometer of Sustainability (IUCN-IDRC, 1997), the total material requirement (EEA, 2001), the Compass Index of Sustainability (AtKisson, 2005), the Living Planet Index (WWF, 2008) and the Happy Planet Index (NEF, 2009).

The ecological footprint is probably the most prominent of these new sustainability indices. As already mentioned in Chapter 1, the ecological footprint measures the amount of natural resources an individual, a community or a country consumes in a given year. It uses official statistics tracking consumption and translates that into the amount of biologically productive land and water area required to produce the resources consumed and assimilate the wastes generated (Redefining Progress, 2010a).

Although these sustainability indices of progress and the underlying frameworks have gained relative prominence and popularity in both the public and private sectors, their effectiveness in influencing actual policy and practices often remained limited (Bartelmus, 2001; Pinter *et al.*, 2005).

There are, however, a number of sustainability indicator initiatives that have gained official endorsements and are being implemented at different spatial and sectoral levels. The following sections give an overview of some of the most prominent initiatives to measure sustainability at the international, national, local and corporate levels.

2.2 Measuring Sustainability at International Level

2.2.1 The UN CDS Indicators[1]

The Brundtland commission that gave us the widely accepted definition of sustainable development (WCED, 1987) was convened by the United Nations (UN), so it should not be surprising that much of the international effort to develop sustainability indicators comes from the UN agencies.

---

[1] Based on the information by the UN ESA (2010) and UN CSD (2007).

The UN initiative on sustainable development indicators started in earnest with The United Nations Conference on Environment and Development held in Rio de Janeiro in 1992 (see Chapter 1). Chapter 40 of Agenda 21, the action plan adopted at the Rio conference, called on countries, as well as international, governmental and nongovernmental organizations, to develop indicators of sustainable development that can provide a solid basis for decision making at all levels. Agenda 21 also called for the harmonization of efforts to develop such indicators.

One of the direct results of the UN Conference on Environment and Development was the formation of the UN Commission on Sustainable Development (CSD) in 1992. At its first meeting, the CSD identified a clear need for a set of standard measures for monitoring progress towards sustainability:

> A measuring stick is required: units by which to distinguish relativity and proximity. This measuring stick should be broad enough to encompass economic, social, environmental, cultural, institutional and other realms of human activity which affect sustainable development. It must also be comprehensive enough to take into account: stresses on economies, ecosystems, and social fabrics; impacts of stresses on the present state of complex systems; and responses to these stresses
>
> *(CDS as quoted in Moldan et al., 1997).*

Since then, a major focus of the CSD work has been on the development and testing of a suite of indicators. Initially, the CSD developed a set of 134 indicators grouped in four major categories: social, economic, environmental and institutional indicators (UN CSD, 1996). Since these initial developments, the indicator set has been revised and the framework modified to reflect latest thinking about sustainability. In the latest (third) edition of the CSD framework, indicators are no longer explicitly categorized into 'four pillars of sustainable development'; that is, social, economic, environmental and institutional. Instead, they are placed in a framework of 14 themes in order to emphasize 'the multi-dimensional nature of sustainable development and reflect the importance of integrating its pillars' (UN CSD, 2007). These are listed in Table 2.1, together with the 96 indicators included in the framework. As can be seen, the UN CSD indicators set is a very comprehensive tool which attempts to measure sustainable development in an integrated manner. Its primary aim is to serve as a reference for countries to develop or revise national indicators of sustainable development.

2.2.2 The EU Sustainable Development Indicators[2]

Much of the work on sustainability indicators undertaken at European Union (EU) level parallels the related UN initiative. The main EU framework and set of sustainability indicators are based on the EU Sustainable Development Strategy (SDS), adopted in 2001 and renewed in 2006 (Council of the European Union, 2006).

The SDS identified seven key sustainability challenges for the EU and called for development of indicators to monitor progress with regard to each particular challenge.

---

[2] Based on the information presented in EC (2009).

Table 2.1   *UN CSD sustainability indicators (UN CSD, 2007)*

Sustainability themes and indicators

Poverty

- Proportion of population living below national poverty line
- Proportion of population below $1 per day
- Ratio of share in national income of highest to lowest quintile
- Proportion of population using an improved sanitation facility
- Proportion of population using an improved water source
- Share of households without electricity or other modern energy services
- Percentage of population using solid fuels for cooking
- Proportion of urban population living in slums

Governance

- Percentage of population having paid bribes
- Number of recorded intentional homicides per 100 000 population

Education

- Gross intake rate into last year of primary education
- Net enrolment rate in primary education
- Adult secondary (tertiary) schooling attainment level
- Life-long learning
- Adult literacy rates

Economic development

- Gross domestic product (GDP) per capita
- Investment share in GDP
- Gross savings
- Adjusted net savings as percentage of gross national income (GNI)
- Inflation rate
- Debt-to-gross national income ratio
- Employment-to-population ratio
- Vulnerable employment
- Labour productivity and unit labour cost
- Share of women in wage employment in the nonagricultural sector
- Number of Internet users per population
- Fixed telephone lines per 100 population
- Mobile cellular telephone subscribers per 100 population

Health

- Under-five mortality rate
- Life expectancy at birth
- Healthy life expectancy at birth
- Percentage of population with access to primary health care facilities
- Immunization against infectious childhood diseases
- Contraceptive prevalence rate
- Nutritional status of children
- Morbidity of major diseases such as HIV/AIDS, malaria, tuberculosis
- Prevalence of tobacco use
- Suicide rate

Demographics

- Population growth rate
- Total fertility rate
- Dependency ratio
- Ratio of local residents to tourists in major tourist regions and destinations

Natural hazards

- Percentage of population living in hazard prone areas
- Human and economic loss due to disasters

Atmosphere

- Carbon dioxide emissions
- Emissions of greenhouse gases
- Consumption of ozone-depleting substances
- Ambient concentration of air pollutants in urban areas

Land

- Land use change
- Land degradation
- Land area affected by desertification
- Arable and permanent crop land area
- Fertilizer use efficiency
- Use of agricultural pesticides
- Area under organic farming
- Proportion of land area covered by forests
- Forest trees damaged by defoliation
- Area of forest under sustainable forest management

Table 2.1 *(Continued)*

Sustainability themes and indicators

- Gross domestic expenditure on research and development as a percentage of GDP
- Tourism contribution to GDP

Global economic partnership

- Current account deficit as percentage of GDP
- Share of imports from developing countries and least developed countries least developed country (LDCs)
- Average tariff barriers imposed on exports from developing countries and LDCs
- Net official development assistance given or received as percentage of gross national income (GNI)
- Foreign direct investment (FDI) net inflows and FDI net outflows as percentage of GDP
- Remittances as percentage of GNI

Consumption and production patterns

- Material intensity of the economy
- Domestic material consumption
- Annual energy consumption, total and by main user category
- Share of renewable energy sources in total energy use
- Intensity of energy use, total and by economic activity
- Generation of hazardous wastes
- Generation of waste
- Waste treatment and disposal
- Management of radioactive waste
- Modal split of passenger transport
- Modal split of freight transport
- Energy intensity of transport

Oceans, seas and coasts

- Percentage of total population living in coastal areas
- Bathing water quality
- Proportion of fish stocks within their safe biological limits

- Proportion of marine area protected
- Marine trophic index
- Area of coral reef ecosystems and percentage live cover

Freshwater

- Proportion of total water resources used
- Water use intensity by economic activity
- Presence of faecal coliforms in freshwater
- Biological oxygen demand (BOD) in water bodies
- Waste water treatment

Biodiversity

- Proportion of terrestrial area protected, total and by ecological region
- Management effectiveness of protected areas
- Area of selected key ecosystems
- Fragmentation of habitat
- Change in threat status of species
- Abundance of key species
- Abundance of invasive alien species

According to the SDS, the key challenges for the EU are:

- climate change and clean energy;
- sustainable transport;
- sustainable consumption and production;
- conservation and management of natural resources;
- public health;
- social inclusion, demography and migration; and
- global poverty.

Table 2.2   *Progress towards sustainable development in the EU since 2000 based on the headline indicators (after EC, 2009)*

Sustainability themes	Headline indicators	EU-27 evaluation change
Socio-economic development	Growth of GDP per capita	☀
Climate change and energy	Greenhouse gas emissions[a]	☁
	Consumption of renewables	☁
Sustainable transport	Energy consumption of transport relative to GDP	⛅
Sustainable consumption and production	Resource productivity	☀
Natural resources	Abundance of common birds[b]	⛅
	Conservation of fish stocks[c]	⛈
Public health	Healthy life years[d]	⛅
Social exclusion	Risk of poverty[d]	⛅
Demographic changes	Employment rate of older workers	⛅
Global partnership	Official development assistance[e]	⛈
Good governance	(No headline indicator)	:

[a]EU-15.
[b]Based on 19 member states.
[c]In North East Atlantic.
[d]EU-25, from 2005
[e]From 2005.
☀   Clearly favourable change/on target path.
⛅   No or moderately favourable change/close to target path.
☁   Moderately unfavourable change/far from target path.
⛈   Clearly unfavourable change/moving away from target path.
:   Contextual indicator or insufficient data.

A set of sustainability indicators (specifically tailored for the EU) to monitor progress towards meeting these challenges was adopted by the European Commission in 2005 and further reviewed in 2007 and 2009 (EC, 2007, 2009). Consistent with the UN CDS model, the EU sustainable development indicators (SDIs) are organized within 10 themes, addressing the seven key challenges mentioned above, and comprising 11 headline indicators (see Table 2.2). There are more than 100 indicators in total, classified into three levels of importance, creating a pyramid structure with Level 1, Level 2 and Level 3 indicators (Figure 2.1). This distinction between the three levels of indicators reflects the structure of the EU SDS (overall objectives, operational objectives and actions respectively) and also responds to different kinds of user needs, with the headline indicators having the highest communication value. Thus, Level 1 or 'headline' indicators (listed in Table 2.2) at the top of the pyramid correspond to the main themes of the framework and monitor the overall objectives of the SDS. They are aimed at high-

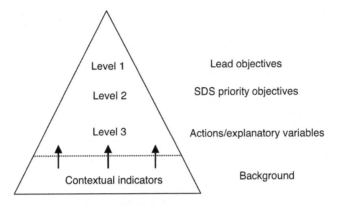

Figure 2.1   *The EU SDI pyramid (after EC, 2009)*

level policy-making and the general public. Level 2 indicators correspond to the sub-themes of the framework (and so the operational or priority objectives of the SDS) and, together with Level 1 indicators, monitor progress in achieving the headline policy objectives. Level 3 indicators relate to various implementing actions in the SDS. These indicators are aimed at further policy analysis and better understanding of the trends and complexities of the issues associated with each theme. They are intended for a more specialized audience. Finally, the three levels are complemented with contextual indicators, which provide valuable background information but which do not monitor directly the SDS objectives.

The main objective of the EU SDI set is to identify EU trends that are unsustainable or potentially unsustainable. The indicators are intended to give an overall picture of whether the EU has achieved progress towards sustainable development in terms of the objectives and targets defined in the EU SDS. The latest EUROSTAT report (EC, 2009) shows a rather mixed picture, as illustrated in Table 2.2.

2.3 National-Level Indicators

Many countries around the world assess progress towards sustainability using suitable national indicators. As an example of national-level indicators, the following section outlines the UK Government's framework for sustainable development indicators.

2.3.1 The UK Sustainable Development Indicators[3]

The UK sustainable development indicators stem from the national sustainable development strategy, *Securing the future*, launched in 2005 (Defra, 2005). A suite of 68 national sustainable development indicators was developed (see Table 2.3) to support the strategy. Included in the suite are 20 'framework indicators' which give an overview of sustainable

---

[3] Based on in the information provided by the UK Government (Defra, 2010b).

Table 2.3   *The UK sustainable development indicators (after Defra, 2010b)*

Sustainability theme and indicators

Greenhouse gas emissions

1. Greenhouse gas emissions[a]	Greenhouse gas and CO_2 emissions, and emissions associated with UK consumption
2. Carbon dioxide emissions by end user	CO_2 emissions from industry, domestic, transport sectors (excluding international aviation and shipping)
3. Aviation and shipping emissions	Greenhouse gases from UK-based international aviation and shipping fuel bunkers

Electricity generation

4. Renewable energy	Renewable electricity generated as a percentage of total electricity
5. Electricity generation	Electricity generated, CO_2, NO_x and SO_2 emissions by electricity generators and GDP

Carbon dioxide and other emissions

6. Household energy use	Domestic CO_2 emissions, domestic energy consumption and household spending
7. Road transport	CO_2, NO_x, PM10 emissions and GDP
8. Private cars	Private car CO_2 emissions, car-kilometres and household spending
9. Road freight	Heavy goods vehicle (HGV) CO_2 emissions, kilometres, tonnes and GDP
10. Manufacturing sector	Manufacturing sector CO_2, NO_x, SO_2, PM10 emissions and output
11. Service sector	Service sector CO_2, NO_x emissions and output
12. Public sector	Public sector CO_2, NO_x emissions and output

Resource use

13. Resource use	Domestic material consumption and GDP
14. Energy supply	UK indigenous energy production and gross inland energy consumption
15. Water resource use[a]	Total abstractions from nontidal surface and ground water, leakage losses and GDP
16. Domestic water consumption	Litres per person per day
17. Water stress	Impacts of water shortages

Waste

18. Waste[a]	Waste: (a) arisings by sector; (b) arisings by disposal
19. Household waste per person:	(a) Arisings; (b) recycled or composted

Natural resources

20. Bird populations[a]	Bird population indices: (a) farmland birds;[a] (b) woodland birds;[a] (c) coastal birds;[a] (d) wintering wetland birds
21. Biodiversity conservation	(a) Priority species status; (b) priority habitat status
22. Agriculture sector	Fertilizer input, farmland bird population, ammonia and methane emissions and output
23. Farming and environmental stewardship	Land covered by environmental schemes
24. Land use (contextual)	Area covered by agriculture, woodland, water or river, urban (contextual indicator)

Table 2.3   (Continued)

Sustainability theme and indicators	
25. Land recycling	(a) New dwellings built on previously developed land or through conversions; (b) all new development on previously developed land
26. Dwelling density	Average density of new housing
27. Fish stocks[a]	Sustainability of fish stocks around the UK
28. Ecological impacts of air pollution[a]	Area of sensitive UK habitats exceeding critical loads for acidification and eutrophication
29. Emissions of air pollutants	NH_3, NO_x, PM10 and SO_2 emissions and GDP
30. River quality[a]	Rivers of good (a) biological and (b) chemical quality
31. Flooding	Number of properties in areas at risk of flooding

Contextual indicators

32. Economic growth[a]	GDP
33. Productivity	UK output per worker
34. Investment	(a) Total investment; (b) social investment relative to GDP
35. Demography	Population and population of working age (contextual indicator)
36. Households and dwellings	Households, single-person households and dwelling stock (contextual indicator)

Society

37. Active community participation[a]	Informal and formal volunteering at least once a month in the last 12 months
38. Crime[a]	Crime survey and recorded crime for (a) vehicles, (b) domestic burglary, (c) robbery
39. Fear of crime	Fear of crime: (a) car theft; (b) burglary; (c) physical attack

Employment and poverty

40. Employment[a]	People of working age in employment
41. Workless households[a]	Population living in workless households: (a) children; (b) working age
42. Economically inactive	Percentage of people of working age who are economically inactive
43. Childhood poverty[a]	Children in relative low-income households: (a) before housing costs; (b) after housing costs
44. Young adults	16–19-year-olds not in employment, education or training
45. Pensioner poverty[a]	Pensioners in relative low-income households: (a) before housing costs; (b) after housing costs
46. Pension provision	Proportion of working age people contributing to a non-state pension in at least three years out of the last four

Education

47. Education[a]	19-year-olds with Level 2 qualifications and above
48. Sustainable development education:	To be developed to monitor the impact of formal learning on knowledge and awareness of sustainable development

Table 2.3   *(Continued)*

Sustainability theme and indicators

Health

49. Health inequality[a]	(a) Infant mortality: differences between socio-economic groups; (b) life expectancy: differences in average life expectancy between local authority areas
50. Healthy life expectancy	Healthy life expectancy: (a) men; (b) women
51. Mortality rates	Death rates from (a) circulatory disease and (b) cancer, below 75 years and for areas with the worst health and deprivation indicators, and (c) suicides
52. Smoking	Prevalence of smoking: (a) all adults; (b) 'routine and manual' socio-economic groups
53. Childhood obesity	Prevalence of obesity in 2–10-year-olds
54. Diet	Proportion of people consuming (a) five or more portions of fruit and vegetables per day and (b) in low income households

Mobility and access

55. Mobility[a]	(a) Number of trips per person by mode; (b) distance travelled per person per year by broad trip purpose
56. Getting to school	How children get to school
57. Accessibility	Access to key services
58. Road accidents	Number of people and children killed or seriously injured

Social justice/Environmental equality

59. Social justice[a]	Social measures to be developed
60. Environmental equality[a]	Populations living in areas with, in relative terms, the least favourable environmental conditions
61. Air quality and health	(a) Annual levels of particles and ozone; (b) days when air pollution is moderate or higher
62. Housing conditions	(a) Social sector homes; (b) vulnerable households in the private sector in homes below the decent homes standard
63. Households living in fuel poverty	Households living in fuel poverty containing (a) pensioners, (b) children, (c) disabled/long-term sick
64. Homelessness	(a) Number of rough sleepers; (b) number of households in temporary accommodation: (i) total; (ii) households with children
65. Local environment quality	Assessment of local environmental quality
66. Satisfaction in local area	Percentage of households satisfied with the quality of the places in which they live: (a) overall; (b) in deprived areas

International

67. UK international assistance	Net official development assistance: (a) percentage of GNI; (b) per capita

Well-being

68. Well-being[a]	Well-being measures

[a] Framework indicators.

development and highlight the four priority areas for the UK:

- sustainable consumption and production;
- climate change and energy;
- natural resource protection and enhancing the environment; and
- creating sustainable communities and a fairer world.

The indicators are first and foremost intended to communicate and highlight progress in key issues for sustainable development in the UK and, along with other evidence, to help identify where action is required.

2.4 Local-Level Indicators

After the World Sustainable Development Summit in Rio in 1992, many local authorities developed Local Agenda 21 (LA21) plans to address local sustainability issues. Subsequently, there have been numerous local-level initiatives to define sets of sustainable development indicators and measurement programmes. These efforts are characterized by broad public participation and a clear focus on community well-being, but in most cases they lack coherent organizing principles in the selection and use of indicators. Their merit often is in the process of how they use measurement tools and indicators.

The following gives an example of local-level indicators, developed in the UK.

2.4.1 The Local Quality of Life Indicators[4]

The local quality of life indicators were developed for use by local authorities in the UK to help them monitor the effectiveness of their sustainable community strategies (The Audit Commission/Defra/ODPM, 2005). The set of 61 indicators complements the UK Government Sustainable Development Strategy and they are organized around eight themes covering the local quality of life. As shown in Table 2.4, the indicators vary tremendously in type and design and rely on a range of different sources and collection methods for the data. Some are based on hard data and are relatively objective, whereas others rely on surveys and subjective opinion.

The main aim of indicators is to provide key measures to help 'paint a picture' of the quality of life in an area covering a range of important environmental, social and economic issues. There is no statutory requirement to use the entire set of indicators, but the UK Government recommends that local authorities use the indicators on a voluntary basis to help monitor the effectiveness of their sustainable community strategies. The data in Table 2.4 provide an example of the use of these indicators to measure the quality of life in London (The Audit Commission, 2010). Similar data are available for a number of other areas in the UK.

As we have seen so far, sustainability indicators are used on all spatial scales – from international to national and local. The ones that we described so far – the UN CSD indicators, the EU and the UK sustainable development indicators and the local quality of

---

[4] Based on the information provided by The Audit Commission (2010) and The Audit Commission/Defra/ODPM (2005).

Table 2.4   *The local quality of life indicators for London (after The Audit Commission, 2010)*

Sustainability themes and indicators	Value (2003–2007)
Community involvement and cohesion	
The percentage of residents who think that people being attacked because of their skin colour, ethnic origin or religion is a very big or fairly big problem in their local area	11.82 %
Percentage of residents who think that for their local area, over the past 3 years, that community activities have got better or stayed the same	91.89 %
Election turnout – at the last European elections	36.97 %
Economic well-being	
Percentage of the working age population who are in employment	83.5 %
Number of Job Seeker's Allowance claimants as a percentage of the working age population	1.5 %
Percentage of Job Seeker's allowance claimants who have been out of work for more than a year	21.1 %
Total number of VAT-registered businesses in the area at the end of the year	13 055
Job density: number of jobs filled to working age population	58.77
Percentage of the population living in the most deprived super output areas in the country	Not available
Percentage of working-age population claiming key benefits: total	0.44 %
Percentage of children that live in families that are income deprived	18.5 %
Percentage of the population over 60 who live in households that are income deprived	10.2 %
Housing	
Total number of new housing completions	2
Affordable dwellings completed as a percentage of all new housing completions	0.0 %
Household accommodation without central heating	4.6 %
The percentage of residents who think that people sleeping rough on the streets or in other public places a very big or fairly big problem in their local area	36.28 %
Percentage of all housing which is unfit	0.0 %
House price to income ratio	6.76
Environment	
Proportion of developed land that is derelict	0.0 %
Percentage of land and highways assessed as having unacceptable levels of litter and detritus	3.0 %
Percentage of land and highways from which unacceptable levels of graffiti are visible	2 %
Percentage of land and highways from which unacceptable levels of fly-posting are visible	2 %
Percentage of land and highways from which unacceptable levels of fly-tipping are visible	2 %
Local estimates of CO_2 emissions (tonnes CO_2) – domestic emissions per capita	2.9 t

Table 2.4   (*Continued*)

Sustainability themes and indicators	Value (2003–2007)
Local estimates of CO_2 emissions (tonnes CO_2) – total emissions per capita	220.3 t
Average annual domestic consumption of gas in kilowatt-hours	14 900 kWh
Average annual domestic consumption of electricity in kilowatt-hours	4649 kWh
Daily domestic water use (per capita consumption, litres)	161 l
Amount of household waste collected per head in kilograms	570.2 kg
Percentage of household waste recycled	28.10 %
Percentage of household waste composted	0.09 %
Percentage of household waste used to recover heat, power and other energy sources	5.28 %
Percentage of household waste landfilled	66.79 %
Area of land designated as a site of special scientific interest (SSSI) within the local authority area	0.00 ha
Percentage area of land designated as an SSSI within the local authority area, which is found to be in favourable condition	Not applicable
Transport and access	
Percentage of the resident population who travel to work by private motor vehicle (car, taxi or motorbike)	9.0 %
Percentage of the resident population who travel to work by public transport	30.3 %
Percentage of the resident population who travel to work on foot or cycle	49.5 %
Percentage of the resident population travelling over 20 km to work	3.6 %
Percentage of residents who think that for their local area, over the past 3 years, that public transport has got better or stayed the same.	74.66 %
Percentage of residents who think that for their local area, over the past 3 years, that the level of traffic congestion has got better or stayed the same.	74.13 %
Estimated traffic flows for all vehicle types (million-vehicle kilometres)	204 million-vehicle km
Community safety	
Domestic burglaries per 1000 households	Value suppressed
Violent offences committed per 1000 population	Value suppressed
Theft of a vehicle per 1000 population	Value suppressed
Sexual offences per 1000 population	Value suppressed
The percentage of residents who think that vandalism, graffiti and other deliberate damage to property or vehicles is a very big or fairly big problem in their local area	9 %
The percentage of residents who think that people using or dealing drugs is a very big or fairly big problem in their local area	22.68 %
The percentage of residents who think that people being rowdy or drunk in public places is a very big or fairly big problem in their local area	43.11 %
Health and social well-being	
Infant mortality rate: deaths up to 1 year per 1000 live births	Data not available
Percentage of households with one or more person with a limiting long-term illness	19.3 %

Table 2.4   *(Continued)*

Sustainability themes and indicators	Value (2003–2007)
Education and life-long learning	
Percentage of half days missed due to total absence in local authority primary schools	5.43 %
Percentage of the working age population who are qualified to NVQ2 and above	Data not available
Percentage of the working age population who are qualified to NVQ4 and above	56.3 %
Culture and leisure	
Percentage of the population that are within 20 min travel time (urban – walking; rural – driving) of a range of three different sports facility types, at least one of which has achieved a quality mark	97.4 %
Percentage of residents who think that for their local area, over the past 3 years, that activities for teenagers have got better or stayed the same	85.35 %
Percentage of residents who think that over the past 3 years, that cultural facilities (e.g. cinemas, museums) have got better or stayed the same	94.72 %
Percentage of residents who think that, over the past 3 years, that facilities for young children have got better or stayed the same	89.77 %
Percentage of residents who think that for their local area, over the past 3 years, that sports and leisure facilities have got better or stayed the same	94.18 %
Percentage of residents who think that for their local area, over the past 3 years, that parks and open spaces have got better or stayed the same	90.78 %

life indicators – are primarily being used to help policy makers measure progress towards international, national or local sustainability goals, targets and objectives.

Increasingly, the indicators are also being used to measure how businesses are performing in the same respect. The following section looks at some of the most conspicuous approaches to measure sustainability at corporate level.

2.5 Measuring Corporate Sustainability

Businesses are under growing pressure from internal and external stakeholders such as employees, customers, investors and local and national authorities for more environmentally and socially responsible, accountable and transparent behaviour aligned with the principles of sustainable development.

Whether a company operates in a socially and environmentally responsible way is becoming an important factor for people when making choices who to work for; which product and/or service to buy and where to invest their funds. Governments and civil society for their part increasingly demand that businesses consider not just their financial performance but also wider economic, environmental and social implications of their activities. For instance, companies' legislation in the UK – after recent changes introduced by the Companies Act 2006 (UK Government, 2006) – requires that quoted companies report information on environmental matters, the company's employees and social and community issues that are material to the company's business, together with information on the company's policies in these areas and the effectiveness of those policies. The Companies Act 2006 also defines a director's duty to promote the success of the company in a way that is consistent with the concept of 'enlightened shareholder value'. In this respect, directors are required to give due regard, among other aspects, to the impact of their decisions on employees, communities and the environment and report the company's performance using key performance indicators (UK Government, 2006).

The regulatory pressures like these, as well as stakeholder concerns, have prompted many businesses to make a commitment to applying the principles of sustainable development to their operations. To meet these commitments, a multitude of policies, plans and programmes have been developed. For instance, many corporations have created sustainable development policies, committed to stakeholder consultation, implemented environmental management systems and produced sustainable development reports (Searcy, 2009).

However, applying the principles of sustainable development in day-to-day decision-making processes requires, among other things, practical and cost-effective ways of assessing sustainability performance and measuring progress (Schwarz *et al.*, 2002). A crucial part of this task is the development and deployment of sustainable development indicators.

The increasing interest in sustainable development indicators in the business community has resulted in a number of approaches to measuring corporate sustainability being developed by various companies, business associations, NGOs and researchers. Some of the approaches are the results of efforts to address environmental issues and focus predominantly on the development of environmental indicators. (For an overview of the development of environmental indicators, see Olsthoorn *et al.*, 2001.)

Other approaches, alongside the environmental, try to include additional factors, mainly economic. One such example is *the eco-efficiency approach*, developed by The World Business Council for Sustainable Development (WBCSD), a global association of some 200 companies dealing exclusively with business and sustainable development. An overview of this approach was provided in Chapter 1; further detail is provided below.

2.5.1 Eco-Efficiency

The eco-efficiency concept focuses on creating more goods and services using fewer resources and generating less waste and pollution. The WBCSD (2000) defines eco-efficiency as being

> achieved by the delivery of competitively priced goods and services that satisfy human needs and bring quality of life, while progressively reducing ecological impacts and resource intensity throughout the life-cycle, to a level at least in line with the Earth's estimated carrying capacity.

The eco-efficiency tool is designed to promote improving both environmental and economic performance at a company level by addressing the whole life cycle of a product or process. According to the WBCSD, the seven measures of eco-efficiency are:

- material intensity of goods and services;
- energy intensity of goods and services;

- toxic dispersions;
- material recyclability;
- sustainable use of renewable resources;
- product durability; and
- service intensity of goods and services.

These measures of environmental performance are normalized with respect to an economic indicator, taken to be value added.

The WBCSD suggests that companies should measure their performance with regard to eco-efficiency by using the 'eco-efficiency indicators'. The eco-efficiency indicators are based on the eco-efficiency formula which brings together two sustainability dimensions – economy and the environment – to relate *product* or *service value* to *environmental influence*.

The eco-efficiency indicators fall into two groups. The first group relates to *product* or *service value* and includes quantity of goods or services produced or provided to customers and net sales. The second group of indicators relates to the *environmental influence* in product or service creation and considers:

- energy, materials and water consumption;
- greenhouse gas emissions; and
- ozone-depleting substance emissions.

As a measurement tool for the business sector, the eco-efficiency approach focuses on measuring *resource efficiency* (minimizing the resources used in producing a unit of output) and *resource productivity* (the efficiency of economic activities in generating added value from the use of resources). It also incorporates the *production of waste*.

The WBCSD suggests that the eco-efficiency concept should be applied throughout all operations of a company: reducing the consumption of resources, reducing the impacts on the natural environment and increasing the product or service value.

Although the WBCSD recognizes the importance of social factors, the eco-efficiency approach integrates only two of the three 'pillars' of sustainability, namely economy and the environment. The third pillar, social progress, is left outside the eco-efficiency's embrace.

There have been attempts to correct this absence of social dimension amongst those who apply the eco-efficiency approach to measure their sustainability performance. One of the more prominent efforts in this direction is BASF's SEEBalance approach.

2.5.2 BASF's Socio-Eco-Efficiency Tool (SEEBalance®)

BASF, one of the world's largest chemical companies, in collaboration with various German academic research institutions, has recently developed the 'Socio-Eco-Efficiency tool – SEEBalance®', which extends the original eco-efficiency framework to incorporate social sustainability of products and processes (BASF, 2010). Thus, the tool enables an integrated sustainability assessment on all three dimensions of sustainable development – economy, society and the environment. This is supported by a variety of tools incorporated within SEEBalance, including environmental life cycle assessment (LCA), economic life

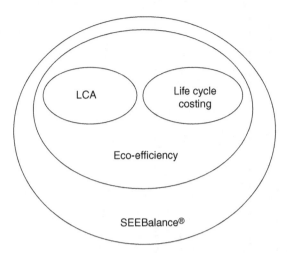

Figure 2.2   *The main components of the SEEBalance tool (adapted from BASF, 2010)*

cycle costing and social indicators. The main components of the tool are illustrated in Figure 2.2.

Within the SEEBalance tool, the social impacts are grouped into five categories (see Table 2.5), each using a set of indicators to address the social aspects that BASF considers important to them and to their stakeholders. As shown in the table, examples of the social indicators considered include the number of employees, occupational accidents and risks to the consumer associated with the use of the product.

In addition to the above two, many other company- and sector-specific approaches have been developed to help measure corporate sustainability (for an overview, see Azapagic and Perdan (2000) for example). As an example of a sector-specific approach, the 'Sustainability Metrics' developed by the Institution of Chemical Engineers (IChemE) for the process industries, is outlined next.

2.5.3 The IChemE Sustainability Metrics

Like SEEBalance, the IChemE's Sustainability Metrics (IChemE, 2002) also covers all three dimensions of sustainability – environmental, economic and social. However, their assessment scope is quite different: while the former takes a life cycle approach to cover all a company's operations from 'cradle to grave', the latter focuses mainly on a company's direct activities; that is, from 'gate to gate'. Although it is possible to take a life cycle approach within the Metrics, this is not a requirement. This is an obvious weakness, as large parts of the supply chain – and sustainability impacts – could be missed in the assessment.

Examples of the indicators included in the Metrics are given in Table 2.6. The environmental indicators estimate the environmental impacts associated with the use of resources and emissions into the environment, while the economic and social indicators measure the creation of wealth or value and the company's attitude to its stakeholders respectively.

Although the Metrics are designed for internal use, companies are encouraged to publish their assessment in whole or in part to demonstrate their commitment to sustainable development. The IChemE also encourages companies in the process sector to report their

Table 2.5 Social indicators considered in SEEBalance (BASF, 2010)

Social sustainability themes and indicators				
Working conditions for employees	International community	Future generations	Consumer	Local and national community
• Working accidents • Fatal working accidents • Occupational diseases • Toxicity potential + transport • Wages and salaries • Professional training (company expenditures) • Strikes and lockouts	• Child labour • Foreign direct investment • Imports from developing countries	• Number of trainees • R&D (company expenditure) • Capital investments • Social security	• Toxicity potential • Other risks and functional product characteristics	• Employees • Qualified employees • Gender equality • Integration of handicapped people • Part-time workers • Family support

Table 2.6 *Examples of sustainability indicators considered in the IChemE Sustainability Metrics (after IChemE, 2002)*

Economic indicators	Environmental indicators	Social indicators
Profit, value and tax	*Resource usage*	*Employment situation*
Sales	Electricity	Number of employees resigned
Value added	Fuels	or made redundant
Gross margin	Water	Number of employees
Net income before tax	Raw materials and	promoted
(NIBT)	packaging	Health and safety
Taxes (total paid to all	Raw material recycled	Lost time accident frequency
taxing authorities)		Expenditure on illness and
		accidents prevention
Investments	*Emissions, effluents and wastes*	*Society*
Average capital	Global warming	Number of meetings with
employed	Acidification	external stakeholders
Return on average capital	Ozone layer depletion	Indirect benefits to the
employed	Photochemical smog	community
Total wages and benefits	formation	Number of complaints
expense	Total solid waste disposal	registered from members of
Total training expense for		the public
direct employees		Number of successful legal
Number of indirect jobs		actions against company or
indirect job		employees
		Discrimination and child
		labour

performance according to the standards recommended by the Global Reporting Initiative (GRI). The GRI is currently one of the most widely used frameworks for sustainability measurement and reporting, and this is the subject of the next section.

2.5.4 Global Reporting Initiative (GRI)

The GRI is a framework for corporate reporting on sustainability performance initiated in 1997 by the US-based NGO 'Coalition of Environmentally Responsible Economies (CERES)' in partnership with the United Nations Environment Programme (UNEP). Since then, the GRI has seen several revisions and has been used by over 1000 companies over the period (GRI, 2010).

The GRI sustainability indicators also cover economic, environmental and social aspects and are divided into 'core' and 'additional' (GRI, 2006, 2010.). Core indicators are those of interest to most stakeholders and are assumed to be material to the business, while additional indicators represent emerging practice or address topics that may be relevant to some organizations but generally not for a majority. While the life cycle approach is not directly mentioned in the framework, most indicators cover direct and indirect impacts, covering the whole supply chain. Currently, there are 79 indicators in the GRI framework, of which 47 are 'core' and 32 are 'additional'. They are listed in Table 2.7.

Table 2.7   *The GRI Performance Indicators (after GRI, 2010)*

Economic	Social
Economic performance	**Social performance: labour practices and decent work**
EC1: Economic value generated and distributed, including revenues, operating costs, employee compensation, donations and other community investments, retained earnings, and payments to capital providers and governments. (Core)	*Employment*
	LA1: Total workforce by employment type, employment contract and region. (Core)
EC2: Financial implications and other risks and opportunities for the organization's activities due to climate change. (Core)	LA2: Total number and rate of employee turnover by age group, gender and region. (Core)
EC3: Coverage of the organization's defined benefit plan obligations. (Core)	LA3: Benefits provided to full-time employees that are not provided to temporary or part-time employees, by major operations. (Additional)
EC4: Significant financial assistance received from government. (Core)	*Labour/management relations*
Market presence	LA4: Percentage of employees covered by collective bargaining agreements. (Core)
EC5: Range of ratios of standard entry-level wage compared with local minimum wage at significant locations of operation. (Additional)	LA5: Minimum notice period(s) regarding significant operational changes, including whether it is specified in collective agreements. (Core)
EC6: Policy, practices and proportion of spending on locally based suppliers at significant locations of operation. (Core)	*Occupational health and safety*
EC7: Procedures for local hiring and proportion of senior management hired from the local community at significant locations of operation. (Core)	LA6: Percentage of total workforce represented in formal joint management-worker health and safety committees that help monitor and advise on occupational health and safety programs. (Additional)
Indirect economic impacts	LA7: Rates of injury, occupational diseases, lost days, and absenteeism, and number of work-related fatalities by region. (Core)
EC8: Development and impact of infrastructure investments and services provided primarily for public benefit through commercial, in-kind or pro bono engagement. (Core)	LA8: Education, training, counselling, prevention and risk-control programmes in place to assist workforce members, their families, or community members regarding serious diseases. (Core)
EC9: Understanding and describing significant indirect economic impacts, including the extent of impacts. (Additional)	LA9: Health and safety topics covered in formal agreements with trade unions. (Additional)

Table 2.7   (Continued)

Environmental	Social

Materials

EN1: Materials used by weight or volume. (Core)

EN2: Percentage of materials used that are recycled input materials. (Core)

Energy

EN3: Direct energy consumption by primary energy source. (Core)

EN4: Indirect energy consumption by primary source. (Core)

EN5: Energy saved due to conservation and efficiency improvements. (Additional)

EN6: Initiatives to provide energy-efficient or renewable-energy-based products and services, and reductions in energy requirements as a result of these initiatives. (Additional)

EN7: Initiatives to reduce indirect energy consumption and reductions achieved. (Additional)

Water

EN8: Total water withdrawal by source. (Core)

EN9: Water sources significantly affected by withdrawal of water. (Additional)

EN10: Percentage and total volume of water recycled and reused. (Additional)

Biodiversity

EN11: Location and size of land owned, leased, managed in, or adjacent to, protected areas and areas of high biodiversity value outside protected areas. (Core)

EN12: Description of significant impacts of activities, products and services on biodiversity in protected areas and areas of high biodiversity value outside protected areas. (Core)

EN13: Habitats protected or restored. (Additional)

Training and education

LA10: Average hours of training per year per employee by employee category. (Core)

LA11: Programmes for skills management and life-long learning that support the continued employability of employees and assist them in managing career endings. (Additional)

LA12: Percentage of employees receiving regular performance and career development reviews. (Additional)

Diversity and Equal Opportunity

LA13: Composition of governance bodies and breakdown of employees per category according to gender, age group, minority group membership and other indicators of diversity. (Core)

LA14: Ratio of basic salary of men to women by employee category. (Core)

Social performance: human rights

Investment and procurement practices

HR1: Percentage and total number of significant investment agreements that include human rights clauses or that have undergone human rights screening. (Core)

HR2: Percentage of significant suppliers and contractors that have undergone screening on human rights and actions taken. (Core)

HR3: Total hours of employee training on policies and procedures concerning aspects of human rights that are relevant to operations, including the percentage of employees trained. (Additional)

Non-discrimination

HR4: Total number of incidents of discrimination and actions taken. (Core)

Freedom of association and collective bargaining

HR5: Operations identified in which the right to exercise freedom of association and collective bargaining may be at significant risk, and actions taken to support these rights. (Core)

Table 2.7   *(Continued)*

Environmental	Social
EN14: Strategies, current actions, and future plans for managing impacts on biodiversity. (Additional) EN15: Number of IUCN Red List species and national conservation list species with habitats in areas affected by operations, by level of extinction risk. (Additional) *Emissions, effluents and waste* EN16: Total direct and indirect greenhouse gas emissions by weight. (Core) EN17: Other relevant indirect greenhouse gas emissions by weight. (Core) EN18: Initiatives to reduce greenhouse gas emissions and reductions achieved. (Additional) EN19: Emissions of ozone-depleting substances by weight. (Core) EN20: NO_x, SO_x and other significant air emissions by type and weight. (Core) EN21: Total water discharge by quality and destination. (Core) EN22: Total weight of waste by type and disposal method. (Core) EN23: Total number and volume of significant spills. (Core) EN24: Weight of transported, imported, exported, or treated waste deemed hazardous under the terms of the Basel Convention Annex I, II, III and VIII, and percentage of transported waste shipped internationally. (Additional) EN25: Identity, size, protected status and biodiversity value of water bodies and related habitats significantly affected by the reporting organization's discharges of water and runoff. (Additional) *Products and services* EN26: Initiatives to mitigate environmental impacts of products and services, and extent of impact mitigation. (Core) EN27: Percentage of products sold and their packaging materials that are reclaimed by category. (Core)	*Child labour* HR6: Operations identified as having significant risk for incidents of child labour, and measures taken to contribute to the elimination of child labour. (Core) *Forced and compulsory labour* HR7: Operations identified as having significant risk for incidents of forced or compulsory labour, and measures to contribute to the elimination of forced or compulsory labour. (Core) *Security practices* HR8: Percentage of security personnel trained in the organization's policies or procedures concerning aspects of human rights that are relevant to operations. (Additional) *Indigenous rights* HR9: Total number of incidents of violations involving rights of indigenous people and actions taken. (Additional) **Social performance: society** *Community* SO1: Nature, scope and effectiveness of any programs and practices that assess and manage the impacts of operations on communities, including entering, operating and exiting. (Core) *Corruption* SO2: Percentage and total number of business units analyzed for risks related to corruption. (Core) SO3: Percentage of employees trained in organization's anti-corruption policies and procedures. (Core) SO4: Actions taken in response to incidents of corruption. (Core) *Public policy* SO5: Public policy positions and participation in public policy development and lobbying. (Core)

Table 2.7 *(Continued)*

Environmental	Social

Compliance

EN28: Monetary value of significant fines and total number of nonmonetary sanctions for noncompliance with environmental laws and regulations. (Core)

Transport

EN29: Significant environmental impacts of transporting products and other goods and materials used for the organization's operations, and transporting members of the workforce. (Additional)

Overall

EN30: Total environmental protection expenditures and investments by type. (Additional)

SO6: Total value of financial and in-kind contributions to political parties, politicians and related institutions by country. (Additional)

Anti-competitive behaviour

SO7: Total number of legal actions for anti-competitive behaviour, anti-trust, and monopoly practices and their outcomes. (Additional)

Compliance

SO8: Monetary value of significant fines and total number of non-monetary sanctions for noncompliance with laws and regulations. (Core)

Social performance: product responsibility

Customer health and safety

PR1: Life cycle stages in which health and safety impacts of products and services are assessed for improvement, and percentage of significant products and services categories subject to such procedures. (Core)

PR2: Total number of incidents of noncompliance with regulations and voluntary codes concerning health and safety impacts of products and services during their life cycle, by types of outcome. (Additional)

Products and service labelling

PR3: Type of product and service information required by procedures, and percentage of significant products and services subject to such information requirements. (Core)

PR4: Total number of incidents of noncompliance with regulations and voluntary codes concerning product and service information and labelling, by types of outcome. (Additional)

Table 2.7   *(Continued)*

	Social
	PR5: Practices related to customer satisfaction, including results of surveys measuring customer satisfaction. (Additional)
	Marketing communications
	PR6: Programs for adherence to laws, standards and voluntary codes related to marketing communications, including advertising, promotion and sponsorship. (Core)
	PR7: Total number of incidents of noncompliance with regulations and voluntary codes concerning marketing communications, including advertising, promotion and sponsorship by types of outcome. (Additional)
	Customer privacy
	PR8: Total number of substantiated complaints regarding breaches of customer privacy and losses of customer data. (Additional)
	Compliance
	PR9: Monetary value of significant fines for noncompliance with laws and regulations concerning the provision and use of products and services. (Core)

As evidenced from the table, there is no doubt that the GRI provides a comprehensive and informative framework for companies and other organizations for assessing their sustainability performance and understanding the impacts (positive and negative) that they can have on sustainable development. The GRI also provides a useful tool for comparing sustainability performance within an organization and between different organizations over time. These are some of the reasons of increasing popularity of the GRI within the business community. A recent survey on corporate reporting, for instance, found that nearly 70 % of the 100 largest companies (by revenue) use the GRI guidelines for their sustainability reporting (KPMG, 2008). The GRI framework itself is constantly evolving, and draws its strength from the development process that seeks consensus through dialogue between stakeholders from business, the investor community, labour, civil society, accounting, academia and others.

2.6 Conclusions

Measurement and indicators play an important part in putting the concept of sustainable development in practice. They help decision makers define sustainable development objectives and targets and assess progress made towards meeting those targets.

Indicators play a key role in the measurement process. They are used to simplify information about complex phenomena, such as sustainable development, in order to make communication easier and, frequently, quantification possible (Hardi *et al.*, 1997).

In recent years we have seen numerous efforts by governments, businesses, communities, international agencies and NGOs aimed at establishing the means to assess and report on progress toward sustainable development. Development of sustainability indicators has been an integral part in this process.

This chapter has outlined some of the approaches that emerged from this process. We looked at some of the methods aimed at producing a 'green' GDP that would take at least the cost of pollution and natural capital depletion into account when assessing progress, as well as the examples of the indicators used to measure sustainability at different levels – from international and national, to local and corporate. Needless to say, the frameworks and indicators outlined in this chapter by no means exhaust the list of sustainability measurement approaches. Those described here are chosen simply to illustrate how the assessment and measurement of sustainability at different spatial and sectoral levels are being approached, not to provide the definitive guide to sustainability measurement.

It is fair to say that, despite some remarkable achievements in the development of sustainability indicators, there is still no broad consensus on the best way to measure progress towards sustainability. Thus, the efforts to produce new and 'better' indicators are continuing. We see constant evolvement and improvement of the existing frameworks as well as emergence of new initiatives. They all attempt to answer that simple question from the beginning of this chapter: How do we measure sustainability? Given the complexity of the concept of sustainable development and the inherent difficulty in measuring what counts for the well-being of both present and future generations, it should not be surprising that the search for the right answer is still very much ongoing.

References and Further Reading

Adriaanse, A. (1993) Environmental policy performance indicators. A study on the development of indicators for environmental policy in the Netherlands, Sdu Uitgeverij Koninginnegracht, The Hague.

AtKisson, A. (2005) Compass index of sustainability. Legacy 2000 report for Orlando and Orange County, Seattle and Boston. http://www.AtKisson.com.

Azapagic, A. and Perdan, S. (2000) Indicators of sustainable development for industry: a general framework. *Process Safety and Environmental Protection Part B: Transactions of Institution of Chemical Engineers*, **78**, 243–261.

Bartelmus, P. (2001) Accounting for sustainability: greening the national accounts, in *Our Fragile World, Forerunner to the Encyclopaedia of Life Support System* (ed. M.K. Tolba), vol. **II**, Eolss Publishers, Oxford, pp. 1721–1735.

BASF (2010) What is the SEEBALANCE®? http://www.basf.com/group/corporate/en/sustainability/eco-efficiency-analysis/seebalance.

Council of the European Union (2006) Review of the EU Sustainable Development Strategy (EU SDS). Renewed Strategy, Brussels, 26 June 2006.

Daly, H. and Cobb, J.B. (1989) *For the Common Good: Redirecting the Economy Toward Community, the Environment, and a Sustainable Future*, Beacon Press, Boston.

Defra (2005) *Securing the Future – the UK Government Sustainable Development Strategy*, HMSO, London.

Defra (2010a) The official UK Government website for sustainable development. Department for Environment, Food and Rural Affairs. http://webarchive.nationalarchives.gov.uk/20100113235321/defra.gov.uk/sustainable/government/.

Defra (2010b) National indicators. Department for Environment, Food and Rural Affairs. http://www.defra.gov.uk/corporate/about/with/localgov/indicators/index.htm.

EC (2007) Measuring progress towards a more sustainable Europe – 2007 monitoring report of the EU Sustainable Development Strategy. Luxembourg: Office for Official Publications of the European Communities. http://epp.eurostat.ec.europa.eu/cache/ITY_OFFPUB/KS-78-09-865/EN/KS-78-09-865-EN.PDF.

EC (2009) Sustainable development in the European Union – 2009 monitoring report of the EU sustainable development strategy. Luxembourg: Office for Official Publications of the European Communities. http://epp.eurostat.ec.europa.eu/cache/ITY_OFFPUB/KS-78-09-865/EN/KS-78-09-865-EN.PDF.

EEA, European Environment Agency (2001) *Total material requirement of the European Union.* European Environment Agency Technical report No 55. Copenhagen. http://reports.eea.eu.int/Technical_report_No_55/en.

ESDI (2010) *The ESDI Approach to Indicators.* http://www.sustreport.org/indicators/esdi_approach.html.

Friends of the Earth (2010) Replacing GDP. http://www.foe.co.uk/community/tools/isew/replace.html.

Global Reporting Initiative (GRI) (2006) Sustainability Reporting Guidelines: Version 3.0, GRI, Amsterdam, The Netherlands.

GRI (2010) Reporting Framework: GRI, Amsterdam. http://www.globalreporting.org/Reporting-Framework/.

Hammond, A., Adriaanse, A., Rodenburg, E. *et al.* (1995) Environmental Indicators: A Systematic Approach to Measuring and Reporting on Environmental Policy Performance in the Context of Sustainable Development. Washington, DC: World Resources Institute.

Hardi, P., Barg, S., Hodge, T. and Pinter, L. (1997) Measuring Sustainable Development: Review of Current Practice. Occasional Paper Number 17, November 1997, Industry Canada, Ottawa.

IChemE (2002) *The Sustainability Metrics Recommended for Use in the Process Industries,* The Institution of Chemical Engineers, Rugby.

IUCN, International Union for the Conservation of Nature and Natural Resources, and IDRC, International Development and Research Centre (Canada) (1997) *An Approach to Assessing Progress toward Sustainability: Tools and Training Series,* IUCN, IDRC, Gland, Switzerland.

Jackson, T., Marks, N., Ralls, J. and Stymne, S. (1997) *Sustainable Economic Welfare in the UK: 1950–1996,* New Economics Foundation, London.

Kennedy, R.,Address, University of Kansas, Lawrence, Kansas, 18 March 1968. http://www.jfklibrary.org/Historical + Resources/Archives/Reference + Desk/Quotations + of + Robert + F. + Kennedy.htm.

KPMG (2008) International Survey of Corporate Responsibility Reporting 2008, KPMG International, Netherlands.

Kuznets, S. (1934) National Income, 1929-1932. Senate document no. 124, 73d Congress, 2d session, 1934.

Moldan, B., Billharz, S.and Matravers, R. (eds) (1997) *Sustainability Indicators: Report on Project on Indicators of Sustainable Development,* Chichester, John Wiley.

NEF (2009) *Happy Planet Index,* New Economics Foundation, London.

Neumayer, E. (2000) On the methodology of ISEW, GPI and related measures: some constructive suggestions and some doubt on the 'threshold' hypothesis. *Ecological Economics,* **34,** 347–361.

Nordhaus, W. and Tobin, J. (1972) *Is Growth Obsolete?* Columbia University Press, New York.

Olsthoorn, X., Tyteca, D., Wehrmeyer, W. and Wagner, M. (2001) Environmental indicators for business: a review of literature and standardization methods. *Journal of Cleaner Production,* **9** (5), 453–463.

Parris, T.M. and Kates, R.W. (2003) Characterizing and measuring sustainable development. *Annual Review of Environment and Resources,* **28,** 559–586.

Pinter, L., Hardi, P. and Bartelmus, P. (2005) Indicators of sustainable development: proposals for a way forward. Discussion Paper prepared under a Consulting Agreement on behalf of the UN

Division for Sustainable Development. United Nations Division for Sustainable Development Expert Group Meeting on Indicators of Sustainable Development, New York, 13–15 December 2005.

Redefining Progress (2010) Genuine Progress Indicator. www.rprogress.org/sustainability_indicators/genuine_progress_indicator.htm.

Redefining Progress (2010a) About the Ecological Footprint, available at: http://www.rprogress.org/ecological_footprint/about_ecological_footprint.htm.

Schwarz, J., Beloff, B. and Beaver, E. (2002) Use sustainability metrics to guide decision-making. *Chemical Engineering Progress*, **98** (7), 58–63.

Searcy, C. (2009) *The Role of Sustainable Development Indicators in Corporate Decision-Making*, International Institute for Sustainable Development (IISD), Winnipeg.

Stockhammer, E., Hochreiter, H., Obermayr, B. and Steiner, K. (1997) The index of sustainable economic welfare (ISEW) as an alternative to GDP in measuring economic welfare: the results of the Austrian (revised) ISEW calculation 1955–1992. *Ecological Economics*, **21**, 19–34.

Talberth, J., Cobb, C. and Slattery, N. (2007) The Genuine Progress Indicator 2006, Report, Redefining Progress.

The Audit Commission/Defra/ODPM (2005) Local quality of life indicators – supporting local communities to become sustainable. London. http://www.areaprofiles.audit-commission.gov.uk/.

The Audit Commission (2010) Area Profiles. http://www.areaprofiles.audit-commission.gov.uk/.

UK Government (2006) Companies Act 2006, Chapter 46. HMSO, London.

UN CSD (1996) Indicators of sustainable development. The Department of Economic and Social Affairs, United Nations, New York. http://www.un.org/esa/sustdev/natlinfo/indicators/methodology_sheets.pdf.

UN CSD (2007) *Indicators of Sustainable Development: Guidelines and Methodologies*, 3rd edn, The Department of Economic and Social Affairs, United Nations, New York.

UN ESA (2010) Indicators of sustainable development. UN Department of Economic and Social Affairs. http://www.un.org/esa/dsd/dsd_aofw_ind/ind_index.shtml.

WBCSD (2000) Measuring eco-efficiency: a guide to reporting company performance. World Business Council for Sustainable Development.

WCED (1987) *Our Common Future*, World Commission on Environment and Development, Oxford University Press, Oxford.

WWF (2008) Living Planet Index. WWF International, Gland, Switzerland, available at: http://assets.panda.org/downloads/living_planet_report_2008.pdf.

3

Assessing Environmental Sustainability: Life Cycle Thinking and Life Cycle Assessment

Adisa Azapagic

The increased awareness of environmental issues and the need to understand better the impacts of human activities on the environment have led to the development of various approaches and tools to help assess environmental sustainability. Life cycle thinking and Life Cycle Assessment (LCA) are examples of such approaches and tools that have gained prominence over the past years. This chapter gives an overview of the LCA methodology and discusses applications of life cycle thinking. Several examples and case studies are presented to illustrate how environmentally sustainable products and activities can be identified.

3.1 Life Cycle Thinking

Environmental issues are characterized by their complexity, wide and far-reaching impacts and their close links with the economic and social aspects of sustainable development. For example, poor urban air quality caused by the emission of pollutants from road traffic affects human health and the quality of life in the local communities and has significant implications for social and economic viability of cities (see Chapter 14). Moreover, environmental impacts of road traffic in cities go well beyond local boundaries, as the emissions from urban transport are one of the major sources of anthropogenic greenhouse gases that cause global warming. And, as the latest estimates and predictions tell us (see Chapter 15), the resulting climate change will affect us all and could have devastating consequences for both humans and the natural environment. Thus, a single environmental issue such as urban air quality appears to be entangled in a web of wide and interconnected impacts.

Sustainable Development in Practice: Case Studies for Engineers and Scientists, Second Edition
Edited by Adisa Azapagic and Slobodan Perdan
© 2011 John Wiley & Sons, Ltd.

Understanding this complex web of environmental outcomes caused by human activities requires a systematic and comprehensive approach that goes beyond single issues and direct impacts.

In an attempt to understand and reduce environmental impacts of industrial and human activities, scientists and engineers have traditionally concentrated on the most immediate and visible outcomes of industrial and human activities. For example, in trying to protect the environment from the emissions from an industrial installation, we have often resorted to end-of-pipe technology to clean up air emissions or liquid effluents. Although clean-up technologies reduce the immediate pollution from the installation, the use of energy and chemicals and the need for further treatment and disposal of wastes generated in the clean-up process often lead to additional pollution further up- or down-stream of that industrial facility. Thus, instead of protecting the environment, we may inadvertently increase the overall impacts from that installation. Similarly, depending on the product, manufacturing may not be environmentally the most important stage in the life cycle; the product use or post-consumer waste may be a 'hot spot' instead.

As these examples indicate, we can only be sure that we are protecting the environment as a whole if we adopt a systems approach that will consider the whole life cycle of an activity. In this way we can obtain a full picture of human interactions with the environment and avoid shifting of environmental impacts from one life cycle stage to another (Azapagic, 2002, 2006).

This systems approach is known as life cycle thinking or a life cycle approach. It is also referred to as a 'cradle-to-grave' approach because it follows an activity from the extraction of raw materials ('cradle') to the return of wastes to the ground ('grave'). This is illustrated in Figure 3.1. Sometimes, the term 'cradle to cradle' is also used to denote the reuse of wastes as raw materials in the same or a different production system.

An important step in trying to understand the impacts of human interactions with the environment is the identification and quantification of environmental impacts of an activity from 'cradle to grave'. Life cycle assessment (LCA) is one of the tools that can help us do that.

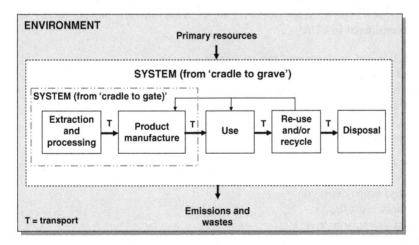

Figure 3.1 *The life cycle of a product from 'cradle to gate' and 'cradle to grave' (adapted from Azapagic, 2006)*

3.2 Life Cycle Assessment

LCA is an environmental management tool that helps to translate life cycle thinking into a quantitative measure of environmental sustainability of products, processes or activities on a life cycle basis. Although life cycle thinking and LCA have been used in some industrial sectors since the 1970s (e.g. nuclear energy), they have received wider attention and methodological development only since the beginning of the 1990s, when their relevance as an environmental management aid in both corporate decision-making and policy became more evident (Azapagic, 1999).

For example, life cycle thinking and LCA are enshrined in various EC Directives, including Integrated Pollution Prevention and Control (IPPC) (EC, 2008), End-of-life-Vehicles (EC, 2000) and Waste Electrical and Electronic Equipment (EC, 2003).

Today, LCA is a well-established tool and is used in a variety of applications in industry, research and public policy. Some of the applications include:

- measuring environmental sustainability;
- identification of environmentally more sustainable options;
- identification of 'hot spots' and improvement options;
- product design and process optimization; and
- product labelling.

A review of LCA applications can be found in, for example, Azapagic 1999, 2002, 2006, 2010. Some examples are presented further below; however, prior to that, the following sections give an overview of the LCA methodology and related aspects.

3.2.1 LCA Methodology

The LCA methodology is standardized by the International Organization for Standardization (ISO, 2006a), which defines LCA as '. . . a compilation and evaluation of the inputs, outputs and the potential environmental impacts of a product throughout its life cycle'.

As shown in Figure 3.1, the following stages in the life cycle of a product or an activity can be considered in LCA:

- extraction and processing of raw materials;
- manufacture;
- use, including any maintenance;
- reuse and recycling;
- final disposal; and
- transportation and distribution.

The LCA methodology comprises four phases (ISO, 2006a, 2006b) :

- goal and scope definition;
- inventory analysis;
- impact assessment; and
- interpretation.

The main steps in each phase and their interactions are shown in Figure 3.2. As shown, the methodology assumes an iterative approach whereby the phases are revisited throughout as

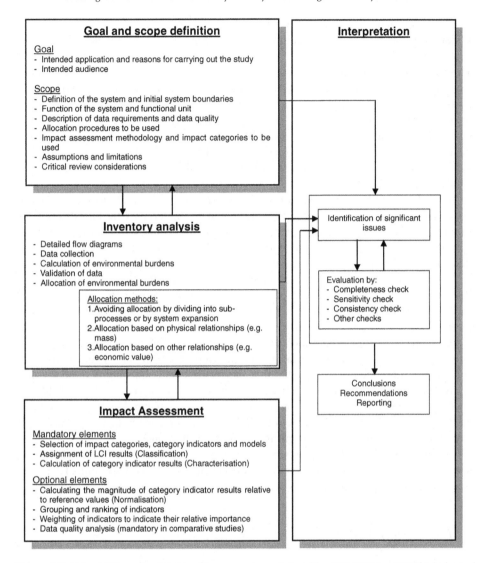

Figure 3.2 *The LCA methodological framework as defined by ISO (2006a, 2006b) (adapted from Azapagic, 2006)*

more information becomes available during an LCA study. The following sections give a brief overview of each phase.

3.2.1.1 Goal and Scope Definition

An LCA starts with a goal and scope definition, which includes:

- statement of the purpose of the study and its intended use;
- description of the system to be studied and definition of system boundaries;

- definition of the functional unit (or the unit of analysis); and
- identification of data quality requirements, the assumptions and limitations of the study.

The process of conducting an LCA study, as well as its outcomes, is largely determined by the goal and scope of the study. For example, the goal of the study may be to identify the 'hot spots' in a manufacturing process and to use the results internally by a company to reduce the environmental impacts from the process. Alternatively, the company may wish to use the results externally, either to provide LCA data to their customers or perhaps to market their product on the basis of environmental claims. In each case, the assumptions, data and system boundaries may be different, so it is important that these are defined in accordance with the goal of the study.

In full LCA studies, the system boundary is drawn from 'cradle to grave', encompassing all stages in the life cycle from extraction of raw materials to the final disposal (see Figure 3.1). However, in some cases, the scope of the study will demand a different approach, where it is not appropriate to include all stages in the life cycle. For example, this is usually the case with intermediate products that can have a number of different uses, so that it is not possible to follow their numerous life cycles after the production stage. As illustrated in Figure 3.1, the scope of such studies can be from 'cradle to gate', as they follow a product from the extraction of raw materials to the point where it leaves the factory gate.

One of the most important elements of an LCA study is a functional unit. The functional unit represents a quantitative measure of the outputs which the system delivers. In comparative LCA studies it is crucial that the systems are compared on the basis of an equivalent function; that is, the functional unit. For example, comparison of different beverage packagings should be based on their equivalent function, which is to contain a certain amount of beverage. The functional unit is then defined as 'the quantity of packaging material necessary to contain the specified volume of beverage'.

This phase also includes an assessment of the data quality and establishing the specific data quality goals. The study goal and scope are constantly reviewed and refined during the process of carrying out an LCA, as additional data become available.

3.2.1.2 Inventory Analysis

The purpose of life cycle inventory (LCI) analysis is to identify and quantify the environmental burdens in the life cycle of the activity under study. The burdens represent materials and energy used in the system and gaseous, liquid and solid waste discharged into the environment. LCI includes the following steps:

- detailed definition of the system under study;
- data collection and validation;
- allocation of environmental burdens in multiple-function systems; and
- estimation of the burdens across the whole system.

Following the preliminary system definition in the goal and scope definition phase, detailed system specification is carried out in LCI to identify the data needs. 'System' is defined as a collection of materially and energetically connected operations which perform some

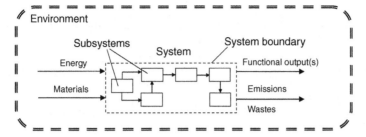

Figure 3.3   *Definition of system, system boundary and the environment*

defined function. The system is 'separated' from the environment by a system boundary; this is illustrated in Figure 3.3.

Detailed system characterization involves its disaggregation into a number of interlinked subsystems; this is represented by flow diagrams (see Figure 3.3). Depending on the data available, the subsystems can represent unit operations (e.g. a chemical reactor) or a group of units (e.g. reactor, pump and compressor). Environmental burdens are then quantified for each subsystem according to the formula

$$B_j = \sum_{i=1}^{I} bc_{j,i} x_i \tag{3.1}$$

where $bc_{j,i}$ is burden j from subsystem or activity i and x_i is a mass or energy flow associated with that activity. A simple example in Box 3.1 illustrates how the burdens can be calculated.

Box 3.1   Calculating environmental burdens and impacts in LCA: an example

The system shown below has one functional output (product) and each activity i from extraction of raw materials to final disposal generates a certain amount of CO_2 and CH_4 emissions. For example, the output from the activity 'Extraction' (x_1) is 2 t of raw materials per functional unit (FU). This activity is associated with the emissions of 0.2 kg of CO_2 and 0.1 kg of CH_4 per tonne of raw materials extracted. The product output from activity 'Use' (x_3) is defined as the functional unit and is equal to 1 t.

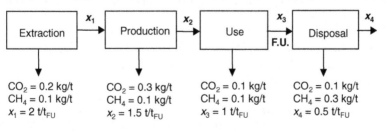

Using Equation 3.1, the total environmental burdens per functional unit related to the emissions of CO_2 and CH_4 are therefore

$$B_{CO_2} = \sum bc_{CO_2} x_i = 0.2 \times 2 + 0.3 \times 1.5 + 0.1 \times 1 + 0.1 \times 0.5 \Rightarrow B_{CO_2} = 1.0 \, kg/t_{FU}$$

$$B_{CH_4} = \sum bc_{CH_4} x_i = 0.1 \times 2 + 0.1 \times 1.5 + 0.1 \times 1 + 0.3 \times 0.5 \Rightarrow B_{CH_4} = 0.6 \, kg/t_{FU}$$

Global warming potential related to these two greenhouse gases can be calculated by applying Equation 3.2 and the classification factors for CO_2 (1 kg CO_2 eq./kg CO_2) and CH_4 (25 kg CO_2 eq./kg CH_4):

$$E_{GWP} = ec_{CO_2} B_{CO_2} + ec_{CH_4} B_{CH_4} = 1 \times 1 + 25 \times 0.6 \Rightarrow E_{GWP} = 16 \, kg \, CO_2 \, eq./t_{FU}$$

If the system under study produces more than one functional output, then the environmental burdens from the system must be allocated among these outputs. This is the case with co-product, waste treatment and recycling systems; such systems are termed 'multiple-function' systems. Allocation is the process of assigning to each function of a multiple-function system only those environmental burdens that each function is 'responsible' for. An example of a co-product system is a naphtha cracker. This produces several products, including ethylene, propylene, butenes and pyrolysis gasoline. The allocation problem here is to assign to each of the products (functional outputs) only those environmental burdens that they have generated. The simplest approach is to use either a mass or economic basis, allocating the total burden (e.g. emission of CO_2) in proportion to the mass output or economic value of each product. The allocation method used will usually influence the results of the LCA study, so that the identification of an appropriate allocation method is crucial. To guide the choice of the correct allocation method, ISO recommends a three-step allocation procedure (ISO, 2006b); this is explained in Box 3.2. Sensitivity analysis should be carried out in cases where the use of different allocation methods is possible to determine the influence of the allocation method on the results.

3.2.1.3 Impact Assessment

In this phase, the environmental burdens are translated into the related potential environmental impacts (or category indicators). Life Cycle Impact Assessment (LCIA) involves the following three steps:

- selection of impact categories, category indicators and LCIA models;
- classification; and
- characterization.

The selection of impact categories, category indicators and LCIA models must be consistent with the goal and scope of the LCA study and must reflect the environmental issues of the system under study.

Box 3.2   The ISO allocation procedure

The international standard ISO 14 044 (ISO, 2006b) prescribes a three-step procedure for avoiding or performing allocation:

1. Where possible, allocation is to be avoided by subdividing the process by analysis at a greater level of detail, or by system expansion.

   Avoiding allocation by subdividing the system is often not possible due to insufficient data, so that system expansion is applied more commonly. System expansion is illustrated on a simple example in the figures below: if System 1 produces products A and B and System 2 produces only product C, and A is to be compared with C, then allocation can be avoided in two ways:

   i. The system can be broadened so that an alternative way of producing B is added to System 2. The comparison is now between System 1 producing A + B and Systems 2 and 3 producing C + B (see Figure i).
   ii. The burdens arising from the alternative way of producing B can be subtracted from System 1, so that now only A is compared with C (see Figure ii). This is also known as the 'avoided burdens' method and is mainly used for systems where a co-product can replace one or more other products; for example, heat from co-generation to substitute heat from oil.

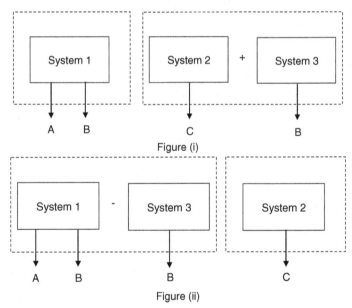

Figure (i)

Figure (ii)

The principal difficulty with system expansion lies in the selection of the additional process 3. Should this be the average of current processes making B, or the current best processes, or likely future processes, or the current least economic processes (on the argument that these are the processes which will be displaced if System 1 is brought into operation)? Appropriate selection of the expanded system depends on the goals and scope of the LCA study; see Weidema (2001).

2. Where allocation cannot be avoided, the environmental impacts should be parti-
tioned between the system's 'different products or functions in a way which reflects
the underlying physical relationships between them' (ISO, 2006b). In other words,
allocation should reflect the way that the system in question actually functions by
allocating an environmental impact to a functional output according to how much the
impact changes with a change in that output while other outputs are kept constant.
This is known as the *marginal allocation* approach. For examples of the application
of this approach, see Azapagic and Clift (1999) and Baumann and Tillman (2003).
3. If neither of these approaches is possible, then allocation should be on a basis 'which
reflects other relationships' between the products. This approach is most commonly
necessary when two or more products must be produced together in fixed proportions; for example, chlorine and sodium hydroxide from electrolysis of brine or beef
and leather from a cow. The 'other relationships' are most commonly the economic
values of the co-products.

Classification involves aggregation of environmental burdens into a smaller number of
environmental impact categories to indicate their potential impacts on human and ecological health and the extent of resource depletion. The aggregation is carried out on the
basis of the potential impacts of the burdens, so that one burden can be associated with a
number of impacts; for example, chlorofluorocarbons (CFCs) contribute to both global
warming and ozone layer depletion.

The identification of impacts of interest is then followed by their quantification in the
next, characterization step using an appropriate LCIA method. An overview of LCIA
methods is given in Section 3.2.2.

In general, the impacts are calculated relative to the characterization factor of a reference
substance as follows:

$$E_k = \sum_{j=1}^{J} ec_{k,j} B_j \qquad (3.2)$$

where $ec_{k,j}$ represents characterization factor k for burden B_j showing its relative
contribution to impact E_k. For example, CO_2 is a reference gas for determining global
warming potentials of other related gases, such as CH_4 and N_2O; therefore, its characterization factor is 1 kg CO_2 eq./kg CO_2, whilst that of CH_4 is 25 kg CO_2 eq./kg CH_4. A simple
example of how to calculate global warming potential (GWP) is illustrated in Box 3.1.
Three further optional steps in LCIA are:

- normalization;
- grouping; and
- weighting of impacts.

The impacts can be normalized with respect to the total emissions or extractions in a certain
area and over a given period of time. This can help to assess the extent to which an activity
contributes to the regional or global environmental impacts.

Grouping involves qualitative or semi-quantitative sorting and/or ranking of impacts and it may result in a broad ranking or hierarchy of impact categories with respect to their importance. For example, categories could be grouped in terms of high importance, moderate importance and low-priority issues.

The final optional stage within LCIA is weighting of impacts, often referred to as valuation. It involves assigning weights of importance to the impacts to indicate their relative importance. As a result, all impact categories are aggregated into a single environmental impact function EI as follows:

$$\text{EI} = \sum_{k=1}^{K} w_k E_k \tag{3.3}$$

where w_k is the relative importance of impact E_k.

A number of valuation methods have been suggested. They are mainly based on expressing preferences by decision-makers, by 'experts' or by the public. Some of these methods include multiattribute utility theory, analytic hierarchy process and cost–benefit analysis.

Valuation is the most subjective part of LCA because it involves social, political and ethical value choices. At present, there is no consensus on how to aggregate the environmental impacts into a single environmental impact function, or even on whether such aggregation is conceptually and philosophically valid. Many argue that valuation should not be carried out at all, as it obscures information and that considering the impacts in a disaggregated form enhances transparency of decision making based on LCA results. The ISO methodology discourages valuation of environmental impacts.

3.2.1.4 Interpretation

The final LCA phase involves:

- identification of major burdens and impacts;
- identification of 'hot spots' in the life cycle;
- sensitivity analysis; and
- evaluation of LCA findings and final recommendations.

Quantification of environmental impacts carried out in LCIA enables identification of the most significant impacts and the life cycle stages that contribute to these impacts. This information can then be used to target these 'hot spots' for system improvements or innovation.

Before the final conclusions and recommendations of the study are made it is important to carry out a sensitivity analysis. Data availability and reliability are some of the main issues in LCA, since the results and conclusions of an LCA study will be determined by the data used. Sensitivity analysis can help identify the effects that data variability, uncertainties and data gaps have on the final results of the study and indicate the level of reliability of the final results of the study.

Finally, the findings and conclusions of the study are reported in accordance with the intended use of the study. The report should give a complete, transparent and unbiased

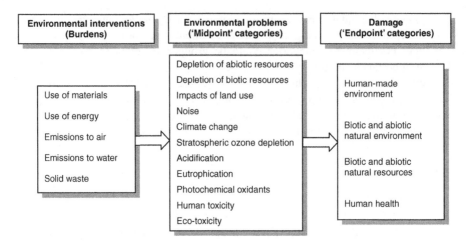

Figure 3.4   *Links between environmental interventions, problems (midpoint categories) and damage (endpoint categories) to the environment and human health (adapted from Azapagic, 2006)*

account of the study as detailed in ISO 14 044 (ISO, 2006b). If the study is used externally, critical review by an independent agent should be carried out.

Further detail on the LCA methodology can be found in the ISO 14 040 and 14 044 standards (ISO, 2006a, 2006b).

3.2.2 Life Cycle Impact Assessment Methods

There are a number of LCIA methods, but, in general, they can be divided into two groups:

1. problem-oriented approaches; and
2. damage-oriented methods.

In the problem-oriented methods, the environmental burdens are aggregated according to their relative contribution to the environmental impacts that they might cause. They are often referred to as 'midpoint' approaches (see Figure 3.4), because they link the environmental burdens somewhere in between the point of their occurrence (e.g. emissions of CO_2) and the ultimate damage caused by that intervention (e.g. GWP). Damage-oriented methods, on the other hand, model the 'endpoint' damage caused by environmental burdens to 'areas of protection', which include human health and natural and human-made environments (Udo de Haes and Lindeijer, 2002). The most-widely used problem-oriented method is the CML 2 method (Guinée *et al.*, 2001); Eco-indicator 99 (Goedkoop and Spriensma, 2001) is the damage-oriented method used most often. A brief overview of each is given below; further detail can be found in Boxes 3.3 and 3.4 respectively.

Box 3.3   CML 2 baseline method: definition of environmental impact categories (Azapagic, 2006)

Abiotic resource depletion potential represents depletion of fossil fuels, metals and minerals. The total impact is calculated as:

$$ADP = \sum_{j=1}^{J} ADP_j B_j \quad (\text{kg Sb eq.})$$

where B_j is the quantity of abiotic resource j used and ADP_j represents the abiotic depletion potential of that resource. This impact category is expressed in kilograms of antimony used, which is taken as the reference substance for this impact category. Alternatively, kilograms of oil equivalent can be used instead.

Impacts of land use are calculated by multiplying the area of land used A by its occupation time t:

$$ILU = A \times t \quad (\text{m}^2 \cdot \text{year})$$

Climate change represents the total global warming potential (GWP) of different greenhouse gases (GHGs), such as carbon dioxide (CO_2), methane (CH_4), nitrous oxide (N_2O) and so on. GWP is calculated as the sum of emissions of GHGs multiplied by their respective GWP factors GWP_j:

$$GWP = \sum_{j=1}^{J} GWP_j B_j \quad (\text{kg CO}_2 \text{ eq.})$$

where B_j represents the emission of GHG j. GWP factors for different GHGs are expressed relative to the GWP of CO_2, which is defined as unity. The values of GWP depend on the time horizon over which the global warming effect is assessed. GWP factors for shorter times (20 and 50 years) provide an indication of the short-term effects of GHGs on the climate, while GWPs for longer periods (100 and 500 years) are used to predict the cumulative effects of these gases on the global climate.

Stratospheric ozone depletion potential (ODP) indicates the potential of emissions of chlorofluorohydrocarbons (CFCs) and other halogenated hydrocarbons to deplete the ozone layer and is expressed as:

$$ODP = \sum_{j=1}^{J} ODP_j B_j \quad (\text{kg CFC-11 eq.})$$

where B_j is the emission of ozone-depleting gas j. The ODP factors are expressed relative to the ODP of CFC-11.

Human toxicity potential (HTP) is calculated by taking into account releases toxic to humans to three different media; that is, air, water and soil:

$$HTP = \sum_{j=1}^{J} HTP_{jA} B_{jA} + \sum_{j=1}^{J} HTP_{jW} B_{jW} + \sum_{j=1}^{J} HTP_{jS} B_{jS} \quad (\text{kg 14-DB eq.})$$

where HTP_{jA}, HTP_{jW} and HTP_{jS} are toxicological classification factors for substances emitted to air, water and soil respectively, and B_{jA}, B_{jW} and B_{jS} represent the respective emissions of different toxic substances into the three environmental media. The reference substance for this impact category is 1,4-dichlorobenzene.

Eco-toxicity potential (ETP) is also calculated for all three environmental media and comprises five indicators ETP_n:

$$ETP_n = \sum_{j}^{J} \sum_{i=1}^{I} ETP_{i,j} B_{i,j} \quad (\text{kg } 1,4\text{-DB eq.})$$

where n ($n = 1$–5) represents freshwater aquatic toxicity, marine aquatic toxicity, freshwater sediment toxicity, marine sediment toxicity and terrestrial ecotoxicity respectively. $ETP_{i,j}$ represents the ecotoxicity classification factor for toxic substance j in the compartment i (air, water, soil) and $B_{i,j}$ is the emission of substance j to compartment i. ETP is based on the maximum tolerable concentrations of different toxic substances in the environment by different organisms. The reference substance for this impact category is also 1,4-dichlorobenzene.

Photochemical oxidants creation potential (POCP) is related to the potential of volatile organic compounds (VOCs) and nitrogen oxides (NO_x) to generate photo-chemical or summer smog. It is usually expressed relative to the POCP of ethylene and can be calculated as:

$$POCP = \sum_{j=1}^{J} POCP_j B_j \quad (\text{kg ethylene eq.})$$

where B_j is the emission of species j participating in the formation of summer smog and $POCP_j$ is its classification factor for photochemical oxidation formation.

Acidification potential (AP) is based on the contribution of sulfur dioxide (SO_2), NO_x and ammonia (NH_3) to the potential acid deposition. AP is calculated according to the equation:

$$AP = \sum_{j=1}^{J} AP_j B_j \quad (\text{kg } SO_2 \text{ eq.})$$

where AP_j represents the acidification potential of gas j expressed relative to the AP of SO_2 and B_j is its emission in kilograms.

Eutrophication potential (EP) is defined as the potential of nutrients to cause overfertilization of water and soil, which can result in increased growth of biomass (algae). It is calculated as:

$$EP = \sum_{j=1}^{J} EP_j B_j \quad (\text{kg } PO_4^{3-} \text{ eq.})$$

where B_j is an emission of species such as N, NO_x, NH_4^+, PO_4^{3-}, P and chemical oxygen demand (COD); EP_j represent their respective eutrophication potentials. EP is expressed relative to PO_4^{3-}.

See Guinée *et al.* (2001) for a full description of the methodology.

3.2.2.1 CML 2 Method

In this approach, environmental burdens are aggregated according to their relative contributions to the environmental problem or impact that they can potentially cause. The following impacts, defined as midpoint categories, are usually considered (see Figure 3.4):

- abiotic resource depletion;
- global warming;
- ozone depletion;
- acidification;
- eutrophication;
- photochemical oxidant formation (summer smog);
- human toxicity; and
- eco-toxicity (freshwater, marine and terrestrial).

The impacts calculated by this method are referred to as potential rather than actual as they are quantified at the intermediate position between the point of environmental intervention and the damage caused, rather than at the endpoint. Box 3.3 provides definitions of the above impacts and the calculation method used in the CML 2 method.

3.2.2.2 Eco-Indicator 99

This method links the midpoint and endpoint impact categories, as shown in Figure 3.4. It is based on European environmental conditions. Three areas of protection or types of damage are considered within this method (Goedkoop and Spriensma, 2001):

- damage to human health, expressed in disability adjusted life years (DALYs);
- percentage damage to ecosystem quality, expressed in terms of potentially disappeared fraction (PDF) of plant species in a certain area over certain time; and
- damage to mineral and fossil resources, expressed as additional energy requirement in megajoules to extract future lower grade ores.

These damage categories are defined in Box 3.4. Their calculation involves three steps:

3. resource, land use and fate analysis;
4. exposure and effect analysis; and
5. damage analysis.

Various empirical fate and exposure models are used within Eco-indicator 99 (see Goedkoop and Spriensma (2001) for details). Damage analysis involves calculation of the damage categories by multiplying the environmental interventions by the appropriate characterization factors. The damage categories are then normalized using the normalization factors for Europe. The normalized results are often divided by the number of people in Europe, to show damage caused by one person per year.

   To indicate the importance or contribution of different environmental impacts to each of the three damage categories, different weighting factors can be applied. The weights are

---

Box 3.4   Eco-indicator 99: definition of the damage (endpoint) categories

1. Damage to human health
   This damage category comprises the following indicators:
   • carcinogenesis;
   • respiratory effects;
   • ionizing radiation;
   • ozone layer depletion; and
   • climate change.
   They are all expressed in disability adjusted life years (DALYs) and calculated by carrying out:
   i. fate analysis, to link an emission (expressed in kg) to a temporary change in concentration;
   ii. exposure analysis, to link the temporary concentration change to a dose;
   iii. effect analysis, to link the dose to a number of health effects, such as occurrence and types of cancer; and finally,
   iv. damage analysis, to link health effects to DALYs, using the estimates of the number of years lived disabled (YLD) and years of life lost (YLL).
   For example, if a cancer causes a 10-year premature death, this is counted as 10 YLL and expressed as 10 DALYs. Similarly, hospital treatment due to air pollution has a value of 0.392 DALYs/year; if the treatment lasted 3 days (or 0.008 years), then the health damage is equal to 0.003 DALYs.

2. Damage to ecosystem quality
   The indicators within this damage category are expressed in terms of potentially disappeared fraction of plant species (PDF) due to the environmental load in a certain area over a certain time. Therefore, damage to ecosystem quality is expressed as PDF m^2 year. The following indicators are considered:
   • Ecotoxicity, which is expressed as the percentage of all species present in the environment living under toxic stress (potentially affected fraction or PAF). As this is not an observable damage, a rather crude conversion factor is used to translate toxic stress into real observable damage; that is, convert PAF into PDF.
   • Acidification and eutrophication, which are treated as one single impact category. Damage to target species (vascular plants) in natural areas is modelled. The model used is for the Netherlands only, and it is not suitable to model phosphates.
   • Land use and land transformation, which are based on empirical data of occurrence of vascular plants as a function of land use types and area size. Both local damage in the area occupied or transformed and regional damage to ecosystems are taken into account.
   For ecosystem quality, two different approaches are used:
   i. Toxic, acid and the emissions of nutrients go through the following three steps:
       • fate analysis, linking the emissions to concentrations;
       • effect analysis, linking concentrations to toxic stress or increased nutrient or acidity levels; and
       • damage analysis, to link these effects with the PDF of plant species.
   ii. Land use and transformation are modelled on the basis of empirical data on the quality of ecosystems, as a function of the type of land use and area size.

3. Damage to resources

   Two indicators are included here: depletion of minerals and fossil fuels. They are expressed as additional energy in megajoules that will be needed for extraction in the future due to decreasing amounts of minerals and fuels. Geostatical models are used to relate the availability of a mineral resource to its remaining amount or concentration. For fossil fuels, the additional energy is based on the future use of oil shale and tar sands.

   Resource extraction is modelled in two steps:

   i.   resource analysis, which is similar to fate analysis, as it links an extraction of a resource to a decrease in its concentrations (through geostatical models);
   ii. damage analysis, linking decreased concentrations of resources to the increased effort for their extraction in the future.

More detail on Eco-indicator 99 can be found in Goedkoop and Spriensma (2001).

---

derived from the cultural theory, taking into account three different general types of people and their perspectives on life: hierarchist, egalitarian and individualist (see Box 3.5). For example, in the human health category, the hierarchist would assign the highest importance to the respiratory effects from inorganic substances, a relatively low importance to carcinogenic effects and almost no importance to radiation effects.

Finally, the damage categories are aggregated into a single environmental impact function – eco-indicator – by using a further set of weights, again applying the hierarchist, egalitarian and individualist perspectives. Therefore, this method involves a two-stage weighting process: first, the impact categories are weighted to aggregate them into the three damage categories, followed by the weighting of the damage categories to derive the eco-indicator. The characteristics of the three perspectives and the respective weights used to aggregate the damage categories into the eco-indicator are summarized in Box 3.5.

3.2.3 LCA Data and Software

Data availability is one of the most important issues in LCA. In general, two types of data can be distinguished:

- foreground or primary data, relating to the specific processes and parts of the system which are of primary interest for the study; and
- background or secondary data relate to the parts of the system which supply materials and energy to the foreground system.

Primary data are preferred but not always available, so background data often have to be used. There are numerous LCA databases providing background data within a software package, including CCaLC (Azapagic *et al.*, 2010) and Gemis (2007), which are freely available, and Ecoinvent (2007), Gabi (PE International, 2008) and SimaPro (PRé Consultants, 2008), which are available commercially.

Table 3.1 *Summary of the cultural perspectives, the most dominant impacts and the weights used to derive the eco-indicator (after Goedkoop and Spriensma (2001)*

Perspective	Time perspective	Management of environmental problems	Required level of evidence of damage	Most dominant impacts	Weighting[a]
Hierarchist	Balance between short and long term	Proper policy can avoid many problems	Inclusion based on consensus	Land use Respiratory effects Fossil fuels	HH – 40 % EQ – 40 % R – 20 %
Egalitarian	Very long term	Problems can lead to catastrophe	All possible effects	Land use Respiratory effects Fossil fuels	HH – 30 % EQ – 50 % R – 20 %
Individualist	Short time	Technology can avoid many problems	Only proven effects	Respiratory effects Minerals Land use Climate change	HH – 55 % EQ – 25 % R – 20 %

[a]HH: human health; EQ: ecosystem quality; R: resources.

Box 3.5   Cultural perspectives used in the eco-indicator method

In the hierarchist approach, the contributions of human health and ecosystem quality to the total eco-indicator are 40 % each. If the egalitarian perspective is applied, ecosystem quality contributes 50 % to the eco-indicator, while human health and damage to resources contribute 30 % and 20 % respectively. In the individualist perspective, human health is by far the most important category, contributing 55 % to the total impact. For all three perspectives, land use, respiratory effects from inorganic substances and fossil fuels are the most important impact categories, while respiratory effects from organic substances (summer smog), ionizing radiation and ozone depletion play an insignificant role. The individual weights for the impact categories for different perspectives can be found in Goedkoop and Spriensma (2001). See Table 3.1 for more detail.

Most databases contain data for Europe and North America only; data for developing countries are still scant. This poses a problem in many LCA studies, given that supply chains are global and that increasingly goods are manufactured in developing parts of the world and imported into developed countries.

3.2.4 Types of LCA Study

Generally, two types of LCA study can be distinguished: attributional and consequential (e.g. Curran *et al.*, 2001; Ekvall and Weidema, 2004). In attributional studies, the impacts are attributed to the system of interest based on the flows in and out of the system as they occur. In consequential LCA studies, the aim is to estimate how the flows to and from the system would change as a result of different potential decisions. The difference between the two approaches is significant, both with respect to the methodology and to the outcomes of the study.

For example, in an attributional LCA of biofuel, impacts from the production of biofuel from wheat would be estimated (attributed) based on the inputs into and outputs from this system, not taking into account what happens with the other related activities in the economy; for example, if the supply of wheat is constrained due to its use for bread production or livestock feed. A consequential LCA of biofuel, on the other hand, would attempt to quantify the impacts of diverting wheat into biofuel production and having to supply food or feed from alternative sources or from elsewhere in the world.

Most LCA studies are based on the attributional approach.

3.3 Using LCA as an Environmental Sustainability Tool: Some Examples

As mentioned at the beginning of this chapter, LCA can be used for different purposes. Some of these applications are illustrated by examples below; further examples and cases studies are provided throughout the book, particularly in Chapters 6, 8, 9, 11, 13 and 14.

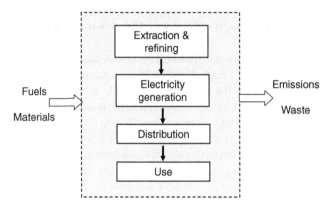

Figure 3.5   *The life cycle of electricity generation*

3.3.1 Measuring Environmental Sustainability and Identifying More Sustainable Alternatives

LCA has been used extensively for measuring sustainability and identifying sustainable alternatives. A typical example of such an application is in the electricity sector, usually to assess the sustainability and compare different fossil-fuel and renewable options on a life cycle basis.

As shown in Figure 3.5, the life cycle of electricity generation involves extraction of fuels and construction materials, conversion of fuels or energy carriers to electricity, its distribution and final use. Each stage in the life cycle is associated with certain environmental burdens, including consumption of resources and various emissions to the environment.

As an illustration, the environmental impacts of several electricity-generating options are compared in Figure 3.6 (global warming potential) and Figure 3.7 (other impacts). The

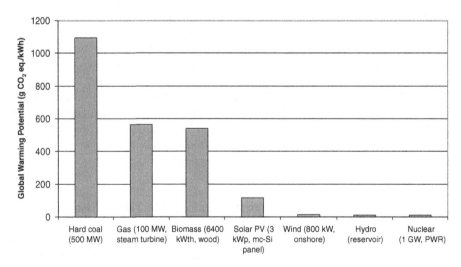

Figure 3.6   *Comparison of global warming potential for various electricity-generating technologies (Data source: Ecoinvent, 2007)*

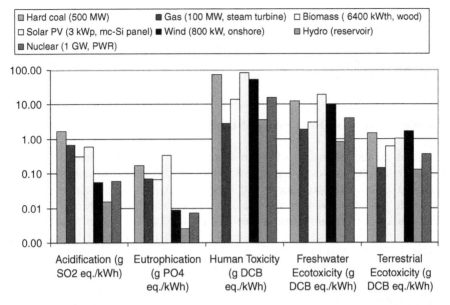

Figure 3.7 *Comparison of life cycle impacts of different electricity-generating technologies (Data source: Ecoinvent, 2007)*

functional unit is 1 kWh and the impacts have been calculated using the CML method (see Section 3.2.2.1). With regard to GWP, the results show that the least sustainable option is electricity from coal, which has a GWP of 1100 g CO_2 eq./kWh; electricity from gas generates around half that amount (560 g CO_2 eq./kWh). It is interesting to note that biomass is comparable to the gas option. The most sustainable options from the GWP point of view are wind, hydropower and nuclear plants, with a GWP of around 10 g CO_2 eq./kWh. With 115 g CO_2 eq./kWh, solar photovoltaic (PV) is also competitive compared with the fossil options. Therefore, if we were only concerned with the carbon equivalent emissions from the life cycle of electricity generation, these four options would help us to become more sustainable. However, if compared for a range of other life cycle impacts, then the order of preference for different technologies changes. This is shown in Figure 3.7.

For several impacts, some of the renewable options come close to or exceed the impacts from the fossil-fuel options. For example, solar PV has the same acidification impact as the gas option. It also has much higher eutrophication impact than either of the fossil fuel options – 2 and 4.7 times respectively. Solar PV and wind are also close to or exceed toxicity of the fossil-fuel options. These impacts occur in the different stages in the life cycle, including the manufacture of raw materials and construction of energy plants.

Thus, this simple example demonstrates how LCA can be used to assess environmental sustainability and compare different alternatives. However, it should be borne in mind that LCA provides information on only one aspect of sustainability – environmental – so that decisions cannot be made on this basis alone, but, as discussed throughout this book, should also include consideration of economic and social sustainability issues. Tools such as life cycle costing (LCC) and social LCA (SLCA), which apply life cycle thinking to estimating economic and social impacts along supply chains respectively, can be used for these purposes (Norris, 2001; Andrews *et al.*, 2009).

Further examples and case studies illustrating the use of LCA for sustainability assessment and comparison of alternatives can be found in Chapters 6 (biofuels), 8 (fuel cells), 9 (nuclear power), 11 (food), and 14 (transport).

3.3.2 Identification of 'Hot Spots' and Improvement Options

In addition to the estimation of environmental impacts from different systems and comparison of alternatives, LCA is also useful for 'hot-spot' analysis as a means of identifying options for improvements within a system. To illustrate this type of application, an example related to a whisky manufacturing system is considered here.

The whisky production system is shown in Figure 3.8. The system boundary in this example is from 'cradle to gate' as the primary interest is in identifying the hot spots associated with the manufacturing process. Thus, the use and product disposal stages are outside the scope of the study. The functional unit is defined as 'production of one litre of pure alcohol'.

To facilitate the hot-spot analysis, the system is divided into foreground and background. The foreground is the system of direct interest; that is, the manufacturing process (malting plant, grain distillery and maturation). The background includes all other activities that supply material and energy to the foreground, including the farming subsystem that provides wheat or maize for the manufacture of whisky. The malting plant provides malted barley used in the distillery plant as a source of enzymes. The whisky produced in the distillery is then matured for a minimum of 3 years and usually up to 8 or 12 years, during which a considerable amount of the product is lost through evaporation (2 % v/v per year). A

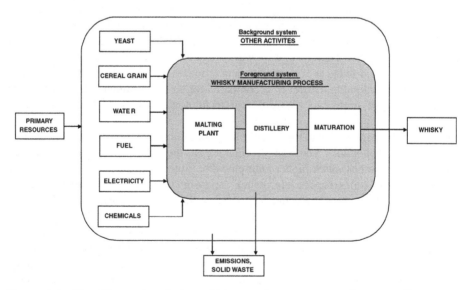

Figure 3.8 The life cycle of the whisky production system from 'cradle to gate' (Azapagic, 2006)

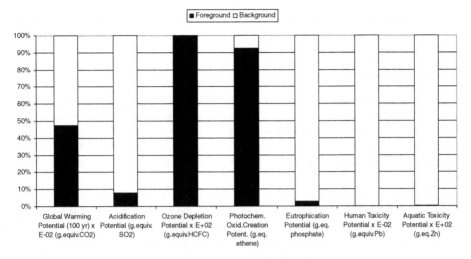

Figure 3.9 *Hot-spot analysis in the whisky system: contribution of the foreground and background systems (Azapagic, 2006). Foreground: whisky manufacturing plant; background: all other inputs into the system, including raw materials and energy*

3-year-old whisky is considered in this example. Further detail on this system can be found in Azapagic (2002).

The results of the hot-spot analysis are shown in Figure 3.9. It is apparent that acidification, eutrophication, and human and aquatic toxicity are mainly attributable to the background system (cultivation of cereal crops). Global warming is contributed equally by the background and the foreground, mainly from distillery and maturation. The latter two processes are also mainly responsible for ozone layer depletion and photochemical smog.

Therefore, this analysis has helped to identify the key stages in the life cycle that should be targeted for maximum improvements, both in the foreground and in the background. The next step is to identify a feasible option for mitigating the hot spots and to carry out further LCA analysis to find out if the alternatives actually lead to improvements and, if so, by how much. In this particular case, for example, replacing the conventional with organic cereal grain as well as various improvements in the distillation process led to almost a complete elimination of human toxicity (as fertilizers and pesticides were no longer used in the system) and a 45% reduction in GWP (owing to the optimized production process) (Azapagic, 2002). The replacement of conventional with organic cereal grain, on the other hand, led to an increase in eutrophication and acidification due to the application of organic fertilizer (manure) and associated emissions of nitrates and ammonia. Therefore, the question is then of prioritizing the impacts – in effect, carrying out a valuation to determine which options would lead to 'optimum' improvements.

3.3.3 Product Labelling

LCA has also been used for product labelling. One of the most prominent eco-labelling initiatives based on LCA is the EU Ecolabel, a voluntary scheme established in 1992 to encourage businesses to produce and market products with lower environmental impacts. Over 1000 products now carry the familiar EU 'flower' logo informing consumers about the life cycle impacts associated with these products (EU, 2010).

Environmental product declaration (EPD) is another example of the use of LCA by manufacturers to communicate the environmental performance of their products. EPDs have to meet and comply with specific and strict methodological prerequisites, following ISO 14 025 (EPD, 2010; ISO, 2006c). EPDs are based on the so-called product category rules (PCRs) which set out general criteria for different product categories, to ensure consistency in calculating the environmental impacts by different manufacturers. Currently, over 150 PCRs have been defined, including for food, construction, and electronic and chemical products (EPD, 2010).

Another emerging application of LCA is for carbon labelling. Driven by the climate change debate, this initiative is spreading fast around the world and is one of the reasons for the renewed interest in LCA. A number of countries and organizations are developing carbon labelling standards and an increasing range of products is being labelled. The labels differ from one country to another, but their aim is to inform the consumer on the life cycle GWP, or carbon footprints, to help them choose climate change 'friendly' products.

In the UK, the carbon labelling initiative is being led by the British Standards Institution (BSI) through the PAS2050 standard (BSI, 2008). PAS2050 is broadly aligned with the ISO 14 044 methodology, although there are some crucial differences, particularly with respect to allocation. However, unlike ISO 14 040, PAS2050 is not a full-LCA standard because it focuses on one environmental impact only (GWP).

There are a growing number of products that have been carbon labelled following the PAS2050 specification.

Figure 3.10 illustrates the scheme on the example of orange juice. It shows the carbon footprints of two types of juice that the consumer can choose from in UK supermarkets: freshly squeezed orange juice and orange juice from concentrate; the latter can either be chilled or stored at ambient conditions. As the results show, the label informs the consumer

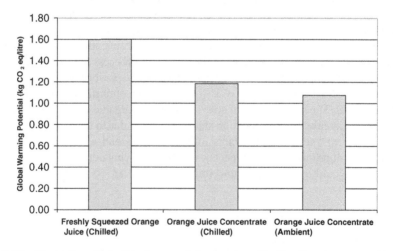

Figure 3.10   *The carbon footprint of orange juice produced in Brazil and consumed in the UK (transport from Brazil to UK included; Data source: Tesco, 2008)*

that they should be buying the orange juice from concentrate kept at ambient conditions if they are to help reduce the impacts of climate change.

At first, these results appear counterintuitive, since more energy is required to produce the concentrate (by dewatering the juice) than the freshly squeezed juice. However, since both types of juice are made in Brazil and transported to the UK, transporting the water in the freshly squeezed juice adds significantly to its overall carbon footprint. Without applying life cycle thinking and conducting an LCA, this information would not have been captured.

However, again, this is just one environmental impact; to make fully informed environmentally motivated purchasing choices, information on other impacts should also be provided to the consumer. Nevertheless, in this particular example and in food applications more generally, criteria other than environmental – most notably taste – may be more important to the consumer. Thus, as in other applications, the challenge is to balance the many factors influencing decisions, be it organizational, public or personal.

3.4 Conclusions

Life cycle thinking and LCA provide a full picture of human interactions with the environment and can, therefore, play an important role in identifying more sustainable products, technologies and human activities. This has been illustrated by several examples discussed in this chapter. Further examples and case studies are presented throughout the book.

However, while information obtained from LCA is useful, it should be borne in mind that it considers only one dimension of sustainability – the environment – and that economic and social criteria should be considered in parallel when evaluating sustainability of different options. Life cycle costing and social LCA, which share the same underlying life cycle philosophy but focus on economic and social aspects of sustainability, could be used for these purposes.

References and Further Reading

Andrews, E.S., Barthel, L.-P., Beck, T. *et al.* (2009) Guidelines for social life cycle assessment of products. United Nations Environment Programme.

Azapagic, A. (1999) Life cycle assessment and its application to process selection, design and optimisation. *Chemical Engineering Journal*, **73**, 1–21.

Azapagic, A. (2002) Life cycle assessment: a tool for identification of more sustainable products and processes, in *Handbook of Green Chemistry and Technology* (eds J. Clark and D. Macquarrie), Blackwell Science, Oxford, pp. 62–85.

Azapagic, A. (2006) Life cycle assessment as an environmental sustainability tool, in *Renewables-Based Technology: Sustainability Assessment* (eds J. Dewulf and H. van Langenhove), John Wiley & Sons, Ltd, London, pp. 87–110.

Azapagic, A. (2010) Life cycle assessment as a tool for sustainable management of ecosystem services, in *Ecosystem Services* (eds R.E. Hester and R.M. Harrison), Issues in Environmental Science and Technology, vol. 30, Royal Society of Chemistry, pp. 140–168.

Azapagic, A. and Clift, R. (1999) Allocation of environmental burdens in multiple-function systems. *Journal of Cleaner Production*, **7**(2), 101–119.

Azapagic, A., Morgan, A., Gujba, H. *et al.* (2010) CCaLC database and LCA software. The University of Manchester.

Baumann, H. and Tillman, A.-M. (2003) *The Hitch-Hiker's Guide to LCA*, Studentlitteratur, Lund.

BSI (2008) *PAS 2050:2008 – Specification for the Assessment of the Life Cycle Greenhouse Gas Emissions of Goods and Services*. BSI, London. http://www.bsigroup.com/Standards-and-Publications/How-we-can-help-you/Professional-Standards-Service/PAS-2050.

Curran, M.A., Mann, M. and Norris, G. (2001) Report on the International Workshop on Electricity Data for Life Cycle Inventories, US Environmental Protection Agency, Cincinnati, USA. http://www.epa.gov/nrmrl/pubs/600r02041/600r02041.pdf.

EC (2000) Directive 2000/53/EC of the European Parliament and of the Council of 18 September 2000 on end-of-life vehicles. *Official Journal of the European Union* (L269), 21.10.2000.

EC (2003) Directive 2002/96/EC of The European Parliament and of the Council of 27 January 2003 on Waste Electrical and Electronic Equipment (WEEE). *Official Journal of the European Union* (L37/24), 13.2.2003.

EC (2008) Directive 2008/1/EC of the European Parliament and of the Council of 15 January 2008 concerning integrated pollution prevention and control (Codified version), *Official Journal of the European Union* (L024), 29/01/2008, 0008–0029.

Ecoinvent (2007) Ecoinvent database, Swiss Centre for Life Cycle Inventories. http://www.ecoinvent.ch/.

Ekvall, T. and Weidema, B.P. (2004) *System boundaries and input data in consequential life cycle inventory analysis. International Journal of Life Cycle Assessment*, **9**(3), 161–171.

EPA (2008) LCA database. US Environmental Protection Agency, Cincinnati.

EPD (2010) Environmental Product Declaration. http://www.environdec.com.

EU (2010) European Ecolabel. http://ec.europa.eu/environment/ecolabel/about_ecolabel/facts_and_figures_en.htm.

GEMIS (2007) GEMIS database and software.

Goedkoop, M. and Spriensma, R. (2001) The Eco-indicator 99: a damage oriented method for life cycle assessment. Methodology report, 3rd edn, 22 June 2001, Pré Consultants, Amersfoort, The Netherlands.

Guinée, J.B., Gorrée, M., Heijungs, R. *et al.* (2001) *Life Cycle Assessment: An Operational Guide to the ISO Standards. Parts 1, 2a & 2b*, Kluwer Academic Publishers, Dordrecht, The Netherlands.

ISO (2006a) ISO/DIS 14040. *Environmental Management - Life Cycle Assessment - Principles and Framework*, ISO, Geneva.

ISO (2006b) ISO/DIS 14044. *Environmental Management – Life Cycle Assessment – Requirements and Guidelines*, ISO, Geneva.

ISO (2006c) ISO 14025:2006. *Environmental Labels and Declarations – Type III Environmental Declarations – Principles and Procedures*, ISO, Geneva.

Norris, G.A. (2001) Integrating life cycle cost analysis and LCA. *International Journal of Life Cycle Assessment*, **6**(2), 118–120.

PE International (2008) Gabi LCA software and database. Stuttgart.

Pré Consultants (2008) SimaPro database and software. The Netherlands.

Tesco (2008) Rolling out carbon labelling. http://www.tesco.com/greenerliving/greener_tesco/what_tesco_is_doing/carbon_labelling.page.

Udo de Haes, H.A. and Lindeijer, E. (2002) The conceptual structure of life-cycle impact assessment, in *Life-Cycle Impact Assessment: Striving Towards Best Practice* (eds H. Udo de Haes, O. Jolliet, G. Finnveden, M. Goedkoop, M. Hauschild and E. Hertwich) SETAC Press, Pensacola, FL.

Weidema, B. (2001) Avoiding co-product allocation in life-cycle assessments. *Journal of Industrial Ecology*, **4** (3), 11–33.

PART 2

4

Translating the Principles of Sustainable Development into Business Practice: An Application in the Mining and Minerals Sector

Adisa Azapagic and Slobodan Perdan

Translating the principles of sustainable development into business practice is not a trivial task and is accompanied by a number of challenges. Meeting these challenges requires an integrated and systematic approach, combining technological solutions and organizational change. This chapter discusses how a corporate management system could be developed and implemented to help companies become more sustainable. The application of the approach is illustrated on a real case study of a company in the mining and minerals sector.

4.1 Introduction

How can a corporation, given its economic 'mission', be managed with appropriate attention to 'the common good'? How can companies improve their contribution to society? Should companies go beyond regulatory requirements and endeavour to raise the standards of social development, environmental protection and respect of human rights?

Sustainable Development in Practice: Case Studies for Engineers and Scientists, Second Edition
Edited by Adisa Azapagic and Slobodan Perdan
© 2011 John Wiley & Sons, Ltd.

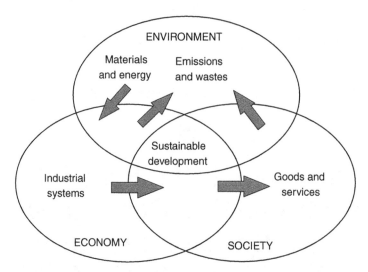

Figure 4.1   *Corporate social responsibility: satisfying human needs in economically viable, environmentally benign and socially beneficial ways*

These are just some of the questions raised in the debate on corporate sustainability or corporate social responsibility (CSR),[1] the concept that is becoming increasingly important for business practice (Azapagic and Perdan, 2003).

In essence, CSR can be regarded as 'a concept whereby companies integrate social and environmental concerns in their business operations and in their interaction with their stakeholders on a voluntary basis' (EC, 2002). In other words, CSR is a way of achieving corporate sustainability by balancing and improving the 'triple bottom line': economic priorities, environmental objectives and social concerns. This is illustrated in Figure 4.1: industrial systems draw on the environment to provide goods and services to society which are eventually discarded as wastes back in to the environment. Currently, all these activities are mainly optimized for economic aspects, but not necessarily for environmental impacts and better quality of life. This exactly is the challenge of sustainable development: as discussed in Chapter 1, moving from a 'three-planet economy' to a 'one-planet economy' will require that goods and services continue to be delivered in an economically viable way, while at the same time minimizing the impact on the environment and maximizing social benefits. Only then can we hope to achieve the development that 'meets the needs of the present without compromising the ability of future generations to meet their needs' (WCED, 1987). For further discussion on the concept of sustainable development and sustainability challenges, see Chapter 1.

However, achieving corporate sustainability is not a trivial task and is accompanied by a number of challenges. Probably the greatest challenge is that it demands a completely new approach to the way business is conducted – a paradigm shift in which CSR is not considered as a mere 'add on' but which is integrated in all parts of business and informs and guides the overall business strategy.

This requires a systematic approach with a structured framework for translating the general principles of sustainable development into business practice through:

---

[1] Corporate sustainability and corporate social responsibility are used interchangeably here.

- identification of key sustainability issues and actions needed to address them;
- performance measurement using sustainability indicators (see Chapter 2) and evaluation to ensure constant improvements; and
- communication of CSR policies and progress to relevant stakeholders.

The following sections outline an integrated CSR management system to illustrate how companies could translate the principles of sustainable development into corporate practice to help balance and improve their triple bottom line. The practical application of the framework is illustrated on a real case study of a company in the mining and minerals sector.

Questions

1. Define corporate sustainability in your own words, using the Brundtland definition as a starting point (see also Chapter 1). Why would companies be interested in becoming more sustainable – what benefits can they derive?
2. Can you provide some answers to the questions asked at the beginning of Section 4.1? Discuss and justify your answers.

4.2 Corporate Sustainability Management System

To facilitate an easier integration into the organizational structure, the CSR management system considered here follows the models of total quality (ISO, 2003, 2008) and environmental management systems (ISO, 1996, 2003) with which most companies are familiar. It is based on the approach developed by Azapagic (2003a) and Azapagic and Perdan (2003).

As shown in Figure 4.2, the CSR management system consists of the following five main steps:

1. policy development;
2. planning;
3. implementation;
4. communication; and
5. performance review.

A brief overview of each step is provided below.

4.2.1 Corporate Sustainability Policy

The first step in setting up the CSR management system is to define a corporate sustainable development policy. The policy should encapsulate the set of core business values agreed by the company and should contain statements of principles or policies on social, economic and environmental responsibilities and stakeholder relationships.

However, before a sustainable development policy can be formulated and put into practice, the following steps have to be carried out:

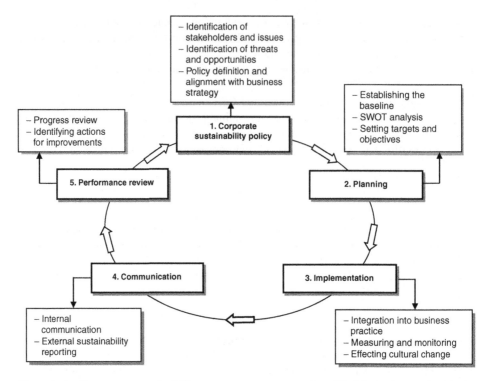

Figure 4.2 *Corporate sustainability management system (modified from Azapagic, 2003a; Azapagic and Perdan, 2003)*

1. identification of stakeholders and sustainability issues; and
2. identification of sustainability threats and opportunities.

4.2.1.1 Identification of Stakeholders and Sustainability Issues

Stakeholder identification and involvement are an integral part of a corporate sustainability strategy. Therefore, each organization needs to think carefully about the many different constituencies upon which its activities and performance have an impact. Understanding interests and concerns of different stakeholders, including investors, customers and local communities, and the time scales over which these interests are important, are the prerequisites for a successful and sustainable business. For example, it is likely that creditors would have a strong interest in a company's economic performance and increasingly a concern for their environmental and social performance. It is expected that the time scale of primary importance to them would be a short-to-medium term (several months to 5 years); however, they may also be interested in a longer term performance (beyond 5 years). This analysis may help businesses to balance the interests of their shareholders and in deciding how to reconcile the different time scales.

The stakeholder analysis is then followed by the identification of key sustainability issues relevant to a company's activities. These should span the whole supply chain from 'cradle to

Figure 4.3 *Measuring the 'triple bottom line': identifying sustainability issues relevant to a company's operations is one of the most important steps towards improving corporate sustainability*

grave', including extraction of raw materials, production and use of the product and end-of-life management (see Chapter 3). Some examples of generic sustainability issues (economic, environmental and social) applicable to many types of industrial activities and companies are given in Figure 4.3.

Economic issues: The main aim of an enterprise is to create value through producing goods and services for society, thereby generating profit as well as welfare for society, particularly through provision of employment. This necessitates consideration of both micro- and macro-economic issues. Micro-issues are directly related to a company's performance and are normally linked to sales, turnover, cash flow, profit and shareholder value. Macro-economic issues put a company's performance in the national and international contexts. They include value added (tax) and contributions to employment and gross domestic product (GDP).

Environmental issues: Most companies already have a good idea of the main environmental issues associated with their business activities, mainly through compliance or as a result of implementation of an environmental management system. In order to understand better the key environmental issues and the ways of addressing them, it is important to identify sources of environmental problems by business activity along the whole supply chains (e.g. processing, products, transport, procurement, etc.) so that they can be targeted for improvements. Tools such as life cycle assessment (LCA) could be used for these purposes (see Chapter 3). Life cycle thinking and LCA are now enshrined in most EU environmental legislation (e.g. the directives on integrated pollution prevention and control (EC, 2008) and on integrated product policy (EC, 2003)) and, therefore, are starting to be used in industry to drive environmental improvements.

Social issues: A socially responsible business has to deal with its position in society in as positive a way as possible and pay careful attention not only to its profit and shareholders, but also to broader social concerns. Therefore, acknowledging and endorsing the wider responsibilities that a business has to communities in which it operates and to society in general, including both present and future generations, plays an important part in the process of developing corporate sustainability (Azapagic and Perdan, 2000).

4.2.1.2 Identification of Sustainability Threats and Opportunities

Once the stakeholders and their main sustainability issues have been identified, it is then easier to identify any threats to the company from unsustainable practices and potential opportunities from more sustainable ways of operating. These may include technical, legislative, environmental, social and other factors, all potentially leading to financial threats or opportunities. Thus, information should be gathered to inform the company on:

- new and proposed legislation;
- industry practices, standards and future trends;
- technical developments, such as clean technologies;
- competitors' strategies; and
- community interests and pressure-group activities.

This preliminary analysis is then used as an input into a more detailed analysis of the strengths, weaknesses, opportunities and threats (SWOT analysis), carried out within the planning stage (see Section 4.2.2.3).

4.2.1.3 Definition of Sustainability Policy

Corporate sustainability policy reflects a company's vision for sustainable development. To be successful, the policy must be aligned with and guided by the business vision and strategy. It should contain statements of principles or policies on social, economic and environmental responsibilities, taking into account stakeholder expectations (GRI,). A sustainability policy can only be successful if there is a clear commitment by the company's senior management. This commitment should be explicitly stated in the policy, as well as shown by direct actions. However, this alone will not guarantee that the policy and strategy will be implemented effectively, as a 'buy in' by all employees is necessary for their successful implementation.

4.2.2 Planning

Policy development is followed by the planning stage to help the company implement its corporate strategy into practice. This involves:

- establishing the baseline;
- analysis of SWOT; and
- setting targets and objectives.

4.2.2.1 Establishing the Baseline

While statements of broad policy on sustainable development are important, the policy statement should be supplemented with a series of specific objectives and targets for sustainability improvements. However, before these can be defined, the company must first establish the baseline to understand where they are starting from and how easy or difficult it may be to achieve their sustainability commitments. The baseline is calculated by using a set of appropriate sustainability indicators, which translate the identified economic, environmental and social sustainability issues into the appropriate quantitative or qualitative measures of performance. The indicators should enable consideration of the whole supply chain and capture the concerns of all relevant stakeholders. They should be quantitative wherever possible; however, for some aspects, particularly of social sustainability, it may be more appropriate to use qualitative descriptions.

As discussed in Chapter 2, a number of companies and organizations are working actively on the development of indicators for different industrial sectors, including the Global Reporting Initiative (GRI,) and the Institution of Chemical Engineers (IChemE, 2002). Further discussion on sustainability indicators for industry can be found, for example, in Azapagic and Perdan (2000) and Azapagic (2003b).

In addition to sustainability indicators, various other tools can be used to help companies put sustainability into practice – SWOT analysis is one of these, as discussed below. Further examples of relevant tools are given in Box 4.1.

Box 4.1   Tools for corporate sustainability

A number of tools can be used to make the corporate sustainability operational. In general, two types can be distinguished:

1. tools for integrating sustainability into business practice; and
2. tools for measuring and improving the level of sustainability.

(1) **Tools for integrating sustainability into business practice**
Several tools are commonly used to achieve cultural change and embed sustainability into business practice. Tools used most widely include corporate strategy, change management programmes and formal risk management procedures (IIED and WBCSD, 2002).

(2) **Tools for measuring and improving sustainability**
The following are some examples of the tools that can be used for measuring and improving sustainability:
- mass and energy balances – used to identify process and energy inefficiencies in the system;
- process optimization – used to identify options for optimum improvements;
- environmental audits and environmental management systems (e.g. ISO14 000) – used to identify environmental inefficiencies and impacts from a company's operations;

- environmental and health and safety risk assessment – used to identify major environmental and health and safety risks associated with a process, product or business activity;
- environmental impact assessment – used to assess environmental impacts of proposed industrial installations; also often necessary for obtaining a planning permission;
- LCA – used to quantify environmental impacts and identify 'hot spots' in the life cycle of a product, process or activity from 'cradle to gate' or 'cradle to grave';
- sustainability indicators – used to measure the level of sustainability of companies, products or human activities.

4.2.2.2 SWOT Analysis

The baseline performance can help the company to understand better the threats and opportunities from sustainability, so that the next stage in the planning process is a detailed SWOT analysis. Following on from the initial analysis of the threats and opportunities, as discussed in Section 4.2.1.2, the outcome should help the company to set realistic targets and objectives to address the major SWOT.

4.2.2.3 Setting Targets and Objectives

As in any other business activities, corporate sustainability strategy also requires setting certain objectives and targets. They should be relevant to the key sustainability issues and the SWOT analysis. For example, objectives and targets may be set for air and water emission levels and for maximum tolerable frequency of work-related injuries. To ensure credibility of the policy and strategy, the targets should be set above legislative limits.

Wherever possible, the objectives should be expressed as measurable targets. This is essential for assessing whether the objectives have been met. Targets also need to be realistic, but challenging and related to certain time scales. Possible obstacles to meeting the objectives and opportunities for exceeding targets should be considered.

Once the planning process is completed, the company can start implementing its sustainability policy and strategy.

4.2.3 Implementation

4.2.3.1 Integrating Sustainability into Business Practice

This is probably the most challenging part of implementation of a sustainability policy and strategy. It involves identifying sustainability priorities and aligning them with business priorities, as well as the identification of specific projects to make business more sustainable. However, more fundamentally, it also involves changing the corporate culture and attitudes. These changes cannot be achieved overnight and normally a 3- to 5-year plan with 1-year milestones will be needed (DTI, 2001).

To enable an easier integration of sustainability into business practice, it is useful to break down the overall business activities into the key activities and areas of interest along the supply chain; for example, resources, production, products, transport, and so on. Specific projects should be identified to help achieve the objectives and targets by addressing the key sustainability issues for each of the key business areas. Examples of projects that demonstrate how different companies have addressed sustainability issues at the practical level are available from WBCSD (2010).

4.2.3.2 Sustainability Measuring and Monitoring

Measuring and monitoring is one way to ensure that the sustainability objectives and targets are being met. Over the years, this will give a good indication of the direction in which the company is going – either towards or away from sustainability. The information obtained by measuring and monitoring can also be used for internal and external communication on progress with respect to sustainability.

4.2.3.3 Cultural Change

Cultural change is critical for a successful implementation of the corporate sustainability management system. The change should be evident throughout the company and among all employees. Awareness raising and training are the main vehicles for effecting the change. For example, the usual training activities (e.g. health and safety) could be broadened to include an introduction to sustainability and its relevance to a particular training activity. Leadership courses could be expanded in a similar way, to encourage management to be innovative and take a lead in corporate sustainability.

Various financial and nonfinancial incentive schemes could be put in place to encourage employees to put forward innovative ideas that could lead to improved levels of sustainability. The increased awareness and participation of employees will not only generate practical ideas, but will also increase enthusiasm for the sustainability programme itself, as most employees enjoy being part of an organization that is committed to operating in a socially and environmentally responsible manner.

4.2.4 Communication

Effective communication is essential for promoting the concept of corporate sustainability, as well as for promoting company's achievements. Therefore, it is important to develop meaningful internal and external reporting procedures.

As already mentioned, internal reporting on a company's achievements with respect to sustainability and the related benefits can have a significant effect on corporate culture. For example, a company could ask line managers to include in their regular reports a statement on whether they have achieved the sustainability targets for a particular period. The board of directors could request similar periodic reports from directors and senior management. A summary of progress should also be communicated to all employees at regular intervals.

In addition to internal reporting, a large number of companies produce external reports on their sustainability performance. Sustainability reporting helps maintain transparency of business dealings by providing relevant information to the stakeholders. Companies who wish to communicate their achievements with respect to sustainability are also using it as a marketing tool. As discussed in Chapter 2, the Global Reporting Initiative (GRI) is the most prominent sustainability reporting standard, followed by over a thousand companies. The GRI gives recommendations and guidelines on both the report structure and the type of sustainability indicators (GRI,) to use for reporting; see Chapter 2 for details.

4.2.5 Progress Review and Corrective Actions

To establish whether the objectives and targets set by the sustainability policy have been met, a progress review should be carried out at regular intervals. The review periods can vary and normally range from 3 months to 1 year. If the targets have not been met, then the reasons should be identified and an appropriate corrective action should follow. Alternatively, the objectives should be reviewed and more realistic targets set. However, if the targets have been met and the achievements clearly communicated, then the process starts again with the policy review and realignment with the business strategy. In this way, the company will be fully aware of their performance and direction in which they are going – towards or away from sustainability.

The review process should ensure continuous improvement and progress towards sustainability. It should also help the company to answer practical questions on what exactly and how much it needs to do to improve its performance in a particular area to become more sustainable. Answering this question is indeed one of the most important aims of developing and implementing a CSR management system, such as the one outlined here. Its application by a company has demonstrated that it provides a powerful approach to corporate sustainability management and that it can provide guidance to companies on what they need to do to become more sustainable. This is presented next.

Questions

1. Describe in your own words the CSR management system shown in Figure 4.2. Discuss its advantages and disadvantages. What improvements to the system would you propose and why?
2. Consider the sustainability issues in Figure 4.3. What other issues can you think of that are relevant for industry? Discuss your answer by referring to the GRI discussed in Chapter 2.
3. How could employees be incentivised to contribute towards CSR in their companies? If you were director of a company, what would you do to encourage your employees to participate in a sustainability programme that your company is implementing?

4.3 Case Study: An Application of the CSR Management System in the Mining and Minerals Sector

An application of the CSR management system outlined in the previous sections is now illustrated on a case study of a company in the mining and minerals sector.[2] The application follows the steps outlined in Figure 4.2. To put this application into context, an overview of the sustainable development challenges for the sector is given first.

---

[2] To preserve confidentiality, the company and their products are not named.

4.3.1 Sustainable Development and the Mining and Minerals Industry

The mining and minerals industry faces some of the most difficult sustainability challenges of any industrial sector (Azapagic, 2003b). To secure its continued 'social licence' to operate, the industry must respond to these challenges by engaging its many different stakeholders and addressing their sustainability concerns. The industry must also be able to measure and assess its sustainability performance and to demonstrate continuous improvements over the long term. The mining and minerals sector has already started responding to some of the sustainability challenges, as demonstrated, for example, by the Mining, Minerals and Sustainable Development (MMSD) project (IIED and WBCSD, 2002). The project identifies numerous benefits of addressing the sustainable development concerns, including:

- **Lower labour costs and more innovative solutions** – providing good working conditions can improve motivation and productivity, result in fewer union disputes, and lower labour absenteeism or turnover.
- **Lower health costs** – a healthy environment for workers and the community improves well-being, which translates into higher productivity, reduced worker and community compensation and damage suits, and reduced costs for social services and medication.
- **Cost savings due to cleaner production methods and innovation** – reducing raw materials use and increasing recycling and recovery can lower production costs. Innovation and technology can introduce new process and product efficiencies.
- **Easy access to lenders, insurers, preferential loans and insurance rates** – lower risks achieved through implementation of a sustainable development strategy may mean lower loan rates or insurance costs.
- **Lower transaction costs** – increased transparency and dissemination of information on a project will build trust among stakeholders and reduce transaction costs. Thorough impact assessments and baseline studies may be useful evidence in case of future liability.
- **Lower closure and post-closure costs** – developing and implementing a clear integrated plan for mine closure can reduce associated financial costs, reduce uncertainties and enable the company more accurately to predict and control terminal liabilities.
- **Higher value for goodwill on the balance sheet** – a commitment to sustainable development may enhance a company's profile and reputation. It will help to attract the best people to join the company. Externally, it could improve its social licence to operate.
- **Best practice influence on regulation** – companies that follow best practice are much better placed than their competitors to influence how standards are set and the direction of regulatory change.
- **Market advantage** – some mineral companies are moving towards integrated management of product chains. This may allow them to build deeper relationships with customers and to capture more value by adding some service elements.
- **Ethical investors** – the rapid expansion of the ethical and socially responsible investment movement poses a new challenge for minerals companies as investors screen out those associated with unacceptable social and environmental performance.

However, there are also a number of challenges associated with addressing sustainability by the industry. One of these is to demonstrate clearly that the minerals sector as a whole contributes to the welfare and well-being of the current generation, without reducing the potential for future generations to do the same (IIED and WBCSD, 2002). This requires

Table 4.1   *Some of the key sustainability issues for the mining and minerals sector (adapted from Azapagic, 2003b)*

Economic issues	Environmental issues	Social issues

• Costs, sales and profits
• Investments
  – capital
  – communities
  – employees
  – pollution prevention
  – mine closure
• Shareholder value
• Value added
	• Resource use and availability
	• Land use, management and rehabilitation
	• Emissions to the environment
	• Biodiversity loss
	• Global warming and other environmental impacts
	• Product toxicity
		• Creation of employment
		• Employee education and skills development
		• Equal opportunities and nondiscrimination
		• Labour/management relationship
		• Employee and citizen health and safety
		• Nuisance (e.g. noise, aesthetics, etc.)
		• Relationship with local communities
		• Stakeholder involvement
		• Human rights and business ethics
		• Bribery and corruption
		• Wealth distribution

addressing its many economic, environmental and social issues (see Table 4.1) in a systematic way (see also Chapter 17). The case study presented in the rest of this chapter illustrates how this could be done by applying the CSR management framework outlined in Section 4.2. Although the application of the framework is specific to a company in the mining and minerals sector, the same approach can be used for any company in the same or other sectors – the difference will be in the specific issues faced by that company or the sector and the types of activity that can be undertaken to improve sustainability performance.

4.3.2 Application of the CSR Management System: Developing Corporate Sustainability Policy

4.3.2.1 Identification of Stakeholders and Sustainability Issues

As discussed in the previous sections, sustainability strategy and policy should address the whole supply chain, rather than just the company's immediate activities. The supply

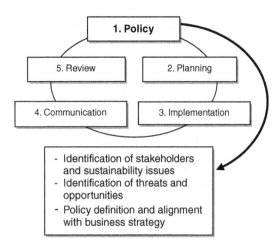

chain for the company considered here is shown in Figure 4.4; this includes all activities from the extraction of primary resources, including the minerals the company is producing, through the production and product transport to the use and recycling of the mineral products.

The company's stakeholders along the supply chain are listed in Table 4.2, together with the importance they place on various sustainability issues and the time scales over

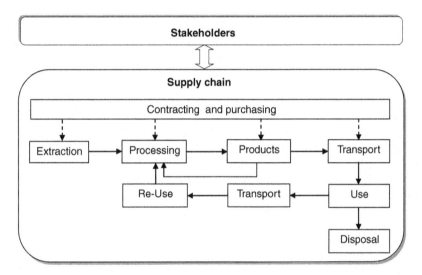

Figure 4.4   *The supply chain related to the company's operations*

Table 4.2   *The company's stakeholders and their concerns*

Stakeholders	Concerns[a]			Time scales[b]	
	Economic	Environmental	Social	Short to medium	Long term
Competitors	☑	✓	✓	●	○
Creditors	☑	✓	✓	●	○
Customers	☑	✓	✓	●	
Employees	☑	✓	☑	●	●
Local authorities	✓	☑	☑	●	○
Local communities	✓	☑	☑	●	●
Non-governmental organizations	✓	☑	☑	●	●
Policy makers	☑	☑	☑	●	○
Shareholders	☑	✓	✓	●	○
Suppliers and contractors	☑	×	×	●	

[a] ☑ strong concern; ✓ some concern; × no concern; ● primary time scales; ○ secondary time scales.
[b] Short to medium: several months to 5 years; long term: 5 years and more.

Table 4.3   *Key sustainability issues for the company (listed alphabetically)*

Economic issues	Environmental issues	Social issues
• Cash flow • Contribution to GDP • Investments (capital, employees, communities) • Profit • Sales • Shareholder value • Turnover	• Biodiversity • CO_2 emissions and global warming • Dust emissions to air • Energy use • Land use, management and restoration • Resources and reserves • Solid waste • Toxic emissions to air • Water use and discharges	• Customer satisfaction • Employee training and education • Employment contribution • Equal opportunities and non-discrimination • Health and safety (employees and citizens) • Noise and visual nuisance • Stakeholder involvement and liaison • Social partnership and sponsorship • Wages and benefits

which these issues are important to them. The key sustainability issues for the stakeholders and the company are summarized in Table 4.3; a more detailed breakdown of environmental issues, showing their impact and source along the supply chain, is given in Table 4.4. This information is then used to decide which aspects of sustainability the company should target in engaging the appropriate stakeholders in the implementation stage. It is also used for identifying the potential threats and opportunities, as discussed below.

Questions

1. Examine the stakeholder list shown in Table 4.2. Discuss the role of each stakeholder in the supply chain and explain why you think they would be interested in the sustainability issues as shown in the table.
2. How can the short-term interests by the stakeholders be reconciled with the long-term scales of sustainable development? Discuss the challenges for the company associated with this issue.
3. Use the information presented in Tables 4.2 and 4.3 to identify which sustainability issues are relevant to what stakeholders. Discuss your answers.
4. How could the company address the environmental issues and impacts given in Table 4.4 along the whole supply chain? Which stakeholders would need to be involved in addressing these issues?
5. Consider a different supply chain – for example, chemicals or food (see chapters 13 & 11). What stakeholders and sustainability issues may be relevant to that sector? How is that different from the mining and minerals sector?

4.3.2.2 Identification of Threats and Opportunities

Table 4.5 gives an overview of the potential threats for the company from unsustainable practices and opportunities from adopting and implementing a sustainable development strategy. These span technical, legislative, environmental and social, all potentially impacting on the economic performance of the company. For example, one of the social threats is

Table 4.4 *Environmental issues, associated impacts and sources along the supply chain*

Environmental issue	Environmental impact	Source in the supply chain
Biodiversity	• Loss (or enhancement) of biodiversity	• Extraction (land use/restoration)
Contribution to global warming (CO_2 emissions)	• Climate change	• Extraction (gas oil combustion in mobile equipment) • Production (fossil fuel combustion for energy generation) • Transport (diesel and petrol combustion)
Dust emissions to air	• Local air pollution	• Extraction • Production (dryers) • Transport (particles generated from diesel combustion)
Energy use	• Depletion of fossil fuel reserves • Climate change (CO_2 emissions) • Local air pollution (SO_2, NO_x particles)	• Extraction (gas oil combustion in mobile equipment) • Production (fossil fuel combustion for energy generation) • Transport (diesel and petrol combustion)
Land use, management and restoration	• Land disturbance • Loss (or gain) of amenity • Destruction or disturbance (or creation) of natural habitats	• Extraction • Production (land occupied by the plant)
Resources and reserves (availability and depletion)	• Non-renewable resource depletion • Future resource availability for the company	• Extraction
Solid waste	• Landfill space • Eco- and human-toxicity (hazardous waste)	• Extraction • Production
Toxic emissions to air (dioxins, heavy metals)	• Eco-toxicity • Human toxicity	• Production (combustion of waste oil)
Transport	• Fossil fuel depletion • Climate change • Local air pollution	• Extraction • Product transport • Business travel
Water use and discharges	• Water loss • Water pollution (pH, suspended solids, oil spills)	• Extraction • Production

Table 4.5   *Opportunities to benefit from sustainability and threats from unsustainable practices*

Aspect	Opportunities and benefits	Potential threats and possible effects
Technical	• Increased production efficiency and product quality through the use of clean technologies, decoupling profits and costs • Increased energy efficiency leading to direct financial benefits	• Continued use of old and inefficient technologies leading to financial and environmental inefficiencies
Legislative	• Improved ability to respond to and influence legislation change through forecasting and better planning • Improved relationships with government and regulatory bodies through proven accountability	• Unprepared to participate in the carbon trading initiative leading to a financial loss • Lack of awareness of the forthcoming legislation
Environmental	• Reduced environmental risks (including reduced risk of a pollution incident) leading to possible reduction in insurance premiums • Identification of inefficiencies in production through environmental monitoring	• Increased environmental incidents through poor planning and management • Lack of understanding of key sustainability issues and areas of business which impact on sustainability
Social	• Increased motivation of staff who are able to see and measure real achievements • Ability to attract and retain good quality people in the company through commitment to staff development and through proven environmental and social responsibility • Improved health and safety leading to lower costs • Trust building with nongovernmental organizations and local communities	• Disputes and conflicts with communities and pressure groups resulting in a lengthy planning process and delays in permit approvals or rejection of planning permissions leading to major financial losses • Poor external image and distrust by communities, NGOs and other stakeholders
Other	• Raised profile and improved reputation • Improved relationship with investors and customers	• Short-term thinking and planning orientated only towards quick pay-backs • Loss of customers

disputes and conflicts with the local communities and pressure groups resulting in delays in permit approvals or rejections of planning permissions, leading to major financial losses. However, at the same time, there is an opportunity to work with the local communities and other stakeholders towards addressing their concerns at an early stage, thus avoiding conflicts and losing the 'social licence' to operate.

Questions

1. Discuss the implications for the company of the threats and opportunities identified in Table 4.5. How could the company turn the threats into opportunities?
2. What other threats and opportunities can you identify for the company, given the sector in which they operate?

4.3.2.3 Definition of Sustainability Policy

Taking into account the key sustainability issues and the stakeholders, as well as the related threats and opportunities, the company have defined their sustainable development policy as:

> The Company and its Board of Directors are committed to contributing to sustainable development by working together as the leading provider of minerals-based solutions for customers. We aim to achieve this through:

> - long-term sustainable growth;
> - development of value-added and environmentally benign solutions;
> - responsible supply of our products and increased customer base;
> - establishment of high performance and socially-responsible culture; and
> - active engagement with our stakeholders and commitment to addressing their concerns.

This top-level sustainable development policy has been developed further to incorporate other relevant company policies, such as those related to environmental issues (including energy, restoration and biodiversity), health and safety, purchasing and community relations. For example, the energy policy has been defined as:

> The Company is committed to the most efficient and sustainable use of energy throughout all of our sites and premises. We aim to achieve this objective through our Sustainable Energy Management System, by targeting the following key areas:

> - reducing our energy consumption and cost;
> - increasing our energy efficiency;
> - reducing our emissions of CO_2 and other environmental impacts arising from our consumption of energy; and
> - investing in renewable and clean energy technologies where practicable.

> We are committed to setting objectives and targets for continuous energy efficiency improvement through a strategic action plan, which will be reviewed and updated each year. We also encourage and support individual voluntary initiatives aimed at increasing the energy efficiency.

Questions

1. Review critically the company's sustainable development policy. Is this policy relevant to their activities and is it going to help address the key sustainability issues that their stakeholders are interested in?

2. Find out how other companies have defined their sustainable development policy (see e.g. the GRI web site). Discuss the differences and similarities between different sustainability policies. Identify the 'best' policy in your opinion and justify your choice.

4.3.3 Planning

4.3.3.1 Developing Sustainability Indicators and Establishing the Baseline

Using the key sustainability issues identified in the previous stage, a set of sustainability indicators has been developed to enable measuring the baseline performance along the company supply chain as well as for monitoring future progress.

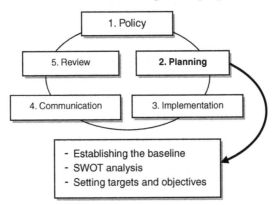

A brief description of the indicators and what they aim to measure is given below. The reader interested in a more detailed exposition on the indicators for the mining and minerals industry may wish to consult the paper by Azapagic (2003b) or GRI (2010).

Economic indicators measure how sustainable the company is financially, but also how much it contributes to society and, through that, to the quality of life. For these purposes, six categories of economic indicators have been defined (see Table 4.6), aiming to capture the key economic issues listed in Table 4.3. For example, the category 'Financial indicators' includes turnover, sales, profit and other indicators usually used to measure the financial performance of a business.

Table 4.6 *Economic indicators and their purpose*

Indicator category	Measures
Products sold	Level of sales and the presence of the business in the economy
Financial indicators (turnover, sales, profit, etc.)	Financial viability of the business and contribution to the national economies
Cost of noncompliance	Whether the company is responsible in terms of economic, environmental and social compliance
Cost of pollution prevention, decommissioning and restoration	Level of investment for these activities; also related to environmental responsibility
Community investment	Social responsibility through charity donations and investment in community projects
Suppliers	Costs of outsourcing and responsibility towards suppliers (e.g. timely payments)

Table 4.7   *Environmental indicators and their purpose*

Indicator category	Measures
Natural resources	Availability and rate of depletion of mineral reserves
Energy	Energy efficiency, use of fossil fuels and contribution to global warming
Materials	Amount of materials used and, related to that, the amount of natural resources
Water	Amount of water used; also loss of the valuable natural resource
Emissions, effluents and wastes	Total contribution to air, water and land pollution
Land use, restoration and biodiversity	Area of land occupied by the extraction activities; the way restoration is carried out and how the biodiversity issues are addressed
Transport and logistics	Transport distances, use of fuels, contribution to global warming and road congestion
Suppliers and contractors	Assessment of suppliers and contractors on environmental sustainability
Products	Product stewardship, LCA of environmental impacts
Compliance and voluntary activities	Environmental responsibility and how proactive the company is

The environmental indicators have been grouped into 10 categories, including resource usage, environmental pollution, land use and biodiversity (Table 4.7). They can help identify environmental 'hot spots' in the supply chain that should be targeted for improvements in the implementation stage (see also Table 4.4).

While the economic and environmental performances are relatively easy to measure and the indicators are generally well developed, measuring the level of social sustainability of a business is not an easy task. One of the reasons is that there are so many aspects of social performance; furthermore, many of them cannot be quantified and qualitative measures must be used instead. For traditionally quantitatively orientated business environments, this may represent a difficulty, particularly if the level of social sustainability cannot be linked to the financial measures of performance. However, without attempting to measure the social performance, it would not be possible to find out whether a company is sustainable and whether the implementation of their sustainability strategy is successful. In this case study, 11 categories of social indicators are considered, each capturing the key social issues identified in Table 4.3. As shown in Table 4.8, they include employment creation, wages and benefits, health and safety, equal opportunities and stakeholder involvement.

Using these indicators, the baseline estimated for the economic, environmental and social performance for two company sites is presented in Tables 4.9–4.11. In total, around 500 employees produced and sold more than 5×10^6 t of minerals, generating a total profit of £12 million. The total energy used was equivalent to 850 000 GJ/year. At Site 2, for example, more than half of the total energy was used for product transport and for business travel. Table 4.10 also shows that the energy use was responsible for 60 000 t of direct emissions of CO_2. Since, in theory, it is possible to offset the CO_2 emissions by sequestration by trees, the number of trees planted by the company at Site 2 in the baseline year has a potential to offset almost completely the total CO_2 emissions from this site.[3]

---

[3] These calculations are based on the Solomon *et al.* (2007) methodology; the assimilation of CO_2 by trees is in the period of 100 years.

Table 4.8   *Social indicators and their purpose*

Indicator category	Measures
Employment	Provision of employment
Wages and benefits	Level of remuneration
Health and safety of employees	Health and safety responsibility towards employees
Health and safety of citizens	Health and safety responsibility towards citizens
Education and training	Investment in human capital
Equal opportunities and nondiscrimination	Attitude towards minorities and whether the child labour is used
Child labour	
Nuisance and accidents	Number of environmental accidents (e.g. accidental releases) and level of noise (related to social responsibility)
Stakeholder involvement	Social responsibility towards stakeholders
Social partnership	
Products and services	Customer satisfaction

Table 4.9   *The baseline economic sustainability performance of the company, showing performance of two different sites [NB: all figures are per year]*

Economic indicators	Unit	Site 1	Site 2
Products			
Total products sold	t/year	999 000	4 234 000
Financial indicators			
Turnover	£/year	45 397 000	16 227 000
Net Profit	£/year	9 754 500	2 320 000
Human capital investment (employee training and education, community education, etc.)	£/year	56 000	25 000
Capital investments	£/year	4 300 000	2 800 000
Return on average capital employed (ROACE)	%	21	n/a
Total wages and benefits	£/year	9 200 000	3 180 000
Total costs of employment as percentage of turnover	%	20	20
Costs of noncompliance			
Total costs	£/year	0	0
Costs of pollution prevention and restoration			
Total costs	£/year	41 000	78 000
Community investment			
Percentage investment in community projects, including charitable donations relative to the total investments	%	0.68	0.14
Suppliers			
Total costs of purchased goods	£/year	20 600 000	n/a

Table 4.10   The baseline environmental sustainability performance of the company, showing performance of two different sites [NB: all figures are per year]

Environmental indicators	Unit	Site 1	Site 2
Resources			
Total material extracted from the ground (minerals and overburden)	t/year	1 685 000	12 413 000
Total minerals extracted	t/year	2 643 000	17 082 000
Percentage of the minerals extracted relative to the total amount of the permitted reserves	%	0.72	10.4
Total energy use (electricity and fuels)	GJ/year	465 900	382 000
Percentage of total energy used for operations	%	n/a	46
Percentage of total energy used for product transport	%	n/a	54
Energy efficiency policy in place?	YES/NO	NO	NO
Materials used (explosives, chemicals, etc.)	t/year	1130	460
Total amount of packaging materials	t/year	1200	60
Total water use	m³/year	160 800	130
Total area of permitted developments (quarries and production facilities)	ha	700	51 000
Total land area newly opened for extraction activities (including overburden storage) during the year	ha	2	2
Percentage of newly opened land area relative to total permitted development	%	0.3	0
Emissions to air			
Total CO_2 emissions	t/year	33 000	27 000
Dust (stacks)	t/year	7	n/a
Water discharges			
Water discharged into waterways	m³/year	6 290 000	65
Solid waste			
Total nonhazardous waste	t/year	298	n/a
Total hazardous waste	t/year	5	33
Environmental accident prevention and/or management plan?	YES/NO	YES	NO
Restoration			
Total area restored in the year	ha	0	13.5
Percentage of land restored compared with the total area open for extraction purposes	%	0	750
Number of sites officially designated for biological, recreational or other interest as a result of restoration	—	0	0
Number of fully grown trees necessary to offset the total CO_2 emissions over 100 years	—	9118	7652
Number of trees planted	—	130	7250
Policy for restoration	YES/NO	NO	YES

(continued)

Table 4.10   *(Continued)*

Environmental indicators	Unit	Site 1	Site 2
Biodiversity			
Biodiversity issues addressed?	YES/NO	YES	YES
Company biodiversity policy?	YES/NO	YES	NO
Transport			
Total number of kilometres for product transport	km/year	n/a	24 330 000
Total amount of products transported to the customer	t/year	n/a	4 234 000
Percentage of product tonnage transported by own fleet	%	n/a	27
Percentage of product tonnage transported by contractors	%	n/a	73
Average distance to customer per tonne product	km/t	n/a	6
Percentage of distance from production facilities to customers covered by:			
road	%	n/a	99
rail	%	n/a	1
waterways	%	n/a	0
Total number of kilometres travelled on business by road	km/year	n/a	200 000
Ratio of product-kilometres and business-travel-kilometres	—	n/a	122
Total kilometres for transport-related activities per tonne of product	km/t	n/a	5.8
Company transport policy	YES/NO	NO	NO
Suppliers and contractors			
Environmental and social issues considered in purchasing and contracting	YES/NO	NO	YES
Assessment of suppliers and contractors on quality/environmental/social performance	YES/NO	NO	YES
Company purchasing and/or contractor policy	YES/NO	NO	YES
Products			
LCA of products	YES/NO	NO	NO
Environmental compliance			
Total number of prosecutions for pollution	—	0	0
Number of reportable environmental incidents (those that must be reported to the regulatory body)	—	23	
Environmentally related voluntary acitivities			
Type	—	Restoration beyond statutory requirements	Restoration activities

n/a: data not available.

Table 4.11 *The baseline social sustainability performance of the company, showing performance of two different sites [NB: all figures are per year]*

Social indicators	Unit	Site 1	Site 2
Provision of employment			
Number of employees	—	400	146
Wages and benefits			
Ratio of lowest wage to national legal minimum	—	1	3
Pension benefits provided to employees (as percentage of total employment package)	%	10	0.40
Health benefits provided to employees (as percentage of total employment package)	%	4	n/a
Health and safety of employees			
Total number of hours of work	—	679 000	302 000
Total number of hours of training regarding health and safety	—	5900	1330
Percentage of hours of training regarding health and safety relative to the total number of working hours	%	1	0.40
Number of fatalities at work	—	1	0
Number of working hours lost per year as a result of accidents at work (lost-time accidents)	—	53	2128
Percentage of working hours lost as a result of accidents relative to the total hours of work	%	0.008	0.70
Percentage of absence-hours on health and safety grounds relative to total hours worked	%	n/a	2.06
Number of compensated occupational diseases	—	0	0
Health and safety of citizens			
Company-level register of external complaints	YES/NO	YES	YES
Total number of external health and safety complaints	—	n/a	0
Education and training			
Percentage of hours of training (excluding health and safety) relative to the total hours of work	%	4	0.40
Percentage of employees sponsored by the company for further education	%	5	0
Percentage of training budget to annual turnover	%	0.1	n/a
Equal opportunities and nondiscrimination			
Percentage of women in senior and middle management ranks	%	<1	30
Percentage of ethnic minorities employed relative to the total number of employees	%	<1	2.74
Child labour			
Verified incidences of noncompliance with child labour national laws	YES/NO	NO	NO
Nuisance and accidents			
Total number of complaints	—	6	0

Table 4.11   (Continued)

Social indicators	Unit	Site 1	Site 2
Stakeholder involvement			
Number of meetings with the stakeholders	—	32	25
Policy for liaison with local communities?	YES/NO	NO	NO
Social partnership			
Involvement in community projects	—	Donations to charities	Improved roads
Time devoted by employees to community projects (percentage of total hours worked per year)	%	n/a	0.25
Products and services			
Customer satisfaction (complaints)	—	n/a	4

n/a: data not available.

A similar analysis for the other sustainability issues helps to give the company an idea where it is starting from and how to set realistic targets and objectives for improvements. Prior to that, it is also useful to revisit the results of the initial analysis of the threats and opportunities and carry out a more detailed SWOT analysis, to inform better the implementation of the sustainability strategy.

Questions

1. Why is it important to establish a sustainability baseline?
2. What data would need to be collected for the indicators in Tables 4.6–4.8? If you were asked by a company to collect the data for them, how would you go about it and where would you get the data from?
3. Examine the results of the baseline analysis given in Tables 4.9–4.11 and discuss the implications for corporate sustainability. What are the hot spots and what can the company do to address them? How do the results between the two sites differ and how could this information be useful to the company?

4.3.3.2 SWOT Analysis

The results of the SWOT analysis are summarized in Table 4.12. Examples of the company strengths include large secured mineral reserves, an opportunity to penetrate into new markets, a good health and safety record and strong partnership with local communities. However, there are a number of weaknesses with respect to sustainability, including short-term economic drivers, emphasis on quantity rather than quality of production, high energy consumption and difficulties in recruiting staff (a generic issue in the mining and minerals sector).

This information, together with the estimation of the baseline sustainability performance, has been used to set the objectives and targets for improvements.

Table 4.12   *Sustainability SWOT analysis*

Current strengths	Current weaknesses
• Large mineral reserves • Possibility to penetrate new markets • Possibility for the production of higher value-added products • Initiatives to move from supplying commodities to providing solutions • Relatively good reputation • Generally, good relationships with local communities • Very good success in obtaining planning permissions • Demonstrated environmental responsibility through restoration works • Bold emphasis on health and safety • The Energy Efficiency initiative • Relatively high interest of employees in the environment and sustainability	• Emphasis on short-term returns and lack of long-term vision (10 years and beyond) • Still emphasis on quantity rather than quality, leading to faster depletion of reserves • Large volumes of potentially useful and profitable products wasted • High energy consumption and emissions of CO_2 • Relatively high number of fatalities and accident-lost time • Majority of products transported by road • Company car policy does not encourage the use of more sustainable cars and fuels • Lack of planning for future succession of the current senior and middle-ranking management • Insufficient internal communication • Low percentage of women and ethnic minorities in senior positions
Opportunities • Further improvement of relationship with local community through demonstration of commitment to sustainability • Improving relationships with government and regulatory bodies through proven track-record • Improving financial and environmental performance through the energy efficiency initiative • Reducing environmental risks and incidents and future liabilities • Improving internal and external communication • Improving public relations • Using the achievements through the adoption of a sustainability strategy as a marketing tool • Increasing motivation of staff and attracting and retaining good quality people to the company	*Potential threats* • Increasingly difficult permitting process • Increasingly stringent legislation • Increased public awareness of sustain ability and pressure-group activities • Disputes and conflicts with communities and pressure groups • Continued lack of understanding of key sustainability issues and areas of business which impact on sustainability • Increased environmental and health and safety incidents and occupational diseases leading to litigation and negative publicity • Inability to penetrate into the new markets in the longer term through poor environmental and social image

Questions

1. How can SWOT analysis inform implementation of a sustainability strategy?
2. Discuss the implications of the SWOT analysis in Table 4.12 for the sustainability of this company. In your opinion, what are the key areas that the company should be focusing on based on this information?

Table 4.13   *Objectives and targets for key sustainability issues*

Objectives	Targets over 3 years
To work with customers to provide value-added solutions	• To increase quality of products by 10%
To maximize efficient utilization of resources at minimum environmental impact	• To reduce energy use and emissions of CO_2 by 3 % annually • To increase recycling of products by 10 % • To reduce the amount of waste by 10 % by increasing the amount of by-products sold
To optimize social and economic contribution to society	• To improve employment opportunities by securing a minimum of 20 new jobs annually
To protect the safety and health of employees and other stakeholders	• To reduce the number of injuries by 50%
To enhance the human potential and welfare of employees and communities	• To increase human capital investment by 1% of the profit annually
To continue active engagement with the stakeholders and commitment to addressing their concerns	• To increase interactions with the stakeholders through meetings, etc. by 15 % • To reduce the number of complaints by the stakeholders by 30 %

4.3.3.3 Setting Targets and Objectives

The objectives and targets set for all the key sustainability issues are listed in Table 4.13. Among others, these include resource use, emissions of CO_2, health and safety, welfare of local communities and stakeholder engagement. For example, the target for energy use and CO_2 emissions is a reduction of 3 % annually over the next 3 years. The implementation of the objectives and targets is discussed next.

Questions

1. Are the objectives and targets set by the company relevant to their sustainability issues? In your opinion, are they ambitious enough to make the company more sustainable? If not, what objectives and targets would you suggest?
2. What should the company be doing in order to achieve the targets and objectives? Develop an appropriate action plan for the company.

4.3.4 Implementation

4.3.4.1 Integrating Sustainability into Business Practice

To help achieve the set objectives and targets, a number of specific projects have been identified by the company. The projects target the 'hot spots' identified for each business area along the supply chain with a specific action plan. A summary of the projects and activities to address the key environmental and socio-economic issues is given in Table 4.14.

As shown, the projects address different parts of the supply chain and business areas (see Figure 4.4); this is discussed below.

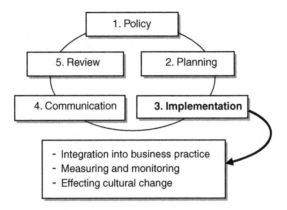

Table 4.14 *Projects and activities to address key sustainability issues*

Environmental issue	Source/target area	Projects and actions
Biodiversity, land-use and restoration	• Extraction (land use/ restoration)	• Continue land restoration and reintroduction of lost species
Energy, CO$_2$ emissions and contribution to global warming	• Extraction (diesel use by mobile equipment)	• N/A
	• Production (electricity)	• Energy efficiency measures (e.g. energy efficient motors, low-energy lighting, etc.) • Switch from diesel to natural gas where possible • 'Green' electricity supply
	• Transport (diesel and petrol use)	• Optimized product transport logistics and increased use of rail • Reduced business travel through car-share and teleconferencing
		• Other measures: Introduction of internal carbon trading schemes to drive company-wide reduction in energy use
Dust emissions to air	• Extraction • Production (dryers)	• Use of 'low-dust' explosives • Improvement of process control and installation of filters
	• Transport (diesel combustion)	• Improvement of equipment and vehicle maintenance
Resources and reserves (availability and depletion)	• Extraction	• Intelligent extraction of reserves with the emphasis on product quality rather than quantity (value-added solutions)

Table 4.14   *(Continued)*

Solid waste	• Extraction	• Maximize use of 'waste' mineral by increasing the amount of by-products sold • Keep different grades of minerals separate to enable their use for different product grades • Recycle waste products
	• Production	• Reuse packaging and use recycled packaging
Toxic emissions to air (dioxins, heavy metals)	• Production (waste oil combustion)	• Improvement of the combustion control for dioxin formation and installation of filters to capture heavy metals
Visual impact	• Extraction	• Screening of the facilities by vegetation • Land restoration and conversion into recreational or other facilities
Water use and discharges	• Extraction • Production	• Introduction of water usage monitoring programmes and improvement of settling systems for removal of suspended solids

Socio-economic issue	Target	Projects and activities
Health and safety	• All operations	• Improvement of the company's health and safety training programmes
Wages and benefits	• Employees	• Enhancement of the pay and benefit schemes • Introduction of reward schemes for innovative ideas related to sustainability
Training and education	• Employees	• Development of new training programmes (including sustainability related) for employees • Increasing further education sponsorship for employees
Noise	• Extraction • Production • Transport	• Replace old noisy equipment where possible • Observe the 'good neighbour' practice (e.g. low-level or no noise and minimized transport during night-time)
Stakeholder partnership	• All stakeholders	• Programmes for stakeholder involvement

Extraction and production: It is fairly obvious that more efficient extraction and production activities lead to an improvement in the economic and environmental bottom lines. This in turn can also improve the social performance of the company. For example, improved energy efficiency results in cost savings and increased profits, while at the same time reducing depletion of nonrenewable (fossil) fuels, local pollution and contribution to global warming. From the social point of view, this demonstrates that the company uses resources in a responsible way, improves quality of the local and global environment and, hence, the quality of life. An example is the switch from oil to a cleaner fuel (natural gas), which leads to reductions in the CO_2 emissions. Another example with respect to energy consumption is the company's energy efficiency initiative, which aims to reduce the use of energy for extraction and production.

Similarly, a sustainable use of mineral reserves with emphasis on product quality, rather than on quantity, prolongs the lifetime of deposits, enhances financial returns through higher value added and usually leads to waste minimization and lower environmental impact overall.

Addressing these issues is also directly linked to the social bottom line, through improved relationships and trust building with the local communities, local authorities, NGOs and other stakeholders. Ultimately, this will reinforce the financial bottom line and help sustain the business over a long period of time.

Transport: Given the total volume of the products, transport has a significant impact on all three components of sustainability through costs, energy use, environmental pollution and in the way it affects the general public. For example, road transport at Site 2 is responsible for more than half of all energy used and CO_2 emissions generated. Obviously, logistics optimization is an important objective in trying to make the business more sustainable. Changing the mode of transport from road to rail or shipping is even more so, provided that the financial and other aspects of sustainability can be balanced.

Products: The vast majority of the mineral products are only slightly processed before being dispatched to the customer. The short production chains mean that the operating costs are relatively low; however, so is the value added. Hence, by concentrating on higher value-added products, the company would develop a more sustainable business.

Solution-based products referred to in the sustainability policy also have a potential to increase the level of sustainability of the company. Rather than selling just the minerals, the company is striving to work together with customers to provide bespoke solutions, thereby adding value, reducing waste and building a long-term relationship with the customer.

Further opportunities to increase the level of sustainability with respect to the products are through utilization of the deposits which contain different minerals that the company is extracting. Previously, only the main mineral was utilized at each company site, with the other minerals considered as waste. This practice has in many cases wasted large amounts of good-quality minerals and has generated huge piles of mixed waste which cannot be utilized. As part of the CSR strategy, the company is changing this practice and starting to utilize all minerals where possible. However, the prohibitively short payback times stipulated by the company are threatening to impede the implementation.

Another interesting sustainability issue is related to the markets in which the products are being sold. Currently, one of the minerals produced by the company in a developing country is exported to developed countries, stripping the country of the valuable resource at little return. To prevent this, the company is considering the opportunities that may help open up the local markets in the future rather than continue to export the mineral.

Health and safety issues related to the production and use of the products are also among the most important sustainability issues. Although the company has a good health and safety record in the developed countries in which it operates, this is less so in the developing countries where it also has facilities. The company is aware that, by adopting different standards and practices in developed and developing countries, they are open to criticism and may lose credentials in a case of an accident.

Purchasing and contracting: Purchasing and contracting also has an impact on the level of sustainability of the company. As a result, the company is switching gradually to cleaner fuels (e.g. gas instead of oil and 'green' electricity), recycled packaging and reuse of wastes from other companies. Suppliers are also being assessed on their level of sustainability. This is consistent with the 'cradle to grave' approach, which considers sustainability of the whole supply chains and is increasingly being adopted by companies.

Workforce: Human capital and its development are one of the central themes of sustainable development. Companies which can demonstrate their commitment to people and their values will raise staff morale and attract and retain the best talent who are more likely to help secure the long-term viability of the business.

Whilst remuneration in attracting high-quality people is important, it is no longer enough. Employees are increasingly considering other aspects, including a company's environmental, social and ethical performances. Here, a link between corporate sustainability and competitive advantage is becoming increasingly clear.

The following are some examples of how the company intends to demonstrate that it is committed to the development of human capital:

- fair remuneration packages, including pension and health benefits;
- equal opportunities and nondiscrimination;
- good health and safety conditions;
- reward schemes for innovative ideas for improvements that lead to financial and environmental benefits;
- training and transferable skills development, including raising sustainability awareness;
- good internal communication (including communication on the level of sustainability of the company);
- succession planning and clear career progression (including mentoring of high-potential individuals being prepared for succession);
- ethical behaviour.

On their part, the employees also have a role to play in making the company more sustainable. The following are some examples of individual work-related actions by employees that can contribute to sustainability:

- implementing the elements of the sustainable development policy relevant to their day-to-day activities;
- choosing cars with low-carbon fuels (e.g. hybrid engines powered by an electric battery and diesel fuel);
- sharing cars for business trips where practicable;
- switching off computers, printers and other office equipment, as well as the office lights, when not in use.

The company is encouraging actively individual activities by employees, as well as innovative ideas related to improvements in the level of sustainability.

Questions

1. Discuss the projects proposed by the company. What sustainability improvements can be expected?

2. Suggest further projects that would help the company become more sustainable.
3. What are other companies doing to improve their level of sustainability? Which company in your opinion is the leader in sustainability? Why?

4.3.4.2 Sustainability Measuring and Monitoring

The establishment of the baseline performance has not only helped the company to set the targets and objectives, but also to develop a system for measuring the performance over the subsequent years. This will be facilitated through the development of a centralized data collection system which will enable acquisition of data from different parts of the company and their integration into sustainability performance datasheets and reports.

Questions

1. What are the challenges that the company may experience in measuring sustainability in future years? How could these challenges be addressed?
2. How could the data collection and estimation of sustainability performance be made easier for companies?
3. Measuring corporate sustainability is voluntary. Should it be made compulsory? Why?

4.3.4.3 Cultural Change

As already mentioned, cultural change is critical for successful implementation of the CSR management system. Although the parts of the system developed and implemented so far provide a good starting point, on its own the system will not bring about the required change throughout the company and amongst all employees. For that reason, the company is stepping up the activities related to awareness raising and training, as the main vehicles for effecting the cultural change. Therefore, as shown in Table 4.14, all training activities involve an element related to sustainability and its relevance to a particular part of the business. All employees are included in training, from labour to senior management. They are encouraged to propose innovative ideas, projects and activities that could lead to an improvement in the company's sustainability performance. Awards are given for best ideas related to sustainability.

4.3.5 Communication

Awareness raising would also improve through internal reports on sustainability performance. Furthermore, the company managers could include in their reports a statement on whether they have achieved the sustainability targets for a particular period. Annual external sustainability reports can be produced once the monitoring system has been in place for a couple of years.

4.3.6 Progress Review and Corrective Actions

To establish whether the objectives and targets have been met, the company should carry out progress reviews annually and take appropriate actions to ensure continuous performance improvement. In this way, they will be aware of their performance and the direction in which they are going – either towards or away from sustainability.

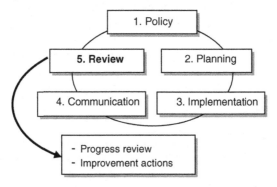

Questions

1. Use the corporate sustainability management system applied in this case study to develop a sustainability strategy for a company of your choosing. Identify the main stakeholders and their sustainability issues and propose an action plan to help the company address these issues.
2. Choose a company that has a sustainability policy and is producing sustainability reports (e.g. see the GRI website for such companies). Critically review the company's policy and performance and suggest improvements. Send your suggestions to the company – they may appreciate it!

4.4 Conclusions

Building a sustainable business is a long-term and multi-level challenge which requires strategic thinking and a change in organization's culture. This change, like all other business activities, must be managed in an appropriate and systematic way.

A CSR management system discussed in this chapter offers a framework for a systematic and structured incorporation of sustainability thinking into corporate practice. Compatible with other management systems, such as environmental management systems, it provides a practical guidance on:

- identification of stakeholders and key sustainability issues;
- development of policies and actions needed to engage the stakeholders and address their issues;
- continuous measurement and evaluation of sustainability performance; and
- communication of progress to relevant stakeholders.

An application of the framework in a company, presented as part of the case study here, has indicated that it provides a powerful approach to managing corporate sustainability and that it can provide guidance to companies on what they need to do to become more sustainable.

However, it must be made clear that a sustainability management system on its own will not make a business sustainable. Whilst it can facilitate this process, it is only an instrument and a tool which will have a limited success without a cultural change needed to make a company more sustainable.

References and Further Reading

Azapagic, A. (2003a) Systems approach to corporate sustainability: a general management framework. *Process Safety and Environmental Protection*, **81**(5), 303–316.

Azapagic, A. (2003b) Developing a framework for sustainable development indicators for the mining and minerals industry. *Journal of Cleaner Production*, **12**(6), 639–662.

Azapagic, A.and Perdan, S. (2000) Indicators of sustainable development for industry: a general framework. *Process Safety and Environmental Protection*, **78**(4), 243–261.

Azapagic, A.and Perdan, S. (2003) Managing corporate social responsibility: translating theory into business practice. *Corporate Environmental Strategy: International Journal of Corporate Sustainability*, **10**, 97–108.

DTI (2001) Sustainable development: improving competitiveness through corporate social responsibility, a directors guide. Department of Trade and Industry, London, May 2001.

EC (2000) Communication from the Commission on Promoting Sustainable Development in the EU Non-energy Extractive Industry. The European Commission, Brussels, 3.5.2000, COM(2000) 265 final.

EC (2002) Communication from the Commission concerning corporate social responsibility: a business contribution to sustainable development. Com(2002) 347 Final, Brussels, 2.7.2002. http://europa.eu.int/comm/enterprise/services/social_policies/csr_communication_en.pdf (3 Oct 2002).

EC (2008) Directive 2008/1/EC of the European Parliament and of the Council of 15 January 2008 concerning integrated pollution prevention and control (Codified version), *Official Journal of the European Union* (L024), 29/01/2008, 0008–0029.

EC (2003) Integrated Product policy: building on environmental life-cycle thinking. Communication from the Commission to the Council and European Parliament. COM(2003) 302 Final. Brussels, 18.06.2003.

Global Reporting Initiative (GRI) (2006) Sustainability reporting guidelines: version 3.0, GRI, Amsterdam, The Netherlands. http://www.globalreporting.org/GRIGuidelines/2002/gri_2002_guidelines.pdf.

Global Reporting Initiative (GR) (2010) Mining and minerals sector supplement, GRI, Amsterdam, The Netherlands. http://www.globalreporting.org/ReportingFramework/SectorSupplements/MiningAndMetals/MiningAndMetals.htm.

IChemE (2002) *The Sustainability Metrics*, The Institution of Chemical Engineers, Rugby.

IIED and WBCSD (2002) Breaking new ground: mining, minerals and sustainable development. Final report on the Mining, Minerals and Sustainable Development Project (MMSD). International Institute for Environment and Development and World Business Council for Sustainable Development 2002. http://www.iied.org/mmsd.

ISO (1996) ISO 14001:1996. *Environmental Management Systems – Specification with Guidance for Use*, International Organization for Standardization, Geneva.

ISO (2003) ISO 9000:2003. *Generic Management System Standards*, ISO, http://www.iso.ch/iso/en/iso9000-14000/tour/generic.html, 2 May 2003.

ISO (2008) ISO 9001:2008. *Quality Management Systems - Requirements, ISO Technical Committee ISO/TC 176, Quality Management and Quality Assurance*, International Organization for Standardization, Geneva.

Solomon, S., Qin, D., Manning, M. *et al.* (eds). (2007) *Climate Change 2007: The Physical Science Basis. Report of Working Group 1 to the Fourth Assessment Report of the Intergovernmental Panel on Climate Change.* Cambridge University Press, Cambridge.

WBCSD (2010) Projects. World Business Council for Sustainable Development. http://www.wbcsd.org/templates/TemplateWBCSD1/layout.asp?type=p&MenuId=Njg&doOpen=1&ClickMenu=LeftMenu.

WCED (1987) *Our Common Future*, World Commission on Environment and Development/Oxford University Press, Oxford.

5

Climate Change and Policy: The Case of Germany

Wolfram Krewitt and Hans Müller-Steinhagen

As a result of worldwide energy consumption patterns, the scarcity of resources, the negative impacts on global climate and the uneven access to affordable energy resources threaten peaceful development of the global society. Therefore, continuing with 'business as usual' clearly is no longer an option. Renewable energies can play a leading role in transforming our energy supply systems towards more sustainable development. While renewable technologies are being developed at an accelerated pace, stronger global efforts are required to increase energy efficiency and to accelerate the market uptake of renewable energy technologies. The German 'Act on Granting Priority to Renewable Energy Sources' has been successful in triggering investment into renewable electricity generation. This chapter describes the mechanism of the support scheme and implications on the electricity market. Scenarios for the deployment of renewables in Germany show that by 2050 renewables could supply more than half of the final energy demand. Owing to the increased use of renewables and the exploitation of efficiency potentials, CO_2 emissions in Germany could be reduced by 80% (compared with 1990) by 2050. Although a significant amount of money is required to support market uptake of renewable energy technologies, scenario analysis shows that a development strategy based on renewable energies ensures that energy supply remains affordable in the future.

Sustainable Development in Practice: Case Studies for Engineers and Scientists, Second Edition
Edited by Adisa Azapagic and Slobodan Perdan
© 2011 John Wiley & Sons, Ltd.

5.1 Energy in the Sustainability Context

Energy plays a crucial role in sustainable development. The balance between its demand and its availability influences practically all fields of social, economical and political activities. Energy consumption patterns affect the environment and the climate and often determine whether nations will live in peace or conflict with each other. The following sections highlight some of the sustainability issues related to energy; further detail can be found in Box 5.1.

Box 5.1   Guidelines for a sustainable energy supply*

1. **Equality of access and distribution for all:** All people shall be assured equal opportunities in accessing energy resources and energy services.
2. **Conservation of resources:** The various energy resources shall be maintained for the coming generations, or comparable options must be created to provide sufficient energy services for future generations.
3. **Compatibility with environment, climate and health:** The adaptability and the regeneration capability of natural systems (the 'environment') may not be exceeded by energy-related emissions and waste. Risks for human health – for example, by an accumulation of problematic pollutants and harmful substances – shall be avoided.
4. **Social compatibility:** The design of energy supply systems shall assure that all people affected by the system are able to participate in the decision-making processes. The system should not restrict the ability of economic players and communities to act and influence, but should rather broaden these abilities wherever possible.
5. **Low risk and error tolerance:** Unavoidable risks and hazards arising from the generation and use of energy shall be minimized and limited in their propagation in space and time. Human errors, improper handling, wilful damage and incorrect use shall also be taken into consideration in the assessment.
6. **Comprehensive economic efficiency:** Energy services shall – in relation to other economical and consumer costs – be provided at acceptable costs. The criterion of 'acceptability' refers, on the one hand, to specific costs arising in conjunction with the generation and use of the energy and, on the other hand, to the overall economic costs while also taking the external ecological and social costs into consideration.
7. **Availability and security of supply:** A steady and sufficient supply of energy must be available to satisfy human needs when and where they arise. The energy supply must be adequately diversified so as to be able to react to crises and to have sufficient margins for the future and room to expand as required. Efficient and flexible supply systems harmonizing efficiently with existing population structures shall be created and maintained.
8. **International cooperation:** The further development of energy systems shall reduce or eliminate potential conflicts between states that are caused by a shortage of resources and also promote their peaceful cooperation by a joint use of capabilities and potentials.

* Compiled by Institute for Technical Thermodynamics (ITT) DLR, Stuttgart.

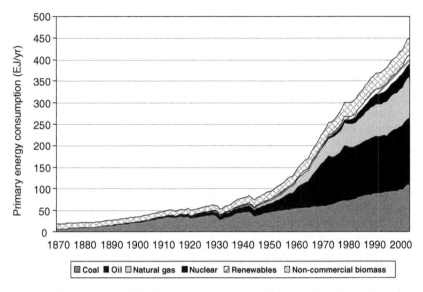

Figure 5.1 *Historic trends for global primary energy consumption (based on data from IEA (2007a))*

5.1.1 Growing Energy Demand and Shrinking Fossil Resources

Since the beginning of industrialization, energy consumption has increased much faster than the number of people on the planet. While the world population has quadrupled since 1870 to 6.3 billion, global energy consumption has increased by a factor of 60 to 475 EJ/year in 2005 (see Figure 5.1). The average person today consumes 15 times more energy than 130 years ago, and those living in the industrialized countries consume significantly more than the average. Temporary drops in energy demand caused, for example, by the two world wars, the oil-price crises, or the serious decline of industrial production in the states of the former Soviet Union interrupted this accelerated growth trend only for short periods of time. As shown in Figure 5.1, the rapid increase in energy consumption started in about 1950; the global energy consumption doubled in just 30 years, between 1970 and 2000.

The traditional use of biomass – that is, the noncommercial use of firewood – in less-developed countries constitutes nearly 9% of the global consumption of primary energy. The other types of renewable energy, mostly hydropower, add up to a share of 4.8%. Nuclear power meets 6.4% of global energy demand. Thus, 80% of the world's energy supply is based on finite fossil fuels. Several hundred million years of photosynthesis were necessary to synthesize these energy-rich carbon compounds. Within just a few centuries humans have consumed most of these valuable resources and polluted the environment with their residues.

Even with rapid changes in the current energy supply systems, fossil-based energy will still be needed for decades to come and possibly to an even greater extent than today. Therefore, the question of which resources are still available, and for how long, is of central importance. The term 'reserves' concerns those quantities of energy which are proven to exist and which are economically exploitable applying today's engineering techniques. The term 'resources' describes either those quantities which have been proven to exist geologically, but cannot yet be exploited economically, or those that are not proven, but presumed to exist in certain areas for geological reasons. The remaining fossil energy reserves are estimated at around 34 000 EJ, corresponding to approximately 75 times the present annual global energy consumption, but only 2.2 times the total amount of fossil energy already consumed. Coal constitutes 60% of these reserves. Conventional mineral oil, representing 20% of the remaining reserves, is already the most-exploited fuel of all fossil energy sources.

A sharp increase in fossil fuel prices is expected once the so-called 'peak oil' point has been reached, a point when the maximum rate of global oil extraction has been reached, after which production starts to decline continuously. There is no agreement as to when the peak-oil point will be reached, ranging from claims that it has already occurred, that it is just about to happen to happening over the next 20–50 years. However, there is an agreement that the peak-oil point will happen. Natural gas alone cannot meet the resulting supply deficit and the reserves of unconventional oil are much more expensive and generate more environmental damage during their exploration. Furthermore, the reserves of oil and natural gas are distributed unequally around the globe. More than 70% of the mineral-oil reserves and more than 65% of natural-gas reserves, are located within the 'strategic ellipse' of countries extending from Saudi Arabia in the south, over Iraq and Iran, up to Russia. Given the recent political circumstances, this may pose future difficulties in energy supply for the countries outside this region. Already today, the secured access to cheap energy resources is of such major significance for the industrial countries that it is contributing to the development and propagation of political and even military conflicts.

5.1.2 Climate Change

The combustion of fossil fuels leads to the emission of CO_2. The concentration of CO_2 in the atmosphere increased from the pre-industrial level of 280 ppm to 386 ppm today, resulting in an increase of global average temperature of $0.6 \pm 0.2\,°C$ (Solomon *et al.*, 2007). Based on these results, the European Council reached political consensus that an increase of $2\,°C$ of the Earth's average temperature above pre-industrial levels is the maximum 'safe' level that can be envisaged. Although uncertainties are still large, current knowledge indicates that the probability of staying within the $2\,°C$ target is rather low for greenhouse gas concentration levels beyond 450 ppm. Various modelling studies suggest that for achieving CO_2 stabilization at this level, global CO_2 emissions need to be cut down to around 10 Gt/year in 2050, which is a reduction of around 60% compared with today's emission levels. To make this challenge more explicit: an expected world population of 9 billion people in 2050, together with an emission target of approximately 10 Gt of CO_2 per year, leaves us with per capita emission rights of around 1 t of CO_2 per year. From Figure 5.2, which shows current annual per capita CO_2 emissions for selected regions, we learn that what is currently emitted in the regions like Africa or India should be our benchmark for a sustainable global per capita CO_2 emission level.

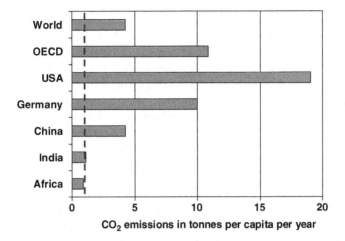

Figure 5.2 *Per capita CO_2 emissions in selected world regions in 2005 (based on data from IEA, 2007a and IEA, 2007b)*

5.1.3 Fair Access to Energy Resources

Another important sustainability issue is the huge disparity in energy consumption between industrialized and developing countries, which has increased rather than decreased in recent years. Today, 18% of the world population in the OECD countries has over 81% of the gross world product at its disposal and is 'responsible' for more than half of the world-wide primary energy consumption and global CO_2 emissions (UN, 2005). While the mean values across groups of countries conceal some of the differences between country-specific indicators, the discrepancies are even more extreme when looking at individual countries. Thus, an average US citizen consumes nearly 12 times more energy than an average African, and almost five times more than the world average. The inhabitants of the poorest countries (Yemen, Haiti and Bangladesh, among others) have to get by with a thirtieth of the energy consumption of a North American. The per capita energy consumption in Europe and Japan is about 50% lower than in North America, indicating that prosperity is only loosely linked to a high level of energy consumption. Nevertheless, at about 175 GJ per capita and year they still consume 2.5 times more than the world average.

The task of achieving fairer access to global energy resources is very important, particularly when considering the long-term economic and environmental consequences. Climate change models (Solomon *et al.*, 2007) suggest that the regions which are most likely to be affected by global climate change impacts are those which contribute least to global greenhouse gas emissions and have the least technical and economic resources for implementing mitigation measures – a fact which might lead to serious social and economic conflicts in the future.

5.1.4 Nuclear Power

Compared with fossil-fuel options, on a life cycle basis, electricity generation from nuclear fission is almost completely CO_2 free. This is the main reason why nuclear power is often considered an important energy option for reducing CO_2 emissions. However, to ensure the long-term avoidance of significant CO_2 emissions, the contribution of nuclear energy to the global energy supply would have to increase several fold. In addition to other issues, such as radioactive waste and potential for proliferation of nuclear weapons, this would pose a challenge with respect to the availability of nuclear fuel, that is, uranium. Estimates on the remaining uranium reserves are uncertain and range from 40 to 100 years, depending on the rate of use. It is also likely that a long-term supply of a large amount of nuclear electricity would require the use of reprocessing and breeding technologies, which are not only more costly, but also involve greater risks than those associated with today's reactors. Already today, it could be argued that nuclear energy conflicts with the basic guidelines on sustainable energy supply (see Box 5.1). Furthermore, nuclear power has been often criticized for being too expensive, particularly due to the low discounting rates used with respect to decommissioning costs. For example, in a recent study for the UK (National Audit Office, 2008), decommissioning costs of existing nuclear power plants were found to exceed the construction costs of fossil power plants by a factor of five (i.e. about €5000–8000 per installed kilowatt). For these reasons, many argue that electricity from renewable sources is already cost competitive with nuclear power. For further discussion on nuclear energy, see Chapter 9.

5.1.5 Renewable Energy

In addition to other options, such as reduction of energy consumption and increased energy efficiency, renewable energies have a potential to play a significant role in moving current energy systems towards a sustainable development path. Solar thermal collectors, photovoltaics (PVs), concentrating solar power systems, heat pumps and geothermal energy are some examples of renewable technologies currently being developed and used (see Table 5.1).

For thousands of years humans relied exclusively on renewable sources of energy, though only at a very low level and with low efficiency. Compared with our ancestors, we now have considerable advantages. Technologies are available today which make renewable energy services possible at almost the same level as fossil and nuclear sources. The associated costs are becoming more affordable and will be more so if these technologies are applied at a large scale (the usual effect of the 'economies of scale'). Moreover, 'costs' must always be judged in relation to the environmental and social 'qualities' of the services provided; that is, considering the external costs and damages that would result from a possible adherence to fossil and nuclear energy systems.

Questions

1. Identify the main environmental, economic and social implications related to the current global energy consumption patterns. Discuss potential long-term consequences. In your opinion, what impacts will be the main driving force for future change in the energy systems and consumption patterns?
2. Analyse to what extent the use of the various energy sources (coal, oil, gas, nuclear, renewables) complies with the key guidelines for sustainable energy supply given in Box 5.1. Try to rank energy supply options according to the sustainability criteria listed. What additional sustainability criteria would you consider?

Table 5.1 *Renewable energy sources*

Primary energy source	Manifestation	Natural energy conversion	Technological energy conversion	Secondary energy
Sun	Biomass	Biomass production	Cogeneration plant/ conversion plant	Heat, electricity, fuel
	Hydropower	Evaporation, pre-cipitation, melting	Hydropower plant	Electricity
	Wind power	Atmospheric motion	Wind turbine	Electricity
		Wave motion	Wave power station	Electricity
	Solar radiation	Ocean currents	Ocean current power station	Electricity
		Heating of Earth's surface and atmosphere	Heat pumps	Heat
			Ocean thermal energy conversion	Electricity
		Solar radiation	Photolysis	Electricity
			Solar photovoltaic cell	Electricity
			Solar collectors	Heat
Moon	Gravity	Tides	Tidal power station	Electricity
Earth	Mainly iso-tope decay	Geothermal	Geothermal cogen-eration plant	Heat, electricity

5.2 From Principles to Practice: Successful Policy Support for Renewable Energy in Germany

5.2.1 Renewable Energy in Germany

Until around 1990, the contribution of renewables to energy supply in Germany was almost exclusively in the form of hydropower and the traditional use of biomass for heating. At that time, their contribution to overall final energy consumption was around 2%. Growth in 'modern' technologies to utilize renewable sources only commenced after 1990, triggered by the German Act on 'Feeding Renewable Electricity to the Grid' adopted in 1991 and the growing levels of public financial incentives provided in the heat sector. Before that, the relative contribution of renewables in the period between 1973, the time of the first oil crisis, and 1990 actually dropped, because of the steep rise in energy demand during that period.

Significant growth in renewable energy output and, hence, in installed capacity started in 1990. This process began with wind power, followed by electricity-generating biomass technologies and, from 2000 onwards, significant contributions from PVs and solar collectors. Figure 5.3 shows the contributions from renewables in Germany over the period from 1975 to 2007 in terms of final energy consumption (electricity, heat and transport fuels). Their contribution reached 224 TWh (807 PJ) at the end of 2007, which corresponds to 8.6% of the total final energy consumption. With 87.5 TWh electricity generation, renewables contributed 14.2% of gross electricity consumption. In the heating sector, renewables reached a share of 6.6% (90 TWh) and in transport fuels the share of renewables was 7.6% (46.5 TWh).

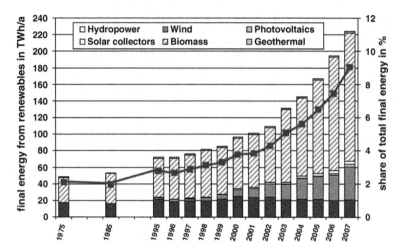

Figure 5.3 *Contribution of renewables to final energy consumption in Germany (Nitsch, 2008)*
Note: the bars correspond to the final energy from renewables; the curve refers to the share of
total final energy

5.2.2 The German Renewable Energy Sources Act

To exploit the potential of renewable energies and to overcome market entry barriers, favourable economic conditions must exist together with appropriate technical, legal and institutional boundary conditions. Financial incentives can help to support market intro- duction and to ensure that the potential for cost reduction is tapped as soon as possible through market learning.

The German Federal Government supports the market development of renewable energies with several different measures. The most important one for promoting renewables in the electricity market is the Act on Granting Priority to Renewable Energy Sources (Renewable Energy Sources Act – in German: *Erneuerbare Energien Gesetz*, EEG). The EEG has been a particularly effective and efficient instrument for promoting the expansion of renewable energies during the transition towards a sustainable energy system. The EEG came into effect in 2000 and was amended in 2004 and 2009. As a result of the EEG, the generation of electricity from renewable sources has nearly tripled from 30 TWh in 1999 to 87.5 TWh in 2007. In 2007, 57 million tonnes of CO_2 were avoided because of the operation of renewable-energy power plants receiving EEG remuneration.

The specific aim of the EEG is to increase the share of renewables in power supply to at least 30% by 2030. It also aims to reduce the costs of energy supply to the national economy, to contribute to avoiding conflicts over fossil fuels and to promote further development of technologies for the generation of electricity from renewable energy sources. The core elements of the EEG are:

- the priority connection of installations for the generation of electricity from renewable energies and from pit gas to the general electricity supply grids;
- the priority purchase and transmission of renewable-generated electricity;

- a guaranteed remuneration for renewable electricity paid by the grid operators over a period of 20 years, which ensures profitable operation of renewable energy power plants;
- the nationwide balancing of the amounts of electricity purchased and the corresponding fees paid; and
- differential costs for renewable-generated electricity are to be passed on to the final consumer.

The following sections explain how the EEG works.

5.2.2.1 Obligation to Purchase and Transmit

Grid-system operators are obliged to give immediate priority to connecting installations for the generation of electricity from renewable energies to their grid and to purchasing and transmitting all the electricity available from these installations. Plant operators have to pay the costs of connection to the grid, while grid system operators bear the costs required for upgrading the grid. These costs will be reflected in the transmission charges.

The EEG creates incentives for operators of renewable energy plants to agree on generation management with the grid system operators in their mutual interest. This is especially relevant for grid upgrading and control energy. This type of agreement can take account of the occasional fluctuations in the electricity supply, thereby minimizing the costs for grid upgrades and reserve energy. To facilitate better integration of renewable energies into the electricity system, installations with a capacity of 500 kW or more are obliged to measure and record their capacity.

5.2.2.2 EEG Fees

The EEG prescribes fixed tariffs which grid-system operators must pay for the feed-in of electricity from hydropower, landfill gas, sewage and pit gas, biomass, geothermal and wind energy and solar radiation. The rate of fees depends on the electricity production costs in each case. The electricity production costs depend on the energy source, the technology and the start of commercial operation of the plant. The minimum fees for each energy source vary depending on the size of the installation and, in the case of wind energy, on the local wind conditions.

The guaranteed payment period is 20 calendar years (except for modernization of hydro-power plants). The tariff valid for the year in which the plant was commissioned remains constant throughout the remuneration period. The only exception to this rule is wind energy, where the 'reference yield model' applies: wind electricity is remunerated at different rates depending on site-specific wind conditions in order to allow the economic operation of wind turbines everywhere in Germany, but at the same time avoiding windfall profits for wind turbine operators at good wind sites. Wind turbine operators can also receive a bonus if the turbine is in a position to provide grid services.

To stimulate innovation and technical progress, the remuneration rates for new installations decrease every year (once a plant is put into operation, the EEG fee is the same over

20 years). The annual degression rate ranges from 1% per year (e.g. onshore wind) to up to 10% per year for large PV systems.

For biomass and biogas power plants, in addition to the basic remuneration, additional fees (bonuses) are applicable if the electricity is exclusively produced from the use of cultivated biomass or from heat and power cogeneration, or if innovative technologies are used (e.g. thermo-chemical biomass gasification, fuel cells, micro gas-turbines, organic Rankine systems, Kalina cycle plants or Stirling engines). The bonuses are intended to offer special incentives for the use of existing biomass potential, efficient heat and power cogeneration and innovative technologies and can be applied cumulatively.

A full list of all payment provisions under the EEG since January 2009 is available from BMU (2008). As an example, Table 5.2 shows the basic fees and the annual degression rates for electricity generation from solar, wind and biomass.

5.2.2.3 The 'Burden-Sharing Mechanism'

Because of the variation in renewable energy resources available in different regions of Germany, electricity consumers would be exposed to different financial burdens resulting from the generation of electricity under the EEG. For example, considerably more electricity is generated from wind power in northern Germany than in southern Germany, due to better wind conditions. To prevent regional inequality in the treatment of electricity consumers, the transmission grid operators are required to balance the electricity volumes

Table 5.2 *Remuneration fees under the EEG 2009 (BMU, 2008)*

	Remuneration €c[a]/kWh	Annual degression rates
Solar radiation		
Roof-mounted PV facilities		
<30 kW	43.01	2010: 8%; from 2011: 9%
30–100 kW	40.91	2010: 8%; from 2011: 9%
>100 kW	39.58	2010: 10%; from 2011: 9%
>1000 kW	33.00	2010: 10%; from 2011: 9%
Free-standing PV facilities	31.94	2010: 10%; from 2011: 9%
Onshore wind		
Initial fee (first 5 years)	9.2	1%
Final fee	5.02	
Offshore wind		
Initial fee (+2 €c/kWh if commissioned by 31 December 2015)	13.00	5% (from 2015)
Final fee	3.5	
Biomass (basic fees)		
<150 kW$_{el}$	11.67	1%
150–500 kW$_{el}$	9.18	1%
500 kW$_{el}$–5 MW$_{el}$	8.25	1%
5–20 MW$_{el}$	7.79	1%

[a] €c – Euro-cents.

purchased under the EEG and the corresponding financial flows across the four control areas in Germany.

5.2.3 Costs of the EEG

As the electricity generated from renewable power plants has a market value in itself – besides the EEG remuneration – the cost to society induced by the EEG is the difference between the EEG fees paid by the grid system operators to the renewable power plant operators and the wholesale electricity purchase costs. The additional costs induced by the EEG are not evenly transferred to all electricity customers: under specific conditions, for energy intensive companies the EEG extra costs are limited to 0.05 €c/kWh. Thus, the additional EEG costs per kilowatt-hour for so-called nonprivileged customers are about 15% higher than if the costs were evenly allocated.

Table 5.3 shows that there was a rise in EEG-induced total cost difference from €0.9 billion in 2000 to €4.3 billion in 2007. Over the same period, the average additional costs per kilowatt-hour in Germany increased from 0.2 to 1 €c/kWh. This increase in the EEG-induced costs is a result of the intended successful expansion of renewable energies in the German electricity supply system. The minimum target of the original EEG that came into force in 2000 was to achieve a renewable share in electricity generation of 12.5% by 2010. Already in 2007 the renewable share was as high as 14.2%. The EEG-induced costs will continue to grow with a rising share of renewable electricity generation until more and more renewable energy technologies gain competitiveness compared with conventional power generation. It is expected that the EEG costs will peak in 2015 at €5 billion to €6 billion per year. Depending on the development of future fossil energy prices, because of the expected cost reduction of renewable energy technologies and the increase in fossil fuel prices and CO_2 emissions allowances, the EEG-induced costs will fall to zero between 2020 and 2030. Afterwards, the society's investment in renewables is expected to pay off.

In addition to the difference between EEG remuneration and electricity wholesale market price, there are other costs that are at least partly caused by the expansion of renewables (Wenzel *et al.*, 2007):

- short-term deviation from the predicted renewable electricity generation leads to an additional demand of balancing capacity;
- the intra-day balancing and the transformation of fluctuating electricity supply from renewables to a so-called uniform monthly 'EEG-band' by the transmission system operator;
- additional fuel costs due to more frequent start-up of conventional power plants or additional operation at partial load;
- the expansion of the electricity grid, which is partly necessary because wind power generation is concentrated mainly in the north of Germany; and
- transmission and distribution system operators' costs for compliance with specific EEG requirements (e.g. audits, publication data on the Internet, etc.).

There are only a few rough cost estimates available for these cost categories. Costs in the year 2006 for the first three items above were estimated to range between €300 million

Table 5.3 Development of EEG costs between 2000 and 2006 (Wenzel et al., 2007, 2008)

	Electricity generation receiving EEG remuneration TWh	Average EEG remuneration €c/kWh	Wholesale electricity price €c/kWh	Total cost difference Billion €	Average EEG additional costs €c/kWh	Additional costs for a reference household (3500 kWh/year) €/month	EEG share of household customer electricity price %
2000	13.9	8.5	1.9	0.9	0.20	0.6	1.4
2004	38.5	9.3	2.9	2.5	0.55	1.6	3.0
2005	44.0	10.0	3.7	2.8	0.63	1.8	3.4
2006	51.5	10.9	4.4	3.3	0.75	2.2	3.9
2007	67.1	11.4	5.0	4.3	1.0	2.9	4.9

and €600 million (Wenzel *et al.*, 2007). The costs of grid expansion for connecting future offshore and onshore wind capacity in Germany are estimated to be around €4 billion. Taking into account depreciation over the financial lifetime of 25 years of the grid infrastructure (€375 million per year) and the electricity transmitted during this period means that the effect of grid expansion on specific transmission charges is only small.

5.2.4 Other Economic Effects from Supporting Renewable Energy

In addition to the direct costs discussed above, there are other, mainly macro-economic, effects resulting from the expansion of renewables that play an important role in the appraisal of renewable energy support policies.

5.2.4.1 Employment Effects

The development of renewable energy resulted in significantly positive employment effects in Germany. The fist-mover advantages are evident through an international, efficient industry which is strong in exports in key sectors of renewable energy. The investment in renewable energy technologies in Germany shows large growth rates and the German industry also benefits from the fast-growing global market (Table 5.4). This market growth has led to the creation of a significant number of jobs (Figure 5.4). In 2007, the renewable energy industry had nearly 250 000 employees, about 40% of them in the biomass sector and 34% in the wind energy sector. Estimates indicate that in 2006 around 134 000 jobs and €14.2 billion in domestic turnover were directly attributable to EEG support (Wenzel *et al.*, 2007).

The direct (manufacturers, operators, service companies) and indirect (supply chain) employment effects triggered by investment in renewable energy systems need to be balanced against the negative effects resulting from substituting conventional power capacity by renewables. Several recent studies confirmed the positive net employment

Table 5.4 *Turnover of the German renewable energy industry (after Kratzat et al. (2008) and Staiß et al. (2006))*

	2004	2006	Change (%)
Investment in equipment for utilization of renewable energies in Germany	€7.0 billion	€11.6 billion	+66
Turnover of German companies due to investment in renewables in Germany	€5.2 billion	€7.5 billion	+44
Turnover of German companies due to renewables outside Germany	€2.0 billion	€4.4 billion	+120
Investment in operation and maintenance	€2.3 billion	€2.6 billion	+13
Turnover from biomass supply	€0.3 billion	€1.1 billion	+267
Turnover from biofuel sales	€0.9 billion	€2.6 billion	+189

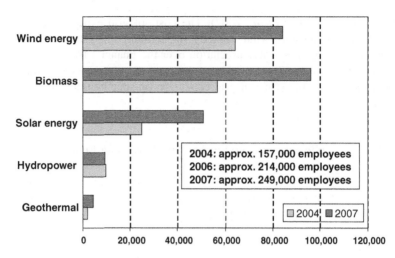

Figure 5.4   *Employees in the renewable energy sector in Germany (based on data from Kratzat et al. (2008) and Staiß et al, (2006))*

effect of renewables in Germany, which amounted to between 70 000 and 80 000 additional new jobs in the year 2006.

5.2.4.2 *External Costs Avoided*

The environmental damage caused by energy conversion can lead to considerable costs for society. These costs, in general, are not borne by the polluter and, thus, are not reflected in the market prices for electricity and heat; thus, they are called external costs. The presence of external effects leads to a number of different effects, most notably to an overexploitation of the environment.

By substituting fossil fuel consumption, the use of renewables in Germany resulted in a reduction of CO_2 emissions of 115 million tonnes in 2007 (Figure 5.5). Nearly 80 million tonnes of CO_2 emissions were avoided by electricity generation from renewables, of which 57 million tonnes were from the facilities receiving EEG remuneration. In addition to reducing CO_2 emissions, a significant amount of particulates, SO_2 and NO_x emissions were avoided. Based on concepts from environmental economics, it is possible to assign a monetary value to environmental impacts, so that the emission reduction can be translated into external costs. In 2007, electricity generation from renewable energies in Germany avoided external costs of about €5.8 billion. Although the quantification of environmental externalities is a matter of major uncertainties, these results suggest that the economic benefits from avoided environmental damage are already now likely to outweigh the costs of the support scheme.

5.2.4.3 *'Merit Order' Effect*

Electricity generation in a supply system takes place in a 'merit order', using the plant that is available to supply power at the least cost first. As an example, Figure 5.6 shows the 'merit

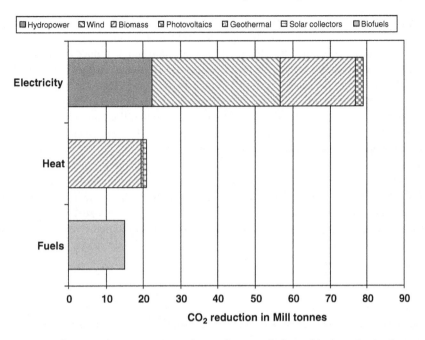

Figure 5.5 *Reduction of CO_2 emissions due to the use of renewable energies in Germany in 2007 (based on BMU (2008))*

order' (or supply) curve for a given capacity of different power plants. When demand is low, only plants to the lower left part of the merit-order curve (e.g. base-load hydro and base-load lignite) are used. As demand increases, plants further up the merit-order curve are brought on stream. The electricity wholesale price in a supply system is determined by the power plant with the highest marginal electricity generation costs that is required to satisfy a given demand. In the example in Figure 5.6, a peak-load gas turbine power plant is needed to

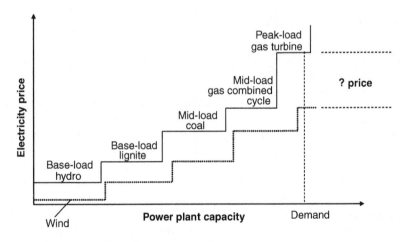

Figure 5.6 *The 'merit order' effect: an example*

satisfy demand; thus, the relatively high electricity generation costs of the gas turbine power plant determine the wholesale electricity price in this situation.

Electricity produced under the EEG feed-in system can help to reduce the average cost of electricity by affecting the wholesale price. Because in Germany the operators of renewable power plants are compensated via the EEG feed-in tariff, the electricity from these plants is available at the spot market 'for free'. As a consequence, the original supply curve (solid line in Figure 5.6) is shifted horizontally to the right (dotted line) and the most expensive power plant at the upper end of the merit-order curve is no longer needed to meet demand, which leads to a reduction of the wholesale price.

The real-world situation is, of course, much more complex, as we are facing continuous fluctuations in supply, demand and electricity prices. Several studies have, however, confirmed the effect of renewable electricity generation under the EEG feed-in tariff system on the spot market electricity prices in Germany (e.g. see Sensfuß *et al.* (2008)). It is estimated that in 2006 renewable electricity generation in Germany resulted in benefits of €3 billion to €5 billion due to reduced electricity wholesale prices.

Questions

1. Describe the key mechanisms of the German support system for renewable electricity generation in your own words.
2. Why do you think the German support system has been successful? Identify the main conditions that are required to trigger investment into new energy technologies.
3. Discuss costs and benefits related to the support of renewable energy sources. To which extent does the introduction of renewables affect society beyond direct impacts on the energy market?
4. Why is the concept of 'external cost' evaluation so important?

5.3 A Long-Term Strategy for Increasing the Use of Renewable Energies in Germany

5.3.1 Policy-Framing Conditions

A set of energy policy-framing conditions on the national, as well as the European, level affects the future development of the German energy supply system, including, for example:

- The decision by the EU Council of Ministers of 9 March 2007 to raise the share of renewable energies in overall energy consumption to 20% by 2020, and the decision to reduce greenhouse gas emissions in the EU by at least 20% by 2020, or by 30% if further industrialized countries participate, from the 1990 baseline.
- The outcomes and recommendations for action produced by the G8 Summit in Heiligendamm 2007 and the Bali Conference of the Parties to the UNFCCC to continue and intensify global climate change mitigation by means of, amongst other things, expanding and improving trade in CO_2 certificates.
- Specific climate and energy policy targets for the year 2020 adopted by the German federal government in 2007, calling for doubled energy productivity (from the 1990

baseline), an increase of the share of combined heat and power in electricity generation to 25% and a share of renewables in electricity generation of 25 to 30%, in heat production of 14% and in fuels of 17%.

- The breakdown of the EU targets for 2020 to the individual Member States, as adopted in January 2008. Germany shall reduce CO_2 emissions by 14% (compared with 2005) from the sectors not participating in CO_2 certificate trading and increase the share of renewables in final energy consumption to 18%.
- The German energy saving act (EnEV) from 2001, to limit energy consumption of new buildings to 130 kWh/(m^2 year) by improved building standards.
- The German Renewable Energies Heat Act (EEWärmeG), which came into effect in January 2009 and the amendment to the Renewable Energy Sources Act (EEG) in January 2009, which set the target shares of renewables for the year 2020 to at least 30% in the electricity sector and 14% in the heat sector. The target share for renewables in fuel consumption was lowered to 12% (energy content).

Achieving these goals requires the adjustment of existing policy measures as well as the implementation of new instruments. Key measures include:

- In parallel with the continuation of the EEG support mechanism, new measures need to be implemented which support a smooth transformation process for renewable energy power-plant operators from the 'EEG-niche' to free-market conditions. In addition, mechanisms for exchanging renewable electricity across European countries need to be established. Also, the import of electricity from solar thermal power plants in the Mediterranean region, in particular from North Africa countries, should be facilitated.
- Effective incentives supporting the use of renewable energies in all segments of the heat market (building stock and new buildings, residential and nonresidential buildings). The existing energy efficiency potentials due to better insulation of houses need to be exploited as fast as possible. Local district heating networks need to be built to allow the economic operation of large-scale geothermal or biomass heating stations or combined heat and power plants and the operation of large solar thermal systems with seasonal storage.
- A consistent strategy for sustainable biomass use needs to be developed. Within the constraints of stringent nature conservation criteria, priority should be given to the use of domestic biomass resources, mainly biomass residues. International trade of biomass should not affect the sustainable, secure and affordable supply of food.

Assuming that appropriate energy policy measures are in place to support the further expansion of renewables in Germany, the German Federal Ministry for the Environment, Nature Conservation and Nuclear Safety developed a set of scenarios to analyse the related technical, environmental and economic implications. The following sections summarize the findings from the main scenario known as the 'Lead Scenario 2008' (Nitsch, 2008).

Question

1. Is there a policy in your country on stimulating the use of renewables? If so, discuss its implications. If not, propose a policy that would help your country to increase the share of renewables in the overall energy system.

5.3.2 Scenario for the Future Use of Renewable Energy in Germany

5.3.2.1 Electricity Generation

In spite of rapid growth of renewables and combined heat and power generation, conventional electricity generation from fossil fuels will still be the dominant source of electricity in 2020 (Figure 5.7). According to the present legislation, the last nuclear power plants in Germany will be closed down in 2023. By 2030, renewables can reach a share of 50% and thus become the dominant source in the electricity sector. By 2050, renewables can provide as much as 80% of gross electricity generation. In order to minimize costs and to ensure security of supply and grid stability, half of the 472 TWh/ year renewable electricity generation in 2050 is from dispatchable sources; that is, biomass, geothermal, hydro and solar thermal power plants. Offshore wind (33% of electricity generation) by nature is a fluctuating energy source, but achieves 3000 to 4000 full load-hours per year which helps to ensure security of supply. Beyond 2030, a trans-European electricity grid gains an increasing importance as it facilitates the exploitation of major cost-effective renewable energy potentials across Europe (offshore and hydro potentials in northern Europe; solar resources in the Mediterranean region) and the capacity levelling of short-term and seasonal fluctuations in supply. Concentrating solar thermal power plants, as depicted in Figure 5.8, play an important role in such a scenario: equipped with a thermal storage system, they can provide dispatchable bulk solar electricity at low costs. Because of the very high solar irradiation, the potential for solar electricity generation in the North Africa/Middle East region is enormous. Electricity transport over large distances at low costs and low transmission losses is feasible by using high-voltage direct current (HVDC) lines (see Figure 5.9).

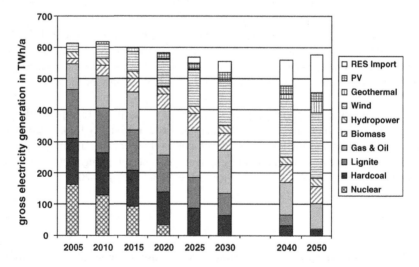

Figure 5.7 *Electricity generation in Germany under the 'Lead Scenario' (Nitsch, 2008)*

Figure 5.8   *Parabolic trough collector of a concentrating solar thermal power plant*

As a result of the electricity sector transformation process, CO_2 emissions from electricity generation in Germany decrease from 309×10^6 t/year today to 248×10^6 t/yr in 2020 and only 32×10^6 t/yr in 2050. In addition to the continuous growth of renewable electricity generation, in particular during the period when nuclear energy is phased out, this reduction of CO_2 emissions is only possible due to the growth in combined heat and power generation, demand-side efficiency improvements, new highly efficient condensing power plants and a shift from coal to gas-fired power plants.

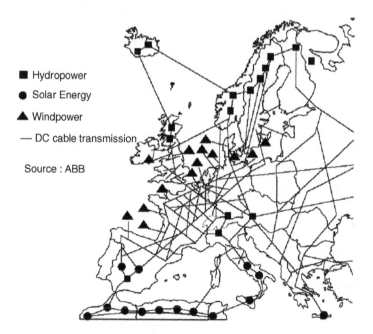

Figure 5.9   *Trans-European HVDC super-grid*

5.3.2.2 Heat Supply

Half of the present German final energy consumption is used for heat provision, generating 40% of energy-related CO_2 emissions. More than a half (55%) of heat is used for space heating, almost 30% for industrial process heat and the remaining 15% is used for hot water and process heat in households and the commercial/public service sector. In contrast to the electricity sector, where renewable energy targets were achieved earlier than expected, the development in the heat sector is lacking behind policy targets. The implementation of support mechanisms for the heat market is more difficult than in the electricity sector. Owing to the many stakeholders involved, the market structure is much more complex: millions of actors – virtually every property owner – make investment decisions which often are not orientated towards optimizing the efficiency of the heating system, but are steered by private peferences, architects' recommendations, the availability of heating networks and so on. Hence, it is difficult to design appropriate and effective instruments which at the same time increase energy efficiency in buildings, the use of combined heat and power generation and the use of renewables in heat supply.

The German Act on the 'Promotion of Renewable Energies in the Heat Sector', which came into effect in January 2009 (BMU, 2009), basically requires that new residential buildings cover at least 15% of the heat demand with renewable energies. Exceptions are possible if the building already complies with stringent efficiency standards. While the Renewable Energy Heating Act is recognized as a helpful first step to accelerate the introduction of renewables in the heat market, it will not create sufficient momentum to reach the German policy targets. The act is restricted to the segment of new residential buildings only, which is too small to accommodate a substantial development of renewables for heating. On average, only 2% of the German building stock is renewed on an annual basis. Hence, future instruments also need to address the existing building stock of residential and nonresidential buildings.

It is expected that final heat energy demand can be halved by 2050 due to more efficient use of energy, in particular better insulation of buildings. In the German 'Lead Scenario', the share of renewables grows from 6.6% today to 14.4% in 2020. By 2050, renewables can meet almost half of the remaining heat demand (Figure 5.10). The exploitation of efficiency measures and the use of renewables result in a reduction of CO_2 emissions of 260×10^6 t/yr in 2050 (compared with 2005). A prerequisite for such a development is a structural change in the heating sector: today almost 70% of the renewable heating systems are stand-alone systems (biomass boilers, solar collectors, heat pumps). To achieve high shares of renewables in a cost-effective way, local heating networks are required that allow the operation of centralized heating stations or the installation of seasonal heat-storage systems together with large solar collector fields (Figure 5.11).

5.3.2.3 Transport Sector

The consumption of energy for transport increased significantly from 1990 to 2000. After that, it has remained approximately constant. It is likely that transport volumes will increase further, in particular in the freight transport and aviation sectors. This increase will largely

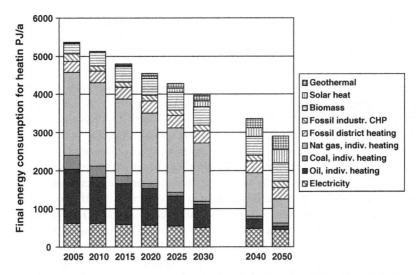

Figure 5.10 *Structure of heat supply in Germany under the 'Lead Scenario' (Nitsch, 2008)*

outweigh the projected efficiency improvements (see also Chapter 15). The trend towards ever larger vehicles hinders a decline in fuel consumption. However, the EU guidelines on the reduction of CO_2 emissions will put increasing pressure on the car industry to reduce specific fuel use. Higher fuel prices will also reinforce the trend towards more

Figure 5.11 *Solar-supported local heating network with seasonal storage, for a solar fraction of 50% (the storage system under construction at the lower left corner) (source: Institute of Thermodynamics and Thermal Engineering (ITW), University of Stuttgart, Germany.)*

energy-efficient vehicles, thus tending to reduce demand for fuel. In the German 'Lead Scenario' it is assumed that total energy demand in the transport sector can be reduced by 27% until 2050 (compared with 2005). The average fuel consumption of the private car fleet will by then be around 3.8 l/100 km.

The provision of fuels from renewable sources is more complex than using biomass in stationary applications. Life cycle energy losses are higher and the greenhouse gas abatement costs are relatively high compared with other CO_2 reduction measures (see also Chapter 6). The introduction of biofuels thus makes sense only in combination with more efficient fuel use. The shift towards hybrid power trains offers a substantial potential for reducing fuel demand. Advantages of hybrid-electric drive trains arise from avoiding inefficient working regimes of the internal combustion engine, recuperation of braking energy and engine displacement downsizing. Fuel consumption of a small-size diesel hybrid vehicle is expected to be at 1.6 litre gasoline-equivalents (l_{ge}) per 100 km in 2050. Battery electric vehicles are even more efficient, with fuel consumption of 0.7 l_{ge}/100 km for small-size cars achievable in 2050. Plug-in hybrids are a combination of conventional hybrids and battery electric vehicles. Fuel consumption depends on system layout and control strategy. Using surplus electricity from fluctuating renewable energy sources for producing hydrogen from water electrolysis at low costs is also an option. However, it is expected that, in spite of the fast market uptake of new propulsion technologies, fossil fuels will still be the dominant energy source in 2050, covering more than half of the total transport energy demand.

5.3.2.4 Economic Effects

Currently, most of the renewable energy technologies are still in a relatively early development phase. Hence, many of them are not yet competitive against conventional energy technologies using fossil fuels. Only by pushing renewables into the mass market and thus moving along their learning curves quickly can we exploit the potential for cost reduction through technical learning and the economies of scale. During the market introduction phase, the expansion of renewables leads to additional costs compared with a business-as-usual strategy. These additional costs may be considered as society's investment into new technologies which hedge against future rising energy costs (and climate change).

In Germany, the market introduction of renewables over the period 2000 to 2007 has resulted in the additional costs of about €30 billion. This considerable amount of money sometimes leads to controversial discussions about the appropriateness of the German policy support schemes. In particular, short- to medium-term projections seem to suggest ever-increasing costs required to bring renewable energies into the market. This suggests that it is important to understand that restructuring of energy supply systems is a long-term process.

It is expected that under the scenario for increasing the use of renewables in Germany described above the additional costs will peak between 2015 and 2020 (Figure 5.12). Assuming that the oil price will rise moderately from $\$_{2005}$ 78 per barrel in 2010 to $\$_{2005}$ 129 per barrel in 2050 (Nitsch, 2008), the cumulative additional costs for exploiting renewables will reach €55 billion by 2010. Of this, €20 billion is attributable to electricity supply excluding PV, €11 billion to PV electricity generation (which today is still quite expensive,

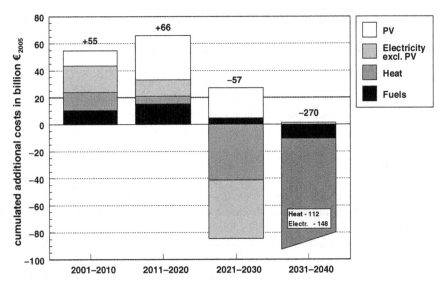

Figure 5.12 *Cumulative additional costs of renewable energy expansion in the German 'Lead Scenario' (Nitsch, 2008)*

but has a large cost reduction potential), €13 billion to heat supply and €11 billion to fuel supply. The cumulative costs continue to grow to €66 billion over the period 2011 to 2020, but growth rate declines. The benefit of the strategy for transforming the energy system becomes apparent after 2020: in the period from 2021 to 2030, the use of renewables saves the German economy €57 billion, which in a business-as-usual development would have been paid for the supply with fossil fuels. The cumulative additional costs of PVs (€22 billion) and of alternative fuels (€5 billion) are more than compensated by some €40 billion benefits from other renewable electricity generation technologies and another €40 billion saved in renewable heat supply. In the period from 2031 to 2040, the deployment of renewables reduces energy expenditures compared with the fossil-based business-as-usual scenario by €270 billion. After 2040, the benefits of using renewables continue to rise substantially.

It is obvious from this analysis that even the relatively high initial funding for PVs is a wise investment decision. This investment leads to reduced energy costs only after 2030, but already earlier contributes to macro-economic benefits by establishing technology leadership and boosting the related export markets. The trend line for additional costs shows that the deployment of renewable energies ensures that energy supply remains affordable in the future. Without such a strategy, the continuous growth of fossil energy prices will pose a serious threat to the German economy at the latest after 2030.

Questions

1. Describe renewable energy options in the electricity, heat and transport sectors.
2. What kinds of policy measures are required to facilitate the long-term transformation process of the current energy supply system towards a more sustainable one?

3. Using the example of scenario analysis presented in this chapter, develop a similar scenario analysis for your country. What would be feasible to assume for the electricity, heat and transport sectors in 2050 in your country? To support your analysis, search for a related work on scenario analysis in your country/region and compare and contrast with your assumptions and findings. Discuss any differences.
4. Discuss the economic, environmental and social implications of your scenario analysis. Based on this analysis, propose the most sustainable future energy mix for your country.

5.4 Conclusions

Business as usual for energy systems is clearly not an option for future generations, as this would have dramatic consequences for the environment, the economy and human society. The German 'Lead Scenario', as well as other national and global scenarios, shows that options for change exist and could be implemented. Among these, renewable energy could play a leading role in the world's energy future. Towards the mid to the end of this century, renewable energy could provide more than half of the world's energy needs, while at the same time ensuring the continuous improvement of global living conditions, particularly in developing regions. There is no need to 'freeze in the dark' for this to happen, but it does require global efforts to increase significantly energy productivity and to accelerate the market uptake of renewable energy technologies.

In the days of a global financial and economic crisis, scenario results offer a positive message: investment in innovative renewable energy technologies contributes to economic growth, to the creation of jobs and in the medium to long term helps to reduce the costs of global energy supply. By moving towards renewable energies, forward-thinking governments can act now to increase employment and investment opportunities whilst at the same time securing future energy supply and mitigating the effects of climate change.

Acknowledgements

The authors gratefully acknowledge the invaluable contributions from Dr Joachim Nitsch on the German 'Lead Scenario' and from Dr Bernd Wenzel on the German Renewable Energy Sources Act.

References and Further Reading

BMU (2008) http://www.feed-in-cooperation.org/wDefault_7/wDefault_7/download-files/documents/National-documents/Germany/2009-EEG-payment-provisions-germany.pdf.

BMU (2008) Erneuerbare Energien in Zahlen. Nationale und internationale Entwicklung. http://www.wind-energie.de/fileadmin/dokumente/statistiken/EE%20Deutschland/BMU_ee_zahlen6-2008.pdf.

BMU (2009) Act on the Promotion of Renewable Energies in the Heat Sector. http://www.erneuerbare-energien.de/inhalt/42351/20026/.

Energy [R]evolution (2008) Energy [R]evolution 2008 – a sustainable world energy outlook. Published by Greenpeace International and the European Renewable Energy Council (EREC), www.energyblueprint.info.

IEA (2007a) Energy balances of OECD countries 2007. IEA, Paris.

IEA (2007b) World energy outlook 2007. IEA, Paris.

Kratzat, M., Edler, D., Ottmüller, M. and Lehr, U. (2008) Kurz- und langfristige Auswirkungen des Ausbaus der erneuerbaren Energien auf den deutschen Arbeitsmarkt. http://www.bmu.de/files/pdfs/allgemein/application/pdf/ee_bruttobeschaeftigung.pdf.

National Audit Office (2008) The Nuclear Decommissioning Authority: taking forward decommissioning. http://www.nao.org.uk/publications/0708/the_nuclear_decommissioning_au.aspx.

Nitsch, J. (2008) Lead Study 2008. Further development of the "Strategy to increase the use of renewable energies" within the context of the current climate protection goals of Germany and Europe. http://www.erneuerbare-energien.de/inhalt/42726/42455/.

Sensfuß, F., Ragwitz, M. and Genoese, M. (2008) The merit order effect: a detailed analysis of the price effect of renewable electricity generation on spot market prices in Germany. *Energy Policy*, 36, 3086–3094.

Solomon, S., Qin, D., Manning, M. *et al.* (eds). (2007) *Climate Change 2007: The Physical Science Basis. Report of Working Group 1 to the Fourth Assessment Report of the Intergovernmental Panel on Climate Change*, Cambridge University Press, Cambridge.

Staiß, F., Kratzat, M., Nitsch, J. *et al.* (2006) Wirkungen des Ausbaus der erneuerbaren Energien auf den deutschen Arbeitsmarkt unter besonderer Berücksichtigung des Außenhandels. Bundesministerium für Umwelt, Naturschutz und Reaktorsicherheit, Berlin. http://www.bmu.de/files/pdfs/allgemein/application/pdf/arbeitsmarkt_ee_lang.pdf.

UN (2005) Report on the world social situation 2005: the inequality predicament. United Nations, New York. http://www.un.org/esa/socdev/rwss/2005.html.

Wenzel, B., Dürrschmidt, W. and van Mark, M. (2007) Background information on the EEG Progress Report 2007. http://www.bmu.de/files/pdfs/allgemein/application/pdf/eeg_kosten_nutzen_hintergrund_en.pdf.

Wenzel, B., Dürrschmidt, W. and van Mark, M. (2008) Electricity from renewable energy sources: What does it cost us? German Federal Ministry for the Environment, Nature Conservation and Nuclear Safety, Berlin. http://www.erneuerbare-energien.de/inhalt/36865/.

6

Sustainability Assessment of Biofuels

Adisa Azapagic and Heinz Stichnothe

This chapter explores the sustainability of biofuels. Derived from bio-based materials, biofuels are seen by some as a major potential contributor to reducing the greenhouse gas emissions from transport as well as providing the security of energy supply. However, there are certain aspects of biofuels, particularly of the first-generation biofuels, which may render them unsustainable, including the increased land requirements and competition with food production. Therefore, sustainability of biofuels should be assessed carefully, considering all relevant environmental, economic and social aspects. To prevent shifting the impacts along the supply chains, sustainability should be assessed considering the whole life cycle of biofuels, including feedstock cultivation and biofuel production processes.

The chapter reviews the current biofuel production routes and illustrates how their sustainability can be assessed on a life cycle basis. It shows that the sustainability of biofuels depends on many technological, economic, environmental and social factors, but above all on policies promoting a more sustainable development of the sector.

6.1 Introduction

Transport accounts for about 13% of the global greenhouse gas (GHG) emissions (Solomon *et al.*, 2007) and these figures are growing faster than for any other sector (The Royal Society, 2008). In the EU and USA, the contribution of transport to GHG emissions is almost double the world average, amounting to approximately 25% (EEA, 2009) and 29%

Sustainable Development in Practice: Case Studies for Engineers and Scientists, Second Edition
Edited by Adisa Azapagic and Slobodan Perdan
© 2011 John Wiley & Sons, Ltd.

(US EPA, 2006) respectively. If the global targets for reducing GHG emissions are to be met, then significant cuts will need to be made in the transport sector.

Biofuels – fuels derived from bio-based materials – are drawing increasing attention worldwide as an alternative to fossil-based transportation fuels to help reduce the GHG emissions as well as address energy security concerns. As a result, world bioethanol production for transport fuel tripled between 2000 and 2007, from 17 billion litres to more than 52 billion litres, while biodiesel expanded 11-fold, from less than 1 billion litres to almost 11 billion litres (Bringezu *et al.*, 2009). Overall, biofuels contributed 1.8 % to the global transport sector in 2007, with the main biofuel-producers being the USA, Brazil and the EU. Globally, investments into biofuels production capacity are probably in the region of $5 billion worldwide and are growing rapidly. Future estimates put the contribution of biofuels at 40–85 EJ/year by 2050; for comparison, the current contribution from fossil fuels totals 388 EJ/year (Bringezu *et al.*, 2009).

Many countries have policies to encourage the supply and use of biofuels, including the EU Renewable Energy Directive (EC, 2009), the German Sustainability Biofuel Ordinance (GFG, 2007), the Swiss Directive on Mineral Oil Tax Redemption for Biofuels (SFG, 2007), the UK Renewable Transport Fuel Obligation (DfT, 2008) and the US Energy Independency and Security Act (USFG, 2007). The principal objectives of these policies are to:

- reduce GHG emissions from transport;
- enhance security of supply; and
- increase employment, particularly in rural areas.

For these purposes, most policies require blending biofuels with conventional fuels, usually between 10 and 15% of bioethanol with petrol and 2–5% of biodiesel with diesel.

Future development of the biofuel sector will depend on many technological, economic, environmental and social factors. This chapter explores some of these, in an attempt to help towards a better understanding of the sustainability issues associated with biofuels. The following sections give an overview of the technological aspects and discuss various environmental, economic and social sustainability issues in the biofuel supply chains.

Questions

1. What are the global targets for reducing the GHG emissions under the Kyoto Protocol? What is the target for your country?
2. What is the contribution of transport to the GHG emissions in your country?
3. Is there a biofuels policy in your country? If so, what are the requirements? Are there any biofuel subsidies?

6.2 Production of Biofuels

As shown in Figure 6.1, biofuels can be produced from a variety of biomass sources and using different production routes. Depending on the type of the bio-feedstock used, they are referred to as first-, second- or third-generation biofuels (OECD and IEA, 2008). Currently, the majority of the global biofuel production is first-generation bioethanol from food crops,

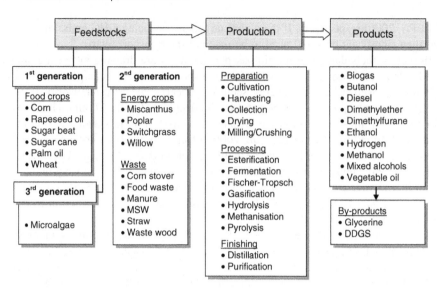

Figure 6.1   *Overview of biofuel feedstocks, processing routes and products (simplified; other feedstocks, production routes and products/by-products possible; DDGS: dark distillers grain with solids)*

representing over 80% of liquid biofuels by energy content (Bringezu *et al.*, 2009); however, the importance of the second- and third-generation fuels is growing. A brief overview of different generations of fuel is given below.

6.2.1 First-Generation Biofuels

First-generation biofuels are produced commercially from conventional food crops, including corn, wheat, sugar cane, rapeseed, sunflower seeds and palm oil. The most common first-generation biofuels are bioethanol, biodiesel and vegetable oil.

Bioethanol is produced from starch- and sugar-based feedstocks, such as wheat, corn and sugar cane, while biodiesel is derived from oil- and fat-containing sources, such as rapeseed, sunflower seeds and palm oil. For example, in the USA, bioethanol is mainly produced from corn and in Brazil from sugar cane; in the EU, biodiesel is produced predominantly from rapeseed oil (Bringezu *et al.*, 2009).

Bioethanol is commonly produced by fermentation and distillation; Figure 6.2 illustrates a typical production process using a cereal crop (grain or straw) as a feedstock. Biodiesel production usually involves catalytic transesterification[1] with alcohols (methanol or ethanol) of oils from vegetable oils or animal fats to produce biodiesel and glycerol.

Although first-generation biofuels have certain advantages, including familiarity with the feedstock, availability of processes and compatibility with fossil fuels, serious concerns about their long-term benefits have been raised. This is due to the competition of biofuel crops with food crops and negative impacts on biodiversity, water and soil, as well as GHG

---

[1] Transesterification is a catalysed chemical reaction between a feedstock and an alcohol (methanol or ethanol) to replace the alkoxy group of an ester by another alcohol.

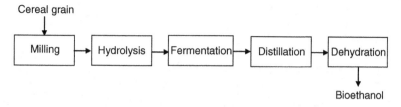

Figure 6.2 *Production of bioethanol from cereal crops*

emissions from land-use change (LUC) (Pimentel and Patzek, 2005; Farrell *et al.*, 2006; Crutzen *et al.*, 2007; Fargione *et al.*, 2008). These issues are discussed in Section 6.3; the advantages and disadvantages of first-generation fuels are listed in Table 6.1.

6.2.2 Second-Generation Biofuels

Second-generation biofuels are produced from nonfood sources and include dedicated energy crops (e.g. perennial grasses, short-rotation coppice willow and other ligno-cellulosic plants) and waste biomass (e.g. agricultural, forestry and municipal solid

Table 6.1 *Some advantages and disadvantages of first-, second- and third generation biofuels*

Advantages	Disadvantages
First-generation biofuels	
• Familiar feedstocks • Well-established production • Scalable processes • Compatibility with fossil fuels • Commercial production and use in several countries	• Competition with food crops • High-cost feedstocks lead to high production costs (an exception is Brazilian sugarcane ethanol) • Modest reductions of fossil fuel use and greenhouse gas emissions (except for sugarcane ethanol from Brazil) • Production of by-products exceeds demand
Second-generation fuels	
• Similar processes to the petroleum/chemical/bio industry • No competition issues with food • Reduction of the amount of waste that needs to be treated/disposed of (if used as feedstock)	• Unfamiliar feedstock and availability uncertain/fluctuating • High capital and energy costs • Processing not optimized for the new feedstocks (e.g. tar formation; syngas clean up, etc.) • Competition for land and water for some energy crops • For anaerobic digestion of waste, only a fraction of waste can be used
Third-generation fuels (microalgae)	
• High oil content • Can be cultivated in a range of systems • A wide spectrum of processing routes and biofuels	• Not commercially available yet • High initial costs • High water content • If cultivated artificially, could require large areas • If exploited from oceans, could impact on the marine life

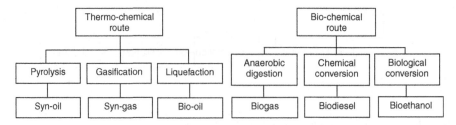

Figure 6.3 *A simplified overview of the thermochemical and biochemical routes for production of biofuels*

waste). Waste biomass is generally preferred to dedicated energy crops as this does not create additional stress on the environment, such as competition for land and water. On the contrary, using nonrecyclable wastes as a biofuel feedstock would support the reuse of resources, save the landfill disposal capacity and lead to a reduction of GHG emissions from disposal sites (Stichnothe and Azapagic, 2009).

The main second-generation biofuels are bioethanol and biodiesel. Other fuels under development include biohydrogen, biomethanol, bio-dimethylfuran (bio-DMF), bio-dimethyether (bio-DME), Fischer–Tropsch biodiesel, biohydrogen diesel and mixed alcohols (Bringezu *et al.*, 2009).

Two main processing routes are used for second-generation biofuels: thermochemical and biochemical (see Figure 6.3).

Thermochemical conversion is carried out at high temperatures and sometimes high pressures and it involves liquefaction, gasification and pyrolysis. Liquefaction is the direct conversion of biomass to liquid fuels at high pressure (50–200 atm) and temperatures (250–450 °C). Gasification is also a high-temperature process carried out in a reduced oxygen atmosphere to produce syngas (mainly carbon monoxide and hydrogen) and char. The syngas is then cleaned to remove CO_2 and passed over a catalyst to produce liquid fuel. Alternatively, syngas can be fermented in the presence of microorganisms to generate bioethanol. Pyrolysis is similar to gasification but is carried out in the absence of oxygen to produce syngas, bio-oil, tars and char. The proportion of gas, liquid and solid products can be controlled by changing the rate of heating and temperature in the pyrolysis chamber.

The biochemical route includes anaerobic digestion and chemical and biological conversion (see Figure 6.3).

Anaerobic digestion is a biological process carried out in the absence of oxygen in which anaerobic bacteria are used to produce biogas from organic matter. Biogas contains about 60% methane and 40% CO_2. The solid and liquid residues (digestate) can be used to improve soil fertility. Different organic matter can be used for anaerobic digestion, including household waste, waste food, garden waste and manure. An advantage of using wastes to produce biogas is that a significant amount of methane emissions is prevented that would otherwise be released from the decay of organic wastes. Other advantages include reduction of odour, volume of waste landfilled and decreased land demand for cultivation of bio-feedstocks. However, using biogas as a transport fuel is not necessarily the best option and it may be better to use it locally to generate electricity and heat. This would save costs of purification, distribution, compression, storage and vehicle modifications (Edwards, 2008a,b).

Chemical conversion involves using chemicals to convert biomass into fuels. The feedstocks include vegetable oil, animal fats, rapeseed, soybean and sunflower seed. As

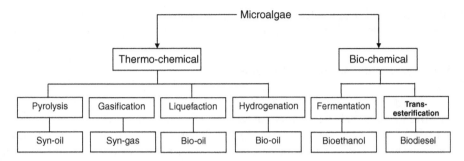

Figure 6.4 *Possible production routes for biofuels from microalgae (after Amin, 2009)*

mentioned previously, transesterification is the most widely used method of producing biodiesel. Waste vegetable oil and animal fats are commonly used for these purposes.

Biological conversion of biomass involves three main steps: conversion of biomass to sugars, fermentation and processing the fermentation products to produce ethanol.

A brief overview of the advantages and disadvantages of second-generation fuels can be found in Table 6.1.

6.2.3 Third-Generation Biofuels

Third-generation biofuels are still under development and the main bio-feedstock being considered is microalgae. They can be cultivated either in purpose-built systems (e.g. fermenters, photo-reactors or ponds) or harvested from oceans. Both thermochemical and biochemical routes can be used to produce biofuels from algae (see Figure 6.4).

Although microalgae have a potential to play a role in biofuels production in the future, currently they are not cost competitive. It is also important to assess these production systems against appropriate sustainability criteria. This is particularly important if they are to be sourced from oceans, given the already negative impacts on the marine environment from overexploitation (The Royal Society, 2008).

Some of the advantages and disadvantages of the microalgae-derived biofuels are summarized in Table 6.1.

Other third-generation biofuels could include alcohols, such as bio-propanol or bio-butanol; however, they are not expected to enter the market before 2050 (OECD and IEA, 2008).

Questions

1. What is the difference between first-, second- and third-generation biofuels?
2. Discuss the difference in the feedstocks and their composition. Which bio-feedstocks can be used for ethanol and which for biodiesel?
3. Which bio-feedstocks are more sustainable and why?
4. What processing routes can be used to produce bioethanol and biodiesel? Describe each route and processes within the routes.

5. Discuss the advantages and disadvantages of different types of biofuel. Which of these do you think are the most important and why? Using these criteria, choose the 'best' biofuel.

6.3 Sustainability Assessment of Biofuels

As discussed in Section 6.1, biofuels have emerged as a potentially more sustainable alternative to fossil fuels for a variety of reasons. One of the major driving forces for the rapid expansion of the biofuels sector has been their potential to reduce the GHG emissions because the biomass from which they are derived is considered 'carbon neutral'.[2] Another attractive feature of biofuels over fossil fuels is that they could provide security of supply, as they can be produced domestically by many countries. Furthermore, they require only minimal changes to the distribution systems and existing production technologies. Biofuels also have a potential to stimulate rural development (Rajagopal and Zilberman, 2007a). Thus, the expectations from biofuels as a source of 'sustainable' energy are high.

However, there are certain aspects, particularly of the first-generation biofuels, which may render them less sustainable. As summarized in Table 6.1, these include:

- additional land requirement and competition with food production systems, leading to increased food prices and in some cases, food poverty (Bird *et al.*, 2008; Fargione *et al.*, 2008; Searchinger *et al.*, 2008; Escobar *et al.*, 2009);
- additional GHG emissions due to the LUC (see Section 6.3.1);
- high capital and in some case operating costs (see Section 6.3.2); and
- various social issues such as health and safety, land-rights issues and child labour (see the Section 6.3.3).

Therefore, sustainability of biofuels should be assessed carefully, considering all relevant environmental, economic and social aspects (The Royal Society, 2008). Furthermore, to prevent shifting the burdens along the supply chains, sustainability should be assessed taking a systems approach and considering the whole life cycle of biofuels, including cultivation of the feedstock, biofuel production processes and their use (Fehrenbach *et al.*, 2007; The Royal Society, 2008; Stichnothe and Azapagic, 2009; US EPA, 2009a; Azapagic and Stichnothe, 2010;). A life cycle approach is also required by various legislative acts related to biofuels, including the EU Renewable Energy Directive (EC, 2009), the German Sustainability Biofuel Ordinance (GFG, 2007), the Swiss Directive on Mineral Oil Tax Redemption for Biofuels (SFG, 2007), the UK Renewable Transport Fuel Obligation (DfT, 2008) and the US Energy Independency and Security Act (USFG, 2007).

As shown in Figure 6.5, the life cycle of biofuels encompasses cultivation and harvesting of biomass (if applicable), its collection and conversion to the biofuel and finally the use of biofuel in vehicles. Transportation of the bio-feedstock and other raw materials and the distribution of the biofuel to the point of consumption are also included in the system. Each stage in the life cycle is associated with several sustainability issues, depending on the type of feedstock, production route and biofuel. Some of these issues are listed in Table 6.2 and are discussed in the rest of the chapter.

---

[2] This is based on the assumption that the amount of carbon released during the combustion of biofuels is equivalent to the amount of carbon sequestered during the growth of biomass from which the fuels were produced.

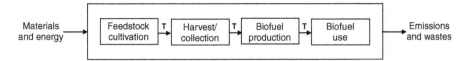

Figure 6.5   *The life cycle of biofuels from 'cradle to grave' (Cultivation and harvest refer to food and energy crops; see Figure 6.1; T: transport/distribution)*

Table 6.2   *Some sustainability issues in the life cycle[a] of biofuels (DfT, 2008; The Royal Society, 2008; Brigenzu et al., 2009; IDB, 2009; Azapagic and Stichnothe, 2010)*

Environmental	Economic	Social
• Global warming potential (GWP)	• Feedstock costs	• Human health
• Land availability	• Investment costs	• Human and labour rights
• LUC	• Biofuel price	• Land ownerships
• Biodiversity	• Local income generation	• Impact on food security
• Water consumption		• Community development
• Other environmental impacts		• Impact on indigenous peoples

[a]The issues are not identified by life cycle stage as many apply to several stages or the whole life cycle.

Questions

1. What are the main sustainability issues associated with fossil fuels and how do they compare with the sustainability issues for biofuels outlined in Table 6.2?
2. Where in the life cycle do the biofuel sustainability issues listed in Table 6.2 occur? How could they be addressed?

6.3.1 Environmental Sustainability of Biofuels

6.3.1.1 Global Warming Potential of Biofuels

Estimation of life cycle GHG emissions or global warming potential (GWP) from biofuels has been subject of many life cycle assessment (LCA) studies internationally, in an attempt to evaluate what savings, if any, can be achieved over fossil fuels (Azapagic and Stichnothe, 2010). Some of these results are presented here. For the generic LCA methodology, the reader can consult Chapter 3; further detail on the LCA methodology for biofuels can be found in Azapagic and Stichnothe (2010).

The life cycle of biofuels is outlined in Figure 6.5. The equivalent life cycle of fossil fuels is shown in Figure 6.6; it encompasses the extraction of crude oil, transportation to the refinery, all refinery processes to produce petrol and diesel and finally the use of the fuels. As in the biofuels system, all material and energy inputs into the system and emissions and wastes from the system are included within the system boundary.

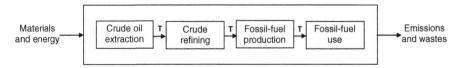

Figure 6.6 *The life cycle of fossil fuels from 'cradle to grave' (T: transport/distribution)*

The GHG emissions or GWP of fuels are usually compared on an energy basis; most studies use 1 MJ of fuel as the functional unit for these purposes so that the GWP is expressed either in grams or kilograms of CO_2 eq./MJ fuel. The methodology for estimating the GWPs from fuels and the GHG savings from biofuels can be found in Box 6.1.

Box 6.1   Calculating global warming potential (GWP) and greenhouse gas (GHG) saving potential from biofuels

The total GWP of a fuel over its life cycle can be calculated as:

$$GWP_{total} = GWP_{production} + GWP_{use} \quad (g\,CO_2\,eq./MJ) \tag{6.1}$$

where GWP_{total} (g CO_2 eq./MJ) is the GHG emissions over the total life cycle, $GWP_{production}$ (g CO_2 eq./MJ) is the GHG emissions for production of fuel, from 'cradle to the point of use' and GWP_{use} (g CO_2 eq./MJ) is the GHG emissions from use (combustion) of fuel.

For biofuels, $GWP_{use} = 0$ since the CO_2 emitted during their combustion is of biogenic nature, having been absorbed from the atmosphere by biomass during its growth. Hence, biofuels are sometimes referred to as being 'carbon neutral'. However, this should not be confused with the whole life cycle CO_2 eq. emissions from biofuels – the 'neutrality' only applies to the use stage of biofuels, not to the whole life cycle, as the emissions associated with crop cultivation (if applicable) and fuel production must be taken into account.

GWP_{use} of fossil fuels, however, must be taken into account. This can be calculated by dividing the GHG emissions from combustion of fossil fuel by its lower heating value and density as follows:

$$GWP_{fossil\ fuel\ use} = \frac{GHG_{emissions}\ (kg\,CO_2\,eq./l)}{LHV\,(MJ/kg) \times \rho(kg/l)} \times 1000 \quad (g\,CO_2\,eq./MJ) \tag{6.2}$$

The GHG savings from biofuels relative to the fossil fuels can be calculated using the following formula:

$$GHG_{saving}(\%) = \frac{GWP_{total\ (fossil\ fuel)} - GWP_{total\ (biofuel)}}{GWP_{total\ (fossil\ fuel)}} \times 100 \tag{6.3}$$

Equation 6.3 is valid in cases where energy efficiency of both fossil and biofuels is the same – that is, the performance of the vehicle engine is not affected by the type of fuel. Otherwise, it should be adjusted to take into account any differences in the efficiency.

Table 6.3 *Life cycle GWP of different fuels (DEFRA, 2007; JRC et al., 2008)*

	Petrol	Diesel	Bioethanol	
			Wheat from Europe	Sugarcane from Brazil[a]
GWP of production (GWP$_{production}$)				
Extraction/cultivation[b] (CO$_2$ eq./MJ)	3.6	3.7	39.4	14.5
Fuel transport (CO$_2$ eq./MJ)	0.9	0.9	0.6	0.8
Fuel production (CO$_2$ eq./MJ)	7.0	8.6	9.5	0.7
Distribution (CO$_2$ eq./MJ)	1.0	1.0	1.5	8.1
Total GWP (GWP$_{production}$) (CO$_2$ eq./MJ)	12.5	14.2	51.0	24.1
GWP of fuel use (GWP$_{use}$)				
Lower heating value (MJ/kg)	43.2	42.5	N/A	N/A
Density (kg/l)	0.74	0.85	N/A	N/A
GHG$_{emissions}$ (kg CO$_2$ eq./l)	2.32	2.63	N/A	N/A
Total (GWP$_{use}$) (CO$_2$ eq./MJ)	72.3	72.6	N/A	N/A
Total GWP (GWP$_{production}$ + GWP$_{use}$)				
Total (GWP$_{Total}$) (CO$_2$ eq./MJ)	84.8	86.8	51.0	24.1

[a]Transported to and used in Europe.
[b]Extraction of crude oil in the case of petrol and diesel; cultivation of crops in the case of bioethanol.
N/A: not applicable.

As an example, Table 6.3 compares the life cycle GWPs of diesel, petrol and bioethanol (DEFRA, 2007). As shown, the use stage (combustion) of fossil fuels contributes 85% to the total life cycle GHG emissions. This indicates that significant improvements in engine efficiency and radical changes in the current fuel consumption patterns would be required to reduce the GHG emissions from fossil fuels (for discussion on the latter, see Chapter 15). Replacing petrol by bioethanol, on the other hand, would result in a 40% saving in GHG emissions in the case of wheat feedstock and 70% in the case of sugar cane (from Brazil). Therefore, at first glance, significant savings could be achieved by fossil-fuel replacement. However, this reduction in GHG assumes a 100% fuel replacement, which is currently not the case as only a small percentage of biofuels is normally added to the petrol–bioethanol blend (5–10%). (The exception to this is Brazil, where 100% bioethanol is used). Therefore, at such low fuel-blend ratios, the GHG savings from biofuels compared with fossil fuels are at best modest and their other sustainability issues – particularly those associated with first-generation biofuels – could outweigh the benefits (see sections below on the economic and social sustainability of biofuels).

It is also interesting to examine the sources of GHG emissions from the life cycle of biofuels. As shown in Table 6.3, most GHG emissions in these systems occur in the cultivation stage: 77% in the case of wheat and 60% in the case of sugar cane. The main sources of these emissions and the contribution of different GHGs are given in Table 6.4. (Note that the values are given per megajoule of wheat and that 1.9 MJ of wheat is needed to produce 1 MJ of bioethanol.)

The largest contributor to the GHG emissions from the cultivation of wheat is nitrogen fertilizer, mainly due to the emissions of CO$_2$ during its production and a subsequent (partial) conversion to nitrous oxide (N$_2$O) during its application on land. The latter alone contributes 64% to the total GWP from cultivation (see Table 6.4). The reason for this is that

Table 6.4 Contribution of different inputs and GHG in the cultivation stage of wheat (PROBAS, 2008)

Inputs	GHG emissions[a]			
	CO_2 (g/MJ$_{wheat}$)	CH_4 (g/MJ$_{wheat}$)	N_2O (g/MJ$_{wheat}$)	GWP[b] (g CO_2 eq./MJ$_{wheat}$)
Diesel	1.65	$<1 \times 10^{-5}$	$<1 \times 10^{-5}$	1.65
N-fertilizer	4.16	0.0090	0.021	10.64
K_2O-fertilizer	0.252	0.0034	1.24×10^{-5}	0.34
P_2O_5-fertilizer	0.311	0.0007	1.74×10^{-5}	0.33
Pesticides	0.70	0.0028	2.57×10^{-5}	0.78
Field N_2O emissions			0.0234	6.97
GWP of cultivation (GWP$_{cultivation}$)				20.72[c]
Contribution (%)	33.9	1.9	64.2	

[a]GHG emissions for the inputs shown on a life cycle basis.
[b]GWP $= \Sigma$GHG$_{emission} \times$ GWP$_{GHG}$; where GWP$_{GHG}$ is the global warming potential of each GHG; GWP$_{CO2} = 1$ kg CO_2 eq./kg CO_2; GWP$_{CH4} = 25$ kg CO_2 eq./kg CH_4; GWP$_{N2O} = 298$ kg CO_2 eq./kg CO_2 – for GWP of other substances, see Chapter 3.
[c]1.9 MJ of wheat is needed for 1 MJ of bioethanol, so that 20.72 g CO_2 eq./MJ$_{wheat} \times 1.9$ MJ$_{wheat}$/MJ$_{bioethanol} = 39.4$ g CO_2 eq./MJ ethanol, as shown in Table 6.3.

cereal crops take up only 20 to 50% of the nitrogen applied to soil (Moshier *et al.*, 2004). The remaining nitrogen is stored in soil for a short time but it quickly leaches into freshwater systems or is converted by microorganisms into atmospheric N_2O, nitrogen (N_2) or ammonia (NH_3). The aquatic emissions of nitrogen lead to eutrophication, while the atmospheric emissions of N_2O and NH_3 cause global warming and acidification respectively (see Chapter 3 for definitions of different environmental impacts). These impacts are further discussed in Section 6.3.1.3.

Further examples of GWP comparison of petrol with biofuels from different feedstocks cultivated in different countries are given in Figure 6.7. As shown, the best-performing biofuel from food crops is the Brazilian ethanol from sugar cane, offering a GHG saving of 70% over petrol (see also Table 6.3). However, overall, the best biofuel is second-generation

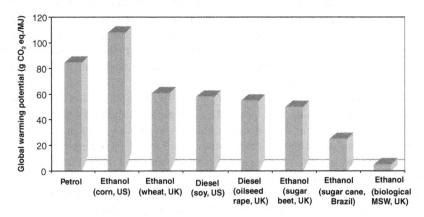

Figure 6.7 GHG emissions from biofuels compared with conventional transport fuels (DfT, 2008; Stichnothe and Azapagic, 2009)

ethanol from biological waste (derived from municipal solid waste), offering a saving of 90% (Stichnothe and Azapagic, 2009). As already pointed out, this option has additional advantages, such as reuse of resources, avoidance of landfilling and the related GHG emissions (Stichnothe and Azapagic, 2009).

On the other hand, ethanol from US corn does not appear to offer any GHG savings over petrol or diesel (as can also be seen in Table 6.3); in fact, its overall GHG emissions are higher than that of petrol and diesel. However, these results depend on the assumptions used in the estimation of GHG emissions, which can lead to a significant variation in the results (Fehrenbach *et al.*, 2007; DfT, 2008; Edwards *et al.*, 2008a,b; JRC *et al.*, 2008; Azapagic and Stichnothe, 2010). Therefore, a careful and thorough evaluation of the GHG saving potential from biofuels is necessary before making irreversible decisions on the future of biofuels. This is further reinforced in the sections on economic and social sustainability of biofuels. Prior to turning our attention to these, it is worth examining further environmental impacts associated with biofuels.

6.3.1.2 Land-Use Change

LUC is probably the most controversial issue associated with biofuels (Fargione *et al.*, 2008). The main concern is related to possible additional GHG emissions when carbon stored in the soil is disturbed and released due to the LUC. Two types of LUC are considered: direct and indirect. Direct LUC involves conversion of existing land from a current use to the cultivation of biomass feedstocks for biofuel production. Indirect LUC is associated with the displacement of existing agricultural activity due to the cultivation of biofuel crops (Searchinger *et al.*, 2008). Whilst the former can be assessed relatively easily (Solomon *et al.*, 2007), the latter is much more difficult as it will depend on many different factors.

An illustration of the influence of direct LUC for biodiesel from rapeseed is given in Table 6.5. Based on the assumptions used in this example (Fehrenbach *et al.*, 2007), biodiesel from rapeseed can provide GHG savings of 48% compared with diesel. However, if direct LUC occurs, the savings drop to below 10%.

In some cases, conversion of land (e.g. managed or wild grassland, forest) to biofuel production will result in GHG emissions large enough to cancel out the potential benefits of biofuels. In addition, there could be other significant negative environmental impacts, particularly on biodiversity. Because of its importance, LUC has to be included when GHG savings from biofuels are calculated.

The UK Department of Transport provides default values that can be used to calculate GHG emissions associated with biofuels if LUC is involved (DfT, 2008). Default values for bioethanol from wheat, sugar cane and sugar beet are shown in Table 6.6.

Table 6.5 *The influence on the GHG emissions with and without direct-land change use for biodiesel from rapeseed oil (Fehrenbach et al., 2007)*

	GHG emissions ($g\ CO_2$ eq./MJ)	GHG savings relative to diesel (%)
Total without LUC	45.2	—
Direct LUC	32.8[a]	47.5
Total with LUC	78.0	9.5

[a]Assumes worst case – conversion of land with high carbon content.

Table 6.6 *Default values for land use change[a] for bioethanol (DfT, 2008)*

Feedstock	Origin	Impact of LUC (g CO_2 eq./MJ biofuel)		
		Land covered by		
		Cropland	Forestland	Grassland
Wheat	Canada	0	977	126
	France	0	329	83
	UK	0	438	116
Sugar beet	UK	0	228	60
Sugarcane	Brazil	0	319	88
	South Africa	0	220	14

[a]The impact of LUC is considered over a 20-year period.

For example, converting rainforest in Brazil to cropland to produce sugar cane, releases 319 g CO_2 eq./MJ of ethanol. Over the period of 20 years (the usual period taken into account when calculating the impacts of LUC), the total GWP will amount to $319 \times 20 = 6380$ g CO_2 eq./MJ. The GWP of bioethanol from Brazilian sugar cane is 24.1 (see Table 6.3), so that the amount of GHG emissions saved over petrol is $84.8 - 24.1 = 60.7$ g CO_2 eq./MJ. Consequently, the payback time is $6380/60.7 = 105$ years. Therefore, it would take 105 years before bioethanol produced from sugar cane grown on converted forest land compensates the CO_2 emissions caused by LUC.

6.3.1.3 Other Environmental Impacts

The following provides brief discussions of other environmental impacts that, in addition to global warming, are associated with biofuel systems.

Biodiversity: Agriculture and forestry have been the main causes of biodiversity loss globally; for example, more land was converted to cropland over 30 years between 1950 and 1980 than over 150 years between 1700 and 1850 (MEA, 2005). Therefore, there is also a potential for biofuel crops to alter local habitats and resources in a way that will affect biodiversity and have adverse impact on native species. These effects will depend on the crop, its density, duration and distribution on the landscape and any regular inputs, including water and chemicals (The Royal Society, 2008). Biodiversity loss can also occur due to direct effects of LUC. For example, if set-aside land in Europe is used to grow biofuel crops, impacts on biodiversity will need to be evaluated because some of these areas are more biodiverse than farmlands (Critchley and Fowbert, 2000). Intensified cultivation of biofuel crops could also lead to new pests and diseases, which could in turn lead to increased use of pesticides/herbicides, causing further environmental damage.

Therefore, it is important that the overall risks and benefits for biodiversity be evaluated appropriately for bioenergy feedstocks. The Royal Society (2008) recommends using a risk assessment framework that covers the following:

- the full life cycle of biofuel production;
- the invasiveness potential of the crop;
- potential interactive effects of the biofuel crop with other pressures in the area (such as drought stress);

- the impacts on ecosystems;
- changes in these risks under a future climate.

However, the lack of data represents a significant barrier in addressing biodiversity on a life cycle basis, as biofuel crops have not yet been assessed for their impacts on biodiversity. Furthermore, currently, there is no agreed methodology on estimating the impacts on biodiversity in LCA.

Water use: Water is used throughout the life cycle of biofuels, from feedstock to biofuel production. So far, water use has not been considered in LCA or other evaluations of environmental sustainability of biofuels. The main reasons are the lack of data and an agreed methodology for estimating the water footprint (Azapagic and Stichnothe, 2010). Although there are some data available on water use for crops, water requirements through the rest of the supply chain are unclear. This is not an issue specific to biofuels only, but also to other systems – as water has emerged as a global issue only relatively recently, the need for information on water consumption in different productive systems has only come to light since. Consequently, no current LCA databases contain reliable data on water consumption so that currently it is not possible to provide reliable estimates of water usage on a life cycle basis (Azapagic and Stichnothe, 2010).

Other impacts: Most LCA studies of biofuels focus on GHG emissions and energy balances. However, as already mentioned, biofuels have wider environmental impacts, including resource depletion, biodiversity, acidification, eutrophication and toxicity. These have rarely been considered in LCA studies to date (Azapagic and Stichnothe, 2010).

As an example, Figure 6.8 compares selective environmental impacts from bioethanol (from wheat) and petrol (Azapagic and Stichnothe, 2010). These results illustrate that,

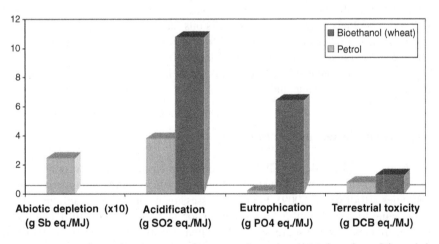

Figure 6.8 *Comparison of environmental impacts of petrol and bioethanol on a life cycle basis (after Azapagic and Stichnothe, 2010). Notes:* Bioethanol is from wheat cultivated in Germany; comparison is made on the basis of the equivalent energy content in petrol and bioethanol; the unit of analysis is 1 l of petrol and 1.6 l of bioethanol (due to the lower energy content of bioethanol compared with petrol); the impacts are expressed per litre for petrol, per 1.6 l for bioethanol; system boundary is from 'cradle to gate' (use stage not included); DCB: dichlorobenzene

while biofuels can provide GHG savings, their other impacts can be higher than those of conventional fossil fuels. For the example considered here, bioethanol has three times higher acidification and 27 times higher eutrophication than petrol (note that the use stage of fuels is not considered). These are mainly due to the use of fertilizers and fuel in the agricultural machinery. Its terrestrial toxicity is 1.6 times higher, again mainly due to the assumed use of chemical fertilizers.

From this and the earlier discussion it is clear that evaluation of environmental sustainability of biofuels should involve consideration of all relevant environmental impacts along the whole life cycle to avoid shifting the burdens along the supply chains and making unsustainable choices.

We now turn our attention to the economic sustainability of biofuels.

Questions

1. Describe the life cycles of biofuels and fossil fuels – what are the main differences in the life cycle stages?
2. How can the environmental performance of biofuels be assessed? What are the main issues that should be considered and why?
3. What are the effects of biofuels on air quality?
4. Is converting forest into cropland a valid option for biofuel production? Why?
5. Calculate the payback time for LUC for one biofuel of your choice. What do you conclude – is that a sustainable option?
6. How would you assess/evaluate the loss of biodiversity? What would need to be taken into account?
7. What would be the total land requirements in your country for production of biofuels? Discuss the implications for food production.
8. Generally, biofuels have lower GHG emissions than fossil fuels; however, their other impacts can be higher. How should the different environmental impacts be traded off? Discuss the implications of the proposed trade-offs.
9. Based on the environmental criteria discussed in this section, which biofuel(s) do you think are more sustainable and why?

6.3.2 Economic Sustainability of Biofuels

While there are many studies on GHG emissions from biofuel systems, economic data are scant and difficult to compare owing to different assumptions for feedstocks and conversion technologies (Bridgwater, 2009). Economic assessments are not available in the public domain owing to confidentiality, as the conversion technologies are still under development. Nevertheless, several sources provide estimates of the economic viability of biofuel systems, as discussed below (Azapagic and Stichnothe, 2010).

On a life cycle basis, the costs of biofuels are mainly contributed by:

- the costs of feedstock cultivation, preparation and delivery;
- the capital costs for manufacturing plants for conversion into biofuels; and
- other costs, such as labour, utilities, maintenance, insurance and so on.

6.3.2.1 Feedstock Costs

The current costs of providing biomass vary greatly depending on the type of biomass and its source. In Europe, for instance, they range from €21 to €180 per tonne of dry matter (DENA, 2006). The variation is due to the different energy and moisture contents, as well as the origin of the feedstocks. Wood chips are at the upper end of the price range, whereas waste wood and agricultural residues are at the lower end; the average feedstock costs are less than €60 per tonne of dry matter. These costs include feedstock storage close to the field or forest (10 km) but not the transport costs to the processing plant. The delivery costs increase with the moisture content and transportation distance.

6.3.2.2 Capital Costs

Estimates of capital costs for biofuel plants (or any other developing technology) are uncertain owing to the many influencing factors. One of the studies puts the cost of thermochemical plants between €525 million and €650 million for plants treating 1×10^6 t of wet biomass and producing 105 000–120 000 t of biofuel per year (DENA, 2006). Figure 6.7 shows the process options considered and Table 6.8 the breakdown of costs. The processing route involving gasification and Fischer–Tropsch synthesis (route 1) appears to be economically the most sustainable option. It is interesting to note that integration into an existing refinery or chemical plant is the most cost-effective option across the different processing routes. Integration into an existing refinery or chemical plant can also accelerate the planning procedure and can lower investment costs by around 25% (DENA, 2006).

Even fewer estimates are available for the capital costs of biochemical plants. A recent study by the US EPA (2009b) estimates the costs for a biochemical plant producing 56 million gallons/year of ethanol from 849 385 dry tonnes/year of corn stover at $133 million/year (for the year 2010). With other costs added (including site development, project contingency and so on), the total project investment costs are estimated at $232 million/year (US EPA, 2009b). For the years 2015 and 2020, the annual costs are predicted to go down to $220 million and $198 million respectively.

6.3.2.3 Biofuel Costs

Estimates of biofuel prices are given in Table 6.9. Although these are uncertain, several general points can be drawn from the estimates (The Royal Society, 2008):

- higher oil prices are beginning to make current biofuels commercially more attractive;
- cost reductions through economies of scale are expected for all biofuels, with lignocellulose technologies anticipated to be in the same range as food-crop technologies;
- the post-tax prices of petrol and diesel fuels in Europe (less so in the USA) are often much higher than the pre-tax costs of biofuels; hence, tax credits or other incentives, for example in the form of reductions in excise taxes on biofuels, would have a large effect on substitution.

Table 6.7 Process options considered in the DENA study (after DENA, 2006)

	Mechanical treatment	Thermal pre-treatment	Gasification	Gas purification	Synthesis	Product conditioning
1	Milling		Entrained-flow gasification	Gas purification	Fischer–Tropsch synthesis	Product conditioning
2	Shredding	Fast pyrolysis	Entrained-flow gasification	Gas purification	Fischer–Tropsch synthesis	Product conditioning
3	Shredding		Fluidized bed gasification	Gas purification	Methanol synthesis	Product conditioning
4	Shredding	Pyrolysis	Entrained-flow gasification	Gas purification	Fischer–Tropsch synthesis	Product conditioning
5	Shredding	Pyrolysis	Entrained-flow gasification	Gas purification	Methanol synthesis	Product conditioning

Row 1: Centralized

Row 2: Decentralized (Mechanical treatment / Thermal pre-treatment); Centralized (Gasification onwards)

Row 3: Decentralized (Mechanical treatment); Centralized (Gasification onwards)

Row 4: Decentralized (Mechanical treatment / Thermal pre-treatment); Centralized (Gasification onwards)

Row 5: Decentralized (Mechanical treatment / Thermal pre-treatment); Centralized (Gasification onwards)

Table 6.8 *Investment costs (million Euro) for different technology options in the DENA study (Bridgewater, 2009; DENA, 2006)*

Case	1	1 Ref	2	2 Ref	3	4	4 Ref	5	5 Ref
Storage and preparation	55	55	60	60	55	50	50	50	50
Pyrolysis	0	0	86	86	0	90	90	90	90
Gasification and cleaning	90	90	79	79	97	90	90	90	90
Gas conditioning	33	33	30	26	68	31	30	31	30
Fischer–Tropsch and conditioning	84	88	78	79	0	84	80	0	0
Lurgi Mt synfuel	0	0	0	0	96	0	0	84	81
Oxygen production	47	0	45	0	54	45	0	45	0
Power plant	24	0	21	0	28	23	0	23	0
Auxiliary plant infrastructure	81	43	131	90	110	89	57	89	56
Planning cost	74	60	90	71	82	71	57	71	57
Contingency	37	35	38	32	39	39	34	39	34
Total	*525*	*398*	*658*	*523*	*629*	*612*	*488*	*612*	*488*
Dry biomass input (t/yr)	700 000	700 000	700 000	700 000	700 000	700 000	700 000	700 000	700 000
Product output, hydrocarbons, t/year	114 000	114 000	106 400	106 400	104 000	118 300	118 300	118 300	118 300

Ref: integrated into refinery; option 3 not considered worthwhile integrating into a refinery.

Table 6.9 *Estimated prices of biofuels compared with the prices of oil and oil products (biofuels exclusive of taxes) (after The Royal Society, 2008)*

Biofuel	2006 (US cents/litre)	2030 (US cents/litre)
Price of oil (US$/barrel)	50–80	
Corresponding pre-tax price of petroleum products	35–60	
Corresponding price of petroleum products with taxes included (retail price)	80 in USA 150–200 in Europe	
Ethanol from sugarcane	25–50	25–35
Ethanol from corn	60–80	35–55
Ethanol from beet	60–80	40–60
Ethanol from wheat	70–95	45–65
Ethanol from lignocellulose	80–110	25–65
Biodiesel from animal fats	40–55	40–50
Biodiesel from vegetable oils	70–100	40–75
Fischer–Tropsch synthesis liquids	90–110	70–85

However, these estimates do not take into account changes in prices and land values that may arise from competing demands from agriculture.

The economic prospects of biofuels will depend on improvements in yields both in the growth of the crops and in the efficiency of the conversion processes. Feedstock costs will also influence biofuel prices.

Questions

1. What are the main aspects determining the costs of biofuels?
2. How could future costs of biofuels be reduced?
3. Which fuels have the greatest potential from the economic point of view and why?
4. Using the economic criteria presented in the previous section, identify the economically most sustainable biofuel. How is your choice different than the choice made based on the environmental criteria (see Question 9 in Section 6.3.1).

6.3.3 Social Sustainability of Biofuels

Although there are numerous social issues along the whole biofuel supply chains, the principal social risks arise at the feedstock cultivation stage (Dufey, 2006; DfT, 2008). As listed in Table 6.2, some of these include human health, human and labour rights, land ownerships, impact on food security, community development and impact on indigenous peoples.

Human health issues can be particularly serious in developing countries. For example, as estimated by the UN, heavy use of pesticides leads to about 2 million cancer cases and 10 000 deaths each year (Quijano *et al.*, 1993).

The issues of human and labour rights, as well as gender discrimination, have also been reported. Women are particularly vulnerable – they receive lower wages and are subjected to longer working hours than men (Rossi and Lambrou, 2008). Furthermore, some studies show that sugar cane cultivation and palm oil plantations, in Brazil and Indonesia respectively, have poor working conditions as well as child and forced labour (Dufey, 2006).

However, as areas of high biomass production are often also areas of low wealth and earnings, socio-economic benefits from biofuels could be significant. Programmes are already underway to ensure that rural and regional economies benefit from the domestic production and use of feedstocks as well as their export (The Royal Society, 2008). For example, policies for social and regional development in Brazil enable biodiesel (from castor oil and palm oil) to gain 'social fuel' certification with associated tax incentives if raw materials are bought from family agriculture and small farms (De Azevedo Rodriques, 2007).

It is important to address social and other sustainability issues while the sector is still developing, before causing irreversible damage. There are numerous initiatives attempting to ensure that the sector develops in a sustainable way. These include transfer of 'appropriate' technologies to developing countries, policies to divert cultivation from highly productive to marginal or abandoned land and increased transparency within the biofuels supply chains.

An example of a biofuel-related policy is the UK's Renewable Transport Fuel Obligation (RTFO) (DfT, 2008). To encourage suppliers to source sustainable biofuels, the Government requires biofuel suppliers to submit reports on both the sustainability of the biofuels they supply and the net GHG saving in order to receive Renewable Transport Fuel Certificates (RTFCs). The reports should address the direct impacts arising from biofuel cultivation that are potentially within the influence of companies sourcing or producing biofuels through effective supply-chain management. Indirect LUC or changes to food and other commodity prices that are beyond the control of individual suppliers, should also be monitored closely. The RTFO commenced on 15 April 2008 and its aim is to reduce up to 3.0 million tonnes of CO_2 per annum by 2010, by encouraging the supply of renewable fuels. The Government also sees the reporting framework as an essential 'stepping-stone' towards a mandatory assurance scheme.

The RTFO reporting guidance focuses on the cultivation part of the supply chain and comprises the seven guiding environmental and social principles given in Table 6.10. It includes a number of related criteria and indicators (as set out in Tables 6.11 and 6.12) to assess the extent to which the feedstock can be considered sustainable.

Table 6.10 *Environmental and social principles (after DfT, 2008)*

Environmental principles	Social principles
1. Biomass production will not destroy or damage large above- or below-ground carbon stocks	6. Biomass production does not adversely affect workers' rights and working relationships
2. Biomass production will not lead to the destruction or damage to high-biodiversity areas	7. Biomass production does not adversely affect existing land rights and community relations
3. Biomass production does not lead to soil degradation	
4. Biomass production does not lead to the contamination or depletion of water sources	
5. Biomass production does not lead to air pollution	

Table 6.11   *Environmental indicators (after DfT, 2008)*

Principle 1: Carbon Conservation	Biomass production will not destroy or damage large above- or below-ground carbon stocks
Criteria	*Indicators*
1.1 Preservation of above and below ground carbon stocks (reference date 30/11/2005)	• Evidence that biomass production has not caused direct LUC with a carbon payback time exceeding 10 years. • Evidence that the biomass production unit has not been established on soils with a large risk of significant soil-stored carbon losses, such as peat lands, mangroves, wetlands and certain grasslands.
Principle 2: Biodiversity Conservation	**Biomass production will not lead to the destruction or damage of high-biodiversity areas**
Criteria	*Indicators*
2.1 Compliance with national laws and regulations relevant to biomass production in the area and surroundings where biomass production takes place	• Evidence of compliance with national and local laws and regulations with respect to: - environmental impact assessment - land ownership and land-use rights - forest and plantation management - protected and gazetted areas - nature and wildlife conservation - land use planning • The company should prove that: - it is familiar with relevant national and local legislation - it complies with this legislation - it remains informed on changes in legislation
2.2 No conversion of high-biodiversity areas after 30/11/2005	• Evidence that production does not take place in gazetted areas • Evidence that production does not take place in areas with one or more high conservation value (HCV) areas • Evidence that production does not take place in any areas of high biodiversity
2.3 The status of rare, threatened or endangered species and high conservation value habitats, if any, that exist in the production site or that could be affected by it, shall be identified and their conservation taken into account in management plans and operations.	• Documentation of the status of rare, threatened or endangered species (resident, migratory or otherwise) and high conservation value habitats in and around the production site • Documented and implemented management plan on how to avoid damage to or disturbance of the above mentioned species and habitats

Table 6.11   (Continued)

Principle 3: Soil Conservation	Biomass production does not lead to soil degradation
Criteria	*Indicators*
3.1 Compliance with national laws and regulations relevant to soil degradation and soil management.	• Evidence of compliance with national and local laws and regulations with respect to: - environmental impact assessment - Waste storage and handling - pesticides and agro-chemicals - fertilizer - soil erosion • Compliance with the Stockholm Convention (list of forbidden pesticides) • The company should prove that: - it is familiar with relevant national and local legislation - it complies with this legislation - it remains informed on changes in legislation
3.2 Application of good agricultural practices with respect to: • prevention and control of erosion • maintaining and improving soil nutrient balance • maintaining and improving soil organic matter • maintaining and improving soil pH • maintaining and improving soil structure • maintaining and improving soil biodiversity • prevention of salinization	• Documentation of soil management plan aimed at sustainable soil management, erosion prevention and erosion control • Annual documentation of applied good agricultural practices with respect to: - prevention and control of erosion - maintaining and improving soil nutrient balance - maintaining and improving soil organic matter - maintaining and improving soil pH - maintaining and improving soil structure - maintaining and improving soil biodiversity - prevention of salinization
Principle 4: Sustainable Water Use	**Biomass production does not lead to the contamination or depletion of water sources**
Criteria	*Indicators*
4.1 Compliance with national laws and regulations relevant to contamination and depletion of water Sources	• Evidence of compliance with national and local laws and regulations with respect to: - environmental impact assessment - waste storage and handling - pesticides and agro-chemicals - fertilizer - irrigation and water usage

Table 6.11   *(Continued)*

	• The company should prove that:
	  - it is familiar with relevant national and local legislation
	  - it complies with this legislation
	  - it remains informed on changes in legislation

4.2 Application of good agricultural practices to reduce water usage and to maintain and improve water Quality	• Documentation of water management plan aimed at sustainable water use and prevention of water pollution
	• Annual documentation of applied good agricultural practices with respect to:
	  - efficient water usage.
	  - responsible use of agro-chemicals
	  - waste discharge

Principle 5: Air Quality	**Biomass production does not lead to air pollution**
Criteria	*Indicators*

5.1 Compliance with national laws and regulations relevant to air emissions and burning practices	• Evidence of compliance with national and local laws and regulations with respect to:
	  - environmental impact assessment
	  - air emissions
	  - waste management
	  - burning practices
	• The company should prove that:
	  - it is familiar with relevant national and local legislation
	  - it complies with this legislation
	  - it remains informed on changes in legislation

5.2 No burning as part of land clearing or waste disposal	• Evidence that no burning occurs as part of land clearing or waste disposal, except in specific situations

Questions

1. Discuss the social aspects of biofuels. How could they be addressed?
2. In your opinion, do the environmental and social indicators in Tables 6.11 and 6.12 cover all the relevant issues? If not, what other issues and life cycle stages should be included?
3. Balancing the economic, environmental and social aspects of biofuels, what do you conclude? Are biofuels sustainable? Why?

6.4 Conclusions

The future development of the biofuel sector will depend on many technological, economic, environmental and social factors. This chapter has explored some of these, in an attempt to

Table 6.12   *Social indicators (after DfT, 2008)*

Principle 6: Workers rights	Biomass production does not adversely effect workers rights and working relationships
Criteria	Indicators
C 6.1 Compliance with national law on working conditions and workers rights	Certification applicant must comply with all national law concerning working conditions and workers' rights
C 6.2 Contracts	Certification applicant must supply all categories of employees (incl. temporary workers) with a legal contract
C 6.3 Provision of information	Certification applicant must show evidence that all workers are informed about their rights (including bargaining rights)
C 6.4 Subcontracting	When labour is contracted or subcontracted to provide services for the certification applicant, the certification applicant must demonstrate that the contractor/subcontractor provides its services under the same environmental, social and labour conditions as required for this standard
C 6.5 Freedom of association and right to collective bargaining	Certification applicant must guarantee the rights of workers to organize and negotiate their working conditions (as established in ILO Conventions 87–98). Workers exercising this right must not be discriminated against or suffer repercussions
C 6.6 Child labour	Certification applicant must guarantee that no children below the age of 15 are employed. Children are allowed to work on family farms if not interfering with children's educational, moral, social and physical development (the work day, inclusive of school and transport time, to be a maximum of 10 h)
C 6.7 Young workers	The work carried out shall not be hazardous or dangerous to the health and safety of young workers (age 15–17). It shall also not jeopardize their educational, moral, social and physical development. All certification applicants must meet basic requirements, including potable drinking water, clean latrines or toilets, a clean place to eat, adequate protective equipment and access to adequate and accessible (physically and financially) medical care. Accommodation, where provided, shall be clean, safe and meet the basic needs of the workers. All certification applicants shall ensure that workers have received regular health and safety training appropriate to the work that they perform.
C 6.8 Health and safety	All certification applicants shall identify and inform workers of hazards, and adopt preventive measures to minimize hazards in the workplace and maintain records of accidents. Wageworkers must be paid wages at least equivalent to the legal national minimum wage or the relevant industry standard, whichever is higher.
C 6.9 Wages/compensation	Workers must be paid in cash, or in a form that is convenient to them and regularly.

Table 6.12   (Continued)

Criteria	Indicators
C 6.10 Discrimination	In accordance with ILO Conventions 100 and 111, there must be no discrimination (distinction, exclusion or preference) practised that denies or impairs equality of opportunity, conditions, or treatment based on individual characteristics and group membership or association like: race, caste, national origin, religion, disability, gender, sexual orientation, union membership, political affiliation, age, marital status, those with HIV/AIDS, seasonal, migrant and temporary workers.
C 6.11 Forced labour	Standards shall require that the certification applicant not engage in or support forced labour including bonded labour as defined by ILO Conventions 29 and 105. The company must not retain any part of workers' salary, benefits, property, or documents in order to force workers to remain on the farm. The company must also refrain from any form of physical or psychological measure requiring workers to remain employed on the farm. Spouses and children of contracted workers should not be required to work on the farm.
Principle 7:	**Biomass production does not adversely affect existing land rights and community relations**
Criteria	Indicators
C 7.1 Land right issues	The right to use the land can be demonstrated and does not diminish the legal or customary rights of other users and respects important areas for local people.
C 7.2 Consultation and communication with local stakeholders	Procedures are in place to consult and communicate with local populations and interest groups on plans and activities that may negatively affect the legal or customary rights, property, resources, or livelihoods of local peoples.

help towards a better understanding of the sustainability issues associated with biofuels. Arguably, however, for the sector to develop in a sustainable way, the 'right' policies will have to be in place promoting sustainable practices along the supply chains around the world. As discussed, there are already some good examples of national and regional policies for sustainable biofuels (e.g. in the EU and UK), but these are still isolated examples. For a more sustainable biofuels sector globally, a concerted action is needed world-wide to ensure that the 'sustainability burden' is not shifted from developed to developing countries and that there is a fair sharing of costs and benefits along the supply chains.

Acknowledgements

Part of the work presented in this chapter has been funded within the project 'Carbon Calculations over the Life Cycle of Industrial Activities (CCaLC)' by the EPSRC, NERC and Carbon Trust (grant no. EP/F003 501/1). This funding is gratefully acknowledged.

References and Further Reading

Amin, S. (2009) Review on biofuel oil and gas production processes from microalgae. *Energy Conversion and Management*, **50**, 1834–1840.

Azapagic, A. and Stichnothe, H. (2010) Life cycle sustainability assessment of Chapter 3, p. 37–60, in *Handbook of Biofuels Production* (eds R. Luque, J. Campelo and J. Clark), Woodhead Publishers.

Bird, D.N., Cherubini, F., Cowie, A., *et al.* (2008) Ten years of analysing the greenhouse balances of bioenergy systems, IEA Task 38, International Energy Agency. http://www.ieabioenergy-task38.org/publications/T38_OC6_2_17_EU_Conf_2009.pdf.

Bridgwater, A.V. (2009) Technical and economic assessment of thermal processes for biofuels. NNFCC Report, York.

Bringezu, S., Schütz, H., O'Brien, M., *et al.* (2009) *Towards Sustainable Production and Use of Resources: Assessing Biofuels*. UNEP Report. http://www.uneptie.org/scp/rpanel/pdf/Assessing_Biofuels_Full_Report.pdf.

Critchley, C.N.R. and Fowbert, J.A. (2000) Development of vegetation on set-aside for up to nine years from a national perspective. *Agriculture, Ecosystems and Environment*, **79** (2), 159–174.

Crutzen, P.J., Mosier, A.R., Smith, K.A. and Winiwarter, W. (2007) N_2O release from agro-biofuel production negates global warming reduction by replacing fossil fuels. *Atmospheric Chemistry and Physics Discussions*, **7**, 11191–11205.

DEFRA (2007) Guidelines for company reporting on greenhouse gas emissions. Defra, London.

Delucchi, M.A. (2004) Conceptual and methodological issues in life cycle analyses of transport fuels. http://www.its.ucdavis.edu/publications/2004/UCD-ITS-RR-04-45.pdf.

DENA (2006) Biomass to liquid – BTL Implementation report (executive summary). Deutsche Erneuerbare Energieagentur (DENA), Berlin.

DfT (2008) Carbon and sustainability reporting within the renewable transport fuel obligation – requirements and guidance. Department for Transport, London.

DfT (2010): *UK Transport and Climate Change Data - Factsheets*, Department for Transport. http://www.dft.gov.uk/pgr/statistics/datatablespublications/energyenvironment/climatechangefactsheets.pdf.

De Azevedo Rodriques, M.C. (2007) Ethanol & Biodiesel in Brazil. Presentation. International Conference on Biofuels Standards. Brussels, 27–28 February 2007. EC-CEN. http://ec.europa.eu/energy/renewables/events/2007_02_27_biofuels_standards_en.htm.

Dufey, A. (2006) Biofuels production, trade and sustainable development: emerging issues. IIED, November 2006. http://www.iied.org/pubs/pdfs/15504IIED.pdf.

E4Tech (2007) Carbon reporting within the Renewable Transport Fuel Obligation – Methodology. Department for Transport, London.

EC (2009) Directive 2009/28/EC of the European Parliament and of the Council of 23 April 2009 on the Promotion of the Use of Energy from Renewable Sources and Amending and Subsequently Repelling Directives 2001/77/EC and 2003/30/EC. European Commission, Brussels. http://eur-lex.europa.eu/LexUriServ/LexUriServ.do?uri=OJ:L:2009:140:0016:0062:EN:PDF.

Edwards, R., Larive, J.-F., Mahieu, V. and Rouveirolles, P. (2008a) Well-to-wheels analysis of future automotive fuels and power trains in the European context. JRC, Eucar and Concawe. V3 November 2008. http://ies.jrc.ec.europa.eu/uploads/media/V3.1%20TTW%20Report%2007102008.pdf.

Edwards, R., Neuwahl, F. and Mahieu, V. (2008b) Biofuels in the European context: facts and uncertainties (ed. G. De Sani), JRC, Ispra.

EEA (2009) Transport at a crossroads - TERM 2008: indicators tracking transport and environment in the European Union. EEA Report, No 3/2009, European Environment Agency, Copenhagen.

Escobar, J.C., Lora, E.S., Venturini, O.J. *et al.* (2009) Biofuels: environment, technology and food security. *Renewable and Sustainable Energy Reviews*, **13** (6–7), 1275–1287.

Fargione, J., Hill, J., Tilman, D. *et al.* (2008) Land clearing and the biofuel carbon debt. *Science*, **319** (5867), 1235–1238.

Farrell, A.E., Plevin, R.J., Turner, B.T. *et al.* (2006) Ethanol can contribute to energy and environmental goals. *Science*, **311**, 506–508.

Fehrenbach, H., Giegrich, J., Gärtner, S. *et al.* (2007) Greenhouse Gas Balances for the German Biofuels Quota Legislation. Methodological Guidance and Default Values. Ifeu, Heidelberg,

Dec 2007. http://www.oeko.de/service/bio/dateien/en/methodology_for_biofuels_default values_ifeu.pdf.

GFG (2007) German Draft Biofuel Sustainability Ordinance. German Federal Government. 5 Dec 2007.

Gwehenberger, G., Narodoslawsky, M., Liebmann, B. and Friedl, A. (2007) Ecology of scale versus economy of scale for bioethanol production. *Biofuels, Bioproducts and Biorefining.*, **1** (4), 264–269.

Halleux, H., Lassaux, S., Renzoni, R. and Germain, A. (2008) Comparative life cycle assessment of two biofuels ethanol from sugar beet and rapeseed methyl ester. *The International Journal of Life Cycle Assessment*, **13** (3), 184–190.

IDB (2009) IDB Biofuels Sustainability Scorecard. Inter-American Development Bank. http://www.iadb.org/biofuelsscorecard/.

Solomon, S., Qin, D., Manning, M. *et al.*. (eds). (2007) *Climate Change 2007: The Physical Science Basis. Report of Working Group 1 to the Fourth Assessment Report of the Intergovernmental Panel on Climate Change.* Cambridge University Press, Cambridge.

JRC, Concawe and EUCAR (2008) Well-to-wheels analysis of future automotive fuels and power-trains in the European context. WELL-TO-TANK Report Version 3.0, November 2008. http://ies.jrc.ec.europa.eu/uploads/media/WTT%20App%202%20v30%20181108.pdf.

Larson, E. (2008) Biofuel production technologies: status, prospects and implications for trade and development. UNCTAD XII, UN Conference on Trade and Development. Accra, Ghana, 20–25 April, 2008. http://www.unctadxii.org/en/Documents/Conference-Documents/.

Lavigne, A. and Powers, S.E. (2007) Evaluating fuel ethanol feedstocks from energy policy perspectives: a comparative energy assessment of corn and corn stover. *Energy Policy*, **35** (11), 5918–5930.

Li, Y.H., Wu, N., Lan, C.Q. and Dubois-Calero, N. (2008) Biofuels from microalgae. *Biotechnology Progress*, **24** (4), 815–820.

MEA (2005) *Ecosystems and Human Well-being: Our Human Planet. Summary for Decision Makers*, Millennium Ecosystem Assessment, Island Press, Washington, DC, www.ifpri.org/pubs/fpr/fpr29.pdf.

Moshier, A.R., Syers, J.K. and Freney, J.R. (eds) (2004) *Agriculture and the Nitrogen Cycle*, SCOPE, vol. **65**, Island Press, Washington, DC.

OECD and IEA (2008) Energy technology perspectives. Scenarios and strategies to 2050. Paris. http://www.iea.org/speech/2006/ramsay/etp_beijing.pdf.

Pimentel, D. (2003) Ethanol fuels: energy balance, economics, and environmental impacts are negative. *Natural Resources Research*, **12** (2), 127–134.

Pimentel, D. and Patzek, T. (2007) Ethanol production: energy and economic issues related to U.S. and Brazilian sugarcane. *Natural Resources Research*, **16** (3), 235–242.

Pimentel, D. and Patzek, T.W. (2005) Ethanol production using corn, switchgrass, and wood; biodiesel production using soybean and sunflower. *Natural Resources Research*, **14** (1), 65–76.

PROBAS (2008) LCA database. www.probas.umweltbundesamt.de.

Quijano, R., Panganiban, L. and Cortes-Maramba, N. (1993) Time to blow the whistle: dangers of toxic chemicals. *World Health*, **46**, 26–27.

Rajagopal, D. and Zilberman, D. (2007a) Review of environmental, economic and policy aspects of biofuels. P. R. W. P. 4341, World Bank. http://www.ncsu.edu/project/amazonia/for414/Readings/biofuels_wb.pdf.

Rajagopal, D., Sexton, S.E., Roland-Holst, D. and Zilberman, D. (2007b) Challenge of biofuel: filling the tank without emptying the stomach? *Environmental Research Letters*, **2** (4), 044004.

Rossi, A. and Lambrou, Y. (2008) Gender and equity issues in liquid biofuels production: minimising the risks to maximise the opportunities. FAO, Rome. http://www.fao.org/docrep/010/ai503e/ai503e00.HTM.

Schmer, M.R., Vogel, K.P., Mitchell, R.B. and Perrin, R.K. (2007) Net energy of cellulosic ethanol from switchgrass. *Proceedings of the National Academy of Sciences of the United States of America*, **105**, 464–469.

Searchinger, T., Heimlich, R., Houghton, R.A. *et al.* (2008) Use of U.S. croplands for biofuels increases greenhouse gases through emissions from land-use change. *Science*, **319** (5867), 1238–1240.

SFG (2007) Amendment of 23 March 2007 of the Mineral Oil Taxation Law (Limpmin). Swiss Federal Government, 23 March 2007.

Stichnothe, H. and Azapagic, A. (2009) Bioethanol from waste: life cycle estimation of the greenhouse gas saving potential. *Resources, Conservation and Recycling*, **53**, 160–184.

The Royal Society (2008) *Sustainable Biofuels: Prospects and Challenges*, The Royal Society, London.

US EPA (2006) Greenhouse gas emissions from the U.S. transportation sector 1990–2003. United States Environmental Protection Agency, Office of Transportation and Air Quality, Washington, DC. www.epa.gov/otaq/climate.htm.

US EPA (2009a) EPA lifecycle analysis of greenhouse gas emissions from renewable fuels. Office of Transportation and Air Quality, EPA-420-F-09-024, May 2009. http://www.epa.gov/OMS/renew-ablefuels/420f09024.pdf.

US EPA (2009b) Draft regulatory impact analysis: changes to Renewable Fuel Standard program, EPA-420-D-09-001, May 2009. http://www.epa.gov/OMS/renewablefuels/420d09001.pdf.

USFG (2007) Energy Independence and Security Act of 2007., Public Law 110–140—DEC. 19, 2007, US Federal Government, http://frwebgate.access.gpo.gov/cgi-bin/getdoc.cgi?dbname=110_cong_public_laws&docid=f:publ140.110.pdf.

7

Scenario Building and Uncertainties: Options for Energy Sources

Richard Darton

In order to develop a strategy for the future, we must have some view of that future in which our current decisions and actions, the components of our strategy, will bear fruit. In this case study we consider how distinct views of the future – scenarios – can be put together so as to influence strategic decisions, and explain how they are used. We concentrate on the key factors which are both highly important and very uncertain. A number of scenarios relevant to global energy supply are discussed, which underline the importance both of techno-logical development and societal change.

7.1 Sustainability and the Need to Look Ahead

As discussed in Chapter 1, many different definitions of sustainability have been offered, but they all have in common that the desire of those of us alive now to enjoy a high standard of living should somehow be balanced against the needs of those who will come after us. Two immediate and difficult questions arise:

1. Can we predict what the future consequences of our present decisions and actions will be?
2. What will be the needs of future generations that we need to take account of now?

Sustainable Development in Practice: Case Studies for Engineers and Scientists, Second Edition
Edited by Adisa Azapagic and Slobodan Perdan
© 2011 John Wiley & Sons, Ltd.

The concept of sustainability thus challenges us to think about the future, not in some vaguely inquisitive way, but with sufficient clarity to alter the choices we are making today. To help us structure our thinking about the future, we introduce here some techniques. Our objective is not to predict the future – an impossible task – but to make our current decisions and strategies robust and in tune with various possible future developments, as far as this is possible.

7.2 Thinking about the Future

Human beings have always wanted to know the future. Early attempts at forecasting were based on mystical inspiration or the ability to interpret various signs (the relative positions of the planets, the appearance of a chicken's entrails when thrown on the ground, or the position of tea leaves in a cup). The value of such methods is questioned by those who cannot see the causality (why *should* they work?), but the casting of horoscopes is still a big business for newspapers and magazines, and they are widely read, if not equally widely believed.

Scientists and engineers are, of course, used to extrapolating into future time. The correct prediction by the Oxford professor of geometry Edmund Halley in 1705 that the comet named after him would return in 1758 was a triumph for the Newtonian system of mechanics, and a historically famous prediction. Halley himself had died in 1742. Such successful applications of the scientific method have given us the confidence to believe that, if we can identify the physical and chemical laws operating in a particular situation, we can forecast how the situation will develop as time passes.

We have even learnt to accommodate uncertainty in such predictive modelling. In some places weather forecasts are now given in these terms 'a 30 % chance of some rain during the day', acknowledging that the physical laws at work are too complicated at present for us to be certain of the prediction. When human affairs are concerned, though, the *scientific* basis for prediction vanishes, and we are frequently reduced to educated guesswork. We may hire a consultant – hoping perhaps that the guesswork will be more educated and thus more likely to prove correct.

Complex systems can of course be modelled, and governments use models of the economy to forecast important features such as their borrowing requirement and rates of economic growth. These forecasts are then frequently used to help determine policy, notwithstanding the fact that they are often found later to have been wrong in the predictions made.

Many assessments of sustainability contain elements of forecasting and are thus susceptible to all the known problems of foretelling the future. The model may be wrong, accidents can happen (including unforeseen geological, biological, technical, meteorological or societal events); the current status may be misunderstood so that the extrapolation starts from the wrong point. Our experience with predictions that have gone wrong in the past should have taught us to be wary: whatever happened to the 'paperless office' or to nuclear power so cheap as to furnish unlimited free electricity?

In practice, though, our thinking about the future mostly relies on guesswork which is heavily influenced by experience of the past and which envisages a single outcome. For the small decisions of daily life this is usually sufficient ('The traffic is light at this time of day so the journey will take about 30 minutes'), and if we have guessed wrong we shrug our shoulders and bear the consequence.

This type of guessing about the future, which is based on short-range extrapolation of the present, is a habit of our daily lives that we tend to carry over into inappropriate situations without thinking.[1] In particular, for large decisions affecting our business or long-term prosperity, extrapolation, and therefore planning on only a single outcome, can be extremely risky. The failure of our expectation can have very serious consequences: the financial pages of almost any newspaper will be found to carry stories about companies whose incorrect expectation of some feature of the business environment, such as sales volume, or raw material price, or the reliability of new technology, or the behaviour of competitors or customers, has brought them into difficulty. We need a more rational approach.

7.3 General Approach to Formulating Strategies

7.3.1 The Problem and its Time Horizon

We will consider the general problem of formulating a strategy which will comprise making decisions and inaugurating actions, in the present. This strategy must take proper account of possible future developments. The objective of the strategy will need to be specified. The problem could be as simple as making a single decision about a matter of personal choice, or as complex as formulating a business plan for the varied activities of a multinational company. In all cases the 'problem' is the formulation of the strategy.

It will also be important to specify the time horizon – the period of time for which the strategy is to be effective. We may think that our problem is easier if the time horizon is short, because there is then less time for unexpected developments, and we may feel more secure in extrapolating current trends. We should be careful of this way of thinking: unexpected events can happen at any time, simply because they are unexpected! Also, by concentrating on the assumed incremental changes of short time horizons we can lose sight of the major changes that are far more important. We should ensure that the time horizon is sufficient to include the time scales of the slowest change processes that are relevant to the strategy. For example, if the problem involves government policy on renewable energy, the time horizon will need to be several tens of years, because of the immense investment needed to make changes in energy and transport infrastructure. That is not to say that all the possible changes and innovations will work on the same time scale, but that if the time horizon is too short, we will miss the effects of those processes that work more slowly.

The general approach we adopt here is thus first to determine the time horizon – the period of time for which our view of the future needs to be drawn. Then we think hard about our problem, to identify what we would like to know about the future exactly, and why – to identify the strategy factors that will affect our decision-making. We rate these factors in terms of uncertainty and importance. We then use the scenario technique to examine ways in which the key factors may change within the time horizon. Finally, we feed the result of this

---

[1] Only in certain defined situations are most people accustomed to think of alternative outcomes, by buying insurance against damage to person or property for example, though insurance company statistics show that many people do not even take this simple measure. The ultimate disregard of future eventualities is perhaps failure to make a will, which is equally common.

analysis back to evaluate the possible consequences of current decisions and actions, so that we can improve our strategy.

7.3.2 Focusing on the Things we Really Need to Know – the Strategy Factors

We have already remarked that some elements of the future can be forecast quite accurately, if the physical laws which govern the circumstances (like gravity determining the movements of the planets) are well understood. Most aspects of strategy and decision-making, though, have to be decided upon with much vaguer ideas about cause and effect. In coming to grips with this sea of uncertainty it is of great importance to decide what it is that we would like to know. That is, we need to select the strategy factors which will influence and guide us. This can be more difficult than it appears – on closer inspection it may well turn out that some of the things we would like to know do not actually affect the decisions we have to take now.

For example, suppose we are trying to decide whether to go for a walk which will last two hours and we do not want to get wet. In this simple example, the strategy factor is 'total local rainfall over the next two hours' – if we only could know the value of this single factor in advance, the decision would be simple.

Now suppose we are facing a somewhat bigger problem – we own a shop selling outdoor clothing and sports equipment and we have to decide what goods to buy to stock our shop for the summer season. Our time horizon is around 6 months, because virtually all the stock has to be sold during this time, in order to make way for the winter range of goods that will be brought in at the end of the summer. An important factor determining how willing our customers will be to spend money in our shop will be their feeling that they have money to spare – what is often called, in shorthand, consumer confidence. Let us suppose that analysis of the business reveals three further factors that will affect our sales – fashion, competition and local interest. If our suppliers introduce new product lines and promote them heavily with national advertising, we know that we will be able to sell a lot of these products because they will be seen as fashionable and desirable. Competition is provided by the local supermarkets, who can easily undercut our prices. However, the supermarkets only ever buy a limited range of products – those that they can sell quickly and with little customer service. For these product lines, though, if the supermarkets do decide to stock them, our own sales will be substantially reduced. The local interest is supplied by a local sporting star who is playing in the national open tennis championship. If she should be successful, then sales of the tennis equipment that she advertises will rise substantially. As shop owners we have thus identified four strategy factors:

1. consumer confidence;
2. promotion campaigns by suppliers;
3. the stocking of our product lines by local supermarkets; and
4. success of a local tennis star in the national championship.

In our assessment of the business, it is these four factors which, if we could only know them in advance by some magical means, would enable us to make a perfect decision – that is, a decision which would enable performance to meet its objective perfectly. In the case of the shop owner, this objective could be the achievement of a target return on the capital employed, say, or the increase in value of the business.

In coming to the short list of four strategy factors we may have rejected many other possible candidates. Let us consider some possibilities:

- *Number and quality of staff serving in the shop.* This is an important feature of the business, but one that we have, normally, under our own control. It does not, therefore, impact the decision, in that, having made our choice of stock, we choose and train the staff appropriately.
- *The weather.* Are there grounds for expecting that the six-month time horizon will yield any different weather from an average summer? If not, then we will simply have to use our expertise to order appropriately for the local climate (in the UK, rather changeable).
- *Disaster* (the shop is struck by lightning, attacked by thieves, drowned in a flood, etc.). Again, are there any grounds for expecting that the risk of disaster is increasing? The possibility should certainly be considered, but it is probably better handled by another measure, like buying insurance, rather than by changing purchasing strategy. The possibility of disaster is thus one of the strategy factors that do not affect our decision of what to buy. (Though having considered the possibility, we may feel that the way we run the business should be adjusted. For example, if there is a genuine concern about theft, we might choose not to have all the new stock delivered to the premises at the same time.)

7.3.3 Uncertainty and Importance of Strategy Factors

In the first of the above examples, the possibility of rain falling within the next two hours determined our decision, and this factor is therefore rated as highly important. In most places such a short-term forecast can be made with a reasonable degree of accuracy, so that its uncertainty level could be rated as low. This combination of importance and uncertainty is shown in Figure 7.1a.

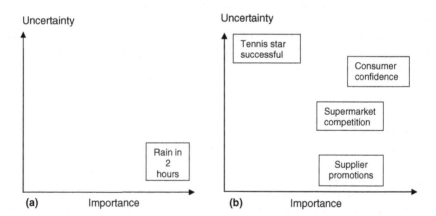

Figure 7.1   *The uncertainty and importance of strategy factors. (a) Affecting the decision on going for a walk. (b) Affecting the purchasing strategy for a shop*

In the second example, illustrated in Figure 7.1b, each of the key factors will have its own uncertainty/importance ranking, and assessing this is a matter of judgement. The following arguments were used to assign the rankings shown in Figure 7.1b. Consumer confidence will affect our total turnover, so it is highly important. It is affected by a wide range of influences, such as taxation and interest rates, house prices, unemployment rates and so on, some of these factors being national and some regional or local in character. For this reason, it is not easy to predict how consumer confidence will change. Our estimate will be based on current trends, with the proviso that many of the influencing factors can change significantly over a 6-month period, and public sentiment is anyway hard to predict – a terrorist bomb or a good football result can equally affect the public mood, in different ways. The degree of uncertainty is, therefore, rated as moderate to high. Promotion campaigns by suppliers will greatly affect the sales of some product lines, but we can find out about them in advance simply by asking the suppliers, who are not likely to change their minds. We could also ask the local supermarkets if they are proposing to stock our product lines, but they are not likely to tell us, and anyway their decisions are taken at short notice, long after we have done our own ordering. Fortunately, only a few product lines will be affected, and we can predict to some extent which lines they will probably be, from our knowledge of their suppliers and their customer profile. The success of our local tennis star must be rated as very uncertain, but again this will only affect a limited range of goods (tennis equipment).

In the first example, only a single strategy factor was of importance. Naturally, as the complexity of the decisions increases, the number of strategy factors increases as well. A good deal of analysis and imagination is then needed to be sure that we have captured all the relevant factors. Even so, we have not (yet) decided on our course of action, only structured our thinking about the problem. The important factors are those that we have placed on the right-hand side of the uncertainty/importance (U/I) diagram, and those requiring particularly careful attention are the factors in the upper right quadrant, as these are both highly important and very uncertain.

Questions

1. Describe a decision that you have taken that you found difficult. List the factors which had an influence on the decision and grade them in terms of importance from 'least important' to 'very important'. Assign uncertainties to each factor, ranging from 'low' to 'high'. Did you take steps to reduce the uncertainty of any of the factors? Was there extra information that you would have liked to have had before you took the decision?

2. You own and run a business, manufacturing moulded plastic cups, plates, cutlery and containers for sale to restaurant chains, fast-food outlets and catering companies. Some 40 % of your product is exported and the rest is sold nationally. Your raw material is plastic, mainly polystyrene and polyvinyl chloride, supplied in particle form by various chemical companies. Your objective is to maximize the economic value of your company. Your time horizon is 5 years, since in 5 years' time you plan to sell the business and retire on the proceeds. Select around 10–15 factors which in your opinion will have an effect on your business over the next 5 years, and perform a U/I analysis to identify the key factors which would influence your business strategy.

7.4 Dealing with Uncertainty: The Scenario Approach

7.4.1 What is a Scenario?

We saw above, in the clothing shop example, that some of the uncertainty concerning strategy factors could be reduced by research. In that example we were able to deduce, at least partially, the likely actions of local supermarkets from our knowledge of their business. We suppose that this knowledge results from previous research into the activities of our competitors. In the case of our own suppliers we could even remove the uncertainty about their plans completely simply by asking them – very easy research! It obviously makes sense to reduce our uncertainty about strategy factors by acquiring more information, where this is feasible.[2] However, even the best information available will still leave us with some strategy factors which have a high degree of uncertainty. Will consumer confidence be high or low over the next 6 months, and will it go up or down?

What we should not do with highly uncertain factors is guess how they will turn out and base a strategy on that single guess – this is the policy of betting on a single horse to win a race. As remarked earlier, the financial press (and the bankruptcy courts) are full of stories about people who did just that. Neither should we attempt to define extreme positions and then average them out, as this is really tantamount to guessing. Similarly, it is not satisfactory to assume that a factor will have the same value over the time horizon as it did over the same period last year or in the last decade – at least not a factor which we have classed as highly uncertain. A more subtle and oblique approach is called for, and the one we shall develop here is based on making scenarios.

In the scenario approach we step back from the problem and attempt to paint a number of self-consistent 'portraits' in words of the different ways in which the different future worlds addressed in the strategy might develop. The particular part of the world in which we are interested is the part that both affects and is affected by our strategy.[3] Each scenario is thus both a separate and distinct view of a possible future and includes one or more paths by which the future can be reached (van der Heijden, 1993; Schwartz, 1997).

Since these futures are not extrapolations of current trends, there is no need to reconcile different opinions about the present, though the threads of the scenarios that are developed must be recognizable in the present situation. The scenarios can, therefore, be rich in incorporating a wide spread of experience about the present. We do not assign a probability to the likelihood of a particular scenario occurring. The future will in any case be different to any single scenario, of that we can be sure. The contrast of this approach with forecasting is shown in Figure 7.2.

We see that in making a forecast the main problem is in selecting the correct rules – those that govern the path into the future. The result is a convergent and mathematically

---

[2] We must be very careful to draw a distinction between the reduction in uncertainty that arises from obtaining hard information (e.g. what the definite plans for sales promotion are, revealed by our supplier) and the much less reliable information contained in a consultant's or expert's opinion.

[3] This, fortunately, limits the magnitude of the challenge facing us. We only need consider those parts of future worlds of relevance to our problem. Thus, in tackling the decision on going for a walk, we only had to consider the rainfall in the local area. In stocking our shop, we only had to consider the sports/clothing business. We must be careful when drawing the boundaries and defining the things to be considered not to leave important elements out, but also not to make the problem unnecessarily large.

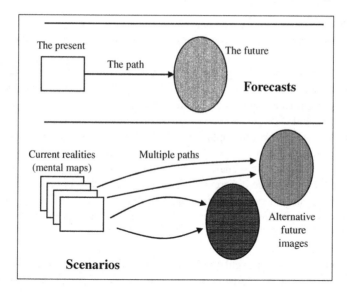

Figure 7.2 *Forecasts and scenarios compared (Darton, 2003)*

sophisticated model, in which doubts about the result tend to be played down, perhaps by incorporating statistical information. In effect the technicians who assembled the model are those determining policy, because the strategy chosen can be tested against the future forecast to predict how the strategy will turn out ('If you do X, then Y will result. Is that what you really want?'). The philosophy of forecasting assumes that it is both possible and useful to attempt to predict the future. Of course, forecasting does have a role to play, in cases where the causality (i.e. the rules connecting the present and the future) is in little doubt. We must be sure, though, that this condition is fulfilled. In most of the interesting problems facing us, particularly in the context of sustainable development, it will not be.

The scenario approach to strategy formulation supposes, on the contrary, that it is neither possible nor useful to predict the future and that we must, therefore, learn to manage the uncertainty. Scenario development is thus a thinking tool that focuses on the most important and uncertain strategy factors and challenges us to consider various alternative outcomes. Whereas forecasting uses our analytical capabilities, scenarios demand our creativity and imagination.

After we have devised our scenarios, then we have to judge the effect of our strategies, and this can include quantitative analysis, as described in the next section.

The scenario approach is in harmony with the precautionary principle (see Chapter 1 for discussion of the precautionary principle). We cannot know what the future will bring, but we can take steps to plan for different eventualities. This is the objective of scenario-driven planning.

7.4.2 Targeting Key Strategy Factors

With respect to the analysis of strategy factors made earlier, it is essential that the scenarios have something to say about these, and particularly about the factors that have been ranked as both highly important and very uncertain. The idea is that the scenarios are used to challenge the strategy, as we develop it, to see how it performs in various possible future worlds.

With regard to our clothing shop example, the U/I analysis shows that the scenarios need to say something about consumer confidence, and the policy of the local supermarkets. The scenarios must, therefore, address the local economic situation – employment, housing, the effects of national taxation and economic policy, and how these might change over the summer months for the sort of people we expect to be our customers, how the customers might react to the provision of low-cost goods by supermarkets, and how supermarkets might exploit the market. The scenarios we might make should arise out of our knowledge of these things. Two or three different scenarios are needed to cover a range of possible futures, and these should be linked to some identifiable, self-consistent themes. As an example, consider the following preliminary brief sketches (the statements refer to possible future events):

1. **Booming business (BB):** Local employment expands as planned and new factories start operations in the spring. Housing demand rises. Local supermarket announces it will expand into home furnishings and furniture. The new public sports centre, which has no shops (and which can thus be expected to generate demand which it is not itself supplying), opens in time for the summer season and is an immediate success with a full programme of events.
2. **National hesitation (NH):** Opening of planned new factories is delayed until autumn as economy slows down. Increase in interest/mortgage rates reduces consumer confidence. Sports centre opens for the summer season but struggles to attract members. Supermarkets compete hard to maintain market share, exploiting every sales opportunity.

Clearly these two scenarios each suggest different effects on the key strategy factors. When the scenarios are fully described and analysed, we should be able to make some clear statements about possible trends in these factors. Our conclusions are summarized briefly in Table 7.1.

Our knowledge of our own business should now enable us to estimate what the best purchasing policies would be, both for the overall volume of stock and for the different lines, for the two different scenarios. We can also judge what the consequences would be of choosing to order stock for one scenario when in fact the other one came about. Of course, we do not know in advance which scenario might be correct, or indeed whether some quite different set of events might happen. However, the analysis does expose what some of the problems and opportunities will be associated with any particular purchasing strategy.

Table 7.1 *Shop-owner scenarios: influence on key strategy factors*

Key strategy factor	Scenario	
	Booming business (BB)	National hesitation (NH)
Consumer confidence	High and rising	Falling
Supermarket competition	Minor	Aggressive

For example, if we decide to purchase for the high business growth of BB, any element of the trend to NH will leave us with unsold stock and possible competition from the supermarkets in selected lines. There may be arrangements we can make in advance to deal with these eventualities; for example, by negotiating resale of unsold stock to a discount store at the end of the season or by entering some agreement with the local supermarkets or sports centre to promote joint sales of some goods. On the other hand, if we decide to purchase for the more difficult conditions of NH and the market turns out better than expected, then we will have to deal with unsatisfied demand. Again, there may be various ways of accommodating this, by taking options on mid-season deliveries of new stock or by purchasing more of the stock that has a longer shelf life, and which could thus be carried over into next season if it remained unsold.

Either way, the consideration of the scenarios:

a. does not make any decisions for us; – it only demonstrates clearly what the consequences and opportunities are, relevant to the different strategies that we have thought up; and
b. it does challenge us to use our ingenuity and knowledge of the problem to think 'outside the box' to generate solutions and options.

7.4.3 The Features of a Good Scenario

Clearly, the usefulness of the scenarios in the process of developing and testing a strategy is dependent on their quality, the extent to which they encapsulate various possible trends and the imagination with which they have been thought through. A scenario which is a limp extrapolation of the current situation is not of much practical use – it must cause us to test the assumptions and extrapolations on which our strategy is based.

A good scenario is also one which picks out and develops features of the current scene. To this end, a high degree of awareness of current developments is obviously important – newspapers and broadcasting are good traditional sources of information on technical, social and political trends, and with the World Wide Web as well there is no shortage of information: the challenge is to select a group of ideas that can be put together into a coherent scenario which addresses the key strategy factors. A scenario must be more than a set of independent assumptions.

Having invented a good scenario, it can then be put to work, using all the modelling and forecasting skills that we can summon up, to make quantitative estimates for those of our strategy factors for which this is appropriate, and possible. These calculations, which must come with all the usual warnings about their being contingent on the validity of the models and that they refer solely to the scenario examined, nevertheless help us to flesh out the future images that we have initially described only in words.

As an example of this, consider the three basic global energy scenarios of the World Energy Council, originally produced in 1990 with a time horizon of 2050 (WEC and IIASA, 2002):

• Case A describes a *high growth* world, in which economic growth is robust so that, despite significant improvement in energy efficiency, energy consumption grows strongly.
• Case B describes a *middle course*.

Table 7.2 *Global energy scenarios: influence on key factors (WEC and IIASA, 2002)*

Key strategy factors	Case A High growth	Case B Middle course	Case C Ecologically driven
World population in 2050	10.1 billion	10.1 billion	10.1 billion
World economic growth to 2050	2.7 % pa	2.2 % pa	2.2 % pa
Energy intensity improvement	medium	low	high
to 2050	−1.0 % pa	−0.7 % pa	−1.4 % pa
Primary energy demand in 2050	25 Gt oe[a]	20 Gt oe[a]	14 Gt oe[a]
Resource availability			
fossil	high	medium	low
nonfossil	high	medium	high
Technology costs			
fossil	low	medium	high
nonfossil	low	medium	low
Technology dynamics			
fossil	high	medium	medium
nonfossil	high	medium	low
CO_2 emission constraint	no	no	yes
Carbon emissions in 2050	9–15 Gt C	10 Gt C	5 Gt C
Environmental taxes	no	no	yes

[a] Gt oe: gigatonne of oil equivalent.

- Case C describes an *ecologically driven* future, in which countries collaborate in nonfossil fuel development and a moderate economic growth is fuelled by an increasingly efficient energy supply, with maximum use of technology innovation.

The way that a number of key strategy factors change under these different scenarios can be tabulated, as we did above in the case of the clothes shop scenarios, in Table 7.1. The difference with the analysis shown in Table 7.2 is that the scenarios now have been further worked through, and, where possible, numerical values have been assigned to the key factors.

Further development of the basic scenarios devised by the WEC and IIASA has led to a number of subdivisions. Not surprisingly, for a problem as large as this, there are an enormous number of alternatives that one could consider.

For example, in exploring the option for increased use of nonfossil fuel, many different assumptions are possible about how the use of nuclear energy might develop. This is partly a question of technology (the potentials for cleaner, easier, cheaper, nuclear power generation and proven, reliable waste disposal) and partly a question of attitudes in society (to risk, to complicated technology and to the association with nuclear weapons programmes). Consideration of this point highlights the aspect of geography, since these problems will certainly be viewed differently in different parts of the world. Summaries such as that presented in Table 7.2 represent the result of an averaging/integration process, by which the consequences of the scenario for each country or region are evaluated, and then all the individual consequences are gathered into the overall picture. The huge geographical variations in economic development and every other aspect of society always have to be kept in mind when looking at global energy scenarios.

Questions

1. The WEC and IIASA scenarios shown in Table 7.2 offer a number of key strategy factors that will be of importance to any consideration of global energy strategy. Suggest some additional factors that might be of interest to a multinational oil company planning its operations with a time horizon of 10 years. Can anything be said about the importance and uncertainty of these additional factors and how they might change in the period up to the planning horizon?

2. Different parties will assess the importance and uncertainty of strategy factors differently. Consider the following participants in the debate about the need to restrain the use of fossil fuels so as to reduce the emission of carbon dioxide:

    i. the US government;
    ii. the government of a small island state which will become submerged and uninhabitable if sea levels rise due to global warming; and
    iii. a group of activists concerned about environmental issues.

    Taking the position of each of these groups in turn, draw up a list of strategy factors for an appropriate time horizon and assign importance and uncertainty ratings to them. Discuss the significance of the differences, for the position that each might take in debate and negotiation on this issue.

7.5 Energy Scenarios: Glimpsing the Future?

Current significant sources of primary energy[4] are

- oil;
- coal;
- natural gas;
- nuclear; and
- hydroelectricity.

In some parts of the world, local energy demand is satisfied by

- traditional biomass (mainly wood, or animal waste products);
- wind power; and
- geothermal energy.

Other renewable energy sources that are being developed, see Boyle (1996), are

- wave power;
- solar (both for direct thermal energy and through photovoltaic conversion);
- crops grown for use as fuel.

Energy sources such as wind can be called renewable since the use of a certain quantity of energy from the source does not deplete the amount available for future generations.

---

[4] By 'primary energy' we mean the energy released by, or extracted from, a natural energy source.

Nonrenewables,such as coal, on the other hand, are taken from finite reserves. The pattern of supply from various different sources is known as the 'energy mix'. Note that primary energy is frequently transformed, before it is consumed by the end-user. For example, in the UK now, nearly all coal is burnt in power stations and converted into electricity. Much electricity also comes from oil and gas combustion and some is from other sources, so that the electricity actually used by the consumer derives from a range of primary energy sources. There are inevitably losses in conversion of energy from one form to another, and these losses are part of the cost of having the energy in a more convenient form.

The utilization of scenarios to help develop and test strategic options was perhaps first exploited by military planners in war games, but the major application by business has been in the area of energy supply. This may be for historical reasons, because of early work with the technique by Shell, but the global energy picture is particularly well suited to scenario analysis. The lead times for investment are long, because of the considerable effort needed to develop new coal mines and new oil and gas reservoirs to the stage of production and because of the complex nature of refinery and gas processing facilities. Investments in large-scale hydroelectricity also require planning and construction times of many years. On the other hand, the energy supply/demand balance has shown itself to be susceptible to sudden shocks, due to war, accident, and political and organizational change.

Figure 7.3 shows the world oil demand from 1960 to 2000, for the geographical area excluding centrally planned economies and eastern Europe (for which reliable data were previously not available). Except in the period before 1973, the demand for this major commodity, which now satisfies around 40 % of primary energy demand, has moved in a rather irregular way. Even before 1973, when demand was steadily rising from year to year, industry experts continually underestimated the rate of growth.

For the whole energy market (all sources of energy) the interaction of supply and demand is thus highly complex, with a great many factors influencing the supply/demand balance.

Two Shell scenarios for the period up to 2050 – *Dynamics as Usual* and *Spirit of the Coming Age* – consider the implications of two different possible routes to a more sustainable energy system (Shell International Limited, 2001). Both scenarios take oil and coal to remain as major sources over this period, and the third major fossil fuel, natural gas, plays a larger role in what is an increasingly diverse supply system. As the world

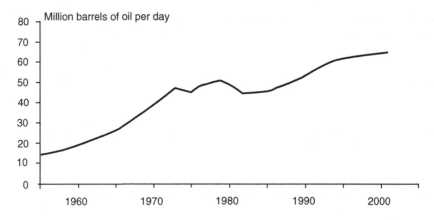

Figure 7.3   *World oil demand (excluding centrally planned economies and eastern Europe)*

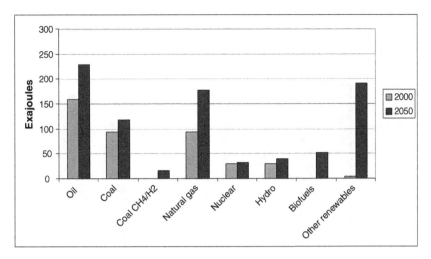

Figure 7.4   *Shell scenario for annual energy demand: 'Dynamics as Usual' (Shell International Limited, 2001)*

population grows from 6 billion to 9 billion over this period of 50 years, the scenarios envisage a quadrupling of world GDP in real terms.

In 'Dynamics as Usual', social priorities for clean, secure and sustainable energy shape the supply system. There is an initial explosive growth in energy demand as major developing countries seek rapid economic growth. In all markets there are advances in communications and materials technologies which enable much more efficient energy usage. The result is shown in Figure 7.4. The total annual demand for primary energy increases over this period from 407 to 852 EJ,[5] and renewable energy comes to supply around one-third of demand.

In 'Spirit of the Coming Age', the efficiency gains from new technology are fewer, and annual energy usage increases to 1121 EJ. Ingenious ways of supplying fuel are developed to meet consumer needs, particularly the continuing need for personal mobility. As shown in Figure 7.5, natural gas plays an even greater role, and there is a significant supply of energy from hydrogen (from coal or natural gas reforming) used in fuel cells. Biofuels, from plants grown sustainably, again become an important energy source, as do other renewables. In this scenario, the sources of primary energy become much more diverse than they were in 2000.

Questions

1. With reference to the current sources of primary energy mentioned in this section, identify situations and communities in which primary energy sources are used without further conversion. For each case, say whether you think that the energy usage is sustainable.

---

[5] In both these Shell scenarios, electrical energy from nuclear, hydro, wind, wave and solar sources is expressed as thermal equivalents.

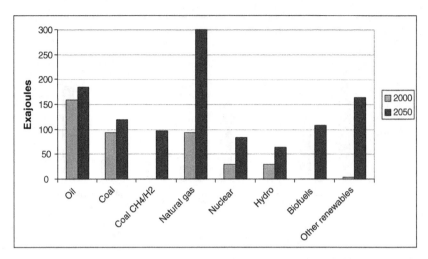

Figure 7.5 Shell scenario for annual energy demand: 'Spirit of the Coming Age' (Shell International Limited, 2001)

2. What is your country's current profile of energy sources for domestic and industrial purposes? Consider what portion of energy comes directly from gas, what portion from electricity and what portion from other sources. What is the distribution of primary sources for electricity generation; that is, what fraction comes from gas, oil, coal, hydro, wind, solar, biomass and so on?
3. What are the main sustainability impacts (economic, environmental and social) associated with each of these sources of primary energy? Distinguish between impacts apparent at a global, regional and local scales.
4. What would be the main advantages and disadvantages accompanying a shift away from fossil-fuel-based energy to renewable forms of energy?

7.6 Implications of Different Energy Scenarios for Sustainable Development

Energy supply is, of course, hugely important to our way of life and economic development, and its impact on the environment has come to be more appreciated in recent years. The global energy situation is thus directly linked to the three major components of sustainability – society, economy and environment. In this section we consider some future consequences for sustainability, derived from scenarios made for the global energy situation.

In constructing our scenarios, we put many thoughts about the possible future into them. It is thus never correct to suppose that the scenarios themselves are making predictions, since features of the scenario only result from the assumptions made in the first place. Nevertheless, by making a coherent vision of a possible future, various insights can be teased out which might not have been obvious from the bare bones of the original world picture.

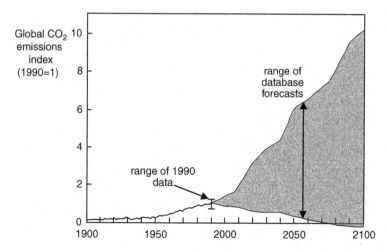

Figure 7.6 *Global carbon dioxide emissions (based on the data from Nakicenovic and Swart, 2003)*

Clearly, scenarios which address the future demand and supply of energy need to consider the possible development of new sources, but the way in which societies might develop is also a crucial strategy factor. Will people adapt their lifestyle to a more sustainable model? Attitudes are important, of course, but technology also has a role to play here. For example, new computer and communications technologies could have a similar impact on lifestyle as the automobile had in the twentieth century – only people would need to travel less, because information can be transferred so much more easily; advanced materials technology and design could mean that goods and equipment are lighter and require less materials and energy in production and use. Carbon fibres could replace steel, and cars could become many times more fuel efficient.

In their 'business as usual' scenario, the IEA (Priddle, 1998) considered a world in which no policies (such as those stipulated by the Kyoto Protocol) were adopted to reduce energy-related emissions of greenhouse gases.[6] The consequence of this scenario was that, whilst energy demand grew by 65 % between 1995 and 2020, CO_2 emissions increased by 70 %. However, the IEA itself has pointed out (Priddle, 1998) that the future will not be 'business as usual', since the Kyoto Protocol obliges signatories to reduce emissions of greenhouse gases over this period, and policies are gradually being adopted to initiate this change. About 90 % of the world's energy is currently supplied by fossil fuels, and the carbon dioxide generated in combustion of these fuels is virtually all discharged to the atmosphere. How quickly and effectively action can be taken to reduce these emissions is, of course, a hugely important unknown feature of the energy scene, and a major difference between many of the energy scenarios now being produced.

The UNs Intergovernmental Panel on Climate Change (IPCC) has collected many of the forecasts from various scenarios, and, as shown in Figure 7.6, they represent a very wide range of possibilities (Nakicenovic and Swart, 2003). This figure demonstrates one of the

---

[6] The International Energy Agency (IEA) regularly updates its World Energy Outlook. The reader is referred to the IEA website for more recent publications.

features of scenario planning – it is not a forecasting tool. Figure 7.6 shows that almost any prediction of carbon dioxide emissions can be found in the IPCC database of scenarios.

The strength of these scenarios is thus not in forecasting, but rather in the clarity of the vision that they reveal to the parties involved in energy supply, including governments. They allow these parties to appreciate what the consequences might be of particular courses of action (or inaction). In this the scenario technique has been very successful, as the publication of these various pictures has drawn attention to the link between energy supply and global warming, and helped to direct international policy development. This has resulted in various moves to encourage the use of renewable energy, such as the imposition of 'carbon taxes' in some countries to penalize the use of fossil fuels, and the introduction of incentives for generators of electricity from wind and other renewable sources.

Energy scenarios like those shown in Figures 7.4 and 7.5 show that a potential shortfall in energy supply within the planning horizon of industry and governments could arise if too much demand is made on the finite supplies of oil and gas. The scenarios of Figures 7.4 and 7.5 show how this might be addressed through developing renewables, to bring supply and demand into balance. Attempting to meet this shortfall by increasing coal production (business as usual) would have significant (intolerable?) impact on global levels of carbon dioxide, and thus on global warming. This has stimulated the search for new energy sources, which must play an increasingly important role as the twenty-first century progresses (Boyle, 1996). One such emerging energy technology – fuel cells – is discussed in Chapter 8.

Several of the scenarios have considered how the explosive growth of global communications, by telephone, television and internet, might change society. There are huge consequences for the sorts of jobs that people do, the companies they work for and the tasks they perform, as commercial and technical information becomes much more readily accessible. There may also be more subtle shifts of power in society, as future generations will be able to decide how they want to live their lives not just by reference to local conditions, but with a vastly improved knowledge of affairs elsewhere in the world. We do not yet know how this will affect aspirations, but these scenarios portray worlds where, for the first time, development issues will be discussed in the light of truly global and public information exchange. The consumers and users – members of the public – who are the stakeholders in so many engineering projects, will be well informed of the issues, and by means of the same communication channels will be able to express their opinions and influence decisions.

One of the major strategy factors for these long-term energy scenarios is the rate at which living standards rise in the less-developed countries. Similarly, another important strategy factor is the extent to which industrialized countries can continue to improve their living standards if they pursue greater sustainability through reducing resource consumption and energy intensity. *Factor 4* (von Weizsäcker *et al.*, 1987) illustrates some approaches to this problem, giving 50 examples which demonstrate a fourfold improvement in resource usage (see also Chapter 1). Technology has a key role to play, of course, but any new technology has to be economically viable. It may be that people will expect their governments to use fiscal and other measures to support sustainable technology which is not yet commercially viable.

With regard to the energy-based industries themselves, the Shell scenarios indicate some areas in which they might develop over the next 50 years. It is evident that throughout this period we will still be distilling oil to make fuel, though biomass grown in sustainably managed plantations could become the new source of feedstock for the distillation. Alternative sustainable fuels could include hydrogen for fuel-cell-powered cars or for generation of electricity, made by reforming bio-oil with subsequent sequestration of carbon dioxide.

Sustainably grown biomass may also support a manufacturing industry extracting and transforming biopolymeric or other natural products to replace those chemicals currently made by a petrochemical route. New industries will have arisen, associated with alternative energy sources, such as photovoltaics, fuel cells and wind farms. A snapshot of the city streets of 2050 would look as strange to us as do photographs of 1950. The challenge to scenario makers is to be able to imagine these images 50 years before they occur.

Questions

1. Assume the following roles and carry out the tasks as described:
    i.   You are a senior energy adviser to the government. Devise an energy strategy for the country, acceptable to the electorate, which will promote sustainable development.
    ii. You are the Chief Executive Officer of your city council. Devise a strategy to implement the principles of sustainable development within the city.
    Note: all elements of a coherent strategy will be driven by the same vision. Make sure you identify the levers available (e.g. legislation, investment, setting of standards, training, public opinion, taxation and tax breaks, etc.), and decide how each will be used. Consider the external pressures and other possible constraints on your actions. Consider also the influence of possible external events and other uncertainties. Where possible, back up your strategy with facts and figures.

7.7 Conclusions

The notion of sustainability requires us to look into the future, both to envisage what the consequences will be of our present decisions and actions and to consider the needs of those future generations who will be affected by them. Our problem is one of formulating a strategy, given that we do not know how the future will turn out. We have shown that our natural habit of guessing, based on limited extrapolation of the present, is not adequate for serious problems. Forecasting is useful only in those special circumstances where the chain of cause and effect is known. In the scenario planning technique described here, we do not attempt to predict the future, but sketch a number of different ways in which the world might develop, and then consider our strategy in the light of these different scenarios. The objective, compatible with the precautionary principle, is to develop a strategy that is robust in a number of possible future worlds.

The scenario technique is widely used by those considering problems of energy supply, and its interaction with the environment, and its effect on social and economic development. Through the use of simple examples we have exposed how the scenarios need to address those key strategy factors that we would, ideally, like to know in advance, and particularly those factors that are both highly important and very uncertain.

Finally, we have considered a number of published global energy scenarios, discussing what key strategy factors they address and what sort of future worlds they envisage.

Consideration of these scenarios underlines the important effects of international agreements on greenhouse gas emissions, of the commercial development of renewable energy sources and new technology, and of changes in lifestyle and human aspirations.

References and Further Reading

Boyle, G. (1996) *Renewable Energy*, Oxford University Press, Oxford.

BP (2003) Statistical review of world energy. Annual reports. http://www.bp.com/centres/energy/index.asp.

Darton, R. (2003) Scenarios and metrics as guides to a sustainable future: the case of energy supply. *Process Safety and Environmental Protection*, **81**(B5), 295–302.

De Wit, B. and Meyer, R. (1998) *Strategy: Process, Content, Context*, 2nd edn, International Thomson Publishing Company, London.

Houghton, J. (1997) *Global Warming*, 2nd edn, Cambridge University Press, Cambridge. http://www.ipcc.ch/.

Houghton, J.T., Ding, Y., Griggs, D.J., Noguer, M., van der Linden, P.J. and Ding, X. (eds) (2001) *Climate Change 2001: The Scientific Basis*, Cambridge University Press, Cambridge.

Jackson, T. (1993) *Clean Production Strategies – Developing Preventive Environmental Management in the Industrial Economy*, CRC Press, Boca Raton, FL.

Jennings, J. (1987) *Sustainable Development – The Challenge for Energy*, Shell International Ltd., London.

Johnson, G. and Scholes, K. (2002) *Exploring Corporate Strategy*, 6th edn, Financial Times Prentice Hall, Harlow, England.

Nakicenovic, N. and Swart, R. (eds) (2000) *IPCC Special Report on Emissions Scenarios*, Cambridge University Press, Cambridge.

Priddle, R. (1999) Achieving sustainable energy – the challenge. *Renewable Energy World*, **2**(3), 23–29.

Schwartz, P. (1998) *The Art of the Longview: Planning for the Future in an Uncertain World*, John Wiley and Sons, Ltd, Chichester.

Shell International Limited (2001) *Energy Needs, Choices and Possibilities, Scenarios to 2050*, Shell International, London.

Sorensen, B. (2000) *Renewable Energy: Its Physics, Engineering, Use, Environmental Impacts, Economy and Planning Aspects*, Academic Press, New York.

Van der Heijden, K. (1996) *Scenarios*, John Wiley and Sons, Ltd, Chichester.

Von Weizsäcker, E., Lovins, A.B. and Lovins, L.H. (1998) *Factor Four, Doubling Wealth, Halving Resource Use*, Earthscan, London.

WEC and IIASA (1995) *Global Energy Perspectives to 2050 and Beyond*, World Energy Council/International Institute for Applied Systems Analysis, London.

8

Fuel Cells in Stationary Applications: Energy for the Future?

Martin Pehnt

Fuel cells represent an old invention which has yet to make a major contribution to the energy economy. However, the time is now ripe for fuel cells to enter widespread use to help reduce emissions of carbon dioxide and other gases emitted from the conventional energy systems based on fossil fuels. In stationary applications, fuel cells offer the possibility of much more efficient generation of electrical power from natural gas or hydrogen. However, assessment of the true benefits of fuel cells must be based on a life cycle approach in which the whole supply chains related to fuel cell systems are considered. This includes fuel extraction, its processing, distribution, conversion into electricity or heat, and energy delivery and use. This chapter and the case study explore some of the benefits of using fuel cells in stationary applications and discuss the life cycle environmental implications of these installations. Economic and social factors influencing commercialization of fuel cells are also addressed.

8.1 Energy Today: Why a Substantial Transformation is Necessary

Fossil and nuclear fuels still dominate electricity production. Unless major changes in the worldwide energy and climate policy occur, global society will still – and increasingly –

Sustainable Development in Practice: Case Studies for Engineers and Scientists, Second Edition
Edited by Adisa Azapagic and Slobodan Perdan
© 2011 John Wiley & Sons, Ltd.

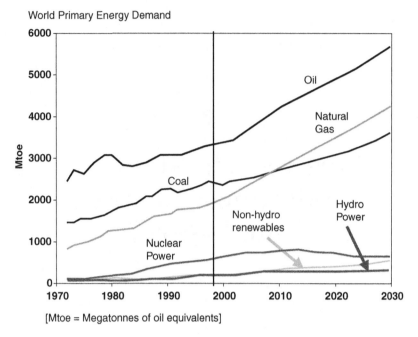

Figure 8.1   *Past and future world primary energy demand according to the reference scenario 'Business as usual' (based on the data from IEA (2002))*

rely on fossil fuels (see Figure 8.1). This is mainly due to the increasing energy demand in developing countries. As the World Energy Outlook 2002 points out, more than 60 % of the increase in world primary energy demand until 2030 will come from developing countries (IEA, 2002). China, already the world's second largest energy consumer, will be a major contributor to that increase. China's energy economy is heavily dependent on coal.

For Europe, dependence on fossil and nuclear energy also implies dependence on external energy resources. According to the EU Green Paper on security of energy supply (EU, 2002), 50 % of the primary energy requirements are already imported. If current trends persist, the predictions are that this will rise to 70 % of the total European energy demand.

When analysing future energy situations, it is important to consider not only energy required for heat and power generation, but also for transportation. Here again, the problem is an ever-increasing demand, particularly in developed countries: there is an almost linear relationship between income and distance travelled per capita. With increasing economic activity in developing countries, the use of vehicles is set to continue growing.

The consequences of the rising energy consumption are potentially serious and irreversible. One consequence is that the CO_2 emissions from burning fossil fuels (i.e. oil, gas or coal) will increase significantly, thus enhancing the anthropogenic greenhouse effect. CO_2 concentration in the atmosphere has already increased by one-third in the past 150 years. By some estimates, the surface temperature of the Earth has risen within the last century by 0.6 °C. There are many more indicators pointing at a climate change on a global level. The Intergovernmental Panel on Climate Change (Solomon *et al.*, 2007) estimated recently that global warming of between 1.4 and 6.4 °C by the end of the twenty-first century is possible.

The consequences of this could be drastic: spread of infectious diseases, water shortages, droughts and famine, changing vegetation, soil erosion, pressure for population migration and so on. For further detail on climate change, see also Chapter 15.

However, global warming is only one of the impacts associated with energy supply. Other environmental impacts also arise from the increasing demand for services, mobility, electricity, communication or heating. These impacts arise through the whole life cycle from primary fuel extraction, through its processing, distribution, conversion into electricity or heat, to energy delivery and use. Some of these impacts, such as acidification caused by nitrogen oxides and SO_2 emitted from power plants, have been reduced considerably in many developed countries over the last 10 years. In Europe, for instance, SO_2 emissions fell by almost 60 %. Several factors have contributed to this positive trend, including the use of cleaner fuels (natural gas) instead of coal, improved combustion and energy efficiency, flue gas treatment, as well as an increased share of renewable energy sources. However, other impacts, such as oil tanker spills and the accumulation of radioactive waste, continue to damage our environment.

Questions

1. Identify the environmental and social impacts associated with the life cycle of electricity generation (i.e. from fuel extraction, through processing, distribution, conversion to electricity delivery and use). Compare these impacts for electricity generated using different fossil (coal, oil, gas) and nuclear fuels. What do you conclude?
2. What measures could be taken to reduce the environmental impacts of electricity supply? Identify examples for each source of electricity analysed in the previous question. Try to rank your suggestions according to feasibility, costs and potential for the reduction of environmental impacts.

8.2 Fuel Cells: An Old Invention

There are numerous approaches to reducing energy demand and, therefore, impact on the environment. However, even if we concentrate on the supply side and take demand as constant, there are still a number of options to reduce environmental impacts associated with energy supply. One possibility is to introduce an efficient, clean energy converter. The fuel cell is often promoted as such a device.

One hundred years ago, the electrochemist Wilhelm Ostwald presented his vision of the twentieth century as the century of electrochemical, combustion-free energy conversion. In the age of coal, his credo 'no smoke, no soot' seemed unrealistic. However, 70 years before Ostwald's statement, the British amateur chemist William Grove and the German Christian Friedrich Schönbein – the latter better known for discovering ozone – had already developed the fuel cell, a device converting the energy of a fuel into electricity without combustion.

One century later, we are much closer to Ostwald's vision. Today, fuel cells are seen by many as a particularly promising technology for clean energy generation and have already attracted much attention, both from industry and the public.

8.2.1 How Does a Fuel Cell Work?

Fuel cells are electrochemical devices which convert chemical energy of the reaction between a fuel (typically hydrogen) and oxygen (normally from air) directly into electrical energy (as direct current, DC). As shown in Figure 8.2, a fuel cell consists of two electrodes which are interspersed with an electrolyte: fuel is oxidized on the anode and oxygen is reduced on the cathode. The role of the electrolyte is to separate the fuel and oxygen to avoid an uncontrolled explosive reaction. Bipolar plates, mounted on the outside of each electrode, feed the fuel and oxygen to the electrodes, collect the electrons and remove the heat of reaction. To achieve higher power outputs, fuel cells typically consist of a number of single cells connected in series. This is called a fuel cell stack.

The reaction between hydrogen and oxygen in the fuel cell generates water and results in an enthalpy change:

$$H_2 + \frac{1}{2}O_2 \rightarrow H_2O_{liq} + \Delta H \qquad \Delta H = -286 \, \text{kJ/mol}$$

The change of enthalpy ΔH which characterizes the 'energy of the reaction' can only partially be transformed into electrical energy. The maximum possible electrical energy that can be obtained is given by the change of Gibbs free energy of formation ΔG. At the pressure of $P = 101\,325$ Pa and temperature $T = 298.15$ K, ΔG for this reaction is equal to -237 kJ/mol. According to the Gibbs function, the difference between ΔH and ΔG is given by $T\Delta S$ (where T is the temperature in the fuel cell and ΔS is the change of entropy in the reaction). Therefore, the maximum (or 'ideal efficiency') thermodynamic efficiency of the fuel cell is given by

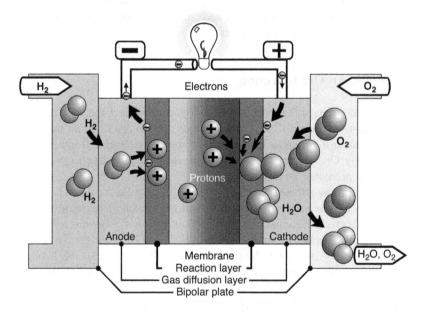

Figure 8.2 *An example of the basic construction of a fuel cell: polymer electrolyte fuel cell (PEFC).*

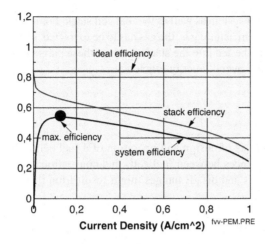

Figure 8.3 *Theoretical efficiency of the PEFC fuel cell stack and the overall system efficiency as a function of the current density.*

$$\eta_{fc} = \frac{\Delta G}{\Delta H} = 1 - T\frac{\Delta S}{\Delta H} \qquad (8.1)$$

That means that with increasing temperature, the efficiency[1] of fuel cell decreases.

The efficiency of a fuel cell also depends on cell voltage and current density. The theoretically possible open-circuit voltage of a fuel cell is determined by ΔG according to the equation

$$E_0 = -\frac{\Delta G}{n_e F} \qquad (8.2)$$

where F is the Faraday constant (96 485 A s/mol) and n_e is the number of electrons. At the standard conditions ($P = 101\,325$ Pa and $T = 298.15$ K), E_0 is 1229 V. However, the theoretically achievable voltage is reduced through various losses in the system. In the fuel cell areas with low current densities, activation losses result from the slow rate of reaction on the surface of the electrodes. In the region of medium current density, ohmic losses reduce the cell voltage, and at high current densities mass transport effects lower the voltage. An example of the resulting change in the cell/stack efficiency (which is proportional to the voltage) with current density of the cell is shown in Figure 8.3.

In addition to the efficiency of the fuel cell and the stack, we also need to consider the efficiency of the whole fuel cell system. The fuel cell system includes fuel and oxygen preparation for use in the stack, power conditioning (conversion from DC to AC current)

---

[1] It is important to note that the thermodynamic efficiency theoretically achievable in a fuel cell is much higher than (the Carnot) efficiency that is theoretically achievable in a combustion process or 'heat engine'.

and a heat management system as well as the fuel cell stack. For instance, in systems where hydrogen is derived from natural gas, the gas has to be extracted, cleaned and reformed into hydrogen before it can be fed into the stack. Each of these parts of the system uses energy and that influences the overall energy efficiency.

Questions

1. Explain the principles of design and operation of a fuel cell in your own words.
2. Describe the differences between fuel cells and conventional power converters. What potential advantages and disadvantages might result from these differences?

8.2.2 Types of Fuel Cell

Fuel cells can be categorized according to the electrolyte used. As described in Box 8.1, there are six types of fuel cell:

- alkaline fuel cell (AFC);
- PEFC, also known as a proton exchange membrane fuel cell (PEMFC);
- direct methanol fuel cell (DMFC);
- phosphoric acid fuel cell (PAFC);
- molten carbonate fuel cell (MCFC);and
- solid oxide fuel cell (SOFC).

Box 8.1 *Fuel cell types*

Alkaline fuel cell (AFC)

Alkaline fuel cells use KOH as electrolyte. The charge transfer in the electrolyte is based on OH^- ions. At the anode, these ions react with hydrogen:

$$H_2 + 2OH^- + 2e^- \Rightarrow 2H_2O \quad (\text{anode})$$

At the cathode, new OH^- ions are formed:

$$\frac{1}{2}O_2 + H_2O \Rightarrow 2OH^- + 2e^- \quad (\text{cathode})$$

AFCs operate at temperatures around $80\,°C$ and have high efficiencies because oxygen reduction in alkaline electrolytes is rapid. One problem with the AFC is that the electrolyte reacts with the CO_2 which is present in the feed air to form carbonates which foul the electrodes. Owing to the advances in PEFC technology, the AFC has been neglected in recent years.

Polymer Electrolyte Fuel Cell (PEFC) (or Proton Exchange Membrane Fuel Cell (PEMFC))

In the PEFC, the electrolyte consists of a proton conducting membrane. This membrane is similar to polytetrafluoroethylene (PTFE or Teflon). Unlike the AFC, in the PEFC the protons (H^+) are the charge-transfer ions. The overall reaction is

$$H_2 \Rightarrow 2H^+ + 2e^- \quad \text{(anode)}$$

$$\frac{1}{2}O_2 + 2H^+ + 2e^- \Rightarrow H_2O \quad \text{(cathode)}$$

The PEFC operates at low temperatures (around $80\,^\circ$C) to avoid melting of the membrane. Therefore, it requires a catalyst to promote the reactions. Typically, platinum group metals are used for this purpose. As they are very sensitive to CO or sulfur contamination, the feed gas must be cleaned appropriately. Water management can be a problem in PEFCs.

Direct Methanol Fuel Cell (DMFC)

A DMFC is similar to a PEFC except that methanol is used as a fuel instead of hydrogen:

$$CH_3OH + H_2O \Rightarrow CO_2 + 6H^+ + 6e^- \quad \text{(anode)}$$

$$1\frac{1}{2}O_2 + 6H^+ + 6e^- \Rightarrow 3H_2O \quad \text{(cathode)}$$

The problems with DMFCs include the high amounts of catalysts required and the crossover (passage) of methanol through the membrane.

Phosphoric Acid Fuel Cell (PAFC)

PAFCs use phosphoric acid as electrolyte. Owing to the acid conditions in the cell, the protons (H^+) are transferred through the electrolyte. The partial reactions are thus identical to those in the PEFC. The PAFC operates at $200\,^\circ$C and is, therefore, less sensitive to CO than the PEFC. The PAFC is the only fuel cell type that has been produced commercially in larger numbers for stationary applications.

Molten Carbonate Fuel Cell (MCFC)

In an MCFC, carbonates (Li_2CO_3, K_2CO_3) are used as electrolyte. These cells are operated at $650\,^\circ$C. The electrodes consist of nickel materials. Carbonate ions which are produced at the cathode are conducted through the electrolyte:

$$CO_2 + \frac{1}{2}O_2 + 2e^- \Rightarrow CO_3^{2-} \quad \text{(cathode)}$$

At the anode, the H_2 reduces these ions to CO_2:

$$H_2 + CO_3{}^{2-} \Rightarrow H_2O + CO_2 + 2e^- \quad \text{(anode)}$$

To supply the CO_2 required at the cathode, the CO_2 from the anode off-gas is recycled back. One problem with the MCFC yet to be solved is corrosion of the electrolyte materials. In addition, the electrodes degrade because the nickel from the electrodes enters the melt and causes short circuits.

The Solid Oxide Fuel Cell (SOFC)

The SOFC operates at the highest temperatures of all fuel cell types. The electrolyte is a ceramic made of zirconia doped with yttrium, which conducts oxygen ions at above 750 °C:

$$H_2 + O^{2-} \Rightarrow H_2O + 2e^- \quad \text{(anode)}$$

$$\frac{1}{2}O_2 + 2e^- \Rightarrow O^{2-} \quad \text{(cathode)}$$

In both the MCFC and SOFC, gases containing CH_4 and CO can be used directly as a fuel. In the low- and medium-temperature fuel cells, a reformer converts natural gas or other hydrogen-containing gases into hydrogen.

The type of electrolyte dictates the operating temperatures in the fuel cell. Thus, PEFCs and AFCs are operated at low temperatures (at around 80 °C); the PAFC is a medium-temperature cell (200 °C) while the MCFC and SOFC are high-temperature cells (operated at 650 °C and >750 °C respectively). Although higher operating temperatures of MCFCs and SOFCs result in decreasing thermodynamic efficiencies (see Equation 8.1), the better kinetics as well as the option to use the high-temperature exhaust gas (e.g. in turbines or for heat supply) more than offset this efficiency reduction. In addition, high-temperature fuel cells offer the advantage of internal reforming – that is, the heat produced in the electrochemical reaction is simultaneously used for reforming natural gas or other fuels into hydrogen, thus decreasing the required cooling effort while efficiently using the heat. Furthermore, high-temperature fuel cells have lower purity requirements for the fuel. Whereas AFCs are sensitive to CO_2 and PEFCs to CO impurities, in high-temperature fuel cells CO_2 acts as an inert gas only, and CO can even be used as a fuel.

8.2.3 Advantages and Applications of Fuel Cells

From the discussion above, two main environmental advantages of fuel cells as energy converters become obvious. On the one hand, fuel cells offer higher efficiencies of conversion into electrical power and thus reduce the amount of fuel required for the production of electricity. This is the *efficiency advantage* of fuel cells.

In addition, the electrochemical nature of the reaction, the low temperature of the reforming reaction and the necessity for removing impurities in the fuel (such as sulfur) result in extremely low local emissions – an important feature, especially in highly populated (urban) areas. There is no open flame and no combustion involved, except for the small burner (to combust unused hydrogen) with extremely low emissions. Furthermore, compared with the conventional energy systems based on fossil fuels, fuel cells generate lower CO_2 emissions, even when hydrogen is derived from fossil fuel. These are the *emission advantages* of fuel cells.

But besides these obvious environmental advantages, other advantages may emerge. These advantages depend on the specific application of fuel cells. Fuel cells can essentially be used in:

- **Stationary applications**: Fuel cells can be used in small systems for domestic energy supply, in larger units for the simultaneous supply of electricity and heat to a district heating system or in large systems for industrial cogeneration. In the long term, the use of fuel cells for more centralized electricity production is of interest, particularly in combination with a gas (or steam) turbine which uses the energy contained in the off-gas. In stationary systems, small distributed power plants help to open up the potential for combined heat and power generation (CHP). Table 8.1 identifies some further potential drivers to use fuel cell systems for stationary applications.
- **Mobile applications**: Fuel cells are attractive energy sources for powering electric drive trains in passenger cars, buses, heavy-duty vehicles, ships, trains or airplanes. In mobile applications, for instance, using fuel cells to replace batteries in electric vehicles increases the driving range and eliminates the need for the gear mechanism.
- **Portable applications**: Small hydrogen fuel-cell systems could be used to replace diesel generators or rechargeable batteries. The cost of fuel cells in these applications is relatively low and offers a potential for further environmental benefits, such as elimination of heavy-metal-containing batteries.

Questions

1. It has taken more than 100 years since its invention for the first practicable fuel cell to be developed. What might have hindered the development of fuel cells this long? Think of the competing inventions (Werner, Siemens, Benz, Edison), but also of historical developments.
2. Discuss and explain possible drivers for fuel cell technology as presented in Table 8.1. Try to identify further advantages not listed here.
3. Why do distributed (smaller scale) fuel cells, and any kind of distributed generation, reduce transmission and distribution losses? Consider that the losses are proportional to the square of the current, to the resistivity (which is a function of temperature and thus again the current), the length of the cable and the inverse of the cross-section of the cable. Typical grid losses are in the order of 6 % of the electricity generated, but they can vary between 3 and 15 %. Given the relationship above, when would the electricity provided by fuel cells be most beneficial: as a base, medium or peak load? Is the grid loss reduction higher on a nonwindy summer day or a cold winter night?

4. Given the information in Table 8.1 and Section 8.2.3, consider the specific motivation of different nations to introduce fuel cells in mobile or stationary applications. What might be the key driver for the following countries to introduce this innovative energy converter:
   - USA, and particularly California;
   - Iceland;
   - Europe;
   - China;and
   - African countries.

   If you are uncertain, try to find out about the key problems related to energy supply and the key environmental issues in the respective countries or regions.
5. The World Energy Outlook 2002 (IEA, 2002) highlights that 1.6 billion people have no access to electricity and four out of five of these live in rural areas. Lack of energy leads to substantial health risks; for example, toxic indoor fumes from biomass stoves (see Chapter 1), carriage of fuel wood over large distances, lack of electricity for water pumps, refrigeration and for hospitals. How could fuel cells help to provide energy in such areas? Where do you see the main barriers for this?

Table 8.1 *Some advantages of using fuel cells in stationary applications*

Environmental	Energy supply
• Higher efficiency, lower CO_2 emissions and resource consumption • Reduced air pollution • Reduced noise and vibration • Simple fuel switching to use less carbon intensive and renewable fuels • Possibility of 'simpler' CO_2 sequestration • Possibility to generate hydrogen from renewable resources	• Increased reliability of distributed generation • Compensation for increased shares of fluctuating renewable energy sources • New options for supply of backup power • Reduced vulnerability of the energy system • New business opportunities for energy companies • Enhanced competition through new opportunities for Integrated Product Policy (IPP)
Technical	*Miscellaneous*
• High power-to-heat ratio • Heat levels suitable to industrial and cooling applications • Lower transmission losses due to distributed generation • Modularity and flexibility of installation • Good partial load characteristics and dynamic response • Lower maintenance costs and increased durability due to a reduced number of moving parts • Reduced requirements for pollution prevention equipment	• Low thermal radiation (particularly suitable for military applications) • Opportunity to promote small-scale cogeneration • Possibility to provide energy in remote areas, particularly in developing countries

8.3 Case Study: Fuel Cells for Distributed Power Generation

In the following case study, we consider the use of fuel cells for distributed power generation to find out if they are more sustainable than conventional power plants. We will concentrate on CHP, also known as cogeneration (see Box 8.2). We will first carry out an environmental evaluation of this fuel cell system and then examine economic and social implications of its use for distributed power generation.

Box 8.2 *What is cogeneration?*

In conventional power plants, only a fraction of the primary fuel input is converted into electricity. The waste heat has to be disposed of and heats up rivers or the air. In cogeneration systems, this heat is not dissipated, but used for various purposes. In industrial cogeneration systems, steam may be generated, agriculture products may be dried, breweries supplied with heat or galvanizing baths heated. In heating cogeneration, the thermal energy is used for space heating and domestic warm water supply.

Various technologies exist for cogeneration, including steam and gas turbines and reciprocating engines. More innovative systems include micro turbines, Stirling engines or fuel cells.

8.3.1 Environmental Considerations

In this case study we assume that, in the next 20 years, stationary fuel cells will mainly be fuelled with hydrogen generated from natural gas. We focus our attention on the emissions of CO_2 and CH_4 as the two most important greenhouse gases generated by the fossil-based energy systems used currently.

As already mentioned, comparison between fuel cells and the conventional energy systems must be based on a life cycle approach. We will, therefore, carry out a (simplified) life cycle assessment (LCA) to quantify the global warming potential (GWP) from the life cycle of the whole fuel cell energy system. We will then compare this GWP with the conventional energy systems to find out if fuel cells are truly more sustainable with respect to greenhouse gases. The analysis is based on the production of 1 kWh of electricity. You may wish to read Chapter 3 on the LCA methodology to help you follow the analysis and carry out the necessary calculations.

A simplified life cycle of the fuel cell system for stationary applications considered here is shown in Figure 8.4. Therefore, in our analysis we will cover the whole supply chain from the exploration and extraction of natural gas, through its processing and delivery to the power plant to the manufacture and the use of the fuel cell system. Note that the blank spaces in Figure 8.4 have been left for you to fill in the results of your calculations using the basic data given in Box 8.3 and the assumptions made in the case study.

Box 8.3   *Some units and properties needed for the case study*

$$1 \text{ kWh} = 3.6 \text{ MJ} = 3.6 \times 10^6 \text{ J}$$
$$1 \text{ TJ} = 10^6 \text{ MJ}$$

GWP of CH_4: 21 kg CO_2 eq./kg (see Chapter 3)
CO_2 emission factors for combustion of diesel and natural gas:

Diesel :   74 g CO_2/MJ
Natural gas :   59 g CO_2/MJ

Lower heating value (LHV) of natural gas: 38 MJ/Nm^3.
All efficiencies and energy data refer to the LHV of a fuel.

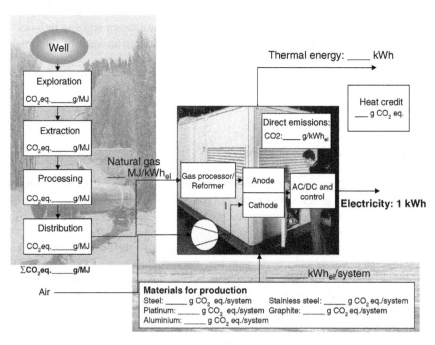

Figure 8.4   *Simplified life cycle of a stationary fuel cell*

Questions

1. It was mentioned that CO_2 and CH_4 are typically the most important greenhouse gases emitted from the energy systems. Consider, however, energy crops as an energy source. Why are the emissions of CO_2 from the combustion of energy crops less important?

Which other greenhouse gas gains in importance? Why? (Taking a life cycle approach, consider the agricultural activities necessary to support the growth of energy crops; for example, the use and production of manure.)
2. When biomass is used to provide fuel for a fuel cell, its life cycle CO_2 balance is almost zero (why?). The same result is found for biomass-derived fuel used in an internal combustion engine. This would point to the conclusion that the high efficiency of the fuel cell system is of no importance for reducing greenhouse gases because, for both the fuel cell and internal combustion systems, these emissions are very low if they use biomass-derived fuel. Why is in this case the fuel cell still of great advantage compared with the internal combustion engine?

8.3.1.1 Natural Gas Supply

Let us start our analysis of the life cycle of the fuel cell system with the supply of natural gas to the fuel cell power plant. Bringing natural gas to the fuel cell involves the following activities.

8.3.1.1.1 Exploration Drillings

We assume here that for drilling a 1 m hole, 0.01 TJ of diesel fuel is used (combusted) by the drilling equipment. Combustion of 1 MJ of diesel leads to 74 g of CO_2 emissions plus 10 g CO_2 for the production of 1 MJ of diesel. Each cubic metre of natural gas may require 4×10^{-6} m drilled.

8.3.1.1.2 Natural Gas Extraction

For extraction, we assume an energy consumption of 1×10^{-9} TJ diesel for each cubic metre of natural gas. As for the exploration stage, the CO_2 emissions per megajoule of diesel used can be assumed to be in total 84 g CO_2/MJ, including diesel production. Owing to leakages, 0.1 % of the gas extracted is emitted into the air at a rate of 0.6 kg CH_4/m^3 of raw natural gas.

8.3.1.1.3 Natural Gas Processing

Gas processing involves drying and desulfurization and requires the use of energy and materials. For simplicity we will only take into account the energy requirement. The assumption is that 0.1 % of the total amount of gas brought in for processing is combusted to produce heat and electricity required for this step.

8.3.1.1.4 Natural Gas Distribution

As a final step, the natural gas is distributed to the customer. The distribution is by pipeline and the assumption is that 2 % of the gas has to be combusted per 1000 km pipeline length to run the pipeline compressors. In our example, we suppose that the power plant is situated in continental western Europe with 20 % of the natural gas brought from Norway (distance of 600 km), 20 % from the Netherlands (200 km), 20 % from Germany (100 km) and 40 % from Russia (5500 km). Owing to pipeline leaks, 200 kg CH_4 is emitted per terajoule of natural gas sourced from Russia; for all other countries this leakage is at the rate of 2 kg CH_4/TJ of natural gas delivered.

Once the natural gas has reached the destination country, no further energy for distribution is required. Just the opposite: some gas suppliers even generate electricity using the pressure gradient from the high-pressure pipeline to the low-pressure distribution system. Owing to a large number of valves, smaller pipes and other infrastructure-related factors, the methane leakage from distribution networks in some countries can be rather high. We assume here modest values of 3 kg CH_4 emissions for delivering 1 TJ natural gas in high-pressure pipelines, 4 kg in medium-pressure pipelines and 5 kg in low-pressure pipelines.

Questions

1. Calculate and add up all CO_2 and all CH_4 emissions for the fuel supply of 1 MJ natural gas to a private household. Convert the CH_4 emissions into CO_2 equivalents using the GWP (GWP) given in Box 8.3. Enter the results in Figure 8.4.
2. What are the 'hot spots' of the natural gas supply according to the results obtained in the previous question? Which other greenhouse gases should have been considered in these calculations?
3. What factors might influence the high gas leakage rates for the Russian pipelines? Can these leakages be reduced or eliminated?

8.3.1.2 Production of the Fuel Cell System

Production of the fuel cell system is very complex and cannot be investigated in detail in this case study. The interested reader can consult Pehnt (2003) for more detail on the subject. However, to get a feel for the relative importance of the production stage in the whole life cycle of the fuel cell system we will consider a simplified PEFC power plant with an output of 200 kW_{el}. Such a system, which can weigh 14 t, consists of thousands of different components and materials so that a detailed LCA is very complicated. For the sake of simplicity, let us assume that the system consists of 70 % steel (of which 20 % is stainless steel), 20 % aluminium, 10 % graphite and 3 g platinum catalyst per kilowatt electric power; 90 % of the platinum used in the fuel cell stack is sourced from recycled platinum.

Supplying these materials is associated with many environmental impacts because the materials have to be extracted, cleaned, processed, transported and formed into components. As we are focusing on the greenhouse gases here, we assume the following emissions of CO_2 eq. per tonne of material used in the fuel cell system:

- 1500 kg CO_2 eq./t of conventional steel;
- 3600 kg CO_2 eq./t of stainless steel;
- 15 kg CO_2 eq./kg of graphite;
- 26 000 kg CO_2 eq./kg of primary (virgin) platinum; and
- 30 00 kg CO_2 eq./t of aluminium.

Except for platinum, all data for CO_2 eq. emissions are based on a mixture of primary and recycled materials. For simplicity, we assume secondary platinum as 'impact free'.

Further CO_2 (and other) emissions are generated from the use of electricity for the manufacture of all fuel cell components. In this case study we assume that a total of 20 000 kWh in used for these purposes, with an average CO_2 emission factor of 480 g of CO_2 eq./ kWh (average European electricity mix).

Questions

1. Calculate the CO_2 eq. emissions from the simplified production process of the fuel cell as described above and enter the results in Figure 8.4. Now calculate the CO_2 eq. emissions per kilowatt-hour electricity by dividing the emissions from the production of the fuel cell system by the kilowatt-hour electricity produced over its lifetime. Assume an average lifetime of 20 years for the system and a yearly electricity production of 5000 h. Neglect at this stage that the fuel cell stack has a shorter lifetime than the rest of the system.
2. Which life cycles stages can be considered as 'hot spots'? Where might improvements be possible?
3. Assume that 10 % of the power capacity in your country would be supplied by PEFCs. Using the platinum recycling rate of 90 % and a lifetime of 20 years (ignoring the fact that the stack has to be replaced within this lifetime), what would the annual national demand for platinum be? Compare this with the world reserves (see for instance the website http://minerals.usgs.gov). When would the world reserves be exhausted? Consider which nontechnical factors influence platinum recycling rate. What happens in the initial growth phase when an increasing number of fuel cells enter the market?
4. What happens if, additionally, 10 % of the vehicles in your country are equipped with similar fuel cells (assume that in mobile applications, 1 g platinum/kW is sufficient). Do you think that, in mobile applications, similar recycling rates can be achieved?
5. What are the competing demands for platinum in other sectors? What follows for future platinum prices? Develop strategies to deal with the issue of platinum under the assumptions used in the previous two questions.
6. If you look at the different fuel cell types in the Box 8.1 and the materials mentioned therein, which of these materials might, on a first glance – without considering the amount needed in fuel cells – be scarce? Discuss how that might influence the potential for fuel cell applications.

8.3.1.3 Operation of the Fuel Cell System

The term 'operation' refers to the conversion of natural gas into electricity and heat. What sounds so simple is actually the interaction of various complex processes. First, the natural gas has to be converted into a gas acceptable to the fuel cell. Whereas high-temperature fuel cells can deal with natural gas directly and convert it internally (inside the stack) into hydrogen, low-temperature fuel cells such as the PEFC used in our case study cannot deal with such gas mixtures. Therefore, the gas has to be desulfurized (because sulfur destroys the catalysts) and then reformed; that is, converted into hydrogen. Different processes can be used for reforming, but steam reforming is the most common method. The reforming process is carried out according to the following reaction:

$$CH_4 + H_2O + heat \Rightarrow CO + 3H_2 \text{ (synthesis gas)}$$

Because CO damages the platinum catalysts, it must be removed by the 'shift' reaction:

$$CO + H_2O \Rightarrow CO_2 + H_2$$

The hydrogen gas must be further cleaned before being introduced into the fuel cell.
All this processing obviously uses energy. Furthermore, oxygen has to be supplied to the cathode of the fuel cell. In many systems, the air must be compressed to increase the oxygen partial pressure. This air compressor is very often one of the main 'parasitic' power consumers of the system and might require 10 or 15 % of the electrical output of the stack. For our calculations, we assume an efficiency of 80 % for the full fuel processing system which (for simplicity) is taken to be more or less constant with varying current densities.

To calculate the stack efficiency, we will assume that designed current density of the fuel cell is 0.4 A/cm^2 (see Figure 8.3) and that the system operates close to that current density all the time.

Finally, the DC has to be converted into AC. This is accomplished in an AC/DC converter, which typically has very high efficiencies. In our case we assume that the efficiency is 96 %.

Our cogeneration system produces both electricity and heat, with the heat used for district heating. The amount of heat that can be extracted depends strongly on the circumstances, particularly on the temperature of the return flow from the heating system. PEFCs are low-temperature fuel cells, so the heat that can be supplied to a household or a district heating system is limited to about 80 °C. In high-temperature fuel cell systems, the heat can be used in the form of steam for industrial purposes or even to drive a gas turbine. The manufacturers' mid-term target for the thermal efficiency is 40 %.

Questions

1. Calculate the electrical efficiency of the system by multiplying the efficiencies together. Compare your result with the 'efficiency curve' in Figure 8.3. How close is your result to that shown in the figure? (Bear in mind that this is a simplified analysis, so the result may not be precisely the same as in Figure 8.3.)
2. The system efficiency curve in Figure 8.3 goes to zero at zero current density. What have we neglected so far that could explain this effect?
3. Calculate the amount of useful heat output produced per kilowatt-hour electricity using the target thermal efficiency of 40 %.
4. Assuming that the system is operated at 0.4 A/cm^2 all the time and taking the electrical efficiency as calculated in Question1, calculate the life cycle CO$_2$ equivalents. Follow the following steps:
   - With the system electrical efficiency found in Question 1, calculate the amount of natural gas necessary to produce 1 kWh of AC electricity.
   - Multiply the CO$_2$ equivalent emissions of natural gas supply (Section 8.3.1.1) with that amount.

- Add the specific emissions for the production of one fuel cell power plant as determined in Section 8.3.1.2.
- Calculate the amount of CO_2 emissions generated in the reformer. This is easy to calculate: each C atom from the natural gas converted in the reformer ultimately leads to CO_2 emissions (see the reforming and shift reactions). Thus, we can take the CO_2 factor of 59 g CO_2 per megajoule natural gas.
- Enter all the results in Figure 8.4.

5. Compare the significance of the fuel supply, production of the system and operation stages. What do you conclude? Which parts of the system are significant with respect to the CO_2 equivalents (i.e. global warming)? In vehicle applications, the production of the system is more significant. Why?
6. What are the advantages and disadvantages of shifting the operating point of a fuel cell power plant from higher to lower current densities? To answer this question, look at Figure 8.3 again. Assuming that the natural gas price may rise in future due to scarcer resources, what does that mean for the rating of such a system?
7. What have been your major problems in carrying out this simplified LCA? What further research have you done to overcome these problems?
8. Comment on the issue of data quality. How robust is the information derived? What could you do if some data points are not reliable? How could you ensure that the statements derived are sufficiently robust?

8.3.1.4 Dealing with the Coproducts

We have now calculated the CO_2 equivalents (i.e. the GWP) for the production of 1 kWh electricity and a corresponding amount of heat by the PEFC system. If you are asked how that compares with the electricity generation by a coal power plant, what would you answer? Well, so far, it would be difficult to answer this question because we have two useful products from the fuel cell system, and we must find a way to calculate the emissions associated with *one* product only.

This kind of problem can arise whenever a system or company produces more than one product. Take a farmer raising cows. The cow produces milk, but eventually it will be slaughtered and converted into meat. How can the farmer allocate the costs of feeding the cow to produce the milk (daily) and the meat (at the end of the cow's life)?

There are two main ways to deal with this problem. One is called *allocation* (see the Appendix on LCA at the end of the book) whereby an appropriate basis is sought for allocating costs between the products. In the case of the farmer, this might be the relative nutritional values of milk and meat, or the prices of the milk and the meat on the market.

For the case of the cogeneration system, one allocation basis could be the energy generated. Take the example of an electrical efficiency of 40 % and a thermal efficiency of 40 %. Thus, for each kilowatt-hour of electricity, 1 kWh of heat is produced. The allocation basis would thus be 50 : 50; that is, 50 % of the CO_2 emissions are allocated to the electrical output and 50 % to the heat output.

However, this allocation basis does not really represent the 'value' of the products. Instinctively, 1 kWh electricity seems more valuable than 1 kWh low-temperature heat. And in fact, as we know from thermodynamics, only a fraction of the heat can be converted into electricity. Therefore, many people use exergy as the allocation basis. Exergy describes the amount of useful energy that is contained within the product; the exergy of electricity is equal to its energy. The exergy of heat, in contrast, is given by the Carnot efficiency multiplied by the energy value.

The second way to deal with coproducts is to estimate the 'avoided burden'. If the cow, for instance, had not produced milk, it would have been necessary to buy some substitute for milk, such as soy milk. The total cost of the feed for the meat would then be the sum of the feed cost over the lifetime of the cow minus the avoided costs for the soy milk.

In the case of the fuel cell system this means that we have to identify the heating systems that would actually be replaced by such fuel cell systems. This will depend on a number of factors; for instance, the country, the type and age of the houses, the preferred fuels and so on. It also depends on the perspective of the decision-maker: from the perspective of a house owner; it is the individual house heating system that might be superseded by a fuel cell system. Boiler manufacturers might compare fuel cells with other modern heating systems. A politician who has to decide which heating system to subsidise financially will have to consider, for instance, a fuel cell domestic energy system or a modern condensing boiler.

Questions

1. Allocate the emissions of CO_2 equivalents between the electricity and heat from the fuel cell system considered in this case study by using exergy as the allocation basis. Assume a temperature of 80 °C for the heat output. The Carnot efficiency is equal to

$$\eta_{Carnot} = 1 - T_s/T$$

   where T is the operating temperature and T_s is the average temperature of the surroundings. Calculate the emissions of CO_2 eq. per kilowatt-hour of electricity by multiplying the calculated allocation factor with the total CO_2 emissions determined in the previous section.
2. Now calculate the CO_2 equivalent emission per kilowatt-hour of electricity using the avoided burden approach. Assume that, as a competing system, a condensing boiler is being replaced and that the production of 1 MJ of heat from the condensing boiler (including the fuel supply and production of the system) leads to the emissions of 75 g CO_2 eq.
3. In the avoided burden approach, when would you assume that a mix of technologies (e.g. the overall electricity mix or an average heat production system) is being substituted and when a single technology (e.g. a coal power plant, a gas combined cycle, or a condensing boiler)? Under what circumstances it is appropriate to base the avoided burdens estimates on future technologies and when on marginal technologies being shut down and leaving the market?
4. Which approach do you consider to be more appropriate: allocation or avoided burden? What are the advantages and disadvantages of the two approaches? Is there the 'best' approach?

5. Now compare your LCA results for CO_2 eq. to the CO_2 emissions from different sources of electricity (see the table below).

Electricity generation system	g CO_2 eq./kWh$_{el}$ (on a life cycle basis)
Coal power plant	980
Gas combined cycle (without cogeneration)	434
Reciprocating engine (cogeneration; avoided burden approach)	370
Wind power	20
River-flow hydroelectric power	20

6. Now assume that instead of the PEFC investigated, you have a 1 MW SOFC system. Such a system might achieve an electric efficiency of 60 % when it is coupled with a gas turbine. The thermal efficiency is then of the order of 20 %. Assume no changes in the CO_2 emissions of the power plant production. How does this SOFC perform with respect to the CO_2 eq.?

8.3.2 Social and Economic Considerations

'Dollars + Time = Fuel cell'

This was the headline in a German newspaper article on the future of stationary fuel cells. This concise quotation highlights the two severe limitations of stationary fuel cells.

Because of their higher efficiencies, and thus reduced fuel costs, fuel cells can still be competitive with higher capital costs than the competing technologies. For example, estimates of capital costs have shown that even with 20–30 % higher costs per kilowatt-hour of electricity fuel cells could still compete with other energy systems. Even so, the costs of current systems are still prohibitively high: fuel cells in stationary applications are still a factor 10–50 too expensive. This is partly due to the current low production volume; if their production increased significantly, learning[2] and economies of scale[3] would lead to a reduction in cost. But in addition to this, research and development are needed to reduce material costs and quantities used, to enhance performance and enable production of more integrated systems with standardized power plant components.

Because of their potential to revolutionize the energy systems, fuel cells have attracted much public attention and raised expectations. These expectations have also been promoted by early announcements by fuel cell manufacturers that the fuel cell systems would be available in the near future. However, as mentioned above, fuel cells need much more technical development and reduction of capital costs and are, therefore, far from commercialization. Another issue yet to be solved is the question of longevity. Owing to

---

[2] 'Learning' curves reflect cost reductions due to increased production and technological innovation as a function of cumulative production.
[3] The economies of scale refer to the relationship between the size of a plant and its capital and operating costs. Normally, the larger the capacity of the plant (i.e. the larger the economies of scale), the lower the capital and operating unit costs.

material and component degradation, the lifetime of fuel cell systems is still well below target. This also means that fuel cells will come too late to enable rapid climate protection measures demanded by the Kyoto Protocol.

Given the marketing efforts of big companies and the good image of fuel cells, it is not surprising that customer acceptance of this technology is high. In some cases, utility companies have been overrun by interested people who wanted to have a fuel cell installed in their home. Customer interviews even showed that a great percentage of people would not refuse a little fuel cell power plant in their own basement.

The fuel cell as a new product also needs new distribution channels. Particularly for small residential applications, but also for larger systems, service contracting will be required; that means that the utility or another service company owns the fuel cell systems and leases it to the customer, to provide a package of services consisting, for instance, of electricity, heat, financing and maintenance of the system. Thus, fuel cells might conceivably lead not only to a technical transformation, but might also fundamentally change the way the heat and electricity markets and domestic energy supply are organized (see Figure 8.5). For instance, utilities might offer fuel-cell-related energy services, in heat supply and district heating systems, and reinforce relationship with their customers by long-term contracts. These new models of commercial relationships also imply new skills needs, with craftsman needing skills which cut across the traditional trades of electrician, plumber and so on. Thus, once fuel cells are sufficiently developed for widespread use, they will need to be supported by the new modes of training.

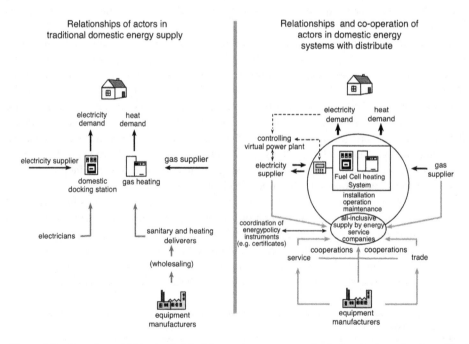

Figure 8.5 *Paradigm shift in the field of domestic energy supply due to the introduction of fuel cells (Pehnt and Ramesohl, 2007)*

Questions

1. What problems arise from the discrepancy between public perception of a product's maturity and its actual readiness for the market?
2. Comment on the readiness of the public to accept fuel cells in 'their backyard'. How does that compare with the public reaction to some other energy technologies, such as incineration and the NIMBY syndrome?
3. Advances in information and communication technology might make it possible for small distributed power systems to act as one large power plant; that is, to be centrally controlled. This is sometimes referred to as a 'virtual power plant' (see Figure 8.5). Discuss the advantages of this concept.
4. Based on your findings in this case study, the information given above and Table 8.1, try to develop a marketing strategy or a commercial case for a fuel cell in an application of your choice. Which aspects would you highlight? How would you visualize this information? Compare this with any advertisements you might have seen with respect to fuel cells or hydrogen.
5. An effective introduction strategy for fuel cells needs to recognize potential bottlenecks or time-limiting factors. Try to design a table similar to Table 8.1 to show the barriers to and challenges for the fuel cells systems.
6. Now imagine you work for a nongovernmental organization dealing with environmental protection. What would be your position with respect to stationary fuel cells? Take into consideration actual and recent political developments, such as the Kyoto Protocol, the Iraq war and events such as tanker oil spills which attract public attention.

8.4 Conclusions

Fuel cells are an emerging energy technology being developed by a number of companies and research organisations worldwide. Currently, fuel cells are much more expensive than the conventional energy systems, and that makes their commercialization difficult and slow. Further problems that are yet to be solved include design improvements, hydrogen storage and provision of infrastructure. However, environmentally, fuel cells appear to offer significant advantages over the competing technologies, despite the fact that they are, at this stage of development, still dependent on fossil fuels. It is expected that in the future the growth of the solar hydrogen economy will make fuel cells even more sustainable.

As in other areas of technology development, the future of fuel cells will not be determined by any one single factor, but rather by a combination of (often unpredictable) technological, economic, environmental and social considerations. Although speculating on the future of anything, and particularly on a technology, is a futile job, one thing at least seems to be certain: fuel cells have come back and are set to continue growing. We await with interest to see whether they grow up.

Acknowledgement

The author would like to acknowledge support for parts of this publication from the German Federal Ministry of Education and Research under the socio-ecological research framework.

References and Further Reading

EU (2000) Towards a European strategy for the security of energy supply. Green Paper, European Commission, COM(2000)769 final.

IEA (2002) *World Energy Outlook 2002*, International Energy Agency, Paris.

Pehnt, M. (2002) *Ganzheitliche Bilanzierung von Brennstoffzellen in der Energie- und Verkehrstechnik (Life Cycle Assessment of Fuel Cells in Stationary and Mobile Applications)*, Fortschritt-Berichte Reihe 6 Nr. 476, VDI Verlag, Düsseldorf, ISBN 3-18-347606-1.

Pehnt, M. and Ramesohl, S. (2003) Market introduction of stationary fuel cells for distributed power: benefits, barriers, and drivers. Study commissioned by the World Wide Fund for Nature (WWF).

Solomon, S., Qin, D., Manning, M. *et al.*. (eds) (2007) *Climate Change 2007: The Physical Science Basis. Report of Working Group 1 to the Fourth Assessment Report of the Intergovernmental Panel on Climate Change*, Cambridge University Press, Cambridge.

9

Sustainability of Nuclear Power

Adisa Azapagic and Slobodan Perdan

As a result of the growing concerns about the increasing emissions of greenhouse gases and security of energy supply, there has been a recent resurgence in interest in nuclear power. This chapter looks at technological, environmental, economic and social aspects of nuclear energy from a life cycle perspective and examines whether nuclear power could provide a sustainable option for our growing energy needs. The extent to which nuclear energy can be shown to be sustainable – or otherwise – will to a significant extent determine its place in the energy supply spectrum.

9.1 Introduction

Energy, and particularly electricity, is vital to human activity and economic growth and, as such, it is an important component of any policy for sustainable development.

It is expected that by 2050 global electricity demand will have increased by about a factor of 2.5 due to the projected 50% increase in the world population and strong economic growth in many developing countries leading to a more energy-consuming lifestyle (IEA, 2006; Solomon *et al.*, 2007). If the current energy policies continue worldwide, this increase will inevitably be met by the rise in the consumption of fossil fuels, as the most of the current electricity generation comes from fossil-fuel burning technologies.

However, growing concerns about environmental, economic and social issues associated with current electricity production, such as climate change, the depletion of fossil resources,

Sustainable Development in Practice: Case Studies for Engineers and Scientists, Second Edition
Edited by Adisa Azapagic and Slobodan Perdan
© 2011 John Wiley & Sons, Ltd.

declining public trust in science and technology and increasing energy prices, have led to a reappraisal of the wider energy scene and of individual energy technologies. Some of the current technologies for providing energy, in particular those based on fossil fuels, are increasingly viewed as unsustainable.

This concern has led to revaluation of the role of nuclear energy in the world's energy future. In the UK, for instance, there has been a radical change in the government policy from a neutral stance towards nuclear power to encouraging actively the private sector to build new nuclear power stations (Greenhalgh and Azapagic, 2009). In 2008, the White Paper on Nuclear Power set out the Government's view that new nuclear power stations should have a role to play in UK future energy mix alongside other low-carbon sources. The White Paper stated that it would be in the public interest to allow energy companies the option of investing in new nuclear power stations, and that the Government should take active steps to facilitate this (BERR, 2008).

Currently, nuclear power provides approximately 19% of the UK electricity generation, which represents 7.5% of total UK energy supplies and 3.5% of total UK energy use (DECC, 2006). In the future, however, its share in the UK electricity generation could significantly increase if the current nuclear ambitions are realized. At the time of writing, there are three main consortia in the UK who, between them, have announced plans to build up to 16 GW of new nuclear capacity. The first new nuclear power stations may begin generating electricity from around 2018 (DECC, 2010).

The UK is not the only country that plans to increase its nuclear power capacity. According to the latest report by OECD Nuclear Energy Agency (NEA), in 2008 there were 41 nuclear power reactors under construction in 14 countries. There are plans for significant further nuclear power plant construction, particularly in China, India, the Russian Federation, the Ukraine and the USA (NEA, 2008).

Currently, nuclear energy supplies 16% of the world's electricity. Worldwide, there are more than 440 nuclear reactors operating in 30 countries, with a total capacity of 387 GWe (see Table 9.1). France, Japan and the USA have 57% of the world's nuclear generating capacity (NEA, 2008). It is projected that global nuclear capacity could increase by a factor of between 1.5 and 3.8, and that the nuclear share of global electricity production could rise from 16% today to 22% in 2050. To achieve this increase, between 2030 and 2050 an average of between 23 (low scenario) and 54 (high scenario) reactors per year would need to be built both to replace plants that are coming to the end of their lifetime and to increase nuclear generation (NEA, 2008).

There are two main global drivers behind this intention to increase the role of nuclear power: concerns about climate change and energy security. The latter is particularly important for countries with little or no fossil fuel resources. For example, these concerns are unequivocally expressed in the UK White Paper on energy (BERR, 2008):

> We need secure, clean and sufficient (energy) supplies if we are to continue to function as a modern society. But we face two long-term challenges:
>
> • Tackling climate change by reducing carbon dioxide emissions both in the UK and abroad;
> • Ensuring the security of our energy supplies.

Nuclear power, according to the UK Government's position, could play a significant role in meeting these long-term challenges because it is a low-carbon, affordable, dependable and safe technology 'capable of increasing diversity and reducing our dependence on any one technology or country for our energy or fuel supplies' (BERR, 2008).

Similar views are expressed by the nuclear industry itself. The industry echoes the above-mentioned concerns by stating that 'the world faces environmental threats from climate change caused by anthropogenic CO_2 emissions and socio-political threats from rising energy prices and the possible lack of secure energy supplies' (NEA, 2008). But the nuclear industry sees this also as an opportunity to prove that 'nuclear energy has a potentially strong role to play in alleviating these problems' (NEA, 2008).

However, as well documented, nuclear energy has its fair share of opponents, so it would not come as a surprise that the views about the 'strong' role of nuclear energy in securing the future energy needs are not shared by everyone. Most of the environmental nongovernmental organizations (NGOs), for instance, are still vehemently opposed to nuclear power and are not enthralled by its latest revival in some quarters. They argue that nuclear energy provides a solution neither to reducing CO_2 emissions nor to energy security. NGOs such as Friend of the Earth (FoE), Greenpeace and WWF argue that nuclear energy is expensive, unsafe, presents security risks, produces dangerous waste, is not 'emissions free' and will not deliver the urgent emission cuts needed to tackle climate change (WWF, 2003; FoE, 2010; Greenpeace UK, 2010). In other words, in the view of its opponents, nuclear energy is not a sustainable option and, as such, should not be pursued.

Amidst these contrasting views from interested parties and anti-nuclear campaigners, nuclear energy remains a contentious issue. This is reflected in public attitudes toward nuclear power which, in general, range from ambivalent to negative; there is, however, a growing public awareness and concern about the impacts of climate change which may start to influence the change in public opinion (Curry *et al.*, 2005; NEA, 2010).

It may be the case that, as its advocates claim, the nuclear option offers a reduction in CO_2 emissions as well as the security of supply. However, it is far from clear how sustainable the nuclear option is overall, compared with other energy generating options. Issues such as health and safety, investment risks, security, public trust and perception must also be considered to understand the full sustainability implications of nuclear generation (Grimston and Beck, 2002). Furthermore, the nuclear power industry is faced with many uncertainties, including financial, technical and regulatory (NEA, 2000). Decommissioning and high-level waste disposal are prime examples of areas where these uncertainties exist (CoRWM, 2006).

Therefore, any decisions about the future of nuclear power will need to consider these and other relevant sustainability issues, taking an integrated, balanced and impartial approach.

This chapter discusses some of the sustainability issues associated with nuclear power. By applying a life cycle approach, it explores the relative environmental, economic, social and political sustainability with an aim of finding out if and under what circumstances nuclear power could contribute to the goals of sustainable development.

Prior to that, we first give an overview of nuclear technologies and their technical characteristics.

Questions

1. What are main drivers behind a recent revival of nuclear energy? Are they the same as in your country?

2. Do you agree with the view that nuclear energy could help mitigate climate change? What are your reasons?
3. What is meant by security of energy supply? How does it affect your country? How could nuclear energy contribute to securing of supply in your country? What other energy options may play a role?
4. Which countries are currently building new nuclear plants?

9.2 Nuclear Power

Unlike power generated from fossil fuels, nuclear power generation does not rely on fuel combustion. Instead, the heat needed to generate electricity is produced through a nuclear reaction – fission or fusion. Currently, all nuclear power is generated by fission; fusion is not expected to be commercially available until 2050 at the earliest. Therefore, fission is the focus of this chapter. The following sections explain the principles of nuclear power generation and give an overview of different reactor designs, following three generations, from the current Generation II to the developing Generations III, III+ and IV. The subsequent sections discuss the life cycle of nuclear power and the related environmental, economic and social impacts.

Questions

1. What is the difference between fission and fusion?
2. Why is fusion not expected to be available until 2050?

9.2.1 The Principles of Nuclear Fission

Nuclear fission is the process of splitting the nucleus of an atom into smaller parts, which releases neutrons and large amounts of heat. In nuclear power plants, this reaction is carried out in controlled conditions in a nuclear reactor, using the uranium isotope U-235 as the fuel. The fusion reaction is illustrated schematically in Figure 9.1. The uranium atom is at first bombarded by an external neutron[1] to generate the short-lived U-236 isotope which then quickly splits into smaller fission products (e.g. krypton and barium):

$$U_{92}^{235} + \text{neutron} \rightarrow U_{92}^{236} \rightarrow Kr_{36}^{92} + Ba_{56}^{141} + 2\,\text{neutrons} + 200\,\text{MeV} \qquad (9.1)$$

The reaction also releases further neutrons which then bombard other uranium atoms to create further fission products and so on. In the presence of enough free neutrons, the chain reaction becomes self-sustaining and the conditions in the nuclear reactor are said to be 'critical'.

---

[1] At a start up of a new nuclear reactor, an external neutron source is needed to start the fission reaction. This is often provided by using beryllium mixed with polonium, radium or other alpha emitter. Alpha particles from the decay cause a release of neutrons from the beryllium as it turns to carbon-12 (WNA, 2010a).

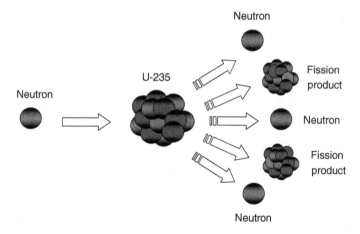

Figure 9.1   *Schematic representation of the nuclear fission reaction*

As the fission reactions continue, the concentration of U-235 in the fuel decreases. Some U-235 atoms will also be converted to atoms of fissile Pu-239, some of which will, in turn, undergo fission and produce heat.

The fission products are retained within the uranium fuel pellets and they become 'poisons', as they absorb neutrons and thus slow the rate of fission and heat generation. The combined effect of the declining concentration of uranium and the increasing concentration of poisons necessitates reactor shutdowns and refuelling.

As shown in Equation 9.1, about 200×10^6 eV of heat is released each time an atom undergoes the fission reaction.[2] By contrast, burning coal releases only a few electron-volts, so nuclear fuel contains at least ten million times more usable energy per unit mass than fossil fuel – hence, its attractiveness as a source of energy.

In most nuclear power plants, the heat released during fission is transferred to water to generate steam and then, via a turbine, electricity. Thus, the thermal part of the electricity generation in nuclear plants is equivalent to that used in fossil-fuel installations.

The amount of energy extracted from nuclear fuel is called 'burn-up', which is expressed in terms of the heat energy produced per initial unit of fuel weight (GWh/tonne of uranium). The early nuclear power stations had a burn-up of about 120 GWh per tonne (GWh/t) of fuel; modern power plants can achieve over 1200 GWh/t (DTI, 2007).

Typically, less than 1% of uranium is burned in a reactor before it is discarded as 'spent fuel'. This is because of the build up of poisons in the fuel from the fission process and because the metal cladding on the fuel weakens over time as it is exposed to radiation (DoE, 2010). The spent fuel can be recycled; however, this option is not practised widely (see Section 9.3.7.1 on waste management).

Questions

1. Explain in your own words the principles of nuclear fission.
2. What is meant by 'critical' condition?

[2] $1 \, eV = 1.602 \times 10^{-19}$ J.

3. Why is the uranium isotope U-235 used in nuclear reactors?
4. What other fuels can be used in a nuclear reactor, in addition to uranium?

9.2.2 Reactor Components

Most nuclear reactors comprise the following main elements:

- fuel assemblies;
- control rods;
- moderator; and
- coolant.

The fuel assemblies consist of the rods filled with the uranium dioxide (UO_2) pellets and inserted in the reactor core.

Both control rods and moderator are used to control the rate of nuclear reaction by absorbing and slowing down the neutrons. Without these, the chain reaction could grow out of control, generating large amounts of heat and leading to an explosion or reactor core meltdown. The control rods are made of a neutron-absorbing material, such as cadmium, hafnium or boron, and are inserted into or retracted from the core to regulate the reaction. The moderator is usually water, but can also be heavy water or graphite.

A coolant in the reactor serves two functions: to facilitate the extraction of heat from the core and to maintain the temperature in the reactor, ensuring safety. Water is normally used as coolant, although gases such as helium (He) or carbon dioxide (CO_2) can also be used. In some reactors (e.g. pressurized water reactors (PWRs) – see Section 9.2.3), water can serve both as moderator and coolant. The coolant normally circulates between the reactor core and a heat exchanger, where it transfers the heat evolved inside the reactor to a secondary circuit (except in boiling water reactors (BWRs); see Section 9.2.3). The heat energy that is transferred generates steam which, in turn, is used to generate electricity in turbines.

The reactor core is housed normally in a robust steel vessel and encased in a thick concrete shield. The structure around the reactor core is housed in a containment building for safety and security reasons.

Questions

1. What are the main components of a nuclear reactor? Describe the role of each.
2. How can the nuclear reaction in a reactor be controlled?
3. What substances and materials can be used as moderators? And as coolants?

9.2.3 Types of Nuclear Reactor

As shown in Figure 9.2, there are many different types of nuclear reactor. They are classified by 'generation', referring to the time frame over which they have developed or are still developing. Generation I reactors are early prototype reactors developed in the 1950s and

---

[2] $1 \, eV = 1.602 \times 10^{-19} \, J$.

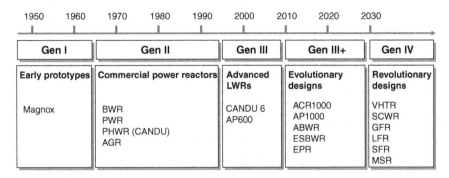

Figure 9.2   *Reactor generations and types (adapted from NEA, 2008)*

1960s; a typical example is Magnox, only ever used in the UK. Generation II reactors were deployed in commercial power plants from the 1970s to the 1990s. They include Boiling Water Reactors (BWRs) and Pressurised Water Reactors (PWRs). Known collectively as light water reactors (LWRs), BWRs and PWRs represent the vast majority (80%) of the installed nuclear power around the world (see Table 9.1). Generation III, or advanced light water reactors (ALWRs), started to be developed from the LWRs in the late 1990s and early 2000s.

Generation III + and Generation IV are still largely under development and are not expected in commercial use until 2020–2030. The latter are being developed by the Generation IV International Forum (GIF), representing 10 countries, who believe that high-temperature fast-reactor[3] designs represent the future of nuclear power. Most include a closed fuel cycle to minimize fuel use and waste. Six designs in particular are considered by GIF as suitable for deployment by 2030:

- very high-temperature reactor (VHTR);
- supercritical water-cooled reactor (SCWR);
- gas-cooled fast reactor (GFR);
- lead-cooled fast reactor (LFR);
- sodium-cooled fast reactor (SFR); and
- molten-salt reactor (MSR).

The principles of operation of some of the above reactors across the four generations are discussed next. As it is not feasible to cover all possible reactor designs, we consider only those that are either currently most widely used or have a potential to be deployed in the future.

Questions

1. What is the difference between thermal and fast neutrons? Therefore, what is the difference between the nuclear reactors using thermal and fast neutrons?
2. Describe the Magnox reactor. How does it work?
3. How many reactors are under construction and in what countries? What type are they?

---

[3] Using fast rather than thermal neutrons, as is the case in most current reactors. Fast neutrons have much higher energy (1 eV) than the thermal neutrons (0.025 eV).

Table 9.1 *Nuclear reactor types in operation around the world (based on WNA, 2010a)*

Reactor type	Main countries	Number	Capacity (GWe)	Fuel	Moderator	Coolant
Pressurized water reactor (PWR) [Generation II]	USA, France, Japan, Russia, China	265	251.6	Enriched UO_2	Water	Water
Boiling water reactor (BWR) [Generation II]	USA, Japan, Sweden	94	86.4	Enriched UO_2	Water	Water
Pressurized heavy water reactor (PHWR or 'CANDU') [Generation II]	Canada	44	24.3	Natural UO_2	Heavy water	Heavy water
Gas-cooled reactor (Magnox, Generation I; AGR, Generation II)	UK	18	10.8	Natural U (metal); enriched UO_2	Graphite	CO_2
Light water graphite reactor (RBMK) [Generation II]	Russia	12	12.3	Enriched UO_2	Graphite	Water
Fast neutron reactor (FNR) [Generation III]	Japan, France, Russia	4	1.0	PuO_2 and UO_2	None	Liquid sodium
Other	Russia	4	0.05	Enriched UO_2	Graphite	Water
	Total	**441**	**386.5**			

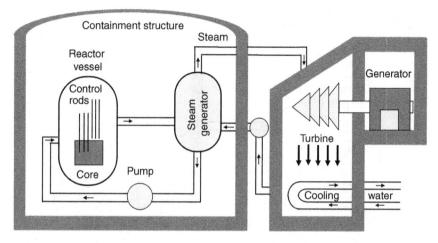

Figure 9.3   *Typical design of a pressurized water reactor (PWR) [adapted from DTI, 2007]*

9.2.3.1 Generation II: Pressurized Water Reactors

PWRs are most common nuclear reactors and with 265 installations and 252 MWe of installed capacity, they provide 65% of the world's nuclear electricity. A typical PWR design is shown in Figure 9.2.

They use enriched UO_2 pellets arranged in fuel assemblies of 200–300 rods each. A large PWR has about 150–250 fuel assemblies with 80–100 t of uranium (WNA, 2010a). Water is used both as coolant and moderator, so that PWRs are classed as LWRs.[4] As illustrated in Figure 9.3, PWRs have a primary cooling circuit which flows through the core of the reactor under a very high pressure (150 atm) and a secondary circuit in which steam is generated to drive the turbine (WNA, 2010a). The high pressure in the primary circuit is necessary to prevent water from boiling, as its temperature in the reactor core reaches about 325 °C. If any of the water turned to steam in the primary cooling circuit, the fission reaction would slow down. This is one of the safety features of PWRs.

In the secondary circuit, the water is at a lower pressure so that it boils in the heat exchangers to generate steam. The steam drives the turbine to produce electricity and is then condensed and returned to the heat exchangers in contact with the primary circuit.

9.2.3.2 Generation II: Boiling Water Reactors

BWRs are second most popular reactors after PWRs, providing 86.4 MWe or 22% of the installed electrical capacity worldwide. A BWR fuel assembly comprises 90–100 fuel rods and there are up to 750 assemblies in a reactor core, holding up to 140 t of enriched UO_2 (WNA, 2010a). They, too, use ordinary water as coolant and moderator.

By design, BWRs are similar to PWRs, except that they have only one cooling circuit (Figure 9.4), with the water boiling in the core of the reactor at 285 °C and pressure 75 atm.

---

[4] Light water refers to ordinary water (H_2O), as opposed to heavy water, which is enriched by deuterium (D_2O).

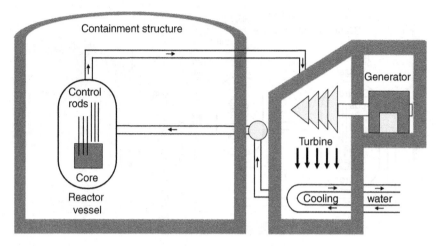

Figure 9.4   *Boiling water reactor (BWR) (adapted from DTI, 2007)*

Owing to this, the water in the turbine is always contaminated with traces of radionuclides, so that the turbine area must be shielded and radiological protection provided during maintenance.

9.2.3.3 Generation II: Pressurized Heavy Water Reactors

Most common pressurized heavy water reactors (PHWRs) are 'CANDU' (Canada deuterium uranium) reactors. They use natural uranium for fuel and heavy water as coolant and moderator. Like PWRs, they also have two coolant circuits, of which the primary is under pressure. As shown in Figure 9.5, the main difference between these two designs is

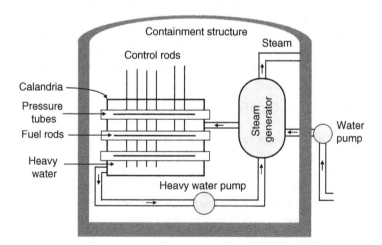

Figure 9.5   *Pressurized heavy water reactor (PHWR) (adapted from DTI, 2007)*

that, instead of a single pressurized reactor vessel, the PHWR has a number of smaller pressurized tubes, one for each fuel assembly, which are housed in a large tank called a calandria (DTI, 2007). New PHWR designs, such as the advanced CANDU reactor (ACR), have light-water cooling and slightly enriched uranium fuel (see Section 9.2.3.6). One of the advantages of the CANDU design is that it can be refuelled during operation, avoiding the need to shut down the reactor, as is the case with other designs.

9.2.3.4 Generation II: Advanced Gas-Cooled Reactors

Developed from the British Generation I Magnox[5] reactors, advanced gas-cooled reactors (AGRs) use enriched UO_2 as fuel, graphite as moderator and CO_2 as coolant. Typically, 115 t of uranium are required per reactor. The plant operates by circulating CO_2 through the core, where it reaches 650 °C, and then passing it through steam-generator tubes within the vessel to generate steam (British Energy, 2006; WNA, 2010a). AGRs have a good thermal efficiency but lower fuel burn-up, and the reactor size needs to be several times larger than a water-cooled design to give the same power output (Royal Society, 1999).

9.2.3.5 Generation III: Advanced Light Water Reactors

These reactors have been developed from Generation II LWRs to improve their safety and fuel technology features. They include the CANDU 6 and AP600 reactor designs (NEA, 2008). The former represents an improved CANDU design with a capacity of around 700 MWe, while the latter is an advanced passive (AP) reactor with an output of 600 MWe. The main characteristic of the AP reactors is their 'passive' design, using the natural laws of gravity, convection and compression for improved safety (SDC, 2006a).

Both of these two types of ALWR have been developed further as Generation III + technologies, as outlined below.

9.2.3.6 Generation III + : Advanced CANDU Reactors (ACR1000)

This 1200 MWe reactor represents an evolutionary development from the previous CANDU designs and, therefore, is classified as a Generation III + reactor. It is still being developed by the Atomic Energy of Canada and its deployment is planned for 2016 (NEA, 2008). Compared with the previous CANDU versions, this reactor uses slightly enriched uranium (2%) rather than natural uranium metal, but it can also use mixed-oxide fuel (MOX).[6] Like the previous designs, it still uses heavy water as moderator; but unlike the previous types, light water rather than heavy water acts as coolant. ACR has a much smaller calandria than the older CANDU design, reducing costs and fuel requirements by 75% (SDC, 2006a).

---

[5] The name is derived from magnesium alloy used in the fuel cladding: 'MAGnesium Non-OXidising'.
[6] MOX can include a mixture of oxides of plutonium and natural uranium, reprocessed uranium or depleted uranium.

The advanced design can achieve very high burn-ups, making it also possible to use spent fuel from other reactors, particularly PWRs. This would, for example, allow for both PWRs and ACRs to operate in parallel (NRC, 2003). However, this so-called 'DUPIC' process is highly complex and currently very expensive (SDC, 2006a).

9.2.3.7 Generation III + : Advanced Passive Reactors (AP1000)

AP1000 was developed by Westinghouse in 2006 as a larger version of the AP600. Rated at 1117 MWe, it is similar to the AP600, except for a taller reactor with a larger number of fuel assemblies and a larger steam generator (SDC, 2006a). Like all PWRs, the AP1000 uses enriched uranium fuel ($\sim$4%), but it can also operate using MOX fuel. The reactor has a modular design, allowing for easier construction. Currently, four AP1000 reactors are being built in China (WNA, 2010a) and it is also under consideration for a new nuclear build in the USA and UK.

9.2.3.8 Generation III + : Advanced Boiling Water Reactors

Advanced boiling water reactors (ABWRs) represent General Electric's evolutionary design of a standard BWR. They are available in four different sizes: 600, 900, 1350 and 1700 MWe. Compared with standard BWRs, the advanced reactors have improved construction and ease of maintenance; however, as in BWRs, water is contaminated by radioactive substances and refuelling is a complex process (SDC, 2006a).

9.2.3.9 Generation III + : Economic Simplified Boiling Water Reactor

Taking the passive concept further, economic simplified boiling water reactors (ESBWRs) are cooled by condensers that take steam from the pressure vessel by natural circulation, condense it by transferring the heat to a water pool and then put the water back into the vessel (NEA, 2008). Also designed by General Electric, they can generate up to 1550 MWe of electricity.

9.2.3.10 Generation III + : European Pressurized Water Reactors

The European pressurized water reactor (EPR) has been designed and developed by AREVA NP (NEA, 2008) and can generate up to 1750 MWe at 37% efficiency (SDC, 2006a). Like some other advanced reactors, it can also use MOX fuel. It is based on active (rather than passive) systems with safety enhancements, such as stronger containment and core capture in the event of an accident (SDC, 2006a). Two EPRs are currently being constructed in Europe – one in Finland and another in France; a further two units are being constructed in China. The first EPR in the USA is expected to be connected to the grid by 2015 (WNA, 2010a).

9.2.3.11 Generation IV: Very High Temperature Reactors

As show in Table 9.2, very high temperature reactors (VHTRs) are graphite-moderated, helium-cooled reactors with modules of 600 MWth or 300 MWe. The core can be built of

Table 9.2 Summary of the characteristics of Generation IV reactors (adapted from WNA, 2010a)

	Neutron spectrum (fast/thermal)	Coolant	Temp. (°C)	Pressure[a]	Fuel	Fuel cycle	Size (MWe)	Uses
Very high temperature gas reactors	Thermal	Helium	900–1000	High	UO$_2$ prism or pebbles	Open	250–300	Hydrogen and electricity
Supercritical water-cooled reactors	Thermal or fast	Water	510–625	Very high	UO$_2$	Open (thermal); Closed (fast)	300–700 1000–1500	Electricity
Gas-cooled fast reactors	Fast	Helium	850	High	U-238[b]	Closed, on site	1200	Electricity and hydrogen
Lead-cooled fast reactors	Fast	Lead or Pb–Bi	480–800	Low	U-238[b]	Closed, regional	20–180[c] 300–1200 600–1000	Electricity and hydrogen
Sodium-cooled fast reactors	Fast	Sodium	550	Low	U-238 and MOX	Closed	30–150 300–1500 1000–2000	Electricity
Molten salt fast reactors	Fast	Fluoride salts	700–800	Low	UF in salt	Closed	1000	Electricity and hydrogen

[a] High pressure = 7–15 MP.
[b] + with some U-235 or Pu-239.
[c] 'Battery' model with long cassette core life (15–20 years) or replaceable reactor module.

prismatic blocks or as a pebble bed. The main difference is that the former uses rods that are vertically inserted into the reactor, while in the latter fuel is in the form of ceramic spheres about the size of a tennis ball. Fuels that could be used in VHTRs include UO_2 and uranium carbide. The high outlet temperatures of between 900 and 1000 °C could enable co-production of hydrogen with electricity. VHTRs have potential for high burn-up and efficiencies of up to 50% (Herranz *et al.*, 2008). Other advantages include completely passive safety, relatively low operation and maintenance costs and modular construction (WNA, 2010a).

One of the promising VHTR designs is pebble bed modular reactor (PBMR) with smaller units, up to 165 MWe. The reactor uses graphite-coated UO_2 spheres of 60 mm; up to 450 000 of these circulate through the reactor continuously, each pebble being used for 6 months and then discarded. Thermal efficiencies of 41% have been claimed (NEA, 2008). Owing to a low power density in the core (one-tenth of that in an LWR), it is inherently safer, as it can withstand temperature excursions if for any reason coolant circulation ceases. This type of reactor was being developed in South Africa, but at the time of writing the project has been put on hold, so its future remains uncertain.

9.2.3.12 Other Generation IV Reactors

This section gives a brief overview of a selection of other Generation IV reactor designs; for further designs, the reader can consult DTI (2007), SDC (2006a), NEA (2008) and WNA (2010).

9.2.3.12.1 Supercritical Water-Cooled Reactor (SCWR)

The SCWR is a high temperature, high pressure water-cooled reactor. It operates above the thermodynamic critical point of water (374 °C, 22 MPa), to give a thermal efficiency of about one-third higher than today's LWRs, from which the design evolves (WNA, 2010a). The supercritical water at pressure 25 MPa and temperature of 510–550 °C drives the turbine directly, simplifying the design.

9.2.3.12.2 Gas-Cooled Fast Reactor (GFR)

Similar to the VHTR, these are also high temperature (850 °C) helium-cooled reactors; however, they use fast neutrons rather than thermal neutrons. They are also suitable for power and heat generation as well as hydrogen production. Unlike VHTRs, they have a closed fuel cycle which reduces the waste produced and allows for a variety of fuels to be used in the process, including plutonium and depleted uranium (SDC, 2006a). They are referred to as 'fast-breeder' reactors, because they generate new fissile material at a greater rate than they consume. This saves nuclear fuel reserves, but also poses challenges, such as plutonium proliferation (for more detail on proliferation, see Section 9.6.4).

Questions

1. Describe the operation of a PWR. How is it different from a BWR? Which reactor do you think is more sustainable and why?

2. Why are passive reactors apparently safer than the active reactor designs?
3. How does graphite work as moderator? Is it better than water or the other way round? Why?
4. What is the main difference between Generation III and Generation IV reactors?
5. What is fast neutron reactor? How is it different from a fast breeder reactor?
6. Which reactor type is in your opinion most sustainable and why? Discuss the criteria that you would need to consider to determine that.

9.3 The Life Cycle of Nuclear Power

The previous sections have given an overview of the various nuclear technologies, both available today and those that may be developed in the future. This section examines the rest of the life cycle of nuclear power generation to find out what activities and operations are involved beyond the nuclear reactor.

The life cycle of nuclear power generation is illustrated schematically in Figure 9.6. It can be divided into two parts: the fuel life cycle and the nuclear plant life cycle. The fuel life cycle start with mining the uranium ore which is then milled to extract UO_2. This is followed by conversion of UO_2 to uranium hexafluoride (UF_6) and the subsequent enrichment of the fissile uranium isotope U-235. The enriched UF_6 is then converted back to UO_2 and manufactured into fuel assemblies for use in the reactor core. The time the fuel spends in the core depends on the type of reactor, but typically the fuel is replaced at intervals of 12–24 months (WNA, 2010a). The spent fuel is highly radioactive, so it usually has to be stored over a long period of time to allow for the decay of radioactive substances. The spent fuel can also be reprocessed for further use as fuel in nuclear reactors. In addition to spent fuel, radioactive waste is generated during mining and fuel preparation, but the level of radioactivity is significantly lower than the spent nuclear fuel. Typically, this waste will be buried back into the mine, discharged into the mine tailings dams or stored at the fuel processing facilities.

The plant life cycle involves construction of the plant, its operation and decommissioning.

The following sections give a brief overview of each life cycle stage involved in both the fuel and plant life cycles.

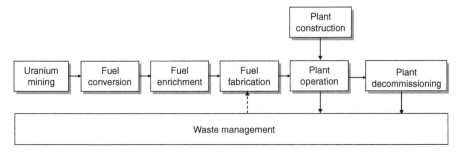

Figure 9.6 *The life cycle of nuclear power generation*

Questions

1. Describe the life cycle of nuclear fuel and a nuclear plant.
2. What are the main sustainability issues associated with the fuel life cycle and the nuclear plant life cycle?

9.3.1 Uranium Mining

Uranium can be obtained from the ground using open-pit mining, underground mining or in-situ leaching. The most common methods are open-pit and underground excavation, which is then followed by milling to extract the uranium. The waste rock is usually used to backfill the extraction site, but it must be separated from the surrounding environment as it is slightly radioactive.

In-situ leaching involves dissolving the uranium in the groundwater and pumping the solution to the surface. To improve the dissolution process, different substances are added to the ground water, including hydrogen peroxide and sulfuric acid. This method eliminates the need for milling the ore and disturbs the landscape much less than the open-pit mining, but it can lead to contamination of groundwater (SDC, 2006a; WNA, 2010a).

As outlined in Figure 9.7, both open-pit and underground mining will involve all or some of the following activities to produce the 'yellow cake' or U_3O_8:

- **Drilling and blasting**: Explosives and manual extraction are used to mine the uranium ore, which is then hauled by trucks or conveyors to the mill for further processing.
- **Crushing and grinding**: The ore is passed through a series of crushers to be ground to a fine powder to which water is added to make a slurry.
- **Leaching**: The slurry is oxidized in large tanks using ferric sulfate and sulfuric acid to dissolve (leach) uranium. The slurry is then passed through a series of thickeners and cyclones to separate the uranium solution from the rest of the slurry. The latter is disposed of in tailings ponds and the uranium solution is either filtered or passed through an ion-exchange column for further purification.

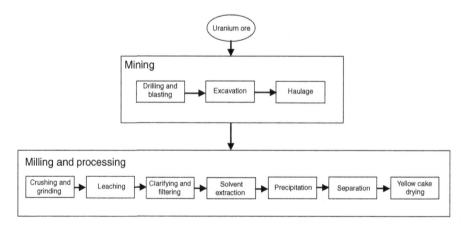

Figure 9.7   *Mining and milling of uranium to produce 'yellow cake' (simplified overview)*

- **Solvent extraction**: The purified and more concentrated uranium solution is then mixed with an organic solvent and subsequently with ammonium sulfate to separate the uranium-rich solution from the mixture.
- **Precipitation and separation**: This solution is treated by gaseous ammonia to precipitate ammonium diuranate $[(NH_4)_2U_2O_7]$, which is then separated out as a yellow paste in a filter or centrifuge.
- **Drying**: The paste is dried to evaporate the ammonia, leaving triuranium octoxide (U_3O_8) or 'yellow cake' (which is in fact khaki in colour). The yellow cake is packed into drums ready for transportation to the next stage – refinement and conversion to UO_2.

The yellow cake product contains between 70 and 90% uranium; this is a large increase from the original ore, which contains typically less than 1% of uranium. Around 200 t of U_3O_8 are required for a 1000 MWe reactor each year (SDC, 2006a).

The remainder of the ore, containing most of the radioactivity and nearly all the rock material, becomes tailings, which are often stored in mined-out pits. Tailings contain long-lived radioactive materials in low concentrations and heavy metals, so they need to be isolated from the environment (WNA, 2010a).

Questions

1. What is the difference between the open-pit, underground and in-situ leaching mining techniques?
2. How is the yellow cake produced?
3. What are the main sustainability issues associated with uranium mining?

9.3.2 Yellow Cake Refinement and Conversion

The yellow cake (U_3O_8) that leaves the uranium mill must be enriched before it can be used as reactor fuel (except for those reactor types that do not require enriched uranium, in which case the U_3O_8 is converted directly to UO_2). The enrichment process requires the material to be in gaseous form, so that the yellow cake must be converted into uranium hexafluoride (UF_6).[7] In preparation for this, the following steps are carried out (Marsh and Eccles, 1996; WNA, 2010a):

- **Purification**: To remove elements similar to uranium and those with large neutron-adsorbing capacities, the yellow cake is dissolved in nitric acid and sent to a solvent extraction process which uses tributyl phosphate dissolved in kerosene. Extracted uranium is washed from the organic solvent using nitric acid and concentrated by evaporation. The solution undergoes thermal decomposition in a fluidized bed reactor to produce UO_3 and is reduced to UO_2 using hydrogen in a rotary kiln at 500 °C.

---

[7] UF_6 is a gas at temperatures above 57 °C.

- **Conversion to tetrafluoride (UF$_4$)**: The UO$_2$ is then reacted with aqueous hydrogen fluoride (HF) also in a rotary kiln at about 450 °C to form UF$_4$.
- **Conversion to hexafluoride (UF$_6$)**: Finally, UF$_4$ is converted to gaseous UF$_6$ using fluorine (F) in a fluidized bed reactor. UF$_6$ is now ready for enrichment.

Questions

1. Why does the yellow cake need to be converted into UF$_6$?
2. What steps are involved in the production of UF$_6$?

9.3.3 Fuel Enrichment

Natural uranium contains only 0.7% of the fissile U-235 isotope and virtually all of the remaining 99.3% is non-fissile U-238 (SDC, 2006a). Fuel enrichment involves increasing the proportion of U-235 to about 3–4%, depending on the type of reactor.

During enrichment of UF$_6$, two streams are generated: one enriched to the required level and the other a waste stream consisting of U-238. The latter is stored for a possible use in some reactor types (as discussed in Section 9.2.3).

Two main enrichment methods are used commercially: gaseous diffusion and gaseous centrifugation. Gaseous diffusion involves forcing UF$_6$ gas under pressure through a series of porous membranes whereby the lighter U-235 molecules diffuse faster through a membrane than heavier U-238 molecules, thus enriching the stream with U-235. Owing to its high energy requirements, this method is gradually being replaced by gaseous centrifugation (Lenzen, 2008; WNA, 2010a).

In gaseous centrifugation, UF$_6$ is fed into a vacuum tube that rotates at very high speeds (Upson, 1996). The centrifugal forces cause the heavier and lighter isotopes to be concentrated on the outside and inside of the tube respectively. The heavier isotopes collect at the bottom of the centrifuge and are removed as a depleted tails stream. The lighter isotopes collect towards the top of the centrifuge and are removed as the enriched U-235 stream.

Between 5 and 20 parallel centrifuge stages may be required to complete the separation. The enriched stream forms the feed to the next centrifuge and the depleted stream returns to the previous stage (WNA, 2010a). Once the desired enrichment level is reached, the enriched UF$_6$ is ready to be fabricated into reactor fuel.

Questions

1. What reactors use enriched uranium and which natural uranium?
2. Why does uranium need to be enriched for use in some reactors?
3. What steps are involved in the fuel enrichment? What is the final product?

9.3.4 Fuel Fabrication

Nuclear fuel has two components: the reactive uranium compound and the metal fuel cladding that surrounds it, providing support and preventing fission products from escaping (Marsh and Eccles, 1996).

The enriched UF_6 is transported to a fuel fabrication plant to be converted into UO_2 powder. The powder is baked at 1400 °C and pressed into pellets which are stacked and encased into thin alloy or steel tubes (the cladding) to produce fuel rods (SDC, 2006a). A number of fuel rods are sealed together to produce 'fuel assemblies' which are then inserted into the nuclear reactor.

The annual fuel requirement for a 1000 MWe LWR is about 25 t of enriched UO_2 (SDC, 2006a). This requires the mining and milling of around 50 000 t of ore to provide about 200 t of triuranium octoxide concentrate (U_3O_8) from the mine.

Questions

1. What is the efficiency of converting uranium from the ore to the final uranium oxide fuel?
2. How is the nuclear fuel fabricated?
3. What form and shape are the fuel assemblies for different reactor types?

9.3.5 Reactor Operation and Electricity Generation

Nuclear reactors are typically base-load systems that work best when operating continuously and at maximum capacity. The operation of a nuclear reactor is characterized, amongst other parameters, by the load or capacity factor and burn-up rate. The capacity factor refers to its annual output level as a percentage of its full rated capacity. For nuclear power plants, this is determined by the amount of 'offline' time due to planned shutdowns or unplanned outages. As already mentioned, the burn-up rate is the amount of energy extracted from the fuel; in modern reactors this is typically 1200 GWh/t fuel (DTI, 1996).

As the nuclear fission reaction proceeds in the reactor core, the amount of U-235 decreases and the amount of fission products, including plutonium-239, increases (see Section 9.2.1). Some of the U-238 content can also be converted to other products, such as actinides. When the concentration of fission products starts to affect the reactor operation – typically the U-235 content will then be below 1% – it is necessary to replace the spent uranium with fresh fuel. On average, every 12–24 months, one-third of the spent fuel is removed from the reactor and replaced with fresh fuel.

Typically, the lifetime of a nuclear reactor and power plant is between 40 and 60 years. After that they have to be decommissioned. And, of course, before they can operate, they need to be constructed. These two stages in the life cycle of nuclear plants are discussed next.

Questions

1. What is the 'burn-up' rate? How is it measured?
2. Why does the nuclear fuel need to be replaced?
3. Explain the mechanism of fuel poisoning in the nuclear reactor.
4. Why are nuclear plants 'base-load' plants? How is that different, for example, from wind power?

9.3.6 Construction and Decommissioning of Nuclear Power Plants

The construction of nuclear reactors takes between 5 and 10 years and requires a large amount of materials (concrete and steel), energy, and financial and human resources. Reducing construction times and costs has been one of the main aims in the development of new reactors.

Decommissioning commences after the permanent closure of the plant and ideally should leave a clear site where the facility had once stood (WNA, 2010a). It involves the safe management of nuclear wastes and materials, decontamination, plant dismantling, demolition and site remediation. Wastes from decommissioning the reactor and the rest of the power plant include radioactive waste and large amounts of concrete, steel, pipework and vessels. There are three internationally adopted decommissioning approaches (WNA, 2010b):

- immediate dismantling, where the entire plant is dismantled and decontaminated soon after the shutdown;
- safe storage, whereby the plant is sealed for around 50 years to allow a decrease in radioactivity; and
- entombment, where the reactor and surrounding area are encased in concrete.

Each of these approaches has its advantages and disadvantages – the choice is very dependent on each individual site and country. For example, entombment is favoured in the USA, while in the UK this is socially an unacceptable option and early dismantling is favoured instead (NDA and DEFRA, 2008).

Options for managing the radioactive waste from nuclear reactors are discussed in the next section.

Questions

1. What does the construction of a nuclear plant involve? Why is it important to reduce the construction times?
2. How can a nuclear plant be decommissioned? What is involved?

9.3.7 Nuclear Waste Management

Radioactive waste is generated at each stage of the nuclear fuel cycle, including mining and milling of the ore, uranium conversion and enrichment, fuel fabrication, the operation of nuclear reactors and the clean up of sites. Radioactive waste is also generated if nuclear fuel is reprocessed. However, the great majority of the radioactivity produced in the nuclear life cycle is contained in the spent fuel (NEA, 2008). The spent fuel can be reprocessed or stored; all other waste is stored until it can be managed safely. These two options are outlined briefly below.

9.3.7.1 Fuel Reprocessing

The spent fuel from a nuclear reactor contains around 95% U-238, 1% U-235, 1% plutonium and 3% radioactive fission products (SDC, 2006a). Initially, it is kept in a pool of water for a period ranging from months to years to allow the radiation levels to decrease. After that it can be reprocessed to recover the uranium and plutonium for reuse as nuclear fuel. This is carried out by dissolving the fuel and the cladding in an acid to separate the components. Uranium can be returned to the conversion plant to be further enriched to 3–4% U-235, whilst plutonium can be used to produce MOX fuel. The remaining 3% of the high-level radioactive waste (about 750 kg per 1000 MW reactor) is vitrified and sealed in cold storage (SDC, 2006a; WNA, 2010a).

Fuel reprocessing takes place in only a few countries in the world, including the UK[8] and France. The following processing steps are typically involved in fuel reprocessing (Denniss and Jeapes, 1996; NDA and DEFRA, 2008):

- **Fuel decladding and dissolution**: The fuel and the cladding are dissolved in nitric acid. Much of the fuel dissolves quickly and the large cladding pieces, along with the cladding fines which settle in the solution, are removed as waste.
- **Clarifying**: Insoluble fission products which impede later processes are removed from the solution by centrifuge.
- **Separation of the fission products**: High-efficiency counter-current liquid–liquid extraction transfers the uranium and plutonium from the solution into a solvent containing 30% tributyl phosphate. Other fission products remain in the nitric acid solution.
- **Separation of the uranium and plutonium**: The plutonium is reduced to Pu(III) using uranium(IV) nitrate stabilized with hydrazine. Pu(III) is insoluble in the solvent and is transferred to the aqueous phase, leaving the uranium behind.
- **Purification of the uranium and plutonium streams**: The plutonium is precipitated in the form of plutonium oxalate by adding oxalic acid. This is dried, calcined and the resulting PuO_2 powder stored. The uranium stream is backwashed into a nitric acid solution, heated to remove the nitrate and the resulting UO_3 powder is stored. All the liquid wastes from the reprocessing separations are treated as radioactive wastes.

While fuel reprocessing saves uranium reserves, it has always been a politically and socially sensitive subject due to the production of plutonium, which could potentially be used for nuclear weapons (see Section 9.6.4).

9.3.7.2 Waste Storage

Most of the radioactive waste arising in the nuclear life cycle is stored. The type of storage depends on the level of radioactivity and the 'half-life'[9] of different components. For example, most of the fission products have half-lives of less than 1 year and the majority of the rest have half-lives of less than about 30 years. In contrast, many of the actinides have significantly longer half-lives of hundreds, thousands or even millions of years (NDA and DEFRA, 2008).

Classification of nuclear waste with respect to the level of radioactivity differs from country to country. Typically, waste is classified into the following categories (SDC, 2006a; DTI, 2007; NEA, 2008; WNA, 2010a):

---

[8] Fuel reprocessing in the UK has ceased and at the time or writing is on hold.
[9] The half-life is the time it takes for a radionuclide to lose half of its own radioactivity.

i.   **High-level waste (HLW):** HLW generates heat as the radioactive isotopes decay. Most of this type of waste is due to the spent fuel and its reprocessing and much of it is in liquid form. After a cooling period of up to 50 years, this waste is normally vitrified in a glass matrix and is stored in steel canisters in ponds or in cooled storage facilities. To vitrify waste from a 1000 MW reactor generated each year, 5 t of glass are required (WNA, 2007).

ii. **Intermediate-level waste (ILW):** ILW exceeds the limits for low-level waste (LLW) but does not have self-heating properties. Most of ILW is due to reprocessing of spent fuel and from the general operation and maintenance of nuclear plant. It consists mainly of metals and organics and it is normally immobilized in cement and stored at ground level in steel vaults. A 1000 MWe reactor generates around $70 \, m^3$ of ILW per year, including the waste from decommissioning (WNA, 2010a).

iii. **LLW:** Most LLW comprises paper, plastic and metal used in the vicinity of a nuclear reactor. Waste from building materials remaining after decommissioning a nuclear plant is also LLW, as is the waste from the mining activities. However, because the latter contains substances with long-lived radioactivity, it has to be managed separately from the other, short-lived waste – it is normally disposed of in tailings dams at the mine. LLW makes up 90% of radioactive waste but contains only 1% of the total radioactivity (WNA, 2010a). It can be stored in concrete vaults just below the ground. To reduce its volume, it is often compacted or incinerated (in a closed container) before disposal. A 1000 MWe nuclear power reactor can be expected to produce around $100 \, m^3$ of LLW every year (WNA, 2010a).

Most countries have no permanent solution for radioactive waste. This is also the case in the UK – although geological disposal[10] has been proposed (CoRWM, 2006) and accepted by the government, no site has been identified as yet.

Questions

1. What is involved in nuclear fuel reprocessing? Why is this waste management option not practised widely? What issues do you envisage are important in fuel reprocessing?
2. How can waste be stored safely?
3. Which countries are considering geological disposal of nuclear waste?
4. How is nuclear waste classified with respect to the level of radioactivity? Why is it important to distinguish between long- and short-lived radioactivity?
5. What is half-life in the context of nuclear waste? How is it measured?
6. Find out the half-lives of different components of radioactive waste and discuss waste management options with respect to that.
7. How much waste is produced over the life time of a 1000 MW reactor? How long will it remain active?

---

[10] Geological disposal involves packing the waste into disposal canisters and permanently sealing them in a repository deep underground.

9.4 Environmental Impacts of Nuclear Power

The previous sections have outlined the life cycle of nuclear power; in this section we examine the environmental impacts arising along the life cycle using life cycle assessment (LCA) as a tool (see Chapter 3 for LCA methodology).

Nuclear power has been promoted on the basis of its relatively low greenhouse gas emissions and the related global warming potential (GWP), particularly compared with the fossil-energy options. Therefore, quite a few LCA studies have focused on GWP from nuclear power and very few report the other environmental impacts. The following sections examine first the GWP from the nuclear life cycle and then discuss some other environmental impacts, in relation to other energy options.

9.4.1 Global Warming Potential

The life cycle greenhouse emissions (GWP) of different reactor types in different countries are given in Figure 9.8. As can be seen, the values range from 4.92 g CO_2 eq./kWh for the BWR operating in Sweden (Vattenfall, 2007) to 15.4 g CO_2 eq./kWh for the CANDU reactor in Canada (Andseta *et al.*, 1998); the average GWP value for the reactors shown is 8.75 g CO_2 eq./kWh. On average, PWRs appear to have lower GWP than BWRs by about 18%.

The difference in the GWPs for the different reactors is due to the different construction and fuel requirements, as these two stages are the 'hot spots' in the life cycle of nuclear power. This is also the reason for the difference in the results for the same reactor type based in different countries. The difference in the results is due to the different electricity mix used for the construction of the plant as well as due to the different sources of the uranium fuel.

The 'hot spots' are illustrated by the examples of BWRs and PWRs in Figure 9.9. On average, 40% of the total GWP is due to the construction and decommissioning of the nuclear plant and 35% is related to the mining activities.

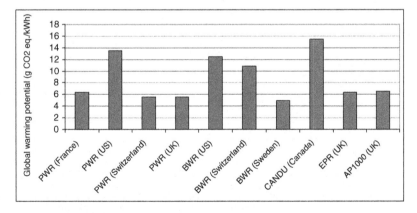

Figure 9.8   *GWP of nuclear power for different reactor types based in different countries. [Data sources: PWR (France, US, Switzerland) and BWR (US, Switzerland): Ecoinvent, 2007; PWR (UK): British Energy, 2006; BWR (Sweden): Vattenfall, 2007; CANDU: Andseta et al., 1998; EPR and AP1000: Matten, 2009.]*

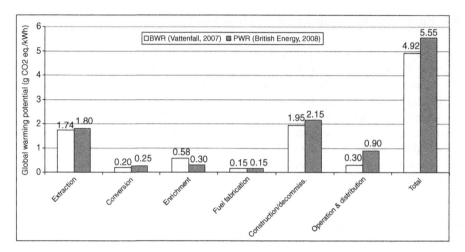

Figure 9.9 *GWP of PWR and BWR as provided in the Environmental Product Declarations (EPDs) by their operators (based on data by British Energy, 2008 and Vattenfall, 2007)*

Despite the variation in the GWP results, nuclear power still appears to have lower GWP than some other generating technologies. As shown in Figure 9.10, its GWP is comparable to that of hydro and wind energy and much lower than the GWP of fossil fuel options, which for coal reaches almost 1100 g CO_2 eq./kWh. Thus, arguably, nuclear is more sustainable than fossil fuel options from the climate change perspective. This, of course, has been one of the major drivers for the latest resurgence of nuclear power, as mentioned in the Introduction.

Let us now examine how sustainable nuclear power is with respect to other environmental impacts.

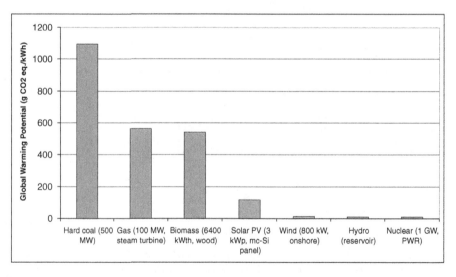

Figure 9.10 *GWP of nuclear power in comparison with other generating technologies (based on data from Ecoinvent, 2007)*

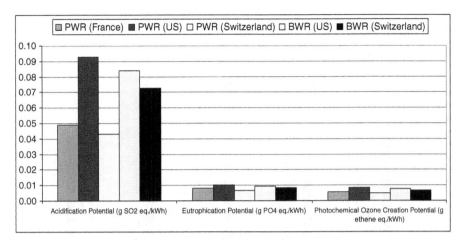

Figure 9.11 *Some environmental impacts from PWRs and BWRs (data source: Ecoinvent, 2007)*

9.4.2 Other Environmental Impacts

This section illustrates some of the environmental impacts associated with PWRs and BWRs used in different countries. It then compares their impacts with some other energy options. The reader may wish to consult Chapter 3 for the methodology on estimating the LCA environmental impacts.

The impacts associated with PWRs and BWRs are given in Figures 9.11 and 9.12. Overall, the highest impacts are noticed for the US PWR and the lowest for the Swiss PWR. The differences in the results between them range from 25% for the eco-toxicity and human toxicity to over 50% for acidification. These are due to the same reasons as for the GWP; that

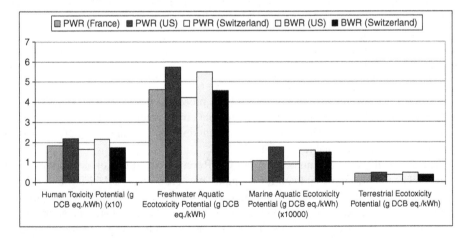

Figure 9.12 *Life cycle toxicity impacts of PWRs and BWRs (Data source: Ecoinvent, 2007)*

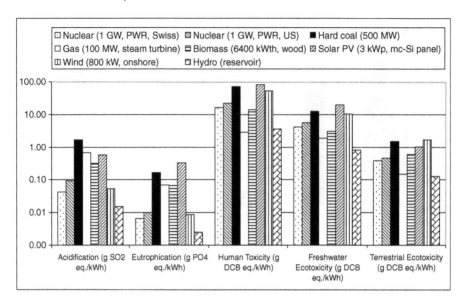

Figure 9.13 *Comparison of nuclear life cycle impacts with other energy options (Data source: Ecoinvent, 2007)*

is, due to the contribution of the 'hot spots' and the different background electricity mix (see the previous section).

The best and the worst nuclear options (PWR and CANDU respectively) with respect to the GWP are compared with other energy options for five environmental impacts in Figure 9.13. The most sustainable option for all the impacts considered is hydro power. The least sustainable option for acidification appears to be hard coal; for terrestrial toxicity, wind; and for the other three impacts, solar photovoltaics. The highest human toxicity impact is from the life cycles of solar photovoltaics and hard coal. Nuclear is comparable to hydro and wind for acidification and eutrophication; for the other impacts it is better than some of the renewables, such as photovoltaics and wind. However, it is less sustainable than the gas option for human, freshwater and terrestrial eco-toxicity.

Questions

1. What do you conclude from the results of LCA presented in this section. Which reactor type would you consider to be most sustainable environmentally?
2. Based on the LCA comparison between different options, in your opinion, is nuclear an environmentally sustainable option? Why?
3. The LCA results show that nuclear has low GWP compared with fossil fuel options, but it has higher toxicity impacts than, for example, gas. How could a decision be made on whether nuclear or gas is a more sustainable option environmentally, given these results? What is more important in your opinion: GWP and the related climate change or human toxicity and eco-toxicity? What would be more important to your government? Discuss your answers.

Table 9.3   *Uranium resources worldwide and projected production of uranium by country for 2007 (based on data from IAEA and OECD, 2007)*

Country	Uranium reserves (@$130/kg U)		Production in 2007 (projected)	
	Tonnes	%	Tonnes	%
Australia	1 243 000	23	7600	18
Kazakhstan	817 300	15	7245	17
Russia	545 600	10	3381	8
South Africa	435 100	8	750	2
Canada	423 200	8	9850	23
USA	339 000	6	2000	5
Brazil	278 400	5	340	1
Namibia	275 000	5	3800	9
Niger	274 000	5	3633	8
Ukraine	199 500	4	900	2
Jordan	111 800	2	—	—
Uzbekistan	111 000	2	2300	5
India	72 900	1	270	1
China	67 900	1	750	2
Other	213 100	5	509	1
Total	**5 468 800**	**100**	**43 328**	**100**

9.4.3 Depletion of Uranium Reserves

In addition to the environmental impacts discussed in the previous two sections, a further impact deserves a special mention, namely depletion of uranium reserves. The amount of uranium available is uncertain, as is indeed its annual usage. Different sources quote different amounts; so, for example, the figures for the annual demand for uranium range from 43 000 t (IAEA and OECD, 2008) to 65 000 t (SDC, 2006b). The IAEA and OECD (2008) estimate that there are almost 5.5 million t of recoverable uranium in the world (see Table 9.3). Assuming their estimated annual consumption of uranium of 43 000 t per year, they predict that known resources could last for around 100 years. More pessimistic sources believe that the uranium will last for a few decades only (SDC, 2006b). For comparison, some estimates put the coal and gas reserves at around 150 and 65 years respectively (BP, 2007).

As discussed previously, fuel reprocessing could reduce pressure on the uranium resources, but various other sustainability considerations, such as transport of waste fuel and potential for terrorist attacks (see Section 9.6.6), make fuel reprocessing an uncertain option for the future. According to NEA (2008), fast breeder reactors could produce enough nuclear fuel to last for 3000 years – but this option raises additional concerns related to nuclear weapons proliferation (see Section 9.6.4).

Another option would be to use thorium[11] instead of uranium, as it is much more abundant in nature – however, currently there are no reactors operating on thorium and the lack of investment in research and development makes it an unlikely candidate to replace uranium in the near future.

---

[11] Although not fissile itself, Th-232 absorbs neutrons to produce U-233, which is fissile.

Questions

1. Why is depletion of uranium an environmental issue?
2. What are the projected reserves of uranium? How does that compare with the reserves of fossil fuels and what are the implications?

9.5 Economic Aspects of Nuclear Power

The economics of nuclear, and any other power generating option, are determined by the following four components:

- capital (construction) costs and the time over which the construction is carried out (the longer the construction time, the higher the costs);
- costs of fuel;
- expenditure on operation and maintenance; and
- decommissioning and waste management costs.

In the case of nuclear power, by far the most dominant component is capital costs, which normally account for 60–75% of the total (SDC, 2006c). For instance, for LWR, 57% of the costs of energy generation are due to capital costs, 30% due to operation and maintenance and 13% are from fuel costs (Tester *et al.*, 2005). On average, capital costs are typically in the region of US$5–10 billion. For example, in 2008, Progress Energy in the USA announced building a power plant with two Westinghouse AP1000 units at $14 billion (WNA, 2010a). At the same time, South Carolina Electric and Gas Co. estimated the costs of their two AP1000 units at $9.8 billion (WNA, 2010a). Both plants are expected on line sometime in 2016–2017, so it remains to be seen how close to the estimated budget they come. The example of the EPR being built in Finland shows how difficult it is to estimate the real costs of nuclear plant and how they can be affected particularly by delays in construction. Originally, the capital costs for this plant were estimated at €3 billion; however, since the project started in 2005, they have escalated to €5.3 billion (in 2009) due to the construction delays (Power, 2009).

The fuel costs contribute from 10 to 20% of the total costs (DTI, 2007; WNA, 2010a). In early 2010, the cost of obtaining 1 kg of UO_2 fuel was equal to US$2555, of which 40% was due to the cost of uranium and just under 50% due to the conversion costs (WNA, 2010a).

In addition to the uncertainty in the construction costs, decommissioning and waste management represent a further source of cost uncertainties. Nevertheless, most agree that decommissioning represents a minor contribution to the total costs of nuclear power (SDC, 2006c). For example, a study by BNFL (Hesketh, 2002) estimated the waste and decommissioning costs to be less than 1% of the generating costs or 0.014 p/kWh (assuming £365 million for the total decommissioning and waste costs). Even if these estimates were to increase by a factor of 10, this would still mean a cost of around 0.14 p/kWh, contributing less than 5% of the total generating cost (SDC, 2006c).

In the UK, the disposal costs for low-level waste are estimated at £2000/m^3 and for high-level waste between £67 000/m^3 and £201 000/m^3 (NEI, 2008). Generally, the ratio of low-level to high-level waste is 80% to 20% (EC, 2007); one reactor produces roughly 12 m^3 of high-level waste annually (OECD, 2008). Table 9.4 gives the volumes of UK legacy waste and radioactive materials.

Table 9.4   *Radioactive materials and waste inventory (data from DEFRA, 2008)*

Materials	Packaged volume		Radioactivity in 2040	
	m^3	%	TBq	%
HLW	1400	0.3	36 000 000	41.3
ILW	364 000	76.3	2 200 000	2.5
LLW	17 000	3.6	<100	0.0
Spent fuel	11 200	2.3	45 000 000	51.6
Plutonium	3300	0.7	4 000 000	4.6
Uranium	80 000	16.8	3000	0.0
Total	**476 900**	**100**	**87 200 000**	**100**

The Nuclear Decommissioning Authority (NDA), responsible for the UK's nuclear waste, estimates the cost of dealing with existing legacy sites at £56 billion (SDC, 2006a). The estimated total cost of the proposed geological disposal option (see Section 9.3.7.2) is in the region of £4.9 billion (NIREX, 2005). It is now also widely accepted that reprocessing adds significantly to costs – for instance, the OECD (1994) study suggested that reprocessing was at least twice as expensive as direct disposal of fuel.

Tables 9.5 and 9.6, as well as Figure 9.15, put the costs of nuclear power in context by comparison with some other energy options. Table 9.5 compares the contribution of the different components to the total generating costs for three energy options: nuclear, combined cycle gas turbine (CCGT) and wind. As shown, for both nuclear and wind the capital costs contribute the largest proportion of the total, while the costs of the gas option are dominated by the fuel.

Table 9.6 compares the total generating costs of nuclear energy with the costs of coal, gas and wind in three different countries (USA, UK and Finland). Two immediate observations

Table 9.5   *Contribution of different elements to the total costs of electricity generation for different energy options (adapted from PIU, 2002)*

	Nuclear (%)	CCGT (%)	Wind (%)
Capital cost[a]	60–75	30–40	85–90
Fuel	5–10	50–65	0
Operation and maintenance	8–15	5–10	5–15
Decommissioning and waste management	<1[b]	0	0

[a] Including interest during construction.
[b] These costs are uncertain.

Table 9.6   *Electricity generation costs in the UK (adapted from NEA, 2008)*

Country	Coal	Gas	Nuclear	Onshore wind	Offshore wind
UK (2003 GB pence/kWh)	3.6–4.0	2.3–2.4	2.8–4.3	3.2–4.2	4.5–5.7
Finland (2006 cents/kWh)	5.2	5.2	2.3	4.55	—
US (2002 US cents/kWh)	4.2	3.8–5.6[a]	4.2–6.7	—	—

[a] CCGT.

can be made from these data: the variation in costs for the same technology and the difference in costs between the different countries. This is mainly due to the data uncertainty associated with costs estimates not only for nuclear, but also for the other options. For example, the costs of nuclear in the UK range from 2.8 to 4.3 GB pence/kWh; in Finland they are 2.3 Euro cents/kWh, while in the USA they are between 4.2 and 6.7 US cents/kWh. Thus, nuclear appears to be cheapest in Finland; the nuclear costs in the UK and USA are quite similar. In the UK, on average, nuclear is competitive with coal and onshore wind but is more expensive than gas. However, some studies show that in some cases nuclear could be the most expensive option. For example, PIU (1994) demonstrates that at 6 p/kWh the Sizewell B (PWR) power station is by far the most expensive energy option for the UK. It should be noted that all cost figures should be interpreted with care due to the uncertainty in estimates as well as the sensitivity to the changing economic conditions – for example, the increase of commodity prices in 2008 makes most of the previous estimates all but obsolete, not just for nuclear, but also for other energy options.

The costs of nuclear are also very sensitive to the discount rates assumed. This is illustrated in Figure 9.14 for a selection of countries (NEA, 2008). The relative increase in costs for the 10% discount rate compared with 5% is around 30% and is characteristic of capital-intensive plants such as nuclear. It is also interesting to note from the figure that the lowest generating costs are in Canada and France, and by far the highest are in Japan.

Figure 9.15 summarizes the cost ranges for nuclear, coal and gas at the 5 and 10% discount rates. At 5% discount, the costs of nuclear power range from 2.1 to 3.5 US cents/kWh; the equivalent prices for coal are between 2.2 and 4.85 US cents/kWh and for gas are from 3.9 to 5.6 US cents/kWh Thus, according to these estimates, nuclear appears to be the least costly option (NEA, 2008). At the discount rate of 10%, both coal and gas become more competitive options, with the average prices for all three options being

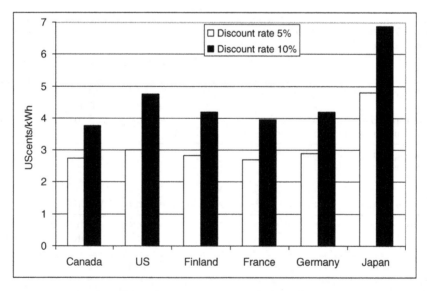

Figure 9.14 *Costs of nuclear electricity at 5% and 10% discount rates (adapted from NEA, 2008)*

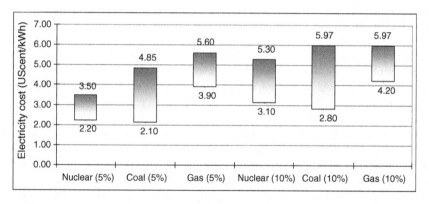

Figure 9.15 *Range of costs for nuclear, coal and gas power plants at 5 % and 10 % discount rates (adapted from NEA, 2008). [The highest and lowest values are excluded from the figure for all three options]*

between 4.2 US cents/kWh for nuclear and 5 US cents/kWh for gas – given the uncertainty in the estimates, these costs are close enough to make the distinction between the options difficult.

We now turn our attention to the social aspects of sustainability of nuclear power.

Questions

1. What is the definition of the 'overnight' cost of energy? And of 'levelized' costs?
2. What is the meaning of 'discount rate?' How does that affect the overall costs of nuclear power?
3. What are main contributors to the total costs of nuclear power?
4. Why is it difficult to predict the real costs of nuclear power?
5. How does nuclear compare with other energy options with respect to economic costs?
6. In your opinion, is nuclear a sustainable option economically? Why?

9.6 Social Considerations

Nuclear energy raises some considerable social concerns. However, this should not be surprising, as all energy technologies have a tendency to create social concerns, controversies and even conflict. Large hydro-energy projects, which have low environmental impacts (as discussed in the previous section), can cause controversy because they affect water availability downstream, inundate valuable ecosystems and may require relocation of population. For instance, the Three Gorges Dam project in China raised serious concerns because of the social and environmental impacts of the massive flooding involved. Some other renewable energy technologies, for example wind turbines, have also come under scrutiny and opposition arising from their perceived visual intrusiveness and noise impacts, as well as the demand on land.

In the case of nuclear energy, the main social concerns include health and community impacts, safety, security, nuclear proliferation and intergenerational equity.

9.6.1 Health Impacts

As with any other major industrial installation, and despite all precautions, nuclear power plants present risks to workers, to people living in the immediate vicinity and, in the case of a very severe accident such as that at Chernobyl, to people living very far away. Usually these risks are analysed in terms of radiological exposure as a result of normal operations and from accidents (NEA, 2005).

Main health concerns with regard to normal operations of nuclear power plants are related to radiological risks from day-to-day discharges of radioactive material both to air and to water. People living near nuclear plants can be affected by these discharges. In principle, discharges of this kind can also affect the human food chain (via locally caught fish or shellfish, for example) and so represent a health hazard to the public.

Workers in the nuclear power industry are another risk group that can be affected by radiation exposure. Traditionally, occupational health risks have been measured in terms of number of accidents and fatalities. However, today, and particularly in relation to nuclear power, there is an increased emphasis on less obvious or delayed effects of exposure to cancer and other ill-effects-inducing substances (WNA, 2008). For example, potential health impacts of long-term exposure to low-level radiation include risks of cancer and childhood leukaemia.

As far as the low-level radiation is concerned, the amount of radiation discharged during the normal operation of reactors is very small; it is the reprocessing of the spent fuel that is the major source of radiation from nuclear reactors – it accounts for 83% of all the radiation attributed to the nuclear industry across the EU (SDC, 2006d). Radioactive doses from nuclear power stations mostly originate from older designs. Dose levels from modern reactors such as PWRs are very low, and are expected to reduce still more for new-build stations.

However, many environmental groups, such as Greenpeace International, advocate an end to all radioactive discharges, based on a precautionary approach to environmental protection (see Chapter 1 for more on the precautionary principle). Greenpeace argue that the effect of continued releases of radioactive material into the environment are unpredictable in the long term, that accumulations may be difficult to reverse and that any detrimental effects may be undetectable until it is too late to reduce their impact. Inherent in their objective of ceasing all releases of radioactive materials is the presumption that all such releases are potentially detrimental. Thus, Greenpeace argue, we should adopt a precautionary approach to radioactive discharges focused on damage prevention, decisions informed by scientific information and a progressive reduction of the presence of environmental stressors (Carroll, 2003).

Radiological protection of both nuclear industry employees and the population in general is covered by a strict legal framework in industrialized countries. In the UK, for instance, statutory dose limits to both groups are a small fraction of naturally occurring levels. The calculated risks to a member of the public developing a fatal cancer due to a new-build nuclear power plant are correspondingly small and considered 'broadly acceptable' by the UK Health and Safety Executive (HSE). According to some recent assessments, there is no evidence of increased rates of childhood cancers, including leukaemia, around any nuclear power station site. It is not expected that this will change with a programme of new-build stations (SDC, 2006e).

However, there are also health risks posed by nuclear accidents. A major nuclear accident may have considerable impacts, including the deaths of individuals (which may occur decades after the accident), and affect people living not only in the vicinity, but also very far away. At Chernobyl, for instance, 31 reactor staff and emergency workers died in the accident or shortly afterwards as a result of receiving acute radiation doses. An IAEA report published in 2005 concludes that up to 4000 people could eventually die of radiation exposure from the accident (IAEA, 2005a). The World Health Organization's report on the Chernobyl accident lists a number of health effects, such as thyroid cancer, leukaemia and non-thyroid solid cancer, cataracts and an increased risk of death from cardiovascular disease in highly exposed individuals. The health impacts were high not only in Ukraine, but also in neighbouring countries. For instance, in Belarus, the Russian Federation and Ukraine nearly 5000 cases of thyroid cancer have now been diagnosed among children who were up to 18 year old at the time of the accident (WHO, 2006).

Potential health impacts from nuclear energy are not limited to nuclear power plant operations only. Every stage in the life cycle of nuclear energy – from cradle (mining) to grave (radioactive waste disposal) – presents some potential health risks of radiation release. For instance, exposure to high levels of radon has been a feature of uranium mines in the early years of nuclear power when exposure of miners to the radon gas led to a higher incidence of lung cancer. However, the industry claims that health risks of uranium mining are very minor today in comparison with a few decades ago. It also claims that, in other parts of the nuclear fuel cycle, radiation hazards to workers are low and industrial accidents are few (WNA, 2008).

Overall, it appears that the health impacts of well-managed nuclear power facilities are small. According to the World Nuclear Association, apart from Chernobyl, no nuclear workers or members of the public have died as a result of exposure to radiation due to a commercial nuclear reactor incident (WNA, 2008). Most of the serious radiological injuries and deaths that occur each year are the result of large uncontrolled radiation sources, such as abandoned medical or industrial equipment, but these are not related to nuclear power generation. Others are due to military or research activities. There have also been a number of accidents in experimental reactors and in one military plutonium-producing pile (at Windscale, in 1957), but, according to industry sources, none of these resulted in loss of life outside the actual plant or long-term environmental contamination – although this is disputed (SDC, 2006e). Also, according to the industry sources, only the Chernobyl disaster resulted in radiation doses to the public greater than those resulting from exposure to natural sources (WNA, 2008).

On the whole, the health impacts of nuclear energy facilities from normal operations appear to be at socially acceptable levels. Nevertheless, the risk of an accident, however small, places nuclear power in a unique category where the low risk of routine activities must be balanced against the very low probability, but potentially high impact, of a serious accident (SDC, 2006g).

Questions

1. What are the main health risks associated with nuclear energy? Who is/can be affected by radiation exposure?

2. What are the statutory dose limits to the workers in nuclear industry for radiation exposure in your country? How do they compare with other occupational doses? What profession is most affected by radiation?

3. What are the statutory dose limits to members of the public for radiation exposure in your country? How do they compare with average doses from other sources of radioactivity, such as natural background radiation and other industrial activities?

4. Could/should a precautionary approach to environmental protection be applied to all radioactive discharges? What would be the implications of such a precautionary approach for the nuclear industry?

5. What were the major health effects of the accident at Chernobyl? Find out what could be the eventual death toll from the accident.

6. Apart from nuclear plant operations, what other stages in the life cycle of nuclear energy could impact on human health? What are their potential health effects? You may wish to revisit Section 9.3 for these purposes.

9.6.2 Community Impacts

The siting, construction and operation of any major facility inevitably have impacts on the local community. These impacts can be both positive and negative.

One of the primary local benefits for communities in the vicinity of a nuclear plant is the creation of local jobs and the direct impacts of salary payments, business taxes and capital expenditure that come with employment.

In the UK, for instance, almost 40 000 people are directly employed by the nuclear industry, with almost as many indirectly dependent upon it. About 20 000 are said to be involved in the production, reprocessing and storage of nuclear fuel, with 15 000 employed in the operation and decommissioning of plants (Cogent SSC, 2005). Many of the jobs are highly skilled, well paid and often in areas where alternative employment opportunities are low. In small communities with a less diverse economic base, the employment effects of a nuclear plant can be significant. In Sellafield in the UK, for instance, two-thirds of the residents are employed at the local reprocessing plant and most others rely indirectly on the nuclear plant demands for services (Blowers and Leroy, 1994).

In addition to local employment, a nuclear facility may bring other positive impacts, such as the development of local supply chains or improvements to infrastructure due to increased demand for services (SDC, 2006f).

However, a nuclear facility could also have negative impacts on a local community. These impacts might include the negative image effect of nuclear power and perceived safety concerns, which may lead to negative outcomes such as a depression in house prices, reductions in tourism or investment, or adverse changes to community character.

Studies have shown that negative attitudes toward facilities which pose health or environmental risks are strong and geographically extensive (Farber, 1998). These attitudes are frequently translated into reduced likelihoods of economic activities, such as tourism, taking a job or locating a business, in regions with such facilities (Slovic *et al.*, 1991).

General distrust of nuclear power and a negative image associated with it may lead to stigmatization of affected communities (Slovic *et al.*, 1991). Stigma may be caused by both scientifically assessed risk and perceived risk and can have both direct and indirect economic impacts. For instance, owing to the negative public perception that follows nuclear energy facilities, companies may leave the affected area or decide not to locate their business there. As nuclear facilities are perceived as the facilities that impose health or amenity risks on the surrounding communities, it is generally expected that these risks will be translated economically into negative effects on adjacent property values. These negative effects may be present even when such facilities possess offsetting advantages, such as employment opportunities, and regardless of whether the source of the perception is quantitative or subjective. As Farber (1998) put it, 'property markets are not behaving irrationally when subjective risk factors enter as price determinants'.

Stigmatization of local community may happen in part due to the concerns about health and ecological risks, but Gregory *et* al. (1996) note that

> stigma goes beyond conceptions of hazard. It refers to something that is to be shunned or avoided not just because it is dangerous but because it overturns or destroys a positive condition; what was or should be something good is now marked as blemished or tainted.

A proposed or existing nuclear facility can also affect the social fabric of the area. Some changes may be triggered by economic factors. For instance, an increasing ratio of industrial to nonindustrial activities in the area, change in the types of homes and businesses, could alter the neighbourhood's character. If these changes are regarded as undesirable, then people who can afford to move out may do so, thereby changing the demographic composition of the area. These changes usually do not happen overnight, but they are likely to be more rapid and destabilizing than the gradual demographic changes that occur in all communities because of births, deaths and migration.

Other changes in the social fabric may be structural; that is, they may concern the formal and informal relationships of groups and individuals in the area. Like other potentially controversial facilities, a nuclear plant is likely to provoke divisions in the affected community among those who are opposed to it, those who favour it and those who do not want the area harmed by a heated, widely publicized conflict.

Local controversies over major facilities can last for years and leave scars and permanently alter formal and informal relationships in the area. As Gramling and Freudenburg (1992) note, 'impacts to social systems occur as interest groups form or redirect their energies, promoting or opposing the proposed activity and engaging in attempts to define the activity as involving opportunities or threats'.

There are also community impacts associated with the nuclear fuel cycle that can affect communities in other countries; for example, in a country when uranium is mined (see Chapter 17).

Questions

1. How can nuclear power plants affect local communities? Discuss both positive and negative community impacts.
2. What is meant by 'community stigmatization?' How can that affect local communities in the vicinity of a nuclear plant or any other industrial installation perceived to be hazardous (see also Chapter 10)?
3. Taking a life cycle approach, discuss how different parts of the nuclear life cycle could affect the local communities.

9.6.3 Safety and Security

Nuclear power stations create some specific safety and security risks. These can arise from the design and operation of the power station itself or from external events. The sort of external influences that could affect a reactor might be natural events, such as flooding, or human made, such as a terrorist attack (DTI, 2007).

9.6.3.1 Safety

In most countries nuclear power plants and other facilities in the life cycle operate under competent regulatory regimes supported by a robust infrastructure of legislation, regulation and standards.

In the UK, for instance, the operators of nuclear plants must conform to the general health and safety standards laid down in the Health and Safety at Work Act 1974 (HSW Act). The HSW Act applies to all employment situations, but nuclear plant operators must also comply with the Nuclear Installations Act 1965 (as amended) and related legislation. Under the Nuclear Installations Act, no site may be used for the purposes of installing or operating any nuclear installation unless a licence has been granted by the HSE. The HSE exercises this responsibility through the Nuclear Directorate (ND), which is the nuclear safety regulator for the UK nuclear industry. Radioactive discharges are regulated by the Environment Agency.

The Nuclear Installation Act requires that no health harm should arise from the operation of the nuclear facility. The ND interprets this in terms of the *acceptability of the risk of accident and the tolerability of its consequences*, and, acting on behalf of the HSE, sets out the general safety requirements to deal with the risks on a nuclear site. Before issuing a licence, the ND must be satisfied that the power station can be built, operated and decommissioned safely, with risks being kept 'as low as reasonably practicable' at all times, (this is known as the ALARP principle). Similar safety regulatory frameworks and requirements are present in many countries utilizing nuclear energy.

While the nuclear regulators have the responsibility to ensure that nuclear safety measures achieve safety objectives, the nuclear industry has, for its part, the responsibility to provide safety features and implement the procedures to meet the safety objectives set by the regulator. This is not a simple task, as nuclear facilities, particularly reactors, are complex systems with a large inventory of radioactive materials. As such, they have the potential to cause significant damage and require comprehensive safety systems.

The main safety concern with nuclear facilities has always been over the possibility of an uncontrolled release of radioactive material, leading to contamination and consequent radiation exposure to workers and people nearby. Modern reactor designs incorporate safety features that reduce the accident risks to very low levels and limit the consequences when failures occur.

The basic technical approach to reactor safety applied by the industry is the 'defence in depth' concept, whereby several different systems perform the same function so that the plant safety does not rely on any single feature. Defence in depth is implemented through the combination of consecutive and independent levels of protection that would all have to fail before harmful effects could be caused to people or to the environment. If one level of protection or barrier were to fail, safety would still be assured through a subsequent level or barrier.

Defence in depth involves three aspects (SDC, 2006e):

- redundancy (multiple ways of shutting a reactor down, providing fuel cooling, or multiple barriers to contain any release);
- diversity (ensuring that systems with the same function are not designed in the same way or do not rely on common features, so that a particular fault on one system does not affect other systems); and
- segregation (reducing the possibility of a common hazard, such as fire, damaging more than one system).

Modern reactor designs are expected to reduce the accident risks still further. New nuclear reactors have passive safety features that can maintain the plant in a safe state, particularly during an unexpected event, without the use of active control (i.e. they do not require operator action or electronic feedback in order to shut down safely in the event of a particular type of emergency). For example, ALWRs and Generation III + reactors (see Sections 9.2.3.5 and 9.2.3.7) employ natural forces, such as gravity flow and natural circulation, to maintain essential cooling. This means that they do not have to rely on the continued operation of engineered safety features, such as pumps circulating coolant, to prevent or limit the effects of plant failures. As a result, new designs of nuclear power stations have a significantly lower risk of plant failures leading to a damaged reactor core, compared with those which are in operation today – which are already acceptable to the nuclear regulators (DTI, 2007).

The reactor design and quality of construction are not the only means of ensuring safety. The analyses of causes and consequences of the two major accidents that occurred with nuclear power reactors – the Three Mile Island in the USA in 1979 and Chernobyl in Ukraine in 1986 – highlighted the need for more attention to human factors, including training and procedures at the operator level and stressed the importance of a safety culture. Safety culture means an overriding priority to safety issues, extending from national legislation at the top, through the regulatory processes, to the senior management of the operating organization and further to each individual having the potential to affect safety.

There is no doubt that nuclear power plants are designed to minimize the potential for accidents and to reduce the consequences to both workers and the general population in the event that they do occur. This is reflected in the international nuclear event statistics, which record very few instances of significant off-site risk or major plant damage.

Nuclear accidents are recorded and ascribed levels of severity using the International Nuclear Events Scale (INES). INES was introduced in 1990 by the International Atomic Energy Agency (IAEA) to explain nuclear and radiological events, their significance and relative importance to the public in simple terms and it is now used by over 60 countries. Events are graded on a scale of 0 to 7 and are assessed against up to three criteria: off-site impact, on-site impact and impact on defence in depth (the extent to which safety protection has been degraded). Level 7, for instance, denotes a major accident with off-site impacts of major release and widespread health and environmental effects. Chernobyl was level 7. By comparison, the vast majority of events in the UK that have been reported against INES criteria have been level 0, 1, or 2 and there have never been any events above level 2 at a UK civil nuclear power plant.

The scale is designed for prompt use following an event, but on occasions it may be necessary to give a provisional rating only. The level is then confirmed, or possibly revised, once the event has been fully assessed. However, critics argue that the INES serves more of a public relations (PR) function than a meaningful index, pointing out that the INES has little meaning because the graduations are not at all linear. Some of the classifications are disputed; for instance, the fire on the Windscale military reactor in 1957 was given the INES level 5 (severe on-site impact but limited off-side impact), although some consider it to have been INES scale 7 (the maximum level). These differences may result from the nonlinear nature of the scale, inviting subjective interpretation of event characteristics (SDC, 2006e).

Safety considerations related to nuclear energy are not limited to the safety of nuclear power plant operations. Transport of nuclear components and materials (uranium, fresh fuel, nuclear spent fuel and plutonium) also raises safety concerns.

Raw uranium and enriched uranium fuel are not very radioactive and the handling and transport of such materials does not pose significant risks. It is only once the fuel has been used in a reactor that it becomes highly radioactive and that significant risks are created for those handling and transporting the spent fuel.

The risks associated with the transport of the radioactive material are reflected in the regulatory requirements. For example, the regulatory requirements for flasks used to transport spent fuel are the most stringent. They are designed to withstand severe accidents without releasing their contents. The industry argues that spent fuel containers are safe as they are very robust and undergo stringent testing, including dropping onto rigid surfaces (the equivalent of a 30 mph impact) and steel spikes, immersion in deep water and an 800 °C fire. This is in accordance with the IAEA 'Regulations on the Safe Transport of Radioactive Materials', which is the basis of the nuclear transportation regulations in most countries. According to industry sources, this regulatory regime has proven its effectiveness by the record established in the last 30 years, in which there has been no known case of significant injury due to radioactivity in the transport of civil radioactive material (NEA, 2008; WNA, 2008).

However, the claims by the nuclear industry that the transport of nuclear materials carries with it very small risks are disputed. Environmental NGOs such as Greenpeace, for instance, argue that the nuclear transport is raising 'profound safety issues' and involves 'significant risks to human health and the environment' (Greenpeace, 2010). The standards for the transportation of spent fuel, according to Greenpeace, do not reflect real accident conditions. While the current international standards require that the spent fuel containers resist temperatures of 800 °C for up to 30 min, studies commissioned by Greenpeace have shown that, in real accidents, for example at sea or in tunnels, fires often burn at temperatures exceeding 800 °C and for considerably longer than 30 min. Average ship fires, for example, burn for 23 h and at over 1000 °C.

As the contentious issue of nuclear transport shows, despite reassurances from industry and (some) governments that nuclear energy is safe, conventional perceptions that nuclear energy poses significant safety risks are difficult to dispel.

While it may not be possible to eliminate all risks, the regulatory requirement is that risks have to be shown to be acceptable and the consequences have to be tolerable and that any accident with potentially large off-site consequences must be shown to have a very low frequency of occurrence.

As a response to the regulatory requirements, modern nuclear power stations are built to high safety standards. As already discussed, they have multiple layers of protection to guard against faults and passive safety features which come into play automatically when a fault condition occurs.

While the nuclear industry safety standards are high and major accidents at nuclear facilities are rare, historical evidence reveals that human error and management lapses are most often responsible – circumstances which undermine public confidence in the industry, even in industrialized countries with tight regulatory regimes (SDC, 2006g). Public confidence in the regulatory regimes for nuclear power stations in all countries, not just developed countries, is also important because unplanned discharges can have serious transboundary effects, as the accident at Chernobyl testifies. This raises a number of problems, including the difficulties of ensuring that the regulatory institutions in less-developed countries are sufficiently resourced and for identifying and dealing with poor health and safety practices which could lead to transboundary environmental or health risks.

9.6.3.2 Security

Security at a nuclear power plant in the event of a terrorist attack has been a focal point for security analysts since the 9/11 event. Nuclear power stations could be attractive targets for terrorist attacks because of the potential impacts such an attack could have on public health and the economy and the publicity it would attract. Transport of nuclear materials could also be a terrorist target.

Since 9/11 there have been concerns about the consequences of a large aircraft being used to attack a nuclear facility with the purpose of releasing radioactive materials. The industry assessment is that attempts at damaging the plant in this way would not succeed, as modern reactor designs have substantial containment buildings which are unlikely to be breached even by a crashing commercial airline. This assessment is based on various studies that looked at the 9/11 style of attack on nuclear power plants. The studies show that nuclear reactors would be more resistant to such attacks than other civil installations because of the large amounts of concrete used in the structures. For instance, a study undertaken by the Electric Power Research Institute and partly funded by the US Department of Energy in 2002 concluded that US reactor structures 'are robust and (would) protect the fuel from impacts of large commercial aircraft' (as quoted in WNA (2008)).

As expected, nuclear security is tightly regulated. At the international level, the main regulatory act is the International Convention on the Physical Protection of Nuclear Material that obligates signatories to the convention to maintain an appropriate security regime with the aim of protecting against the theft of civil nuclear material and protecting such material and civil nuclear facilities against sabotage (IAEA, 2005b). In implementing this obligation, signatories are required to maintain a legislative/regulatory framework, designate a regulatory authority and apply a number of fundamental principles. Implementation of the convention has led to the development of comprehensive legal and regulatory frameworks in the countries that are signatories to the convention, including the UK. The main regulatory body in the UK is the Office of Civil Nuclear Security (OCNS), which regulates security arrangements for the protection of nuclear and radioactive material on civil nuclear sites and while being transported between sites. It requires site operators to develop security plans according to the 'defence in depth' principle (discussed previously), with several layers and methods of protection that have to be overcome or circumvented, thereby providing appropriate detection, assessment, delay and response to malicious acts.

The arrangements detailed include physical security measures, policing and guarding, the protection of sensitive nuclear information and the trustworthiness of staff with access to the site, nuclear material and sensitive nuclear information (DTI, 2007).

All nuclear power stations in the UK are protected by armed officers from the Civil Nuclear Constabulary (CNC), as well as civilian security guard forces. The CNC, a specialist police force, funded by the nuclear industry, protects nuclear sites and materials. Officers in the CNC have full police powers within 5 km of a licensed nuclear site and anywhere else they need to be to protect nuclear material. Access to nuclear power stations is tightly controlled. Measures to prevent or at least delay unauthorized access include (DTI, 2007):

- double lines of fencing with razor wire, high-intensity lighting and CCTV linked to a permanently manned security building;
- turnstiles at personnel access points where entry and exit is only possible with a site-specific electronic pass;
- random searches of personnel and vehicles;
- double barriers at vehicle access points and chicanes to prevent the barriers from being rammed at high speed;
- additional barriers within the station to protect sensitive areas such as the reactor building, to which only certain personnel will have access.

OCNS supervises a comprehensive personnel clearance programme ('vetting'), which is undertaken to minimize the possibility of stations being infiltrated by untrustworthy individuals. Vetting encompasses all personnel working within the perimeter fence of a nuclear power station (including secretarial, administrative and cleaning staff, amongst others), not just those requiring access to a radiologically controlled area or inner security barrier. Personnel without such clearance are not permitted unescorted access to site (SDC, 2006e).

However, despite these strict security measures, there have been instances of intrusions by groups protesting about nuclear power (e.g. Greenpeace), who have used such events to highlight supposed breaches in nuclear security.

Possible use of nuclear fuel (reactor-grade and spent fuel) by terrorists is also raised as a security concern. Shipments of spent fuel for reprocessing, for instance, could be attacked en route from the station to the reprocessing plant, either with the intention to spread contamination over a wide area or to steal the material for future use in a nuclear weapon. Reactor-grade fuel could be used to make a 'dirty bomb' (SDC, 2006e). The industry assessment is that spent fuel containers are robust and undergo stringent testing and that the spent fuel pellets they contain are not easily dispersed even under severe impact and fire (WNA, 2008). But an alternative view is that stolen spent fuel would be valuable as a dirty bomb in itself and is, therefore, of value to terrorists. It would appear, therefore, that the potential use of nuclear fuels by terrorists remains a risk and, therefore, a concern (SDC, 2006e).

To sum up, there are already high levels of security at nuclear power stations which have been under constant review since 9/11 and provisions have been strengthened as deemed necessary. Modern nuclear power plants appear to be resistant to external attack and the industry is confident that standard shutdown procedures would minimize or eliminate altogether the risks of any serious damage being done. However, it remains difficult to fully predict the mode of a terrorist attack and the capacity of terrorists to exploit weaknesses in the design, operation or security of nuclear power stations and associated infrastructure.

Despite reassurances from the industry and governments with respect to security of nuclear power stations, their potential vulnerability to terrorism, as the latest surveys of public attitudes show, remains one of the main security concerns amongst the general public. These are discussed further below, but prior to that, we examine another related issue:, namely a potential for nuclear weapons proliferation.

Questions

1. What are main safety and security risks associated with nuclear power plants?
2. How is nuclear safety regulated internationally? And in your country?
3. How is safety addressed through the design of nuclear plants?
4. Explain the 'defence in depth' concept.
5. Explain the design features of nuclear plants that could minimize the impacts of a terrorist attack.
6. Describe the main security measures undertaken at the UK nuclear facilities. How is that different or similar to the security measures in your country?
7. The nuclear industry claims that the transport of nuclear materials carries with it very small risks for safety and security. Do you agree or disagree with this view? Why?

9.6.4 Proliferation Risks

One of the major social concerns related to nuclear power is that sensitive nuclear material, in particular highly enriched uranium and plutonium, as well as the technology and equipment used for civilian activities, could be diverted to military or terrorist purposes.

The most important instrument for discouraging the production or diversion of weapon-grade materials is the permanent Treaty on the Non-Proliferation of Nuclear Weapons (NPT) (IAEA, 1970). The treaty commits 187 countries and carries an explicit commitment by the non-nuclear-weapon states to receive the benefits of peaceful nuclear technology in return for agreeing to forego nuclear weapons. The compliance with the latter commitment is being verified by an international safeguards regime, administered by the IAEA. Through its safeguards system, the IAEA can verify that nuclear activities in non-nuclear-weapon states, party to the NPT, are being used exclusively for peaceful purposes. The effectiveness of safeguards controls has been strengthened recently in order to enable the IAEA to provide credible assurances about the non-diversion of declared nuclear material and the absence of undeclared nuclear material and activities.

In parallel, in the EU, nuclear safeguards are required under the Euratom Treaty and implemented by the European Commission. To avoid duplication, safeguards arrangements in the EU countries are harmonized between the IAEA and European Commission inspectorates.

This system of safeguards requires operators of nuclear facilities to have a detailed nuclear material accounting and control system and to make regular reports on inventories of nuclear material. Verification inspections of the declared location and quantities of nuclear material by the internal safeguards inspectorates aim to detect any diversion of significant quantities of such material from peaceful use (DTI, 2007).

Specific safeguard arrangements at civilian nuclear facilities vary from site to site. For example, a power station with onsite storage of spent fuel could be subject to accountancy verification of fresh and spent fuel as well as containment and surveillance measures. One could, for instance, include CCTV monitoring as well as seals on the reactor and the packaging to detect clandestine removal of irradiated fuel. These safeguard systems are designed to provide timely detection of the diversion of nuclear material and, thus, deter any such attempt. The industry's view, shared by governments such as the UK's, is that the safeguards in place are capable of detecting any attempts by civilian operators of nuclear power stations to divert nuclear materials for clandestine nuclear weapon purposes (NEA, 2008).

However, terrorist organizations, by definition, operate outside national and international law and, therefore, safeguards to protect against proliferation are almost irrelevant to such groups. Similarly, it is very difficult to protect against civil nuclear power being developed into a military nuclear capability where motivations are strong enough, as has been shown in a number of countries (SDC, 2006e).

Risk of nuclear proliferation raises not only social and political concerns, but also poses important moral and legal questions. Industrialized countries intend to develop new nuclear capacity, arguing that nuclear power is necessary, even critical, in reducing emissions of greenhouse gases. However, they simultaneously claim that a country like Iran should not be permitted to follow the same course of action. As the UK Sustainable Development Commission (SDC, 2006h) points out, countries such as the UK need to be fully aware of the implications of developing new nuclear capacity, particularly in the context of international treaties such as the UN Framework Convention on Climate Change (UNFCCC). Under the terms of the UNFCCC, developed countries are legally obliged to help other countries develop appropriate carbon abatement technologies. In fact, the UNFCCC explicitly encourages 'the development, application and diffusion, including transfer of technologies, practices and processes that control, reduce or prevent anthropogenic emission of greenhouse gases' (UNFCCC, 1992: Article 4.1c). If nuclear power is part of the UK's chosen solution to climate change, argues the Sustainable Development Commission, then it would be considered a suitable solution for all countries. A decision to develop nuclear power in the UK essentially removes the UK's ability, both morally and legally, to deny the technology to others (SDC, 2006h).

As the results of recent surveys of public attitudes show (see Section 9.6.6), proliferation remains a matter of high public concern. Many believe that an expansion of nuclear power programmes will increase the risk of more countries acquiring nuclear weapons capability. As can be seen from the historical record, it is impossible to guarantee, over time, that any civil nuclear programme will not be developed into a military capability.

The main concerns expressed in this respect are (SDC, 2006e):

- the difficulties of enforcing international treaty obligations;
- proliferation risks associated with the widespread use of nuclear technologies in countries with very diverse systems of governance;
- the capacity and resources available to enforce international obligations in a potentially growing number of states with a nuclear capacity; and

- how to deal with states that withdraw from treaties or develop nuclear capability outside of them.

In the global environment that we inhabit today, such considerations are important to the deliberations about the role nuclear power can play in meeting our energy needs.

Questions

1. What international safeguards are in place to prevent the proliferation of nuclear weapons from the nuclear materials used in and arising from civil power stations?
2. Is your country a signatory to the Treaty on the Non-Proliferation of Nuclear Weapons? If so, what are the obligations under the treaty?
3. What are the main concerns about the proliferation issue?
4. Why is fuel reprocessing of concern for proliferation?

9.6.5 Intergenerational Issues

As emphasized in Chapter 1, an integral part of the concept of sustainable development is the need to safeguard the interests of future generations. The concept of sustainable development consistently stresses the obligations of one generation to all future generations, both in terms of access to environmental resources, systems and services and in terms of not passing on the direct or indirect costs of development to those who have no share in the benefits of that development. This has often been referred to as 'intergenerational equity' (see Chapter 1).

Nuclear technologies pose complex ethical dilemmas in this regard. On the one hand, nuclear energy, as its advocates point out, could play a significant role in reducing emissions of CO_2 and, thus, preventing climate change – for the benefits of future generations as well as of our own. As the most devastating effects of climate change are predicted for the future, one could argue that we have a moral duty to future generations to use all technologies at our disposal to mitigate these effects. Since nuclear energy is a low-carbon technology we are, one could argue, duty bound to pursue some kind of nuclear option.

On the other hand, it is well documented that high-level nuclear waste remains dangerously radioactive for hundreds of thousands of years and that nuclear reactors will need to be secured for decades whilst decommissioning takes place. Future generations, who were neither responsible for the decisions to build nuclear reactors in the first place, nor enjoyed the benefits of electricity from those reactors during their lifetime, will nevertheless have to bear both risks and costs of nuclear waste management and decommissioning. Considering the current uncertainties over total costs and the science of long-term waste management, one could find it difficult to reconcile these issues with the sustainable development principles.

The fact that nuclear technology poses ethical dilemmas should not be surprising. Almost all decisions about complex technologies, however scientific and 'fact based' they may appear at one level, have an ethical dimension – in terms of prospective 'winners' and 'losers' and wider impacts on people and society. Nuclear power, however, appears to be particularly charged with such considerations, as its waste legacy has clear intergenerational impacts. Its potential to harm or benefit future generations must, therefore, be taken into account when assessing whether nuclear power presents a sustainable energy option.

Questions

1. What is intergenerational equity? How is that different from intragenerational equity?
2. What are the potential impacts of nuclear energy on future generations? How could they be minimized or avoided?

9.6.6 Public Attitudes Towards Nuclear Energy

There is no doubt that the technical, economic, environmental and social considerations described above (or, at least some of them) shape public attitudes towards nuclear power.

Analysis of recent public opinion surveys, both quantitative and qualitative, suggests that overall public attitudes and opinion toward nuclear energy – as the primary way of meeting future energy needs – are currently broadly unfavourable. There is only limited public support for a new programme of nuclear power plants, particularly when compared with renewable technologies. But, there are some signs that the climate change issues may be encouraging new reflection (SDC, 2006g; NEA, 2010).

Nuclear energy is a controversial issue and a difficult topic for an opinion poll. While respondents tend to have a general opinion about nuclear energy, many surveys have revealed that they also feel uninformed about nuclear issues and lack detailed knowledge of specific topics, such as radioactive safety or radioactive waste. Another particularity of this subject is that it tends to provoke attitudes that are not necessarily linked to people's level of knowledge or awareness of current affairs. This can be assumed to be particularly the case for risk perceptions of nuclear energy. Even if people are aware of the advantages of nuclear energy and of the safeguards in place, it does not automatically erase their fears (EC, 2007a, 2007b).

Among recent studies of public opinion on nuclear power, the Eurobarometer surveys have been most comprehensive, in particular 'Eurobarometer on Energy Technologies: Knowledge-Perception-Measures' (EC, 2007a), 'Europeans and Nuclear Safety' (EC, 2007b), and 'Europeans and Radioactive Waste' (EC, 2005). The results provided by the Eurobarometer surveys are widely respected owing to the sample size (over 27 000 respondents) and the way the surveys were constructed and conducted. A summary of the findings from these surveys is given below.

Europeans do not seem to see nuclear energy as a solution to the current or future energy challenges; in fact, only one in five EU citizens supports the use of nuclear power. The largest segment of the European population (39%) would like to reduce the share of electricity produced by nuclear power; almost as many Europeans would like to keep it the same as at present (34%), while only 14% of respondents would increase the share of nuclear energy in the mix of all energy sources. In relation to the present energy structure in their countries, Europeans are reluctant to accept the use of fossil fuels (less than half of them are in favour of gas, oil and coal) but are much more favourable about renewable energies (all forms, 55% or over) than the nuclear option.

European public opinion on nuclear energy and nuclear safety is divided between countries which have nuclear power plants and countries which do not. Countries that have nuclear power plants perceive nuclear power in a more positive light than countries that do not have them. For instance, the absolute majorities of citizens in Austria (80%), Greece (73%) and Cyprus (70%) are opposed to the use of nuclear power in their country. These countries do not have nuclear power plants in operation. Swedish (41%), Slovakian (37%) and Lithuanian (37%) respondents are mostly in favour of the use of nuclear power in their country. This is understandable, since 70% of energy in Lithuania, 56% in Slovakia and 47% in Sweden is produced by nuclear power.

Europeans have a slightly more positive perception of the value of nuclear energy in terms of the contribution it makes to energy independency (69%), more stable energy prices (50%) and the fight against global warming (46%). A significant proportion (47%) also thinks that replacing nuclear energy would not be an easy task.

Despite these observations, increasing the share of nuclear energy is not seen as the answer to Europe's energy challenges, namely the increasing demand for energy or the fight against global warming.

The potential danger posed by nuclear power is usually found to underlie people's reluctance to support it. The absolute majority of Europeans (53% against 33% who say the opposite) think that the risks posed by nuclear power outweigh its advantages, and exactly the same percentage of citizens believes that nuclear power plants represent a risk to themselves and their families (53% against 38%). These fears appear to be connected primarily with the threat of terrorism, the possible misuse of radioactive materials and the unresolved question of radioactive waste. On the other hand, Europeans seem fairly confident about the safe functioning of nuclear power plants, the sufficiency of national legislation and the functioning of their national authorities regarding nuclear safety. Even if Europeans on average have a fair level of knowledge of nuclear issues, particularly whether or not there are nuclear power plants in their countries, they feel unfamiliar with the issue of nuclear safety (ranging from 56 to 90%). The vast majority in every country admit that they are not informed about this topic. The most trusted sources for acquiring information are scientists and environmental NGOs, while national nuclear safety authorities and international nuclear energy organizations also enjoy the confidence of a fair share of Europeans. The least trusted sources of information are the media and national governments.

As expected, attitudes towards nuclear energy are influenced by socio-demographic factors such as gender and level of education. Males and those with a high level of education tend to have more positive attitudes towards nuclear energy. They are also more knowledgeable of nuclear issues and feel more informed about nuclear safety than females and respondents who finished their education before the age of 20.

The findings of the Eurobarometer studies illustrate that nuclear power remains a controversial issue and holds an unfavourable status among the general public. An analysis of opinion polls and surveys on nuclear energy by the NEA (2010) indicates that messages derived from the Eurobarometer studies appear to be generally applicable to a wider spectrum of countries, not only in the EU.

Some relatively recent surveys in the UK generally convey the same message: a new programme of nuclear power stations enjoys only a limited support (less that 30%) and, although there is some sign that the climate change issue may be encouraging a new perspective, this is overshadowed by the continuing concerns over secure radioactive waste disposal, decommissioning and industrial secrecy (SDC, 2006g).

As indicated at the beginning of this chapter, public trust and perception must be considered to understand the full sustainability implications of nuclear energy. Opinion polls may be imprecise, but they are the only readily available tools to allow an understanding of public views. As the recent poll findings presented here suggest, the factors that reduce public support for nuclear energy are concerns with respect to terrorism, radioactive waste and the misuse of nuclear materials.

Whilst some of the findings suggest that 'new' factors – such as climate change, security of supply and decommissioning – may play an important role in shaping public attitudes, current perceptions appear to be influenced by pre-existing and latent understandings of both nuclear energy and the nuclear industry.

Many people assess the merits of possible new nuclear power plants in the light of the unresolved issues of safe disposal of radioactive waste and secure decommissioning of existing facilities. Recurrently, satisfactory solutions to these issues emerge as preconditions for looking more favourably on any new nuclear proposals.

Public perceptions of new nuclear energy investment appear also to be influenced strongly by a widespread lack of trust in governments and industry either to tell the truth or to take adequate responsibility, should something go wrong (Poortinga and Pidgeon, 2003).

Alongside such ongoing concerns there is also some evidence of public appreciation of potential benefits of nuclear energy, including security of supply, cleaner air and reducing the emissions of greenhouse gases.

Questions

1. What are the predominant public attitudes towards nuclear energy in Europe? And in your country?
2. In your opinion, will the concerns about climate change and energy security influence the opinion of those who are opposed to nuclear energy? Why?
3. Are there any other issues or information that was not mentioned in the chapter that you believe need to be considered when assessing the sustainability of nuclear power?
4. Putting together the technological, economic, environmental and social issues, in your opinion, is nuclear energy a sustainable solution for our energy needs? Why?

9.7 Conclusions

Sustainability of nuclear energy is a contentious issue. For some people, nuclear energy is not compatible with the principles of sustainable development, while others see it as one of the most sustainable solutions for our energy needs. As discussed in the chapter, some would argue that it is expensive, unsafe, poses great environmental and health risks, makes society more vulnerable to acts of terrorism, increases the chances of nuclear proliferation and burdens future generations with high environmental and economic costs. Others would point out that nuclear energy is affordable, low carbon, with better environmental and safety records than most of the current energy technologies. They would argue that there is no way out of our current energy predicaments, such as climate change, rising prices and security of supply, without having recourse to the nuclear option.

Some people are fiercely opposed to nuclear energy; others are genuinely enthusiastic about it. This controversial status of nuclear energy makes an examination of its sustainability even more demanding.

This chapter has looked at the relevant technological, economic, environmental and social aspects of nuclear energy. It shows that most nuclear power plants in the industrialized countries are built and operated to the highest safety and security standards. However, the same level of confidence cannot always be applied to other countries, and this remains a cause for serious concern. The health impacts of a well-regulated nuclear power industry appear to be low. However, the risk of a low-probability, but high-impact accident must be considered, especially in the context of the international concerns mentioned above. In addition, nuclear power facilities and processes are vulnerable to exploitation by terrorist groups and, although safety and security standards may be high, this does not rule out the possibility of a successful strike. The proliferation of nuclear materials is equally a cause for concern in this context. As industrialized countries show strong intentions to expand their nuclear capacity this essentially removes their ability, both morally and legally, to deny the technology to others. And that raises further concerns, as the widespread adoption of nuclear power would greatly increase the chances of nuclear proliferation, both through the efforts of nation states and possibly terrorist organizations. Finally, the impacts of the legacy of nuclear waste on future generations raises ethical concerns of intergenerational equity. Considering the current uncertainties over the total costs and long-term waste management, it may prove difficult to reconcile these issues with the sustainable development principles.

Therefore, the issues associated with nuclear power are complex and numerous and, as in many other systems discussed in this book, there are no simple answers to the question of sustainability. Yet, it is important that answers to this question are sought, as the extent to which nuclear energy can be shown to be sustainable – or otherwise – will determine its place in future energy supply.

Acknowledgements

Part of the work presented in this chapter has been funded by the UK Engineering and Physical Sciences Research Council (EPSRC) within the project 'Sustainability Assessment of Nuclear Power: An Integrated Approach (SPRIng)' (grant no. EP/F001444/1). This funding is gratefully acknowledged.

References and Further Reading

Andseta, S., Jarell, J. and Pendergast, D. (1998) CANDU reactors and greenhouse gas emissions. Proceedings of the 19th Annual Conference, 18–21 October 1998, Canadian Nuclear Society, Toronto, Canada.

BERR (2008) Meeting the Energy Challenge – A White Paper on Energy. Cm 7124. Department for Business Enterprise and Regulatory Reform. The Stationery Office, Norwich.

Blowers, A. and Leroy, P. (1994) Power, politics and environmental inequality: a theoretical and empirical analysis of 'peripherilisation'. *Environmental Politics*, **3**, 197–228.

BP (2007) British Petroleum statistical review of world energy. www.bp.com.

British Energy (2006) How an AGR power station works. http://www.british-energy.com/documents/ How_an_AGR_power_station_works.pdf.

British Energy (2008) *Environmental Product Declaration of Electricity from Sizewell B Nuclear Power Station - Technical Report*, AEA Energy & Environment, London.

Carroll, S. (2003) Expectations for the protection of the environment: Greenpeace perspectives. Proceedings of the Third International Symposium on the Protection of the Environment from Ionising Radiation (SPEIR 3), Darwin, Australia. IAEA, Austria.

Cogent SSC (2005) Industry profile. http://www.cogent-ssc.com/industry/nuclear/industry_profile.php.

CoRWM (2006) Independent scrutiny and advice. Committee on Radioactive Waste Management. http://www.corwm.org.uk/.

Curry, T., Reiner, D., de Figueiredo, M. and Herzog, H. (2005) A Survey of public attitudes towards energy & environment in Great Britain. MIT, Laboratory for Energy and Environment, Cambridge MA, MIT.

DECC (2010) *Climate Change Action Plan*, Department of Energy & Climate Change, London.

Denniss, I. and Jeapes, A. (1996) Reprocessing irradiated fuel, in *The Nuclear Fuel Cycle* (ed. P. Wilson), Oxford University Press, Oxford.

DoE (2010) Nuclear power and the environment. Nuclear Issues Paper. Department of Energy, USA. http://www.eia.doe.gov/cneaf/nuclear/page/nuclearenvissues.html.

DTI (2007) The future of nuclear power: the role of nuclear power in a low carbon UK economy. Consultation document, Department of Trade and Industry, London, http://www.bis.gov.uk/files/file39199.pdf.

EC (2005) Special Eurobarometer – Europeans and radioactive waste, European Commission.

EC (2007) Management of spent nuclear fuel and radioactive waste. Amended proposal for a Council Directive (Euratom) on the management of spent nuclear fuel and radioactive waste COM(2004) 526 final. http://europa.eu/legislation_summaries/energy/nuclear_energy/l27048_en.htm.

EC (2007a) Special Eurobarometer – Energy technologies: knowledge-perception-measures, European Commission.

EC (2007b) Special Eurobarometer – Europeans and nuclear safety, European Commission.

Ecoinvent (2007). Ecoinvent Database, Swiss Centre for Life Cycle Inventories, http://www.ecoinvent.ch/

Farber, S. (1998) Undesirable facilities and property values: a summary of empirical studies. *Ecological Economics*, **24**, 1–14.

FoE (2010) Is nuclear power the answer to our energy needs? Friends of the Earth. http://www.foe.co.uk/resource/faqs/nuclear_energy2.html.

Gramling, R. and Freudenburg, W.R. (1992) Opportunity-threat, development, and adaptation: toward a comprehensive framework for social impact assessment. *Rural Sociology*, **57** (2), 216–234.

Greenhalgh, C. and Azapagic, A. (2009) Review of drivers and barriers for nuclear power in the UK. *Environmental Science Policy*, **12** (7), 1052–1067.

Greenpeace UK (2010) Nuclear power, Greenpeace UK. http://www.greenpeace.org.uk/nuclear.

Greenpeace (2010) Transport. Greenpeace International. http://www.greenpeace.org/international/campaigns/nuclear/waste/transport.

Gregory, R., Slovic, P. and Flynn, J. (1996) Risk perceptions, stigma, and health policy. *Health and Place*, **2** (4), 213–220.

Grimston, M. and Beck, P. (2002) *Double or Quits – the Future of Civil Nuclear Energy*, Earthscan Books, London.

Hesketh, K. (2002) *Reactor Economics, BNES Seminar*. BNFL Research and Technology, 15 May 2002.

Herranz, L.E., Linares, J.I. and Moratilla, B.Y. (2008) Power cycle assessment of nuclear high temperature gas-cooled reactors. *Applied Thermal Engineering*, **29**, 1759–1765.

IAEA (1970) Treaty on the Non-Proliferation of Nuclear Weapons. IAEA INFCIRC/140.

IAEA (2005a) Chernobyl's legacy: health, environmental and socio-economic impacts. IAEA.

IAEA (2005b) Nuclear Security – measures to protect against nuclear terrorism. Amendment to the Convention on the Physical Protection of Nuclear Material. http://www.iaea.org/About/Policy/GC/GC49/Documents/gc49inf-6.pdf.

IAEA and OECD (2008) *Uranium 2007: Resources, Production and Demand*, OECD, Paris. http://www.oecdbookshop.org/oecd/display.asp?sf1=identifiers&st1=9789264047662.

IEA (2006) *Energy Technology Perspectives 2006: In Support of the G8 Plan of Action*, International Energy Agency, Paris, France.

Lenzen, M. (2008) Life cycle energy and greenhouse gas emissions of nuclear energy: a review. *Energy Conversion and Management*, **49**, 2178–2199.

Marsh G. and Eccles, H. (1996) Fuel fabrication, in *The Nuclear Fuel Cycle* (ed. P. Wilson), Oxford University Press, Oxford.

Matten A. (2009) The sustainability of nuclear power. MEng Research Project, The University of Manchester.

NDA and DEFRA (2008) The 2007 UK Radioactive Waste Inventory: a review of the processes contributing to radioactive wastes in the UK. DEFRA/RAS/08.004. NDA/RWMD/006. NDA and DEFRA, March 2008, London. http://www.nda.gov.uk/ukinventory/documents/Reports/loader. cfm?url=/commonspot/security/getfile.cfm&pageid=10355.

NEA (2000) Nuclear power in competitive electricity markets. Nuclear Energy Agency, OECD, Paris.

NEA (2005) Nuclear energy today. Nuclear Energy Agency, OECD, Paris.

NEA (2008) Nuclear energy outlook 2008. Nuclear Energy Agency, OECD, Paris.

NEA (2010) Public attitudes to nuclear power. Nuclear Energy Agency, OECD, Paris.

NEI (2008) Buried costs. *Nuclear Engineering International*. http://www.neimagazine.com/story. asp?storyCode=2049209.

NIREX (2005) Technical note: Cost estimate for a reference repository concept for UK high-level waste/ spent nuclear fuel. Report Number: 484281. NIREX. http://www.nda.gov.uk/documents/upload/ Technical-Note-Outline-Design-for-a-Reference-Repository-Concept-for-UK-High-Level-Waste-Spent-Fuel-2005.pdf.

NRC (2003) AECL: ACR-700 Technical Description, Ref: ML032030391. http://www.nrc.gov/ reading-rm/doc-collections/fact-sheets/next-gen-reactors.html.

OECD (1994) *The Economics of the Nuclear Fuel Cycle*, Nuclear Energy Agency, Paris.

OECD (2008) Nuclear energy data. OECD, Paris. http://www.oecdbookshop.org/oecd/display.asp? K=5KZK0CBTJQZT&CID=&LANG=en.

PIU (2002) The energy review; working paper on the economics of nuclear power. Performance and Innovation Unit, Cabinet Office, UK.

Poortinga, W. and Pidgeon, N. (2003) Public perceptions of risk, science and governance: main findings of a British survey of five risk cases. Centre for Environmental Risk, University of East Anglia.

Power (2009) AREVA suffers hefty losses from delays in Finnish EPR project. *Power*, 2 September 2009. http://www.powermag.com/POWERnews/AREVA-Suffers-Hefty-Losses-from-Delays-in-Finnish-EPR-Project_2151.html.

Royal Society (1999) Nuclear energy – the future climate. http://royalsociety.org/Nuclear-energy—the-future-climate-full-report/.

SDC (2006a) The role of nuclear power in a low carbon economy. Paper 1: An introduction to nuclear power – science, technology and UK policy context. An evidence-based report by the Sustainable Development Commission, March 2006, London.

SDC (2006b) The role of nuclear power in a low carbon economy. Paper 8: Uranium resource availability. An evidence-based report by the Sustainable Development Commission, March 2006, London.

SDC (2006c) The role of nuclear power in a low carbon economy. Paper 4: The economics of nuclear power. An Evidence-Based Report by the Sustainable Development Commission, March 2006, London.

SDC (2006d) The role of nuclear power in a low carbon economy: Paper 7 – public perceptions and community issues. Sustainable Development Commission, London, March 2006.

SDC (2006e) The role of nuclear power in a low carbon economy: Paper 6 – Safety and security, Sustainable Development Commission, London, March 2006.

SDC (2006f) The role of nuclear power in a low carbon economy: Paper 3 – Landscape, environment and community impacts of nuclear power, Sustainable Development Commission, London, March 2006.

SDC (2006g) Is nuclear the answer? A commentary by Jonathon Porritt Chairman Sustainable Development Commission, London, March 2006.

SDC (2006h) The role of nuclear power in a low carbon economy – Position Paper, Sustainable Development Commission, London, March 2006.

Slovic, P., Layman, M., Kraus, N. *et al.* (1991) Perceived risk, stigma, and potential economic impacts of a high-level nuclear waste repository in Nevada. *Risk Analysis*, **11** (4), 683–696.

Solomon, S., Qin, D., Manning, M. *et al.* (eds) (2007) *Climate Change 2007: The Physical Science Basis. Report of Working Group 1 to the Fourth Assessment Report of the Intergovernmental Panel on Climate Change*. Cambridge University Press, Cambridge.

Tester, J., Drake, E., Driscoll, M. *et al.* (2005) *Sustainable Energy Choosing Among Options*, MIT Press, Cambridge, MA.

UNFCCC (1992) The United Nations Framework Convention on Climate Change, UN, New York. http://unfccc.int/essential_background/convention/background/items/1362.php.

Upson, P. (1996) Isotopic enrichment of uranium, in *The Nuclear Fuel Cycle* (ed. P. Wilson), Oxford University Press, Oxford.

Vattenfall (2007) Certified environmental product declaration EPD of electricity from Forsmark nuclear power plant. S-P-00021. Vattenfall AB Generation Nordic.

WHO (2006) Health effects of the Chernobyl accident: an overview. World Health Organization. www.who.int.

WNA (2008) Environment, health and safety in electricity generation, World Nuclear Association. http://www.world-nuclear.org.

WNA (2010a) Nuclear power reactors. World Nuclear Association. http://www.world-nuclear.org.

WNA (2010b) Decommissioning Nuclear Facilities.. World Nuclear Association. http://www.world-nuclear.org.

WWF (2003) Position statement: nuclear power, May, 2003, WWF International, Gland, Switzerland. www.panda.org.

10

Municipal Solid Waste Management: Recovering Energy from Waste

Adisa Azapagic

Municipal solid waste (MSW) management is one of the most important and challenging issues for sustainable development. It is also one of the most controversial issues and the subject of an ongoing debate between different stakeholders. A particularly 'difficult' issue is MSW incineration, which has in many countries become a socially unacceptable option for dealing with solid waste. On the other hand, the increasing amounts of waste require timely and practical solutions to the problem which currently cannot be solved by recycling alone. This chapter addresses the problem of MSW and, after an introduction to this vast and complex subject, presents a case study related to using MSW for energy generation. The subject of the case study is a proposal by a waste management company for an energy-from-waste (EfW) plant. The study shows the complexity and a multidisciplinary nature of the problem by guiding the reader through the issues involved, from the technical and design aspects, through environmental assessments of different technologies to social concerns of the stakeholders. Through that, the case study examines the role of engineering design, scientific assessments and people's opinions in decision making for a more sustainable MSW management.

10.1 Introduction

Management of household and commercial waste, collectively known as municipal solid waste (MSW), is one of the major challenges of sustainable development. As societies are

Sustainable Development in Practice: Case Studies for Engineers and Scientists, Second Edition
Edited by Adisa Azapagic and Slobodan Perdan
© 2011 John Wiley & Sons, Ltd.

Table 10.1   *MSW generation in the world (adapted from Rand et al. (2000)*

Area	Range (kg/capita year)	Mean (kg/capita year)	Growth rate (%)
OECD-total	263–864	513	1.9
North America		826	2.0
Japan		394	1.1
OECD-Europe		336	1.5
Europe (32 countries)	150–624	345	N/A
Eight Asian capitals	185–1000	N/A	N/A
South and West Asia	185–290	N/A	N/A
Latin America and the Caribbean	110–365	N/A	N/A

becoming wealthier, the amount of waste tends to grow. For example, in 1990, each person in the world produced on average 250 kg of MSW, or around four times our body weight, generating in total 1.3 billion tonnes of solid waste (Beede and Bloom, 1995). Ten years later, this amount of waste had almost doubled, reaching 2.3 billion tonnes produced worldwide. In the EU countries, over 220 million tonnes of municipal waste are produced each year and, with an annual growth of 3%, MSW has outpaced GDP growth over the last decade.

With each person producing on average 500 kg of solid waste per year, developed countries generate on average twice as much MSW as countries in the developing world (see Table 10.1). In the UK alone, every person generates 10 times their own body weight in household waste every year.

By 2020, the OECD estimates we could be generating 45% more waste than we did in 1995. Obviously, we must reverse this trend if we are to avoid being submerged in rubbish. The EU, for example, wants to reduce the quantity of waste going to landfill by 20% from 2000 to 2010, and by 50% by 2050. Currently, around 50 % of solid waste is landfilled in EU countries.

Solid waste creates a number of problems. First, the large amounts of waste generated each year require a large space for its storage and disposal. MSW is currently predominantly disposed of in landfills, but in many countries landfill space is at premium as the amount of land available for these purposes is diminishing. Second, landfilling waste generates a number of environmental problems, including emissions of carbon dioxide (CO_2) and methane (CH_4) into the atmosphere and leaching of chemicals into the soil and ground-water. Landfilling also represents a waste of valuable resources which could otherwise be recycled to recover materials or energy. For example, it has been estimated that, in the UK alone, the MSW waste generated annually has a potential energy value equivalent to 30 million tonnes of coal, which is around 10% of the UK's primary energy demand. Only about 1.5% of that energy potential is utilized (Barron, 1995).

Therefore, the main challenge associated with the MSW is how to manage the waste in the most sustainable way. Following the widely adopted waste management hierarchy shown in Figure 10.1, it is clear that reducing waste generation in the first place is the most sustainable option. However, the wealthier societies in particular have not been very good at achieving this goal so far; so, at present, we are left with an ever-increasing pile of waste each year. Reusing and recycling waste to recover materials would also be a sustainable way to deal with the problem of MSW; however, various factors, such as lack of appropriate

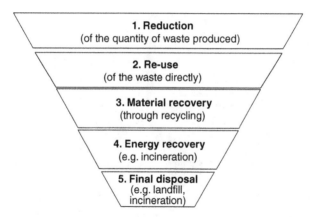

Figure 10.1   *Solid waste management hierarchy in a decreasing order of desirability*

technologies, high costs of collection, sorting and recycling of waste, as well as insufficient public participation, make recycling difficult (Azapagic *et al.*, 2003). A further MSW management option is to recover energy from waste; for example, through incineration. The final and least desirable option is to incinerate the waste without energy recovery or to landfill it.

This chapter explores one of the options for MSW management – energy recovery by incineration, which can be used when all other more desirable options in the waste management hierarchy have been exhausted. This option is particularly interesting to explore in the context of sustainable development for several reasons. First, from a resource point of view, recovering energy from waste is a more sustainable option than the currently most-practised MSW management option, namely waste landfilling. Second, if an appropriate, modern incineration is used, energy recovery by incineration could be economically profitable as well as environmentally safe. However, incineration is one of the areas where the public tend to mistrust or reject a technological solution owing to its potential risks to human health and the environment. For this reason, in most countries in Europe and in the USA, it is now almost impossible to obtain planning permission for a new incinerator.

Therefore, the case study presented here explores some of the sustainability issues surrounding MSW incineration for energy recovery. The case study is based on a real design and a planning application for a new MSW incinerator in England; however, to preserve confidentiality, the names of the place and the company are not mentioned.

Prior to introducing the case study, we give a brief overview of MSW management options in general and specific practices around the world. This is followed by an overview of the technical, environmental, economic and social aspects of energy recovery by incineration, to help the reader understand the scope of the problem and the main sustainability issues involved in the case study.

10.2 Integrated MSW Management

MSW comprises waste from households and commercial activities and includes waste paper, glass, plastics, food scraps and garden waste and other, normally, nonhazardous types of waste. An example of a typical composition of MSW is shown in Figure 10.2.

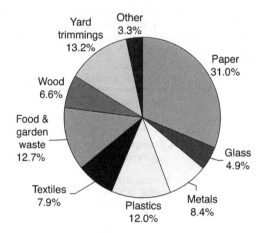

Figure 10.2   *Typical MSW composition by material (based on the US MSW composition; EPA, 2010)*

Sustainable management of MSW demands an integrated approach based on the waste management hierarchy shown in Figure 10.1. It is unlikely that a single waste management option would be sufficient to deal with the problem of MSW, so that normally a combination of several options would need to be considered. Some of these options are shown in Figure 10.3. Clearly, the first and most preferable option is prevention and reduced generation of MSW.

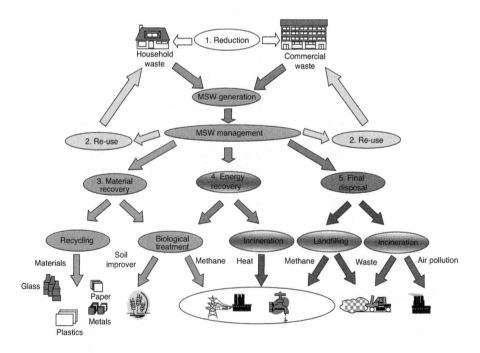

Figure 10.3   *MSW management options (adapted from Romero-Hernández et al. (2003))*

If generation of waste cannot be prevented, then as many of the materials as possible should be recovered, preferably by recycling. Many countries have introduced recycling targets for materials recovery. For example, the European Commission has defined recovery and recycling targets for packaging waste (EC, 1994), end-of-life vehicles (EC, 2000a) and electrical and electronic waste (EC, 2003a).

A further option for materials recovery is aerobic composting of organic waste, such as food scraps and garden waste, to produce minerals and humus which can be used as soil improvers. Anaerobic digestion of organic waste, on the other hand, generates biogas – CH_4 – which can be used to generate either heat or electricity. This is the next option in the MSW management hierarchy, related to energy recovery. Further energy recovery options include incineration to generate heat or electricity or both (see Figure 10.3).

Final disposal of waste by landfill or incineration without energy recovery should only be used as a last resort. Both these methods need close monitoring because of their potential to cause environmental damage. However, it is also important to bear in mind that the other waste management options, such as materials and energy recovery, will also generate some environmental impacts, due to the collection and transportation of waste, recycling processes, incineration and other related activities. Applying life cycle thinking (see Chapter 3) can help identify the environmental impacts associated with each of the waste management alternatives from 'cradle to grave' and choose the most sustainable options. The life cycle of the integrated MSW management is outlined in Figure 10.4.

To help us understand the current trends, the following section gives a brief overview of the MSW management practices in different regions in the world.

10.2.1 MSW Management in the EU

The EU countries generate in total around 220 million tonnes of MSW each year. Table 10.2 shows the amount and the composition of waste in different EU countries.

The waste management systems in the EU are designed around the waste management hierarchy described in the Introduction. However, there is some variation in the waste management priorities within the EU countries: for example, the northern European nations give the recovery of materials a higher priority than energy recovery, while France considers them as equal. Figure 10.5 shows the percentage of different MSW management options used in some of the EU countries.

Overall, the recycling rates are increasing in the EU countries, with the amount of landfill falling steadily. Some countries, such as Sweden, have banned landfill altogether. An example of this declining trend is shown in Figure 10.6 for the UK. The data show an increase in recycling and composting of waste (by 55%) and in incineration with energy recovery (by 41%) in the period from 1996 to 2002; however, over the same period, the total amount of waste increased by 15%, so that the amount of waste sent to landfill decreased only by 8%.

Waste management is legislated extensively at the EU level, and legislation is based on the following main principles, known as the 'five Ps' (EC, 2003b):

1. **prevention principle:** waste prevention and minimization should be given the highest priority;

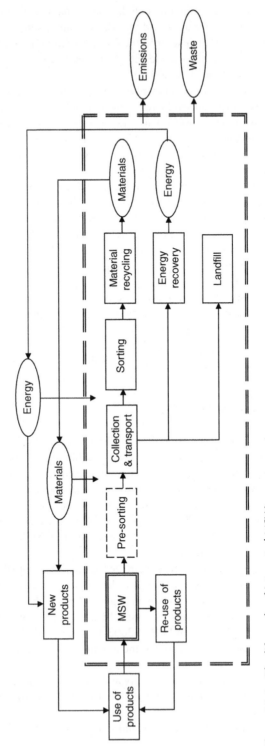

Figure 10.4 *The life cycle of integrated MSW management*

Table 10.2   *MSW generation and composition by weight in Europe (EC, 2006)*

	1999 or latest available year							
	Amount (1000 t)	Paper	Textiles	Plastics	Glass	Metals	Food and garden waste	Other
Belgium	5 462	17	4	6	3	4	20	46
Denmark	3 141							
Germany	44 390							
Greece	3 900	18	4	10	3	3	51	11
Spain	24 470	21	5	11	7	4	44	8
France	37 800	25	3	11	13	4	29	15
Ireland	1 933	33	2	10	6	3	24	22
Italy	26 846							
Luxembourg	184							
Netherlands	9 359	28	2	5	6	3	39	17
Austria	5 270	24	3	15	9	7	29	13
Portugal	4 364							
Finland	2 510	33	2	3	2	5	33	22
Sweden	4 000							
UK	28 000							
Iceland	189							
Norway	2 650	36	4	9	3	4	30	14
Switzerland	4 555							
Bulgaria	3 197	11	4	7	6	4	41	27
Cyprus	369	29	7	12	1	2	42	7
Czech Republic	3 365	8	2	4	4	2	18	62
Estonia	569							
Hungary	4 376	20	5	15	4	3	31	22
Latvia	292	14	3	7	8	4	48	16
Lithuania	1 236	1	1	0	2	19	40	37
Poland	12 317							
Romania	5 699	18	6	10	6	5	53	2
Slovak Republic	1 700	13	3	9	6	8	26	35
Slovenia	1 024	15		10	5	7	32	31

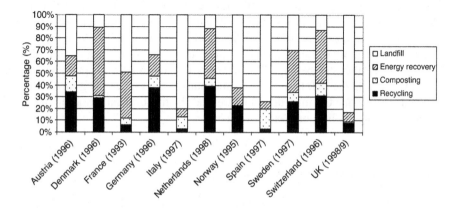

Figure 10.5   *MSW management in the EU (based on the data from EC (2006))*

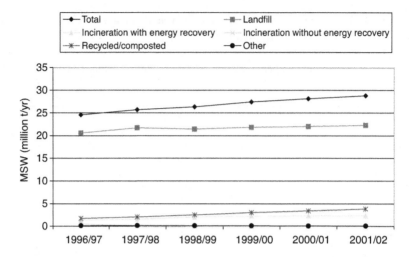

Figure 10.6   *MSW generation and management in the UK from 1996 to 2002 (based on the data from DEFRA (2003))*

2. **proximity principle:** waste should be disposed of as close as possible to where it is produced;
3. **producer responsibility principle:** waste producers should bear full 'cradle to grave' (see Figure 10.4) responsibility for any damage caused by the waste that they produce;
4. **polluter pays principle:** polluters (including waste producers), rather than society in general, should bear the full cost of the safe management and disposal of waste;
5. **precautionary principle:** waste management strategies should not pose risks (if there is even a small chance of a major problem, that option should be avoided).

Some examples of the EC legislation in the area of waste management include the directives on environmental impact assessment, incineration, landfilling, packaging waste, electronic and electrical waste equipment and end-of-life-vehicles. Some of the waste-related directives are listed in Box 10.1. The responsibility for the implementation of these directives rests with the national governments of the member countries. A number of the EU waste directives and many national waste laws and regulations are linked to the planning processes, so that most waste management programmes and facilities require planning permission before they can be built. The authority for granting the planning permissions varies widely within the EU. For example, in countries like France this process is highly centralized, while in the UK most decisions are made by the local authorities for the region where the planning application has been made.

10.2.2 MSW Management in the USA

Approximately 250 million tonnes of MSW were generated in the USA in 2008, or 2 kg per person each day (EPA, 2010). The recovery rate for material recycling (including

---

Box 10.1   EU legislation on solid waste (EC, 2003b)

Waste framework

- Framework Directive on Waste (Council Directive 75/442/EEC as amended by Council Directive 91/156/EEC);
- Hazardous Waste Directive (Council Directive 91/689/EEC as amended by Council Directive 94/31/EC).

Specific wastes

- Disposal of waste oils (Council Directive 75/439/EEC);
- Directives on waste from the titanium dioxide industry (Council Directives 78/176/EEC, 82/883/EEC and 92/112/EEC);
- Batteries and accumulators containing certain dangerous substances (Council Directive 91/157/EEC);
- Packaging and packaging waste (Council Directive 94/62/EC);
- The disposal of polychlorinated biphenyls (PCBs) and polychlorinated terphenyls (Council Directive 96/59/EC);
- Protection of the environment, and in particular of the soil, when sewage sludge is used in agriculture (Council Directive 86/278/EEC).

Processes and facilities

- Reduction of air pollution from existing municipal waste-incineration plants (Council Directive 89/429/EEC);
- Reduction of air pollution from new municipal waste-incineration plants (Council Directive 89/369/EEC);
- Incineration of hazardous waste (Council Directive 94/67/EC);
- Directive on the landfill of waste (Council Directive 99/31/EC).

Transport, import and export

- The supervision and control of shipments of waste within, into and out of the European Community (Council Regulation EEC No 259/93);
- Rules and procedures applying to shipments of certain types of wastes to non-OECD countries (Council Regulation No 1420/1999 and Commission Regulation No 1547/99.

Table 10.3   Generation and recovery of materials in MSW in 2000 (EPA, 2010)

Material	Generated (million tonnes)	Recovered (million tonnes)	Recovered (%)
Paper and paperboard	77.42	42.94	55.5
Glass	12.15	2.81	23.1
Steel	15.68	5.29	33.7
Aluminium	3.41	0.72	21.1
Other nonferrous metals[a]	1.76	1.21	68.8
Plastics	30.05	2.12	7.1
Rubber and leather	7.41	1.06	14.3
Textiles	12.37	1.89	15.3
Wood	16.39	1.58	9.6
Other materials	4.50	1.15	25.6
Food, other[b]	31.79	0.80	2.5
Yard trimmings	32.90	21.30	64.7
Miscellaneous inorganic	3.78	—	—
Total MSW	249.61	82.87	33.2

[a] Includes lead from lead–acid batteries.
[b] Includes recovery of other organics for composting.

composting) was 32.3%, or around 0.6 kg per person per day, with the highest recycling rates achieved for paper, nonferrous metals and garden waste (see Table 10.3). Of the remaining waste, 12.6% was incinerated for energy recovery and 54.2% was landfilled.

The US Environmental Protection Agency (EPA) has adopted an integrated waste management hierarchy similar to that in the EU. The hierarchy includes the following three components, listed in order of preference (EPA, 2010):

1. source reduction (or waste prevention), including reuse of products and onsite, or backyard, composting of yard trimmings;
2. recycling, including offsite, or community, composting;
3. disposal, including waste combustion (preferably with energy recovery) and landfilling.

Although the EPA encourages the use of strategies that emphasize the top of the hierarchy whenever possible, all three components remain important within an integrated waste management system.

Most states and provinces in the USA have solid waste management plans that define the goals and agenda for regional waste management action within the integrated waste management hierarchy. Some laws require local governments to set up recycling centres or programmes that will achieve specific levels of recycling; other laws impose recycling responsibilities on industries and businesses.

Local governments have primary responsibility for managing MSW in the USA. However, there are minimum national-level design and operating standards for landfills, incineration and materials recovery facilities which must be adopted at the state level and implemented by local governments and private firms (UNEP, 1996). In some states and provinces, the economic and environmental pressures of waste disposal are causing the responsibility for waste management to shift from the local to the state/provincial level.

10.2.3 Asia and Pacific

Solid waste management policies and practices in the countries in Asia and the Pacific are normally related to the level of public awareness and interest in the waste issues and to the existing quality of the environment. Waste management is much more advanced in the industrialized countries of the region than in the developing countries. In Japan and Australia, for example, laws and regulations have banned the disposal of substances such as batteries, waste oil, tyres, CFC gases, PCBs and so on (UNEP, 1996). There is a mandatory deposit/take-back requirement for some goods, such as mercury oxide batteries, aluminium and plastic containers, tyres and nondegradable plastic bags. In Japan, to ensure that separation of wastes is carried out properly, households are required to use transparent plastic bags for waste disposal so that collection crews can see the contents. A major issue for MSW planning in these countries is public resistance to the siting of disposal facilities (UNEP, 1996).

The most common MSW management problems in developing countries of the region are financial constraints, outdated legislation and its inadequate enforcement, as well as the shortage of experienced specialists in the field. The additional problem is that, in many cases, the new waste regulations are directly copied from industrialized countries without any serious study of the social and economic conditions, the technology, the level of skill required and the local administrative structure. As a result, they prove to be unenforceable (UNEP, 1996). To help overcome this problem, the UNEP has defined a set of criteria for evaluation of MSW management options (see Box 10.2) to guide decision makers in choosing the most appropriate waste management alternative or a combination of alternatives for their specific conditions.

Box 10.2   Criteria for evaluation of waste management options (UNEP, 1996)

For each technology or policy under consideration, decision makers should ask a number of questions designed to facilitate comparison of the available alternatives:

- Is the proposed technology likely to accomplish its purpose in the circumstances where it would be used? More specifically, is it technologically feasible and appropriate, given the financial and human resources available?
- Focusing on the financial aspects of the practice, is it the most cost-effective option available?
- What are the environmental benefits and costs of the practice?
- Could the environmental soundness of the proposed practice be significantly enhanced by a small increase in costs? If so, do the environmental benefits justify budgeting for these costs?
- Conversely, would it be possible to reduce the cost of the practice significantly with only a small detriment to environmental soundness? If so, should that cost-reducing option be chosen, perhaps with the aim of more fruitfully investing society's resources in environmental quality improvement or toward other ends?
- Is the practice administratively feasible and sensible?

- Is it practical in the given social and cultural environment?
- How would specific sectors of society be affected by the adoption of this technology or policy? Do these effects promote or conflict with overall social goals of the society?

In many large cities in developing countries a particular problem is MSW management in the poor areas or 'slum cities' which are often treated by authorities as illegal and denied waste collection services. In many such places the accumulation of waste in open areas represents a health hazard.

Municipalities in most South Asian countries operate under the health, environment or local government ministries of the central or regional governments. In the central part of the region and in some countries in the north, health ministries are expanding to oversee municipal corporations more directly. In the Indian subcontinent, on the other hand, there is a movement toward decentralization, with municipalities being expected to raise their own funds and take on more responsibilities (UNEP, 1996).

10.2.4 Africa

Similar to the problems in other developing countries, MSW management in African countries is also constrained by a lack of financial resources, trained staff and poor enforcement of legislation.

Responsibility for MSW management in African countries rests either with the Ministry of Environment, the Ministry of Health or the Ministry of Planning and Development. Under the national ministry, various municipal agencies are responsible for planning and urban affairs in the country's major cities. Inefficient administration is often quoted as one of the reasons for poor waste management practices in Africa (UNEP, 1996).

10.2.5 Latin America and the Caribbean

In this region, MSW technologies are fairly well developed but the quality of services is dependent on improving the present management systems (UNEP, 1996). Throughout the region, local governments are responsible for management of solid wastes within their jurisdiction. However, enforcement programmes are practically nonexistent, as legislation on MSW management is weak and the local governments lack resources.

Questions

1. Compare the typical composition of MSW in the USA and the EU countries. What do you conclude in terms of the materials used in the households in these countries? Compare these with the waste composition in your country and discuss any differences.
2. Based on the typical composition of MSW in the USA and the EU countries, which MSW management options shown in Figure 10.3 would be most suitable for each type of

MSW? Why? Which options would be suitable for the waste composition in your country?

3. Find out how much MSW is generated in your town or city and in your country and how much of that is recycled for material and energy recovery and how much is landfilled.

4. Taking the life cycle approach (see Figure 10.4), describe the life cycles of each of the MSW management options shown in Figure 10.3 and discuss the advantages and disadvantages of each.

5. Describe the MSW management hierarchy in your country (if any) and discuss the current waste management practices.

6. Use the UNEP evaluation criteria in Box 10.2 and the MSW management options shown in Figure 10.3 to devise an integrated MSW management strategy for your town or city. Justify your choice of MSW options. Do they correspond to the current practice? Discuss any differences.

10.3 Energy Recovery from MSW

The previous two sections have provided an introduction and an overview of MSW and options for its integrated management. As the subject of this chapter and the case study is energy recovery from MSW by incineration, the next sections focus on this waste management option to examine the general technical and sustainability issues associated with it.

10.3.1 Technical Considerations

As illustrated in Figure 10.7, an energy-from-waste (EfW) plant typically comprises the following parts:

- waste handling facility, including waste reception and pretreatment;
- incinerator and boiler;
- energy recovery and energy generation plant;
- air pollution control plant; and
- ash treatment facility.

As shown in more detail in the block diagram in Figure 10.8, depending on the type of incineration technology, fuel pretreatment can include sorting and/or mixing and shredding of waste. Incineration involves burning of waste at high temperatures (normally from 980 to 1090 °C) to generate heat. The heat can then be recovered as hot water or as steam by heating water in the boiler. The hot water can be used directly or in a district heating system, whilst the steam can be utilized directly or it can be used to turn a turbine which drives a generator to produce electricity. The type of energy recovered determines the total energy efficiency of the plant and, therefore, influences its economic and environmental sustainability. As shown in Table 10.4, combined heat and power (CHPs) plants are the most efficient systems, recovering up to 85% of the original energy contained in the waste. Generating electricity alone, on the other hand, recovers only 35% of energy.

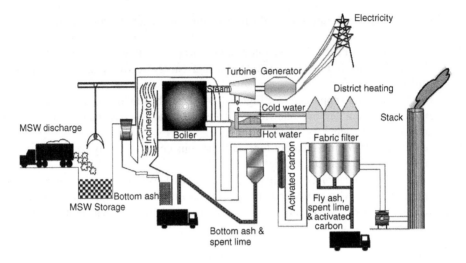

Figure 10.7 *A schematic representation of an EfW plant generating both electricity and heat (adapted from Romero-Hernández et al. (2003))*

In addition to the useful product – heat, electricity or both – the incineration process also generates flue gases, containing various air pollutants, such as carbon oxides (CO and CO_2), sulfur oxides (SO_2 and SO_3), nitrogen oxides (NO and NO_2), hydrogen chloride (HCl), heavy metals and dioxins and furans. A certain amount of ash is also generated, equivalent to about one-quarter of the original weight of the waste and approximately 90% of its volume. Both the flue gases and the ash must be treated in an appropriate way before they can be discharged into the environment.

To choose and design a sustainable EfW system, a number of technical factors must be considered, including waste composition and its energy content, type of incineration technology and energy recovery system. These factors are discussed briefly below.

10.3.1.1 Waste Composition and Characteristics

One of the most important factors to consider in recovering energy from MSW is its suitability for combustion. The following chemical and energy properties determine whether the waste is suitable for combustion:

- moisture content;
- flammable fraction (volatile matter plus fixed carbon);
- content of elements (C, H, O, N, S);
- noncombustible fraction (ash); and
- lower and higher heating values.

The waste is theoretically suitable for combustion without additional fuel when the moisture content $W < 50\%$, the ash content $A < 60\%$ and the content of carbon $C > 25\%$ (Rand *et al.*, 2000). This 'combustible' region is represented by the shaded area on the Tanner diagram shown in Figure 10.9.

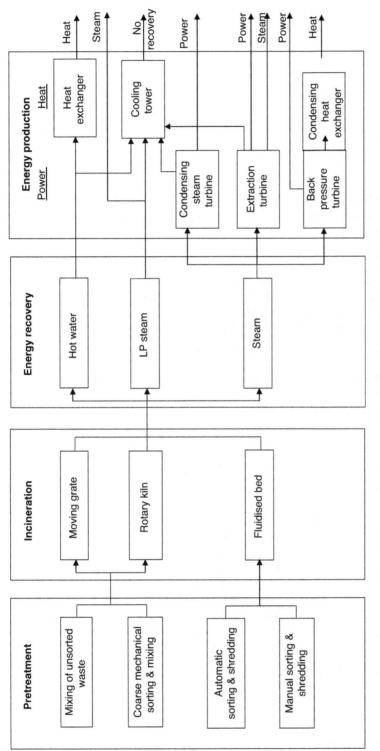

Figure 10.8 *Generating energy from MSW: a technology overview (adapted from Rand et al. (2000))*

Table 10.4   *Energy efficiency of different EfW systems*

Energy system	Energy recovery	Overall efficiency[a]
Heat only	Heat 80 %	80 %
Steam only	Steam 80 %	80 %
Power only	Power 35 %	35 %
Combined steam and power	Steam 75 % Power 35 %	35–75 %
Combined heat and power (CHP)	Heat 60–65 % Power 20–25 %	85 %

[a] Efficiency defined as usable energy related to the energy content (LHV) of waste.

The lower and the higher heating values determine how much thermal energy can be recovered from the waste. The higher heating value (HHV) of MSW can be determined using the equation:

$$HHV = 337C + 1419(H_2 - 0.1250_2) + 93S + 23N \tag{10.1}$$

where HHV (MJ/kg) is the higher heating value (heating value without water and ash) and C, H, O, S, N are the percentages by weight of each element obtained by ultimate analysis. Typically, the HHV of MSW is about 20 MJ/kg (Kiely, 1996).

The lower heating value (LHV) of waste, can be calculated as:

$$LHV = HHV \times B - 2.445W \tag{10.2}$$

where LHV (MJ/kg) is the lower heating value, B is the flammable fraction (volatile matter plus fixed carbon) by weight obtained in proximate analysis and W is the moisture content fraction by weight obtained by proximate analysis.

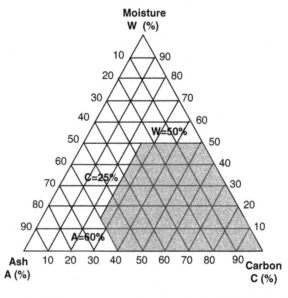

Figure 10.9   *Tanner triangle for assessment of combustibility of MSW (after Rand et al. (2000))*

Table 10.5 *Typical energy content of MSW (Kiely, 1996)*

Material	Moisture	Volatiles	Fixed carbon	Ash	LHV	HHV
		% by weight			MJ/kg	
Paper and card	10.2	76	8.4	5.4	15.7	18.7
Plastics	0.2	96	2	2	32.7	37.1
Textiles	10	66	17.5	6.5	18.3	22.7
Glass	2	—	—	96–99	0.2	0.15
Food	70	21	3.6	5	4.2	16.7
Metals	2.5	—	—	94–99	0.7	0.7

An alternative formula for calculating the LHV of MSW has been proposed by Khan *et al.* (1991):

$$\text{LHV} = 0.051(F + 3.6\text{CP}) + 0.352(\text{PLR}) \tag{10.3}$$

where F is the percentage of food by weight, CP is the percentage of cardboard and paper by weight and PLR is the percentage of plastic and rubber by weight.

Typical LHV and HHV values for MSW are given in Table 10.5. Obviously, the higher the heating values, the higher the amount of energy that can be recovered from waste. Table 10.6 shows that the production of steam drops dramatically with a decrease of the heating value of MSW, as well as with the increase in moisture and the fraction of incombustibles in the waste. In addition, the amount of energy recovered will also depend on the type of EfW technology chosen and on the incinerator design. These factors are discussed next.

10.3.1.2 EfW Technologies

There are many types of incineration plant currently in use for energy recovery from MSW, but they can be divided into three general categories (UNEP, 1996):

Table 10.6 *Steam production related to the quality of MSW as a fuel (Vesilind, Worrell and Reinhart, 2002)*

	LHV (kJ/kg)				
	15 000	14 000	11 500	9 300	7 000
MSW properties					
Moisture (%)	15	18	25	32	39
Noncombustibles (%)	14	16	20	24	28
Combustibles (%)	71	66	55	44	33
Steam generated (t/t MSW)	4.3	3.9	3.2	2.3	1.5

- mass-burn plants;
- modular plants; and
- refuse-derived fuel (RDF) plants.

Mass-burn systems generally consist of either two or three combustion units ranging in capacity from 50 to 1000 t/day per unit. Hence, the total mass-burn plant capacity ranges from about 100 to 3000 t/day. These plants can accept waste that has undergone little preprocessing other than the removal of oversized items, such as refrigerators and sofas. Most of the mass-burn systems generate both electricity and heat.

Modular combustors have relatively small capacities burning between 5 and 120 t of waste per day. Typical plants have between one and four units for a total plant capacity of about 15 to 400 t/day. The majority of modular units produce steam as the only energy product. Because of their small capacity, modular combustors are generally used in smaller communities or for commercial and industrial operations. On average, investment (capital) costs per tonne of capacity are lower for modular units than for mass-burn and RDF plants (UNEP, 1996).

RDF refers to solid waste that has been mechanically processed to produce a storable, transportable and more homogeneous fuel for combustion. A large majority of RDF combustion facilities generate electricity. On average, capital costs per tonne of capacity are higher for RDF combustion units than for mass-burn and modular units (UNEP, 1996). The production of RDF is relatively more common in the USA and Scandinavia, where it is co-fired with other wastes, but less so in other EU countries.

In addition to the established incineration-based EfW technologies, two new MSW thermal treatment techniques are being investigated: pyrolysis and gasification. The former involves decomposition of MSW by heating with no oxygen and the latter with a reduced amount of oxygen, compared with the normal combustion conditions. The products of pyrolysis and gasification include carbon monoxide, hydrogen, oils, tars, carbon and noncombustible residues. Carbon monoxide and hydrogen (also known as syngas) can be used either as fuels or raw materials (e.g. for methanol production), whilst oils, tars, carbon and the other products can be used as raw materials in different industrial sectors. Therefore, pyrolysis and gasification comprise both materials and energy recovery. Although there are more than 100 facilities operating or ordered around the world, these technologies are still considered unproven.

With regard to the incinerator designs, there are three common types (see Figure 10.8):

- moving grate or mechanical stoker;
- fluidized bed; and
- rotary kiln.

The majority of mass-burn incinerators have a moving-grate design. The moving grate pushes the waste through the incinerator and deposits the ash into the tank at the bottom of the incinerator. A typical design of a moving-grate incinerator is shown in Figure 10.10. This technology is well developed and commercially available from a number of manu-facturers. It is the dominant technology, with many plants providing heat, electricity or both.

In a fluidized-bed combustor, instead of a grate supporting the waste, the furnace contains a bed of sand on an air distribution system. The air keeps the sand bed and the waste fluidized and so increases mixing and combustion efficiency. The fluidized-bed design is particularly

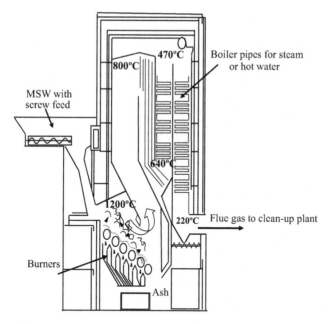

Figure 10.10 *Schematic representation of a typical moving-grate (mechanical stoker) incinerator (Azapagic et al., 2003)*

suited for RDF, as these types of incinerator require preprocessing of waste. A comparison of the technical performance of a fluidized-bed and a moving-grate incinerator is given in Table 10.7.

In a rotary kiln combustor, waste is rotated in a cylindrical furnace as it burns; the air is supplied through the perforations along the length of the furnace to ensure complete combustion. Rotary kilns provide the most turbulence of any grate system and thereby enhance the rate and completion of combustion. This technology is not widely used for MSW (White *et al.*, 1995).

Questions

1. Draw a flow diagram of a typical EfW facility and describe each part.
2. Why is a CHP plant so much more efficient than a plant that generates electricity only? In your opinion, what is the reason that CHP plants are still relatively rare in many countries compared with the electricity generating plants?
3. Which characteristics of waste must be considered in determining its suitability for energy recovery?
4. What is the difference between HHV and LHV? Write down the formulae for calculating both HHV and LHV and explain the differences by analysis of the formulae.
5. What is the difference between the proximate and ultimate analysis of waste? If you have a chemistry background, describe how each type of analysis can be carried out.
6. List the main incineration technologies and describe the suitability of each depending on the amount of waste to be treated.

Table 10.7   *Comparison of fluidized-bed and moving-grate incinerators (adapted from White et al. (1995))*

	Moving-grate incinerator 1200 t/day	Fluidizedbed incinerator 350 t/day
Max. capacity		
Combustion		
Mixing	Mild agitation	Turbulent
Burn out	Often incomplete	Complete
Air ratio	1.8–2.5	1.5–2.0
Load	200–250 kg/(m² h)	400–600 kg/(m² h)
Fuel size	75 cm	50 cm
Combustion residue		
Unburnt carbon	3–5 % by wt.	0.1 % by wt.
Volume	larger	smaller
State	wet	dry
Iron recovery	difficult	easy
Fly ash		
Volume	smaller	larger
Unburnt carbon	3–7 % by wt.	1 % by wt.
Flue gas		
Volume	larger	smaller
NO_x control	post-combustion	in-combustion

7. Describe the difference between incineration, pyrolysis and gasification of MSW.
8. What are the main differences between a moving-grate furnace and a fluidized-bed combustor? Which one would you choose based on their technical performance?
9. Suppose that your friend who has no engineering or science background has asked you to explain how an EfW plant operates. Using words and sketches, explain on one A4 page how such facilities work from taking the waste in to generating electricity. Now ask your friend to explain it back to you. Have you been able to explain that to them so that they understood? If not, try again.

10.3.2 Environmental Considerations

As already mentioned, incineration of MSW can be environmentally damaging mainly because of the air pollution and solid waste (bottom and fly ash) generated during the combustion process. Dust, heavy metals, dioxins and furans as well as acid gases, such as SO_x, NO_x and HCl, are some of the air pollutants that can be present in the flue gas. Dioxins and furans in particular are a subject of an ongoing debate and opposition of the public to incineration due to the potential of dioxins and furans to cause cancer. CO_2 is also generated in the combustion of MSW, thus contributing to global warming and climate change. However, it should be noted that MSW contains biogenic material (e.g. garden waste and paper), so that a proportion of the CO_2 in the flue gas will be biogenic and, therefore, not increase the net carbon emissions into the atmosphere. Thus, only the carbon derived from fossil-based materials (e.g. plastics) will be counting towards the CO_2 emissions from incineration. The composition of waste, incineration technology and the combustion conditions all influence the formation of these pollutants, including the amount of fossil

Table 10.8 *Typical emission levels from MSW incinerators before flue gas clean-up (Kiely, 1996)*

Pollutant	Typical emissions $(mg/m^3$ at 9 % $O_2)$
Dust	1500–1800
SO_2	400
HCF	500
HF	5
NO_x	300
CO	100
Organic vapours	5
Hg vapours	0.05–0.5
Ni + As + Pb + Cr + Cu + Mn	0.05–0.5

CO_2. Typical air emission levels from MSW incinerators before flue gas treatment are shown in Table 10.8.

Liquid effluents and water pollution can also be generated in cases where the treatment of flue gases involves the use of an absorption liquid.

Clearly, energy recovery from MSW can only be considered a sustainable option if the environmental impacts of incineration do not exceed the benefits of energy recovery. Hence, it is important to minimize the potential environmental damage from incineration by preventing and controlling air and water pollution as well as by appropriate disposal of the bottom and fly ash. The following section gives an overview of the techniques used for the prevention and control of pollution from incineration.

10.3.2.1 Air Pollution Prevention and Control

The following air pollutants can be generated in the combustion of MSW:

- nitrogen oxides, NO_x (NO and NO_2);
- sulfur oxides, SO_x (SO_2 and SO_3);
- carbon oxides, CO_x (CO and CO_2)
- particulate matter, PM (dust and particles of various sizes);
- metals, metalloids and their compounds;
- halogens and their compounds, including HCl and HF; and
- organic compounds, including dioxins and furans.

Discussion of the formation mechanisms and control of these pollutants is outside the scope of this chapter. The interested reader can consult, for example, Kiely (1996) and Vesilind *et al.* (2002) for an overview of the subject.

Two types of measure can be used to control air pollution from combustion of MSW: primary and secondary. The primary measures are those used in the furnace to prevent the formation of the pollutants and the secondary measures use clean-up technologies to remove air pollutants.

Primary measures – in-combustion control: The formation of pollutants such as particulates, NO_x, CO, hydrocarbons, including dioxins and furans, can be reduced significantly by controlling the combustion conditions within the furnace and the boiler. These measures can, for example, include:

- a control system for the supply of primary and secondary air (to control emissions of CO, NO_x and dioxins); and
- control of temperature and residence times in the combustion chamber, boiler and flue treatment units (to prevent formation of dioxins and NO_x).

For example, running the incinerator with a lower excess of air decreases the amount of nitrogen oxides formed during combustion by lowering the flame temperature and the amount of nitrogen and oxygen available for the formation of NO_x; however, this measure also increases the amount of CO and hydrocarbons due to the incomplete combustion. Table 10.9 lists several of the primary measures and summarizes their effects on NO_x, CO, hydrocarbons and dioxins, as well as on the bottom ash (clinker) and energy efficiency. The control mechanisms for dioxins, furans and heavy metals are summarized in Box 10.3. The technically minded reader may wish to consult a paper by Acharya *et al.* (1991) which provides a good overview of the dioxin formation and control mechanisms.

Secondary measures – cleaning up the air pollution from incineration: As illustrated in Figure 10.7, a flue gas treatment system can include a combination of the following:

Table 10.9   *Effect of primary measures (in-combustion control) on the formation of air pollutants*

Primary measure	Furnace temperature	O_2	CO and HCs	Total NO_x $(NO + NO_2)$	Remark
Low excess air	Decrease	Decrease	Increase	Decrease	Reduced bottom ash burn out and increase of dioxins; reduced potential for recycling of bottom ash
Increased excess air	Decrease	Increase	Decrease	Increase	Improved bottom ash burnout but the furnace temperature must be controlled carefully to prevent formation of dioxins
Increased air preheat	Increase	No effect	Decrease	Increase	Improved bottom ash burnout and decrease of dioxins; increased potential for recycling of bottom ash
Less air preheat	Decrease	No effect	Increase	Decrease	Reduced thermal efficiency
Load reduction (lower MSW throughput)	Decrease	No effect	No effect	Decrease	Reduced thermal efficiency

---

Box 10.3   Controlling emissions of dioxins, furans and heavy metals

Dioxins and furans represent a combination of a number of organic compounds called polychlorinated dibenzodioxins andpolychlorinated dibenzofurans respectively. There are two primary mechanisms responsible for the presence of dioxins and furans in flue gases from incineration:

- Direct emissions from materials containing dioxins and furans introduced into the incinerator as part of the waste feed, which have not been removed before being fed to the furnace or which are not destroyed during combustion.
- Formation by *de novo* synthesis from chlorinated precursors, including PVC and PCBs. This process typically occurs as the combustion gas is cooled or passed through the flue gas clean-up equipment, or both.

   The formation of dioxins and furans can be minimized by controlling waste feed rate and its composition, combustion temperature (minimum of 850 °C), residence time of the flue gas in the combustor, CO and hydrocarbon levels and so on. As an additional measure to remove dioxins and furans formed during the combustion process, the flue gas can be passed over activated carbon.

   To prevent *de novo* synthesis of dioxins and furans, the combustion gases should be cooled rapidly to below 200 °C before entering the flue gas clean-up equipment and the residence time in the cooler regions of the stack should be limited to less than 2 min. Cooling the gas also has the advantage of causing the low volatility metals (antimony, arsenic, beryllium and chromium) and semi-volatile metals (lead and cadmium) to condense out, along with some of the heavier organics, thus promoting the removal of the heavy metals from the flue gas.

- scrubbers, for the removal of acid gases such as HCl, HF, SO_2;
- cyclones, electrostatic precipitators or fabric filters for fly ash removal;
- activated carbon for removal of heavy metals and dioxins;
- selective catalytic reduction (SCR) of NO_x with ammonia; and
- selective noncatalytic reduction (SNCR) of NO_x with ammonia or urea.

   The choice of a particular type of equipment and treatment method will depend on many factors, including their removal efficiency, their capital and operating costs and their ease of operation and maintenance. The average removal efficiencies of some of the control techniques are summarized in Table 10.10. Further detail on the air pollution control equipment can be found, for example, in Vesilind *et al.* (2002).

10.3.2.2 Solid Waste Disposal: Bottom and Fly Ash

Two types of ash are generated from MSW incineration: bottom and fly ash. The bottom ash consists of the ash part of the burnable materials, such as paper and plastics, and the incombustible matter, such as glass and metals. The mixture of ash and the partially fused

Table 10.10   *Removal efficiency of different air control equipment*

	Efficiency	Remark
Acid gases		
Scrubbers		Relatively simple designs and inexpensive; the need to dispose of the spent adsorption/absorption medium
Dry	Up to 65 %	
Semi-dry	~70 %	
Wet	>90 %	
Particulate matter		
Dry cyclones	Up to 90 % for particles >5 μm	Simple design and inexpensive, can operate at high temperatures and pressures; ineffective for smaller particles; pressure drop 100–2000 Pa
Fabric filters	Up to 99.9 % for particles >1 μm 90 % for particles <1 μm	Require high capital costs and regular maintenance; sensitive to acid gases; pressure drop 1000–2000 Pa
Electrostatic precipitators	Up to 99 % for particles >1 μm Up to 99.99 % for particles <1 μm	Require high capital costs and regular maintenance; pressure drop ~250 Pa; efficient with very small particles, down to 0.01 μm
Nitrogen oxides		
SNCR	30–65 %	Optimum temperature 900–1090 °C; maintaining the optimum temperature difficult; emissions of ammonia ('slip') and N_2O into the atmosphere
Selective catalytic reduction, SCR	80–90 %	Optimum temperature 300–400 °C; safety problems with handling anhydrous ammonia; ammonia 'slip'

residues from the furnace is often referred to as clinker. A small fraction of the bottom ash ends up as a fly ash, which comes off in the flue gas. Typically, burning 1 t of MSW waste generates 200 kg of bottom ash and 30–40 kg of fly ash (Kiely, 1996).

The main environmental concerns associated with the bottom and fly ash are heavy metals and dioxins. For example, some of the heavy metals, such as lead, remain in the bottom ash, while the more volatile mercury concentrates in the fly ash. However, while the heavy metals in the bottom ash are not prone to leaching, they seem to be more leachable in the fly ash. Furthermore, dioxins and furans are concentrated in the fly ash, so that the fly ash should only be disposed of in secure landfills. This is not always the case, and fly ash has been used as an additive to asphalt and other road products (UNEP, 1996). This practice has been discontinued in many countries as awareness has grown of the presence and the leachability of the toxic constituents of these materials, particularly dioxins. The bottom ash could be utilized with care, for example, in road construction.

Questions

1. List the air pollutants that are generated by incineration of MSW and describe the mechanisms for their formation.

2. Describe the methods for primary and secondary control of the air pollutants you listed in the previous question and discuss their advantages and disadvantages.
3. How can *de novo* synthesis of dioxins and furans be prevented?
4. Applying life cycle thinking and using the information on the primary and secondary air pollution techniques summarized in Tables 10.9 and 10.10 respectively, which techniques would you choose to control air pollution from MSW incineration? Explain and justify your choices.

10.3.2.3 Environmental Legislation

Most countries have very strict environmental legislation for control of gaseous, liquid and solid discharges from MSW incineration. For example, in the EU, proposals for new EfW plants are subject to at least six EC directives, including:

- Integrated Pollution Prevention Control (IPPC) Directive;
- Environmental Impact Assessment Directive;
- Framework Directive on Waste;
- Landfill Directive;
- Waste Incineration Directive; and
- Ambient Air Framework Directive.

In addition to the EC regulations, EfW activities are also subject to national legislation in each EU country. The situation is no less complex in other regions, including the USA, Australia and Japan. Therefore, attempting to given an overview of MSW-related legislation worldwide would not be feasible for the purposes of this chapter. Given that the case study considered here is based in the EU region and specifically in the UK, the relevant legislation is discussed later, within the case study.

Questions

1. Describe the legislative framework for MSW management and EfW plants in your country.
2. If you were to make an application for a planning permission for a new EfW plant in your town, which authority would you apply to? What kind of documentation would you have to prepare?

10.3.3 Economic Considerations

The EfW plants require high capital investments as well as operating and maintenance costs. Hence, the resulting cost per tonne of waste incinerated can be rather high compared with the other options, such as landfilling. For example, in the USA, incineration costs range from about $400–$550 per tonne of waste, while landfilling costs are between $60 and $270 (McKinney and Schoch, 2003). These costs are much lower in developing countries; for example, in the South East Asia the incineration costs range from $25 to $100 per tonne of

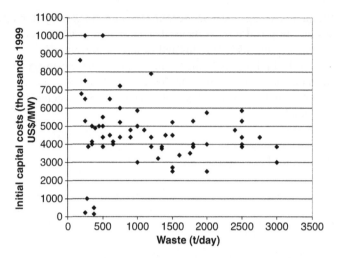

Figure 10.11   *Capital costs of EfW plants in the USA for different plant capacities (based on the data from EIA (2001))*

waste, with an average cost of $50 per tonne, while the landfilling costs range from $10 to $40 (Rand *et al.*, 2000).

The following sections give a brief overview of the capital and operating costs in different countries.

10.3.3.1 Capital Costs

Capital costs of an EfW plant depend on a wide range of factors, including the type and size of combustor, waste throughput, heating value of the waste, type of energy recovered and environmental legislation. Figure 10.11 shows the influence of the plant size on the capital costs: the usual economies of scale apply, so that the smaller plants are more expensive per tonne of waste incinerated. For example, an EfW facility which burns 500 t/day of waste costs on average £6000/MW, which is 1.5 times more expensive than a facility burning 2000 t/day of MSW.

Building a typical mass-burn incinerator in the USA that can treat around 500 t/day of waste would cost around $120 million, whilst the plant treating 2000 t/day would cost between $160 and $200 million.

Capital costs of EfW plants in the EU countries are shown in Table 10.11. The costs are based on the 1990 data, so that the costs for the latter years are projections rather than the actual data.

10.3.3.2 Operating Costs

Operating costs include fixed and variable costs. The former comprise cost of administration and salaries while the latter include costs of chemicals for the flue gas cleaning system, cost of electricity (which will be offset if the plant is producing electricity), cost of

Table 10.11 Costs and technical performance of EfW plants (adapted from EC (2006))

Parameter	1980	1985	1990	1995	2000	2005	2010
Typical unit size (MWe)	4–7	4–11	5–18	10–27	11–29	15–30	15–30
Availability factor (%)	80	80	85	85	90	90	90
Fuel efficiency (%)	14	16	18	20	22	23	24
Energy consumption rate (% of output)	10	10	12	12	15	15	15
Construction time (years)	2	2	2	2–3	2–3	2–3	2–3
Economic lifetime (years)	20	20	20	20	20	20	20
Capital cost (£[1990]/kW)	3153–3941	3448–3621	2759–3678	1931–2483	1856–2445	1343–2359	1276–2241
Operation and maintenance cost (£[1990]/kW)	268–315	234–280	184–245	145–166	131–151	116–129	110–123
Fuel cost (£[1990]/kWh)	–(0.01 to 0.03)	–(0.01 to 0.06)	–(0.01 to 0.07)	–(0.01 to 0.09)	–(0.01 to 0.1)	–(0.02 to 0.1)	–(0.02 to 0.1)
Cost of energy derived from above data, using 8 % discount rate (pence [1990]/kWh)	6–8	2.3–8	1–7.5	0.9–7.5	0.5–3.7	0.47–3.26	0.47–2.8

Conversion rate: £1 = 2.145 ECU (1990).
Assumptions underlying the cost and technical performance data for MSW incinerators:

1. During the 1980s a significant proportion of the facilities (about 35 %) were just incinerators (no power recovery) and, compared with later facilities, with low throughput capacities. Further, the gas cleaning equipment was rudimentary – usually only dust control. Power generation efficiencies were also low (about 350 kWh/t compared with 500 kWh/t for modern plant). Capital costs per kilowatt are, therefore, comparatively high.
2. The newer facilities require a greater capital investment because of gas cleaning requirement and so on, but have increased throughput to be more cost effective, and are more efficient power generators – hence the lowering in costs on a per kilowatt basis.
3. The fuel cost is negative, as this is effectively the waste disposal fee which, in the early years, was relatively low, about £(1990)2–9/t, but now ranges from £(1990)5/t to £(1990)42/t. In future, the lower costs are expected to rise more quickly than the higher ones, such that by 2010 the costs will range from £(1990)14/t to £(1990)52/t.
4. The impact of this increase in waste disposal cost, taken together with better power generation efficiencies and lower capital costs per kilowatt, is to reduce the energy costs from a high of about 8 pence(1990)/kWh to a value in the range 0.47–2.8 pence(1990)/kWh for the future.

Table 10.12 *Estimates of externalities of landfill and incineration (The UK Government, 1995)*

Waste management option	Externalities (£/t waste)
Incineration with energy recovery	−£4.00
Incineration without energy recovery	£5.00
Landfill with energy recovery	£1.00
Landfill without energy recovery	£3.50

[Note: Derived from 'Externalities of Landfill and Incineration' by Powell, 1993].

water and handling of waste water and cost of residue disposal. Additional operating costs are related to maintenance, which comprise costs to maintain the equipment and the buildings. Finally, waste collection and transportation also contribute to the total operating costs. For example, the average operating costs in Europe are around £70/t (Juniper, 2000) or £140 000/MW (EC, 2006). The average transportation costs are around £10/100 km.

The operating costs of EfW plants are offset by an income from the energy recovered and through the tipping fees, which are paid by the local authorities to the operators of EfW plants to treat the waste.

10.3.3.3 Externalities

The capital and operating costs are known as 'internal' costs and they represent direct costs associated with incineration. However, it is also important to know the total cost to the environment and society of waste management. These are known as 'externalities' and take into account environmental damage caused by a waste management option. However, they are very difficult to estimate and are associated with large uncertainties. Nevertheless, some estimates of externalities have been made and these are listed in Table 10.12. These data should be interpreted with care and only as a relative indication of what it might cost the environment and society to incinerate the waste rather than to landfill it. The estimated externalities include emissions of greenhouse gases (CH_4 and CO_2), acid gases (sulfur dioxide and nitrogen oxides), volatile organic compounds (VOCs), leachates, transport-related impacts and pollution displacement from the energy recovery. The emissions of dioxins from incinerators are not included. The negative values for incineration with energy recovery show the importance of pollution displacement which would have otherwise been generated through the use of conventional fuels.

For example, a municipal incinerator which burns 135 000 t of MSW a year, producing about 34 MW of heat for 3500 dwellings, saves around 170×10^6 kWh of fossil fuel energy and 30 000 t of CO_2 each year, which would have been produced by burning fossil fuels.

Questions

1. Explain how capital and operating costs can be calculated for an EfW plant.
2. Use the cost data given in Figure 10.11 and Table 10.11 to compare the costs of incineration in the USA and Europe. What do you conclude?
3. What are the capital and operating costs of EfW plants in your country? Discuss the sources, age and reliability of the cost data.

4. Explain the meaning of 'externalities' in the context of MSW management and particularly the EfW option. How are these externalities calculated?

10.3.4 Social Considerations

There are a number of different stakeholder groups whose interests and concerns must be taken into account when considering EfW systems. As shown in Table 10.13, in addition to the plant operators, other stakeholders include local communities, citizens, nongovernmental organizations (NGOs), waste-handling companies and energy producers. 'Scavengers' are also important in developing countries, as they are involved in collection and sorting of waste for reuse and recycling.

The interests and concerns raised by these stakeholders are often diametrically opposed. For example, the waste-handling and plant operators have an active interest in building new EfW facilities, as they wish to maintain or expand their business. On the other hand, community groups, neighbours, NGOs and the general public are likely to be against proposals for new EfW plants.

Table 10.13 Typical stakeholders for the EfW systems

Stakeholders	Stakeholder interests	Possible stakeholder influence
Neighbours and community groups	Concerned that the proposed EfW plant would lead to an increase in noise, dust, traffic and visual impact and a reduction of property prices; on the other hand, interested in increased employment opportunities	Delay, change in specification of the EfW plant and/or refusal of planning permission due to protests
NGOs	Interested in reducing the impact of waste management on the environment; primarily promoted minimization of waste and recycling	Delay, change in specification of the EfW plant and/or refusal of planning permission due to protests
Scavengers	Concerned that changed waste management practices may affect or eliminate their source of income	Scavengers' activities may affect the properties and amounts of waste; in some countries they have a strong political influence opposing EfW plants
Waste-handling companies	Interested in collection and transport of waste for EfW plants in order to maintain or expand their business	Can dictate the collection, transportation and tipping fees and increase the operating costs of EfW plants
EfW operators	Wish to maintain or expand their business; interested in reliable and increasing waste streams	Can lobby local authorities and influence the planning process
(Large) energy producers	Opposition to purchase of energy from smaller external producers (such as EfW plants)	Can be a barrier to sale of energy at local market prices; can dictate the price of energy

In fact, public acceptability of incineration is a very important issue and is often the main obstacle in building new EfW plants. There are two main reasons for this: the not-in-my-back-yard (NIMBY) syndrome and the concern related to pollution from incineration and the impacts on human health and the environment. Dioxins and furans in particular are a subject of a continuing debate between the proponents and opponents of EfW systems over the levels of emissions and the related human toxicity. The issue of dioxins is very serious indeed and, as shown in the UK, it can have very serious consequences (see Box 10.4). Furthermore, some stakeholders object to the visual impact, odour and noise from EfW facilities, increased transport activities in their area associated with waste handling and the effect on their own property's value. On the other hand, the local communities may also be interested in the new employment opportunities that the EfW systems provide, both during their construction and operation.

Box 10.4   Dioxin pollution: the case of the Byker incinerator in Newcastle, UK

The following *Guardian* (2003) article illustrates the scope of the problem and the controversy caused by the use of mixed bottom and fly ash from the Byker incinerator as a 'soil improver' over the allotments in Newcastle upon Tyne in the northeast of England.

Dioxins in city may be worst case in UK

David Hencke, Westminster correspondent, *Guardian*
  Tuesday, Feb 13, 2001
  The spreading of poisoned incinerator ash over allotments in Newcastle upon Tyne's poorest area was one of the worst cases of dioxin contamination in Britain, an independent investigator said yesterday.
  The consumption of eggs, poultry and vegetables produced on 22 allotments in the city was banned last year after 2,000 tonnes of incinerator ash was spread in Byker, in the constituency of the agriculture minister, Nick Brown.
  The report, by Alan Watson, an independent scientist, was commissioned by residents. Separate reports by the environment agency and the food standards agency released last night confirmed high levels of metal contamination and the presence of high levels of dioxins – which can cause cancer – in the eggs of hens raised on the allotments. The environment agency has also revealed that the allotments were already highly polluted before the ash was spread. A fourth report, by Newcastle University, analysed the findings.
  The disclosure of the findings, which had been held back for six months, provoked a big row between residents and the city council at a meeting in Byker last night. Newcastle council and the Newcastle and North Tyneside health authority have agreed to continue the ban on the consumption of eggs and poultry raised on the allotments as 'a precautionary measure'. But they claimed that, although the level of dioxins was high, it was not a serious danger to health.

Last year the council removed all the ash – which had been there for up to eight years – from the allotments, footpaths and bridleways in the city. Toddlers were prevented from playing on the allotments in case they ate the ash.

The council and Cambridge-based Combined Heat and Power face 19 charges between them of illegally disposing of toxic waste.

Dr Watson's report said: 'The contamination of allotments in Newcastle by high levels of dioxins and heavy metals from the Byker incinerator could be one of the most serious dioxin contamination events in the UK … this is because it is nearly unprecedented to have high levels of dioxin-contaminated material being introduced so directly on to land used for personal food supplies including eggs for a large number of people.'

He accused the food standards agency and environment agency of not doing a thorough job. He said they had failed to assess the dioxin intakes of children under the age of 10 and had ignored the effect of dioxins on people who might have eaten the contaminated hens. He said there could be other contaminated sites in Newcastle that had not been identified. 'In at least some of the cases the allotments will need to be cleared completely, with new topsoil being supplied.'

Last night Newcastle council condemned Dr Watson's findings. A spokesman said: 'He is the only person who seems to have drawn such a conclusion – neither the food standards agency nor the environment agency are saying that the risk to health is so serious.'

The reports from the two agencies and the analysis by Newcastle University all confirm heavy contamination. The University revealed that severe soil contamination with heavy metals and arsenic was found in more than half the allotments – and warned that other sources as well as the incinerator could be responsible. It also found that many of the eggs tested had dioxin levels 'well in excess of levels found in supermarket barn eggs'.

Both the environment agency and the food standards agency thought that people would have to have consumed huge quantities of produce to run a serious risk.

In many countries, the opposition by some stakeholders to new incineration plants is very strong and can often lead to a refusal of the planning permission for a new plant. These groups advocate waste minimization and recycling instead, arguing that new incinerators encourage increased consumption and generation of waste. However, one problem with waste minimization and recycling is that it has so far failed to reduce the amount of solid waste significantly because of the lack of public participation and inadequate recycling facilities. A survey on public perception of MSW and recycling carried out in the UK confirms that recycling is important but will not on its own be able to achieve the targets for reducing the amount of MSW that is disposed of in landfills (see Box 10.5).

Therefore, we have to find alternative ways of dealing with the growing amount of MSW waste, and EfW may be one of these alternatives within an integrated waste management strategy. However, this can only be an alternative if EfW plants can be designed and operated in a sustainable way. The following case study illustrates what needs to be taken into account in an attempt to achieve this goal by considering relevant technical, environmental, economic and social issues. It also illustrates the complexity of the problem, which involves a number of stakeholders with different and often opposing interests.

Box 10.5   Public perception of MSW and recycling (EA, 2002c)

This survey, carried out by the Environment Agency for England and Wales, found out the following:

- On the whole, people would participate in recycling if the councils provided a means of sorting waste for recycling, but time is an issue.
- Some 28 % people feel that they do not have time to sort their rubbish – a view that is most strongly held among younger, convenience-food-using people.
- Potential for waste is exacerbated by two-for-one offers in supermarkets. Usually, economizing triumphs over environmental responsibility – even among environmentally responsible people.
- On the whole, people do not think recycled products are of inferior quality, but a third do perceive them as being more expensive than nonrecycled products.
- People see the point in recycling and claim to mend or repair broken/worn out possessions and buy more durable products.
- It seems that willingness to mend/repair and purchase of more durable products is economy driven, not conscience driven.
- Though people know that avoiding products with lots of packaging will significantly reduce waste, relatively few do so.
- Significant recycling is limited to newspapers and glass – items that are easily recycled because the council either collects or provides street recycling points.
- Although people recycle newspapers (58 %), only a small proportion (33 %) recycles cardboard boxes.
- Hardly anyone recycles plastic packaging (11 %); a greater, yet still small (22 %), proportion recycles plastic bottles. This compares with 60 % for glass bottles and 35 % for drinks cans.
- Charging by amount of rubbish produced was unpopular – 58 % opposed such an idea.
- Some 90 % would be certain or very likely to sort rubbish for recycling if their local council provided containers. Similar proportions claim that they would sort if they were charged varying amounts of £10 per year to £100 per year, suggesting that fees may do little to increase participation.

Conclusions of the survey

- The concept of sorting and recycling is favourably received by the public – the majority claim they would recycle more if they were provided easier means to sort rubbish.
- The public has a reasonable degree of knowledge of recycling issues, but remain uncertain as to the environmental advantages and disadvantages of landfilling versus incinerating, and how to dispose of more 'difficult' products, such as paint, household chemicals and pesticides.
- However, there is a significant minority, of between a fifth and a quarter, who are not willing to participate in responsible waste management. These tend to be younger, non-environmentally committed, time-starved people, those living in rented accommodation and more elderly households.

Starting with the choice of the technology and design of the plant, the case study guides the reader through the environmental, economic and social assessment of the EfW plant, as required by the planning application process in many countries.

Read on to find out which stakeholder group – the proposers or the opponents – won the argument and if the planning application for this EfW plant has been successful.

Questions

1. Emissions of dioxins are one of the main objections of the public to incineration and EfW plant. However, dioxins are also emitted from open fires, such as home fireplaces. It is known that the effect on human health of fireplaces is greater than that from incinerators (why?). Discuss why you think that people accept this health risk and yet they object to incinerators.
2. Comment on the Byker incineration case outlined in Box 10.4. What is your view on the affair? Explain and justify your position.
3. Find out what the NGOs in your area or country do with respect to incinerators. Compare that with the Greenpeace action – visit their website for more information.
4. You are the managing director of an EfW plant. Your plant manager calls you at home in the early morning in panic to inform you that several members of Greenpeace have climbed the stack of the plant and chained themselves to it. The press has already arrived to the site. What actions do you take?

10.4 Case Study: A Proposal for a New EfW Plant

This case study is based on a real proposal for a new EfW in England. The following describes the development of the case, from design, through sustainability assessment to the final decision of the local authority on whether to grant the planning permission. The names of the place and the actors have been concealed to preserve confidentiality.

10.4.1 Problem Definition

A county council (CC) in England is considering various options for MSW management. Following the waste management hierarchy discussed in Sections 10.1 and 10.2, the CC has already put in place a strategy for waste reduction and materials recovery through recycling. However, although improving, the strategy is not helping to reduce significantly the amount of MSW disposed in the regional landfills. Currently, out of almost 600 000 t of MSW generated each year within the county, only 13% is recycled and the remaining 87% is landfilled. Even if the recycling rates are increased to the target 25% set by the EU, the county will still have 450 000 t of waste per year to treat or dispose of by other means.

In the meantime, the region is running out of landfill space with the predictions that the last licensed landfill site will reach its capacity in 3 years' time. It is unlikely that a new landfill site will be opened due to the increasing objections by the public to new landfill facilities. The CC, therefore, is willing to consider energy recovery as one of the longer

term options that could help it deal with the increasing amounts of waste generated each year. However, the CC is aware that this is going to be a very contentious issue, as the local population and other stakeholders are likely to oppose the proposal for an EfW plant, particularly as this would be the first incinerator in the whole county.

Nevertheless, given its own pressures related to MSW management, the CC has identified an existing industrial site as a possible location for an MSW incinerator and has invited a reputable, locally based waste management company 'WEnergise' to put together a proposal for an EfW plant. The company's task is to design a sustainable EfW system which will be able to handle 225 000 t of waste per year.

To accomplish this task, WEnergise has put together a design team consisting of three engineers and an environmental scientist. In addition, the company lawyer has been made available to the design team for guidance and advice on the planning process and environmental legislation. Furthermore, the company has also contracted an environmental consultancy firm to help the design team with the environmental assessments of the proposed plant as required by the relevant EU and UK legislation.

Having examined a number of options, the design team has put forward a design for an EfW plant generating, on average, 20 MW of electricity. The team has also considered the use of heat for district heating in addition to electricity generation, but has decided against it because of the lack of the district heating infrastructure. However, they have designed the plant so as to enable an easy modification, should district heating become a feasible option at a later stage.

In putting the proposal together, the team has evaluated the level of sustainability of the following five design options:

- **Base case:** Moving grate furnace with SNCR for NO_x removal and semi-dry removal of acid gases.
- **Option 1:** Fluidized bed furnace with dry removal of acid gases.
- **Option 2:** Moving grate with SNCR for NO_x removal and dry removal of acid gases.
- **Option 3:** Moving-grate furnace with semi-dry removal of acid gases.
- **Option 4:** Moving-grate furnace with SNCR for NO_x removal and wet removal of acid gases.
- **Option 5:** Moving-grate furnace with SCR for NO_x removal and semi-dry removal of acid gases.

As required by the EU Directives on Integrated Pollution Prevention and Control (IPPC) and Environmental Impact Assessment (EIA), the design team has assessed these options with the help of the environmental consultancy on the technical, economic, environmental and social performance and have concluded that the base case is the most sustainable EfW option.

Following this decision, and as required by the EU and UK law, WEnergise has submitted the required documentation for a planning permission to the CC, including an application for the IPPC Authorization and the EIA Statement.

As expected by both the CC and WEnergise, the proposal has attracted a considerable public interest with the local residents vigorously opposing the proposal and organizing an anti-incinerator movement. As a result, the CC has solicited written opinions from the various stakeholders to try to resolve the issue. The following sections recount this whole process, from the design of the incinerator, through the sustainability assessment of the options to the issues raised by the public and other stakeholders, and the final decision of the CC on whether to grant a planning permission for this EfW application. The reader is invited to participate in this process by challenging both the design and sustainability assessment of the plant carried out by the WEnergise team and the environmental consultancy, as well as the arguments and opinions of the other stakeholders.

Questions

1. If you were a managing director of WEnergise and had to put a design team together to design an EfW plant, which professions would you want to include in the team and why?
2. Use Table 10.13 to identify the stakeholders for the proposed EfW plant and try to predict their position on the proposal.

10.4.2 Design Considerations

10.4.2.1 Overview of the Base Case Design

The base case design of the EfW plant as proposed by the WEnergise design team is shown in Figure 10.12. The proposed plant consists of four parts:

1. waste handling facility;
2. incinerator and energy recovery plant, including the incinerator, turbine and generator;
3. air pollution prevention and flue gas treatment plant; and
4. bottom ash treatment facility.

As this is a complex system, the team has built the design step by step, by first considering each part separately and then connecting and optimizing them in an integrated design. The design process is discussed in more detail further below.

10.4.2.1.1 Waste Handling Facility

This part of the plant consists of the waste reception and storage areas. The waste will be weighted on arrival and then tipped into the storage bunker. Waste in the bunker will be mixed regularly to homogenize it, identify noncombustible items and avoid malodorous (anaerobic) decomposition.

10.4.2.1.2 Incinerator and Energy Recovery Plant

Waste from the storage bunker will be transferred by overhead cranes to the feed hoppers of the mass-burn moving-grate incinerator. To be able to process the predicted throughput of 225 000 t/year of waste, the team has chosen two incinerator units with the total capacity of 28.6 t/h or 14.3 t/h each. With an estimated average LHV of 9800 kJ/kg, this amount of waste will be generating 20 MW of electricity.

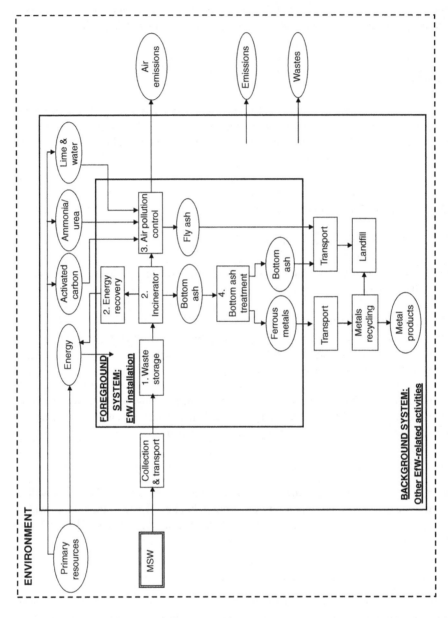

Figure 10.12   *Block diagram of the proposed EfW plant from 'cradle to grave' (excluding construction of the plant)*

10.4.2.1.3 Air Pollution Prevention and Control Plant

In this proposed design, SNCR will be used to remove nitrogen oxides by injection of either aqueous ammonia or dry urea into the incinerator. The formation of dioxins and furans during combustion will be prevented by an online control of the combustion temperature and the residence time of the flue gas in the combustor, as well as by a subsequent rapid cooling of the combustion gases to below 200 °C to prevent the formation of these pollutants by *de novo* synthesis. Acid gases, such as SO_2, HCl and HF, will be scrubbed in a semi-dry cyclone with lime slurry, $Ca(OH)_2$. A proportion of the larger particles will also be removed in the cyclone, while the fly ash particles will be removed in a fabric filter following the semi-dry cyclone. The design team has estimated that, depending on the composition of the waste, the amount of fly ash captured will be around 8300 t/year, all of which will be disposed in a licensed landfill.

In addition to these air pollution control measures, activated carbon will be injected into the flue gas between the cyclone and the filter to remove mercury and other metals, as well as any dioxins formed during the flue gas treatment. Further amounts of these pollutants will also be adsorbed within the filter onto the lime particles which remain in the flue gas after the cyclone. The cleaned flue gas will then be discharged through a 70 m high flue stack.

10.4.2.1.4 Bottom Ash Treatment Facility

Depending on the waste composition, the plant will produce on average 47 800 t of bottom ash residue per year. The ash will represent approximately 25% by weight or 8% by volume of the original waste and will contain less than 3% unburned carbon. It will be discharged from the bottom of the incinerator by an ash discharger onto vibrating conveyors, which will deliver the ash residue into a residues bunker. A drum magnet above the conveyor will extract ferrous materials, which will be recycled.

10.4.2.2 Technical Challenges

The design team is well aware that burning MSW to recover energy poses many technical challenges. Some of these are related to its variable composition, heating value and water content, which influence the amount of energy that can be recovered, as well as the flue gas emissions and related requirements for pollution prevention and control. Therefore, they first have to determine these variables and the extent to which they may vary so that the designed plant can cope under different operating conditions.

The next task for the design team is to estimate the following parameters:

- total heat released by combustion of the waste;
- efficiency of the turbine and the efficiency of energy conversion – from heat into electricity;
- material and energy balances of the plant, including the flow rates of the steam.

The following section discusses some of these parameters that have been calculated by the team. Owing to space limitations, it is not possible to discuss the calculations in detail, so that in most cases only the final result is given. However, the reader is invited to complete the calculations and check the accuracy of the results obtained by the design team.

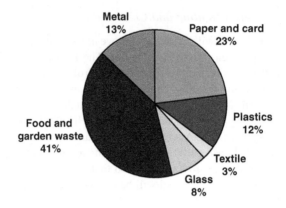

Figure 10.13   *Average composition of the MSW to be used in the EfW plant (composition by weight)*

10.4.2.2.1 Quantity and Composition of Waste

The average amount of waste that will be available for collection and incineration is estimated at 225 000 t of MSW per year. Figure 10.13 shows the expected average composition of the MSW, while Tables 10.14 and 10.15 give the average results of proximate and ultimate analyses of waste. The design team has used these data to determine on the Tanner triangle (Figure 10.9) whether the waste is suitable for combustion.

Table 10.14   *Composition of waste by weight on a wet basis (proximate analysis) and its energy content*

	Composition (% by wet weight)				Heating value (MJ/kg)	
	Moisture	Volatiles	Fixed carbon	Ash	LHV	HHV
Paper and card	6	80	11	3	15.5	24
Plastics	0.1	97	2	1	32.7	39
Textile	6	70	21	3	18.3	23
Glass	1	0	0	99	0.2	0.2
Food and garden waste	55	40	3	2	4.2	21
Metal	4	0	0	96	0.7	1

Table 10.15   *Composition of waste on a dry basis (ultimate analysis)*

	Composition (% by dry weight)					
	Carbon	Hydrogen	Oxygen	Nitrogen	Sulfur	Ash
Paper and card	57.5	6	30	0.3	0.2	6
Plastics	68	7	23	0	0	2
Textile	67.8	4	18	5	0.2	5
Glass	0.5	0.1	0.3	0.1	0	99
Food and garden waste	60	6	26	2.5	0.5	5
Metal	1.5	0.6	1.8	0.1	0	96

Using the results for LHV and HHV for each component of the waste shown in Table 10.14, the team has estimated that the LHV of waste is about 9800 kJ/kg and the HHV is around 19 600 kJ/kg.

Questions

1. Use the results of the proximate and ultimate analysis shown in Table 10.14 and Table 10.15 to find on the Tanner diagram (Figure 10.9) the point which defines this waste. What do you think the design team concluded about the suitability of the waste for incineration?
2. Examine the waste composition and heating values of the waste given in Figure 10.13 and Tables 10.14 and 10.15 and answer the following questions:
   - i. Which materials in the MSW will contribute to energy generation and which materials have little energy value?
   - ii. Use the data in Tables 10.14 and 10.15 to check that the design team have calculated correctly the LHV and HHV respectively for the waste composition given in Figure 10.13.
   - iii. Use Equations 10.1–10.3 to check how well the LHV and HHV that you calculated above agree.
3. How does the waste composition shown in Figure 10.13 differ from the waste composition in your region? Is the waste in your region suitable for incineration and energy recovery? Why?

10.4.2.2.2 Energy Efficiency

As already mentioned, to be able to process 225 000 t/year of waste, the design team has chosen an incinerator with a total capacity of 28.6 t/h of waste. This capacity is based on an estimated availability of the plant of 7867 operating hours per year. Two incineration units will be used, each with the capacity of 14.3 t/h of waste. The waste will be incinerated in the presence of 47.6 t/h of primary air and 31.7 t/h of secondary air. The primary air will be heated to about 100 C in the furnace air preheater before entering the furnace; secondary air will go directly to the furnace without preheating. To ensure maximum oxidation of dioxins and other organic pollutants, after the last injection of air, the flue gas will be held at the temperature above 850 °C for at least 2 s in the presence of at least 6% of oxygen.

For these operating conditions, the team has estimated the total heat release of 77.9 MW, which will be utilized in the boiler to raise steam. The energy efficiency is estimated at 31.7 %.

However, the team knows that this is well in excess of the heat load that will actually be passed to the steam due to heat losses. Furthermore, they also have to take into account situations whereby some very wet or otherwise incombustible waste has been fed to the incinerator so that the use of additional fuel (oil or natural gas) may be necessary.

Questions

1. Show that burning 28.6 t/h of waste with the lower heating value of 9800 kJ/kg will release 77.9 MW of heat.
2. If the EfW plant is producing 20 MW of electricity and 15% of that is used to run the plant, calculate the net export of electricity from the site.

3. Calculate how much coal is saved each year in a power station, equivalent to the net exported electricity generated by burning MSW. Repeat the same calculation for oil and natural gas. Use the following lower heating values of the fuel and the heat-to-electricity conversions:
   - Coal: LHV $= 17$ MJ/kg, $\eta = 33\%$;
   - Oil: LHV $= 42$ MJ/kg, $\eta = 40\%$; and
   - Gas: LHV $= 35$ MJ/m^3, $\eta = 42\%$.
4. Discuss the implications of burning wet waste and the use of additional (fossil) fuel to maintain combustion of the wet waste.
5. Given the total amount of waste to be burnt per day, which incineration technology would you chose (see Section 10.3.1.2) and with how many units? Is your choice different from the choice of the WEnergise team?
6. Why is it desirable to preheat the primary air before combustion? How would you preheat it?
7. The energy efficiency for the design proposed by the design team is 31.7%. Can you propose a configuration that is more energy efficient? Their proposal is based on a closed-feed heater to preheat the boiler water up to about 137 °C, combined with the intermediate pressure (IP) steam sub-cooling to about 56 °C to take the advantage of the fact that IP steam is condensed at about 46 °C so that more energy can be recovered from the system.

10.4.2.2.3 Pollution Prevention and Control

In addition to designing for different waste composition and energy efficiency, the design team must also make sure that the plant is optimized on environmental performance. The following air pollutants will be formed in the combustion process:

- nitrogen oxides (NO and NO_2);
- sulfur oxides (SO_2);
- carbon oxides (CO and CO_2);
- hydrogen chloride and hydrogen fluoride (HCl and HF);
- particulates (fly ash);
- heavy metals and their compounds;
- organic compounds, including dioxins and furans.

To prevent the formation and control the emissions of these pollutants, the team has decided to combine both the primary and secondary measures for the prevention and control of air pollutants (see Section 10.3.2.1 for an overview of these measures). The layout of their proposed design of the air pollution prevention and control plant is given in Figure 10.14.

Primary measures: After a careful consideration of the options and their effects on the air pollutants as summarized in Table 10.9, the team has chosen the primary air preheat to reduce the formation of CO and hydrocarbons, including dioxins, and to improve the potential for bottom ash recycling (e.g. in the construction applications). However, the air preheat will increase the formation of NO_x, which will be controlled by SNCR, as explained further below.

Furthermore, the constant movement of the grate will continuously rotate the burning waste, enabling the formation of a homogeneous bed and promoting the burnout of waste.

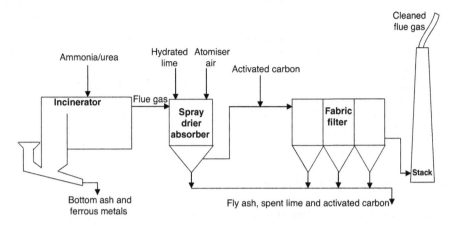

Figure 10.14   *The air pollution prevention and control plant*

This will in turn ensure the destruction of dioxins, furans and other volatile organic compounds and improve the potential for recycling of the furnace bottom ash.

Secondary measures: As shown in Figure 10.14, the proposed flue gas clean-up plant comprises:

- SNCR of NO_x to nitrogen and water by injection of ammonia or urea into the boiler;
- semi-dry scrubber for removal of acid gases with lime slurry;
- fabric filters for removal of particulates (fly ash);
- system for removal of waste/recycled product from the filters and the absorber; and
- injection of activated carbon to remove dioxins, furans and metals.

After the rapid cooling of the flue gas within the boiler, the gases exit the boiler and enter a cyclone spray dryer where a lime slurry is atomized into the gas stream. The temperature of the flue gas will be maintained at 130–150 °C by water injection, to prevent the formation of dioxins by synthesis *de novo*. The temperature drop may also cause condensation of certain metals (for example, mercury and organic compounds) onto the lime particles. Some lime particles will be collected at the bottom of the cyclone, while the finer particles will be collected on to a fabric filter, which is installed downstream from the semi-dry system. The expected lime usage is between 15 and 21 kg/t of waste burned, depending on the HCl content.

However, before the flue gas is passed into the fabric filters to collect the fly ash, the activated carbon is injected upstream of the filter to promote the removal of dioxins, gaseous mercury and some other heavy metals.

Depending on the content of the acid gases, the operating temperature of the filter will be held at around 140 °C or slightly above the acid dew point to prevent the condensation of the acid gases and the resulting damage to the filter fabric.

Questions

1. Consider the effects of different primary measures on the formation of the pollutants shown in Table 10.9. Which of these measures would you use to control pollution from

the EfW plant considered in this case study and why? Is your choice different from the choice made by the design team? If so, why?

2. Which secondary air pollution measures would you choose and why? Discuss their advantages and disadvantages.
3. Why is the acid dew point important for the operation of fabric filters? Find out how the content of acid gases such as SO_2 and HCl affect the acid dew point. What happens if the acid dew point is above 200 °C and how does that affect the design of the air pollution control plant?

10.4.3 Environmental Considerations

Having designed the EfW plant, the next task for the WEnergise team is to carry out an environmental assessment of their proposed design. Since the proposed EfW plant is subject to both the IPPC and EIA directives, the team has to identify and quantify all potential releases to air, water and land from the construction and operation of the plant, together with the measures that will be used to prevent or reduce these releases. Their assessment, carried out in collaboration with the contracted environmental consultancy, is summarized in the sections below.

Both the IPPC and EIA directives require quantification of environmental impacts during the construction and operation of the plant. Although the information required by the IPPC and EIA is similar and proposers can use parts of the IPPC documentation for the EIA and vice versa in their application for a new EfW plant, further work is needed for both types of application and normally involves a significant effort to carry out.

Space precludes detailed considerations of both types of application, so that this section focuses on the IPPC requirements. The EIA findings are presented at the end of the section.

One of the requirements of the IPPC Directive is that the emissions and discharges into the environment of the prescribed and other substances from the proposed EfW installation should be prevented or controlled by using best available technique (BAT). The BAT should be based on the balance between environmental benefits and economic costs and should consider the impacts of both the foreground system (i.e. the installation) and the background system (other related activities). Furthermore, identification of the BAT must be based on a life cycle approach, including the use of energy and raw materials and pollution from both the foreground and background systems, as shown in Figure 10.15 (note that this diagram is based on a more detailed system outline shown in Figure 10.12).

10.4.3.1 The Foreground System: The EfW Plant

10.4.3.1.1 Energy and Raw Materials

In addition to generating energy, the EfW plant will use some energy to run the pumps, air-cooling fans, conveyors, air pollution control equipment and so on. The design team have estimated that the plant will use 15% of the energy generated.

The raw materials will include lime, water, ammonia or urea and activated carbon. The estimated quantities of the raw materials that will be used in the EfW plant are listed in Table 10.16.

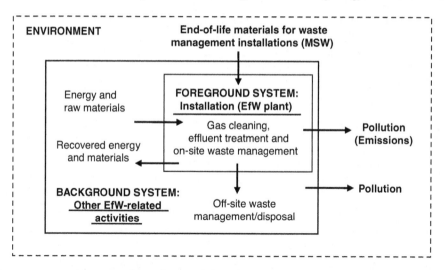

Figure 10.15 *The system boundary and the life cycle stages considered within an IPPC application for a new EfW plant (adapted from Nicholas et al. (2000))*

10.4.3.1.2 Gas Cleaning, Effluent Treatment and On-Site Waste Management

The emissions of the prescribed substances for air will be controlled by the air pollution prevention and control plant described in Section 10.4.2.2.3 (Pollution prevention and control).

10.4.3.1.3 Pollution (Emissions)

Air pollution: To estimate the air emissions from the EfW plant, the WEnergise design team and the environmental consultancy have used two main sources of information:

- the average air emission factors for the construction and operation of an EfW plant, as shown in Table 10.17;
- the air emission limits from incinerators as prescribed by the EC Waste Incineration Directive and summarized in Table 10.18.

Using the maximum emission limits listed in Table 10.18, the team has estimated the total annual air emissions which are summarized in Table 10.19.

Table 10.16 *Raw materials used in the EfW plant*

Raw material	Quantity (t/year)
Towns water	74 250
Lime	3375–4500
Activated carbon	100
Ammonia	370

Table 10.17 *Average emissions from EfW plants during construction of the plant and from combustion (EC, 2003c)*

Air pollutant	Emission factor (kg/TJ)
Combustion	
CO_2 (non-biomass)	99 850
SO_2	697
NO_x	843
Particulates	73
VOCs	47
Construction	
CO_2	1251
SO_2	10
NO_x	4

Table 10.18 *Air emission limit values from incinerators: Waste incineration directive 2000/76/EC (EC, 2000b)*

Daily average values (mg/m³)		
Total dust		10
Total organic carbon		10
Hydrogen chloride		10
Hydrogen fluoride		1
Sulfur dioxide		50
NO and NO_2 expressed as NO_2		
existing plant with capacity exceeding 6 t/h or new plant		200
existing plant with capacity of 6 t/h or less		400
Half-hourly average values (mg/m³)		
Total dust		30
Total organic carbon		20
Hydrogen chloride		60
Hydrogen fluoride		4
Sulfur dioxide		200
NO and NO_2 expressed as NO_2		
existing plant with capacity exceeding 3 t/h or new plant		400
Average values (mg/m³) over sample period:	min. 30 min	max. 8 h
Hg	0.05	0.1
Cd + Tl	0.05 (total)	0.1 (total)
Sb + As + Pb + Cr + Co + Cu + Mn + Ni + V	0.5 (total)	1 (total)
Average values (ng/m³) over sample period: min 6 h, max 8 h		
Dioxins and furans	0.1 (total)	
Carbon monoxide		
Daily average value (mg/m³)		50
10 min average value (mg/m³)		150
Half-hourly average values taken in any 24 h period (mg/m³)		100

Table 10.19 Assessing the significance of different air emission categories to identify BAT for air pollution prevention and control

Substance	Maximum daily mean release (g/s)	Maximum yearly mean release (kg/yr)	Long-term contribution				Short-term contribution			
			PCᵃ (μg/m³)	EALᵇ (μg/m³)	1% of EAL (μg/m³)	Significant	PC (μg/m³)	EAL (μg/m³)	10% of EAL (μg/m³)	Significant
Particulate matter (PM)	0.434	12 290	0.11	40	0.4	No	0.5	50	5	No
Hydrogen chloride (HCl)	0.434	12 290	0.11	20	0.2	No	5.7	800	80	No
Hydrogen fluoride (HF)	0.0434	1230	0.011	—	n/a	n/a	0.57	250	25	No
Sulfur dioxide (SO₂)	2.168	61 400	0.56	50	0.5	Yes	47	267	26.7	Yes
Nitrogen oxides (as NO₂)	8.674	245 660	2.24	40	0.4	Yes	96	200	20	Yes
Cadmium (Cd)	0.0022	62	0.0006	0.005	0.00005	Yes	0.028	1.5	0.15	No
Mercury (Hg)	0.0022	62	0.0006	0.25	0.0025	Yes	0.028	7.5	0.75	No
Antimony (Sb)	0.022	623	0.006	5	0.05	No	0.0028	150	15	No
Arsenic (As)	0.022	623	0.006	0.2	0.002	Yes	0.0028	15	1.5	No
Lead (Pb)	0.022	623	0.006	0.5	0.005	Yes	0.0028	n/a	n/a	n/a
Chromium (as CrVI)	0.022	623	0.006	0.1	0.001	Yes	0.0028	3	0.3	No
Cobalt (Co)	0.022	623	0.006	0.2	0.002	Yes	0.0028	6	0.6	No
Nickel (Ni)	0.022	623	0.006	1	0.01	No	0.0028	30	3	No
Vanadium (V)	0.022	623	0.006	5	0.05	No	0.0028	1	0.1	No
Carbon dioxide	3.6	102 895 000	—	n/a	n/a	n/a	n/a	n/a	n/a	n/a
Dioxins and furans	4.34 × 10⁻⁹	0.0001	1.12 × 10⁻⁹	n/a	n/a	n/a	n/a	n/a	n/a	n/a

ᵃ Process contribution
ᵇ Environmental assessment levels

To ensure that the emission of the air pollutants will not result in a significant decrease of air quality around the plant as required by the Ambient Air Framework Directive on the air quality standards (AQS) (see Table 10.20 for the AQS in the EU and UK), the design team has carried out air dispersion modelling to calculate the ground concentrations of the emitted air pollutants. Their results are shown in Table 10.21, also indicating the percentage of the contribution of the plant to the ground concentrations of the prescribed pollutants, relative to the prescribed AQS.

Water pollution: No process water will be released from the plant during normal operation so that no liquid effluent will be released to the surface or ground water except for the sewage, which will be discharged directly to the sewer.

Land pollution: The main types and quantities of solid waste that will arise from the combustion process are given in Table 10.22.

The expected composition of the bottom and fly ash estimated by the design team is shown in Table 10.23. Ferrous metals will be recycled in the background system; therefore, they will not be disposed of as waste.

Bottom ash can be recycled; however, initially at least, it is envisaged that the bottom ash will be landfilled together with the fly ash, spent lime particles and activated carbon.

Questions

1. Use the air emission results in Table 10.19 and air emission limits according to the EC Directive on Incineration shown in Table 10.18 to calculate the volume of the flue gas from the incinerator (R: 156 240 m^3/h).
2. Use the CO_2 emission factors shown in Table 10.8 and the LHV you calculated in question 2 in Section 10.4.2.2.1 (Quantity and composition of waste) to calculate the emissions of CO_2 and the equivalent contribution to global warming from the EfW plant. Note that the biogenic-derived CO_2 (e.g. CO_2 from burning paper and organic waste) is not counted in the total emission of CO_2. The global warming potential of CO_2 is equal to 1 kg CO_2 eq./kg CO_2 (see Chapter 3 for the calculation of global warming potential).
3. According to the US EPA (1999), the average emissions of CH_4 and CO_2 from decomposition of waste in landfills are 113 kg/t and 311 kg/t of MSW respectively. Calculate the contribution to global warming from landfilling of the 225 000 t/year of waste. Use the global warming potential of CH_4 over 100 years, equivalent to 25 kg CO_2 eq./kg CO_2. Compare that with the global warming from incineration of the same amount of waste that you calculated in the previous question. What do you conclude in terms of this impact? Is it better to landfill or incinerate?
4. Use the CO_2 emission factors below to calculate the savings or the increase in the CO_2 emissions from MSW incineration, compared with the electricity generated from a fuel mix and the electricity produced using coal only. What do you conclude? Is MSW incineration a better option for generating electricity in terms of the emissions of CO_2?

Table 10.20   *Environmental quality standards for air pollutants – the Ambient Air Framework Directive (99/30/EC)*

Substance	Reference period	EC Directive (99/30/EC) Limit value	To be met by	UK Air Quality Regulations Standards Limit value
Sulfur dioxide	Hourly mean	$350\,\mu g/m^3$ Exceeded no more than 24 times a year	1 Jan 2005	$350\,\mu g/m^3$ Exceeded no more than 24 times a year
	Daily mean (24 h)	$125\,\mu g/m^3$ Exceeded no more than 3 times a year	1 Jan 2005	$125\,\mu g/m^3$ Exceeded no more than 3 times a year
	15 min mean			$266\,\mu g/m^3$ Exceeded no more than 35 times a year
Particulate matter (PM10)	Daily mean (24 h)	$50\,\mu g/m^3$ Exceeded no more than 35 times a year	1 Jan 2005	$50\,\mu g/m^3$ Exceeded no more than 35 times a year
		$50\,\mu g/m^3$ Exceeded no more than 7 times a year	1 Jan 2010	
	Annual mean	$40\,\mu g/m^3$ $20\,\mu g/m^3$	1 Jan 2005 1 Jan 2010	$40\,\mu g/m^3$
Nitrogen dioxide	Hourly mean	$200\,\mu g/m^3$ Exceeded no more than 18 times a year	1 Jan 2010	$200\,\mu g/m^3$ Exceeded no more than 18 times a year
	Annual mean	$40\,\mu g/m^3$	1 Jan 2010	$40\,\mu g/m^3$
Ozone		$120\,\mu g/m^3$ Exceeded no more than 20 days a year averaged over 3 years	2010	
	Daily maximum of running 8 h mean			$100\,\mu g/m^3$
				Not exceeded more than 10 times a year
Carbon monoxide	8 h mean Running 8 h mean	$10\,\mu g/m^3$	1 Jan 2005	$11.6\,\mu g/m^3$
Benzene	Annual mean Running annual mean	$5\,\mu g/m^3$	1 Jan 2010	$16.25\,\mu g/m^3$
Lead	Annual mean	$0.5\,\mu g/m^3$	31 Dec 2004	$0.5\,\mu g/m^3$ $0.25\,\mu g/m^3$
1,3-Butadiene	Running annual mean			$2.25\,\mu g/m^3$

Table 10.21   *Summary results of the air quality impact assessment for the proposed EfW plant*

Substance	Reference period	Ground air concentration ($\mu g/m^3$)	UK Air Quality Standard (AQS) ($\mu g/m^3$)	Percentage of the AQS (%)
Sulfur Dioxide	Hourly mean	22	350	6.3
	Daily mean (24 h)	6	125	4.8
	15 min mean	47	266	18
Particulate matter (PM10)	Daily mean (24 h)	0.3	50	0.6
	Annual mean	0.11	40	0.3
Nitrogen dioxide	Hourly mean	48	200	24
	Annual mean	1.12	40	2.8
Benzene	Running annual mean	0.11	$16.25\,\mu g/m^3$	0.7
Lead (+ other heavy metals)	Annual mean	0.006	$0.5\,\mu g/m^3$	1.2
			$0.25\,\mu g/m^3$	2.4

Table 10.22   *Solid wastes arising and materials recovered from the EfW plant*

Material	Quantity (t/year)
Bottom ash	47 800
Fly ash	8 300
Spent lime	4 000
Ferrous metals	28 000
Activated carbon	100

Table 10.23   *Expected composition of the bottom and fly ash*

Major constituents	Bottom ash (% by weight)	Fly ash (% by weight)
Aluminium as Al_2O_3	7.2	2.3
Calcium as CaO	14.0	47.6
Copper as CuO	0.2	
Iron as Fe_2O_3	9.7	7.9
Lead as PbO	0.1	0.4
Magnesium as MgO	1.6	0.7
Phosphorus as P_2O_5	5.3	2.0
Potassium as K_2O	1.0	1.0
Silicon as SiO_2	42.9	5.4
Sodium as Na_2O	3.1	1.2
Titanium as TiO_2	0.8	0.4
Zinc as ZnO	0.1	1.4
Chloride as Cl	0.1	11.8
Sulfate as SO_3	0.2	0.6
Sulfate as SO_2	<0.1	0.6
Hydroxide as OH		11.5
Other, including heavy metals	0.2	0.3

	CO_2 emission $(kg/MW_{th})^a$	Efficiency of electricity generation (%)
Electricity (mix of different fuels, including nuclear energy)	166	38
Coal	300	33

[a] Note that the CO_2 emission factors are shown for the primary energy (i.e. per MW_{th}), which means that you need to divide these factors by the efficiency (fraction, not percentage) of electricity generation to obtain the emission of CO_2 per megawatt of electricity (MW_{el}).

5. Use the results in Table 10.23 to calculate the total yearly amounts of individual components of the bottom ash and fly ash that will have to be disposed of.
6. Use Figure 10.12 to show the inputs and outputs of materials and energy into and out of the EfW system, as well as their flows through the system.
7. Compare the predicted ground air concentrations of different pollutants with the AQSs, both given in Table 10.21. Is air pollution from the proposed EfW plant going to be significant? Why?

10.4.3.2 The Background System: Other Related Activities

10.4.3.2.1 Recovered Energy and Materials

The plant will generate 20 MW of electrical energy, all of which will be sold to the national grid, except for the energy used to run the plant, which has been estimated at 15% of the total energy generated.

On average, around 28 000 t of ferrous metals will be recovered from the plant and sold to a metals recycling company. As already mentioned, bottom ash could also potentially be reused, but currently it is envisaged to landfill it.

10.4.3.2.2 Off-Site Waste Management and Disposal

As already mentioned, 47 800 t/year of bottom ash and 8300 t/year of fly ash will have to be disposed of in a landfill. The ash will be transported together with the spent lime particles and activated carbon to the nearby landfill site every 5 days to reduce the impact of transport on the neighbourhood.

10.4.3.2.3 Pollution: Emissions to Air, Water and Land

Various emissions to air, water and land will be released in the background system. These include the emissions related to the collection and transport of waste to the foreground system, recycling of metals and disposal of the bottom and fly ash as well as the spent lime and activated carbon. Further impacts include the upstream impacts associated with the life cycle of the transport, recycling and waste disposal systems.

Questions

1. List the air and water emissions and solid waste that will be generated in the background system associated with this EfW plant. How easy would it be to quantify these emissions?

2. Which impacts do you think are more significant: those from the foreground or those from the background system? Why?
3. If you have access to LCA software, carry out an LCA of this EfW plant. Divide your system into the foreground and background and compare the impacts from each. What do you conclude?
4. On the basis of technical design and environmental assessment of the EfW plant carried out by the design team, do you think the planning permission for this plant should be granted? Justify your decision.

10.4.3.3 BAT Appraisal of Air Pollution Control Options

To justify their choice of the base case design of the EfW plant as the BAT among the six options they have considered, the design team has had to carry out a full BAT appraisal as prescribed by the IPPC Directive. For these purposes, they have followed the IPPC H1 Guidance on Environmental Assessment and Appraisal of the BAT for different air pollution control options (EA, 2002a). The results of their appraisal are shown in Tables 10.19–10.25. The BAT appraisal process is illustrated in Figure 10.16 and summarized in Box 10.6.

Comparison between the options is based on 'significant' air, water and land impacts which are identified following the procedure explained in Box 10.6. As shown in Tables 10.19 and 10.24, the team has found that the significant air pollution criteria on which the different options should be assessed are:

- sulfur dioxide (SO_2);
- nitrogen oxides (as NO_2);
- cadmium (Cd);
- mercury (Hg);
- arsenic (As);
- lead (Pb);
- chromium (as Cr(VI)); and
- cobalt (Co).

Table 10.24   Long- and short-term environmental quotients for air pollutants for the base case design

'Significant' substance	Long-term EQs[a]			Short-term EQs		
	EAL	PC	EQ = PC/EAL	EAL	PC	EQ = PC/EAL
Sulfur dioxide (SO_2)	50	0.56	0.011	267	47	0.176
Nitrogen oxides (as NO_2)	40	2.24	0.056	200	96	0.48
Cadmium (Cd)	0.005	0.0006	0.120	1.5	0.028	0.019
Mercury (Hg)	0.25	0.0006	0.002	7.5	0.028	0.004
Arsenic (As)	0.2	0.006	0.030	15	0.0028	0.000
Lead (Pb)	0.5	0.006	0.012	n/a	0.0028	n/a
Chromium (as Cr(VI))	0.1	0.006	0.060	3	0.0028	0.001
Cobalt (Co)	0.2	0.006	0.030	6	0.0028	0.000
Total EQ$_{air}$			0.322			0.680

[a] EQ - Environmental quotients

Table 10.25 BAT appraisal of different design options for the EfW plant

	Options					
	Base case	1	2	3	4	5
Furnace						
Moving grate	×		×	×	×	×
Fluidized bed		×				
Air pollution control						
SNCR for NO_x removal	×		×		×	
SCR for NO_x removal						×
Dry removal of acid gases		×	×			
Semi-dry removal of acid gases	×			×		×
Wet removal of acid gases					×	
Total power used (kWh/t waste)	75	80	71	74	88	109
Energy use relative to the base case (%)	0	7	−5	−1	17	45
Total annualized cost of options in £k	7200	7560	7308	7056	7416	8244
Total cost relative to the base case (%)	0	5	1.5	−2	3	14.5
Average air EQ $[EQ_{air} = (EQ_{air\ long\ term} + EQ_{air\ short\ term})/2]$	0.50	0.79	0.57	0.73	0.43	0.23
Average air EQ relative to the base case (%)	0	58	14	46	−14	−54
Photochemical ozone creation potential (POCP), t ethylene eq./year	983	1590	1131	1141	835	467
POCP relative to the base case (%)	0	62	15	16	−15	−52

As the options are similar for the other environmental impacts, including waste, global warming potential, noise, odour and visual impact, as well as for the potential for accidents, the team has not compared them on these impacts.

Therefore, the team has based their comparison between the options on the environmental quotient (EQ) for air (EQ_{air}) alone (see Box 10.6 for calculation of EQ_{air}). These results indicate that Option 5 is the BAT, with the EQ_{air} 54% lower than the proposed base case design (see Table 10.25). This option also has the lowest potential for tropospheric ozone creation. However, in terms of energy use, Option 5 uses 45% more energy than the base case. With respect to this criterion, Option 2 is the BAT.

To be able to make a final decision on the BAT, the design team also has to examine and assess the total costs of the options. However, prior to discussing this BAT criterion, they have summarized their findings on the environmental sustainability of the proposed EfW plant in Tables 10.26 and 10.27. This summary matrix shows the environmental impacts from both the construction and operation of the plant as required by the EIA.

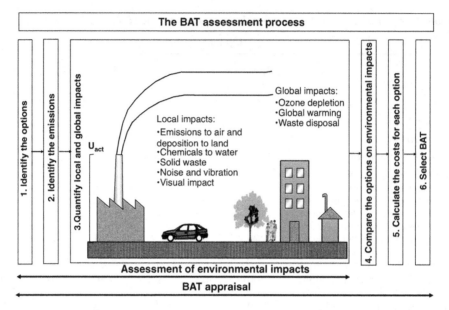

Figure 10.16   *The BAT appraisal of EfW options under the IPPC regulations (adapted from EA (2002a))*

Box 10.6   Summary of the BAT options appraisal process (EA, 2002a)

Step 1. Identify the options

This step involves description of the options to be compared (see Section 3.4.1 for the description of the options for the proposed EfW plant).

Step 2. Identify the emissions

The aim of this step is to produce an inventory of sources and releases of polluting substances from each option. Owing to space limitation, the results of this step are shown for air pollutants for the base option only in Table 10.19 as maximum daily mean releases in grams per second. They are referred to as 'release rate' (RR).

For the air pollution, the so-called effective height of release from the stack must be calculated using the formula:

$$U_{\text{eff}} = 1.66H\left(\frac{U_{\text{act}}}{H} - 1\right) \tag{10.4}$$

where U_{eff} (m) is the effective height of release of the flue gas and air pollutants, H (m) is the height of the tallest building within five stack heights (m) and U_{act} (m) is the actual height of the stack.

The effective stack height will then be used to calculate the ground concentrations of air pollutants. The reference conditions for releases to air from point sources are temperature 273 K (0 C) and pressure 101.3 kPa (1 atm) with no correction for water vapour or oxygen.

Step 3. Quantify local and global impacts

The aim of this step is to quantify local and global impacts associated with each option and then to identify those impacts which are significant and for which the options should be compared. The significance of each impact is assessed by comparison with the available benchmark values for that impact.

Again, owing to space limitations, we consider here only the methodology for air. The estimates of impacts are based on the ground concentrations of the air pollutants. These emissions are referred to as 'process contribution' (PC) and are expressed in micrograms per cubic metre. They can be obtained either by using sophisticated mathematical dispersion modelling or by the simplified method developed by the Environment Agency, using the formula:

$$PC = DF \times RR \qquad (10.5)$$

where PC ($\mu g/m^3$) is the process contribution, RR (g/s) is the release rate and DF [($\mu g/m^3$)/(g/s)] is the dispersion factor, expressed as the maximum average ground-level concentration per unit mass release rate, based on annual average for long-term release and hourly average for short-term releases. A table of dispersion factors is provided below; linear interpolation can be used for stacks of different height than those given in the table.

	Dispersion factor, DF [($\mu g/m^3$)/(g/s)]	
Effective height of release (U_{eff})	Long term: maximum annual average	Short term: maximum hourly average
0	148	3900
10	32	580
20	4.6	161
30	1.7	77
50	0.52	31
70	0.24	16
100	0.11	8.6
150	0.048	4.0
200	0.023	2.3

Air pollution PCs obtained for the proposed EfW plant by air dispersion modelling are summarized in Table 10.19. Two types of PC are distinguished: long term and short term. The former are based on the annual averages and the latter on the hourly averages. The PCs are considered to be 'significant' if:

- $PC_{long term} > 1$ % of the long-term environmental benchmark;
- $PC_{short} > 10$ % of the short-term environmental benchmark.

The environmental benchmarks are based on either environmental quality standards (EQSs) or environmental assessment levels (EALs), depending on the availability of the data. Like PCs, both the EQS and EAL are expressed as the long- and short-term values. The EALs for the air pollutants relevant in this case study are shown and compared with the PCs in Table 10.19.

Step 4. Quantify local and global impacts

The next step involves listing all substances emitted to air that have not been screened as insignificant. This should be done for long-term emissions only. The PCs should then be normalized for each substance against the appropriate benchmark, either EQS or EAL for that substance using the formula:

$$EQ_{substance} = PC_{substance}/EAL_{substance} \qquad (10.6)$$

The normalized values $EQ_{substance}$ are then summed up for all air pollution substances to obtain a total cumulative air impact:

$$EQ_{air} = EQ_{substance1} + EQ_{substance2} + \cdots \qquad (10.7)$$

The results of these calculations for the proposed EfW plant are shown in Table 10.24.

A similar methodology is also used to quantify emissions to air deposited to land and for water emissions. The IPPC also provides guidance on calculating the impacts of noise, odour and accidents, visual impact, the photochemical ozone creation potential and global warming potential. Further detail on these methodologies can be found in EA (2002a). The EA has also developed freely available software to help with the calculations of the impacts.

Step 5. Compare the options on environmental impacts

The aim of this step is to compare the overall performance of each option for all the environmental considerations assessed in step 4, to identify which option has the lowest impact on the environment as a whole. The appraisal results for the proposed EfW plant for the air pollutants are given in Table 10.25.

If it is obvious which option is best, then the appraisal process can stop here. If however, the applicant wishes to justify their choice on the basis of costs, then they should proceed to the next step.

Step 6. Calculate costs for each option

The aim of this module is to estimate the costs of implementing each of the options carried forward from step 5, so that a balanced judgement of the costs of controlling releases of pollution against the environmental benefits can be made. Both capital and operating costs should be considered and the total expressed as annualized costs. The guidance note explains the methodology in detail (EA, 2002a).

The costs of different air pollution control options for the proposed EfW plant are compared with the environmental performance in Table 10.25.

Step 7. Select the BAT

The aim of this module is to identify the BAT from the candidate options, by balancing the environmental benefits of each option against the costs of achieving them. In our case, the base option has been identified as the BAT by the design team.

Table 10.26   *Environmental impacts from the construction of the combustion plant*

Aspect	Impacts during the construction stage		
	Impact	Nature	Significance
Geology, ground and surface water	Change to the run-off characteristics of the site	—	No or negligible impact
	Mobilization of contaminants	—	No or negligible impact
	Localized excavation into the ground water	—	No or negligible impact
Waste management	Disruption to existing waste management operations during construction	—	No or negligible impact
Ecology	Temporary loss of habitat for certain bird species	—	No or negligible impact
	Temporary loss of water bodies and marshy grassland on application site	—	No or negligible impact
	Temporary disturbance to wildlife using the site	Adverse	Slight
Air quality	Dust arising from construction	Adverse	Slight
Noise	Noise arising from construction	Adverse	Slight
Transport	Additional traffic generation for periods during construction	Adverse	Slight
Cultural heritage	Potential damage or destruction to archaeological features or deposits	Adverse	Slight
	Increased knowledge of the archaeology of the area	Beneficial	Moderate
Socio-economic	Reduction in unemployment within the construction sector	Beneficial	Slight
Land use	The land which is within an industrial site is currently not used for any other purpose	—	No or negligible impact
Landscape	Temporary effect of construction activity on landscape character and views	Adverse	Slight

Table 10.27 *Environmental impacts from the normal operation of the plant*

Aspect	Impacts from the plant operation		
	Impact	Nature	Significance
Geology, ground and surface water	Changes to surface water drainage	—	No or negligible impact
Waste management	Sustainable change to long-term waste management within the county	Beneficial	Significant
	Disposal of ash residue within the context of sustainable strategy for the county	—	No or negligible impact
Ecology	Provision of enhanced habitat for certain bird species	Beneficial	Slight
	Provision of replacement aquatic habitat	Beneficial	Slight
	Build-up of pollutants within defined habitat	Adverse	No or negligible impact
Air quality	Net reduction in greenhouse gases	Beneficial	Slight
	Slight increase in atmospheric pollution but remaining well within relevant guidelines and standards both individually and cumulatively	Adverse	Slight
	Emission from lorry traffic	—	No or negligible impact
Noise	Noise from lorry traffic	—	No or negligible impact
	Net change in the noise environment as a result of the operation of the site	—	No or negligible impact
Transport	Increase in vehicle movements to the site	Adverse	Slight
	Number of lorry movements during an average week-day	—	No or negligible impact
Cultural heritage	Archaeological potential	—	No or negligible impact
	Impact on the town's conservation area	—	No or negligible impact
Socio-economic	Reduction in unemployment in the local area	Beneficial	Slight
	Creation of skill shortages or wage increase	—	No or negligible impact
Land use	Conformity with development plan policy but some conflict with non-statutory guidance	Beneficial	Moderate
	Perception of impact from the adjacent industrial estate and the recreational park	Adverse	Slight
Landscape	Effect on landscape character and views from the existing industrial estate	Beneficial	Moderate

Table 10.27   (Continued)

Aspect	Impacts from the plant operation		
	Impact	Nature	Significance
	Effect on landscape character and views from within the site itself	Beneficial	Slight
	Effect on landscape character of the river corridor and adjacent residential areas and views from the nearby nature reserve and river corridor	Adverse	Moderate
	Effect on views from residential areas	Adverse	No or negligible impact/slight

Overall, based on their findings and the summary matrix, the design team has concluded that the negative environmental impact from the proposed EfW plant would be insignificant. In the worst case, the plant will have a slight impact on the air quality, land use and the landscape. On the other hand, they believe that the plant would have a significant positive impact on waste management.

Questions

1. If the actual height of the stack for the proposed incinerator is 70 m, use formula (10.4) in Box 10.6 to calculate the effective height of the stack; that is, the height at which the flue gas and the air pollutants will be released into the environment taking into account the specifics of the site where the incinerator would be situated. The height of the tallest building within five stack heights is 38 m.
2. The PCs to the air emissions have been calculated using air dispersion modelling software. In cases where such software is not available, then, according to the IPPC guidance notes, the PC can be calculated using formula (10.5) in Box 10.6. Use this formula and the DF shown in the table in the textbox to calculate the PCs for different air pollutants and compare your results with those of the design team, shown in Table 10.19. How well do the results agree?
3. Compare your results for PCs with the EALs given in Table 10.24 to determine the significance of the pollutants that will then be used for the BAT appraisal of the six air pollution control options. Which air pollutants are significant in your case? Do your results correspond to the results of the design team?
4. Use your results to calculate the EQs for the significant air pollutants using the following formula:

$$EQ_{substance} = PC_{substance}/EAL_{substance}$$

5. Now calculate the total environmental burden for both long- and short-term releases as

$$EQ_{air} = EQ_{substance\,1} + EQ_{substance\,2} + \cdots$$

Compare your result for the base case design with that of the design team. Are the results similar? If not, explain the differences.

6. Use the emission factors in Table 10.8 to estimate the total yearly emissions of the air pollutants from the proposed EfW plant. Compare these figures with the estimated annual releases shown in Table 10.19 and calculate the required efficiency of the air pollution control plant to maintain the release rates at the level required by the EU Incineration Directive. Do you think these efficiencies are realistic? Comment on the ability of the operator to maintain the emissions of the air pollutants at the level required by the EU Incineration Directive (see Table 10.18).

7. How does your base case design compare with the other five options with respect to the EQ_{air}? Which option would you choose if you were to consider the air pollution alone? Justify your choice.

10.4.4 Economic Considerations

10.4.4.1 Plant Costs

The annualized plant costs for the six design options investigated by the design team are given in Table 10.25. The costs include the initial capital and financing costs (which are theoretically spread over the estimated life of the technology) and the maintenance and supply costs, taking into account the revenue gained from energy recovery. The team has estimated that the base case design would cost £7.2 million per year. The least expensive options is Option 3 which is 2% cheaper than the base design. However, this option is 14% worse on air pollution than the base design and is, therefore, not a BAT candidate. On the other hand, the environmentally best Option 5 is 14.5% more expensive than the base case and would be difficult to justify as the BAT. On balance, taking into account both the environmental and cost criteria, the design team believes they can justify their choice of the base case design as the BAT and are confident that they can convince the CC that their choice conforms to the BAT principles.

The final step that remains to be carried out by the design team before they can submit their application for the IPPC authorization and planning permission is social assessment of their proposed plant. These considerations are discussed next.

10.4.5 Social Considerations

10.4.5.1 Employment

The design team estimates that the proposed plant will result in the creation of a number of temporary construction jobs as well as permanent jobs during the operation of the plant. The number of construction workers that will be working on site in any one month is estimated around 320 over the 3-year period of construction. Once fully operational, the plant is predicted to create around 55 new permanent jobs for local people.

Table 10.28   *Uptake of dioxins and furans via inhalation, vegetation and locally produced food (milk and beef)*

	Estimated daily intake (pg/kg day)	TDI[a] (pg/kg day)	Percentage of TDI (%)
Inhalation	2.86×10^4	1–4	0.007–0.03
Vegetation	1.8×10^2	1–4	0.45–1.8
Milk	1.28×10^3	1–4	0.03–0.13
Beef	8×10^5	1–4	0.002–0.008

[a] Tolerable dioxin intake

10.4.5.2 Human Health Impact Assessment

In order to assess the potential public health implications of the release of the pollutants from the proposed EfW plant, the design team has considered the possible pathways for these substances into the human population through the atmosphere (inhalation) and through contaminated vegetation or food (ingestion), including milk and beef from locally reared cattle.

A key aspect of health impact assessment is a dose estimate for the exposed population. Because of the large uncertainty in determining the exposure dose, it is common practice to take the precautionary principle and assume a worst-case scenario with a hypothetical individual exposed to a maximum dose from all sources over a lifetime of 70 years. The design team realizes that this approach will produce an overestimate, but it will also guarantee that if, under these circumstances, the health impact is insignificant, then it will also be insignificant under the realistic actual dose conditions.

The results of the dose estimates carried out by the design team for the dioxins and furans are shown in Table 10.28. The estimated intake from the EfW source is 0.02 pg/day of dioxins and furans. The World Health Organization (WHO) defines tolerable daily intake (TDI) of dioxins and furans between 70 280 pg I-TEQ/day for a 70 kg adult[1]. The contribution from the EfW, therefore, is between 0.007 and 0.03% of the TDI.

The estimated intake of dioxins and furans from the ingestion pathway through vegetation consumption is 0.018 pg/(kg day), which represents 0.45–1.8% of the TDI. The dioxin uptake via locally produced cattle through milk and beef is estimated at 1.28 pg/(kg day) and 0.08 pg/(kg day) respectively, which represents 0.03–0.13% and 0.002–0.008% of the TDI respectively.

The total daily intake for the metals is estimated to be 0.12 µg/day. The US EPA reference dose (RD) for the metals that will be emitted from this EfW is equal to 131 mg/day, so that the contribution from the EfW plant is less than 0.0003%.

Using these estimates, the design team has concluded that the potential human health impacts are insignificant under the worst assumed conditions and that they will, therefore, be even more insignificant under the actual dose conditions.

---

[1] I-TEQ: international toxic equivalents – expresses the overall toxicity of a mixture of dioxins and similar substances as a single number.

10.4.5.3 Odour and Noise

The MSW management facilities must be designed so as to control the odour that is generated by decomposition of MSW. The design team has ensured that the design of the plant enables odorous materials to be processed rapidly to prevent decomposition and the production of odours. Containment of any odour that may develop will be achieved through the maintenance of a negative pressure in the hall. This will be achieved by the combustion air-fans drawing air from the bunker hall into the furnace to feed the combustion process. As a result, potential odour arising from the tipping, mixing and furnace loading operation will be retained within the bunker or carried out into the furnace rather than escaping to the outside.

Regarding the noise levels, the background noise is already relatively high due to the proximity of a busy motorway in the area where the EfW plant is proposed to be built. The traffic levels are likely to increase regardless of the proposed development because of the increased influx of population in the area, therefore leading to a gradual increase in the background noise. However, the proposed EfW is likely to contribute further to the traffic and to the noise levels, both during the construction and operation phases. The design team claims that the plant has been designed to ensure that the noise levels generated are below the level that could be heard at the nearest housing at the quietest part of the night or day. This has been achieved by placing many of the noisier operations, such as fans and condensers, inside a single building and using silencing on other parts of the process.

10.4.5.4 Visual Impact

The proposed development could have a visual effect on both the local landscape and on views from important viewpoints. The local landscape is characterized by a diverse landscape with open, rolling heathland and coniferous woods. The river corridor is generally attractive, with mature trees which prevent long distance views. Heavily populated areas also exist with development focused in transport corridors. The landscape quality is affected, however, by the nearby motorway, the electricity pylons, mobile-phone masts and the industrial estate. The latter, which is the proposed siting of the EfW plant, is influenced by the usual character of industrial sites – it is generally unattractive and dominated by car parks, open storage and so on. Resembling an aircraft or a space ship, the architectural design of the EfW plant itself is very modern, almost futuristic, and in that respect the plant would stick out from the surrounding industrial buildings and particularly from the nearby housing estates with red-brick terraced houses. The stack, although not particularly tall, would be visible from various viewpoints in the area.

10.4.5.5 Transport

The design team has estimated that the construction and operation of the EfW plant will lead to a slight increase in traffic. In the construction phase, this increase will be around 2.5 % compared with the current situation. It is predicted that, when fully operational, the development will generate 1300 heavy goods vehicle movements during weekdays with a total of 85 on Saturdays.

10.4.5.6 Cultural Heritage

The area has a number of archaeological sites and remains from the Neolithic, bronze, iron and Roman periods. Field evaluations will be undertaken during construction works to ensure that none of the archaeological sites is damaged. The team anticipates no effects to these sites during the operation phase.

Questions

1. Describe the human health effects of the air pollutants that will be emitted from the proposed plant. What are the main exposure pathways for the public for each of these pollutants emitted from an EfW plant? Discuss in particular the effects of VOCs, dioxins and furans.
2. Use the results in Tables 10.19 and 10.21 and the estimated atmospheric exposure doses given in Section 10.4.5.2 to determine if the human health effects from the air pollution are likely to be significant. Discuss your conclusions.
3. Using the predicted process contribution of $PC = 1.12 \times 10^{-9} \, \mu g/m^3$ for dioxins and furans and the metals concentration of $0.006 \, \mu g/m^3$, and assuming a typical pulmonary ventilation rate of $20 \, m^3/day$, calculate the total lifetime dose (over 70 years) to a hypothetical individual from the atmospheric exposure route. Do you think these amounts are significant? Why?
4. Examine the predicted composition of the bottom ash and fly ash given in Table 10.23. Which of the components are harmful to humans and the environment and how would you dispose of the ash?
5. In your opinion, is the daily number of heavy goods vehicle movements (1300) needed to deliver waste to the EfW significant? Why? How would you optimize transport logistics so that the impact of waste deliveries is reduced?
6. Summarize and discuss the social impacts from the EfW plant, both positive and negative. Are there any impacts that the design team has not considered that you think are important?

10.5 Final Considerations: Stakeholders' Views and the County Council Decision

Having prepared very detailed assessments in support of the planning and the IPPC authorization application as described above in a summarized form, WEnergise has submitted the documentation to the CC. The application has quickly attracted the attention of a number of stakeholder groups in the local area who, by law, have access to the planning application documentation. The stakeholder groups include the local residents, NGOs and political parties. The following summarizes their views on the proposed development.

10.5.1 Local Residents

Having examined the application in some detail, the local residents formed an association and started a very active campaign against the proposed EfW plant. Their objections included the following:

- the plant will be visually intrusive with its dimensions of 138 m × 101 m, 40 m high with the stack 70 m high;
- it will cause deterioration of the air quality in the area, particularly due to the increase in the concentrations of NO_x and particulate matter;
- it will put the health of local residents at risk due to the emissions of dioxins and heavy metals;
- it will increase noise due to the air cooling condensers;
- it will generate odours, including ammonia;
- it will generate further solid waste and ash residues;
- it will generate heavy traffic flows, increasing an already high congestion in the area;
- it will pose a threat to the economy of the town because businesses and employees would be deterred by a large polluting industrial installation;
- it will undermine the recreational and amenity value of the river corridor and the local nature reserve;
- it would prejudice recycling by burning material that is capable of being recycled;
- the proposed design has not been proven to be the BAT, as it has to be assessed along side waste minimization, recycling, composting, digestion and other techniques, using life cycle assessment;
- the plant would waste energy because of the lack of CHP generation, which is an absolute requirement and its absence places this application low down the waste hierarchy; and
- waste from other regions would be imported to be burnt in this plant.

The local residents have stressed that they believe that the incinerator is the wrong solution and the location is too sensitive. They have argued that they want to reduce waste and recycle instead. They have demanded that the CC initiates kerbside collections of waste that would be pre-sorted to help the recycling process. They have also demanded a moratorium on incineration in the county. Furthermore, the residents have demanded to be consulted on waste policy in the county before any decision is taken on the need for, let alone the location of, an incinerator.

They have concluded their objections to the development by asking that this application be refused and more environmentally acceptable and sustainable waste solutions be explored.

10.5.2 Other Stakeholders

The local residents have been supported by both the environmental NGOs and an opposition political party. The NGOs have argued that incineration wastes resources, causes pollution and does not solve the problem of landfill, as ash still has to be disposed of. They, too, wanted to see the waste strategy based on a properly resourced kerbside recycling system and other sustainable waste management initiatives.

The opposition political party wanted consideration of the alternative technologies for EfW plants, including pyrolysis. Like the local residents and the NGOs, they also wanted to see the recycling rate improve to meet the government target of 25% waste recycled.

10.5.3 The County Council Decision

Having received over 20 000 letters of objection by the local residents and other stakeholders, the proposal for the EfW plant has been rejected by the CC. The explanation given
is that the proposal involves built development on a substantial scale and form which will
have a significant material adverse impact on the adjacent river, green belt town centre and
nearby residential and business properties. It would also have a negative visual effect.

Questions

1. Analyse the stakeholders' views on the proposed EfW plant and summarize their
   objections. In your opinion, which of the points raised are 'right' and which are 'wrong'?
   In answering this question, try to put yourself in the role of each of the stakeholder
   groups.
2. What could have the design team and WEnergise done to ensure that the planning
   permission is granted? Where do you think they went wrong?
3. If you were the managing director of WEnergise, what would you do to ensure that the
   company obtained the planning permission for this EfW plant?
4. There is another case of an EfW plant in England – SELCHIP, situated in South East
   London. The proposers of this CHP plant were successful with their proposal for the
   development and the project was granted planning permission without much opposition
   by the local communities. Find out how this project developed and the reasons why the
   proposal for the plant was successful. Compare and contrast the case of SELCHIP with
   the case study presented in this chapter. What are the main differences and what is the
   lesson that could be learnt from both of these cases?

10.6 Conclusions

MSW is an important problem for sustainable development which can only be solved by
taking an integrated approach to waste management. Ideally, we need to avoid generating
waste in the first place, as this, in addition to reducing the use of resources, also avoids the
need to deal with the waste. However, whilst we should strive to minimize waste generation
as much as possible, on the practical level, it looks unlikely that we will succeed completely,
at least not in the short term, so that the problem of waste will persist for some time to come.

   We have different possibilities to deal with the waste once it has been generated,
including the use of waste to recover materials or energy. Alternatively, we can dispose of
waste in landfills, which of course is the least sustainable option. Which option we choose to
deal with MSW will depend on many factors, including technical, economic, environmental
and social. This case study has tried to illustrate the complexity of the problem and some of
the factors which determine the sustainability and acceptability of an MSW management
option. Admittedly, the chapter considers one of the most controversial options for waste
management there is – but this was on purpose. The lesson to be learnt from this case is that
engineers and scientists can produce technically, economically and even environmentally
the most efficient designs possible, but, if they are deemed socially unacceptable, these
designs will never become real installations.

References and Further Reading

Acharya, P., DeCiccco, S.G. and Novak, R.G. (1991) Factors that can influence and control the emissions of dioxins and furans from hazardous waste incinerators. *Journal of the Air & Waste Management Association*, **41** (12), 1605–1615.

Azapagic, A., Emsley, A. and Hamerton, I. (2003) *Polymers, the Environment and Sustainable Development*, John Wiley and Sons, Ltd, Chichester.

Barron, J. (1995) *An Introduction to Waste Management*, 2nd edn, Chartered Institution of Water and Environmental Wastes, London.

Beede, D.N. and Bloom, D.E. (1995) Economics of the Generation and Management of Municipal Solid Waste. NBER Working Papers 5116, National Bureau of Economic Research, Inc. http://netec.mcc.ac.uk/WoPEc/data/Papers/nbrnberwo5116.html (Aug 2003).

DEFRA (2003) Municipal Waste Management Statistics 2001/2. http://www.defra.gov.uk/environment/statistics/wastats.

EA (2002a) Integrated Prevention and Control. Environmental Assessment and Appraisal of BAT. Horizontal Guidance Note H1. The Environment Agency for England and Wales, Environment and Heritage Service and Scottish Environmental Protection Agency. www.environment-agency.gov.uk.

EA (2002b) Solid Residues from Municipal Waste Incinerators in England and Wales, May 2002. www.environment-agency.gov.uk.

EA (2002c) Environment Agency Household Waste Survey 2002. The Environment Agency for England and Wales. http://www.environment-agency.gov.uk/subjects/waste.

EA (2010). The Environment Agency for England and Wales. http://www.environment-agency.gov.uk/subjects/waste.

EC (1994) Council Directive 94/62/EC of 20 December 1994 on packaging and packaging waste. *Official Journal of the European Communities* (L365), 10–23, (31.12.1994).

EC (1999) Council Directive 1999/31/EC of 26 April 1999 on the landfill of waste. *Official Journal of the European Communities* (L182), 1–19, (16.7.1999).

EC (2000a) Directive 2000/53/EC of the European Parliament and of the Council of September 18, 2000 on end-of-life vehicles. *Official Journal of the European Communities* (L269) (21.10.2000).

EC (2000b) Directive 2000/76/EC of the European Parliament and of the Council of 4 December 2000 on the incineration of waste. *Official Journal of the European Communities* (L332), 0091–0111, (28.12.2000).

EC (2003a) Directive 2002/96/EC of the European Parliament and of the Council of 27 January 2003 on waste electrical and electronic equipment. *Official Journal of the European Communities* (L37/24) (13.2.2003).

EC (2003b) *Handbook on the Implementation of EC Environmental Legislation. Section 4: Waste Management Legislation*. European Commission, Brussels.

EC (2003c) Municipal Solid Waste Combustion. http://europa.eu.int/comm/energy_transport/atlas/htmlu/mswtech.html.

EC (2006) Directive 2006/12/EC of the European Parliament and of the Council of 5 April 2006 on waste, *Official Journal of the European Union*, (L 114/9) (27.4.2006).

EIA (2001) The Impact of Environmental Regulation on Capital Costs of Municipal Waste Combustion Facilities: 1960–1998. In: Renewable Energy 2000: Issues and Trends. Energy Information Administration, Department of Energy, USA, February 2001. http://tonto.eia.doe.gov/ftproot/renewables/06282000.pdf, pp 41–73.

EPA (1999) *State Workbook: Methodologies for Estimating Greenhouse Gas Emissions*, 2nd edn, Environmental Protection Agency, USA, chapter 5.

EPA (2010) Municipal Solid Waste in the United States: 2008 Facts and Figures. US EPA. http://www.epa.gov/epawaste/nonhaz/municipal/pubs/msw2008rpt.pdf.

Juniper (2003) *Pyrolysis and Gasification of Waste*, Juniper Consultancy Services Ltd, Gloucestershire, England.

Khan, Z., Ali, M. and Abu-Ghurrah, Z.H. (1991) New approaches for estimating energy content in MSW. *ASCE Journal of Environmental Engineering*, **117** (3), pp. 8–13.

Kiely, G. (1996) Solid waste treatment. *Environmental Engineering*, McGraw Hill, Maidenhead, England, chapter 14.

McKinney, M.L. and Schoch, R.M. (2003) *Environmental Science: Systems and Solutions*, 3rd edn, Jones and Bartlett Publishers, Boston.

Nicholas, M.J., Clift, R., Walker, F.C. *et al.* (2000) Determination of 'Best Available Techniques' for integrated pollution prevention and control: a life cycle approach. *Transactions of the Institution of Chemical Engineers; Part B (Process Safety and Environmental Protection);*, **78** (3), 193–203.

Powell, J. (1993): Externalities of Landfill and Incineration, CSERGE, Warren Spring Laboratory & EFTEC - Report for the DoE, HMSO, London.

Rand, T., Haukohl, J. and Marxen, U. (2000) Municipal Solid Waste Incineration: Requirements for a Successful Project. World Bank Technical Paper no. WTP462. http://www-wds.worldbank.org.

Romero-Hernández, O., Lázaro-Ruiz, A. and Ruiz-López, P. (2003) Feasibility Evaluation to Incorporate Waste-to-Energy Processes in Mexico. Working Paper. Instituto Tecnológico Autónomo de México, ITAM. México.

The UK Government (1995) Making Waste Work. A Strategy for Sustainable Waste Management in England and Wales. HMSO, London.

UNEP (1996) International Source Book on Environmentally Sound Technologies (ESTs) for Municipal Solid Waste Management (MSWM). UNEP, Nov 1996. http://www.unep.or.jp/ietc/estdir/pub/msw/index.asp.

Vesilind, P.A., Worrell, W.A. and Reinhart, D.R. (2002) *Solid Waste Engineering*, Brooks/Cole Thompson Learning, USA.

White, P.R., Franke, M. and Hindle, P. (1995) *Integrated Solid Waste Management, A Life Cycle Inventory*, Blackie Academic & Professional, London.

11

Sustainability Issues in Food Provisioning Systems

Adisa Azapagic, Heinz Stichnothe and Namy Espinoza-Orias

Meeting the food needs of the world's growing population faces enormous challenges, including demographic and dietary changes, food security, climate change, bio-energy development and natural-resource constraints. This chapter discusses some of these challenges along the food supply chains. Two case studies are presented – bread and chicken meat production – as an illustration of the sustainability issues that would need to be addressed in this sector.

11.1 Introduction

Food is central to the survival of humans. And yet, more than 1 billion people suffer from chronic hunger (FAO, 2009a). One of the challenges of sustainable development is to provide food security for these people, but also to be able to feed the growing world population, projected to exceed 9 billion by 2050 (UN, 2008). To achieve this, global food production would need to increase by 40% by 2030 and 70% by 2050 compared to 2007 (OECD-FAO, 2009).

Meeting the increasing demand for food is facing several challenges, including demographic and dietary changes, climate change, bio-energy development and natural-resource constraints (Tilman *et al.* 2002; FAO, 2009a). For example, income growth in developing economies is already starting to show a dietary shift towards higher meat consumption. In China alone, the consumption of meet increased fourfold in the last 30 years, from 14 kg

Sustainable Development in Practice: Case Studies for Engineers and Scientists, Second Edition
Edited by Adisa Azapagic and Slobodan Perdan
© 2011 John Wiley & Sons, Ltd.

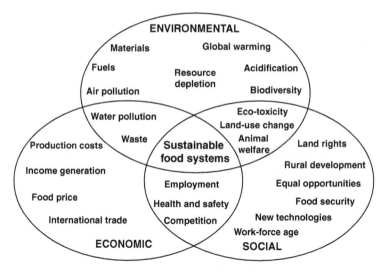

Figure 11.1   *Sustainability issues for food production systems*

per person in 1980 to 60 kg per person in 2005 (FAO, 2009a). If current trends continue, the production of livestock will increase by 70% by 2050 (Rosegrant and Thornton 2008), also requiring a significant increase in the production of cereal grain to feed the livestock. These and related activities will cause further pressure on the already constrained natural resources, such as land, water, fossil fuels and biodiversity. As a result, the impacts of climate change and environmental pollution are also likely to increase, leading to a range of socio-economic issues, including competition for resources and food security. Some of the sustainability challenges associated with food provision are illustrated in Figure 11.1.

Food systems consist of complex and increasingly global supply chains, involving agricultural activities to produce livestock and crops and their processing to produce various food products, which are then packaged and distributed to consumers around the world. A simplified food supply chain is shown in Figure 11.2. Each part of the supply chain is associated with a range of sustainability issues, some of which are explored in the rest of the chapter.

Questions

1. What are the global challenges in meeting food needs? How could they be addressed at the international level?
2. What are the main reasons that 1 billion people suffer from chronic hunger? How could food be provided to those people and what are the main challenges? How could developed countries help address this issue?
3. Discuss the implications of the globalization of food supply chains for sustainable development. Which sustainability issues shown in Figure 11.1 are affected by globalization of food systems? Identify any other issues that you think are important.
4. What are the main food-related issues in your country? How could they be addressed?

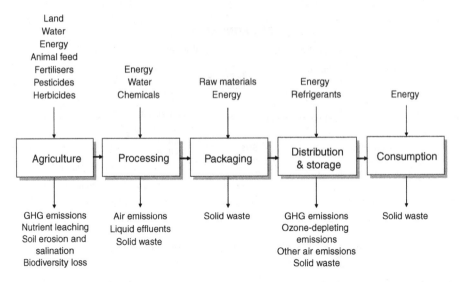

Figure 11.2 *Food production systems from 'cradle to grave' showing some environmental issues in the life cycle of food production*

11.2 Environmental Issues

Food production is associated with a wide range of environmental issues, such as resource depletion, greenhouse gas (GHG) emissions, pollution, waste and loss of biodiversity.

The largest environmental impacts in the food sector are generated in the agricultural stage. As shown in Figure 11.2 and Figure 11.3, the main issues in this stage include the increasing use of water, fertilizers, pesticides and herbicides. For example, since the 1960s, the use of water has doubled while the use of pesticides and nitrogen fertilizers has increased 10-fold. At the same time, the production of meat and cereals grew only by 50% and 35% respectively (McIntyre *et al.*, 2009). This and other agricultural activities, such as land-use change, have led to various impacts, including climate change, soil erosion and biodiversity loss. For example, agriculture contributes 13% to the global emissions of GHGs, mainly due to methane (CH_4) from livestock enteric fermentation, nitrous oxide (N_2O) from the use of fertilizers and manure management, as well as carbon emissions from land use and land-use change (Solomon *et al.*, 2007; FAO, 2009a). As shown in Figure 11.4, global GHG emissions from livestock production are estimated at 7 Gt CO_2 eq. per year, the majority of which is from land use and land-use change (36%), manure management (31%) and enteric fermentation (27%).

Climate change and other sustainability issues in agriculture and other parts of the food supply chain are discussed below.

11.2.1 Land and Soil-Related Impacts

Amongst other factors, productivity of agricultural systems depends on the content of nutrients in soil. Nutrients can be supplied either by synthetic (nitrogen, potassium or

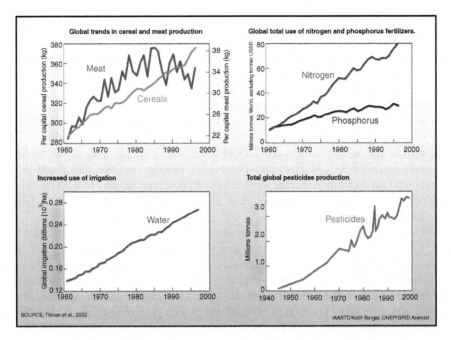

Figure 11.3 *Global trends for meat and cereal production and the related use of water, fertilizers and pesticides (reproduced by permission from IAASTD ())*

phosphorus-based) or organic (manure) fertilizers. Owing to a relatively poor uptake by plants, a significant proportion of nutrients applied to soil, particularly nitrogen, is released back into the environment. For this reason, in Europe for example, agriculture is a major source of environmental impacts from nutrients (EEA, 2005). Particularly

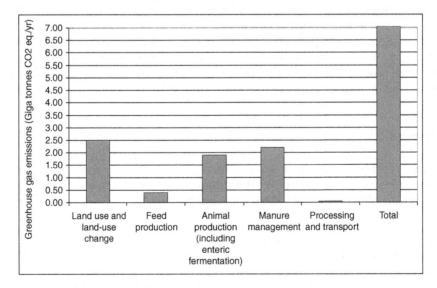

Figure 11.4 *Estimated GHG emissions in the animal production chain (based on FAO (2009a))*

significant is the contribution of nitrous oxide (N_2O) from nitrogen,[1] which has a global warming potential (GWP) 300 times that of carbon dioxide (CO_2) so that agriculture contributes the majority of N_2O emissions globally (Solomon *et al.*, 2007). A further impact is caused due to the leaching of nutrients to aquatic systems which leads to eutrophication (see Chapter 3 for definition of this and other environmental impacts) and biodiversity loss of aquatic species.

In addition to the environmental impacts, a further issue related to the use of fertilizers is depletion of rock-phosphate reserves, which at the current rate of consumption could be exhausted in the next 50–100 years (OECD-FAO, 2005). As phosphorus has no known substitute, it could be considered an absolutely limiting resource that could lead to international competition to secure the sources of phosphate supply (EC, 2009). Already in 2008 the price of phosphate rock saw a 700% increase from US\$50 to US\$350 (EC, 2009).

Soil loss through erosion is also an issue in agriculture, mainly caused by tillage.[2] More than 10×10^6 ha of cropland are lost annually through soil erosion (Preiser, 2005). Furthermore, tillage contributes to the release of CO_2 by exposing organic matter buried in the soil, thus contributing to climate change. Conservation tillage,[2] on the other hand, could contribute to carbon sequestration of 0.1–1.3 t of carbon per hectare annually and could feasibly be adopted on up to 60% of arable land (Solomon *et al.*, 2007). Organic farming techniques could also reduce soil erosion and lead to increased formation of soil humus, which often results in considerable carbon gains (40–2000 kg of carbon per hectare per year) (EC, 2009).

Another agricultural activity contributing to climate change is land-use change. In many parts of the world, the expansion of agricultural land is achieved by conversion of forests and grassland into pastures and cropland, leading to the release of carbon stored in soils. For example, converting Brazilian forest to annual cropland releases 37 t of CO_2 eq. per hectare per year (Solomon *et al.*, 2007). Additionally, land-use change results in habitat and biodiversity loss (Meir *et al.*, 2006; Canadell *et al.*, 2007; FAO, 2009a).

Agricultural systems not only contribute to climate change, but are also affected by it. In addition to the changing weather patterns due to climate change which affect yields, the rising atmospheric CO_2 concentration influences the quality of crops. Wheat and rice are particularly vulnerable, as their protein concentration is reduced by up to 15% at current atmospheric concentrations of CO_2 (Taub *et al.*, 2008). Incidentally, current food production systems are mainly dependent on these two crops.

Questions

1. How do different agricultural practices (e.g. application of synthetic or organic fertilizers, conventional or conservation tillage, crop rotation, set-aside land, irrigation) affect environmental impacts from crop cultivation?

---

[1] N_2O is formed either directly from oxidation of nitrogen or indirectly from volatilization and redeposition of ammonia (NH_3) and nitrogen oxides (NO_x) (Van der Gon *et al.*, 2005).

[2] Tillage is the process of soil preparation which can involve ploughing and harrowing; it is also used for the removal of residues in the soil from the previous crop. Conservation tillage leaves a minimum of 30 % of crop residue on the soil surface to reduce soil erosion.

2. Discuss the direct and indirect effects of agriculture on biodiversity.
3. What sustainability issues related to agriculture are important for your country?

11.2.2 Water Use and Related Impacts

Water use in farming accounts for 70% of global water withdrawals, of which rice accounts for 21% and wheat for 12% (OECD-FAO, 2008). The livestock sector uses about 8% of global water use, but that is primarily due to irrigation of feed crops (FAO, 2009a). Figure 11.5 shows how much water is needed for different agricultural products; for example, rice has a 'water footprint' of 3900 l/kg, while production of beef requires four times that amount (including the water needed to produce feed crops) (Hoekstra, A.Y. and Chapagain, A.K., 2008).

Water use is also an issue in food processing, owing to the large amounts of water used for preparation of food, washing of the equipment and the related waste water discharges.

As indicated by the historical trends (see Figure 11.3), meeting the increasing food demand will necessitate further increases in water consumption. It has been estimated that an additional 15–20% of water will be needed for agriculture over the next 25 years (Global Vision on Water, 2000). This is particularly an issue in water-stressed areas. Currently, one-fifth of the world's population – around 1.2 billion people – live in areas of water scarcity and 500 million people are approaching this point (IWMI, 2007). Most water-stressed areas are in West Asia, North Africa or sub-Saharan Africa (UNEP, 2010).

An important issue related to water use in agriculture is soil salination. Each year 10×10^6 ha of cropland are being lost because of salination caused by irrigation leading to loss of productivity and income (OECD-FAO 2008).

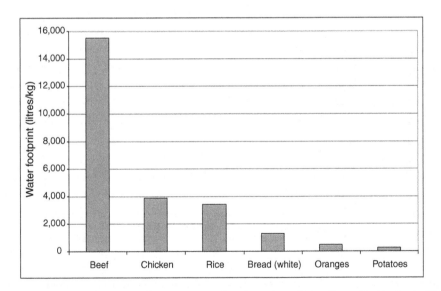

Figure 11.5 *Water footprint of various agricultural products (Waterfootprint Network, 2008)*

Questions

1. Why is water an issues in agriculture? Discuss the implications of water use in agriculture in water-stressed regions.
2. Which countries are most water stressed? Is water an issue in your country and if so, why?
3. How can irrigation lead to salination? How does salination affect crops?
4. How is the 'water footprint' calculated? What kind of water or sources of water should be counted when calculating water footprint?
5. Water is also an issue in food processing. Discuss how and why.

11.2.3 Energy Use and Related Impacts

World food supply is heavily dependent on fossil fuels used along the whole supply chains, from agriculture, to food processing, distribution and consumption. As an illustration, Figure 11.6 shows the use of energy in different parts of the food supply chain in the UK: out of the total 337 MJ of energy required to produce food from 'field to fork' to feed one person per week, half is used in the agricultural and food processing stages and around 30% during home storage and cooking. Packaging uses 6.5% of the total energy and the overall transport and distribution 8.5%. The energy the average person gets from food is 73 MJ per week, or only 20% of the energy that went into its production.

In addition to depleting fossil fuel reserves, energy used in food production leads to the emissions of GHGs and related climate change impacts. These and other environmental impacts are discussed further in the case studies (Section 11.5). Here we continue to examine the economic and social issues of food provisioning systems.

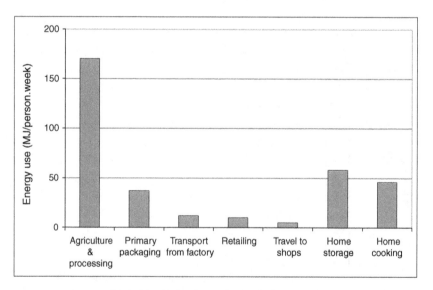

Figure 11.6 *Energy use in food supply chains (megajoules per person per week) (UK data; based on INCPEN (2009))*

Questions

1. What are the main environmental impacts related to the use of energy?
2. Identify and discuss the main methods for industrial food processing and discuss the energy and water needs for each technology.
3. Follow the stages outlined in Figure 11.2 and discuss how the use of energy could be minimized along the food supply chains.
4. What role can renewable energy play in 'greening' the food supply chains, from agriculture to processing to waste management? Discuss what renewable energy options would be feasible for your country.
5. What are the major environmental issues associated with food productions systems? Explain the impacts of food production on (a) climate change, (b) resource depletion and (c) biodiversity loss.

11.3 Economic Issues

Some of the most significant economic issues associated with food production include food prices, production costs and income generation along the supply chains (see Figure 11.1).

In 2008, the prices of basic foods reached their highest levels for 30 years, threatening food security of the poor worldwide and pushing an additional 115 million people into chronic hunger (FAO, 2009b). Many factors contributed to this dramatic price increase, including record oil prices, adverse weather conditions, increased production of biofuels, rapid economic growth of some regions, notably China and India, and the related increase in demand for meat. Although food prices have fallen since, they still remain higher than historically expected.

Figure 11.7 shows both the historical and projected food prices in 2007–2008 and 2009–2018 respectively, relative to 1997–2006. As shown, from 1997–2006 to 2007–2008

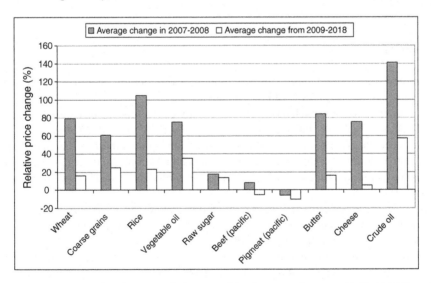

Figure 11.7 *Historical and projected changes of food prices relative to 1997–2006 (based on data from OECD-FAO (2008))*

the average prices of most food products have increased in real terms (adjusted for inflation). The price of rice increased most, doubling over the period; the prices of butter, wheat and vegetable oil increased by about 80%.

While it is difficult to forecast future food price trends accurately, most analysts agree that, in the short to medium term, prices will remain higher than in the recent past and that increased price volatility will become the norm (IFPRI, 2007; OECD-FAO, 2008; World Bank, 2008a). Assuming the economy recovers and the price of oil goes down, food prices are projected to decrease in the period up to 2018 (OECD-FAO, 2009). This varies by commodity, but average crop prices are expected to be 10–20% higher in real terms relative to 1997–2006. Meat prices are not expected to increase, and if the economic crisis continues, then there may be a shift towards cheaper meat, favouring poultry over beef and lamb. Rising vegetable oil prices will also drive upwards the prices of diary products; for example, the average price of butter is expected to go up by 15%.

The impact of high food prices is obviously most severe for the poor, for whom food can account 50–80% of the budget (FAO, 2009b). Thus, higher prices affect not only the quantity and quality of their food consumption and, therefore, their health, but also their ability to afford other basic needs, such as energy and housing. The most visible indicator of this negative economic impact was the social unrest around the world triggered by the soaring food prices (FAO, 2009b), including in Mexico, Haiti and several countries in Africa and Asia.

While high prices of food clearly affect consumers negatively, they should, at least in theory, have a positive effect on producers along the supply chain, including farmers. However, the increasing costs of production, which led to the increased food prices, also work against improvements in profit and may cancel it out. It appears that, in particular, farmers in developing countries did not benefit from the increased food prices. Most producers in these countries are far distanced from what happens on the international markets that increasing food prices there do not necessarily mean higher profits for them (FAO, 2009b).

Questions

1. Identify and discuss factors affecting food prices. Which of these are in your opinion most important and how could they be addressed?
2. In your opinion, how much will the increasing food prices impact on consumer demand? Which world regions and sections of society are likely to be affected most?
3. The need to protect consumers from higher food prices must be balanced against incentives to food producers along the supply chain to continue meeting the increasing demand for food. Discuss what policy measures would be needed in place to ensure this balance.
4. Many developing countries need international support to overcome budgetary constraints and to identify and implement appropriate policies. Discuss what developed countries could do to help towards this.
5. Discuss the impacts of international trade on food prices and availability. Discuss the role of both developed and developing countries.
6. What proportion of family budget is spent on food in your country? How does that affect different sections of society?

11.4 Social and Ethical Issues

Food security and poverty, human health and concerns about animal welfare and new technologies are just a few of the social and ethical issues associated with food production systems (see Figure 11.1). They all pose enormous challenges and have been the subject of many international activities and publications. Hence, they cannot possibly all be discussed here, so that we only give a brief overview of several social and ethical issues below. The interested reader can consult the reference list for further in-depth reading and analysis of these issues.

Among social sustainability aspects, food security is arguably the most critical issue that requires concerted international action. In 2009, more than 1 billion people were suffering from chronic hunger. Historically, the number of people without food has been rising steadily, from 830 million in 1995–97 to today's 1 billion (see Figure 11.8). At this rate, the World Food Summit's goal to halve the number of people who suffer from hunger by 2015 (FAO, 2009c) will not be met. At the same time, there are 1 billion people worldwide who are overweight or obese (WHO, 2010), posing an altogether different challenge to society.

Theoretically, more than enough food is produced to feed everyone in the world if the food produced were distributed equitably among the world population (Millstone and Lang, 2008). In an attempt to address this issue, in 2008 the right to adequate food was recognized as a basic human right and enshrined in international law (FAO, 2009c). It establishes the right of every person to have continuous access to the resources necessary to produce, earn or purchase enough food not only to prevent hunger, but also to ensure health and well-being. The right-to-food framework provides guidelines to national governments on how to ensure that all vulnerable groups have access to adequate food.

As already mentioned, another relevant issue related to food is obesity. Currently, more than 1 billion people are overweight, with 300 million clinically obese (WHO, 2010). For example, 33% of adults in the USA and 22% in the UK are obese.

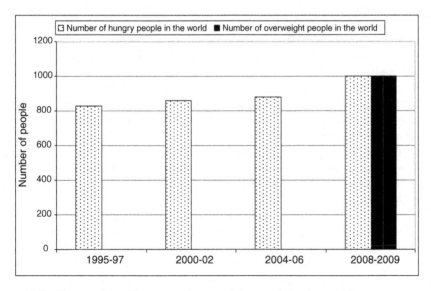

Figure 11.8   *The number of hungry and overweight people in the world*

Obesity is not only a problem in developed countries, but also affects developing countries, including some African nations. Whilst obesity also depends on a range of lifestyle factors, the changing food consumption patterns and diets, as well as convenience, are important contributing factors.

Convenience in particular has become the main driver for the way we purchase and consume food. The food industry has responded accordingly, providing a huge range of pre-processed and pre-prepared food to cater for the changing lifestyles and more-demanding consumer expectations. This means that we eat more heavily processed food, which in turn can lead to obesity and affect our health in various other ways. Food is also being increasingly transported long distances to provide all-year round availability that the modern consumer has come to expect. Furthermore, owing to inefficient processing, storage and transport, up to 40% of food harvested is lost before it reaches the consumer. Post-consumer food waste is also growing; an estimated 30% of perfectly usable food is thrown away by consumers in Europe (EC, 2009). All of these activities add to the environmental stresses from food production systems, as discussed in the case studies presented in the next section.

However, alternative approaches to food production and consumption are also emerging, including organic farming and fair trade. The latter recognizes the need for fair terms of trade for farmers and workers in the developing world. The market for these products is still small but growing fast, in response to the environmental, health and ethical concerns associated with globalized, intensive food production systems. In the UK, for example, ethical food sales increased fivefold from £1 billion in 1999 to £5.4 billion in 2005 (Defra, 2008a).

Other important drivers for alternative production systems are ethical concerns over animal welfare and health and the penetration of new technologies into food provisioning. The latter include the use of genetically modified organisms (GMOs), nanotechnology and animal cloning (EC, 2009). For the risks and potential benefits of these technologies, see Chapter 1.

Although animal welfare is legislated in Europe (EC, 1998) and some other parts of the world, serious concerns remain over the way animals are treated in the so-called 'factory farms'. A typical example is 'battery chickens', which are usually kept in very small cages with no freedom of movement; they are fast-fed for rapid weight gain so that they can enter the retail market much sooner than they would have done otherwise. Free-range and organic chicken farming represent alternative ways of providing chicken meat wth improved animal welfare conditions; however, they are still a niche market and, therefore, more expensive than the 'battery chickens', so that the latter remain the main source of chicken meat worldwide.

Animal health is also of primary concern, particularly as some of the diseases, such as 'mad cow disease', 'bird flu' and 'swine flu', are jumping species and affecting humans. The latter, caused by the A(H1N1) virus, has been declared a worldwide pandemic by the World Health Organization.

The growing power of international food corporations and retailers is also creating some socio-economic and ethical concerns. The dominance of large retailers is growing particularly fast (Farnworth *et al.*, 2009). While belonging to a global supply chain can open big opportunities, it may also create high barriers to entry into market for smaller producers (EC, 2009). It can also create economic and social dependencies which may make smaller producers vulnerable to any changes in the supply chain.

Questions

1. Discuss how the right-to-food framework could help to address the hunger.
2. What are the advantages and disadvantages of 'convenience food?' Discuss its impacts on the environment and society.
3. Discuss the role of consumer behaviour in making food systems more sustainable.
4. What role could organic farming play in providing food more sustainably? Discuss the implications of organic farming replacing conventional farming – what would be the environmental, economic and social consequences globally?
5. How do producers and retailers affect the food production systems? Discuss their respective roles and any interdependences.
6. What are the main concerns about GMOs? And nanotechnology? Are these an issue in your country?
7. Why is animal welfare an issue? Discuss how different production systems affect animal welfare.

11.5 Case Studies

This section explores some of the sustainability issues raised in the previous sections using two case studies as examples: bread and chicken meat production. They have been chosen as representative examples of plant- and meat-based systems respectively to illustrate any differences and highlight the main issues.

11.5.1 Bread

Bread is a staple diet around the world. It can be produced from a variety of cereal grain, including wheat, corn, barley and rye. Bread from wheat is most common and is the focus of this case study. We follow a loaf of bread from 'cradle to grave' to discuss its sustainability aspects along the supply chain. The focus is on the impact on climate change as an illustration of environmental impacts caused by bread production. Other environmental impacts, as well as socio-economic issues, are also discussed.

11.5.1.1 The Life Cycle of a Loaf of Bread

The life cycle of a loaf of wheat bread is sketched out in Figure 11.9. It involves cultivation and milling of wheat, bread making, packaging, distribution, storage, consumption and final

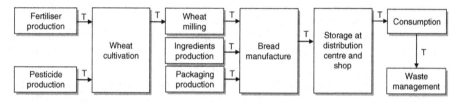

Figure 11.9   The life cycle of bread from 'cradle to grave' (T: transport)

Table 11.1   *Resources used to produce 1 t of wheat in west Canada and the UK (CFI, ; Korol, 2002; Defra, 2008b; Environment Canada, 2008)*

Resource	UK	West Canada
Yield (kg/ha)	8000	2690
Land (ha)	0.13	0.37
Seed (kg)	25.00	50.19
Calcium ammonium nitrate, as N (kg)	0.13	—
Ammonium nitrate, as N (kg)	17.81	—
Ammonium sulfate, as N (kg)	1.03	1.82
Ammonia, as N (kg)	—	11.77
Urea, as N (kg)	4.75	11.77
Monoammonium phosphate, as P_2O_5 (kg)	—	10.83
Triple superphosphate, as P_2O_5 (kg)	3.88	—
Potassium chloride, as K_2O (kg)	4.94	7.92
Limestone (kg)	34.88	—
Dolomite (kg)	1.90	—
Pesticide (kg)	0.59	0.37

disposal. Each stage is discussed briefly, followed by the discussion of their contribution to climate change and other environmental impacts. Life cycle assessment (LCA) has been used to estimate the environmental impacts (see Chapter 3 for the LCA methodology).

Wheat cultivation: This stage includes wheat cultivation and post-harvest operations such as grain drying and grain storage. Conventional wheat cultivation (considered here) relies heavily on the use of fertilizers and pesticides. As an illustration, Table 11.1 shows the typical amounts used for wheat cultivation in the UK and Canada and the related wheat yields. As shown in the table, despite about a 35% higher amount of fertilizers used for the Canadian wheat, the yield is much higher in the UK (8000 kg/ha) than in Canada (2690 kg/ha). This is mainly due to the different land areas used for cultivation in the two countries, as well as to the climatic conditions and farming practices.

Cultivation of crops is associated with a range of environmental impacts, as discussed in Section 11.2. Here, we consider one of these –GWP; for the methodology for calculating GWP, see Chapter 3. For example, despite the lower yields and higher consumption of fertilizers and pesticides per tonne of wheat, the Canadian wheat has a lower GWP (470 kg CO_2 eq./tonne) than UK wheat (600 kg CO_2 eq./tonne). The main reason for this is the type of fertilizer used and the more intensive farming practices in the UK. This is demonstrated in Figure 11.10. However, in both cases, the 'hot spots' in the cultivation stage are emissions from soil (N_2O from the use of fertilizers and carbon release due to tillage), followed by the emissions due to the agricultural activities (CO_2 emissions from fuels used in farm machinery) and CO_2 emissions in the production of fertilizers.

As demonstrated by this example, the GWP of wheat cultivated in different countries can differ considerably depending on the above-mentioned factors. This is illustrated in Figure 11.11. For example, wheat cultivated in Spain has twice the GPW of that grown in Canada. Organically grown wheat in Switzerland has the same GWP as conventionally cultivated wheat in France, while the UK organic wheat has a slightly lower impact than either. This example demonstrates the complexity associated with environmental impacts from farming – they can differ enormously not only between different countries, but also even between adjacent farms, depending on the type of soil, farming inputs and practices,

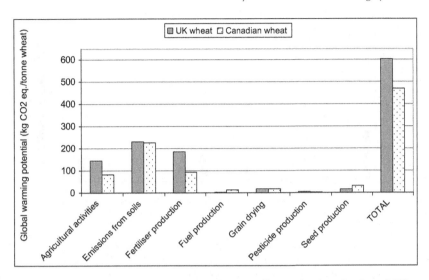

Figure 11.10 *GWP from wheat cultivation in the UK and Canada: Contribution of different life cycle stages*

climatic conditions and so on. Therefore, these factors must be understood properly if more sustainable solutions are to be identified and implemented in agriculture.

Other life cycle stages: Following wheat cultivation, the next stage in the life cycle of bread is wheat milling to produce flour (Figure 11.9). Depending on the wheat components included, three basic flour types can be produced: white, brown or wholemeal. White flour contains typically 75% of the grain, brown 85% and wholemeal flour is made from the whole grain. Flour is then distributed to bakeries, food processors and retailers to manufacture bread.

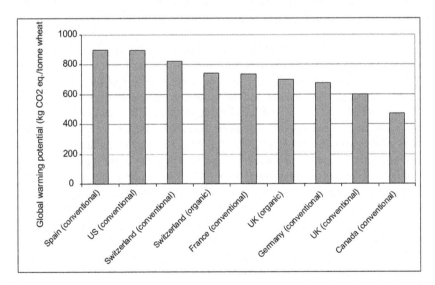

Figure 11.11 *GWP of wheat cultivated in different countries (based on data from Ecoinvent (2007), Defra (2008b) and Environment Canada (2008))*

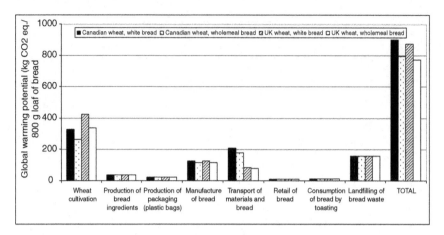

Figure 11.12   *GWP of a loaf of white and wholemeal bread from the UK and Canadian wheat. Assumptions: bread is manufactured and consumed in the UK; half of the bread is consumed as it is and the remaining half is toasted; all bread is packaged in plastic bags; 30 % of post-consumer bread is discarded as waste and landfilled*

In addition to flour, other main bread ingredients are yeast, salt and various additives, including iron, thiamine, niacin and calcium. Bread making includes dough preparation using some or all of these ingredients, followed by proving and baking. Some breads are sliced and then packaged into either polyethylene or paper bags. Bread is then distributed to the consumer, normally first going through distribution centres and then to retail shops. Bread can be consumed as it is or toasted, depending on the type of bread and consumer preferences. Finally, post-consumer waste is disposed of, including packaging and waste bread. Estimates show that a significant amount of bread is thrown away – in the UK, for example, 30% of bread is discarded by the consumer and landfilled (WRAP,). Other life cycle stages also generate waste, either due to spoilage of bread in the distribution chain or due to the processing inefficiencies.

Figure 11.12 shows the GWP of white and wholemeal bread made from the UK and Canadian wheat. The results indicate that wholemeal bread has a lower GPW than white bread regardless of the source of the wheat. This is because of the use of the whole grain, which reduces the amount of wheat needed and the waste discarded from the grain, compared with white bread. Overall, the wholemeal bread made from the UK wheat has the lowest GWP (770 g CO_2 eq. per 800 g loaf of bread), despite the fact that the UK wheat has a higher GWP than the Canadian wheat (see Figure 11.11). This is mainly due to the additional impacts from the transportation of wheat from Canada to the UK, where the bread is made and consumed (under the assumptions of this case study – Figure 11.12 details the assumptions). At 900 g CO_2 eq. per 800 g loaf of bread, white bread from the Canadian wheat has the highest GWP of the breads considered here.

For all types of bread considered here, wheat cultivation, bread manufacture, landfilling of waste bread and overall transport (also known as 'food miles') represent the carbon 'hot spots'. Other life cycle stages, including the manufacture of ingredients and packaging, as well as toasting, contribute little to the total GWP.

Thus, the results of the above analysis would suggest that switching to wholemeal bread would help to reduce the impact on climate change. However, climate change is just one

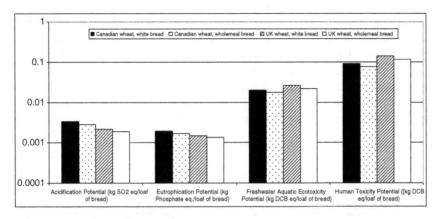

Figure 11.13 *Environmental impacts of a loaf of white and wholemeal bread from the UK and Canadian wheat*

environmental impact, albeit a very important one. It is thus also worth examining how the different bread options compare for other environmental impacts.

As shown in Figure 11.13, the preferred bread option is now less obvious. For acidification and eutrophication, both the wholemeal and white breads from the UK wheat are better than the breads from the Canadian wheat. The opposite is true for the freshwater and human toxicity.

Therefore, identification of an environmentally sustainable bread becomes more difficult if multiple environmental impacts are considered. Arguably, this is necessary to ensure that we do not make decisions which reduce one impact at the expense of another. Indeed, broader sustainability aspects should be considered, including consumer preferences which drive the production chains and determine the market share of products. For example, in the UK, 87% of bread flour is white and only 8.7% is wholemeal (Defra, 2009), despite the fact that the government promotes wholemeal bread as a healthier option (FSA, 2010).

Cost of bread is also an important factor. Generally, white bread tends to be cheaper, one of the reasons being the economy of scale related to its share of the market. Some retailers also sell white bread below the real market price as a way of attracting consumers in the hope that their other purchases will compensate for the loss of revenue from bread (and other staple food such as milk).

These are only some of the sustainability issues that would need to be considered in this relatively simple supply chain. We now turn our attention to a much more complex food provisioning system – production of chicken meat.

Questions

1. What are the main sustainability issues associated with bread production? Discuss each stage in the life cycle with respect to different environmental, economic and social aspects.
2. What are the main carbon 'hot spots' in the life cycle of bread and how could they be addressed to minimize the impact on climate change?

3. In this case study, transport, or 'food miles', has been shown to be a significant contributor to the GWP. In general, how much do food miles contribute to the GWP of a product? How does that change with the type of product (e.g. vegetables/fruit/cereals versus meat) and the distance to which they are transported?
4. According to this case study, packaging does not contribute significantly to the GWP of bread. In general, is packaging an important contributor to the environmental impacts of a product? Discuss how this varies for different product categories, including meat and drinks.

11.5.2 Chicken Meat

World production of chicken meat stood at 72×10^6 t in 2009 and is projected to continue growing (USDA, 2009). As already mentioned, the chicken production industry is affected by several sustainability issues, including animal welfare (see Section 11.4). In this case study we examine some of these issues, notably the environmental impacts in the life cycle of chicken meat production. Other sustainability issues are also discussed. The focus is on the intensive production systems or 'battery chicken'. The study is based on the UK conditions.

11.5.2.1 The Life Cycle of Chicken Meat Production

In this case study we follow the life cycle of chicken meat from 'cradle to gate' as outlined in Figure 11.14 This encompasses the production of chicken feed, broodstock rearing, egg incubation and hatching, broiler rearing and finally slaughtering of chickens.

The type of chicken considered in this case study is the hybrid broiler chicken. These chickens are a product of selective breeding and are suitable for intensive rearing and efficient feed-to-weight conversion, typically in the order of 1.7–2 kg feed per kilogram of chicken meat (RACEnvironment Ltd, 2006). Chickens are fed feed mixtures prepared at feed mills and specially formulated to satisfy the basic nourishment needs and stimulate rapid weight gain. They include cereals (wheat, barley, oats), pulses (beans, peas) and oil seeds (soy beans, rape seed, sunflower).

Broiler chickens are considered finished when they reach the standard weight of 2.2 kg, usually at around 37 to 42 days of age. They are then transported in cages to slaughterhouses. After that, chicken meat can be distributed for retail as whole chickens or undergo further processing, producing meat cuts and a range of value-added fresh, frozen and

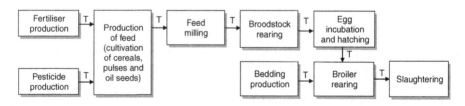

Figure 11.14   *The life cycle of chicken meat production from 'cradle to gate' (T: transport)*

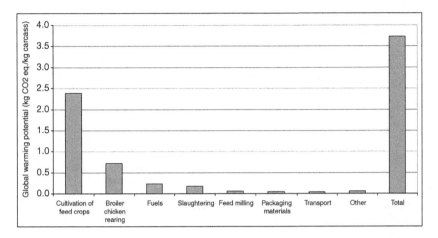

Figure 11.15 *GWP from the life cycle of chicken meat production (from 'cradle to gate')*

cooked products, such as ready meals, coated chicken, chicken nuggets, chicken burgers and roasted chicken.

The LCA results in Figure 11.15 show that the GWP of the production of chicken meat in the UK is equal to 3.7 kg CO_2 eq. per kilogram of chicken carcass, or 3.7 times its weight. The largest contributor to the GWP is cultivation of the feed (65%). This is perhaps not surprising, as the amount of feed required is twice the amount of chicken meat produced, and half of the feed is wheat. As discussed in the bread case study, the GWP from the cultivation stage is mainly due to the agricultural activities, carbon release from soil and application of fertilizers.

The second significant stage contributing to GWP is broiler rearing (20%), mainly due to the emissions of CH_4 and N_2O from chicken manure. Methane emissions arise from anaerobic decomposition of the manure during storage, treatment and application to land. The combination of nitrification and denitrification of nitrogen contained in the manure causes emissions of N_2O. Nitrous oxide is also generated due to the losses of volatile nitrogen in the form of ammonia and nitrogen oxides.

The production of fuels and slaughtering contribute 5–6% each to the total GWP and the remaining stages 1% or less each. Hence, the chicken feed and manure are the two life cycle stages where opportunities for reducing the GHG emissions should be sought.

In addition to GWP, other sustainability issues are pertinent to this sector, notably animal welfare and human health – this was discussed in Section 11.4. Although a lot of consumers are concerned about these issues, the majority continue to enjoy cheap chicken meat from 'battery farms'. This remains one of the main obstacles to a switch to more sustainable chicken (and other food) production systems.

Questions

1. What are the main environmental impacts from chicken meat production? Identify the 'hot spots' and discuss how they could be mitigated.

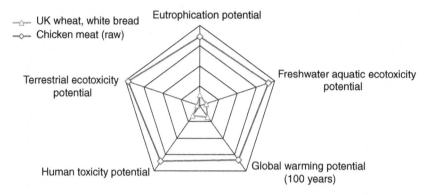

Figure 11.16 *Environmental impacts of white bread and chicken meat normalized to the calorie intake of 100 kcal*

2. Draw the life cycle diagram of an organic chicken production system. What would be the main environmental impacts and how do they compare with the impacts from conventionally produced chicken meat? Discuss these along the whole supply chain.
3. How could the issues of animal welfare and meeting the growing demand for chicken meat be balanced?

11.5.3 Environmental Impacts Versus Nutritional Content of Food

It is also interesting to examine the environmental impacts of food relative to their nutritional value. Figure 11.16 shows the results for the bread and chicken case studies considered in the previous sections, normalized to the calorie intake of 100 kcal. Although bread and chicken meat cannot be compared directly, as they have different nutritional compositions (see Table 11.2), the results suggest that bread has on average 11 times lower environmental impact than chicken (note that the results for chicken are for uncooked meat, so its impact would be even higher with the cooking energy included).

Questions

1. Compare the life cycle impacts of bread and chicken meat. What do you conclude?
2. Can products as different as bread and chicken be compared? Why? How could different meat products be compared on an equivalent basis? Discuss the different functions that

Table 11.2 *Nutritional composition of 100 g of white bread and chicken meat (USDA, 2008)*

Nutrient	Unit	White bread	Chicken meat (roasted)
Energy	kJ	1113.0	795.0
Energy	kcal	266.0	190.0
Proteins	g	7.6	28.9
Carbohydrates	g	50.6	0.0
Fibre	g	2.4	0.0
Fat	g	3.3	7.4

different products provide, including taste, and identify an appropriate unit of analysis (functional unit).

11.6 Conclusions

The food sector faces enormous sustainability challenges. Among these, food security should remain at the top of the international political agenda. Other priority issues include mitigation of the climate change impacts, improved human health and animal welfare and fair treatment of producers and suppliers. Consumer behaviour could have a transformational impact on the future development of the food sector. However, consumers are both influenced and constrained by the food industry, which would need to play a much more proactive role towards more sustainable food provisioning systems.

Acknowledgements

Part of the work presented in this chapter has been funded within the project 'Carbon Calculations over the Life Cycle of Industrial Activities (CCaLC)' by EPSRC, NERC and Carbon Trust (grant no. EP/F003 501/1). This funding is gratefully acknowledged.

References and Further Reading

CFI (2001) Nutrient uptake and removal by field crops – Western Canada 2001. Canadian Fertilizer Institute, Canada.

Canadell, J.G. Pataki, D. and Pitelka, L. *et al.* (eds) (2007) *Terrestrial Ecosystems in a Changing World*, Springer, Heidelberg.

Cordell, D. Drangert J-O., and White S. *et al.* (2009) The story of phosphorus: global food security and food for thought. *Global Environmental Change* Volume 19, Issue 2, May 2009, pp. 292–305.

Defra (2008a) Ensuring the UK's food security in a changing world. Discussion paper. July 2008, London.

Defra (2008b) UK wheat milled and flour production. https://statistics.defra.gov.uk.

Defra (2008c) The British survey of fertiliser practice. Fertiliser use on farm crops for crop year 2007. Department for Environment, Food and Rural Affairs (DEFRA), London.

Defra (2009) UK wheat milled and flour production. Department for Environment, Food and Rural Affairs.

FAO (2009a) The state of food and agriculture. Food and Agriculture Organisations of the United Nations, Rome. http://www.fao.org/publications/sofa/en/.

FAO (2009b) The state of agricultural commodity markets: high food prices and the food crisis – experiences and lessons learned. Food and Agriculture Organisations of the United Nations, Rome. http://www.fao.org/docrep/012/i0854e/i0854e00.htm.

FAO (2009c) The state of food insecurity in the world: economic crises – impacts and lessons learned. Food and Agriculture Organisations of the United Nations, Rome.

EC (1998) Council Directive 98/58/EC of 20 July 1998 Concerning the Protection of Animals Kept for Farming Purposes. *Official Journal of the European Communities*, (L221/23), 8 August 1998, pp. 0023–0027.

EC (2009) New challenges for agricultural research: climate change, food security, rural development, agricultural knowledge systems. 2nd SCAR Foresight Exercise. European Commission, Brussels.

Ecoinvent (2007) Ecoinvent database, Swiss Centre for Life Cycle Inventories. http://www.ecoinvent .ch/.

EEA (2005) Source apportionment of nitrogen and phosphorus inputs into the aquatic environment. European Environmental Agency, Brussels.

Eggleston, S., Buendia, L., Miwa, K. *et al.* (eds). (2006) *2006 IPCC Guidelines for National Greenhouse Gas Inventories*, IGES, Japan.

Environment Canada (2008) National Inventory Report 1990–2006. Greenhouse gas sources and sinks in Canada. Environment Canada, Quebec.

Farnworth, C.R., Jiggins, J. and Thomas, E.V. (eds). (2009) *Creating Food Futures. Trade, Ethics and the Environment*, Gower Publishing Ltd, Aldershot, UK.

FoB (2007a) UK bread market. The Federation of Bakers www.bakersfederation.org.uk.

FoB (2007b) Industry statistics – bread production. The Federation of Bakers http://www .bakersfederation.org.uk.

Fresco, L.O. (2009) Challenges for food system adaptation today and tomorrow. *Environmental Science & Policy*, **12** (4), 378–385.

FSA (2010) Eat well be well. Food Standards Agency, UK http://www.eatwell.gov.uk/asksam/ healthydiet/sfq/.

Global Vision on Water (2000) A vision of water for food, Global Vision on Water, Life and the Environment in the 21st Century. http://www.riob.org/forum2/WFVFinal.pdf.

Hoekstra, A.Y. and Hung, P.Q. (2005) Globalisation of water resources: international virtual water flows in relation to crop trade. *Global Environmental Change Part A*, **15** (1), 45–56.

Hoekstra, A.Y. and Chapagain, A.K. (2008) Globalization of water: Sharing the planet's freshwater resources, Blackwell Publishing, Oxford, UK.

IFPRI (2007) The World Food Situation. New Driving Forces and Required Actions. Food Policy Report, IFPRI, December 2007, Washington D.C.

INCPEN (2009) Table for one – the energy cost to feed one person. INCPEN, July 2009.

IWMI (2007) *Water for Food, Water for Life: A Comprehensive Assessment of Water Management in Agriculture*, Earthscan, London and International Water Management Institute, Colombo.

Jones, P. (2005) Nitrogen UK. Biffaward Programme on Sustainable Resource Use, Biffaward, London.

Korol, M. (2002) Canadian fertilizer consumption, shipments and trade 2001/2002. Agriculture and Agri-Food Canada, Canada.

McDonough, W., Braungart, M. Anastas T., *et al.* (2003) *Peer reviewed: applying the principles of green engineering to cradle-to-cradle design. Environmental Science & Technology*, **37** (23), 434A–441A.

McIntyre B., Herren HR, Wakhungu J., *et al.* (eds). (2009) *Agriculture at Crossroads. International Assessment of Agricultural Science and Technology for Development (IAASTD)*, Island Press, Washington.

Meir, P., Cox, P. Grace J., *et al.* (2006) *The influence of terrestrial ecosystems on climate. Trends in Ecology & Evolution*, **21** (5), 254.

Millstone, E. and Lang, T. (2008) *The Atlas of Food*, Earthscan, London.

Mintel Group (2006) Market intelligence food and drink: poultry UK.

Mintel Group (2007) Bread – UK – February 2007. Market Intelligence Report.

NABIM (2008) The UK flour milling industry. National Association of British and Irish Millers www .nabim.org.uk.

OECD-FAO (2005) Statistical databases. OECD, Paris.

OECD-FAO (2008) Agricultural Outlook 2008–2017., OECD Paris.

OECD-FAO (2009) Agricultural Outlook 2009–2018. OECD, Paris.

Preiser, R.F. (2005) Living within our environmental means: natural resources and an optimum human population. http://dieoff.org/page50.htm.

RACEnvironment Ltd (2006) Poultry UK. Mass balance of the UK poultry industry. Biffaward Programme on Sustainable Resource Use, Mass Balance Projects. http://www.massbalance.org/ downloads/projectfiles/1639-00390.pdf.

Rosegrant, M.W. and Thornton, P.K. 2008. *Do higher meat and milk prices adversely affect poor people?* id21 insights, issue No. 72, February 2008. http://www.eldis.org/go/topics/insights/2008/

the-growing-demand-for-livestock-will-policy-and-institutional-changes-benefit-poor-people/
how-do-higher-meat-and-milk-prices-affect-poor-people.

Solomon, S., Qin, D., Manning, M. *et al.* (eds). (2007) *Climate Change 2007: The Physical Science Basis. Report of Working Group 1 to the Fourth Assessment Report of the Intergovernmental Panel on Climate Change.* Cambridge University Press, Cambridge.

Taub, D. Miller, B. and Allen, H., (2008) Effects of elevated CO_2 on the protein concentration of food crops: a meta-analysis. *Global Change Biology*, **14** (3), 565–575.

Tilman, D., Cassman, K.G. Matson P.A., *et al.* (2002) Agricultural sustainability and intensive production practices. *Nature*, **418** (6898), 671.

UN (2008) World Population Prospects. The 2008 Revision Population Database. www.esa.un.org/unpp.

UNEP (2010) Environmental knowledge for change. Grid-Arendal. http://maps.grida.no/go/graphic/increased-global-water-stress.

USDA (2008) National nutrient database for standard reference – Release 21. United States Department of Agriculture http://www.nal.usda.gov/fnic/foodcomp/search/.

USDA (2009) Livestock and poultry: world markets and trade. Foreign Agricultural Service/USDA Office of Global Analysis, October 2009 http://www.fas.usda.gov/dlp/circular/2009/livestock_poultry_10-2009.pdf.

Van der Gon, D. and Bleeker A. (2005) Indirect N_2O emission due to atmospheric N deposition for the Netherlands. *Atmospheric Environment*, **39**, pp. 5827–5838.

WHO (2010) Global strategy on diet, physical activity and health. World Health Organization http://www.who.int/dietphysicalactivity/publications/facts/obesity/en/.

Williams, A.G., Audsley, E. and Sandars, D.L. (2006) Determining the environmental burdens and resource use in the production of agricultural and horticultural commodities. Main Report. Defra Research Project IS0205. Defra, London.

World Bank. 2008a. *Rising food prices: policy options and World Bank response*. World Bank, Washington, DC.

WRAP (2008) The food we waste. Waste and Resources Action Programme Banbury, Oxon www.wrap.org.uk/thefoodwewaste.

12

Providing Sustainable Sanitation

Richard Fenner and Amparo Flores

Providing sanitation to everyone on the planet is one of the most pressing challenges of the twenty-first century. The UN Millennium Development Goals specify a target of reducing by half the proportion of people without sustainable access to safe drinking water and sanitation by 2015. To meet these goals, alternative approaches to conventional sanitation need to be developed and evaluated. These should have the following sustainable features: encourage decentralized systems, allow waste flow stream separation, emphasize water conservation, provide nutrient, organic and energy recovery and allow for water reuse, as well as minimizing waste by-products such as sludge.

This chapter classifies a range of alternative systems according to their function (collection, treatment and utilization) and form of wastewater (e.g. faeces, urine, grey-water[1]) and analyses their potential operational sustainability features. A range of tools are described which have been used by others to evaluate sanitation systems, with most focusing solely on the environmental dimension of sustainability. A case study based on a rural/peri-urban municipality in South Africa is described and used to demonstrate how a set of socio-cultural/institutional, economic and environmental indicators can be used to make a comparison of alternative types of sanitation solutions and so provide a better evaluation of the options available.

---

[1] Greywater is generated from domestic activities, such as laundry, dishwashing and bathing and can be recycled for on-site use.

Sustainable Development in Practice: Case Studies for Engineers and Scientists, Second Edition
Edited by Adisa Azapagic and Slobodan Perdan
© 2011 John Wiley & Sons, Ltd.

12.1 Providing Sustainable Sanitation Solutions

Sanitation is the removal and/or treatment of wastes to create hygienic conditions and prevent disease. This chapter focuses on the liquid waste generated by households (domestic wastewater). The following sections give an overview of the current status of sanitation worldwide and the scope of the sanitation challenge.

12.1.1 Meeting the Sanitation Challenge

Each year 1.6 million children younger than 5 years old die because they lack access to safe water and basic sanitation. This is eight times more than the number of people who were killed by the Asian tsunami of 2004. The statistics are harsh: presently, around 1.1 billion people do not have access to an improved source of drinking water, 84% of whom live in rural areas. Even more starkly, 2.6 billion people defecate in the open or in unsanitary places (WHO and UNICEF, 2006; see Figure 12.1). This represents 40% of the world population, again with rural dwellers disproportionately affected. In 2004, rural sanitation was less than half the urban sanitation coverage (WHO and UNICEF, 2006).

Current trends in rapid urbanization have resulted since 2007 in more people living in urban areas than rural areas, and this growth of people living in poor sanitary conditions in slum areas is likely to grow in Africa, Asia and Latin America. The movement of people from rural to urban areas presents a series of major problems, including the pressing need to extend water and sanitation facilities to peri-urban areas so as to avoid the spread of cholera and other water-related diseases amongst the poorest city dwellers in these often overcrowded places. Challenges also arise from high population density and the associated concentrated demand on resources and production of wastes, limited space and the need to work with existing infrastructure, which in peri-urban slum areas in developing countries is usually unplanned and, therefore, chaotic.

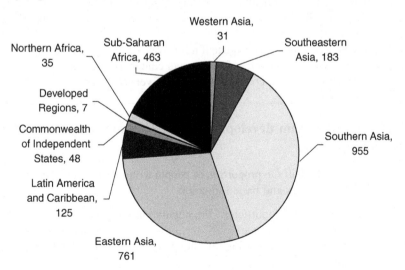

Figure 12.1 *Population (millions) without improved sanitation by region in 2004 (after WHO and UNICEF (2006))*

The World Health Organization (WHO) estimates that poor sanitary conditions and practices cause 80–95% of diarrhoeal diseases in developing countries (Prüss-Üstün *et al.*, 2004) and 1 billion people suffer from soil-transmitted helminth (parasitic worms) infections (WHO, 2004) which are perpetuated by the unsanitary disposal of faeces. These public health impacts result in decreased productivity, which then prevents economic and social development and perpetuates the cycle of poverty. Poverty, in turn, prevents families from affording water and sanitation services.

Sanitation in peri-urban areas is generally much lower than the average for urban areas. Often, any facilities that do exist are communal and these do provide a better level of provision than practices such as disposing of faecal matter with solid waste or open defecation. The WHO recommends that, where possible, the aim of urban sanitation development should be to provide sustainable solutions such as small bore and condominial sewerage with provision for effective wastewater treatment (WHO and UNICEF, 2006). This is applicable where drinking water is provided by piped distribution systems. These options, however, are not always feasible, and so on-site methods of sanitation, such as pit latrines[2] or dry compost toilets, must be considered. In contrast to the aim of providing toilets connected to simplified sewerage systems in urban areas, for rural settings the social marketing of a range of design options for on-site sanitation is equally important.

12.1.2 Millennium Development Goals

The Millennium Development Goals (MDGs) emerged from the largest ever gathering of world leaders at the United Nations Millennium Summit in New York in September 2000. The MDGs represent an integrated set of time-bound targets for tackling the most pressing issues facing developing countries and making real progress by 2015 relative to 1990 (UN Millennium Project Task Force, 2005). These include eradicating extreme poverty and hunger, achieving universal primary education, promoting gender equality, reducing child mortality, improving maternal health, combating major diseases and improving environmental sustainability. Targets for water and sanitation are embraced in the MDG 7, as outlined in Box 12.1.

The WHO considers sanitation adequate if it is private or shared (but not public) and if it hygienically separates human excreta from human contact (Gleick, 2006).

Table 12.1 summarizes what constitutes improved versus unimproved sanitation.

Box 12.1   Millennium development goal 7: ensure environmental sustainability

Target 10: Reduce by half the proportion of people without sustainable access to safe drinking water and basic sanitation.

> *Indicator 30:* Proportion of the population with sustainable access to an improved water source.
> *Indicator 32:* Proportion of the population with access to improved sanitation.

---

[2] Pit latrine is a hole dug in the ground.

Table 12.1   *Improved versus unimproved sanitation facilities (WHO and UNICEF, 2006)*

Improved sanitation	Unimproved sanitation
Flush or pour-flush to: sewer system, septic tank, pit-latrine	Flush or pour-flush elsewhere
	Public or shared facilities
Covered simple pit latrine	Open pit latrine
Ventilated Improved Pit (VIP) latrine	Bucket latrine
Composting toilet	Hanging latrine
	Open defecation

The target is formidable, as it means providing improved sanitation to 440 000 people *every day* from 2001 until 2015 (Mara, 2005). To make things even more challenging, can an additional 1.6 billion people be provided with improved sanitation facilities not just by 2015, but with improved facilities that are sustainable and will be in use for the next 10, 15 or perhaps 20 years?

Progress towards meeting these targets for sanitation are unequal across the world, with sub-Saharan Africa and Southern Asia making the least progress. If current trends continue up to 2015, the absolute number of people without improved sanitation will decline by 221 million. However sub-Saharan Africa will end up with 91 million *more* people without access to sanitation facilities than in 2004. This demonstrates that the global targets matter less than national targets set by individual countries. For example, significant progress in China and India alone could achieve the global target, without there being any progress in sub-Saharan Africa (UN Millennium Project Task Force, 2005).

The 2006 UN Human Development Report (UNDP, 2006) notes that some regions will miss the water and sanitation target (Figure 12.2). Sub-Saharan Africa will miss the sanitation target by more than two generations, with Southern Asia missing the sanitation target by 4 years. Overall, 74 countries are off-track and on current trends will fail to meet

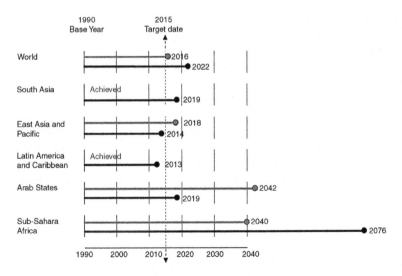

Figure 12.2   *Regions off-track for reaching the MDGs by 2015 (UNDP, 2006)*

the sanitation target by 430 million people, leaving 2.1 billion still lacking access to sanitation by 2015.

12.1.3 Integration with Wider Issues – Water, Health and Hygiene

This chapter focuses on how sanitation systems can be developed sustainably. However, such solutions must be delivered in practice as part of a wider integrative approach to water, health and hygiene issues. These comprise several interrelated components (Prüss-Üstün *et al.*, 2008), including: consideration of potential transmission of pathogens through water supplies; the provision of suitable infrastructure to provide water and sanitation services, as well as solid waste management and irrigation systems; the behaviour of the communities being served with respect to domestic and personal hygiene practices; and the use of natural resources and impacts on ecosystems through creation of environmental stress. Therefore, policy integration at this wider level will be important if specific initiatives in providing sanitation are to be maximized.

There are many political, institutional and financial constraints on achieving these goals, which are too complex to deal with in this chapter, so the reader is referred to the References and Further Reading for more insight into these problems. One reason, however, that sanitation is not higher up the agenda for local and national governments is that the poor simply have more pressing priorities, such as food, water and basic shelter. This means that many of the bottlenecks to the provision of basic water and sanitation services lie outside the sector itself. Where government provision has not been forthcoming, partly because of competing budget priorities, solutions can be instigated through community-led sanitation programmes.

There are also technical challenges which must be met, and whilst there are several options to choose from, it is vital that the most suitable solutions are adopted, which can deliver the required level of service reliably and sustainably in any particular local situation. Many lessons have been learnt about the installation of systems that have been too complex or expensive for communities to maintain or that have taken insufficient account (if any at all) of community preferences or customs. Furthermore, flexible design standards are needed which are appropriate for disperse rural areas or congested urban communities and squatter settlements on marginal lands. The condominial and simplified sewerage approach has been pioneered in Latin America, in which the minimum slope is based on the peak flow at the start of the design period and the pipe diameter relates to the peak flow at the end of the design period (see Box 12.2).

This is an example of an innovative technology that has eventually supplanted technical standards for sewers (Mara, 1996). However, a key element in reaching the sanitation targets in the MDGs is to focus on sustainable service delivery, rather than on the construction of facilities alone. Conventional approaches to sanitation have been found to have limitations and drawbacks (see Section), and so the rest of this chapter will discuss the nature of alternative approaches and how they can contribute to greater sustainability in sanitation provision.

Questions

1. Why are the MDG targets for sanitation unlikely to be met by 2015?
2. Compare the problems of providing improved sanitation in urban and rural areas.

Box 12.2   Simplified sewerage design

Like conventional sewerage, simplified sewerage is designed to transport unsettled wastewater; however, its design is based on a minimum tractive tension or boundary shear stress of $1 \, N/m^2$ rather than a minimum self-cleansing velocity. Additional key features of simplified sewerage are (Mara, 2005): (a) a peak flow factor (equal to daily peak wastewater flow/daily mean wastewater flow) of only 1.8; (b) a minimum peak flow of 1.5 l/s in any stretch of the sewer (this approximates the peak flow induced by a single flush of a WC); (c) pipeline diameter based on the peak flow at the end of the design period with a minimum sewer diameter of 100 mm (compared with 150 mm for conventional sewers); (d) use of a wide range of the proportional depth of flow in the sewer (d/D – that is, the depth of flow d divided by the sewer diameter D): 0.2–0.8; (e) calculation of the minimum sewer gradient based on the peak flow at the start of the design period; and (f) routing of sewers through backyards, front yards and sidewalks and not through roads, as shown below. Conventional sewerage is expensive and more disruptive to construct because pipelines need to be buried deeper to protect them from road traffic and roads need to be excavated and rebuilt.

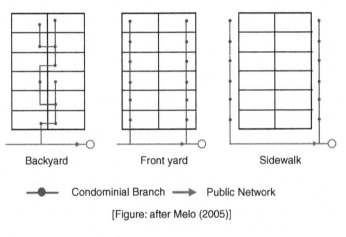

Backyard   Front yard   Sidewalk

●— Condominial Branch ⟶ Public Network

[Figure: after Melo (2005)]

3. Using the principles of simplified sewerage design (refer to Box 12.2) and the assumptions and formulae below, how many people can be served by a 100 mm sewer laid at a minimum gradient (I_{min})?

Water consumption	60 l/person/day
Peak factor	$k_1 = 1.8$
Return factor (wastewater flow/water consumed)	$k_2 = 0.9$
Peak flow	$q = k_1 k_2 pw/86\,400$ (p: population; w: per capita water consumption)
Minimum gradient	$I_{min} = 5.64 \times 10^{-3} q^{-6/13}$ (q is peak flow in litres per second)
Diameter D (mm)	$D = 23 q^{3/8} (I_{min})^{-3/16}$

(Reference: Mara (1996))

4. For the regions shown in Figure 12.1, investigate the latest WHO and UNICEF predictions for changes in population without access to improved sanitation by 2015 (in millions). How many regions are expected to have (a) an increase and (b) a decrease in the number of people without access to sanitation?

12.2 The Need for Alternatives to Conventional Sanitation

Traditional approaches to sanitation in developed countries require the waterborne transport of human waste and excreta often, but not always, to some central downstream wastewater treatment facility. This provides separation of the wastewater from the user, but mixes faeces, urine, water used for toilet flushing (up to 9 l of clean water to move 1 l of waste) with greywater, stormwater and sometimes industrial effluents in extensive sewer pipeline networks underground (see Box 12.3).

End-of-pipe separation of these wastes of varying levels of contamination and volumes at wastewater treatment facilities or sewage treatment plants then becomes a highly energy-intensive process and has consequences for the pollution of the downstream environment.

Sewered sanitation systems contribute to the environmental degradation of water bodies through discharges of organic matter, nutrients, heavy metals, endocrine-disrupting compounds and other contaminants, including gross solids released at times of high flow from sewer overflows. They often rely on high-quality drinking water supplies – which are becoming increasingly limited in many parts of the world – to dilute and transport waste. Properly built and operated conventional wastewater systems designed to remove solids and organic matter are very expensive and unaffordable by most developing country standards. Advanced or tertiary treatment to remove nutrients is unaffordable even for many regions in industrialized countries. Conventional systems in developed countries are reaching their capacity in densely populated and fast-developing regions, with receiving waters becoming less able to assimilate large volumes of wastewater without serious environmental impacts. Finally, the end-of-pipe treatment and discharge model of conventional wastewater systems is based on a linear concept of material flows, an approach that is inherently unsustainable.

In many developing countries, the conventional approach to sanitation is the pit latrine, a deep hole dug in the ground that is used as a receptor for human excreta, and often other human waste, and abandoned when full. Collection, treatment and disposal all happen on site within the pit latrine. Unlike the centralized or off-site model of sanitation in developed countries, this alternative is inexpensive, requires little or no infrastructure and is highly decentralized (commonly managed at the household or community level). A toilet or some other pedestal may be fitted over the hole and a superstructure may be built for privacy. Unfortunately, poorly operated – or inappropriately sited – pit latrines can fail to contain pathogens and nutrients contained in the excreta, with the potential for them to seep into groundwater, which is often a source of drinking water in developing countries. Pit latrines may also be prone to flooding and releasing their contents. If not managed properly, they can quickly become smelly and infested with flies, mosquitoes and other disease vectors, becoming a continuing source of disease and pollution. More practically, they are unsuited to rocky and sandy places, or areas with a high groundwater table.

Box 12.3   What is 'wastewater'?

Wastewater is made up of: human excreta (faeces and urine) and toilet flush water (collectively called black water); water from kitchens, showers/baths and washing machines (greywater); used water from industries; and rainwater that runs off roofs, roads and so on (stormwater). The various components are produced in different magnitudes, contain different types of contaminant and, therefore, require different levels of treatment (UNESCO-IHP and GTZ, 2006).

Wastewater	Typical production rates	Characteristics
Faeces	50 l of faeces per capita per year	Consists of organic matter, nutrients, trace elements and micro-organisms from the intestinal tract, when derived from infected people, highly contaminated with pathogens (e.g. bacteria, worm eggs). Requires treatment to prevent spread of disease and to protect surface waters from eutrophication.
Urine	500 l per capita per year	Contains most of nutrients – nitrogen (N), phosphorus (P), potassium (K) – found in domestic wastewater; may contain hormones and pharmaceutical residues; generally sterile. Nutrients may need to be removed prior to discharge into surface water.
Greywater	25–100 000 l per capita per year	May contain a variety of substances (oils, detergents, etc.) but generally safe from a health perspective. Treatment requirement depends on discharge/reuse process. May not require treatment for certain reuse applications (e.g. flushing toilets).
Industrial wastewater	Site specific, depends on local industries	Magnitude and type of contamination depends on industrial process; pretreatment may be required before discharge into a common sewer system
Stormwater	Site specific, depends on climate and infrastructure (especially impervious surface area)	Generally contaminated with pathogens from faeces left on the ground (from dogs, birds, humans, etc.), chemicals found on ground surfaces (e.g. fertilizers, pesticides, heavy metals) and suspended solids.

History has shown that replacing pit latrines with centralized treatment plants is not sustainable. Over the last few decades, international organizations such as the World Bank have supported the construction of conventional wastewater treatment plants in developing countries as exported from developed countries. Such projects often failed. For example, Wright (1997) notes that more than 90% of such plants in Mexico quickly became nonfunctional. Aside from cost, conventional treatment plants are generally not appropriate in developing countries because they: (1) require complex equipment that generally cannot be manufactured locally; (2) require expertise to operate and maintain; (3) rely on plentiful water supplies; (4) require a stable and large amount of energy; (5) are focused on the removal of organics, which are a secondary concern in developing countries, where the removal of pathogens is of paramount importance; and (6) are not suited to operation in the hot climates of many developing countries.

Finally, where resources are scarce, the potential to recover organic matter and nutrients from human excreta is an important driver for the alternative forms of sanitation. Conventional sanitation systems are generally not designed to maximize resource recovery.

Questions

1. Discuss the reasons why local management of wastewater should be the preferred option when considering ways of improving sanitation facilities.
2. What different categories of pollutants are found in wastewaters?

12.3 Incorporating Sustainability Considerations into Sanitation Provision

As noted in the previous section, certain features of conventional forms of sanitation limit their sustainability and, consequently, their potential for contributing to the long-term achievement of the MDGs. How, then, can sanitation systems be made more sustainable?

Figure 12.3 presents a methodology for the incorporation of sustainability considerations in the design and selection of sanitation systems. This methodology is suitable for both

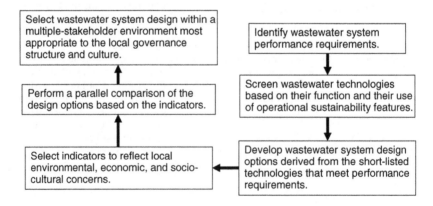

Figure 12.3 *A methodology for sustainable wastewater or sanitation system provision*

developed and developing country scenarios, but this chapter focuses on its application to developing countries. The following sections discuss specific aspects of this methodology in more detail.

12.4 Sustainability Features of Sanitation Systems

From an environmental perspective, the following sustainability principles are relevant to wastewater systems: adaptability to local conditions, resource conservation, resource recovery and waste minimization. In a wastewater management context, these can be translated into the operational features listed below. While the concept of sustainability has increasingly become mainstream, sanitation provision in developing countries currently still focuses primarily on just one or two of the features discussed below (e.g. the use of locally available and affordable resources and water conservation). A broader list of considerations is needed to make greater progress towards the sustainability of wastewater systems. Note that the operational features listed below all have the potential to contribute to sustainability, but some of these features may actually be double-edged; that is, they can also contribute to unsustainability. For example, decentralization may mean that there are no benefits from economy of scale and the system may become financially unsustainable. As discussed later in this chapter, these *net* effects can (and should) be evaluated from a multidimensional perspective using appropriate sustainability indicators.

12.4.1 Decentralization

The conventional wastewater management paradigm for urban and peri-urban areas involves the construction of extensive sewer networks that connect households, industries and so on to a centralized wastewater treatment plant. While such centralized systems can benefit from economies of scale and perhaps more efficient management, they are not suitable for all places. An extensive sewer network with a centralized plant is capital-intensive, expensive and, thus, often unaffordable for low-income regions. Such centralized systems are also generally more suitable in areas that have the institutional capacity for handling municipality-wide services. Finally, centralized systems may not be appropriate for areas that are very heterogeneous physically (geologically, topographically, etc.), culturally or politically.

Decentralization – while not a requirement of sustainability – does allow for reduced wastewater infrastructure and pumping (energy) costs, adaptation to local conditions and sanitation management at the household or community level. The option for household- or community-level management is particularly relevant in parts of developing countries where the city government may not have the capacity or the will to provide sanitation services. In developed countries, a decentralized system may be necessary to treat wastewater from new development in areas where the local wastewater treatment plant has reached its capacity. Decentralized systems can contribute towards sustainability by: (1) keeping nutrient and water cycles small, thus facilitating resource recovery at the local level; (2) facilitating source stream separation, allowing for separate treatment and reuse of the different waste streams (Green and Ho, 2005).

12.4.2 Waste Flow Stream Separation

Waste flow stream separation can contribute towards sustainability by preventing cross-contamination and allowing for treatment appropriate to the wastewater quality, which can lead to reduced chemical and energy consumption and improved treatment. It also facilitates the recovery of nutrients and organic matter (UNESCO-IHP and GTZ, 2006). Since faecal matter is the most contaminated portion of wastewater and, therefore, has the most adverse impact on public health, containing it and keeping its volume small may make its treatment more efficient and manageable. Urine is generally sterile and is the source of up to 90% of the N and 55% of the P in wastewater; therefore, separate collection of urine would significantly facilitate nutrient recovery (UNESCO-IHP and GTZ, 2006; Larsen and Lienert, 2007). It is important to note, however, that, in practice, separation of faeces and urine can be challenging. On the other hand, separate greywater collection is more easily achieved. Greywater is generally of good quality and can be reused for flushing toilets, watering gardens and so on and/or can be treated minimally before being discharged. It represents the largest fraction by volume of domestic wastewater.

Industrial wastewater can contain a variety of contaminants, such as heavy metals and organic chemicals, which may require special treatment; mixing industrial wastewater with domestic wastewater can, therefore, complicate treatment and reuse. The same is true for stormwater – the runoff from roads, farms and other surfaces that often contain micro-organisms, organic matter, heavy metals, pesticides and other substances. An additional complication with stormwater is that it is generated intermittently and in large volumes; in parts of the world where storm drains are connected to the sewer system, surges in stormwater flows often result in the overload of the treatment plant capacity and subsequent discharge of untreated wastewater into water bodies.

12.4.3 Water Conservation

It is estimated that 48 countries will be classified as water scarce or water stressed by 2025, and 54 countries by 2050 (WHO, 2006). These figures do not include countries where water is available but poorly distributed and where certain areas may be water scarce or water stressed. Accordingly, water conservation in such areas is a critical feature of any sustainable sanitation system. Furthermore, water extraction, treatment and delivery processes consume materials and energy; therefore, minimizing water consumption is a sensible step towards sustainability regardless of location.

12.4.4 Nutrient and Organic Matter Recovery

In conventional sanitation practice, the nutrients and organic matter in wastewater are viewed as major pollutants that require considerable amounts of resources to treat. When discharged to surface water, nutrients stimulate excessive growth of algae and/or aquatic plants, which can result in the decline of the surface water quality in a process known as eutrophication. High levels of organic matter in discharged wastewater also cause water quality problems; micro-organisms consume oxygen as they decompose organic matter, resulting in decreased oxygen levels in the receiving body.

However, nutrients and organic matter are not fundamentally bad for the environment; in fact, they are valuable resources that are critical to agriculture. When applied to plants as fertilizer, nutrients such as N, P and K enhance their health and productivity. When applied to soil, organic matter makes conditions favourable for root growth and increases drought tolerance by improving the soil's water-holding capacity. The recovery of nutrients and organic matter from wastewater thus not only provides a renewable source of these valuable resources, but also eliminates/minimizes their negative environmental impacts. The use of wastewater-derived nutrients and organic matter can be especially beneficial in parts of developing countries where land has been severely damaged by erosion and overfarming and where artificial fertilizer may be unaffordable.

12.4.5 Water Recovery

As noted previously, the increasing scarcity of water supplies is a well-recognized problem with various uses of water – agricultural, industrial, domestic and environmental – competing with each other. Wastewater is a renewable water resource that can ease the demand on limited fresh water supplies. The recovery of water from wastewater, often called water reclamation, can be described as 'the treatment, storage and distribution of wastewater for some kind of beneficial use or reuse application' (WEF, 2006). Depending on local regulations, highly treated wastewater can be used to recharge groundwater or surface water systems that supply water to a water treatment plant; note, however, that this level of treatment often requires large inputs of energy. It can also be used to recharge groundwater to mitigate salinity intrusion. Wastewater can be used directly as a nonpotable water supply (preferably after some treatment) for irrigation of agriculture and landscapes and industrial applications (e.g. boiler water). Reclaimed wastewater can be used for environmental purposes, such as the construction of wetlands; in this case, the wetlands may even be designed to be part of the treatment process. At the household or community levels, greywater may be reused with or without treatment. The level of treatment required for each type of reuse application varies depending on the risks to public health and the potential environmental impacts.

12.4.6 Energy Recovery

The organic matter in wastewater can be used as a renewable short-term cycle carbon energy source. In practice, this is often done through anaerobic digestion of sludge; incineration of sludge can also be used.

12.4.7 Minimization of Waste Sludge

Sludge from wastewater treatment is often viewed as a waste, even though it can actually be a valuable source of nutrients, organic matter and energy. Disposal of waste sludge may involve application to a landfill; however, this practice is becoming increasingly restricted because of the environmental impacts of landfills and reduced land availability. For example, effective in 2005, landfill disposal of organic waste was made illegal by Swedish legislation in accordance with EU Directive 99/31 (Lundin *et al.*, 2004). Incineration is also a common disposal method, with or without energy recovery. Sanitation systems that treat sludge as a resource rather than waste contribute to sustainability by reducing its environmental impacts and by reducing the demand on other nonrenewable sources of nutrients, organic matter and energy.

Question

1. Using Table 12.4, suggest which indicators are suitable for evaluating each of the sustainability features identified in Sections 12.4.1–12.4.7.

12.5 Sanitation Technologies

Using the operational sustainability features listed above to screen options for developing countries, a list of alternative (i.e. nonconventional) systems/components is generated as shown in Figure 12.4 and Table 12.2. The sanitation technologies that might be considered are presented in Figure 12.4, which classifies them based on whether they are used for collection (and transport), treatment and/or utilization and what form of wastewater they

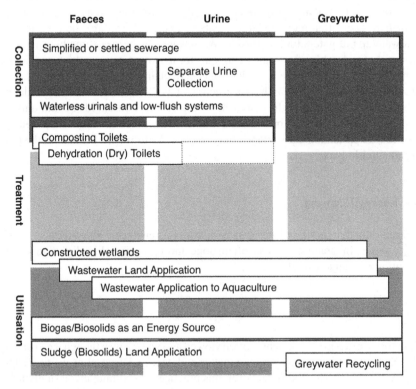

Figure 12.4 *Sanitation systems and components classified according to function and form of wastewater (after UNESCO-IHP and GTZ (2006))*

Table 12.2 *Examples of alternative sanitation components and systems and their potential operational sustainability features*

Sustainability feature	Decentralization	Waste flow stream separation	Water conservation	(Facilitates) resource recovery				Minimization of waste sludge
				Urine nutrients	Faecal nutrients and organics	Water	Energy	
Dehydration (dry) toilets	✓	✓	✓		✓		✓	✓
Composting toilets	✓	✓	✓		✓			✓
Separate urine collection		✓		✓				✓
Waterless urinals and low-flush systems		✓	✓	✓				
Greywater recycling	✓	✓	✓			✓		
Constructed wetlands	✓			✓	✓	✓		
Wastewater land application				✓	✓			
Sludge (biosolids) land application				✓	✓			✓
Wastewater application to aquaculture			✓	✓	✓	✓		
Biogas/biosolids as an energy source					✓			✓
Simplified and settled sewerage	✓							

✓: may or may not be applicable depending on specific design.

handle. Table 12.2 translates environmental sustainability *principles* into *physical infra-structure*, noting which operational sustainability features the various technologies embody. Note that while many advocates of the 'ecological sanitation' or 'ecosan' model of sanitation promote the sustainability features in Table 12.2, they have tended to focus primarily on the application of the first few technologies listed in this table. Table 12.2 is intended to demonstrate that, in fact, a wide range of technological options exists, with applications possible in diverse local conditions. For more detailed information about these technologies, refer to UNESCO-IHP and GTZ (2006), Winblad and Simpson-Hebert (2004), Metcalf and Eddy Inc. (2005), and Mara (1996).

In developing sanitation options, incorporating those components or systems from Table 12.2 – especially those with higher number of sustainability features – is a first step towards integration of environmental sustainability principles into the wastewater system. Any option developed should, of course, meet the local technical requirements (e.g. flow rate capacities, minimum treatment standards). The next steps are then to evaluate and compare the overall sustainability of the design options in the local context.

Question

1. Which sanitation components/systems might be considered for the following locations:

   i.   a dense peri-urban informal settlement bordering a large city with piped water supply in Brazil;

   ii. a rural village in Malawi with no piped water supply and electricity and where residents rely on subsistence farming;

   iii. a new city being constructed in a water-stressed region in northern China with requirements for local food supply for the new residents?

12.6 Sustainability Evaluations of Sanitation Systems

Various tools have been used to evaluate the sustainability of engineered systems, including sanitation systems. They are often used together, with one providing the input to the other, or used in parallel to address the various dimensions of sustainability. Many of the tools are based on a systems analysis approach (e.g. exergy analysis, materials flux analysis, and environmental life cycle assessment (LCA)); that is, they use a comprehensive approach based on mass and energy balances that include substance/material use, emissions, costs and required land area (Balkema *et al.*, 2002). Table 12.3 lists and describes the various tools applied to sanitation systems, and identifies the sustainability dimensions they attempt to address.

Once the sanitation options have been screened and selected (using Table 12.2 as a guide), an evaluation of their relative sustainability can be performed. From the list of tools presented in Table 12.3, the use of sustainability indicators is recommended for this purpose, as it allows for a comprehensive evaluation of environmental, economic and socio-cultural dimensions. It requires input from other tools. For example, LCA can be used as the quantitative basis for the environmental indicators. It is a well-established and compre-hensive tool with international standards, and recommended by the United Nations

Table 12.3   *Tools used to evaluate the sustainability of sanitation systems*

Tool and description	Sustainability dimension addressed		
	Environmental	Economic	Socio-cultural
Exergy analysis: Quantifies all exergy (useful fraction of energy that can be used to perform mechanical work (Hellstrom and Karrman, 1997)) inputs and outputs; results then used to compare system efficiencies and quantify consumption of physical resources; gives insight into process efficiency, but does not result in a complete accounting of environmental impacts (Balkema *et al.*, 2002).	✓		
Material flow analysis(MFA). System analysis-based quantitative calculation of flows of materials and substances, pollutants and products (Assefa *et al.*, 2005); results allow for estimates of exergy consumption and production, costs, revenues and environmental impacts associated with each material flow.	✓	✓	
Material intensity per unit service(MIPS). Material input per total unit of services delivered by product over its lifetime, from resource extraction to final waste disposal (Schmidt-Bleek, 1999); used to calculate 'ecological rucksack': $\sum$ material input (kg) of natural material − weight of product, represents stress exerted by goods on the environment, a potential indicator of its sustainability impact.	✓		
Life cycle assessment(LCA). Well-established tool for evaluating environmental impacts − from use of land, water, materials such as minerals, energy and their associated emissions to land, water and air − over the life cycle of a product/service/process; standardized approach consists of goal and scope definition, life cycle inventory, life cycle impact assessment, and interpretation (ISO, 2006a, 2006b; see Appendix of this book for more detail).	✓		
Ecological footprint analysis(EFA). Generally, EFA calculates land area (in global acres of biologically productive space) needed to sustain human consumption and absorb its ensuing wastes (Redefining Progress, 2005); can be tailored to evaluate environmental impacts of a specific service/product, such as wastewater management; requires information on material and energy flows, and direct land use requirements.	✓		

Table 12.3   *(Continued)*

Tool and description	Sustainability dimension addressed		
	Environmental	Economic	Socio-cultural
Economic analysis. As a sustainability assessment tool, evaluates whether the system can pay for itself, with costs not exceeding benefits (Balkema *et al.*, 2002); all costs and benefits (e.g. financial, socio-cultural and environmental) ideally included in the analysis, but it is often difficult to quantify nonfinancial concerns objectively in monetary terms.		✓	
Integrated Model: Organic Waste Research Model (ORWARE/URWARE). Developed for quantifying and comparing the environmental impacts, energy balances, and economics of municipal waste management schemes (Assefa *et al.*, 2005); uses MFA to quantify material flows, subsequently used for estimating energy balances, costs and revenues; LCA guides delineation of system boundaries and assessment of potential environmental impacts; life cycle costing used to valuate financial and environmental costs.	✓	✓	
Sustainability indicators. Relies on evaluation of indicators selected according to the specific project goals; indicators are parameters used to define/describe a condition, usually to be measured against a benchmark or a target; for wastewater systems, indicators can be selected to characterize sustainability based on public health, environmental, socio-cultural, economic and engineering considerations (e.g. Lundin and Morrison, 2002).	✓	✓	✓

Environment Programme (UNEP, 2003). The economic dimension can be evaluated based on both financial and economic analyses, which can take into account factors such as ability to pay and potential business generation effects. The socio-cultural issues can be addressed qualitatively through detailed interviews, focus groups, general surveys and first-hand observations.

Note that, in addition to its usefulness as a planning tool, indicators can also be employed as an *ex-post* evaluation tool to determine potential improvements to the sustainability of existing systems. Indicators should always be developed to address the specific goals of a project, taking into account the local context. In developing countries, for example, where high unemployment rates and poverty are common, employment and local business generation effects are important considerations for having a more comprehensive impact on sustainable development.

Further detail on sustainability indicators can be found in Chapter 2.

The next section presents a case study to illustrate how sustainability indicators can be used to evaluate and compare two sanitation options.

Questions

1. Identify the data required for each of the sustainability tools described in Table 12.3.
2. Draw a life cycle diagram of a sanitation system in general and discuss the sustainability (economic, environmental and social) aspects associated with each stage. Choose a developing country in which this system could be installed and discuss sustainability issues in the context of that country.
3. What types of question/issue can be addressed by the various sustainability tools listed in Table 12.3? For example, for what type of project would you choose to use an ecological footprint analysis?

12.7 Case Study: Rural/Peri-Urban Provision of Sanitation in eThekwini Municipality, South Africa

12.7.1 Background

The eThekwini Municipality (ETM) is responsible for providing water and wastewater services to over 3 million people in the city of Durban on the eastern coast of South Africa, as well as to the surrounding wider metropolitan area consisting of urban, peri-urban and rural areas. The Durban area has a mild subtropical climate with an annual rainfall of 1009 mm; it is very hilly, with a few flat areas in the Durban downtown and harbour areas.

Box 12.4   A historical look at the evolution of ETM's sanitation programme

The evolution of the ETM's current sanitation programme is closely tied to major events in the history of South Africa, particularly its transition from apartheid (DWAF, 2002). During the apartheid era between 1948 and 1994, whites, blacks, Indians and coloureds lived in segregated areas in the city of Durban, ruled by a white government, as well as the surrounding mainly peri-urban and rural areas. By early 1995, 95 % of Durban was sewered; small urban sections of the surrounding areas were also sewered. Parts of Durban were served by two deep marine outfalls that discharged raw wastewater – with only oils and grit removed – into the sea. The rest of Durban's wastewater underwent secondary treatment for surface water discharge. Outside of Durban, sanitation consisted mainly of open defecation (rural areas), simple pit latrines and the 'bucket system', in which containers of human excreta were manually collected two to three times per week for emptying into designated dump sites connected to the sewage reticulation system. Pre-1995, many of the nonwhite undeveloped areas outside Durban were managed by a variety of agencies. When apartheid officially ended in 1994, government was restructured to unify the country and correct historic inequalities.

Consequently, Durban was incorporated with surrounding areas previously overseen by approximately 40 local authorities to form the ETM; the area overseen by the unified municipality ultimately expanded by more than 10 times to 2000 km^2 and became a diverse landscape of urban, peri-urban and rural areas. Thus, in 1995, the ETM faced the challenge of managing a complex patchwork of unconnected water and wastewater systems that were previously managed separately, often with very different levels of service.

Consistent with the national government's goal to provide at least the minimum acceptable level of sanitation to all South Africans by 2010 (DWAF, 2001), in 1995 the ETM began to plan for providing universal sanitation coverage to its service area. Note that this is a much more ambitious target than that set by the MDGs. The ETM's efforts focused mainly on the rural and peri-urban areas and the emerging informal settlements in the urban areas, most of which did not meet the minimum acceptable level of service defined as a ventilated improved pit (VIP) latrine or equivalent by the national government (DWAF, 2002). The ETM also recognized that it would have to develop an alternative to VIPs for unserved areas. Emptying VIPs every 5 years or so is labour intensive and expensive, and a pit emptying backlog for existing VIPs (inherited from previous agencies) quickly developed. This is because many VIPs were located on steep hillsides with no road access and, therefore, had to be emptied manually. Furthermore, a significant amount of space (2 m × 3 m × 1 m) is required to make on-site burial of pit contents a viable option; ground conditions and lack of space often precluded this from taking place. From a construction perspective, the ETM also recognized that VIPs had limited applicability in areas with rocky surfaces and high groundwater tables (they require pit depths of 2 to 3 m). For example, in Umzinyathi, one of the pilot areas targeted by the ETM in the late 1990s/early 2000s, the ETM found that, based simply on hydro-geological considerations, only 40% of the households could be served by VIPs. Considering pit-emptying access issues, this proportion dropped to 20%.

In their search for an alternative, the ETM ultimately decided that a dual pit urine diversion dehydrating (UDD) toilet was the best option for peri-urban/rural areas. In addition, the householder would receive a reticulated basic supply of potable water. The ETM's UDD toilet is designed with two ventilated 1 m^3 chambers and a moveable toilet seat (see Figure 12.5). When the active chamber is full, the pedestal is moved above the empty chamber; the filled chamber is then closed and its contents are allowed to dry and undergo hygienization while the other chamber fills (designed for approximately a 12-month period for a household of eight). Once the second chamber is filled, the contents of the first chamber are removed and buried by the household (or a contractor); the freshly emptied chamber is now ready for use again. Theoretically, the UDD toilet can be used indefinitely and completely managed at the household level, presenting significant advantages over the VIP; it can also be constructed where there are hydro-geological conditions unsuitable for VIPs.

The decision to switch from VIPs to UDD toilets was primarily based on maintenance and cost considerations by the ETM, but how do the two systems compare when considering

Figure 12.5   *ETM's UDD toilet*

a broader and more multidimensional sustainability perspective? And how would the results of the selection process change?

For illustration purposes, the indicator approach is applied to ETM's rural/peri-urban sanitation programme to evaluate and compare the two alternatives; the results are presented in Table 12.4 and are discussed below.

For this case study example, the indicators were chosen based on a literature review and a consideration of local issues of concern in the ETM. For example, the indicator 'local development, business and income-generation effects' is particularly important in South Africa – and in many developing countries – where poverty alleviation is often a key goal of government-sponsored programmes.

Ideally, the indicators would be selected through a stakeholder consultation process to ensure that the interests of all of the stakeholders, particularly the users, are represented. If required, some indicators can be assessed more quantitatively. Note that there is less experience associated with UDD toilets and, therefore, there is much to learn about their real-life performance; research projects are currently underway (e.g. at the University of KwaZulu-Natal) to evaluate the UDD toilets more systematically and quantitatively. This underlines the notion that sustainability evaluations should not be treated statically and absolutely – new information and experiences should be integrated into the evaluation as they emerge to continue to make progress towards sustainability.

Table 12.4 *Results of sustainability comparison of the alternative sanitation systems installed in peri-urban/rural areas in the ETM*

Indicators[a,b]	VIPs	UDD toilets
Socio-cultural/institutional		
User acceptability	Medium	Medium
Adaptability to different age, gender and income groups	Medium	Medium
Current legal acceptability and institutional compatibility	Low	Medium
Exposure to pathogens and risk of infection	Medium	Low
Risk of exposure to hazardous substances	Medium	Low
Health benefits due to improved hygiene, food production, nutrition, status, livelihood	Medium	Medium (*potentially greater with safe excreta reuse for agriculture*)
Effects of system failure	Medium	Low
Robustness of system	High	Low
Possibility to use local competence for construction and O&M	High	High
Ease of system monitoring	Medium	Medium
Durability	Medium	High
Complexity of construction and O&M	Low	Medium
Compatibility with existing systems	High	High
Economic		
Capital cost/1000 people/year (construction only)	$2000–6200	$8000
O&M cost/1000 people/year (pit emptying only)	$6200	$0 (household) or $1900–2100 (contractor)
User ability to pay (annualized cost as % income)[c]	1.7 %	0–0.8 %
Financial benefits from reuse	None	None (*but with future potential*)
Potential for local development, business and income-generation effects	High (construction and pit emptying service)	High (construction and pit emptying service)
Environmental		
Use of natural resources (construction and O&M)		
Land (Toilet and material disposal requirements (solids)	8 m^2	10 m^2
O&M energy	None (unless off-site disposal required)	None
% Renewable energy (O&M)	None	None
Water consumption (O&M)	None	None
Water discharges		
BOD/COD discharge to water bodies[d]	None–Low	None
N and P discharge to water bodies[d]	None–Low	None
Air emissions		
GWP (construction materials) in kg CO_2 equivalent per household/toilet	702	1200
Odour	Medium	Medium (but less than VIPs)

Table 12.4   *(Continued)*

Indicators[a,b]	VIPs	UDD toilets
Land discharges		
Hazardous substances: heavy metals (e.g. Cd, Pb, Cu and Hg), persistent organic compounds, and so on.	Medium (excreta are land-applied)	Medium (excreta are land-applied)
Resources recovered		
Nutrients applied to agriculture	None	Household-dependent[e]
Energy	None	None
Organic matter	None	Household-dependent[e]
Water	Household-dependent	Household-dependent

[a]Indicators were developed and modified based on UNESCO-IHP and GTZ (2006), Balkema *et al.* (2002), and Lundin and Morrison (2002).
[b]Assumes an average of 4.3 people/household.
[c]For incomes of 1000 ZAR/household/month.
[d]There is potential for leaching into groundwater if there is insufficient distance between the pit bottom and the groundwater table.
[e]ETM currently does not recommend recycling of the UDD chamber contents.

12.7.2 Socio-Cultural/Institutional Dimensions

From a socio-cultural/institutional perspective, the VIPs and UDD toilets confer some similar advantages, but also differ in some respects. The UDD toilets perform better from an institutional perspective (both are acceptable by national standards, but the UDDs are supported by the ETM because of the perceived greater ease of maintenance, particularly to the ETM). They also perform well from a risk perspective: exposure to pit contents due to flooding is problematic with VIPs and the viability of pathogens in the pits is theoretically higher than in the UDD chambers, although more scientific evidence is needed to support this. Lastly, they work well from a durability/lifetime perspective because of much lower material volumes and potentially higher degradation rates; space requirements are lower for UDD toilets; and they theoretically can operate indefinitely.

VIPs perform better from system robustness and ease of monitoring perspectives: they are less complex to use, as urine and faecal separation is not required, and even some water in the VIPs is acceptable. They are also favoured from a complexity of construction and operation and maintenance (O&M) perspective – UDD toilets have a more sophisticated design due to the two chambers and the urine separation requirements, and operation requires more user discipline. The two systems perform similarly from user acceptability, adaptability, health benefits and compatibility with existing systems viewpoints.

12.7.3 Economic Dimensions

From an economic perspective, the two systems also perform similarly based on the higher end of the total annualized capital and O&M costs (see Table 12.4). The O&M costs associated with UDD toilets confer advantages, in that they can drop to zero for both the user and the municipality if households carry out the emptying themselves. Note that the areas currently served by the UDDs are indigent and the full capital cost of the units are, therefore, subsidized by the ETM. Other municipalities with insufficient funding may find the VIPs more economically sustainable from their perspective, as simpler models can be built for lower initial costs. However, the cost of pit emptying may then be unsustainable for the users. The ease of emptying the UDD toilets is one of their key advantages compared with VIPs. It remains to be seen, however, whether households will be comfortable in the long term with emptying the chambers themselves; interviews with users reveal that they are generally uncomfortable with the idea of emptying the chambers. More experience and surveys of long-term UDD toilet users are needed to determine what proportion will do the emptying themselves and what the ultimate cost will be to the users.

Another potential advantage of the UDD toilets – untapped in the case of ETM – is that they create the possibility of deriving economic value from the collected excreta. In other countries (e.g. Burkina Faso and Malawi), dehydrated or composted faeces and separately collected urine from similarly designed toilets are used as soil conditioner and fertilizer, leading to increased crop yields and/or reduced artificial soil conditioner/fertilizer costs to the households. Excreta reuse is currently not being promoted by the ETM.

12.7.4 Environmental Dimensions

From an environmental emissions perspective, the main difference between VIP and UDD toilets is the potential for N and P contamination of groundwater by the VIP, as it allows for stormwater and washwater infiltration into the porous pit, which can mobilize contaminants. Otherwise, the two systems function similarly, in that urine and faeces are ultimately discharged to land and not to water bodies, thus preventing the microbial contamination of surface water supplies and minimizing the potential for eutrophication. In the case of the UDDs, faeces are isolated from land for some time (approximately 1 year) before eventually being buried. In the case of VIPs, urine, faeces and washwater (and other solid waste discharged into the pits) are in contact with the soil from the start of use. Note that the land requirements of the two options turn out to be similar.

It is important to note that both the VIPs and UDD toilets are only designed for blackwater (mainly urine and faeces) management; they do not provide for greywater management. Greywater disposal is generally done via land disposal, sometimes via irrigation of vegetable gardens. In the ETM, greywater reuse is dependent on the household, and at least some reuse often occurs for cleaning or dust control. In both cases, the structures are not material intensive and generally require similar amounts of construction materials (primarily brick, blocks, cement mortar, wood for the door and tin for the roofing).

12.7.5 Case Study Conclusions

Based on the sustainability indicators considered in this analysis, the two options are not too dissimilar overall. The key differences lie in the *potential* for resource recovery (nutrients and organic matter) in the case of the UDDs, which can have environmental, economic and socio-cultural impacts, and in the O&M requirements, which have both economic and socio-cultural impacts. The biggest challenges of the UDD toilets are related to the education/training of the users on their proper operation and maintenance and the potential need for a service provider, which is affordable to users, to empty the chambers for households who do not want to empty the chambers themselves. The ETM is already working on addressing these challenges, which are not insurmountable; there could even be the benefit of contributing to local economic development through recovery of nutrients.

Questions

1. What indicators would you use if you were doing this analysis?
2. How would you weigh the various indicators? Which ones would you consider to be most important and why?
3. How would you make the choice between the two alternatives?
4. How would changes to the results of the individual indicators affect the overall decision?

12.8 Conclusions

The methodology presented in the case study provides a systematic and explicit way of incorporating multidimensional sustainability considerations into the development of wastewater options for developing countries and an evaluation and comparison of these options. Appropriate technologies for developing countries were screened based on their function and their use of operational sustainability features. This list of technologies can then be used to develop design options. Indicators are used to enable a parallel comparison of the options from socio-cultural/institutional, economic and environmental perspectives. This is intended to avoid a decision-making process, wherein one factor (e.g. O&M cost) and/or one perspective (e.g. a regulator's) ends up driving a programme that has wide-ranging effects on a variety of stakeholders from public health to the economic viability of municipalities.

The ultimate selection of the most sustainable option rests on the shoulders of the stakeholders, who will need to decide how to take into account the various indicators based on the local issues of concern. There are formal and informal methods of so-called multicriteria decision making (for examples, see Hurley *et al.* (2008). The approach taken should reflect the local conditions, particularly the local governance structures and culture. Whilst, in practice, limited budget and time for project implementation often pose significant constraints on the decision-making process, to make progress towards sustainability, the process should be as deliberate and stakeholder inclusive as possible.

In bringing improvements in sanitation to many parts of developing countries all over the world, the overriding goals are not the building of the physical systems themselves, but ultimately the health benefits they bring to the communities being served. Whilst the provision of a service or facility where none may have existed before may seem to be an obvious positive step forward along this road, mistakes can be (and have been) made which can lead to a rapid discontinuation of use. The broader sustainability aspects of sanitation services need to be considered so that the selected sanitation system is one that meets each individual community's needs and aspirations, provides opportunities for resource recovery and, of course, serves as an effective public health barrier. The MDGs represent a starting point in many regions, with a focus on sustainable service delivery, rather than the construction of facilities alone, being the key to future success.

Acknowledgments

The authors would like to thank the Gates Cambridge Trust and St John's College for their funding support. They are also grateful to the staff, particularly John Harrison and Teddy Gounden at the ETM and Professor Chris Buckley at the University of KwaZulu-Natal for their assistance with the case study research in the ETM.

References and Further Reading

Assefa, G., Bjorklund, A., Eriksson, O. and Frostell, B. (2005) ORWARE: an aid to environmental technology chain assessment. *Journal of Cleaner Production*, **13**, 265–274.

Balkema, A.J., Preisig, H.A., Otterpohl, R. and Lambert, F.J.D. (2002) Indicators for the sustainability assessment of wastewater treatment Systems. *Urban Water*, **4**, 153–161.

Drangert, J.-O. (2005) A tool for selecting sustainable sanitation arrangements. Paper presented at 3rd at Third International Ecological Sanitation Conference, 23–26 May 2005, Durban, South Africa, http://conference2005.ecosan.org.

DWAF (Department of Water Affairs and Forestry) (2001) White Paper on Basic Household Sanitation.

DWAF (Department of Water Affairs and Forestry) (2002) The Development of a Sanitation Policy and Practice in South Africa.

Gleick, P.H. (2006) *The World's Water 2006–2007: The Biennial Report on Freshwater Resources*, Island Press, ISBN 1-59726-106-8.

Green, W. and Ho, G. (2005) Small scale sanitation technologies. *Water Science and Technology*, **51** (10), 29–38.

Hellstrom, D. and Karrman, E. (1997) Exergy analysis and nutrient flows of various sewerage systems. *Water Science and Technology*, **35** (9), 135–144.

Hurley, L., Ashley, R. and Mounce, S. (2008) Addressing practical problems in sustainability assessment frameworks. *Proceedings of the Institution of Civil Engineers, Engineering Sustainability Journal*, **161** (ES1), 23–30.

International Standards Organization (ISO) (2006a) ISO 14040. *Environmental management – Life cycle assessment – Principles and framework*.

International Standards Organization (ISO) (2006b) ISO 14044. *Environmental management – Life cycle assessment – Requirements and guidelines*.

Larsen, T.A. and Lienert, J. (2007) Novaquatis final report: NoMix – a new approach to urban water management. Eawag, 8600 Duebendorf, Switzerland.

Lundin, M. and Morrison, G.M. (2002) A life cycle assessment based procedure for development of environmental sustainability indicators for urban water systems. *Urban Water*, **4**, 145–152.

Lundin, M., Olofsson, M., Pettersson, G.J. and Zetterlund, H. (2004) Environmental and economic assessment of sewage sludge handling options. *Resources, Conservation and Recycling*, **41**, 255–278.

Mara, D. (1996) *Low-Cost Urban Sanitation*, John Wiley & Sons Ltd, Chichester.

Mara, D.D. (2005) Water supply and sanitation options for small towns and large villages in developing countries. Background Paper for the 2nd UN-Habitat Global Report on Water and Sanitation.

Melo, J.C. (2005) The experience of condomininial water and sewerage systems in Brazil: Case Studies from Brasilia, Salvador and Parauapebas. World Bank Water and Sanitation Program – Latin America. Lima, Peru.

Metcalf and Eddy Inc. (2003) *Wastewater Engineering: Treatment and Reuse*, 4th edn (revised by G. Tchobanoglous, F.L. Burton and H.D. Stensel), McGraw-Hill Inc.

Prüss-Üstün, A., Bos, R., Gore, F. and Bartram, J. (2008) *Safer Water, Better Health: Cost, Benefits and Sustainability Interventions to Protect and Promote Health*, WHO, Geneva, Switzerland, ISBN 978 92 4 159643 5.

Prüss-Üstün, A., Kay, D., Fewtrell, L. and Bartram, J. (2004) Unsafe water, sanitation and hygiene, in *Comparative Quantification of Health Risks: Global and Regional Burden of Disease Attribution to Selected Major Risk Factors* (eds M. Ezzati, A.D. Lopez, A. Rodgers and C.J.L. Murray), WHO, Geneva, Switzerland, pp. 1321–1352.

Redefining Progress (2005) Ecological Footprint of Nations – 2005 Update. Oakland, California, USA, http://www.ecologicalfootprint.org/ (accessed 4 July 2007).

Schmidt-Bleek, F. (1999) The Factor 10/MIPS-Concept: bridging ecological, economic, and social dimensions with sustainability indicators. United Nations University, Zero Emissions Forum. ISSN 1609-493X (Online).

UNDP (United Nations Development Programme) (2006) *Human Development Report – Beyond Scarcity: Power, Poverty and the Global Water Crisis*, Palgrave MacMillan, New York, ISBN 0-230-50058-7.

UNEP (United Nations Environment Programme) (2003) *Evaluation of Environmental Impacts in Life Cycle Assessment. Meeting Report, Brussels, 29–30 November 1998, and Brighton, 25–26 May 2000.* UNEP, ISBN 92-807-2144-5.

UNESCO-IHP (United Nations Educational, Scientific, and Cultural Organization – International Hydrological Programme) and GTZ (Deutsche Gesellschaft fur Technische Zusammenarbeit GmbH) (2006) Capacity building for ecological sanitation: concepts for ecologically sustainable sanitation in formal and continuing education. UNESCO Working Series SC-2006/WS/5.

UN Millennium Project Task Force on Water and Sanitation (2005) *Health, Dignity and Development: What Will it Take?* Stockholm International Water Institute and UN Millenium Project, New York, ISBN 91-974183-8-2.

WEF (Water Environment Federation) (2006) *Membrane Systems for Wastewater Treatment*, WEF Press, McGraw-Hill Inc., New York, USA.

WHO (World Health Organization) (2004) *The Sanitation Challenge: Turning Commitment into Reality*, WHO, Geneva, Switzerland, ISBN 92 4 159162 5.

WHO (World Health Organization) (2006) *Guidelines for the Safe Use of Wastewater, Excreta and Greywater*, WHO, Geneva, Switzerland, ISBN 92 4 154686 7.

WHO (World Health Organization) and UNICEF (United Nations Children's Fund) (2006) *Meeting the MDG Drinking Water and Sanitation Target: The Urban and Rural Challenge of the Decade*, WHO, Geneva, Switzerland, ISBN 92 4 156325 7.

Winblad, U. and Simpson-Hebert, M. (eds) (2004) *Ecological Sanitation*, revised and enlarged edn, SEI, Stockholm, Sweden.

Wright, A. (1997) Toward a strategic sanitation approach: improving the sustainability of urban sanitation in developing countries. UNDP–World Bank Water and Sanitation Program, IR www.wsp.org.

13

Sustainable Process Design: The Case of Vinyl Chloride Monomer (VCM)

Adisa Azapagic

This chapter illustrates how different sustainability criteria can be integrated within a common framework to guide the design of more sustainable processes and chemical plants. Applying life cycle thinking, the chapter follows process design from project initiation, through preliminary to detailed design. The case study shows how to identify relevant sustainability criteria, how to assess the level of sustainability of a process design and how to use the obtained information to make the design more sustainable.

13.1 Design, Systems and Life Cycles

Process design is normally based on technical and micro-economic considerations to ensure that the proposed plant is 'fit for purpose' and that it maximizes economic returns to the company. Some of the environmental (e.g. emissions from the plant) and social (e.g. health and safety) criteria are also considered during design. However, this is often done as an 'afterthought', once the technical and economic components of the design have been finalized. Such an approach can lead to a suboptimal environmental performance of the plant, because design choices are more limited in the latter stages of design and may not allow consideration of more environmentally sustainable process alternatives. Moreover, even if included in the design stage, environmental criteria are usually considered at the

Sustainable Development in Practice: Case Studies for Engineers and Scientists, Second Edition
Edited by Adisa Azapagic and Slobodan Perdan
© 2011 John Wiley & Sons, Ltd.

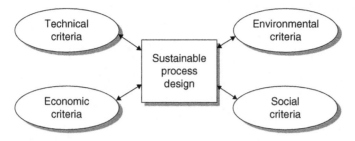

Figure 13.1 *Integrating sustainability criteria into process design*

minimum level required by legislation and are almost invariably related to direct environmental interventions from the plant without considering the upstream or downstream impacts. Thus, the designer can design a plant which reduces the environmental impacts from that particular process, but increases the impact upstream, perhaps through a choice of unsustainable energy and materials, or downstream; for example, through waste management and disposal.

Therefore, designing sustainable processes, plants and facilities requires a systems approach whereby sustainability is not considered as an 'add on' but is integrated systematically into the design. This means that, in addition to the traditional technical and economic factors, environmental and social components must be considered simultaneously during design (see Figure 13.1). This is by no means a trivial task and will require a range of 'hard' science and engineering skills, but also the use of 'soft' theories and approaches, drawing on the knowledge and input from environmental and social scientists. Therefore, a multidisciplinary approach to design is essential.

Process engineers are familiar with the systems approach because this is the approach that underpins design: the process of interest is defined as a system around which a system boundary is drawn to include all of its constituent elements and their interactions (see Figure 13.2). However, the system boundary is drawn around the process itself, usually without considering any upstream and downstream activities. For example, although material and energy inputs into the process and waste and emissions from the process are accounted for in the design, their upstream origin and downstream destination are usually not included within the system boundary. As already mentioned, this can lead to a design which optimizes the performance inside the system boundary but is suboptimal outside it.

Furthermore, design is often focused on the operation stage and is usually not concerned with the other stages in the life cycle of the plant; that is, construction and decommissioning.

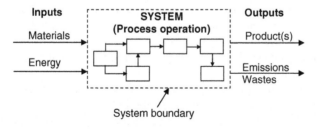

Figure 13.2 *System definition and system boundary in conventional process design*

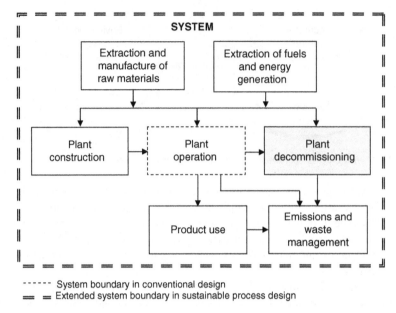

Figure 13.3   *Sustainable process design: the extended system boundary encompassing the life cycles of process and product*

However, these stages can often have significant economic, environmental and social impacts. For example, decommissioning chemical plants can be costly and environmentally challenging, particularly for polluting processes – not accounting for this at the design stage can lead to much higher environmental impacts and costs at the end of the plant's useful life.

Thus, the whole life cycle of a plant, from construction through operation to decommissioning, should be taken into account during design to ensure that all relevant sustainability aspects have been taken into account over the lifetime of the plant (see Figure 13.3). Furthermore, the drive for broader corporate social responsibility (e.g. see Chapters 2 and 4) also demands consideration of the life cycle of the product to be manufactured by the plant, including its use and subsequent disposal. The rest of the chapter demonstrates how this can be done in practice.

Questions

1. What is meant by 'sustainable process design'?
2. What is the systems approach? Why is it important for process design?
3. Explain why it is important to integrate technical and economic with environmental and social criteria in sustainable process design.
4. What are the advantages of sustainable process design and what might be the difficulties associated with it?
5. What is meant by the 'life cycle approach to process design'? Why is it important to take a life cycle approach in design for sustainability?
6. Sustainable design requires multidisciplinary team work. What disciplines do you think need to work together in designing more sustainable processes? Explain why and what

kind of knowledge and skills these disciplines bring together. What might be the difficulties of working in multidisciplinary teams?
7. Give some examples of sustainability criteria that you think could be relevant in process design.

13.2 Sustainable Process Design

Approaches to design vary and no two designers will design a complex process in exactly the same way, following exactly the same steps. However, regardless of the approach, the design process normally involves the following stages:

1. project initiation;
2. preliminary design;
3. detailed design; and
4. final design.

As shown in Figure 13.4, each of these four stages consists of a number of steps. A detailed explanation of the design procedure and these steps is beyond the scope of this chapter; the interested reader can find excellent descriptions in, for example, Ulrich (1992), Douglas (2003), Ray and Johnston (2000), Sinnott (2001) and Seider *et al.* (1999). Instead, only a brief overview of the major design stages is given below, followed by a detailed discussion of the sustainability aspects of design. In Figure 13.4 the design stages related to sustainability are *in italics* so that they can be distinguished from the stages which are part of conventional design; the section headings below relating to these sustainability aspects are indicated with an asterisk. Final design is not considered here, as it would not normally involve further sustainability considerations.

13.2.1 Project Initiation

i. Identifying the Need
All engineering projects, and therefore process designs, are typically initiated as a result of an identified economic opportunity and/or social need. For example, a chemical company may identify a consumer need for a certain product which can be produced profitably. The role of the designer is to design a process or product that will fulfil this need. In the context of sustainable development, however, this need must be fulfilled in a socially and environmentally responsible way, while at the same time providing economic benefits to the company which will manufacture the product.

Thus, the designer is confronted with the sustainability challenge at the outset of the project. How successfully that challenge is tackled will depend on many factors. Some of these will be 'external' and outside the designer's control; for example, physical and thermodynamic laws will limit process efficiencies and, hence, the level of environmental sustainability. Other, 'internal', factors, such as the choice of process and operating conditions, will be under the control of the designer; however, the limitation here may be the designer's skills and experience.

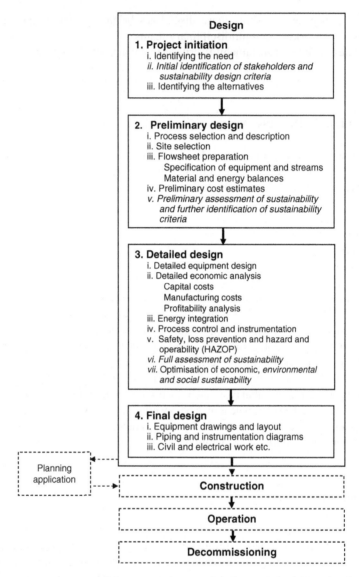

Figure 13.4   *Stages in sustainable process design, also showing the life cycle of a plant from design to decommissioning*

ii. Initial Identification of Stakeholders and Sustainability Design Criteria

As discussed in the previous section, sustainable design requires a systems approach based on life cycle thinking. Thus, identification of sustainability criteria must be done by considering all activities in the system from 'cradle to grave' (see Figure 13.3). At this initial stage of the project specification, when it is still not clear what design alternatives exist and which sustainability issues may be relevant for each alternative, particularly when

Table 13.1 *Examples of sustainability criteria relevant for process design*

Economic criteria	Environmental criteria	Social criteria
Micro-economic:	Energy use	Provision of employment
Capital costs	Water use	Employee health and safety
Operating costs	Emissions to air	Citizens' health and safety
Profitability	Emissions to water	Customer health and safety
Decommissioning costs	Solid waste	Nuisance (odour, noise,
	Abiotic reserve depletion	visual impact, transport)
Macro-economic:	Global warming	Public acceptability
Value added	Ozone depletion	
Taxes paid, including	Acidification	
'green' taxes (e.g.	Summer smog	
carbon tax)	Eutrophication	
Investment (e.g. pollution	Human toxicity	
prevention, health and	Eco-toxicity	
safety; decommission-		
ing; ethical		
investments)		
Potential costs of		
environmental liability		

designing completely new processes, the designer can only identify and use sustainability design criteria that are generally applicable to most processes. Some examples of these criteria that can be used to evaluate and screen the alternatives in the next design step are listed in Table 13.1. In identifying the specific sustainability criteria, the designer should be aware of the relevant stakeholders and the sustainability issues that will be of interest to them. Typically, the stakeholders will include employees of the company which will own and operate the plant, investors, neighbouring communities and citizens, nongovernmental organizations (NGOs) and government. Each stakeholder group will have their own interests in the life cycle of the project, and these interests will often be diametrically opposite (see Chapter 17, for example). The designer must be aware of these issues and try to balance them appropriately.

In addition to the technical design variables, some of the sustainability criteria listed in Table 13.1 are already used routinely in conventional design, particularly the micro-economic (e.g. costs and profits) and some of the environmental (e.g. energy and water use) and social criteria (e.g. employee health and safety). Others, such as value added, ethical investments and provision of employment are usually not addressed in the conventional design, and particularly not within the extended system boundary from 'cradle to grave'. The interested reader can consult Azapagic and Perdan (2000) for a more detailed discussion on process-related sustainability criteria. Here, only a brief overview of general economic, environmental and social criteria is given; Section 13.2 shows how they can be applied in the case of VCM.

It should be noted that sustainability criteria are considered at the qualitative level at this stage, by identifying advantages and disadvantages of different alternatives, with respect to these criteria. They will be translated into the more concrete and largely quantitative measures of sustainability performance in the preliminary stage of design, as discussed further in Section 13.2.2.

Economic Criteria

Economic viability of industrial activities is at the heart of sustainable development. Only competitive and profitable enterprises are able to make a long-term contribution to sustainable development by generating wealth and jobs and, through that, contributing to social welfare. Therefore, the aim is to design profitable processes and facilities which will benefit both the company and the society at large. Hence, two types of economic criteria are relevant for sustainable process design: micro- and macro-economic criteria. The former are related directly to the economic performance of the company and include the usual financial measures, such as capital and operating costs, cash flow and return on investment. Macro-economic criteria demonstrate social responsibility of the company through the financial returns to society from the taxes paid and other socially responsible investments, including investment in pollution prevention and health and safety, ethical investments, investment in decommissioning and so on.

Environmental Criteria

As mentioned above, quantifying environmental emissions and wastes from process plants is already an integral part of design, mainly because of the legislative constraints imposed on the their operation. However, the emissions and wastes are rarely translated into the potential environmental impacts, which is what ultimately matters. The environmental impacts listed in Table 13.1 represent typical environmental impacts considered in environmental analysis of industrial activities; hence, most of them should be applicable to process design. In the context of sustainable process design, the environmental impacts should be considered from 'cradle to grave' using life cycle assessment (LCA) as a tool. The environmental criteria listed in Table 13.1 are also considered routinely in LCA studies. The LCA methodology is outlined in Chapter 3, which also shows how to translate the environmental burdens (i.e. the use of energy and materials and emissions to air, water and land) into potential environmental impacts.

Social Criteria

Social accountability is related to wider responsibilities that companies have to employees and to communities in which they operate. The social criteria in Table 13.1 take into account both the interests of employees and those of the neighbouring communities by addressing health and safety issues associated with the construction, operation and decommissioning of the plant, as well as with the product use and post-use waste management. Furthermore, they also take into account potential nuisance that the plant can cause to the neighbouring communities through unpleasant odour, noise and visual impact, as well as through transportation activities associated with the construction and operation of the plant. Associated with these criteria is the public acceptability of both the plant and the product and the so-called 'social licence to operate'. Without it, it will not be possible to proceed with the project, however good the design, so that the public acceptability issues must be considered at an early stage. The issue of public acceptability and its influence on engineering projects is discussed in detail in Chapters 10 and 17.

This initial choice of sustainability design criteria will be further refined in the later stages of design. It is possible that, as the design progresses, some of the criteria will become redundant while additional criteria are identified. It is important, therefore, that the designer is fully aware of the dynamic nature of the design process and is able to use a flexible approach which enables incorporation of new criteria as well as elimination of the criteria which initially appeared relevant but later turned out to be of no importance for a particular design configuration.

iii. Identifying the Alternatives

In many cases there will be a number of alternative solutions to a design problem. These will include alternative processing routes, technologies, raw materials, energy sources and so on. To identify feasible design solutions, it is necessary to describe the alternatives, specifying the processing routes, the availability of technologies, raw materials, products and by-products. The sustainability criteria identified in the previous stage are then used to evaluate the alternatives by identifying their main advantages and disadvantages and screening out those that are less promising at this stage.

This initial screening is often carried out on a qualitative basis and requires experienced designers. Simple flowsheets can be used to make initial comparisons between the alternative processes. A large number of alternatives may require a more formal approach, perhaps using a simple table or a decision tree to rank the suitability of an alternative for each of the initially identified design criteria. For a smaller number of alternatives, screening can be carried out through discussions among a group of informed and interested stakeholders. Ideally, the outcome of this stage should be the identification of the most promising alternative; however, in practice, it is more likely that there will be several feasible and potentially sustainable process alternatives. The final process selection is then made in the next, preliminary design stage.

Questions

1. Use the Brundtland definition to explain the link between sustainable development and initiation of a design project.
2. Draw your own list of sustainability criteria that you think should be used in process design for sustainability and compare it with those listed in Table 13.1. Explain any differences.
3. Explain the link between the micro- and macro-economic design criteria. Support your explanations with examples.
4. Explain the links between economic, environmental and social design criteria. Give examples which illustrate these links.
5. Why is it important to identify sustainability criteria before specifying the design alternatives? What would happen if we did it the other way round?

13.2.2 Preliminary Design

Design problems are usually solved by first developing very simple design configurations and then adding successive layers of detail. There are a number of approaches to doing this, the review of which is outside the scope of this chapter. One of the approaches widely used in conventional design is the hierarchical method developed by Douglas (2003), whereby the design is developed by following a certain decision hierarchy, starting from the selection of a continuous or batch process, through the development of the input–output and recycle structure of the flowsheet to the development of the general structure of the separation system and the heat-exchanger network. This is then followed by a preliminary economic evaluation, to enable a more detailed development of the process.

In sustainable process design, in addition to the economic evaluation, the system is also evaluated on environmental and social sustainability (see Figure 13.4). This then enables the final identification of sustainability criteria which will be used in detailed design. These stages are described briefly below, with the emphasis on the stages related to sustainability.

i. Process Selection and Description

The final selection of an appropriate process is an important decision which will determine all the subsequent work (Ray and Johnston, 1989). It is important, therefore, that this decision is made by considering as many decision criteria as possible, using the technical, economic, environmental and social criteria identified in the preceding design stage. The final choice will usually be based on trade-offs between the advantages and disadvantages of the alternatives, as it is unlikely that any one process will possess all the positive sides and no negative sides.

The chosen process should then be described in enough detail to enable the flowsheet preparation in the next design step. This should include a description of the chemistry involved in different stages, the operating conditions of the process, the feeds and energy used and intermediates, products and by-products produced. The type of emissions and solid wastes should also be specified.

However, prior to that, it is important to choose an appropriate site for the proposed plant.

ii. Site Selection

The issue of site selection only arises in the design of completely new plants and is not a consideration for process additions to an existing integrated plant (apart from where exactly on the existing site it is going to be built). Selection of an appropriate site for a new plant is important for several reasons. First, from the operational and economic point of view, it is important that the site is accessible, has fundamental infrastructure and is close to the raw material, utility and the labour supply, as well as that it is reasonably well connected to the anticipated markets. Second, it is important that the site is suitable from the environmental and social points of view so that the proposed plant does not cause opposition from the public and planning authorities. For example, the proposed development could be close to a nature or recreational spot or too close to the local communities. In many countries an environmental impact assessment (EIA) of new and modified processes is required by law, so that the designer must take into account the requirements of the EIA in choosing an appropriate site in order to minimize the relevant environmental and social impacts. An example of an EIA statement for a proposed (incineration) plant is given in Chapter 10.

iii. Flowsheet Preparation

Flowsheet is a process 'blueprint', which shows the process sequence, individual equipment, material and energy balances and serves as a framework for cost estimation. Different flowsheeting packages are available to assist in flowsheet preparation and process simulation; some examples include ASPEN PLUS (Aspen Technology, 2003), CHEMCAD (Chemstations, 2002) and HYSIM (Hyprotech, 1988). Further detail on flowsheet preparation can be found in, for example, Ulrich (1992), Sinnott (2001) and Seider *et al.* (1999).

iv. Preliminary Cost Estimates

This stage involves a preliminary calculation of capital and operating costs which are normally within ± 20–30% of the actual costs (Ray and Johnston, 1989). This information is used to determine the economic feasibility of the chosen process or to help choose between design alternatives. Detailed and more accurate cost estimates are only required in the detailed design, after the design and sizing of all equipment and specification of pipework and instrumentation have been completed. Further discussion on cost estimates is outside the scope of this chapter and the interested reader can consult, for example, Ulrich (1992) and Sinnott (2001) for more detailed economic analyses of chemical processes.

v. Preliminary Assessment of Sustainability and Further Identification of Sustainability Criteria

As already mentioned, the qualitative sustainability criteria identified in the first design stage need to be translated into the appropriate measures of economic, environmental and social performance. These measures of performance are usually referred to as sustainability indicators or metrics (see Chapter 2). The quantitative indicators can be expressed in monetary, mass, energy or other suitable units, whilst the qualitative indicators are presented as descriptive statements. For example, the profitability criterion is usually translated into the economic indicators such as cash flow and net present value, which are expressed in monetary units. On the other hand, the criterion 'public acceptability' would be represented by a set of qualitative indicators which describe the issues of concern raised by the neighbouring communities, NGOs and other stakeholders.

Further reading on industry-related sustainability indicators can be found, for example, in Azapagic and Perdan (2000) and IChemE (1988).

Assessing Economic Sustainability

The economic evaluation in conventional design is normally based on the micro-economic indicators, such as net present value, discounted cash flow analysis, returns on capital invested and so on. This evaluation is carried out for the whole lifetime of the plant, normally 25–30 years. These indicators are also used in sustainable design; however, as shown in Table 13.1, here the additional economic indicators must also be considered, including costs of decommissioning, value added, costs of pollution prevention and environmental liabilities. In many cases these costs will be difficult to estimate, particularly the future decommissioning costs and costs of potential environmental liability. Nevertheless, it is important that they be considered at this stage, albeit at a very crude level, as this analysis may help to improve the economic sustainability of the plant.

In conventional process design, if the preliminary economic evaluation is favourable, the project is then authorized either on the basis of that information or after a further, more detailed estimate (with an accuracy of ±10–15%). However, in sustainable process design, before the project can proceed to the detailed design stage, it is necessary to evaluate the process on the other two dimensions of sustainability: environmental and social.

Assessing Environmental Sustainability

Environmental sustainability of a process can be assessed using two types of quantitative indicators: environmental burdens and impacts. The former include the use of materials and energy, emissions to air and water and the amount of solid waste. They are obtained directly from the flowsheet and material and energy balances. The information on the burdens can then be used to calculate the environmental impacts. In sustainable process design, the environmental burdens and impacts are calculated from 'cradle to grave' (see Figure 13.3) using LCA as a tool. The LCA methodology is explained in Chapter 3.

Quantifying the environmental burdens and impacts helps to assess the environmental sustainability of a design, as well as to identify the most significant impacts. It also helps in the identification of the 'hot spots' in the system; that is, the parts of the system with the highest contribution to the environmental impacts that should be targeted for improvements in the detailed design stage.

An LCA software and database will normally be required for the assessment of environmental sustainability (see Chapter 3 for examples of LCA software). A more detailed account of using LCA for process design and optimization can be found in Azapagic (1999).

Assessing Social Sustainability

Social sustainability criteria can be translated into both quantitative and qualitative indicators (see Table 13.1). For example, provision of employment and some health and safety issues can be expressed in quantitative terms as the 'number of employees' and 'number of injuries' respectively. Others can only be expressed qualitatively; for example, the visual impact of the plant on different people. Dealing with qualitative information can be challenging in process design, where most information and decisions are based of quantitative data. However, for most of the socially related criteria that are relevant in process design, various quantitative methods have been developed. For example, to evaluate a health hazard related to the toxicity of materials used in the manufacture of chemicals, the LD50[1] values or occupational exposure limits (OELs) are normally used; or to calculate a potential safety risk from fire and explosion, the Dow fire and explosion index (Sinnott, 2001) can be used, and so on.

As in the environmental analysis, evaluation of social sustainability also enables identification of the most significant design criteria and the 'hot spots' in the system. This information is fed in to the next, detailed stage of design.

Questions

1. List the steps involved in preliminary design and briefly describe each. Which of these steps are related to sustainability?
2. Which process variables would you need to include in describing the selected process in detail?
3. Why is the site selection important? Why is it important to select the site before the design of flowsheets starts?
4. Using the Douglas (2003) approach to conceptual design, describe the decision hierarchy used in preliminary design and flowsheet preparation.
5. What is included in the estimation of capital and operating costs? How do we know if a process design is economically viable?
6. Describe the procedure for sustainability process assessment. Why is it carried out and what are the outcomes?
7. What is the difference between sustainability design criteria and sustainability indicators? How can the criteria be translated into the indicators? See also Chapter 2.
8. How can we deal with the qualitative social indicators in the quantitatively based design process? How would you go about it?

---

[1] LD50: lethal dose at which 50 % of the test animals are killed.

9. Examine the sustainability metrics developed by the Institution of Chemical Engineers (IChemE) (IChemE, 2003). These sustainability indicators are suitable for use by chemical and process companies to assess their level of sustainability. Which of these indicators could also be relevant for assessing sustainability of chemical processes? Discuss your findings.

13.2.3 Detailed Design

After all the preliminary work has been completed, the detailed design work can begin. In conventional design, this stage will normally involve:

i. detailed equipment design, including reactors, distillation columns, heat exchangers and so on;
ii. detailed economic analysis (with an accuracy of $\pm 5-10\%$), including capital and manufacturing cost estimation and profitability analysis;
iii. energy integration;
iv. process control and instrumentation; and
v. safety, loss prevention and hazard and operability (HAZOP) and Control of Substances Hazardous to Health (COSHH) assessments.

Space precludes further discussion of these design steps; the interested reader can find more detail on the subject in, for example, Sinnott (2001) and Ray and Johnston (1989).

vi Full Assessment of Sustainability

In sustainable design, before the work on the detailed design can proceed further, one additional step must be carried out: full assessment of process sustainability. This involves an integrated assessment of economic, environmental and social performance and is aimed at ensuring that all relevant sustainability criteria have been identified so that they can be addressed appropriately. As the full assessment is based on the preliminary assessment already carried out, it will normally not involve much more additional work. Detailed economic assessment and some aspects of the social assessment will have been carried as part of the conventional detailed design (e.g. steps *ii*. and *v*. respectively), so that the additional amount of work is negligible. The environmental assessment will require a more detailed LCA study, which, once carried out, requires only a marginal effort, particularly if LCA software is used.

These data are then used in the next design stage, which is aimed at optimizing the system to improve its overall performance.

vii Optimization of Economic, Environmental and Social Sustainability

Although the purpose of design is to produce an optimal solution to the design problem so that some process optimization is applied throughout, it may also be necessary to use more formal optimization approaches in detailed design to fine-tune the final flowsheet. There are a number of optimization techniques in use, ranging from simple analytical methods to sophisticated mixed-integer nonlinear programming (e.g. see Edgar and Himmelblau (1988) and Floudas ()). The general procedure in optimization is to define an objective function and optimize the system on it, subject to a range of constraints, including materials and energy balances, capacities and operating conditions. In conventional process design, the main aim is to minimize costs and maximize profitability, so that the objective functions are defined as costs and profit. In sustainable process design, the additional objective functions must be considered, to reflect the environmental and social aspects of sustainability. The environmental objectives are usually defined as environmental burdens or impacts (such as those listed in Table 13.1) which must be minimized (Azapagic, 1999). Similarly, the social objectives are defined to include the relevant social indicators, so that the social benefits from the process can be maximized. However, formulating some of the social objectives may be difficult; for example, those related to social perceptions.

Therefore, optimization for sustainability is a complex and challenging task, both mathematically and also in terms of how we deal with social objectives and priorities. The mathematical challenge is to develop robust procedures for solving multiobjective optimization problems; that is, the models where a number of objectives must be considered and optimized simultaneously. This is a task for scientists and engineers. However, dealing with social objectives and priorities is not a challenge that can or should be tackled by engineers alone; it is a challenge which requires participation and involvement of all relevant stakeholders and must be addressed in a wider social context.

Questions

1. Give a brief overview of the steps included in detailed process design.
2. What is involved in detailed sustainability assessments? Why is it necessary to have a detailed assessment if the preliminary assessment has already been carried out? What is the outcome of a detailed sustainability assessment?
3. Which optimization techniques can be used for process optimization?
4. What is the difference between conventional process optimization and optimization for sustainability?
5. What are the main challenges in process optimization for sustainability?
6. The discussion here has been focused on sustainable process design. How would you apply this methodology to product design? Discuss any differences between the two approaches.

13.3 Case Study: Designing a More Sustainable Vinyl Chloride Monomer (VCM) Process

The methodology for sustainable process design outlined in the preceding sections is now illustrated on a case study of a vinyl chloride monomer (VCM) plant. The case study aims to illustrate what kind of sustainability criteria are relevant and should be considered in process design; how to carry out sustainability assessment of the process; how to identify 'hot spots' and how to make design choices to improve the level of process sustainability.

This is a hypothetical study, based on the type of design projects set by the IChemE as the final part of the Institution's qualifying examinations for professional chemical engineers. Because it is a hypothetical study, it should be borne in mind that some of the assumptions and design decisions may not necessarily be realistic. For the same reason, the case study goes only as far as the preliminary design, with some discussion of the detailed design related to sustainability assessment and optimization. As in the previous section, the emphasis is on the design steps that are concerned with sustainability rather than on the conventional design stages, as it is assumed that the reader is familiar with the latter.

13.3.1 Project Initiation

i. *Identifying the Need*

With over 35 million tonnes of VCM produced per year worldwide, the VCM industry is well established. Virtually all VCM produced globally (99%) is used for the production of polyvinyl chloride (PVC), so that the demand for VCM is closely linked with the demand for PVC.

However, VCM and PVC are highly cyclical industries in terms of price and profitability. When conditions are favourable (i.e. when the raw materials – ethylene and chlorine, – prices are low and the selling price of VCM is high), the industry is very profitable. Such conditions only occur about every fourth year. Hence, it may not be very profitable to build a stand-alone plant producing solely VCM. To reduce the financial risk, it is often better to integrate the VCM plant either upstream into the production of ethylene (and co-products) and chlorine/caustic soda or downstream into the PVC production. However, the PVC business is also very competitive, particularly in western Europe, where it has to compete with imports from the lower cost areas such as the Middle and Far East. In addition to this, as discussed later in this case study, many environmental NGOs in Europe and some other regions are campaigning for a ban on PVC products because of the potential of PVC to cause human health and environmental damage.

Nevertheless, the increasing worldwide demand for PVC is set to increase the demand for VCM, so that there appears to be a (social) need for its increased production. Although financially and environmentally it can be a risky business, an international PVC company called PlasticFuture has carried out a pre-feasibility study and believes that they can design a plant to produce VCM profitably by integrating the VCM process with the existing plant for the production of PVC situated in the UK. The PVC plant is on an industrial site where two other companies produce chlorine and ethylene, the raw materials used in the production of VCM. PlasticFuture, therefore, have decided to initiate the project and have put a multi-disciplinary design team together to help them realize this opportunity.

The company's board of directors is committed to sustainable development, and they give the design team the following simple but ambitious brief:

The project: Design a plant to produce VCM in the most sustainable way. The capacity of the plant should be 15 000 kg/h with a projected output of 130 000 t/year.

Questions

1. Find out who the largest producers of VCM are and where they are situated. What is the average output for these VCM plants? How does that compare with the capacity that PlasticFuture is designing for? Can you work out from the VCM capacity their production capacity for PVC?

2. Why do you think a company like PlasticFuture would want to build their own VCM plant?
3. Who are the main competitors to PlasticFuture in terms of PVC in the UK and in Europe? Do you think they will be able to compete with the producers in Middle and Far East?
4. How do you think the increased recycling of PVC would affect the VCM producers and particularly a company like PlasticFuture?
5. Find out why some NGOs are campaigning for the ban on PVC products.

ii. *Initial Identification of Sustainability Criteria*

The first task for the design team is to produce a list of initial sustainability criteria that will guide their decision-making in the preliminary design stage. As explained in Section 13.2, at this stage it is still not clear what process alternatives exist, so that the design team decide to use the general sustainability criteria listed in Table 13.1 as the decision-making criteria for screening the alternatives. These will be refined further in the preliminary design after an initial sustainability assessment (see Section 13.3.2).

Question

1. List sustainability criteria that you would use in design of the VCM process. Are your criteria different from the criteria used by the PlasticFuture team, and if so then why?

iii. Identifying the Alternatives

The VCM processing route is well established, so that there are few choices to be made at this stage with respect to the processes, technologies and raw materials. As shown in a simple block diagram in Figure 13.5, VCM is produced from ethylene (or ethane) and chlorine in five main steps:

- Direct chlorination: reaction of ethylene (or ethane) and chlorine to produce ethylene dichloride (EDC).
- Oxy-chlorination: reaction of recycled HCl with ethylene (or ethane) and oxygen (or air) to yield more EDC.
- EDC purification: removal of impurities from EDC to minimize the by-products from the cracking process and corrosion of the equipment.
- EDC cracking: pyrolysis of EDC to produce VCM and HCl.
- VCM purification: separation of VCM, HCl and uncracked EDC, after which VCM is taken out as a product and HCl and EDC are recycled back into the process.

The VCM process is explained in more detail further on. Here, however, the focus is on the process alternatives.

Although the process for VCM production is well established and is carried out according to the above description, several process alternatives are used or are being investigated with the aim of improving production efficiencies, costs, health, safety and

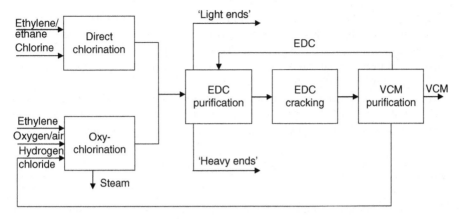

Figure 13.5   *Simplified flow diagram of the VCM process*

environmental performance. Here, for illustration, we concentrate on the alternatives related to the:

- feedstocks; and
- processes.

Feedstock Alternatives

One of the feedstock-related alternatives is to replace the expensive ethylene with a relatively inexpensive ethane feedstock in the direct chlorination stage (Clegg and Hardman, 2003; Marshall *et al.*, 2003). However, this alternative can lead to a loss of ethane, mainly through its combustion and the formation of CO_2 (Clegg and Hardman, 2003).

Another feedstock-related alternative is to use air instead of pure oxygen in the oxy-chlorination stage. Using air could be advantageous economically, as air is freely available while oxygen must be produced by an air separation process and paid for. However, there are certain advantages to using pure oxygen in the process, including smaller equipment size, lower energy use, lower operating temperature, higher process efficiencies and product yield.

Processes Alternatives

One of the problems in direct chlorination is that EDC can be easily contaminated, either by iron (from the $FeCl_3$ catalyst) or through the formation of β-trichloroethane (generated in further chlorination of EDC). To control this contamination, two different processes are possible:

- sub-cooling, where EDC is maintained below its normal boiling temperature (at 60 °C); and
- boiling, where EDC is maintained at the normal boiling point (84 °C).

The sub-cooled process produces EDC with less β-trichloroethane but is iron contaminated. The boiling process generates more β-trichloroethane, but EDC can, in principle, be obtained iron free. The boiling process would eliminate the need to wash and dry the EDC stream, which must be done before cracking if it contains iron. However, because of the higher proportion of β-trichloroethane in the boiling process, the reactor needs to be constructed from a material that is resistant to erosion and corrosion, as opposed to the sub-cooled process where carbon steel can be used.

Therefore, before proceeding on to the preliminary design stage, the task of the design team is to make a choice between the alternative feedstock materials and direct chlorination processes, using the sustainability criteria identified in the previous step.

Questions

1. Find out and compare the costs of ethylene and ethane. What would be the saving in operating costs from using ethane rather than ethylene for a production of VCM of 130 000 t/year? Assume complete conversion of ethylene/ethane into VCM.
2. What are the disadvantages of using ethane? In your opinion, does the cost saving justify the use of ethane, regardless of the disadvantages?
3. Describe the process differences between an air- and an oxygen-based system. What are the advantages and disadvantages of the two alternatives?
4. Apply life cycle thinking to decide which of the following alternatives would be more sustainable:
   • the ethylene- or ethane-based process; and
   • the air- or oxygen-based system.
Discuss and justify your choices for each alternative.
5. Discuss the equipment, energy use, costs and health and safety implications of the sub-cooling and boiling process alternatives in direct chlorination. Which one appears to be favourable and why?
6. An activated carbon bed is normally used to strip EDC and traces of the other hydrocarbons present in the process water from both the direct chlorination and oxy-chlorination sections. An alternative technology to this is to use a live steam stripping for this purpose. Describe these two processes and discuss their differences. Which option is in your opinion more sustainable and why?
7. Use the preliminary sustainability criteria to evaluate the alternative feedstock materials and process options in direct chlorination. You may wish to use an example table shown below to represent relative advantages and disadvantages of the options as ' + ' and '−' respectively.

| Alternatives | Economic criteria | | | Environmental criteria | | | Social criteria |
	Capital cost	Operating cost	...	Air emissions	Water emissions	...	...
Ethylene	no	−	...	...	...	...	...
Ethane	difference	+					
Oxygen	+	−	...	...	...	...	...
Air	−	+					
Sub-cooling	...	...	...	...	...	...	...
Boiling	...	...	...	...	...	...	...

8. Based on your analysis and evaluation of the alternatives, which feedstock and process options would you choose? Explain how you made your choices, particularly if one alternative scored better for some criteria but worse for the others.

13.3.2 Preliminary Design

i. Process Selection and Description

Having considered and traded off the advantages and disadvantages of the alternative process feeds, the design team decide to choose ethylene over ethane and oxygen over air. They also decide to choose the sub-cooled reactor over the boiling. Their next task is to describe the process in enough detail to enable preparation of the more detailed flowsheets.

Question

1. Compare your choice of the feedstocks and processes with those of the PlasticFuture design team. Are they different? If so, explain your choices and why you think the design team made their choices.

VCM Process Description

As shown in Figure 13.5, VCM is produced first by reacting ethylene and chlorine to make EDC, followed by its cracking to obtain equimolar amounts of VCM and HCl. The process is carried out according to the following summary reaction:

$$C_2H_4 + Cl_2 \rightarrow C_2H_4Cl_2 \rightarrow C_2H_3Cl + HCl$$

Chlorination   EDC   Cracking

As already discussed, EDC is produced in both direct chlorination and oxy-chlorination of ethylene. These stages and the relevant process variables are described in more detail below.

1. Direct Chlorination

Gaseous ethylene and chlorine are reacted to produce EDC by the following reaction:

$$C_2H_4 + Cl_2 \rightarrow C_2H_4Cl_2$$

This highly exothermic reaction occurs in liquid EDC in the presence of iron chloride (FeCl$_3$) as a catalyst and, as already discussed, can be carried out in either a sub-cooled or boiling reactor. This design considers a sub-cooled reactor, where the reaction occurs at a temperature of 60 °C. Owing to the further chlorination, β-trichloroethane is also formed:

$$C_2H_4 + 2Cl_2 \rightarrow C_2H_3Cl_3 + HCl$$

The sub-cooling process will generate iron contamination, but the amount of β-trichloroethane will be reduced.

The reaction of ethylene and chlorine proceeds very rapidly. The rate limiting factor is believed to be the solution of ethylene in EDC. Therefore, the reactor, whether sub-cooled or boiling, must be designed to provide adequate residence time for the gas dissolution. This is commonly achieved by using bubble column reactors with the reacting gases being introduced separately into the reactor through small orifices and a high sparging velocity (~100 m/s). To ensure the complete reaction, the process is also operated in the presence of a slight excess of ethylene (0.5–1.0%) relative to the amount of chlorine.

With respect to the vent gases, precautions must be taken against a breakthrough of chlorine due to loss of ethylene feed or any other reason. It is normal to provide a large scrubbing tower with sodium hydroxide solution permanently recycled through it and capable of neutralizing the full chlorine inventory in the system. Furthermore, the presence of oxygen in the chlorine feed is a flammability hazard which must be eliminated by using a suitable inert.

Questions

1. Why is the formation of β-trichloroethane highly undesirable?
2. The formation of β-trichloroethane is dependent on three major variables:
   - temperature of reaction;
   - presence of the $FeCl_3$ catalyst; and
   - amount of dissolved O_2.

   Find out and discuss how these process variables affect the formation of β-trichloroethane.
3. Discuss the advantages and disadvantages of the sub-cooled and the boiling process for the direct chlorination stage.
4. Discuss the environmental, health and safety issues that are associated with direct chlorination. What are the potential risks from this process?
5. How can the flammability risk from the presence of oxygen in the chlorine feed be reduced? Which inerts would you use for these purposes?

2. Oxy-Chlorination

In this stage, ethylene and hydrogen chloride (recycled from the VCM purification stage) react with oxygen to produce EDC and water. The exothermic reactions take place in either a fixed- or a fluidized-bed reactor with a cupric chloride ($CuCl_2$) catalyst on an alumina support:

$$C_2H_4 + 2HCl + \tfrac{1}{2}O_2 \rightarrow C_2H_2Cl_2 + H_2O$$

In addition to the EDC, other chlorinated hydrocarbons are also formed: 'light ends' ($CHCl_3$, CCl_4, C_2H_5Cl, $C_2H_2Cl_2$, C_2HCl_3) and 'heavy ends' ($C_2H_3Cl_3$, $C_2H_2Cl_4$, C_2Cl_4). These impurities are removed by distillation, in the EDC purification stage (see Figure 13.5).

In parallel with the main oxy-chlorination reaction, a direct oxidation of ethylene to CO_2 also occurs, although this reaction only accounts for a few per cent of the ethylene converted. Catalyst activity increases with temperature, but an increased temperature favours oxidation to CO_2 at the expense of oxy-chlorination. There is, thus, an optimum temperature which depends on the type of reactor chosen. A fluidized-bed reactor is normally operated at temperatures of 220–245 °C (and pressures of 150–500 kPa), while a fixed-bed reactor is operated at 230–300 °C (and 150–1400 kPa). Temperature in fluidized-bed reactors is controlled by internal cooling coils and in fixed-bed reactors by multitube heat exchangers.

The choice of the material of construction used for the reactor is one of the most important decisions to be made in designing this part of the process due to the complex erosion and corrosion mechanisms that occur in oxy-chlorination. Although running the reactor above the dew point of the gas mixture can help reduce the effects of corrosion, experience shows that corrosion occurs at temperatures well above the theoretically calculated dew point. The key parameter is the partial pressure of steam in the reactor product gas mixture, because this controls the gas dew point.

The reactor must contain means of properly introducing the main feeds, bearing in mind the necessity not to premix ethylene and oxygen outside the reactor.

On leaving the reactor the gases have to be quenched and condensed and the residual HCl neutralized, normally with sodium hydroxide. The organic and aqueous phases are separated; the former is then sent to an azeotropic drying column and the latter to a stripping column to recover dissolved EDC. Catalyst particles entrained into the reactor exit gases must also be removed and recycled to the reactor before the gas is discharged to the atmosphere.

If an air-based process is chosen, the vent gases leaving the system will need to pass through equipment to recover as much EDC as is practical before being vented to the atmosphere. If an oxygen-based process is chosen, most of the vent gases will be recycled to the reactor to achieve the desired gas partial pressures and only a small amount vented after cleaning to maintain pressure. The CO_2 and the excess water vapour produced in the reactor are also vented to the atmosphere.

Questions

1. Write down the reaction for direct oxidation of ethylene to CO_2. Why is this reaction undesirable from both the process and environmental points of view? How can the formation of CO_2 be minimized?
2. Discuss the differences between the fluidized- and fixed-bed reactors with respect to the operating temperature and direct oxidation of ethylene. Given the exothermic reaction, which reactor type would be more appropriate and why?
3. Why must oxygen and ethylene not be premixed outside the reactor?
4. How would you remove the catalyst particles from the reactor exit gases? Why is this cleaning-up process necessary?
5. Discuss the advantages and disadvantages of the air- and oxygen-based systems with respect to the reactor vent gases.
6. Discuss the environmental, health and safety issues that are associated with oxy-chlorination. What are the potential risks associated with this process?

3. **EDC Purification**

The EDC must be treated to remove impurities before being converted into VCM in the cracking stage. The cracking process is highly susceptible to inhibition and fouling by trace impurities in the feed, so that EDC must be of a very high purity, normally greater than 99.5% by weight. It is also important that the EDC is dry (containing less than 10 ppm H_2O) in order to prevent downstream corrosion.

The EDC from direct chlorination is already of high purity (99.5% wt), so that little further purification is required. If a sub-cooled reactor is chosen, as is the case in this design, then the EDC product must be washed to remove iron chloride. This is preferably done in two stages, the first stage using water and the second dilute sodium hydroxide. In each stage the volumes of aqueous and organic phases continuously in contact should be approximately equal. The wet EDC must then be dried by azeotropic distillation. If a boiling reactor is chosen then there is no need to wash the EDC; hence, no drying is required. However, the products from the boiling reactor have to be processed in a distillation column to remove β-trichloroethane.

The EDC from the oxy-chlorinator is much less pure than the EDC from direct chlorination, as it contains chlorinated hydrocarbons and water which must be removed by distillation. However, prior to distillation, the EDC must be washed with water and then with a sodium hydroxide solution to remove any chlorine impurities. The wet EDC stream is then sent to the azeotropic distillation column, to be dried together with the wet EDC from a sub-cooled direct chlorinator.

In the distillation process, the EDC is processed to separate the hydrocarbons with the low ('light ends') and high boiling points ('heavy ends'). As shown in Figure 13.5, the 'light ends' are taken off from the top of a distillation column while the EDC is collected with the 'heavy ends' at the bottom. This stream is then passed to a second distillation column. The 'heavy ends' are collected at the bottom while the EDC is taken off at the top of the column and passed to the cracking section of the plant.

Questions

1. Why is it necessary to use the azeotropic distillation for drying the EDC?
2. List the gaseous and liquid effluents from the EDC purification stage. Discuss the possible treatment and disposal options and the environmental implications of each.

4. **EDC Cracking**

In this stage, EDC is first vaporized and then normally cracked by pyrolysis into VCM and HCl. This is an endothermic reaction, normally carried out as a homogeneous noncatalytic gas-phase reaction at elevated temperature (475–525 °C) and pressure (1.4–3.0 MPa) in a direct-fired furnace. This reaction can be summarized as

$$C_2H_4Cl_2 \rightarrow C_2H_3Cl + HCl$$

A significant number of by-products are also formed during cracking, including acetylene, chloroprene and dichlorobutenes. Vinylidene chloride is also formed by partial pyrolysis of the β-trichloroethane impurity in the EDC feed. Empirical data indicate that ratio of β-trichloroethane converted to EDC converted is roughly 0.4.

The aim of cracking is to produce VCM as pure as possible by minimizing the formation of the by-products. A number of process parameters influence the formation of the by-products in cracking. They include operating pressure, the level of impurities (especially iron) in the EDC feed, residence time of gases in the cracking reactor and the material used for the tubes in the reactor. However, the fractional conversion of EDC per one pass through the reactor (known as 'depth of crack') is the dominating parameter. The quantity of by-products formed per tonne of VCM produced increases rapidly as the depth of crack increases. Some of these by-products foul the tubes of the reactor, reducing the rate of heat transfer and increasing the pressure drop to such an extent that the reactor must be shut down for cleaning or 'decoking'.

Therefore, a low depth of crack is desirable to minimize by-product formation. However a low crack implies increased steam usage later in VCM purification. This means that there will be an optimum depth of crack, which is normally between 0.53 and 0.63. This crack, combined with a gas residence time of around 2–30 s, results in a cracking selectivity to VCM of greater than 99%.

Questions

1. Find out how the operating pressure, the level of impurities in the EDC feed, the residence time of gases in the cracking reactor and the tube wall material used in the reactor influence the formation of by-products. What are the optima for these operating parameters?
2. Which fuels would you use in the cracking furnace? Why?
3. To minimize the by-product formation and reactor coking, it is important to quench the cracker effluent gases quickly. To save energy, this is normally achieved by direct contact with the cold EDC liquid. Explain the cooling mechanism and how you would carry out this energy integration in the most cost- and environmentally-efficient way?
4. The Le Chatelier principle suggests that because the cracking reaction involves break up of one molecule (EDC) and the formation of two molecules (VCM and HCl), a low operating pressure is desirable. Why is this a misleading statement?
5. Which parameters have to be considered in determining the appropriate operating pressure in the cracking section?
6. Discuss the environmental, health and safety issues that are associated with cracking. What are the potential risks from this process?

5. VCM Purification

The mixture of VCM, HCl and uncracked EDC obtained form the EDC cracking is then separated to obtain pure VCM product. The purification is carried out by rapidly cooling the hot gases and then passing the two-phase mixture to distillation columns to separate the components. Normally, the HCl is removed first as an overhead product and returned back into the process to be utilized in the oxy-chlorination stage. This is followed by the separation of the VCM and EDC in a second column. The EDC is then recycled back in the process for further utilization, while the VCM product is sent to storage.

Questions

1. Why is it necessary to cool the hot gases rapidly from the EDC cracking?
2. The HCl taken off the top of the distillation column is passed through a condenser which is normally refrigerated. Which refrigerant would you choose for these purposes and why? Discuss the environmental, health and safety implications of the chosen type of the refrigerant.
3. Identify all major gaseous, liquid and solid waste streams from the whole VCM process and discuss their potential impact on the environment if released. Which of these will have to be treated before their release into the environment and how do you propose to do that?

ii. Site Selection

This VCM process will be a part of an integrated installation which also produces PVC. As already mentioned, the (hypothetical) plant is situated in the UK so that its design, construction and operation will be subject to UK and EC legislation. This means that, amongst others, the design team will have to take into account the EC Directive on the Integrated Pollution Prevention and Control (IPPC) (EC, 2008), which requires the use of best available techniques (BATs). The plant will also be subject to an EIA so that a detailed EIA statement will have to be prepared after the design has been finalized and submitted to the competent authority as a part of the application for planning permission.

Therefore, in preparing the flowsheets and producing a preliminary design of the plant, the design team will have to consider the BAT and EIA requirements (see Chapter 10) in order to minimize the environmental and social impacts of the proposed plant. It is important that these aspects are considered at the preliminary design stage to minimize the design time and costs, which could otherwise increase considerably if the plant did not comply with these requirements and had to be redesigned at a later stage.

Questions

1. Detail the relevant legislation affecting process plants in your country.
2. If you are based in the EU region, discuss the general requirements of the IPPC Directive. Compare and contrast the requirements of the EIA Directive.
3. Which projects require an EIA according to the EC EIA Directive? Why does this proposed project require one?
4. How would you go about preparing an EIA for this plant following the legislative requirements in your country? Which activities in the life cycle of the project should be considered and what information would you need to carry out an EIA?

5. According to the EIA requirements in the EU (or in your country), which environmental aspects of the normal and abnormal (start-up, shutdown and emergencies) operation should be considered in the case of the proposed VCM plant?

iii. Flowsheet Preparation

The next task for the design team is to prepare the process flowsheets. This will involve specifying the equipment and streams and performing the mass and energy balances. Having examined the process, the chemistry and the process variables, the team decide to work towards the design specification given in Box 13.1.

The team are using the flowsheeting software CHEMCAD (Chemstations, 2002) and after several iterations have produced a detailed process flowsheet, which is shown in Figure 13.6a and b. To simplify the analysis for the purposes of this writing, this flowsheet is simplified and shown as a process flow diagram (PFD) in Figure 13.7. The simplified mass balances and energy requirements in the process are shown in Table 13.2; they correspond to the simplified PFD given in Figure 13.7. A summary of the input materials and utilities and the output of gaseous and liquid flows from the process is shown in Table 13.3. Because of the high content of the chlorinated hydrocarbons, including dioxins and furans, the waste streams must be treated before they can be discharged into the environment. In this design, incineration is chosen as a method to destroy the chlorinated hydrocarbons. However, care must be taken to design and operate the incinerator so as to prevent further formation of dioxins during and after the incineration. Furthermore, because of the chlorine present, HCl is also formed during the combustion process. The flue gas from the incinerator, therefore, must be cleaned up before being discharged into the environment. The design team choose a sodium hydroxide scrubber for these purposes, which will absorb HCl, CO_2 and NO_x.

Like the HCl from the incinerator flue gas, the aqueous HCl stream from the EDC purification is also neutralized with sodium hydroxide. Therefore, after the treatment of the gaseous and liquid streams, in theory, very few pollutants would be discharged into the environment. Assuming high absorption efficiencies in the scrubber, there would be almost no discharges of gaseous pollutants (although, in reality, some HCl and CO_2 would still be released). The only liquid discharge would be the wastewater containing salts after the neutralization of HCl and absorption of CO_2. In addition to this, some solid waste will also be generated periodically, from the spent catalysts and the activated sludge from the wastewater treatment plant.

Questions

1. Use the design specifications in Box 13.1 to generate your own VCM process flowsheet. How does your design differ from the one shown in this case study? Explain the differences.
2. Carry out material and energy balances for your design. Specify material and energy inputs and potential discharges to the environment.
3. Identify and quantify the gaseous, liquid and solid streams generated in the process which must be treated before being discharged into the environment.

Box 13.1   Design specification

Feeds

Ethylene: 8.0 bara and ambient temperature containing up to 400 ppm v/v
                  ethane

Chlorine: Available either as cell gas at 3.0 bara containing:
                  oxygen: 2.0 % v/v;
                  nitrogen: 0.5 % v/v;
                  hydrogen: 0.1 % v/v; and
                  carbon dioxide: 0.15 % v/v,
                  or as re-vaporized liquid at 3.0 bara which can be assumed 100 %
                  pure

Oxygen   Purity better than 99 % v/v

Product

VCM: Should contain not more than 100 ppm by weight total impurities.

Intermediate stream

EDC: As cracker feed should have a minimum purity of 99 % w/w.
                  Specific impurity maxima are:
                  C_1 lights: 2000 ppm w/w;
                  C_2 lights: 4000 ppm w/w;
                  C_4 lights: 100 ppm w/w;
                  C_2 heavies: 1000 ppm w/w with up to 500 ppm w/w
                  β-trichloroethane;
                  C_4 heavies: 50 ppm w/w;
                  water: 0.002 mol%; and
                  Fe: 1 ppm w/w.

HCl   Separated from cracked gas should contain less than 200 ppm w/w
                  VCM.

EDC   Separated from cracked gas should contain less than 200 ppm w/w
                  VCM.

Utilities

LP steam:	3.1 bara and 155 °C	Town's water:	8.0 bara and 20 °C max.
IP steam:	15.0 bara and 225 °C	Cooling water:	4.0 bara and 22 °C
HP steam:	42.4 bara and 270 °C		
Natural gas:	4.5 bara and 35 °C containing:		

Natural gas: 4.5 bara and 35 °C containing:
                  94% v/v methane;
                  4% v/v ethane; and
                  2% v/v nitrogen.

Emissions, effluents and solid waste

All gaseous emissions, liquid effluents and solid wastes must be below the limits
prescribed by legislation. The BAT should be used for the prevention and control of
environmental pollution.

4. Explain what you have done to minimize the use of materials and energy and to prevent emissions to the environment.

5. Write down the reactions in the sodium hydroxide scrubber where the flue gas from the incinerator is cleaned up. Calculate the required amount of sodium hydroxide for the

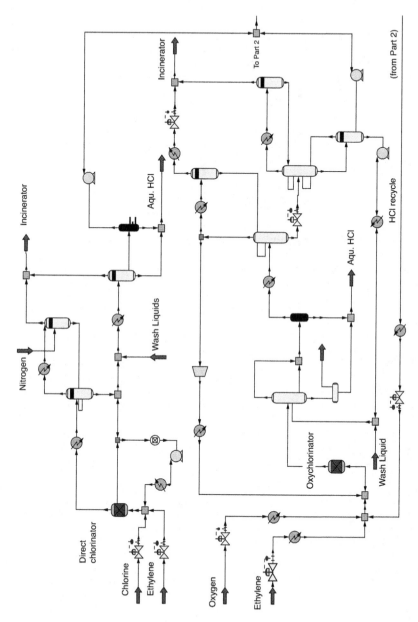

Figure 13.6 *VCM process flowsheet. Part 1: direct chlorination and oxychlorination*

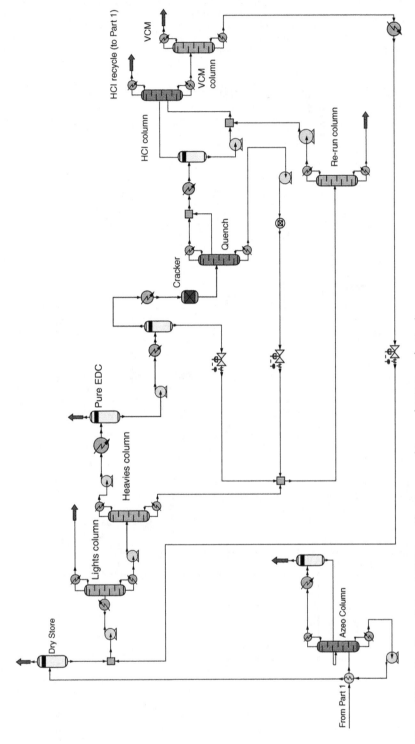

Figure 13.6   *(Continued) Part 2 (EDC purification, cracking and VCM production)*

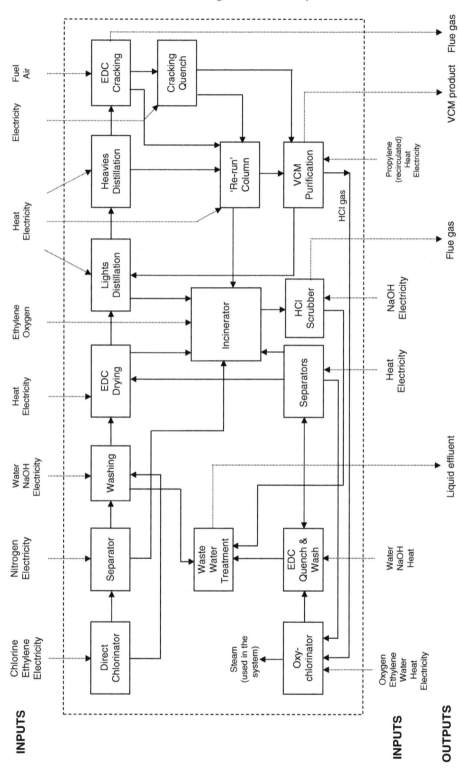

Figure 13.7 *Simplified process flow diagram for the VCM plant*

Table 13.2 Simplified material balances and energy requirement in the VCM process (basis: production of 15 000 kg/h VCM)

	Material in	kg/h	Material out	kg/h	Energy use (MJ/h)
Direct chlorination					
Direct chlorinator	Chlorine	9204	'Direct' EDC	12 530	746
	Ethylene	3625	'Direct' HCs	299	
Oxy-chlorination					
Oxy-chlorinator	Oxygen	2493	Oxy EDC	19 792	5664
	Ethylene	3479			
	HCl recycle	8959			
	CO$_2$ recycle	4861			
EDC purification					
Separators (direct chlorinator)	'Direct' HCs	299	'Direct' EDC	108	73
	Nitrogen	840	'Separators' HCs	1 032	
Washing (direct chlorinator)	'Direct' EDC	12 638	NaCl	353	10
	NaOH (100 %)	1	'Direct' EDC	12 646	
	Water	360			
EDC quench and wash (oxy-chlorinators)	'Oxy' EDC	19 792	'Oxy' EDC	20 857	1 155
	Water	90	NaCl	2 778	
	NaOH (100 %)	176			
	Water recycle	3 577			
Separators (oxy-chlorinator)	'Oxy' EDC	20 857	'Oxy' EDC	11 899	324
			'Oxy' HCs	519	
			Water recycle	3 577	
			CO$_2$ recycle	4 861	
EDC Drying	'Direct' EDC	12 646	'Dry' HCs	5	3 808
	'Oxy' EDC	11 899	'Dry' EDC	24 522	
	'Dry' EDC	24 522			
Lights distillation	EDC recycle	24 842	Light ends	247	29 499
	EDC and heavy ends	49 118	EDC and heavy ends	49 118	
Heavies distillation			'Pure' EDC	48 270	49 878

Input streams

Process unit	Stream	Flow
EDC cracking		
EDC cracker	'Pure' EDC	48 270
Cracking quench	'Cracked' EDC	48 270
	Quench heavies	750
'Re-run' column	Heavy ends	848
	VCM and HCl	47 520
VCM purification	'Re-run' VCM and HCl	1 315
	Refrigerant (propylene; recirculated)	0.17
Wastewater treatment	'Direct' NaCl	352
	'Oxy' NaCl	2 778
	'Oxy' HCs	519
Incinerator	'Separators' HCs	1 032
	'Dry' HCs	5
	Light ends	247
	'Re-run' heavies	283
	Oxygen	576
	Ethylene and ethane	10

Output streams

Stream	Flow	Flow
		848
'Cracked' EDC	48 270	33 192
Quench heavies	750	611
VCM and HCl	47 520	
'Re-run' heavies	283	1 020
'Re-run' VCM and HCl	1 315	20 535
VCM	15 034	
EDC recycle	24 842	
HCl Recycle	8 959	
Refrigerant (propylene; recirculated)	0.17	
Treated wastewater	3 130	n/a
Flue gas containing:		n/a
HCl	2 672	
CO_2	443	
Chlorine	1 153	
Chlorinated HCs	3	
NO_x	Traces	
Water vapour	8.5×10^{-3}	
Nitrogen and oxygen	110	
	963	

Table 13.3 *Summary of the materials and energy used in the VCM process (basis: production of 15 000 kg/h VCM)*

	Direct chlorination	Oxy-chlorination	EDC purification	Cracking and VCM purification	Total
Chlorine (kg/h)	9 204				9 204
Ethylene (kg/h)	3 625	3 479	10		7 104
Oxygen (kg/h)		2 493	576		3 069
Sodium hydroxide[a] (100 %) (kg/h)	1	176			177
Nitrogen (kg/h)	840				840
Water (kg/h)	360	90			450
Electricity (MJ/h)	746	474	1835	7 451	10 506
Heat (natural gas) (MJ/h)		5 190	82 440	47 907	135 537

[a] Sodium hydroxide used in the scrubber to treat the incinerator flue gas is not included in this table.

absorption of HCl, CO_2 and NO_x. Assuming absorption efficiencies of 95%, calculate the emissions of HCl and CO_2 to the atmosphere. Is the absorption efficiency of 95% realistic?

6. Dioxins and furans are formed in the manufacture of VCM and this is a concern because they are carcinogenic. Use the stream and components specification lists in your design to find out where in the process the dioxins and furans are generated and at what level. Are their concentrations below the limit allowed by legislation in your country? If not, how would you reduce the amount of dioxins reaching the environment?

7. Incineration has been used in this case study to prevent the emissions of hydrocarbons into the environment. However, incineration of chlorinated hydrocarbons not only can destroy dioxins, it also generate them. Explain how you would design and run the incinerator so that the dioxins are not formed during or after the combustion.

8. In addition to the dioxins, incineration also generates carbon dioxide and nitrogen oxides. Considering only the quantities, use the components list to compare the amount of hydrocarbons destroyed in incineration to the amount of CO_2 generated. Is the incineration justified? Can we use the quantities alone to make such a comparison? Why?

9. Now, compare the potential environmental impacts from the emissions of the hydrocarbons if discharged directly into the atmosphere with the impacts of CO_2 and dioxins (if formed) generated during incineration. Is the incineration still justified? Is it possible to compare these different impacts? If so, explain how you have compared them. If you think they cannot be compared, then explain why.

iv Preliminary Cost Estimates

The design team use the process flowsheets and the material and energy balances to carry out a preliminary economic assessment of the proposed design. Following the specification for economic assessment given in Box 13.2, the team calculate the capital and operating costs, which are shown in Tables 13.4-13.7.

Box 13.2   Economic basis for design (September 2002 prices)

Feeds

Chlorine (as cell gas):	£76/t
Ethylene:	£305/t
Oxygen:	£32/t

Product

VCM:	£315/t

Utilities

NaOH (50 % solution):	£60/t	Electricity:	£38/MWh
Nitrogen:	£23/t	Heat (natural gas):	£1.37/GJ
Water:	£0.37/m^3		
Cooling water:	£0.07/m^3		

Other information

Equipment shipping costs:	8 %
Tankage investment:	20 % of on-site investment costs
Off-site investment:	10 % of on-site investment costs
Corporation tax rate:	30 %
Depreciation allowance:	100 % in first year of operation
Operating personnel:	Five shifts
Labour cost (one shift position):	£300 000 (including overheads)
Annual maintenance cost:	3 % of capital costs
Other annual costs (supplies, rates, supervision, administration, etc.):	2.6 % of capital costs

---

Capital Costs

Following Coulson and Richardson's guide to chemical engineering design (Sinnott, 2001) and the IChemE's (1995) guide to capital cost calculation, the design team estimate the equipment costs at £6 023 000 and the total capital costs at around £35 709 000 (see Table 13.4).

Operating Costs

The fixed and variable operating costs, estimated using the specification in Box 13.2, are shown in Tables 13.5 and 13.6 respectively. The former include the costs of labour, maintenance and other annual costs, such as overheads, while the variable costs include the costs of raw materials and utilities. The team work under the assumption that each year the plant would be shut down for 3 days for routine maintenance and every third year it would require a major shutdown, assumed to last 21 days. This means that in a normal year there will be 8688 h of operation, whilst in a major shutdown year the plant will operate for 8256 h. They also assume that a plant of this size will need four operators per each shift, with each shift position costing £300 000 per year. The PVC

Table 13.4 Summary of the equipment and total capital costs

Equipment items	Cost (£)
Pumps	1 386 643
Packed columns	51 951
Distillation columns	227 087
Heat exchangers	1 090 539
Tanks	308 073
Drums	290 412
Reactors	862 821
Incinerator	142 810
Compressors	22 332
Quenches	101 946
Refrigeration unit	828 889
Catalysts	263 252
Total equipment costs	**5 576 755**
Total delivered cost of equipment	**6 022 895**
(assuming shipping costs at 8 % of the equipment costs)	
Estimated capital costs	**27 468 468**
(using the Lang factor of 4.56)	
Total capital costs	**35 709 000**
(incl. 20 % for tankage and 10 % for off-site investments)	

Table 13.5 Fixed operating costs

	Cost (£/year)
Annual maintenance	1 071 270
Other annual costs	928 435
Labour	1 200 000
Total	*3 199 705*

Table 13.6 Variable operating costs

Raw materials and utilities	Amount	Cost	Normal-operation year (£/year)	Shutdown year (£/year)
Chlorine	9204 kg/h	£76/t	6 077 291	5 775 105
Ethylene	7104 kg/h	£305/t	18 824 463	17 888 440
Oxygen	3069 kg/h	£32/t	853 231	810 805
Total raw materials			**25 754 985**	**24 474 350**
Sodium hydroxide[a] (50% solution)	354 kg/h	£60/t	184 533	175 357
Nitrogen	840 kg/h	£23/t	167 852	159 506
Process water	450 kg/h	£0.35/m^3	1370	1300
Cooling[b] water	1000 m^3		350	350
Electricity	10 506 MJ/h	£38/MWh	963 470	915 563
Heat (natural gas)	135 537 MJ/h	£1.36/GJ	1 601 462	1 521 831
Total utilities			**2 919 037**	**2 773 907**

[a] Not including the amount used in the scrubber to treat the incinerator flue gas.
[b] Cooling water is recirculated, so the figure shown is an approximate total requirement over the lifetime of the plant.

Table 13.7 Summary of annual operating costs (fixed and variable)

	Normal-operation year (£/year)	Shutdown year (£/year)
Fixed costs	3 199 705	3 199 705
Raw materials	25 754 985	24 474 350
Utilities	2 919 037	2 773 907
Total	**31 873 727**	**30 447 962**

plant has a combined heat and power (CHP) plant run on natural gas, so that the steam will be supplied from the CHP. Therefore, the cost of natural gas is used to calculate the cost of the steam (although, in reality, the cost of steam would be higher than the cost of natural gas).

Therefore, it will cost £35 709 000 to build the plant and around £31 874 000 per year to operate it in a normal-operation year. This gives the design team a basis for the economic evaluation of the plant, which involves calculating the cash flow, the breakeven point and the profit that the plant will make over a certain period of time. The economic evaluation is carried out in the next design step, as part of the preliminary sustainability assessment.

Questions

1. Using the economic data and assumptions made in this study, carry out your own estimates of the capital and operating costs, based on your design. How do they compare with the costs obtained by the PlasticFuture design team? Discuss any major differences in costs.
2. This design does not include the operating costs associated with the incinerator scrubber. How would the operating costs change if these costs were included?
3. The estimate of the use of heat in this design is based on the cost of natural gas rather than the actual cost of steam. Assuming the cost of HP steam of £5.5/GJ and the cost of IP of £4.3/GJ, calculate the real cost of heat supply.
4. What is your confidence level in the estimated costs? How does that compare with the usual 20–30% confidence level for the preliminary costs? What would you do (if anything) to improve the accuracy of the costs at this stage?

v. *Preliminary Assessment of Sustainability and Further Identification of Sustainability Criteria*

As discussed in Section 13.2, before proceeding from a preliminary to a detailed design, it is first necessary to assess the level of sustainability of the proposed process design. This involves assessments of the economic, environmental and social sustainability, as illustrated below.

Assessment of Economic Sustainability

Using the economic sustainability criteria listed in Table 13.1 to evaluate the plant on economic sustainability, the team's first task is to carry out a profitability analysis. For these

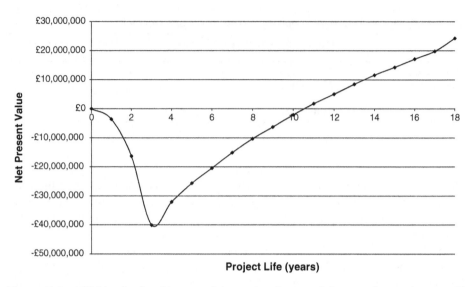

Figure 13.8 *NPV for the first 18 years of the project (assumed discount (interest) rate: 6 %)*

purposes, they make the following assumptions. The design and construction phase of the plant will take 3 years: the total fixed capital for the plant will be spent at a rate of 10% in the first year, then 30% and finally 60% in the third year. Also spent in the third year is the working capital for the project, which is spent on items like stocks of raw materials and for building up a product inventory; as such, this money is recoverable at the end of the project. This figure is assumed at 15% of the fixed capital.

The plant will start producing VCM at the beginning of year four, incurring the operating costs, but also bringing income from the sales of the product. Assuming the sale price of £315/t VCM, the projected income is £41 050 800 per year for a normal-operation year and £39 009 600 per year for a year with a major shutdown. The profit from this income is subject to a corporate tax at a rate of 30%, although tax rebates may be claimed to account for the depreciation in value of the plant. The major shutdowns will also incur a cost every 3 years, which is taken to be 30% of the annual maintenance costs.

Using the above assumptions, the design team carry out the discounted annual cash flow analysis to obtain the net present value (NPV) of the plant, showing the payback time and the overall profit at any given time during the lifetime of the plant. The NPV profile for a discount (interest) rate of 6% is shown in Figure 13.8. The figure shows that, at the assumed interest rate, the plant has a payback time of just over 10 years and after 18 years it will be making an overall profit of around £24 240 000.

The results of the cost and profitability analyses are summarized in Table 13.8. In addition to these, the team also calculate value added[2] to find out how much the operation increases the value of purchases from other companies, including raw materials, energy, goods and services. For this design, the value added amounts approximately to £12 377 000

---

[2] Value added is the value of sales less the cost of goods, raw materials, energy and services purchased.

Table 13.8 Using economic indicators to evaluate the level of economic sustainability of the VCM plant (based on the normal-operation year)

Economic criteria	Value
Total capital costs	£35 709 000
Operating costs	£31 873 727/year
Profitability (as NPV):	
Breakeven point	10 years
Profit after 18 years	£24 235 730
Value added	£12 376 778/year
Value added per unit value of sales	£0.30/£
Value added per unit amount of product	95 £/t
Taxes:	
Income tax (@30 %)	£2 753 000/year
Climate change levy tax	CHP plants exempt
Landfill tax	~£10 000/year
Investment (as % of capital investment)	
Pollution prevention	1 %
Health and safety	2 %
Decommissioning	Uncertain (from 20 to 60 %); not accounted for here
Potential costs of environmental liability (as % of capital investment)	Potentially large

per year, or £95 per tonne of VCM produced. Per unit sales, the value added is £0.30 per pound.

The other information that the team wishes to analyse is profit-related tax, but also the 'green' taxes, which have been introduced by the government to protect the environment. The corporate tax paid on the profits at the rate of 30% is equal to £2 753 000 per year. They also estimate the climate change levy (CCL) that taxes the industrial users in the UK for the use of fossil-fuel-derived energy. Electricity use is taxed at 0.43 pence/kWh, while using natural gas costs 0.15 pence/kWh, so that the total cost to the company from the CCL would be around £600 000 per year. However, the team are relieved to find out that the use of CHP is exempt from the CCL. In addition to the CCL, the team also calculate the cost of landfill tax which, at approximately £10 000, is relatively small and reflects a relatively small amount of solid waste being landifilled.

Finally, they analyse the investments and find out that, by design, approximately 1% of the capital will have been invested in the environmental protection and 2% into health and safety. The former does not include the costs of the incinerator scrubber, so that this figure is expected to be higher when the (high) costs of sodium hydroxide and energy have been added. Furthermore, the design does not take the decommissioning costs into account, but the team estimate that they could add anything from 20 to 60% to the cost of the investment. Although decommissioning should have been considered in the preliminary design, because of the lack of reliable information, the team are unable to incorporate these costs at this stage and decide to address this issue later, in the detailed design.

Thus, based on their findings, they decide that the project is economically (just) sustainable. However, they realize that there is a potential to improve the design to reduce costs and improve profitability. This will be their task in the detailed design, whereby the preliminary design will be optimized on costs. However, prior to that they still need to evaluate the project on the other two dimensions of sustainability.

Questions

1. Carry out an evaluation of economic sustainability of your design and compare your results with the results obtained in this case study. Which design is more economically sustainable, yours or that of the PlasticFuture? Why?
2. The breakeven point of the PlasticFuture's plant is 10 years, which is a relatively long time. How would you reduce this time to increase the profitability of the plant and, therefore, its economic sustainability?
3. The economic analysis performed by PlasticFuture is only for 18 years of the plant's life. What profit could be expected over 25 years, which is an assumed lifetime of a chemical plant? What would the profitability look like with a different interest rate, say 8% or 10%? Which interest rate is more realistic to use in your country?
4. The PlasticFuture preliminary design does not take into account the costs of decommissioning. Can you include that in your design? Is there enough information available to carry out these estimates and can you use 'guesstimates?' Discuss your findings and reliability of the results.
5. Calculate the costs of scrubbing the incinerator effluent. What do you conclude – are the incineration and scrubbing justified economically? If not, how else would you prevent releases of chlorinated hydrocarbons and HCl into the environment?
6. Find out which 'green' taxes are used in your country and calculate the costs to the project. What design improvements could you implement to decrease or avoid paying these taxes?
7. Use the economic sustainability indicators used by the PlasticFuture design team to make an overall evaluation of your design. Do you think the plant as designed is going to be economically sustainable? Discuss your findings.

Assessment of Environmental Sustainability

As discussed in Section 13.1, in sustainable process design, environmental sustainability should be assessed from 'cradle to grave', using LCA. The design team have used the data from the mass and energy balances and the simplified PFD in Figure 13.7 to perform an LCA study of the proposed VCM plant. Using the methodology given in Chapter 3, they consider the life cycle environmental impacts of the raw materials and utilities (including energy) and the impacts from the VCM plant itself. A simplified life-cycle flow diagram of the VCM plant is shown in Figure 13.9. To identify the 'hot spots', the system is divided into 'foreground' and 'background' subsystems. The former is the VCM plant itself, while the latter includes the raw materials and utilities. The functional unit is defined as 'the production of 130 000 t/year of VCM' and the system boundary is from 'cradle to gate'; that is, from the extraction of primary resources to the point where the VCM is produced and ready to leave the factory gate. The LCA environmental impacts of the foreground system are calculated using the design data, while the impacts from the background sub-ystem are calculated using the an LCA database.

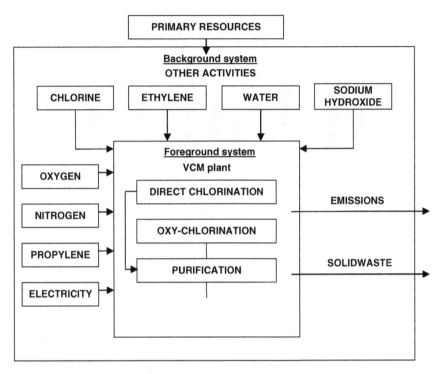

Figure 13.9 Simplified life cycle diagram of the VCM plant

The LCA results are shown in Figure 13.10. The environmental burdens and impacts shown in the figure represent environmental indicators, which correspond to the environmental criteria identified earlier in the design process and listed in Table 13.1. In addition to these, the design team use a number of additional environmental indicators, to ensure that

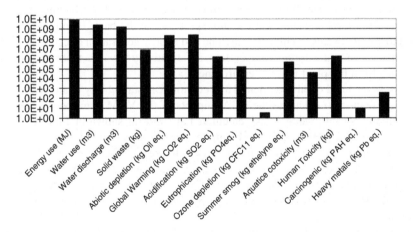

Figure 13.10 The LCA results showing the environmental burdens and impacts associated with the proposed VCM design (all burdens and impacts expressed per functional unit '130 000 t/year VCM produced')

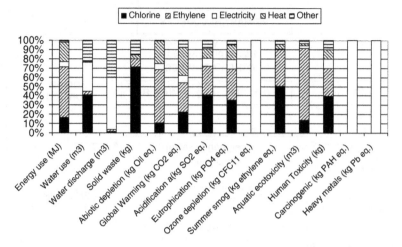

Figure 13.11 *Contribution of different parts of the VCM process to the total life cycle environmental impacts*
[Legend:
  – 'Chlorine', 'ethylene', 'electricity' and heat represent the life cycles of chlorine, ethylene, electricity and heat;
  – 'Other' includes the foreground system and the life cycles of all other parts of the VCM system shown in Figure 14. 9, apart from chlorine, ethylene, electricity and heat]

all relevant environmental criteria have been identified. Out of these, two further environmental indicators appear to be relevant: carcinogenic potential related to VCM (as discussed in Section 13.3.2.5.3 on social sustainability below) and the amount of heavy metals emitted from the system into the environment. They are also shown in Figure 13.10.

The next task for the design team is to identify the 'hot spots' in the system; that is, the parts of the VCM system that contribute most to the impacts. Their findings are given in Figure 13.11, which indicates that the 'hot spots' are in the background and are mainly related to the life cycles of chlorine, ethylene and energy generation (electricity and heat). The impacts from the foreground system are relatively low, as there are few direct discharges from the plant into the environment.

To assess the level of environmental and economic sustainability in an integrated way, the design team also calculate the LCA impacts of the VCM plant per tonne of VCM produced and per unit value added, calculated at £95/t (as shown in Table 13.8). These results are shown in Table 13.9. For example, the results reveal that to make a tonne of VCM product, on a life cycle basis it is necessary to use 62.5 GJ of energy, which depletes 1.5 t of fossil fuels (expressed as oil equivalents) and generates 2 t of CO_2. Linking the environmental and economic performance, for every pound of value added per tonne of VCM, 658 MJ of energy is used, depleting 15.8 kg of oil eq. and generating 34 kg of CO_2 emissions.

Having analysed and discussed the results, the design team proceed to the final stage of sustainability assessment to find out if their proposed design is sustainable from a social point of view.

Table 13.9 *Using environmental indicators to assess environmental and economic sustainability of the VCM plant*

Environmental criteria	Expressed per tonne of VCM	Expressed per value added
Energy use	62 484 MJ/t	658 MJ/£
Water use	19 474 m^3/t	205 m^3/£
Water discharge	11 254 m^3/t	118 m^3/£
Solid waste	53 kg/t	0.6 kg/£
Abiotic reserves depletion	1502 kg oil eq./t	15.8 kg oil eq./£
Global warming	2029 kg CO_2 eq./t	34 kg CO_2 eq./£
Acidification	11 kg SO_2 eq./t	0.1 kg SO_2 eq./£
Eutrophication	1 kg PO_4 eq./t	0.01 kg PO_4 eq./£
Ozone depletion	2.5×10^{-5} kg CFC11 eq./t	2.6×10^{-7} kg CFC11 eq./£
Summer smog	3 kg ethylene eq./t	0.03 kg ethylene eq./£
Aquatic ecotoxicity	0.3 m^3/t	3.2×10^{-3} m^3/£
Human toxicity	14 kg/t	0.15 kg/£
Carcinogenic potential	6.7×10^{-5} kg PAH eq./t	7.1×10^{-7} kg PAH eq./£
Heavy metals	2.9×10^{-3} kg Pb eq./t	3.1×10^{-5} kg Pb eq./£

Questions

1. Carry out an LCA of your VCM plant configuration and compare the results with the results obtained by the PlasticFuture design team. Discuss and explain any differences between your and their results. Which design is more environmentally sustainable, yours or theirs? Why?
2. Calculate the LCA impacts per tonne of VCM produced (in t/kg, m^3/kg or MJ/kg) and then per unit value added (t/£, m^3/£ or MJ/£). Compare your results with the respective results shown in Table 13.9 and discuss any differences.
3. How do you think different LCA databases used to calculate the environmental impacts from the background system (e.g. for ethylene, chlorine and energy) influence the total LCA results?
4. Draw flow diagrams to show the life cycles of the raw materials and energy generation.
5. Identify the 'hot spots' in the system. Explain why you consider them to be the 'hot spots' and discuss their relative contribution to the total impacts.
6. Identify the sources of each environmental impact for each 'hot spot'. For example, where in the life cycle of ethylene does aquatic toxicity come from? Or, which part of the life cycle of chlorine is responsible for solid waste?
7. Based on the LCA results, which environmental impacts do you consider to be most significant? Why? Explain how you identified the 'significant' impacts.
8. Which parts of the VCM system contribute most to the most significant impacts? What do you conclude from these results: which parts of the system should be targeted for improvements? How would you do that?
9. If ethylene and energy were supplied from renewable sources, how do you think that would influence the environmental sustainability. See Chapters 3 and 6 for the data.
10. Using the economic and environmental criteria and the results of the LCA and economic analysis so far, is it possible to make any conclusions at this stage on whether this design is sustainable? If so, what do you conclude? If not, why?

Table 13.10   *Using social indicators to assess social sustainability of the proposed VCM design*

Social criteria	Issues addressed
Provision of employment	Plant operators and contractors
Employee health and safety	Injuries, fatalities, noise, VCM exposure
Citizens' health and safety	Emissions into the environment, VCM exposure
Customer health and safety	VCM exposure
Nuisance	Odour, noise, visual impact
Public acceptability	VCM, PVC and dioxins

Assessing Social Sustainability

To assess social sustainability of their proposed design, the design team use the social criteria listed in Table 13.1. Their (mainly qualitative) findings are shown in Table 13.10 and discussed below. Some of these preliminary findings will serve as a starting point for a detailed safety study and loss prevention study, including HAZOP, in the detailed design stage.

Provision of Employment

The team have already found out in the economic analysis that the proposed VCM process will provide full-time employment to 20 operators over the lifetime of the plant. In addition to this, an estimated 25 full-time contractors would be employed during the construction phase, which is projected to last for 3 years.

Employee Health and Safety

Occupational health and safety is an important issue for any chemical plant, but particularly in the case of VCM. In addition to the usual health and safety concerns such as injuries, fatalities, exposure to noise and vibration, there are several other issues that the design team need to consider here. First, production of VCM requires the use of hazardous materials, such as chlorine, ethylene, sodium hydroxide and oxygen, so that the design must ensure that the risks from these materials are minimized.

Second, exposure to VCM has been linked to liver and other types of human cancer (Rahde, 1998). For this reason, the occupational exposure limits for VCM have been reduced significantly over the years from several thousand milligrams per cubic metre in the 1940s and 1950s to today's value of $2.6 \, \text{mg/m}^3$ or 1 ppm (expressed as 8 h time-weighted average, TLV-8h TWA). The short-exposure limit (15 min) must not exceed 5 ppm; direct contact with liquid VCM must be avoided. Although these are operational issues, the preliminary design, and then later the detailed design, must ensure that the exposure to and contact with VCM are minimized as far as possible.

This is particularly important, as the design team are aware that exposure to VCM and the associated occupational hazards are still a subject of dispute between the industry, government and NGOs. For example, in the Veneto region in Italy, three chemical companies producing chlorine, VCM and PVC are being prosecuted for the death of 157 and poor health of over 100 employees. It is alleged that the deaths and poor health are due to a long-term exposure to VCM. In addition to these charges, the companies are also accused for the environmental damage caused to the Venice lagoon, due to the emissions of dioxins, furans and other toxic substances.

Dioxins and furans are another health and safety concern associated with the production of VCM. Exposure to these substances can cause cancer and other toxicological effects. As already mentioned, the manufacture of VCM generates a certain amount of dioxins (mainly contained in the 'heavy ends'), which must be destroyed or minimized in the waste streams. The design team have for that reason chosen to incinerate the waste streams containing chlorinated hydrocarbons and dioxins, but they are also aware of the fact that incineration can generate further amounts of dioxins (as discussed in Chapter 10). They have, therefore, made sure that the design and operating conditions in the incinerators are such that the formation of dioxins is prevented.

Citizens' Health and Safety

The design team must also make sure that exposure to VCM of the general public living in the vicinity of the plant is prevented or minimized. Some studies suggest that daily VCM inhalation rates range from $4\,\mu g$ to more than $100\,\mu g$ per person per day for populations living in the immediate vicinity of VCM plants (ECETOC, 1998). Therefore, the design must ensure that the loss of the VCM product through evaporation is minimized.

Customer Health and Safety

All the VCM produced will be used on-site for the manufacture of PVC, so that the customer in this case is the PlasticFuture company itself. In addition to the safe storage of the VCM product which the team must build into the design, they also need to be aware of the downstream customer health and safety issues. For example, as VCM is a human carcinogen, it is important that PVC contains as little residual monomer as possible. During the latter part of the 1970s, the production process was significantly improved to address this problem, so that now PVC is routinely produced with less than 5 ppm of VCM.

Nuisance

The design must also ensure that noise, odour and visual impact of the plant are minimized to prevent causing nuisance to the neighbouring public. Because this VCM plant is an addition to an existing plant on an industrial estate, the design team estimate that the additional noise and odour levels will be relatively small and will probably not cause significant public nuisance. The visual impact will be minimal, as the plant will blend in with the other surrounding installations.

Public Acceptability

As discussed in Chapters 9 and 10, public acceptability is one of the most important factors which can ultimately determine whether an industrial installation gets a planning permission or keeps its licence to operate. The design team are aware that some of the above concerns, such as citizens' health and safety issues and nuisance, may cause objections to building the proposed plant. They must, therefore, ensure that the above issues are addressed adequately in the design, so that the objections to the planning proposal are minimized.

However, there are also public acceptability issues further downstream in the life cycle of VCM, related to PVC. Many people object to the production and use of PVC because it will eventually end up as waste and, if incinerated, it can contribute to the formation of dioxins. This is one of the main reasons for the public objection to incineration, so that in many parts of the world it is now almost impossible to obtain planning permission to build a new incinerator (as shown in the case study in Chapter 10).

Therefore, envisaging that the objections to PVC incineration could lead to a reduced demand for PVC, and hence VCM, the design team decide to build into the design a possibility for PVC recycling. They then need to revisit the flowsheet to make the necessary design modifications. This is their next task before proceeding to the final design stage.

This is where we leave our design team; but before we do that, let us have a quick look at what the rest of their job will be before they hand it over to the planning application team.

Questions

1. List and discuss the health and safety hazards associated with the materials used in the VCM production.
2. What are the dioxin emissions limit in your country?
3. At which operating conditions can the formation of dioxins from incinerators be prevented?
4. How would you prevent the loss of the VCM product so that the exposure of the public to VCM is prevented?
5. What can the VCM plant designer do to ensure customer health and safety?
6. Because this VCM plant is going to be integrated into an existing installation, the additional noise, odour and visual impact may not be significant to cause nuisance. Discuss how this would change if the plant were a stand-alone installation in the countryside, surrounded by villages. What would be the main objections by the neighbouring communities to building the plant?
7. Find out why Greenpeace is opposed to the VCM and other chlorine-related industries. Do you agree with their view? Why?
8. As an engineer or scientist, what could you do to reduce the environmental, health and safety concerns associated with the VCM and PVC? Based on that, how would you try to argue your 'case' to Greenpeace?
9. Based on all of the above consideration, carry out a social sustainability assessment of your VCM design and discuss the results.
10. How would you redesign the VCM plant to allow for recycling of waste PVC? What modifications would be necessary for that? You may wish to consult the book by Azapagic *et al.* (2003) for the PVC recycling technologies.

13.3.3 Detailed and Final Designs

After completing the preliminary design, the team begin to work on detailed design. As discussed at the beginning of this chapter, this design stage will involve detailed equipment

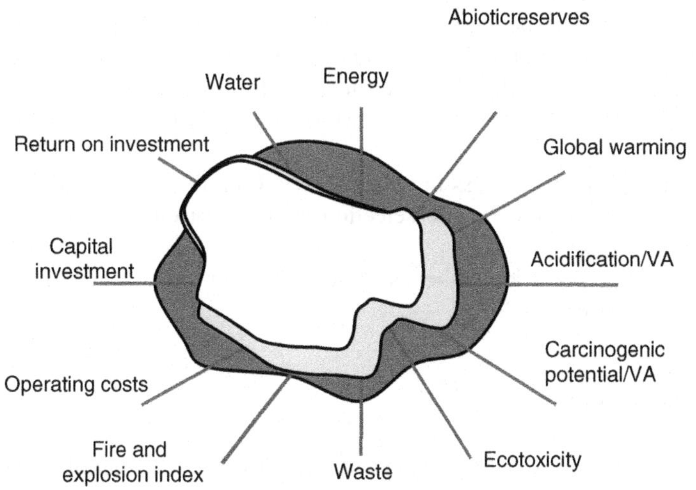

Figure 13.12 *Optimizing on sustainability and identifying the most sustainable VCM design*

design and economic analysis, process control and instrumentation and safety and prevention, including HAZOP studies. The team will then carry out a full sustainability assessment to ensure that all relevant sustainability factors have been identified and addressed appropriately in the design. These findings can then be used to further optimize the design on the economic, environmental and social performance. This will require a choice of the appropriate objective functions to reflect the most significant sustainability issues, as identified in the sustainability assessments. The team will have to think carefully as to how to tackle mathematically this complex multiobjective nonlinear optimization problem and also how to formulate some of the social objectives. Design optimization is by no means a trivial task and can take considerable time and resources to perform. However, it is also a powerful approach which can help the design team to identify the most sustainable design out of a number of feasible design options. Figure 13.12 illustrates how their optimization may progress, improving sustainability at each optimization and arriving at the design configuration with the smallest 'sustainability footprint'.

Once the most sustainable design has been identified, the team is then ready to proceed to the final design stage to produce equipment drawings and layout, piping and instrumentation diagrams and so on. They then hand over the project to the planning application team and, if their design is successful in obtaining the planning permission, to the construction team.

Questions

1. Carry out a detailed design of one or more parts of the VCM plant. If feasible, combine your work with the work of the rest of your design team to produce an overall detailed design of the VCM plant.
2. How would you perform the optimization of your design? List the main steps in optimization and describe how you would carry out each one for your VCM design. You

may wish to use the books by Edgar and Himmelblau (1988) and Floudas () for optimization theory and Lakshmanana *et al.* (2003) for a VCM optimization case study.

3. How would you choose the objective functions for optimization? Why?
4. How would you use the optimization results to identify the most sustainable design? Why?
5. Describe the planning process in your country. Link that with the EIA requirements discussed earlier within the site selection step and discuss the role of EIA in the application process.
6. What would you do as a member of the design team to make sure that the planning application is successful?

Acknowledgements

The author is grateful to Alan Millington and Aaron Collett, who contributed to a previous version of this chapter.

References and Further Reading

Aspen Technology (2003) ASPEN PLUS. Aspen Technology Inc., Cambridge, MA. http://www. aspentec.com.

Azapagic A. (1999) Life cycle assessment and its application to process selection, design and optimisation. *Chemical Engineering Journal*, 73, 1–21.

Azapagic, A. (2002) Life cycle assessment: a tool for identification of more sustainable products and processes, in *Handbook of Green Chemistry and Technology* (eds J. Clarkand D. Macquarrie), Blackwell Science, Oxford, pp. 62–85.

Azapagic, A. (2003) Systems approach to corporate sustainability: a general management framework. *Transactions of IChemE, Part B*, 81, 303–316.

Azapagic, A., Emsley, A. and Hamerton, I. (2003) *Polymers, the Environment and Sustainable Development*, John Wiley & Sons, Ltd, Chichester.

Azapagic, A. and Perdan, S. (2000) Indicators of sustainable development for industry: a general framework. *Transactions IChemE (Process Safety and Environment Protection), Part B*, 78 (B4), 243–261.

Chemstations (2003) CHEMCAD. Chemstations Inc., Houston, TX. http://www.chemstat.net.

Clegg, I. and Hardman, R. (1998) Vinyl chloride production process. Patent: US5728905.

Douglas, J.M. (1988) *Conceptual Design of Chemical Processes*, McGraw Hill, New York, p. 601.

EC (2008) Directive 2008/1/EC of the European Parliament and of the Council of 15 January 2008 concerning integrated pollution prevention and control (Codified version), Official Journal of the European Union (L024), 29/01/2008, 0008–0029.

ECETOC (1988) The mutagenicity and carcinogenicity of vinyl chloride: a historical review and assessment. Technical Report No. 31. European Chemical Industry, Ecology and Toxicology Center (ECETOC), Brussels. (Quoted in: Rahde, A.F. (1992)).

Edgar, T.E. and Himmelblau, D.M. (1988) *Optimization of Chemical Processes*, McGraw Hill, New York.

Floudas, C.A. (1995) *Nonlinear and Mixed-Integer Optimization: Fundamentals and Applications*, Oxford University Press, Oxford.

Hyprotech (2003) HYSIM. Hyprotech Ltd., Calgary. http://www.hyprotech.com.

IChemE (2003) The sustainability metrics: sustainable development progress metrics recommended for the use in process industries, Institution of Chemical Engineers, Rugby.

IChemE (1998) A guide to capital cost estimating. IChemE, Rugby.

Jebens, A. and Kishi, A. (2000) Vinyl chloride monomer (VCM). CEH Report. http://ceh.sric.sri.com/ Public/Reports/696.6000/ (9 March 2003).

Lakshmanana, A., Rooney, W.C. and Biegler, L.T. (1999) A case study for reactor network synthesis: the vinyl chloride process. *Computers & Chemical Engineering*, 23, 479–495.

Marshall, K., Henley, J., Reed, D. *et al.* (2001) Process for Vinyl Chloride Manufacture from Ethane and Ethylene with Secondary Reactive Consumption of Reactor Effluent HCl. US Patent No. WO0138272. 31 May 2001.

Rahde, A.F. (1992) Vinyl Chloride International Programme on Chemical Safety. IPCS Poisons Information Monograph 558, http://www.inchem.org/documents/pims/chemical/pim558.htm.

Ray, M.S. and Johnston, D.W. (1989) *Chemical Engineering Design Project. A Case Study Approach*, Gordon and Breach Science Publishers, London, p. 357.

Seider, W.D., Seader, J.D. and Lewin, D.R. (1999) *Process Design Principles. Synthesis, Analysis and Evaluation*, John Wiley and Sons, Inc., New York, p. 824.

Sinnott, R.K., (2000) *Coulson & Richardson's Chemical Engineering*, 3rd edn, vol. 6 (Design), Pergamon Press, Exeter.

Ulrich, G.D., (1984) *A Guide to Chemical Engineering Process Design and Economics*, John Wiley and Sons, Inc., New York, p. 472.

14

Urban Sustainability: The Case of Transport

Slobodan Perdan and Adisa Azapagic

Urban transport, in particular the ever-increasing dependence on car use, contributes significantly to unsustainable trends in urban development. This chapter describes the main environmental and social impacts of urban transport, including greenhouse gas emissions, air pollution, noise exposure, and adverse health, safety and community impacts. It identifies car dependency as the main cause of unsustainable trends in urban transport. Drawing on social research on consumption, the chapter shows that the car culture is closely linked with the issue of (un)sustainable consumption and the symbolic role consumer goods play in society. The role of the car as a 'positional good' (that is, as a symbol of social status and identity) is then examined and its environmental and wider social implications demonstrated using the example of growing popularity of sport utility vehicles (SUVs) among city dwellers. In the concluding section, the chapter argues that changing the car-dependency culture and making urban transport sustainable require a wide spectrum of measures, from technological innovations to 'soft' and 'hard' measures to encourage behaviour change.

14.1 Introduction

Half of the human population now lives in cities and it is expected that within two decades nearly 60% of the world's people will be urban dwellers (UN-HABITAT, 2000).

Sustainable Development in Practice: Case Studies for Engineers and Scientists, Second Edition
Edited by Adisa Azapagic and Slobodan Perdan
© 2011 John Wiley & Sons, Ltd.

Cities play a central part in economic, social and cultural life, generating the major share of the world's wealth and knowledge. They are principal drivers of economic growth and provide significant benefits to human society in terms of commercial economies of scale, accessibility of services and social cohesion.

However, current trends in urban development, such as the growth of road transport, the drive for more housing and rising household consumption of natural resources, place severe pressure on the environment, human health and the quality of life. Poor air quality, high levels of greenhouse gas (GHG) emissions, generation of large volumes of waste and waste water, high levels of traffic and congestion, high levels of ambient noise, urban sprawl and derelict land are some of the common environmental problems facing urban areas (EC, 2006; RCEP, 2007; UN-HABITAT, 2000). These are serious pressures which have significant consequences for the quality of life and health of people living in cities and the economic performance of the cities themselves.

Urban transport contributes significantly to these pressures.

There is no doubt that transport plays a key role in the economy and quality of life of cities. It enables access to people, goods and services and, as such, is critical to the economic and social viability of urban areas. However, transport is also a major source of urban pollution, emitting pollutants that damage the natural environment, buildings and human health. In areas where there is heavy road traffic, congestion imposes costs on the economy and seriously reduces the quality of life. In many urban areas traffic dominates the streets, squeezing out other road users and intimidating pedestrians and thereby severing connections between communities. People with cars become more dependent on them, while those without them are kept apart from jobs, services and facilities (RCEP, 2007).

Current trends in urban transport are characterized by increased car ownership and traffic volumes. In Great Britain, for instance, urban traffic levels have increased by 10% over the period 1994–2004, with the volume of motor traffic (excluding motorcycles) in urban areas expected to grow by approximately 40% by 2031 (DfT, 2005). Across the country, road traffic volume (measured as total car-kilometres travelled) increased by 20% between 1990 and 2007 (Defra, 2009).

Over the same period, car ownership has increased significantly, too; so, now, nearly a third of households in the UK have access to two or more cars (DfT, 2009). Similar trends are registered in the EU. Between 1995 and 2006, car ownership levels in the EU increased by 22% (equivalent to 52 million cars), and passenger car use increased by 18% (EEA, 2009).

Official transport statistics data for the UK and EU show the dominance of car use, even for short-distance trips, which indicates a high degree of dependency on this mode of transport (DfT, 2009; EEA, 2009). At the same time, walking and cycling for travel purposes have both generally declined. This trend in urban transport applies not only for the UK and EU, but also to the rest of the developed countries, and a similar pattern is emerging in the developing world as well (UN-HABITAT, 2000).

The increasing dependence on car use has significant implications for environmental and social sustainability of urban areas. These implications are presented in Figure 14.1. As can be seen from the figure, there is a complex web of connections between increased car ownership and car use in urban areas and a whole range of environmental and social issues which determine urban (un)sustainability. The next sections explore these issues in more detail.

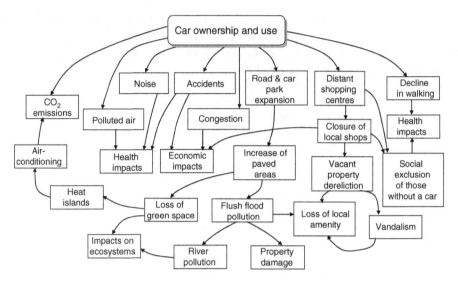

Figure 14.1 *Interconnections between car use and environmental and social impacts in cities (adapted from RCEP, 2007)*

Questions

1. Why is transport important for sustainability of urban areas?
2. How is the increasing car use related to environmental and social sustainability of urban areas? Discuss the interconnections shown in Figure 14.1.

14.2 Environmental and Social Impacts of Urban Transport

Urban transport has significant environmental impacts, including emissions of GHGs, air pollution, noise exposure, fragmentation of habitats and impacts on wildlife. As already indicated (see Figure 14.1), many of the environmental impacts of urban transport are interlinked with major social issues such as health, safety, poverty and the community well-being. For instance, transport has direct impacts on health and safety in terms of air quality and traffic accidents, but it has also become an important factor in the design of urban areas and, thus, leads to indirect effects on the well-being of urban residents and communities. Such effects include noise pollution, reduced opportunities for exercise, which can contribute to obesity and cardiovascular disease, and impacts on communities and urban landscapes, which can adversely affect well-being (RCEP, 2007). Urban transport could also exacerbate the segregation of certain income and age groups, as those living in households without a car are deprived access to employment opportunities, services and facilities, thus presenting a significant barrier to social inclusion.

14.2.1 Contribution to Climate Change: Greenhouse Gas Emissions from Transport

Globally, 13% of GHG emissions (for an overview of GHGs, see Box 14.1) come from transport (Solomon *et al.*, 2007). In the developed world, in particular Europe and the USA, transport's share of GHG emissions is even larger. The EU transport, for instance, contributes approximately one-quarter of all GHG output (EEA, 2009); in the USA, transportation sources account for approximately 29% of total US GHG emissions (EPA, 2006).

Box 14.1   Climate change and greenhouse gases

There is no doubt that climate change is the most important environmental challenge we face today. A growing body of scientific evidence shows that the release of GHGs into the atmosphere by human activity is the primary cause of climate change (Houghton *et al.*, 2001; Solomon *et al.*, 2007). Although there is some uncertainty in the predictions, the general scientific consensus is that the enhanced greenhouse effect is causing a rise in average global temperature which is likely to cause major changes in climatic patterns. The Intergovernmental Panel on Climate Change predicts a rise in mean global temperatures of between 1.4 and 5.8 °C by the end of the twenty-first century as a result (Solomon *et al.*, 2007).

GHGs, such as carbon dioxide (CO_2), methane (CH_4), nitrous oxide (N_2O) and water vapour (H_2O), occur naturally in the Earth's atmosphere. They help to keep the planet hospitable to life by trapping some of the Sun's heat and reradiating it back into the atmosphere. Without this 'greenhouse effect' the Earth's average surface temperature would be about 33 C cooler than it is currently (Houghton *et al.*, 2001).

Human activities release GHG emissions and contribute to increasing concentrations of GHGs in the atmosphere. The principal GHG emitted by human sources is CO_2. Other significant GHGs are CH_4, water vapour and nitrous oxide (N_2O). Other gases, although present in small concentrations, are nevertheless potent heat absorbers and, therefore, contribute to the greenhouse effect: they include chlorofluorocarbons (CFCs), hydrofluorocarbons (HFCs), other halons, perfluorocarbons, sulfur hexafluoride (SF_6) and tropospheric ozone[1] (O_3) (Houghton *et al.*, 2001; Azapagic *et al.*, 2004).

Like most GHGs, CO_2 is produced both by natural and human activities and can be removed from the atmosphere through natural processes (Houghton *et al.*, 2001). However, increased production of CO_2 by human sources has caused total GHG emissions to exceed natural absorption rates, resulting in increased atmospheric concentrations. Since the beginning of the industrial revolution, atmospheric concentrations of CO_2 have increased by nearly 30%, CH_4 concentrations have more than doubled and N_2O concentrations have risen by approximately 15% (Houghton *et al.*, 2001).

Because CO_2 is the most prevalent of all GHGs, GHG emissions are typically reported in terms of CO_2 equivalent (CO_2 eq.) to provide a common unit of measure. Other GHGs are converted into CO_2 equivalent on the basis of their global warming potential (GWP),

---

[1] Ozone generated in the lower layer of the atmosphere, known as troposphere. This is the layer immediately above the ground, stretching up to 10 km above the Earth.

which is defined as the cumulative radiative forcing[2] effect of a gas over a specified time horizon in comparison with CO_2. Therefore, the GWP of CO_2 is unity and that of CH_4 and N_2O, for example, is 25 kg CO_2 eq./kg CH_4 and 298 kg CO_2 eq./kg N_2O respectively.

Although, on an equal mass basis, CO_2 is a less potent global warming agent than the other GHGs, the quantity of CO_2 emissions is so large that it remains the main contributor to global warming. It is estimated that CO_2 emissions account for around 80% of the global total GHG emissions (Solomon *et al.*, 2007). Combustion of fossil carbon-based fuels – coal, oil and gas – used for energy generation and for transport is the main source of CO_2 emissions.

Emissions of GHGs from transport are growing everywhere. In the USA, for example, transport is the fastest growing source of GHGs, accounting for 47% of the net increase in total US emissions since 1990. Transportation GHG emissions increased by a larger amount than any other economic sector over this period, growing from 1509.3 Tg CO_2 eq. in 1990 to 1866.7 Tg CO_2 eq. in 2003, an increase of 24% (EPA, 2005). It is worth noting that these estimates of US transportation GHGs do not include emissions from additional life cycle processes, such as the extraction and refining of fuel and the manufacture of vehicles, which are also a significant source of domestic and international GHG emissions.

As illustrated in Figure 14.2, the life cycle of transport involves extraction and processing or raw materials and fuels, vehicle manufacture and their use for transport. Each life cycle stage is associated with a number of different environmental impacts – some of these are generated within the city due to the direct emissions from vehicles, while others are generated elsewhere. The life cycle GHG emissions of different city transport options, estimated using life cycle assessment (see Chapter 3), are compared in Figure 14.3. For example, on average, a petrol car generates 181 g CO_2 eq. per person and kilometre travelled; an equivalent diesel car emits slightly less, 178 g CO_2 eq. As shown in the figure, taking a bus halves the amount of GHG emissions per person and kilometre travelled. The most sustainable options from the climate change perspective, however, are trams and local trains. It is interesting to note from Figure 14.3 that adding bioethanol to petrol may not always result in lower GHG emissions, depending on the source of the ethanol (see also Chapter 6) and the efficiency of the vehicle.

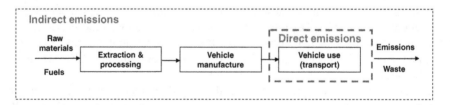

Figure 14.2 *The life cycle of transport*

---

[2] Radiative forcing is the change in balance between radiation entering the Earth's atmosphere and radiation being emitted back into space. A 'positive radiative forcing effect' means that the ratio of incoming to outgoing radiation increases, generally resulting in a warming of the Earth. Conversely, a 'negative radiative forcing effect' generally results in cooler Earth temperatures.

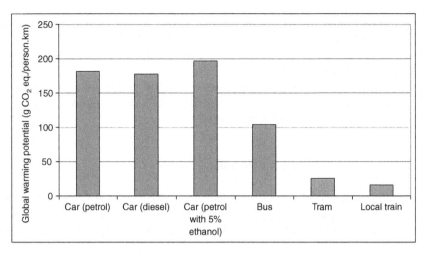

Figure 14.3 *Life cycle emissions of GHGs from different vehicles and transport options (data source: Ecoinvent, 2008)*

However, when these transport options are compared for some other environmental impacts, the picture changes – this is discussed in the next section. Here we continue to consider the emissions of GHGs from transport.

CO_2 emissions make up the majority of GHG emissions from transport, and are increasing due to the growth in traffic volumes. In the EU, for instance, growing transport volumes have driven emissions up by 27% between 1990 and 2006 (excluding the international aviation and marine sectors) (EEA, 2009). It is estimated that, if current trends continue in the EU, CO_2 emissions from transport will be some 40% higher in 2010 than in 1990 (EC, 2007).

The majority of CO_2 emissions from transport sources come from road transport. In the UK, for instance, out of estimated 533 million tonnes of total CO_2 emissions from transport in 2008, 90% came from road transport (DfT, 2009).

Transport sources emit other GHGs, including CH_4 and N_2O (during fossil fuel consumption) and HFCs (due to leakage in vehicle air conditioning and refrigeration systems). However, these GHGs are released in much smaller quantities than CO_2; nevertheless, they are much more potent global warming agents (see Box 14.1).

There are several other compounds emitted from transport that are believed to have an indirect effect on global warming but are not considered GHGs. They include ozone, carbon monoxide (CO) and aerosols. Scientists have not yet been able to quantify their impact with certainty, so that these compounds are not usually included in the official transportation GHG emissions estimates.

Questions

1. Describe the mechanisms of global warming and the potential consequences.
2. What is GWP? List as many GHGs as you know and find their GWPs in the literature. Which GHGs are the most potent with respect to global warming and what is their contribution to GHG emissions globally?

3. Which countries are the greatest emitters of GHGs? Are they signatories to the Kyoto Protocol? Discuss the implications.
4. Summarize the requirements of the Kyoto Protocol. What is the commitment of your country under this protocol?
5. How do the CO_2 emissions from transport compare with other sectors globally?
6. What are the options for reducing emissions of CO_2 from transport? Which of those would be suitable for your region/country?

14.2.2 Transport and Urban Air Pollution

Transport, in particular road traffic, contributes significantly to urban air pollution (see Box 14.2). Many air pollutants emitted from transport sources remain in the atmosphere for long periods of time and often travel long distances, thus affecting both the local and global environment.

Box 14.2   Pollutants in urban areas and related environmental impacts

In many parts of the world, and particularly in large cities, the local atmosphere is becoming increasingly polluted from road vehicles, local industrial activities and household heating. A wide variety of substances can contribute to local air pollution, most notably SO_2, NO_x, CO_2, CO, volatile organic compounds (VOCs), unburned hydrocarbons and solid particles of dust, ash and soot. In addition to causing the global and regional effects such as global warming, ozone depletion, and water and soil acidification, the combined effects of these pollutants can cause a number of local air pollution effects. Of these, 'winter' and 'summer' smog are the two effects most often encountered in the urban atmosphere (Azapagic *et al.*, 2004).

The main constituents of winter smog are SO_2 and particles, whose emissions increase in the winter months in the areas which use coal for heating; hence the name. The synergistic effect of particles and SO_2 can have deleterious impact on the environment and particularly on human health. A direct link between these pollutants and increased illness and mortality was first established in the 1950s in London, where, in one week alone, 4000 people died due to the prolonged winter smog episodes.

Summer or photochemical smog, on the other hand, occurs in the summer months due to the reactions between NO_x, VOCs and unburned hydrocarbons in the presence of UV radiation from sunlight. These pollutants, emitted mainly from vehicles, react to generate photochemical oxidants such as peroxylacetylnitrate and tropospheric ozone. Photochemical smog and photo-oxidants can cause respiratory problems and eye irritation in humans and can also affect vegetation through oxidation processes. Tropospheric ozone can also act as a GHG (Azapagic *et al.*, 2004).

For definitions of other environmental impacts, see Chapter 3.

Air pollution from road traffic stems from a number of sources, including exhaust pipe emissions and contributions from friction processes and resuspended road dust. This results in a complex mixture that includes particulate material and gaseous pollutants, such as nitrogen oxides (nitric oxide and nitrogen dioxide), CO and VOCs, all of which pose risks to health (Krzyzanowski *et al.*, 2005).

Particulate matter is one of several types of pollutant that come from exhaust gases and includes carbon- and metal-based particles with a diameter of 10 μm or less, known as PM10. Owing to the probable detrimental impact on human health, there is particular concern over ambient levels of ozone and fine particles (PM2.5 with a diameter of 2.5 μm or less).

The combustion of vehicle fuels (petrol and diesel) is one of the major sources of nitrogen oxides (NO_x) emissions, which, among other environmental impacts, cause acidification. They also interact with unburned hydrocarbons from combustion to generate photochemical smog (see Box 14.2). In the UK, for instance, road transport emitted about 441 000 t of NO_x emissions in 2007, which accounted for around 30% of total NO_x emissions (Defra, 2009).

Road traffic may also contribute to high levels of benzene and poly-aromatic hydrocarbons (PAH) in some urban areas (EC, 2007).

As a further illustration of the impacts generated from transport, in addition to the GWP discussed in Section 14.2.1, Figure 14.4 shows the acidification and photochemical smog potentials for different city transport options. For both impacts, travelling by tram or local train has the lowest impact, as was also the case for the GWP. The worst option with respect to acidification is travelling by bus, which in the case of GWP was the second-best option. For photochemical smog, driving a petrol car is the worst alternative, as it was for the GWP. However, the diesel car is now the second-best option, together with the bus.

Thus, as illustrated in this example, identifying more sustainable transport options is not a trivial task, as some options are better for some impacts but worse for the others. Furthermore, as transport technologies are constantly evolving, some of the options that currently have higher impacts could be improved through various technological advances.

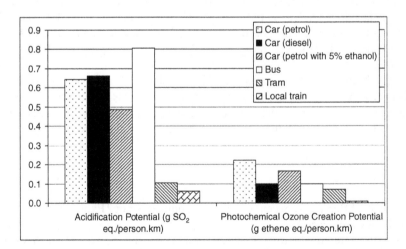

Figure 14.4 *Life cycle acidification and photochemical (summer) smog creation potentials for different vehicles and transport options (data source: Ecoinvent, 2008)*

The latter has been one of the main reasons for the decline of the emissions of some air pollutants from transport sources in recent years. In the UK, for instance, PM10 emissions from road transport steadily increased from 1980, peaking at over 44 000 t in 1995. By 2007, however, emissions had reduced to 25 000 t, 19% below the 1980 level (Defra, 2009). NO_x emissions from road transport followed a similar trajectory – they peaked at over 1×10^6 t between 1988 and 1993 and have fallen by 59% since 1990 to around 441 000 t in 2007 (Defra, 2009; DfT, 2009).

In part, the decline in emissions has been due to the requirement for cleaner engine combustion and the compulsory fitting (in most developed countries) of catalytic converters to all new petrol-fuelled cars, which have been highly effective, especially for reducing emissions of CO and VOCs.

Other technical measures to reduce air pollution have also been effective. The diesel vehicles are a substantial contributor to emissions of particulate matter and nitrogen oxides, and particle filters have been successfully introduced to reduce particulate emissions. However, they also have some undesirable side effects, as they result in a higher ratio of NO_2 to NO in exhaust emissions, which is more damaging to health. A report by the Air Quality Expert Group for Defra concluded that the rise in proportion of primary NO_2 emissions from road transport relates to the increasing numbers of light-duty diesel vehicles, especially those fitted with oxidation catalysts and, in the case of heavy-duty vehicles, particle filters (AQEG, 2004).

However, the rate of improvement in emissions of NO_x and particulates from road transport has slowed in recent years and in some cities levels are rising again. The reasons for this are not fully known, but are likely to include the rising volume of traffic, higher background concentrations of pollutants from sources other than transport and an increase in diesel vehicles (RCEP, 2007).

A recent EU transport strategy paper concluded that air quality is still a problem across Europe and that, despite falling emissions of regulated air pollutants from vehicles, concentrations remain high in some urban areas. The paper pointed out that in many European urban areas there have been no significant improvements in concentrations of fine particulates (PM10) and nitrogen oxides (NO_x), which have a major impact on air quality and human health. It singled out traffic emissions of particulate matter (PM10 and PM2.5) and NO_x as the local pollutants of most concern, since the daily limit value of PM10 and the annual limit value for NO_2 have been exceeded most extensively in European cities (EC, 2007).

Though situations may differ from one city to another and from one country to another, the rising volume of traffic seems to undermine the benefits achieved by technological progress in terms of energy efficiency and road vehicles emissions, and urban transport, in particular road traffic, continues to have a detrimental environmental effect.

Questions

1. What is the difference between 'winter' and 'summer' smog? Explain the mechanism by which they are generated.
2. What is the difference between stratospheric and tropospheric ozone? Are they generally beneficial or generally harmful? Explain the role of NO_x in the generation of tropospheric ozone.

3. What are the major sources of air pollution in your town or city? Find out how much SO_2, NO_x and particles they emit per year.
4. Describe air pollution legislation in your country and list the major acts which regulate air pollution.
5. What is the contribution of transport to air pollution in your region/country?
6. Why does a car using petrol–bioethanol blend, shown in Figure 14.4, have a lower acidification potential than the petrol-only car? Discuss where in the life cycle the acid gases causing acidification are emitted and how that may differ between petrol and ethanol.
7. What substances cause photochemical (summer) smog? Why does a petrol car have the highest summer smog potential of the options considered in Figure 14.4? Where in the life cycle of a petrol car would the photochemical oxidants be emitted?
8. How would you deal with the problem of air pollution from transport in urban areas? What would be sustainable options for your city/area?

14.2.3 Noise Pollution from Transport

Most urban dwellers are affected by noise pollution. Roads, railways and airports are the main sources of ambient noise, which can affect the quality of people's lives.

The World Health Organization (WHO) recommends that day- and night-time exposure to noise pollution in dwellings should not exceed 55 dB and 45 dB respectively (WHO, 1999). Urban traffic noise levels in most cities in Europe, however, usually exceed these guidelines set for the protection of health (EC, 2007).

The latest assessments suggest that around 20% of the EU population suffer from noise levels that scientists and health experts consider to be unacceptable, whereby most people become annoyed, their sleep is disturbed and adverse health effects are to be expected (WHO, 2008). An additional 40% of people are living in so-called 'grey areas', where noise levels are such as to cause serious annoyance during the daytime. In the UK, around half the population may be exposed to levels above the WHO guideline of 50–55 dB (RCEP, 2007).

Road traffic is by far the main source of transport noise. In Europe, for example, almost 67 million people (i.e. 55% of the population living in urban areas with more than 250 000 inhabitants) are exposed to daily road noise levels exceeding 55 dB (the WHO benchmark for excessive noise officially accepted in the EU) (EEA, 2009).

Exposure to high-level noise has decreased in some countries in the last decades due to technological measures, noise barriers and adapted spatial planning. However, some of these achievements are likely to be offset by the expected growth in traffic.

Questions

1. What are the main sources of noise pollution in urban areas?
2. How is noise pollution measured? What are the recommended daytime and night-times limits? Compare these with the typical noise levels in your area.
3. How can noise pollution from transport be reduced?

14.2.4 Health Impacts of Urban Transport

Transport affects health both directly (e.g. through air- and noise-pollution or traffic accidents) and indirectly (e.g. through its impacts on neighbourhoods and community life). It can have both positive and negative impacts on health. For example, transport policy can promote access to shops selling fresh food or facilitate walking and cycling and, therefore, have a positive effect on health. On the other hand, traffic can be a hazard to all road users, leading to accidents, and air- and noise-pollution caused by traffic can have seriously adverse health impacts. Some of the health impacts from transport are discussed next.

14.2.4.1 Transport, Air Pollution and Health

One important reason for our concern about air quality lies in the effects of air pollution on human health. Some of these effects are immediate and obvious, whilst the others can develop over time. In either case, it is not easy to establish a direct link between air pollution and human health effects because of the many other factors that also have an influence (Azapagic *et al.*, 2004).

However, there is growing scientific evidence that air pollution can have serious effects on people's health. For example, an EU study (Spix *et al.*, 1998) analysed a number of epidemiological studies carried out in 15 large cities across the EU. The study concluded that the rate of hospital admissions varied depending on the concentrations of different pollutants: increases of $50\,\mu g/m^3$ in NO_2 levels above the background level were estimated to lead, within hours or a few days, to an increase of 2.6% in hospital admissions for asthma treatment. The same increase in NO_2 levels leads to a 1.9% increase in admissions for lung conditions. A UK-based study showed that mortality rates follow a similar trend: deaths from all causes (excluding external causes such as accidents) are increased by 3.5% for every increase of $100\,\mu g/m^3$ in daily average NO_2 level (COMEAP, 1998).

Scientific evidence points out that exposure to air pollution can have a long-term effect on health, associated in particular with premature mortality due to cardiopulmonary (heart and lung) effects. In the short term, high pollution episodes can trigger increased admissions to hospital and contribute to the premature death of those people that are more vulnerable to daily changes in levels of air pollutants. Current official estimates for the UK are that air pollution reduces the life expectancy of every person in the UK by an average of 7–8 months (Defra, 2007). According to the WHO's global assessment of the burden of disease due to air pollution, more than 2 million premature deaths each year can be attributed to the effects of urban outdoor and indoor air pollution (WHO, 2002).

Recent research indicates that air pollution stemming from transport is an important contributor to these adverse effects of air pollution on human health (Dora and Phillips, 2000; Krzyzanowski *et al.*, 2005). Traffic fumes are a particular cause of ill-health: nitrogen dioxide (NO_2) at relatively high concentrations causes inflammation of the airways and long-term exposure may affect lung function; particulate matter can affect respiratory and cardiovascular systems (for example, asthma) and accelerate mortality. Exposure to CO reduces the capacity of the blood to carry oxygen and deliver it to tissues. SO_2 causes constriction of the airways and may cause acute mortality. Exposure to high levels of lead (Pb) affects the haemoglobin, the kidneys, gastrointestinal tract, joints and reproductive

Table 14.1   *Reduction of air pollution concentration and the resulting health and costs benefits (Department of Health, 1999)*

	Effect per 1 µg/m³ reduction of pollutant (based on urban population)		
	Particulate matter (PM10)	Sulfur dioxide	Tropospheric ozone (summer only)
Number of premature deaths avoided per year	340	270	170
Number of hospital admissions avoided per year (respiratory diseases)	280	180	145
Annual average savings for the 'tax payer' (1996 prices)	£0.62 m	£0.43 m	£0.37 m

system and damages the nervous system (Greater London Authority, 2002; Krzyzanowski *et al.*, 2005; UNEP, 2007).

There are particular health concerns about the levels of particulate matter in urban areas. A recent UK review indicated that the levels of airborne particles could reduce average life expectancy in the country by around 8 months (AEA Technology, 2004). According to recent estimates for the EU, exposure to particulate matter, particularly PM2.5, in the EU countries reduces average statistical life expectancy by approximately 9 months. This equates to approximately 3.6 million life-years lost or 348 000 premature mortalities per annum. The associated health costs of particulate matter amount to several billions of euros per annum (EC, 2007).

As the latter statistics on health impacts of particulate matter indicate, air pollution costs not only human health and lives, but also money. A UK report estimated that in 1996–97 the cost of admissions to hospitals for respiratory diseases related to air pollution cost the Government (and the tax payer) in total £566 million, or £1400 per person per spell in hospital (Department of Health, 1999). These estimates were based on 407 000 hospital admissions in that year, with an average length of stay of 7.7 days. The report also concluded that the relationship between pollution and health was linear and reversible over the pollution ranges considered, so that reductions in pollution levels would reduce both hospital admissions and premature deaths.

Table 14.1 summarizes these reductions and the estimated health and cost benefits for the three pollutants – particulate matter (PM10), SO_2 and tropospheric ozone – for which the information is most reliable. The figures suggest that 780 fewer people would die per year from air-pollution-related illnesses and this could potentially save £1.42 million of tax payers' money per year.

More recent data for the UK suggest that the national cost of air pollution in terms of health impacts is up to £20 billion each year (Defra, 2007).

14.2.4.2 Health Impacts of Noise Pollution

Epidemiological studies show that noise exposure in urban environments causes annoyance and sleep disturbance in adults (Dora and Phillips, 2000). Epidemiological studies also suggest a higher risk of cardiovascular diseases, including high blood pressure and myocardial infarction, in persons chronically exposed to high levels of road traffic noise, such as those that occur in urban areas.

Persistent environmental noise above 40–55 dB causes annoyance, levels of 40–60 dB disturb sleep, while levels of 65–70 dB increase the risk of ischaemic heart disease. Noise levels above 75 dB contribute to hearing impairment. (For comparison, the level of noise in a library is around 40 dB and from a home refrigerator 50 dB.) Studies have also reported adverse effects of aircraft and traffic noise on mental health, the cardiovascular system, and school performance in children (WHO, 2002; WHO, 2004; RCEP, 2007).

14.2.4.3 Other Health Impacts of Urban Transport

Some of the health impacts of transport are more difficult to assess than others. For instance, it has been well established by the medical profession that cycling and walking can help greatly in reducing obesity; however, owing to many other contributing factors involved in the issue of obesity, it is virtually impossible to reliably estimate the contribution of transport. There are, however, some studies that establish a firm link between obesity and transport. Adams (2005), for instance, shows that more and more children are becoming overweight at an early age because they are being increasingly confined to indoors and depending on adults for mobility.

Other health impacts have also been well documented. Traffic noise has been shown to induce nervousness, depression, sleeplessness and undue irritability, but other aspects of transport also cause irritation and frustration. Regular exposure to traffic congestion is shown to impair health, psychological adjustment, work performance and overall satisfaction with life (Novaco *et al.*, 1990). Congestion constrains movement, which increases blood pressure and frustration tolerance. This phenomenon not only reduces the well-being of those experiencing it, but can also lead to aggressive behaviour and increased likelihood of involvement in a crash. Aggressive behaviour on the road is common and appears to be increasing. For instance, one study found that 25% of young drivers aged 17–25 would chase another driver if they had been offended (WHO, 2008); another reported that 60% of study participants behaved aggressively while driving (Joint, 1995).

Among other health impacts of transport, it is worth mentioning that high traffic density affects children's development. Fewer and fewer children are being allowed to walk or cycle even short distances, because parents are worried about accidents. Several studies point out that the space within which children can move freely shrinks significantly as street traffic increases in the immediate environment (WHO, 2004). Children have become more dependent and less physically active, and this reduction in physical activity not only has longer term effects on physical well-being but can also affects children's stamina, alertness at school and academic performance.

Post-traumatic stress disorder, phobic travel anxiety and other accident-related psychological problems registered in the road-crash victims should also be added to the list of adverse health impacts from transport.

Questions

1. What are the most important health impacts of urban transport?

2. What are the WHO health-based air quality guidelines for transport-related pollutants? Find out whether the guidelines are exceeded in your local area or in your country and, if so, for which pollutants?
3. What are the WHO guidelines for exposure to road and rail noise? Find out whether these guidelines are met where you live.
4. What are the health impacts of transport in children? How could they be avoided?

14.2.5 Safety

In addition to direct and indirect health impacts, traffic itself is a significant physical hazard in the urban environment.

Statistics shows that each year thousands of people are killed or maimed in traffic accidents. For instance, the WHO estimates that around 1.2 million deaths worldwide come from road traffic injuries (WHO, 2004). Two-thirds of overall road accidents and one-third of overall road deaths occur in urban areas. In cities, pedestrians and cyclists are frequently victims of road accidents, representing one-third of the deaths from road traffic injuries.

Children are particularly vulnerable because their ability to cope with traffic is generally limited until around 10 years of age. They are more at risk in conditions with heavy or fast traffic, limited visibility or when a driver's attention is focused elsewhere rather than on pedestrians or cyclists. According to the WHO, road traffic injuries are the leading cause of death of children and young people (age of 5–29 years). In Europe, for instance, traffic causes 6500 deaths per year among children aged 0–14 years (WHO, 2004).

Real and perceived safety concerns are also quoted as the most important barrier preventing many people from choosing walking and cycling as means of transport (WHO, 2004). Road traffic accidents can also have an indirect effect on the entire community when these events occur, through changing people's perceptions of safety. Fear from traffic dangers, for instance, has led to an increase in the number of parents who drive their children to school, and this may limit children's capacity for social interaction and exercise (Dora and Phillips, 2000; Hunt *et al.*, 2000). Poor perceived road safety may also reduce the number of adults who would otherwise engage in walking and cycling, which in turn may affect their health.

Concerns over road safety may be a barrier to people's mobility and, therefore, reduce their access to family, friends, shops and other services. A perception of poor road safety may also contribute to the negative views about a locality in general.

Questions

1. How do concerns about road safety influence people's mobility?
2. Do safety concerns predominantly deter people from using more sustainable forms of transport (i.e. walking, cycling, public transport) or are there other, more important reasons why people opt for travelling by car?
3. In which way can concerns about road safety affect human health?
4. How could road safety be improved?

14.2.6 Social Exclusion

Social inclusion is a concept which is closely linked to poverty, but has a broader meaning and refers to a process which places people on the margins of social and community life (Shaw *et al.*, 1999). It can be a consequence of poverty, but people can be socially excluded without being poor. For instance, they can be excluded because of their sexuality, race or because of where they live. Access to resources such as education, employment, social networks and support, healthcare services and recreational facilities forms a basis to social inclusion.

Access to transport is a key element of social inclusion. Not all members of society have fair and equal access to public transport. For example, poorer people may not be able to afford public transport, people with disabilities may find it difficult to access buses and trains, and infrequent public transport may make certain localities more isolated. Thus, poor access to the resource of transport is, of itself, a social exclusion.

'Transport poverty' describes the lack of real travel choice for those who experience exclusion from transport and, as a consequence, lack choice in their destinations and activities (DfT, 2000). There is a growing body of evidence (SEU, 2003) to suggest that people on low incomes and in particular those living in households without a car are unable to meet their human needs and, thus, have a reduced opportunity to secure a reasonable quality of life.

There is also strong evidence that adverse transport impacts are worse in more deprived areas, which in turn exacerbates existing social exclusion and increases inequality (SEU, 2003). People living in more deprived areas tend to suffer the worst impacts from transport – road accidents, pollution and severance. For instance, an analysis of mortality in Ireland for the period 1989–1998 showed a clear social class gradient for death from transport accidents, with the poorest suffering most (Balanda and Wilde, 2001). On the other hand, they are the people least likely to cause these problems, as deprived people are less likely to own or have access to a car. Without a car they are also much more dependent on public transport, cycling and walking to get around. However, public transport is often expensive, inadequate or unpleasant, and, with the increasing traffic volumes, cycling and walking have become more dangerous. With the urban sprawl, distances to services have also increased – as witnessed in many countries by the growth of out-of-town superstores at the expense of local shops. Many people, particularly those without access to a car, find it difficult, therefore, to get to the services they need. The adverse impacts are greatest for elderly people, women and disabled people (Kavanagh *et al.*, 2005).

Poor accessibility is also linked with low educational achievements. The SEU (2003) study suggests that children in low-income households are more likely to attend the nearest school because of the lack of transport or the expense of travel cost. This can give rise to inequalities in educational outcomes where the nearest school is considered to be poorly performing. It also reduces parental choice among households who are least likely to be able to move in order to secure better educational opportunities. The evidence-base is stronger for linking poor transport and high travel costs with the low take-up of further education and college dropout rates (Lucas and Brooks, 2005).

To sum up, the lack of affordable access to resources such as education, health, shopping, leisure and so on can, therefore, be a significant barrier to social inclusion, and could exacerbate the segregation of certain income, ethnic and age groups.

Questions

1. What is social exclusion?
2. Describe 'travel poverty'. What are the most vulnerable groups in terms of travel poverty?
3. In which way can transport exacerbate social exclusion?

14.2.7 Community Life

Effects of transport on community life are varied and range from impacts it has on social contacts within a community to determining the attractiveness of the local environment and influencing views about the safety in the community.

For instance, the flow of traffic can break social networks and change the quantity or quality of support they can provide. It could lead to community severance; that is, separation of different areas within a community (McCarthy, 1999).

Roads and traffic create real and perceived barriers to social contact. For example, children may not be allowed to visit friends unaccompanied because of parental concern over road traffic accidents. A landmark study in San Francisco (Appleyard, 1981) found a direct correlation between lower traffic flows and speeds and increased levels of social interaction – including the higher number of local friends and acquaintances, the number of 'interactions between neighbours', levels of walking and the size of an area considered by residents as their home territory.

A similar study in Ireland found that, compared with people living in 'car-dependent' localities,[3] people who lived in 'walkable',[4] pedestrian-orientated localities were more likely to know and trust their neighbours and to participate in organizations (Leyden, 2003).

Neighbourhoods which are built to be pedestrian friendly may encourage people 'bumping into' each other. This process protects and promotes social networks and encourages a greater number of people to use public space and local services, which altogether influences the quality of life in the community. Neighbourhoods that revolve around car usage, on the other hand, could lead to deterioration in community relationships. While car mobility enables people to maintain social networks not confined by spatial restraints, a consequence for local neighbourhoods can be that they become anonymous and lack trust. This can lead to public spaces being perceived as unsafe and even hostile, which impedes civic life (WWF, 2008).

Access to green spaces is related to this aspect. Green spaces are frequently making ways for transport infrastructure; for instance, school playing fields have been sold and gardens redeveloped or paved over to provide parking. However, green spaces in urban areas are part of distinctive urban ecosystems which provide not only important environmental services, such as drainage, flood mitigation, biodiversity and climate regulation, but also deliver important social and health benefits for people and communities (Tiwary *et al.*, 2009). They offer elements of physical comfort, such as shading, cooling, fresh air and places to rest, and provide opportunities for formal and informal social interactions, recreation and exercise

---

[3] Designed to be negotiated in cars, with amenities spread out over a large area and emphasis on roads and parking over pavements.

[4] With pedestrian areas, sidewalks, meeting spaces and local shops.

that could make communities more attractive and healthier places. Replacing green spaces with transport infrastructure deprives local communities from these environmentally and socially valuable resources.

Questions

1. How does transport affect community life and well-being?
2. What is 'community severance' and in which way does this issue affect urban communities?
3. Why are parks, playing fields, gardens and other green spaces important for urban communities?

So far, this chapter has shown that current modes of urban transport, in particular road traffic and the ever-increasing car dependence, have serious negative environmental and social impacts, including climate change, air and noise pollution, health, safety and community effects. The degree to which the current transport habits damage or impair the urban environment and human health has raised great concerns about the sustainability of current transport trends.

However, the car-number trends show every sign of continuing to grow, despite overwhelming evidence of serious environmental and social impacts of road traffic. As already pointed out, this growing factor in car ownership and the resulting increase in traffic volumes continuously undermine the benefits generated by technological progress in the field of energy efficiency, emissions or noise from road vehicles.

Clearly, the car remains the mode of choice for the majority of the population. According to the latest statistics, the proportion of households in Great Britain with access to a car increased from 52% to 75% between 1971 and 2007. Over the same period, the proportion of households without access to a car almost halved, from 48% to 25% (Office for National Statistics, 2009a, 2009b).

It is not only that three-quarters of us live in households with access to a motor vehicle – we tend to use those vehicles frequently and in ways that weave car use into the fabric of our lives. Once we own the car and it is outside the door, the car tends to become the 'default choice', used for every journey, no matter how short it might be.

This increasing car dependency is at the heart of sustainable transport issues. The following sections examine the issue of car dependency and its implications for sustainability of urban transport in more detail.

14.3 Car Dependency and its Implications for Sustainability of Urban Transport

As evidenced by numerous surveys, forums, and so on, there is little doubt that most people are nowadays aware of the environmental impact of cars and the need for cleaner, 'greener' ways of getting around. People often talk about the need for more accessible, more reliable public transport and are generally aware of the advantages of walking and cycling more. However, evidence suggests that they often find themselves with little choice but to continue with travel patterns that are inherently unsustainable (SDC and NCC, 2006). Where no public transport is available, the car is often the only choice for the decisions on how to travel to shops and work places and on where and how to travel to holiday destinations. As more and more shops are located outside our towns, car use for shopping purposes inevitably increases. Even if people are eager to choose a green transport mode, they are stuck with high-impact choices.

However, people also often express their personal attachment to cars and the concept of car ownership (SDC and NCC, 2006). This emotional attachment to cars – together with the perceived unreliability of public transport and the concerns for safety of walking and cycling – leaves people struggling to reconcile environmental concerns with the need to cut back on driving.

This indicates that, at a deeper level, sustainable choices do not always resonate with people's deeply held aspirations. In our consumer society the car has become far more than a means of getting from one place to another – it is now an extension of people's living space as well as an index of prosperity and status in society. These forces operating at the very core of consumer behaviour constitute a huge challenge to addressing the car culture (Mont and Emtairah, 2007).

However, without addressing this challenge, a modal shift to alternative, more sustainable modes of transport will be impossible. Looking beyond the functional use of cars and understanding the symbolic value the car plays in our lives could provide us with resources on which to build change. Relevant research on sustainable consumption could provide us with some insights with respect to this issue. This is the subject of the next section.

Questions

1. If you own a car, what purposes do you use it for? How could you reduce the use of car?
2. Are there alternative modes of transport available to you for commuting, shopping and leisure activities? How do they compare with the car travel in terms of convenience, speed, safety and costs?
3. What would motivate you to change your current mobility habits; that is, to switch from driving a car to cycling or using public transport for commuting/shopping/leisure activities?
4. What incentives and policies would help to reduce the use of car and promote public transport in your area/country?

14.3.1 Consumption and the Symbolic Role of Cars

The general notion that certain kinds of consumer goods, such as cars, are used to advertise status, power and social position has been explored extensively in the scientific literature on consumption. The research on this subject is very rich and includes disciplines as diverse as consumer research, psychology, sociology, social philosophy, anthropology and economics.[5]

---

[5] Miller (1995), Røpke (1999), Edwards (2000), Michaelis (2000), Sanne (2002), Jackson (2004) and Mont and Emtairah (2007) provide good overviews and supporting accounts of this research.

There are at least a couple of significant lessons we can draw from this vastly rich and complex consumption literature. The first lesson is that material goods such as cars are important to us, not just for their functional uses but also because they play other important symbolic roles in our lives.

All consumer goods and services play a huge variety of roles in people's lives. Some of these roles are purely functional. Cars satisfy a need for transport, food satisfies a need for subsistence, housing for basic protection and so on. But consumer goods also play vital symbolic roles in our lives. This symbolic role of consumer goods facilitates a range of complex, deeply engrained 'social conversations' about status, identity, social cohesion, group norms and the pursuit of personal and cultural meaning (Jackson, 2004). As social anthropologist Mary Douglas (Douglas and Isherwood, 1979) pointed out: 'An individual's main objective in consumption is to help create the social world and to find a credible place in it'.

The consumption literature frequently refers to the concepts of 'conspicuous consumption' and 'positional goods' to suggest that consumption is implicated in processes of identity formation, social distinction and identification.

The term 'conspicuous consumption' was introduced by Thorstein Veblen in his 1899 book *The Theory of the Leisure Class* (Veblen, 1994) to describe the lavish spending on goods and services acquired mainly for the purpose of displaying income or wealth. After Veblen, the term 'conspicuous consumption' has been broadly applied to individuals and households with expendable incomes whose consumption patterns are prompted by the utility of goods to show their status rather than any intrinsic utility of such goods.

Fred Hirsch's concept of 'positional goods' provides a more general variation on Veblen's idea of conspicuous consumption. Hirsch (1995) suggested that once our material needs are met, we are led to consume 'positional goods', goods that have the characteristic of allowing us to 'position' ourselves socially with respect to our fellows. The defining quality of such goods is their social scarcity; and it is this scarcity that provides the vehicle for social positioning. If the goods were freely available, their value in positioning us in relation to our fellows would be diminished. Once enough people possess these goods, moreover, their value in positioning us ahead of the crowd declines, and those wishing to stay ahead must engage in a search for new goods with social scarcity. In this way, Hirsch argues, the positional economy engages us in a never-ending struggle. 'It is a case of everyone in the crowd standing on tiptoe and no-one getting a better view', he suggests (Hirsch, 1995). At the start of such a process, a few individuals gain a better view by standing on tiptoe. But the upshot is that others are forced to follow just so that they can maintain their original position. However, 'if all do follow. . . everyone expends more resources and ends up with the same position' (Hirsch, 1995). The vigorous pursuit of positional consumption, according to Hirsch, turns out to be nothing more than a kind of 'zero sum game'.

It is obvious that 'conspicuous consumption' and 'positional goods' have serious implications for sustainability of consumption. The dynamic nature of this kind of consumption forces us to consume more and more precisely because our competitors are also engaged in the same race. As Hirsch pointed out, it is 'a Red Queen effect' – like the Red Queen in Lewis Carroll's *Through the Looking Glass*, we must run faster and faster to stay in the same place (Hirsch, 1995).

Another important lesson from social research on consumption is that, far from being able to exercise deliberative choice about what to consume and what not to consume, for much of the time people find themselves 'locked in' unsustainable consumption patterns.

In fact, according to some consumption researchers, conspicuous and status-seeking aspects of consumer behaviour have been overemphasized (Shove and Warde, 1997; Gronco and Warde, 2001). Ordinary, everyday consumption, argue these authors, is not particularly orientated towards display. Rather, it is about convenience, habit, practice and individual responses to social and institutional norms. Far from being willing partners in the process of consumerism, consumers are seen as being 'locked-in' a process of unsustainable consumption over which they have very little individual control.

Consumer 'lock-in' occurs in part through economic constraints, institutional barriers, inequalities in access and restricted choice (Darnton, 2004). But it also flows from habits, routines, social norms and expectations and dominant cultural values. Sometimes we act unsustainably out of sheer habit; sometimes we do so because that is what everyone else does (SDC and NCC, 2006).

The insight that consumer goods play vital symbolic roles in our lives has a popular resonance. Most people recognize that we value goods not just for what they can do, but for what they represent to us and to others. There are few places where this process is more obvious than in the case of cars.

Cars have long been recognized as far more than a means of getting from one place to another. They have come to symbolize (for their owners at least) a wide variety of 'cultural goods': social status, sexual prowess, personal power, freedom and creativity (Freund and Martin, 1994). Like many other consumer goods, they are now deeply imbued with cultural meaning.

Questions

1. Explain the concepts of 'conspicuous consumption' and 'positional goods'. How do they apply to transport/mobility issues?
2. Explain how available (or unavailable) infrastructure and urban planning decisions lock people into unsustainable travel choices.

14.3.1.1 The Car as a Positional Good – the Case of SUVs

Few would argue against the idea that, for their owners, cars have 'positional value' (as opposed to *functional* value) because they 'increase' their social status. It is important, however, to understand how this positional value of cars influences urban transport and its environmental and social implications.

Consider, for instance, the case of increasing popularity of sport utility vehicles (SUVs) amongst city dwellers.

SUVs are enormously popular in the USA, where more than a half of all new vehicle sales are in this category (NHTSA, 2003). SUVs are also becoming more popular in other parts of the world. In the UK, for instance, SUV sales have gone up significantly over recent years. Demand in London alone has doubled, and in the period 1998–2006 one in every seven cars bought there was an SUV (Young Foundation, 2006).

As SUVs are designed for rough terrain rather than urban tarmac, it is obvious that in cities the actual need for an SUV is limited. The increasing demand for SUVs among city dwellers, therefore, has more to do with status, perceived safety and image than the functional need. The nickname given to SUVs in the UK – 'Chelsea tractors' (in reference to the size and bulkiness of the vehicle and to a wealthy borough of Chelsea in London in which this type of vehicle is particularly popular) – expresses public recognition of their real function. The expression is commonly used to describe any expensive large four-wheel-drive vehicle that is driven in an urban environment as a status symbol for ordinary, day-to-day purposes (typically for the school run) and will never be driven off-road.

SUVs may indeed provide some functional benefits compared with cheaper and more practical vehicles. These benefits may include increased reliability, durability and safety and more pleasurable driving. However, much of an SUV's attraction is undoubtedly in their 'positional value'.

Importantly, this positional value of SUVs results in some significant environmental and social impacts. For example, in city traffic SUVs emit up to four times more CO_2 than standard cars (Young Foundation, 2006), thus considerably increasing urban air pollution. In 2006, the *Observer* ran a story under the heading 'Chelsea choked by its tractors', in which it highlighted the impact SUVs had on local air pollution. The article reported that the pollution monitors in Chelsea registered an average annual level of NO_2 that was 2.5 times the recommended WHO maximum. The increase in pollution levels was ascribed to the growth in the use of SUVs in the area. The article also revealed that traffic was restricted on the Albert Bridge (a major route across the River Thames that connects Chelsea with Battersea) for some periods after it was found that 4×4 vehicles were seriously damaging its structure (The Observer, 2006). At the time of writing, the Albert Bridge was being closed for 18 months for restoration.

Generally, 'positional' features of SUVs, such as larger size, increased performance, off-road capability and additional accessories, make these vehicles less fuel efficient, which ultimately leads to increased resource consumption (Verhoef and Bert van Wee, 2000).

The increasing use of SUVs in the urban environment also has important implications for road safety. People who opt to buy SUVs rather than a more conventional vehicle often cite safety as their paramount concern. Driving inside one of these tall, bulky road vehicles, which towers over the other cars on the road, gives the drivers the feeling that they are less vulnerable than other road users. However, some recent transport studies have shown that this feeling may not be fully justified. In fact, the belief that SUVs provide additional safety to their drivers may be completely misplaced.

Although SUVs are heavier than normal cars, and so might be expected to be more resilient in the event of a crash, official statistics in the USA show that SUVs are involved in a disproportionately high number of fatal car accidents. In 2003, for example, a driver of an SUV was 11% more likely to be killed in a traffic accident than someone in a standard car. One of the key reasons is the extra height of the vehicles, which gives them a higher centre of gravity and makes them more prone to roll over in a collision or even a sharp road manoeuvre (NHTSA, 2003).

As well as posing a danger to their own drivers, research has shown that SUVs present a far greater threat to other road users. Pedestrians who get knocked down by an SUV are twice as likely to die as those hit by a normal vehicle. The reason for this higher mortality rate lies not only in the sheer mass of a typical SUV, but the design of the vehicles as well. Their blunt and broad frontal geometry makes injuries to the heads and neck regions of pedestrians far more common than is the case with normal car impacts, which, because of a car's lower and more aerodynamic bearing, more frequently result only in leg injuries (Acierno *et al.*, 2004).

The SUVs' impact on other motorists is not any better. If you are travelling in a car which is involved in a collision with an SUV, you, too, are twice as likely to die as you would have been if you had been struck by another car. The US transport statistics show that SUVs and light tracks (representing about 36% of all registered vehicles) are involved in about half of all fatal two-vehicle crashes with passenger cars. In these crashes, over 80% of the resulting fatalities are to occupants of the passenger cars (NHTSA, 2003).

In the case of collision with a standard car, the extra weight of the SUV contributes to its greater destructive potential, but design is also a key factor. A typical SUV rides so high that its bumper will make no contact with the bumper of a car when the two are involved in a frontal collision. In a sideways impact, the SUVs bulky front end tends to strike the occupants of a car in the vulnerable upper body area, increasing the likelihood of fatality (Acierno *et al.*, 2004).

It is fair to say that the manufacturers have taken steps to address these safety concerns about SUVs. Some models have been redesigned – to lower their bumper heights, for example – and more attention has been paid to rollover resistance in the design of new models. However, despite significant improvements in standards between 2006 and 2009, the latest reports indicate that the safest SUVs are still more likely to roll over than the least safest standard cars.

As the case of SUVs illustrates, embodying cars with status results in some unintended environmental and social outcomes. It also has wider social implications.

14.3.2 Social implications of Car Dependency

As the car turns into more than a means of getting from one place to another and is converted into a symbol of prosperity and status in society, travel by car becomes a socially preferred mode of transport while other forms of travel are perceived as inferior and, in same cases, undesirable and, as such, often stigmatized. Stigma that is sometimes attached to non-car transport is well illustrated by the statement attributed to Margaret Thatcher: 'A man who, beyond the age of 26, finds himself on a bus can count himself as a failure'.[6]

This statement reflects the underlying current of the car culture and indicates its wider social implications. In a society in which the car ownership becomes a norm and cars are used to display social status and identity, those who do not own a car are considered 'nobodies' or, as Margaret Thatcher might have put it, 'failures'.

In a car-dependent society, non-drivers are facing the risk of being increasingly marginalized. Businesses, for instance, often decide to locate to sites with better access by car rather than other transport modes, as driving is considered the preferable mode of transport for employees and customers. This may present practical problems to non-drivers and deprive them from access to important social resources. As pointed out earlier in the chapter, in a car-dependent society, non-drivers may suffer from the reduced access to resources such as education, employment, social networks and support, healthcare services and recreational facilities, which in turn could exacerbate social exclusion.

Embodying car with the status value also motivates some people to increase their vehicle ownership beyond what they would otherwise choose (Steg, 2005). For example, a lower income person might be best off overall relying on a combination of walking, cycling,

---

[6] Margaret Thatcher in 1986, as quoted in Commons debates, 2003-07-02, column 407.

public transport and rented cars, but chooses instead to own a car because of the status it conveys. Once a person owns a vehicle they are motivated to use it in order to maximize the value of its expense. The status value of vehicle ownership, therefore, shifts people from the multi-modal lifestyle (i.e. using various modes of transport) to car dependency. As a consequence, other modes of transport, such as bus travel, walking and cycling, may decline. As these modes experience significant economies of scale, reductions in their demand reduce their quality of service. This, in turn, could lead to further practical problems for non-drivers, such as inadequate walking and cycling conditions, poor public transport service, and unpleasant stops and station waiting areas.

Questions

1. What environmental and social implications could be associated with embodying cars with status value?
2. Should the car culture be changed? Could it be changed? If so, how would you go about changing it?

14.4 Measures to Promote Sustainable Transport

A shift from the polluting and car-dependent urban transport to a more sustainable urban mobility requires a spectrum of measures, from technological innovations to measures that allow people to change attitudes and behaviours in a more fundamental way.

Technological measures are at the near end of this spectrum. Simple technological interventions, such as catalytic converters, have had a very positive impact on reducing air pollution. Other technological innovations could also significantly benefit the urban environment – for example, next-generation vehicle technology, such as electric power (including battery-electric vehicles, plug-in hybrid electric vehicles and hydrogen fuel-cell electric vehicles).

Technological measures may require less in terms of intervention and active behavioural change, yet even here people's attitudes and inclinations play a significant part. Take, for instance, the case of electric/hybrid cars. Whether or not these less-polluting, low-carbon vehicles will become universally acceptable depends not only on their technical capabilities and/or environmental credentials, but also on whether they can fulfil other roles the car plays in social life. As emphasized in the previous section, for many people the car is not only a means of getting from one place to another, but also represents a personal symbol of status and identity. Making low-carbon cars 'desirable' would provide an opportunity to work *with* the grain of people's pride in their cars and address their underlying attachment to cars. The Toyota Prius provides a good case study in this respect.

When the Toyota Prius won the 'Car of the Year' award at the 2005 Paris and Detroit motor shows, it became a new must-have. The fact that the Prius has strong environmental credentials but is also a desirable model means that their owners can have all their aspirations from their car met while still buying into environmentally advanced technology (SDC and NCC, 2006). As Yutaka Matsumoto, general manager of strategy at Toyota, put it in a recent interview for the *Sunday Times*: 'If a car is not attractive or fun, people will not buy it, no matter how green it is'. (Sunday Times, 2009a).

However, a shift towards the use of low-emission cars will not happen by itself. Another prominent businessman, Sir Terry Leahy, chief executive of Tesco, has recently emphasized the point that this change needs to be actively encouraged (Sunday Times, 2009b):

> You can't tax petrol more than we have already but people are still driving around in great big gas guzzlers. It is not until you incentivise and motivate them through information and choice that your get them to say it is cool to drive a small car or it is cool to drive a low-carbon one.

In a recent transport report, the UK Sustainable Development Commission (SDC) suggested a product roadmap for mainstreaming low-carbon cars (SDC and NCC, 2006). The SDC recommends several measures to achieve a shift towards low-carbon vehicles, including the introduction of a £0 bottom band of vehicle excise duty for vehicles with emissions below $100\,g\ CO_2/km$ and removing financial disincentives to low-emission vehicles. These measures, the SDC believes, would dramatically improve the market demand for highly fuel efficient vehicles such as hybrid cars.

However, as much as the shift to low-carbon cars is highly desirable, it is worth noting that low-carbon cars are not necessarily a completely environmentally benign technology. While they reduce or eliminate direct emissions in cities, on a life cycle basis they still contribute significant impacts in the hinterland. For example, electric cars rely on electricity which needs to be generated using a mix of fuels; depending on the national grid, this may have higher or lower GHG emissions than the direct emissions from transport. Hybrid cars still depend on fossil fuels, so their life cycles must also be considered when assessing the environmental impacts.

At the other end of the spectrum of measures for sustainable transports are so-called 'smart and soft' mobility management measures.

People's attitudes and behaviours directly influence the way they travel; attitudes and behaviour, therefore, are key aspects to be considered by urban transport policies. To address these aspects, a number of 'smart and soft' mobility management measures have been suggested (see, for instance, EC, 2006; EC, 2007; WWF, 2008; EEA, 2009). Their aim is to help people reduce their car use by providing better information and opportunities while enhancing the attractiveness of alternatives.

'Smart and soft' measures include: travel awareness campaigns, public transport information and marketing, school, green and personalized travel plans, car clubs, car sharing and car pooling schemes, telecommuting, video-conferencing and home shopping. As transport measures, they are fairly new, mostly relatively uncontroversial and often popular.

It is suggested that, if successfully implemented, these measures could result in considerable environmental and social benefits such as:

- 'Smart and soft' mobility management measures could reduce car traffic in Europe by 11% over a decade (EC, 2007).
- Car sharing could save a lot of valuable public space and offer a number of other advantages, such as reducing the average annual car mileage and related CO_2 emissions. For instance, in Bremen (Germany), where such a scheme has been successfully implemented, each 'shared car' replaced four to ten privately 'owned cars' and each car-sharing user reduced their car-related CO_2 emissions by at least 39% and by up to 54% (EC, 2007).

- Schemes such as 'teleworking' from home can improve employee performance, bring social benefits, such as reduced stress, and contribute to stronger family ties and unity (Johnson, 1994).
- Videoconferencing enables companies to reduce long-distance travelling and, as such, offers huge carbon savings opportunities, especially for service companies, for whom 50% or more of their carbon footprint stems from business travel (WWF, 2008a).

'Smart and soft' measures are aimed at either reducing transport demand growth or reducing transport demand altogether. In general, most countries favour these soft measures over stronger regulatory approaches, like congestion charging, to make their transport systems more sustainable (EEA, 2009).

The 'smart and soft' measures mentioned here may indeed eventually work, and result in a change in people's travel behaviour. However, changing people's behaviour is notoriously difficult. Providing information, for instance, does not necessarily change attitudes, and changing attitudes does not necessarily cause a change in behaviour. How we behave is determined by many factors. Individual behaviours are deeply embedded in social situations, institutional contexts and cultural norms. As mentioned in the previous sections, people often find themselves 'locked in' unsustainable behaviours by a combination of habit, disincentives, social norms and cultural expectations. Trying to bring about behaviour change in an environmentally beneficial direction is thus often inherently difficult.

'Smart and soft' measures aimed at behaviour change will work better if supported by 'hard measures', such as: congestion charging and parking charges, reallocation of road space and road pricing schemes, restricting access for the most polluting road vehicles (low emission zones), fostering the use of cleaner, quieter and lower CO_2 road vehicles and so on. In this way, the benefits of behaviour change measures would not be eroded by induced traffic.

It is important that the measures aimed at promoting sustainable transport are applied in an integrated manner and are mutually supportive. Otherwise, benefits brought about by measures in favour of cleaner vehicles, for instance, can be undermined by car traffic growth brought about by decisions related to land use, parking or public transport. Sustainable solutions can only be worked out if all aspects are carefully taken into consideration, if all legal and administrative authorities concerned and all relevant stakeholders (including the public and the NGOs) are involved in the solution-finding processes.

Questions

1. How would you improve the transport situation in your town/city? What would be more sustainable transport options than currently used in your city?
2. Which arguments would you use to persuade the local government in your town/city to adopt and develop more sustainable transport policies?

14.5 Conclusions

Making urban transport more sustainable is not a trivial task. It requires concerted efforts to address car dependency and associated growth in road traffic, as well as a wide range of measures to promote alternative, more environmentally and socially beneficial modes of transport. Technological innovations such as low-carbon vehicles and alternative, less-polluting fuels have a significant role in finding a solution to the problems of urban transport. However, successful implementation of sustainable solutions for urban transport will require not only technical measures, but also understanding and encouraging behavioural change.

Acknowledgements

Part of the work presented in this chapter has been funded by the UK Engineering and Physical Sciences Research Council (EPSRC) within the project 'Pollutants in the Urban Environment (PUrE)' (grant no. EP/C532651/2). This funding is gratefully acknowledged.

References and Further Reading

Acierno, S., Kaufman, R., Mock, C. *et al.* (2004) Vehicle mismatch: injury patterns and severity. *Accident Analysis and Prevention*, **39**, 761–772.

Adams, J. (2005) Hyper-mobility: a challenge to governance, in *New Modes of Governance: Developing an Integrated Policy Approach to Science, Technology, Risk and the Environment* (eds C. Lyall and J. Tait), Ashgate, Aldershot.

AEA Technology (2004) The evaluation of the air quality strategy. Report to Defra. Publication No. ED50232.

Air Quality Expert Group (AQEG) (2004) Nitrogen dioxide in the United Kingdom. Report for Defra.

Appleyard D. (1981) *Liveable Streets*, University of California Press, Los Angeles, CA.

Azapagic, A., Duff, C. and Clift, R. (2004) Integrated prevention and control of air pollution: the case of nitrogen oxides, in *Sustainable Development in Practice: Case Studies for Scientists and Engineers*, 1st edn (eds A. Azapagic, S. Perdan and R. Clift), John Wiley & Sons, Ltd, Chichester.

Balanda K.P. and Wilde, J. (2001) *Inequalities in Mortality – A Report on All-Ireland Mortality Data*, The Institute of Public Health in Ireland, Dublin.

COMEAP (1998) *Quantification of the Effects of Air Pollution on Health in the United Kingdom*, Committee on the Medical Effects of Air Pollutants, Department of Health, The Stationary Office, London.

Darnton, A. (2004) Driving public behaviours for sustainable lifestyles. Defra/COI Sustainable Development Desk Research Report 1, Defra, London.

Defra (2009) *Sustainable Development Indicators in your Pocket 2009*. Department for Environment, Food and Rural Affairs. HMSO, London.

Department of Transport (DfT) (2000) Social inclusion and the provision of public transport. Department of Transport, London.

Department for Transport (DfT) (2005) *Transport Statistics Great Britain 2004*, The Stationary Office, London.

Department for Transport (DfT) (2009) *Transport Statistics Great Britain – 2009 Edition*, Department for Transport, The Stationary Office, London.

Department of Health (1999) *Economic Appraisal of the Health Effects of Air Pollution*, Ad-Hoc Group on the Economic Appraisal of the Health, Effects of Air Pollution, The Stationary Office, London.

Dora, C. and Phillips, M. (2000) *Transport, Environment and Health*, WHO regional publications, European series; No. 89, WHO Regional Office for Europe, Copenhagen.

Douglas, M. and Isherwood, B. (1979) *The World of Goods: Towards an Anthropology of Consumption*, Penguin, Harmondsworth.

Edwards, T. (2000) *Contradictions of Consumption: Concepts, Practices and Politics in Consumer Society*, Open University Press, Milton Keynes.

EPA (2005) Inventory of U.S. greenhouse gas emissions and sinks: 1990–2003. United States Environmental Protection Agency, Washington, DC.

EPA (2006) Greenhouse gas emissions from the U.S. transportation sector 1990–2003, United States Environmental Protection Agency, Office of Transportation and Air Quality, Washington, DC, www.epa.gov/otaq/climate.htm.

European Commission (EC) (2007) Sustainable urban transport plans preparatory document in relation to the follow-up of the thematic strategy on the urban environment. Office for Official Publications of the European Communities, Luxembourg, 25 September 2007.

European Commission (EC) (2006) Communication from the Commission of 11 January 2006 on a thematic strategy on the urban environment, COM(2005) 718, final, Not published in the *Official Journal*. http://ec.europa.eu/environment/urban/pdf/com_2005_0718_en.pdf.

European Environment Agency (EEA) (2009) Transport at a crossroads – TERM 2008: indicators tracking transport and environment in the European Union, EEA Report, No. 3/2009, Copenhagen.

Freund, P. and Martin, G. (1994) *The Ecology of the Automobile*, Black Rose Books.

Greater London Authority (2002) *Cleaning London's air: The Mayor's Air Quality Strategy*, Greater London Authority. ISBN 1 85261 403 X.

Gronco, J. and Warde, A. (2001) *Ordinary Consumption*, Routledge, London.

Hirsch, F. (1995) *Social Limits to Growth*, Revised edition, Routledge, London.

Hunt, R., Davis, A., Falce, C. *et al.* (2000) *Health Update – Environment and Health; Road Transport*, Health Education Authority, London.

Houghton, J.T., , Ding, Y., Griggs, D.J. *et al.*, (2001): Climate Change 2001: The Scientific Basis. International Panel on Climate Change (IPCC), Third Assessment Report, Cambridge, UK.

Jackson, T. (2004) Negotiating sustainable consumption: a review of the consumption debate and its policy implications. *Energy and Environment*, **15**(6), 1027–1053.

Johnson, R.P. (1994) Ten advantages to telecommuting: in the areas of conserving energy, protecting the environment, promoting family values, and enhancing worker safety. http://www.orednet.org/venice/rick/telecommute/telebenefits.html.

Joint, M. (1995) *Road Rage*, Public Policy Group, Road Safety Unit, Automobile Association, Basingstoke.

Kavanagh, P., Doyle, C., and Metcalfe, O. (2005): *Health Impacts of Transport: A Review*. The Institute of Public Health in Ireland, Dublin.

Krzyzanowski, M., Kuna-Dibbert,B. and Schneider J. (eds) (2005) *Health Effects of Transport-Related Air Pollution*, World Health Organization, Geneva.

Leyden, KM. (2003) Social capital and the built environment: the importance of walkable neighbourhoods. *American Journal of Public Health*, **93**, 1546–1551.

Lucas, K. and Brooks, M. (2005) 'Social indicators', appraisal of sustainability project report, Institute for Transport Studies. www.its.leeds.ac.uk/projects/sustainability/project_outputs.htm.

McCarthy, M. (1999) Transport and health, in *Social Determinants of Health* (eds M. Marmot and R.G. Wilkinson), Oxford University Press, Oxford.

Michaelis, L. (2000) *Sustainable Consumption: A Research Agenda*, Oxford University Press, Oxford.

Miller, D. (ed.) (1995) *Acknowledging Consumption – a Review of New Studies*, Routledge, London.

Mont, O. and Emtairah, T. (2007) Systemic changes for sustainable consumption and production, in Proceedings: Changes to Sustainable Consumption, 20–21 April 2006, Copenhagen, Denmark. Workshop of the Sustainable Consumption Research Exchange (SCORE!) Network.

NHTSA (National Highway Transport Safety Administration) (2003) Statement for House hearing on SUV Safety – February 26, 2003, The honourable Jeffrey W. Runge, M.D. administrator, National Highway Traffic Safety Administrator before the Committee on Commerce, Science, and Transportation, United States Senate. http://www.nhtsa.dot.gov/nhtsa/announce/testimony/SUVtestimony02-26-03.htm.

Novaco, R.W., Stokols, D., and Milanesi, L. (1990) Objective and subjective dimension of travel impedance as determinants of commuting stress. *American Journal of Community Psychology*, **18**, 231–257.

Office for National Statistics (2009a) National travel survey. Department for Transport; Family Expenditure Survey, Office for National Statistics.

Office for National Statistics (2009b) general household survey (longitudinal). Office for National Statistics.

Paul, K., Doyle, C. and Metcalfe, O. (2005) *Health Impacts of Transport: A Review*, The Institute of Public Health in Ireland, Dublin.

Røpke, I. (1999) The dynamics of willingness to consume. *Ecological Economics*, **28**(3), 399–420.

RCEP (2007) The urban environment. Royal Commission on Environmental Pollution, Twenty Six Report, London, 2007.

Sanne, C. (2002) Willing consumers – or locked in? Policies for sustainable consumption. *Ecological Economics*, **43**(2–3), 127–140.

Shaw, M., Dorling, D. and Davey-Smith, G. (1999) Poverty, social inclusion and minorities, in *Social Determinants of Health* (eds M. Marmot and R.G. Wilkinson), Oxford University Press, Oxford.

Shove E. and Warde, A. (1997) Noticing inconspicuous consumption, paper presented to the European Science Foundation TERM programme workshop on Consumption, Everyday Life and Sustainability, Lancaster.

Social Exclusion Unit (2003) Making the connections: final report on transport and social exclusion, ODPM.

Solomon, S., Qin, D., Manning, M. *et al.* (eds). (2007) *Climate Change 2007: The Physical Science Basis. Report of Working Group 1 to the Fourth Assessment Report of the Intergovernmental Panel on Climate Change.* Cambridge University Press, Cambridge.

Spix, C., Anderson, H.R., Schwartz, J. *et al.* (1998) Short-term effects of air pollution on hospital admissions of respiratory diseases in Europe: a quantitative summary of APHEA study results. (Air pollution and health: a European approach). EU Project in the Environment and Climate Programme, http://europa.eu.int/comm/research/success/en/env/0267e.html (October 2003).

Steg, L. (2005) Car use: lust and must. Instrumental, symbolic and affective motives for car use. *Transportation Research A*, **39**, 147–162.

Sunday Times (2009a) Toyota brings fun to its hybrid cars. *Sunday Times*, London, 26 April 2009.

Sunday Times (2009b) Tesco turns itself into a green giant. *Sunday Times*, London, 31 May 2009.

The Observer (2006) Chelsea choked by its tractors. *The Observer*, Sunday 20 August 2006.

The Sustainable Development Commission (SDC) and the National Consumer Council (NCC) (2006) I will if you will – towards sustainable consumption. Sustainable Consumption Roundtable Report, May 2006, London.

Tiwary, A., Sinnett, D., Peachey, C. *et al.* (2009) An integrated tool to asses the role of new planting in PM10 capture and the human health benefits: a case study in London. *Environmental Pollution*, **157**, 2645–2653.

UNEP (2007) Liveable cities – the benefits of urban environmental planning, Washington DC.

UN-HABITAT (2008) *State of the World's Cities 2008/2009 – Harmonious Cities*, Earthscan, London/Sterling, VA. www.unhabitat.org.

Veblen, T. (1994) *The Theory of the Leisure Classes*, Dover, New York.

Verhoef, E. T. and Bert van, Wee (2000): "Car Ownership and Status: Implications for Fuel Efficiency Policies from the Viewpoint of Theories of Happiness and Welfare Economics", *European Journal of Transport and Infrastructure Research*, Vol. 0, Is. 0 pp. 41–56.

WHO (1999) Guidelines for community noise. WHO Regional Office for Europe, Copenhagen, available at, http://www.who.int/docstore/peh/noise/guidelines2.html.

WHO (2002) World health report 2002. Reducing risks, promoting healthy life. World Health Organization, Geneva.

WHO (2004) Transport-related health effects with a particular focus on children: towards an integrated assessment of their costs and benefits. State of the art knowledge, methodological aspects and policy directions. WHO Regional Office for Europe, Copenhagen.

WHO (2008) Transport, health and environment: trends and developments in the UNECE–WHO European region (1997–2007). WHO Regional Office for Europe, Copenhagen.

WWF (2008) One planet mobility – a journey towards a sustainable future. Report, World Wild Fund, Godalming.

WWF (2008a) Travelling light – Why the UK's biggest companies are seeking alternatives to flying. One Planet Future. http://www.wwf.org.uk/filelibrary/pdf/travelling_light.pdf.

Young Foundation (2006) Positional goods – new inequalities and the importance of relative position. C Presentation, Seminar: Positional Goods and Luxury Fever, The Smith Institute, London, September, 2006.

Veblen, T. (1994) *The Theory of the Leisure Classes*, Dover, New York.

15

Aviation and its Response to Environmental Pressure

Alice Bows and Kevin Anderson

The aviation sector is just one of many producing greenhouse gas and other emissions that are damaging to the global climate. Reducing emissions in line with avoiding 'dangerous climate change' by ensuring that global mean surface temperatures do not exceed a 2 °C rise above pre-industrial levels is necessary across the aggregate of all sectors. Therefore, if the aviation industry's emissions continue to grow, other sectors will have to reduce more to compensate. However, in the longer term, it is likely that global emissions of carbon dioxide in particular will need to be reduced to zero. This chapter explores the aviation sector in the context of the climate change challenge.

15.1 Aviation and its Response to Environmental Pressure

The aviation industry has, for many years, responded to environmental pressure from grass-roots activists, national or international regulation or through rising economic cost. However, at no other time in the industry's history has the political focus been so clearly on the aviation industry. The ongoing climate change debate has become increasingly concerned with the issue of growing emissions from the aviation sector, taking aviation on a journey from a 'darling' industry to an environmental 'villain'. This transformation has drawn attention to the conflict between a rapidly growing sector with few technological options for decarbonization, set against a world striving for the dramatic and urgent emission reductions necessary to avoid 'dangerous climate change'. This chapter explores this conflict in addition to potential climate change responses.

Sustainable Development in Practice: Case Studies for Engineers and Scientists, Second Edition
Edited by Adisa Azapagic and Slobodan Perdan
© 2011 John Wiley & Sons, Ltd.

15.1.1 Aviation and Sources of Pollution

15.1.1.1 Noise and Local Pollution

Environmental pressures and concerns are not new to the aviation industry. The issue of aircraft noise disturbing people's sleep, disrupting school children's concentration and, in extreme situations, causing structural damage (particularly to house roofs) is a well-established concern that has driven technology in a particular direction (for further health effects of aviation, see Chapter 16). In response to grass-roots activists, public consultations and subsequent EU regulations on noise around airports, manufacturers have developed noise-reducing technologies particularly for aircraft engines. However, these technologies increase the overall weight of the aircraft and, as such, lead to an increase in the aircraft fuel burn. While oil prices were relatively low and climate change was yet to inform the aircraft innovation debate, such a trade-off was less of a concern. This is no longer the case. Not only have climate change and reducing the emissions of carbon dioxide (CO_2) risen rapidly up the political agenda, but the price of oil has started to increase sharply. As long as efforts to reduce noise increase the weight of the aircraft, and as long as aircraft are powered by fossil fuels, manufacturers will have to carefully balance research and development of more carbon-efficient engines, airframes and operation with concerns over noise pollution. The latter is particularly important due to the health effects, as discussed in Chapter 16.

Aircraft pollution around airports specifically is not restricted to noise. The combustion of kerosene-based aircraft fuels releases volatile organic compounds (VOCs) along with various oxides of nitrogen and sulfur (NO_x and SO_x respectively); these are particularly significant during aircraft landing and taking-off (LTO) cycles and are closely linked with localized health problems such as breathing difficulties. Reducing NO_x emissions can be achieved by reducing the temperature of combustion within the engines. However, in a not dissimilar way to the noise solution, lowering the temperature of combustion reduces the overall efficiency of the engine. Therefore, efforts to reduce locally polluting emissions through reduced combustion temperature will again be at the expense of increased emissions of the greenhouse gas CO_2. How to prioritize the various environmental hazards is inevitably problematic, with the industry being driven more by the regulatory environment and responsibilities to shareholders, whilst those living around airports are more concerned about immediate health, social and environmental impacts. However, whatever the priorities, local pollution and noise concerns continue to play an important role in moulding aircraft and engine design.

The unavoidable local noise and emissions burdens associated with aero-engines are significantly exacerbated by how the airport operates and is used by passengers and other consumers. Like any building, airport terminals require heat and electricity to function, each of which leads to emissions of greenhouse gases and other pollutants, both directly and in the rest of the life cycle. In terms of land-based modes of transport, the airport requires a number of 'airside' vehicles to fuel the aircraft, transport baggage between the aircraft and terminal, maintain the aircraft and meet the catering requirements of the airlines. Transport to and from airports for passengers and freight is another carbon-intensive activity. Although some airports have good links to rail services, most rely heavily on passengers travelling by car or taxi before taking their flight. All this additional activity necessary to service and maintain a customer base for the aviation industry brings with it environmental and social costs. However, within this chapter, the principal focus is on the climate change impact of the aircraft themselves, rather than these additional, but nonetheless, important burdens.

Measures to alleviate emissions associated with local pollution and airport terminals are already well established, if not always implemented, whereas addressing the climate change impact of the aircraft has only recently begun in earnest. Arguably, the new analytical focus has, to some degree, shifted away from noise and local pollution towards climate change. Considering how and why this has come about helps understand the aviation sector within the broader climate change context.

15.1.1.2 Climate Change Emissions

The combustion of kerosene within an aircraft engine releases emissions of CO_2, nitrogen oxides (NO_x), black carbon (BC), sulfur dioxide (SO_2), VOCs and water vapour (H_2O) (see Equation 15.1). Approximately 70% of the resulting emissions are CO_2, 29% water vapour, with the remaining 1% making up the rest.

$$C_xH_y + O_2 + N_2 \rightarrow CO_2 + H_2O + VOCs + BC + NO_x + SO_2 \tag{15.1}$$

The altitude at which these emissions are released means that, in some cases, the emissions cause warming or cooling impacts that would not have occurred had the emissions been released at ground level.

To estimate the warming (or cooling) impact of emissions, a measure known as 'radiative forcing' is often used. Radiative forcing is the incoming minus outgoing radiation at the tropopause – the boundary layer between the troposphere and the stratosphere (at approximately 10 km above the Earth). Therefore, in the case of aviation, it is the change in incoming minus outgoing radiation when a molecule of CO_2 or one of the other emissions is released. The radiative forcing brought about by the different emissions varies due to the radiative properties of the emission in addition to where the emission is released. For example, NO_x emissions react chemically at particular levels of the atmosphere to produce ozone and deplete methane. Ozone and methane are both greenhouse gases with different radiative properties; hence, their associated climate change impacts do not necessarily cancel out.

Water vapour, BC and SO_2 emitted by aircraft can lead to the formation of condensation trails or 'contrails' as they are familiarly known. Contrails tend to be very short lived when compared with greenhouse gas emissions such as CO_2, but have a strong positive radiative forcing associated with them. In addition, contrails are a localized phenomenon, whereas CO_2 emissions become well mixed within the atmosphere due to their long half-life – of the order of 100 years. Aircraft emissions also contribute to cirrus cloud formation. Cirrus clouds are the very high clouds in the atmosphere made up primarily of ice crystals. However, attributing a cirrus cloud to an aircraft is problematic, as cirrus clouds are also formed naturally, unlike contrails. Consequently, the radiative forcing associated with aviation-induced cirrus clouds is particularly difficult to calculate, with any estimates subject to considerable uncertainty.

The impact of aviation on the climate since its beginnings is presented in a number of reports and publications, including in Penner *et al.* (1999) and Sausen *et al.* (2005). From Figure 15.1, a 'radiative forcing index', or 'uplift factor', can be deduced, where the

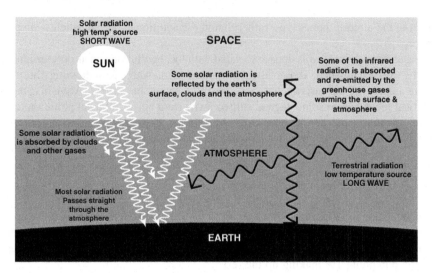

Figure 15.1   *The greenhouse effect illustrating sources of shortwave and longwave radiation (Sausen et al., 2005)*

'radiative forcing index' refers to how much more warming than the CO_2 alone can be attributed to other climate changing emissions. It is essential to note that 'radiative forcing indices', or 'uplift factors', are a measure of historical warming; as such, they should not be used as a simple policy tool for considering and comparing future emissions.

For the year 2000, for example, Sausen *et al.* (2005) estimates that, since the early days of aviation, the other emissions have contributed to just under twice as much warming as the CO_2 alone (excluding the cirrus cloud contribution). However, this measure does not allow for a calculation of the climate change impact of a particular flight or indeed for future climate change impacts, as this will be affected by how much the industry grows as well as by technical or operational measures to reduce one emission relative to another. This issue is discussed in detail by Forster *et al.* (2006), who show that, even if the aviation sector does not grow from where it is today, the CO_2 emissions will continue to accumulate in the atmosphere because of their long lifetime, whereas the contrails formed will remain at the same level, as they dissipate within hours. Therefore, over time, even for a stagnant aviation sector, the CO_2 emissions become a greater proportion of the industry's overall climate change impact due to the cumulative effect of the emissions. In order to appreciate more fully the role of emissions from a growing aviation sector, it is important to understand the broader climate change context. This is discussed in the next section.

Questions

1. Name the three principal areas of environmental concern with relation to aviation and provide a brief description of each.
2. What are the sources of local airport pollution associated with the groundside of aviation? (See also Chapter 16.)
3. Outline and describe briefly the climate change implications of reducing noise and/or local air pollution from aircraft.

4. What measures can be taken to alleviate the noise and local pollution impact of air travel?
5. Name the emissions released when kerosene is combusted by aircraft and describe their relative environmental impact.
6. Summarize how radiative forcing is calculated and the appropriateness or otherwise of current radiative forcing indices and uplift factors for informing future aviation and climate change policy.

15.2 Climate Change and Evolving Context

15.2.1 Greenhouse Effect

The global atmosphere's composition is dominated by nitrogen and oxygen, with just 1% left for all of the other 'trace gases'. Some of these trace gases have a minimal impact (for example, argon and neon), whereas others, particularly CO_2, ozone, water vapour and methane, are essential for life on Earth – principally from how they interact with incoming or outgoing radiation. For example, ozone in the stratosphere absorbs considerable amounts of very shortwave incoming ultraviolet radiation from the sun, thereby offering some protection against skin cancer. CO_2, water vapour, methane and ozone in the troposphere absorb the longwave or terrestrial radiation emitted by the Earth's surface, clouds or other gases and subsequently warm the atmosphere. These gases are known as the greenhouse gases, and without them the 'global mean surface temperature' would be $-18\,°C$, whereas with them the average temperature is 15 °C (Figure 15.1). The Earth's atmosphere delicately balances the incoming and outgoing radiation to maintain long-term thermal equilibrium. However, human activities, particularly in relation to the burning of fossil fuels, are releasing additional greenhouse gas emissions into the atmosphere, altering this fine balance.

15.2.2 Greenhouse Gas Emissions

Fossil fuels, fertilizers, industrial processes and agriculture all contribute to the production of greenhouse gas emissions. Although a proportion of these emissions, particularly those of CO_2, are absorbed by the Earth's soils, vegetation and oceans, some remain in the atmosphere, increasing the concentration of those gases. For example, the CO_2 concentration in the atmosphere has risen from around 280 parts per million by volume (ppmv) in 1750 to around 386 ppmv today (Figure 15.2) – the highest level recorded during the past 420 000 years according to ice-core records.

The other gases show similar patterns (Solomon *et al.*, 2007). Furthermore, the ability of the Earth and oceans to absorb ever-increasing amounts of CO_2 is questionable, with scientists recently suggesting limitations and a fear that, at very high concentrations, the land could become a source rather than a sink for CO_2 and that oceans could become too acidified, affecting the aquatic life within.

Rising concentrations of greenhouse gases in the atmosphere impact on the radiative balance, thus causing a warming. The magnitude of this warming is difficult to predict due to the chaotic and complex nature of the atmosphere. Were the Earth not rotating,

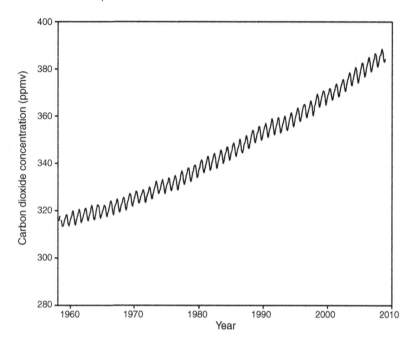

Figure 15.2   *Vostok ice-core data for the CO_2 concentration within the atmosphere (Source: www.esrl.noaa.gov/gmd/ccgg/trends)*

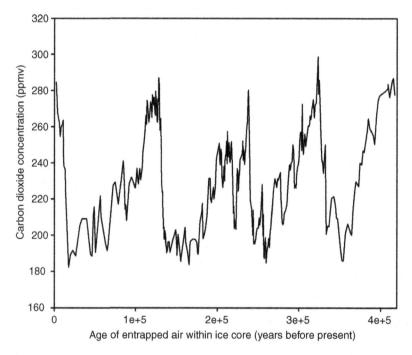

Figure 15.3   *CO_2 concentration from air entrapped within ice-core data from 400 000 years ago onwards (Barnola et al., 2003)*

calculating the radiative impact of a change in the greenhouse gas concentration would be much less demanding. However, the Coriolis effect arising from the Earth's rotation produces complex dynamical heat transfer patterns around the globe. To help understand the natural system, large and complex computer models are used to explore the relationship between temperatures and, for example, a doubling of the greenhouse gas concentration in the atmosphere. The best estimate from the analysis to date suggests a doubling of the greenhouse gas concentration from 280 ppmv to around 560 ppmv would result in a 3 °C globally averaged temperature increase. This correlation between temperature and a doubling of the greenhouse gas concentration is known as the 'climate sensitivity'. However, current emission trends demonstrate close links between greenhouse gas production and global gross domestic product (GDP) growth and, in the absence of radical and urgent reductions in emissions, put global society on a course towards a 4 °C temperature increase (Anderson and Bows, 2008). A 4 °C global temperature increase would likely be devastating for many ecosystems and have fundamental repercussions for the human race; even a 2 °C temperature increase is considered by many to be entering the realm of 'dangerous climate change'. Therefore, taking measures to mitigate greenhouse gas emissions across all sectors of the economy is now an urgent and necessary requirement to avoid 'dangerous climate change'.

15.2.3 Climate Policy in Relation to Aviation

To address globally increasing levels of greenhouse gas emissions, world governments came together to develop the Kyoto Protocol in 1997. Under the protocol, EU nations agreed to reduce their emissions, on aggregate, by 8% by between 2008 and 2012. Within this agreement, all 'domestic' sectors of the economy are included for each nation. In other words, greenhouse gas emissions associated with the household sector, industry, transport, the energy sector, services and public administration that occur within a nation's boundaries are included. Consequently, the greenhouse gas emissions associated with domestic flights are included, whereas those associated with international aviation and shipping are excluded. Instead, the Kyoto Protocol states that the emissions associated with international aviation are to be pursued through the International Civil Aviation Organization (ICAO) and international shipping through the International Maritime Organization (IMO). However, the EU Commission has been unimpressed with the progress made by ICAO in developing policies for mitigating the climate impact of aviation and has subsequently developed proposals for including international aviation within its own EU emissions trading scheme (ETS).

A legacy of international aviation being omitted from national emissions accounting is its subsequent omission from national climate change policies. For example, in the year 2000, the Royal Commission on Environmental Pollution (RCEP) conducted a study into how the UK could play its 'fair' part in ensuring the global mean surface temperatures do not rise by more than 2 °C above the pre-industrial levels (RCEP, 2000). It concluded that the UK should reduce its CO_2 emissions by 60% by 2050 to achieve such a goal. However, its calculations explicitly omitted international aviation and, as a consequence, when the UK Government adopted the recommendations from the RCEP, its own target and Energy White Paper of 2003 omitted emissions from international aviation and international shipping (DTI, 2003). Furthermore, in the subsequent development of a UK Climate

Change Bill of 2008, the emissions from international aviation remain external to the accounting procedures adopted for the other sectors. This omission essentially renders obsolete the climate change goal of ensuring global mean surface temperatures do not exceed 2 °C, because the sum of the sectors included would not, if aggregated to the global scale, result in complete global emission coverage (Anderson and Bows, 2007).

In addition to the failure to account adequately for aviation and shipping emissions, the long-term emission reduction targets adopted by the UK Government have not, until recently, paid sufficient attention to emissions reductions in the short term. Given it is the cumulative emissions of CO_2 that are important, the earlier they are reduced, the less stringent emission reductions need to be in the medium term. Conversely, the longer that emissions remain high, the more severe the reductions will be required in the longer term. In other words, the long-term (2050) emission target has little relevance to the global temperature goal, given it is highly dependent on the short-term emission trajectory (Anderson *et al.*, 2008). Therefore, to comprehensively aim for the UK to play its 'fair' role in avoiding 'dangerous climate change', its targets must include all emissions and take account of emission pathways in the short term. In adopting 5-year emission budgets, the UK's Climate Change Act (OPSI, 2008) goes some way towards addressing this concern.

Questions

1. List the 'global warming potential' of the different greenhouse gases compared with CO_2 over 100 years.
2. Describe the range of constituents within the Earth system that interact with shortwave radiation.
3. Describe the range of constituents within the Earth system that interact with longwave radiation.
4. What would the temperature on the Earth be if the greenhouse gases did not exist?
5. Why are cumulative emissions important in relation to CO_2?
6. What are the Kyoto targets for the EU, USA, China and Australia? What is your opinion about these targets? Are they 'right'?

15.3 Aviation and Evolving Context

The aviation industry has evolved dramatically in recent decades from its position as a 'darling' industry associated with luxury, chandeliers and exclusivity, to becoming a routine means to an end, facilitating regular business links, geographically distributed families and more 'exotic' celebrations (Randles and Mander, 2009). The number of people who fly has increased dramatically over the previous decades, as flights have become more affordable and individuals have become more comfortable with foreign travel. However, the rapid growth of the low-cost airline industries has taken aviation to another level entirely. Not only has this opened up air travel to some lower income travellers, but it also facilitated frequent flying, particularly by the 'middle classes' within the EU.

The practices ordinarily conducted 'at home', such as sporting competitions, retirement celebrations or Christmas shopping trips, are now commonly happening at the destination flown to by a short- and medium-haul low-cost flight. As such activities become widespread, so does the use of air travel. Consequently, although the industry is relatively mature within nations such as the UK, growth rates continue to outstrip the other transport modes, and ordinarily lie a small percentage above GDP growth rates. If this sector within the UK were to be demonstrating rapid improvements in fuel efficiency, or the adoption of low-carbon fuels, relatively high growth may be sustainable within a climate change context. However, as described in the next section, the aviation sector is bounded by considerable technological challenges that set it aside from other sectors in terms of emission mitigation. Furthermore, as industrialized nations like the UK continue to experience rapidly growing aviation industries, industrializing nations such as China and India are on another level altogether.

In recent years, China's aviation industry has been growing at some 14% per year in terms of passenger numbers, with its economy growing at around 10% per year. In addition, the majority of Chinese people do not currently have the opportunity, or indeed the inclination, to fly; therefore, the potential for further growth is enormous. Rapid growth for the aviation sector within the UK with its 60 million population causes significant concerns for climate change mitigation, but if China with its 1.3 billion population were to demonstrate a similar predilection for flying, then the challenge would be an order of magnitude more demanding. Furthermore, the low-cost airline model has already made inroads into China, albeit in a somewhat modified form (Liang and James, 2009). Consequently, the issue of aviation and climate change will be one of the world's major climate change challenges for many years to come.

15.3.1 Barriers to Aviation Mitigation

What sets the aviation industry somewhat apart from other sectors of the economy, particularly compared with other modes of transport, is the very long time lag in developing new technology and updating the global fleet. In general, aircraft are flown for around 30 years, with new designs often being manufactured for 20 to 30 years. As such, aircraft technology designed today could lock the industry into a future design that will change little over the coming 60 years. Given the current designs are for high-carbon fuels, these technological barriers are problematic for carbon mitigation.

15.3.1.1 Technological Solutions

New airframe designs do make it onto the drawing boards, but even when their efficiency is shown to be significantly greater than those currently in existence, this understandably highly risk-adverse industry demonstrates reluctance to role them out. The fuel savings that could be made and financial returns on such designs are currently not enough to instigate radical step change. Therefore, designs such as the blended wing body (BWB) aircraft for long-haul flights remain a distant notion for civil aviation. This is not to say that technological development is stagnant in the aviation industry, but more that there are

inadequate incentives or drivers to encourage a step change that will benefit the climate specifically and sustainability more generally.

Technologies that would improve aircraft efficiency include more widespread use of composite materials within the airframe, wing-tips to improve the aerodynamic flow around the wings to reduce drag, laminar flow to reduce the drag on the aircraft and more radical airframe designs such as the BWB, or highly efficient wing-in-ground effect planes (WIGs – by flying some 6 m above the ground the lift to drag ratio is improved) (Greener by Design, 2005).

Engine technology also has a role to play in relation to improving the fuel efficiency of the aircraft, or indeed ultimately in designs for lower carbon fuel sources. Over the years, engines have improved significantly in terms of their overall efficiency, but the technology currently in use is relatively mature and there have been no step changes in recent years. As a consequence, engines tend to improve in fuel efficiency at a rate of about 1% per year. If carbon mitigation is to take a step change in development, new designs will be required. In the meantime, open rotor and turbo-prop engines are again receiving serious consideration, with both being more fuel-efficient at the expense of noise pollution.

15.3.1.2 Low-Carbon Fuels

In addition to improving the technological efficiency of the aero-engine and airframe, the use of low-carbon fuels would reduce the carbon intensity of the aviation sector (Bows *et al.*, 2008). However, unlike other transport modes, such developments are in their infancy and, furthermore, face considerable barriers to their widespread implementation. For example, for land-based transport modes, electricity could be provided through a lower carbon electricity grid incorporating increasing amounts of low-carbon supply; hybrid petrol–electric cars are already on the market, while fuel cells and biodiesel are already being used.

Some of the most commonly considered possibilities for aviation include bio-kerosene and biodiesel mixed with kerosene and hydrogen. Biodiesel would likely take the form of a kerosene extender. In other words, it would be mixed with mineral kerosene to produce a new, lower carbon-emitting fuel. Biodiesel proportions may be limited to 10–20% of a given aviation fuel, as in higher proportions the biodiesel alters the crystallization properties of the aviation fuel at low temperatures. Advantages of biodiesel over conventional kerosene include its lower polluting emissions, biodegradable nature and relatively simple production from major bio-crop feedstocks. However, mixing mineral kerosene with biodiesel compromises kerosene's ability at the low temperatures experienced at altitude. An additional, but extremely important issue is that first-generation biofuels have considerable negative sustainability implications (see Chapter 6). Second- and third-generation biofuels may help to provide a more practical solution.

One alternative to mixing biodiesel with kerosene is to produce kerosene from a biomass feedstock using the Fischer–Tropsch chemical conversion process, thus providing fuel-cycle CO_2 benefits compared with mineral kerosene and eliminating oxides of sulfur. Bio-kerosene is physically and chemically similar to standard kerosene and broadly compatible with current fuel storage and engines. However, its lack of aromatic molecules and the fact that it is virtually sulphur free lead to poor lubricity. Its energy density is also lower than standard kerosene, which would impact on long-haul flights, requiring more fuel. A few modifications could, on the other hand, improve its lubricity, making it fit for use. This type of kerosene is likely to be a medium-term development for the aviation industry, although significant sustainability concerns remain.

Hydrogen is another possibility, but brings with it considerably more barriers than the bio-options. First, it would require fundamental changes to the jet design due to its low energy density. Larger fuel tanks would be necessary in addition to a world-wide hydrogen supply at airports. On the other hand, there would be a weight advantage due to aircraft carrying lighter fuel, but this would be offset to some degree by the weight of a larger fuel tank itself. As the volume of hydrogen carried is some 2.5 times that of the equivalent kerosene, the airframe would need to be larger, with correspondingly higher drag. The combination of higher drag and lower weight would require flight at higher altitudes. If hydrogen were to be used as an aviation fuel, it would most likely be used in large long-haul, high-altitude aircraft. Aside from problems of hydrogen storage, transportation and the need for new infrastructure world-wide, hydrogen's main by-product is water vapour – which is a greenhouse gas in the upper troposphere. Therefore, the sensitivity to cruising altitude would likely be large and would impact on radiative forcing. Further research is required to ensure that any advantage gained in reducing CO_2 emissions would not be exacerbated by an increase in climate impacts due to enhanced water vapour production. Table 15.1 lists the impact of emissions at different levels in the atmosphere.

15.3.1.3 Air Traffic Management and Operations

While many of the technological solutions are bounded by considerable time delays in their implementation, measures on the operational or management side of air travel could improve the fuel efficiency and, hence, the carbon intensity of the fuels more rapidly. Currently, aircraft frequently circle prior to landing or spend additional time taxiing or queuing on runways with engines running. Tackling congestion would lead to the more efficient use of aircraft; therefore, the building of new runways and terminals is one policy that may, in the short term, reduce the overall carbon intensity per passenger-kilometre being travelled. However, if the overall growth in air travel is in excess of the improvement

Table 15.1 Emissions from aviation and the primary temperature impacts at the earth's surface (based on Penner et al., 1999)

Emission	Role	Primary effect at the Earth's surface
Carbon dioxide	Greenhouse gas	Warming
Water vapour	Greenhouse gas	Warming
	Contrail formation	Warming
Nitrogen oxides	Forms ozone (greenhouse gas)	Warming
	Depletes methane (greenhouse gas)	Cooling
Sulfur oxides and sulfuric acid	Reflects sunlight	Cooling
	Contrail formation	Warming
	Increased cirrus cloud cover	Warming
Soot	Reflects sunlight	Warming
	Contrail formation	Warming
	Increased cirrus cloud cover	Warming

in carbon efficiency, then emissions from aviation will continue to grow. Therefore, there is some fear that the provision of additional airport capacity could lead to a rebound effect, whereby the efficiency gains in the short term are rapidly offset by increases in growth rates in the medium term. This issue of rebound is not particular to the aviation sector, but must be considered in all aspects of reducing the carbon emissions across energy-consuming sectors. However, given that within industrialized nations the aviation sector's growth tends to outstrip other sectors and that it faces the technological barriers highlighted previously, the rebound effect is of particular importance.

Additional operational methods for reducing the carbon intensity of air travel include increasing the load factor and seat density of aircraft. Load factor refers to how full an aircraft is and seat density to how many seats are placed within a particular model of aircraft. For example, an aircraft with 50% spacious business traveller seats and a 30% overall load factor will result in considerably more emissions per passenger than the same model aircraft with 100% economy filled to 30% load factor. Introducing sophisticated ticketing arrangements that encourage airlines to team up when flying partially full aircraft to the same destination could lead to an increase in the mean load factor. An incentive for this is already provided through cost savings, in addition to carbon reductions. Alternatively, implementing a charge per flight to the airlines could incentivize higher load factors.

Larger aircraft, such as the new Airbus A380, could reduce the emissions per passenger-kilometre if they replace two older aircraft flying the same route. However, again, guards against a rebound effect allowing for a continuation of high growth are necessary if emissions are actually to reduce in the short to medium term.

Questions

1. Where in the atmosphere do aircraft typically cruise and what are the implications of cruising at that altitude?
2. What would be the implications of aircraft flying lower within the troposphere or higher within the stratosphere?
3. How do emissions from aircraft differ in terms of the climate change impact compared with other transport modes?
4. How do NO_x emissions from aircraft cruising in the tropopause relate to climate change?
5. Explain the formation of contrails and their implications for climate change.
6. Describe the variety of operational and managerial measures that could be taken to improve the fuel efficiency of air travel.
7. Taking a life cycle approach, discuss the greenhouse gas emissions from different life cycle stages of an aircraft, including its manufacture and operation. Where do you think the 'hot spots' in the life cycle are and how would you reduced them?

15.4 Aviation and Climate Change Conflict

Conflicting policies within the UK in relation to climate change and aviation came to light in 2003 with the publication of two diverse White Papers. The Energy White Paper of 2003: Our Energy Future – Creating a Low Carbon Economy (DTI, 2003) – reaffirmed the UK

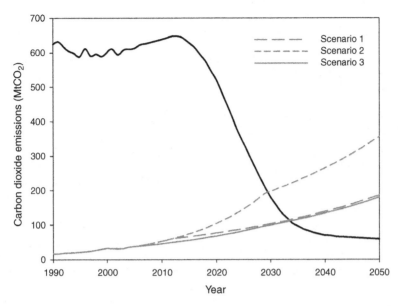

Figure 15.4 *Aviation emission scenarios for CO_2 compared with a UK emission budget commensurate with the 2°C target (black line) (Bows et al., 2006)*

Government's commitment to climate change with its 60% carbon reduction target. However, the Aviation White Paper published around the same time presented the UK Government's plans for the expansion of the aviation industry (DfT, 2004b). Despite the forecasts for CO_2 emissions from the documentation accompanying the Aviation White Paper (DfT, 2004a) appearing to be somewhat conservative (Bows *et al.*, 2006), they still result in this one industry consuming a very large proportion of the UK's carbon budget by 2050 (Bows and Anderson, 2007). Alternative scenarios for aviation emissions out to 2050 suggest that the aviation industry could consume the entire carbon budget for the UK, if the industry continues to grow at rates typical of the past decade (Figure 15.4).

15.4.1 EU Aviation and Climate Change Targets

More passengers pass through UK airports than through any other country in Europe; therefore, the UK's proportion of total national emissions is larger than those experienced by other EU nations. However, the story within the EU is not too dissimilar. As long as the aviation industry within the EU continues to grow rapidly and the EU maintains its commitment to ensuring global mean surface temperatures do not exceed 2 °C, aviation will inevitably consume a greater proportion of the overall emissions (Figure 15.5).

Concern with regard to aviation's growing emissions has prompted the European Commission to develop proposals to incorporate the emissions associated with international aviation into the EU's ETS. Currently, this scheme includes high-emitting installations, such as power stations and cement factories, and allows them to trade emissions rights within an emissions cap. By including aviation in the scheme, airlines will be able to trade with these other installations, with the most likely outcome being an

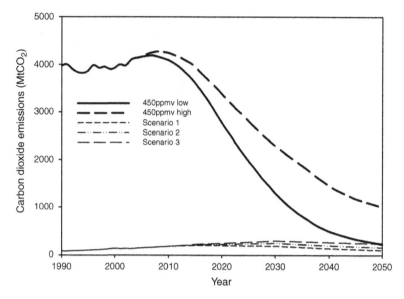

Figure 15.5 *Aviation emission scenarios for CO_2 compared with a range of EU emission budgets commensurate with the 2 °C target (black full and dashed line) (Anderson et al., 2007)*

increased cost to the sector given the rapid growth in emissions. However, as it stands, the EU ETS cap is unlikely to stimulate carbon price levels sufficiently to impact significantly on aviation emissions growth in line with the EU's commitment to contributing to global mean surface temperatures not exceeding the 2 °C threshold between acceptable and dangerous climate change (Bows and Anderson, 2008).

Questions

1. Describe the EU's emission trading scheme and the consequences of including aviation in it.
2. Outline possible conflicts between the UK's aviation and energy white papers of 2003.
3. What policies under the EU's jurisdiction influence the environmental impact of the aviation industry?
4. What economic instruments could be employed to reduce the aviation industry's climate change emissions?
5. What is emission apportionment and how can it assist with climate change policy development in relation to the aviation industry?
6. If an aircraft flies from London via Amsterdam to Hong Kong, discuss possible methods of allocating the greenhouse emissions burden. Who is responsible for these emissions?

15.5 Global Context

The aviation industry within the USA and the EU is well developed and, as such, contributes a larger proportion of total greenhouse gas emissions within those nations than the global average. At the global scale, the emissions from aviation accounted for some 2.4% in 2004, while the figures were closer to 4% and 6% for the EU and UK respectively. These figures reflect the higher propensity to fly within industrialized nations. However, this situation is changing rapidly, with many industrializing nations not only experiencing very high growth in terms of passengers travelling, but beginning also to develop their own aviation manufacturing industries and expertise. As a consequence, and without significant technological opportunities for low-carbon aviation in the short to medium term, future global emissions generated by aviation will likely be an increasing proportion of total global greenhouse gas emissions – particularly if other sectors are mandated with reducing their emissions. The implications of a rapidly increasing emission burden from aviation are stark when put within the context of the emission reductions necessary for a reasonable chance of not exceeding the 2 °C threshold. Figure 15.6 illustrates the severity of the challenge by presenting emission scenarios or pathways for energy and industrial process CO_2 emissions that fit within a budget aimed at not exceeding the 2 °C warming above pre-industrial temperatures.

For global mean surface temperatures not to exceed the 2 °C threshold, global greenhouse gas emissions must peak and then swiftly begin to decline as a matter of urgency (Anderson and Bows, 2008). The challenge for all sectors of the economy cannot be overstated. However, almost all of the other sectors have a variety of opportunities to decarbonize, whereas the aviation industry is in a much more challenging position.

Figure 15.6 compares the emission pathways with typical emission scenarios for the CO_2 produced by the aviation industry out to 2050. Given that the aviation industry is growing rapidly with few technological options to decarbonize, it is predicted by many that emissions will continue to rise during the coming decades. However, for global emissions

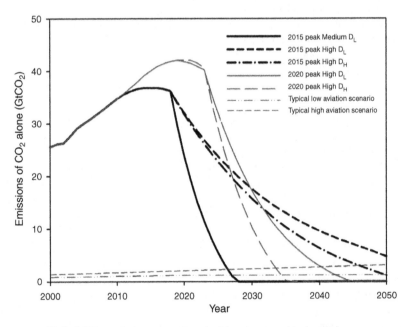

Figure 15.6   *Global CO_2 emissions associated with energy and industrial processes commensurate with the not exceeding 2 °C compared with a low and high CO_2 emission scenario for global aviation*

to remain within the budget required to avoid 'dangerous climate change' (as illustrated in Figure 15.6), total decarbonization could be necessary as early as 2030. It is essential, therefore, that the aviation industry begins to reduce its emissions within the coming decades. Otherwise, the situation presented in Figure 15.6, where the aviation sector breaks the carbon budget available, will occur. Emissions trading cannot solve this dilemma at the global scale. If current technology or management practices do not make a step change in the short to medium term, then increasing numbers of passengers and flights will not be compatible with avoiding 'dangerous climate change'. Certainly for the UK, EU and most OECD nations, it is difficult to envisage annual aviation growth in passenger-kilometres of over 2% being compatible with making their fair contribution to the climate change agenda. Consequently, for these nations, demand management is a prerequisite of their aviation sector's contribution to achieving meaningful emission reductions.

Questions

1. How does current aviation and aviation growth in OECD nations compare with non-OECD nations and what does this imply for reconciling aviation with emission reductions necessary to meet the 2 °C threshold between acceptable and 'dangerous' climate change?
2. What proportion of the world's population currently flies? How does that compare with your country? And you personally?
3. Where are the biggest areas of potential growth globally for the aviation industry?
4. How does the low-cost airline model operate and what would make it potentially different if operating within China?
5. Why do emission reductions globally to avoid 'dangerous climate change' need to reduce so rapidly in the coming years?
6. What would be the outcome by 2100 of allowing greenhouse gas emissions to continue to rise indefinitely?

15.6 Conclusions

The aviation industry has historically responded to environmental concerns through the implementation of new technologies, engine modifications and moderated operational practices. The past domination of noise and local pollution in terms of environmental issues is changing, however, and climate change has risen rapidly to the top of the agenda. The climate change challenge faced by all greenhouse-gas-producing sectors is so severe that, currently, it would appear unlikely that global policies will avoid global temperatures rising by more than 2 °C above pre-industrial levels. Even avoiding a 3 °C rise is likely to be extremely difficult. Consequently, all sectors will be required to play their part in the short to medium term.

The difficulty for the aviation industry lies in an absence of opportunities for techno-logical low-carbon step changes in this short- to medium-term timeframe. However, without such developments, it will be necessary to curb growth through demand manage-ment in the industry to mitigate its CO_2 and other non-greenhouse gas emissions, such as NO_x, soot and sulfuric acid. Such a conclusion is unpalatable for an aviation industry that typically has growth rates a small percentage in excess of GDP growth. Despite the urgency of addressing growing sources of emissions, the price of oil plays a much more significant role currently in influencing carbon-intensive industries like aviation than any emission-related policy instrument in place. This is a telling sign for policymakers who consider themselves to be serious about tackling rising greenhouse gas emissions. If reductions in emissions compatible with avoiding 'dangerous climate change' are to be achieved, then the price mechanism on which most policies currently rely must be complemented with a stringent and urgent regulatory framework.

Acknowledgments

The authors would like to thank NERC, EPSRC and ESRC for funding the Tyndall Centre for Climate Change Research at the University of Manchester where this research was carried out. In addition, the authors would like to thank contributions to knowledge from Dr Sarah Mander and Dr Sally Randles.

References and Further Reading

Anderson, K. and Bows, A. (2007) A response to the Draft Climate Change Bill's carbon reduction targets. Tyndall Centre Briefing Note 17, Tyndall Centre for Climate Change Research, from http://www.tyndall.ac.uk/publications/briefing_notes/bn17.pdf.

Anderson, K. and Bows, A. (2008) Reframing the climate change challenge in light of post-2000 emission trends. *Philosophical Transactions A*, **366**(1882), 3863–3882.

Anderson, K., Bows, A. and Foottit, A. (2007) Aviation in a low-carbon EU. Report for Friends of the Earth, Tyndall Centre Manchester.

Anderson, K., Bows, A. and Mander, S. (2008) From long-term targets to cumulative emission pathways: reframing UK climate policy. *Energy Policy*, **36**(10), 3714–3722.

Barnola, J.-M., Raynaud, D., Lorius, C. and Barkov, N.I. (2003) Historical CO_2 record from the Vostok ice core, in *Trends: A Compendium of Data on Global Change*, Carbon Dioxide Information Analysis Centre, Oak Ridge National, Laboratory, US Department of Energy, Oak Ridge, TN.

Bows, A. and Anderson, K. (2008) A bottom-up analysis of including aviation within the EU's emissions trading scheme. Tyndall Centre Working Paper 126.

Bows, A., Anderson, K. and Upham, P. (2006) Contraction & convergence: UK carbon emissions and the implications for UK air traffic. Tyndall Centre Technical Report 40. Tyndall Centre for Climate Change Research, Norwich.

Bows, A., Anderson, K. and Upham, P. (2008) *Aviation and Climate Change: Lessons for European Policy*, Taylor & Francis, London.

Bows, A. and Anderson, K.L. (2007) Policy clash: can projected aviation growth be reconciled with the UK Government's 60% carbon-reduction target? *Transport Policy*, **14**(2), 103–110.

DfT (2004a) Aviation and global warming. Department for Transport, The Stationery Office, London.

DfT (2004b) The future of air transport. Aviation White Paper. Department for Transport, HMSO, London.

DTI (2003) Our energy future – creating a low carbon economy. Energy White Paper. Department of Trade and Industry, The Stationery Office, London.

Forster, P.M.d.F., Shine, K.P. and Stuber, N. (2006) It is premature to include non-CO_2 effects of aviation in emission trading schemes. *Atmospheric Environment*, **40**(6), 1117–1121.

Greener by Design (2005) Mitigating the environmental impact of aviation: opportunities and priorities. Air Travel – Greener by Design, Royal Aeronautical Society.

Solomon, S., Qin, D., Manning, M. *et al.* (eds). (2007) *Climate Change 2007: The Physical Science Basis. Report of Working Group 1 to the Fourth Assessment Report of the Intergovernmental Panel on Climate Change.* Cambridge University Press, Cambridge.

Liang, L. and James, A.D. (2009) The low-cost carrier model in China: the adoption of a strategic innovation. *Technology Analysis & Strategic Management,* **21**(1), 129–148.

OPSI (2008) Climate Change Act. Office of Public Sector Information. http://www.opsi.gov.uk/acts/acts2008/ukpga_20080027_en_1#Legislation-Preamble.

Penner, J.E., Lister, D.G., Griggs, D.J., *et al.* (eds) (1999) *Aviation and the Global Atmosphere; A Special Report of IPCC Working Groups I and III,* Cambridge University Press, Cambridge.

Randles, S. and Mander, S. (2009) Aviation, consumption and the climate change debate: "Are you going to tell me off for flying?" *Technology Analysis & Strategic Management,* **21**(1), 93–113.

RCEP (2000) Energy – the changing climate. 22nd report, CM 4749. The Stationery Office, London.

Sausen, R., Isaksen, I., Grewe, V., *et al.* (2005) Aviation radiative forcing in 2000: an update on IPCC (1999). *Meteorologische Zeitschrift,* **14**(4), 555–561.

16

Health Impact Assessment of Urban Pollution

Zaid Chalabi and Tony Fletcher

It is now well recognized that urban pollution has a harmful effect on the health of an urban population. In an urban environment, pollution (of air, soil or water) is generated from multiple sources and humans can be exposed to this pollution via a number of pathways, including inhalation, ingestion and dermal contact. To guide the formulation of evidence-based policies for mitigation of the impact of pollution on health, it is imperative to quantify the ill-health effects of pollution via epidemiological analyses and/or risk modelling. This chapter reviews some of these methods and illustrates how they can be applied. A case study of the health impacts of an airport on the local community is used for these purposes.

16.1 Introduction

The steady rise of the number of people living in cities and the evolving demands and lifestyle of the urban population have contributed significantly to the increase of anthropogenic urban pollution over the last few decades. Although the types, causes and trends of urban pollution differ between developed and developing countries, the urban pollution problem is of concern to all regions of the world. There are numerous types of urban pollution characterized by source or media (air, water, soil, etc.). These include air and noise pollution generated by increased use of vehicles and road freight, soil pollution caused by urban waste and soil pollution associated with the legacy of past industrial sites.

Sustainable Development in Practice: Case Studies for Engineers and Scientists, Second Edition
Edited by Adisa Azapagic and Slobodan Perdan
© 2011 John Wiley & Sons, Ltd.

Over the years, alarms have been raised on the harmful health effects of urban pollution and public-health policy makers have accordingly set standards on the maximum acceptable concentration levels of a number of pollutants, aimed at minimizing or preventing risks to health. Policies to reduce urban pollution, and by implication their detrimental effect on health, have been implemented. Because of the complexity of the urban environment, the manner in which the environment affects health and the lack of real data, public-health policy makers need to rely on a number of health impact assessment tools to estimate the health impacts of urban pollution.

The next section gives a brief overview of these models. This is followed by a review of their use for the estimation of health impacts of pollution commonly found in cities, including noise, air and soil pollution from both single and multiple sources. The final part of the chapter demonstrates for a real case study of Schiphol Airport, Amsterdam, what health impacts can be expected from city airports and how to assess them.

16.2 Health Impact Assessment

A health impact assessment (HIA) can include the following:

1. **epidemiological analyses** to unwrap the empirical evidence to distinguish the health effects of urban pollutants in the presence of other unrelated exposure factors which might obscure or exaggerate apparent risks of pollution (known as 'confounding');
2. **risk assessment** models to calculate the potential health impacts of pollution where there is no direct empirical evidence; and
3. **decision support models** to help evaluate and compare alternative options for reducing the health effects of urban pollution, based on a number of criteria.

16.2.1 Epidemiological Analyses

The empirical evidence on the association between elevated levels of urban pollution and ill health has been gathered over the years through conducting epidemiological studies. These studies essentially compare the prevalence or incidence of a disease (e.g. cancer, respiratory disease episodes) in one group of the urban population exposed to a higher level of a pollutant with the prevalence or incidence of the same disease of another population exposed to a lower level of the pollutant. The contrast can be over time, comparing changes in pollution levels from day to day, or geographically between areas with contrasting pollution.

Statistical models (e.g. Poisson regressions for health event counts or logistic regression for studies comparing exposure in cases to exposure in disease-free controls) are then fitted to the disease outcome and exposure data whilst adjusting for any 'confounders' which might also be risk factors for the disease. The confounders could be demographic characteristics (e.g. age, socio-economic status) or exposure (e.g. other pollutants, smoking habits).

The results of the epidemiological analyses are formulated in terms of concentration–response relationships, which associate increased risk of an individual developing the disease with increased level of pollutant concentration. These relationships are mostly expressed as either linear, with risk rising in proportion to exposure, or threshold–linear,

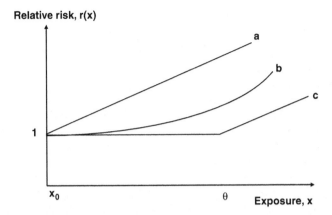

Figure 16.1 *Exposure–response relationships: (a) linear; (b) nonlinear; (c) threshold–linear relationship; x_0 is the baseline or minimum exposure level (e.g. in rural areas); θ is the threshold level for the threshold–linear relationship; $r(x)$ is the relative risk at exposure x (defined as the risk of developing the disease at exposure x divided by the risk of developing the disease at the r baseline exposure value x_0)*

where risk rises above a threshold with no concentration–response below the threshold. There may be circumstances, too, where the relationship is curved, but for typical urban pollution situations the linear relationships generally fit well. These relationships are shown in Figure 16.1.

In the case of urban air pollution, there has been a wealth of epidemiological studies linking increased levels of mortality and morbidity (e.g. increased hospital visits for respiratory disease) with increased levels of air pollution (Samet and White, 2004). This evidence was invaluable in setting up air quality standards. Likewise, but to a lesser extent, there have been epidemiological studies carried out to study the impact of increased levels of urban noise on the health (e.g. sleep disturbance, hypertension) of urban populations (Stansfeld *et al.*, 2000).

Questions

1. Why is an HIA important? What can it tell us?
2. What is epidemiological analysis? What does it involve?
3. What is relative risk?
4. In calculating relative risk of disease, the risk of disease is compared between groups. How might the groups differ?
5. In a concentration–response relationship, what is meant by a threshold?

16.2.2 Risk Assessment Models

In the absence of direct empirical evidence, risk models can be used to assess the potential health risk of exposure to urban pollution. Risk assessment models integrate models of population exposure with concentration–response relationships obtained

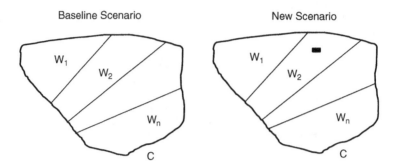

Figure 16.2   *A schematic diagram of a city C with and without the processing plant. The square symbol shows where the plant is to be located; W indicates the population wards; baseline and new scenarios represent the city with and without the industrial development respectively*

from epidemiological studies. For example, Hough *et al.* (2004) assessed the potential health risk of heavy metal exposure from home-produced vegetables in an urban area. They integrated models of metal uptake of vegetables with exposure–response relationships obtained from epidemiological studies on health impacts from ingestion of metals.

The health impact calculations in a risk assessment model can be described by a number of steps. To simplify the description, let us consider one pollutant exposure (e.g. $PM_{2.5}$, arsenic or noise) and a single health outcome (e.g. incidence of asthma, cancer or death). Furthermore, to put the calculation steps in context, consider a scenario whereby an HIA is required for a new industrial development in a city (e.g. a waste management plant). The operation of the plant is believed to cause an increase in an exposure e (relative to the baseline) which is known to be associated with the incidence of a particular disease d.

Figure 16.2 shows the baseline and the new scenarios, respectively, for the hypothetical city C. The city is divided into n population wards ($W_1 \ldots W_n$).

Estimating the risk from this industrial development would involve the following steps:

- **Step 1**. Obtaining from national databases the baseline incidence of disease d in city C and the population size in each of the wards.
- **Step 2**. Modelling the changes in exposure e in each ward between the new scenario and the baseline scenario.
- **Step 3**. Obtaining from the epidemiological literature the relative risks of incidence of disease d associated with a unit increase in exposure e.
- **Step 4**. Determining the expected excess number of cases of disease d attributable to the increase in exposure in each ward, taking into account ward population sizes.
- **Step 5**. Summing up the total number of cases of disease d across all wards to obtain the total health impact.

Assuming that different exposures have independent health impacts, the above steps can be repeated for impacts associated with more than one exposure and more than one health outcome, and the total impact summed up. For a more mathematically inclined reader, Box 16.1 provides a mathematical model for estimation of health risks.

Box 16.1   Risk assessment model

In general, health risks from exposure to a pollutant can be calculated as follows.

If we denote the distribution of the population by exposure level by $p(x)$ and by $y(x)$ the relative risk of developing a disease at exposure x, where x is the concentration of the pollutant of interest, then the excess rate of disease incidence (above the baseline rate) is given by

$$\delta = \lambda \int_X (y(x)-1)p(x)\,\mathrm{d}x \qquad (16.1)$$

Where λ is the baseline rate of incidence of the disease and X is the range of exposure

Equation gives the health impact for one pollutant. If there are n pollutants in which each is a risk factor for this disease, then the number of individuals developing the disease above its baseline rate is given by

$$\Gamma = \sum_{i=1}^{n} \delta_i = \lambda \sum_{i=1}^{n} \int_{X_i} (y_i(x_i)-1)p_i(x_i)\,\mathrm{d}x_i \qquad (16.2)$$

where δ_i is the additional disease event rate attributable to pollutant i, y_i is the disease relative risk associated with pollutant i, p_i is the modelled distribution of the population by exposure level x_i of pollutant i and X_i is the range of exposure of pollutant i.

Equation assumes that the health impacts are additive.

Questions

1. What does risk assessment involve and what does it tell us?
2. What is the difference between epidemiological analysis and risk assessment? How reliable is each method?
3. Why is it important to know the distribution of the population by exposure level in risk assessments?
4. Where would you search for information needed in Steps 1 and 3 of risk assessment? Is it easily available for your country or area where you live?

16.2.3 Decision-Support Tools

Public-health policy makers are often faced with a number of options for reducing the harmful health effects of urban pollution. These options are usually either policies and standards regulating the permissible exposure levels or interventions aimed at reducing the exposure. In either case, the decision problem is to determine the preferred option (i.e. policy or intervention) based on a single criterion or a set of criteria. If health is the only criterion to be taken into account, the decision is obvious: the option which has the least harmful effect on health is the preferred one. If health and costs are the two criteria, then the option which is the most cost effective could be considered as the preferred option. However, if the comparison between options is to be made across a number of criteria, such as health, costs, impact on the environment, impact on the economy and so on, then the problem becomes much more complex. In such cases, multi-criteria decision analysis (MCDA) can be used as a decision-support tool to help identify a more sustainable option.

There are several types of MCDA method which can be used for decision support (Saaty, 2000; Belton and Stewart, 2002; Figueira, Greco and Ehrqott, 2005). Most of them involve the following elements:

1. The set of decision options which are available to choose from.
2. The set of decision criteria on which to compare the different options.
3. The (subjective) weights that are attached to each criterion to express their relative importance.
4. Models to calculate the impact on each criterion of adopting each option.
5. A method to integrate the impacts and the weights into a single score for comparative evaluation between the options. The option with the highest score is the option to choose.

MCDA has been applied widely in many areas of decision making related to health management (e.g. Steele *et al.*, 2009), air quality policy (e.g. Phillips and Stock, 2003) and road transport (e.g. Kollamthodi, 2005).

Questions

1. What is the role of MCDA in public-health decision making? Discuss its usefulness or otherwise in health-related applications.
2. What criteria do you consider important in public-health decision making? Why?
3. What criteria do you think would be important to different groups of stakeholders, including (i) government, (ii) citizens and (iii) industry, when considering different options for reducing health impacts of a population? Discuss different perspectives and priorities they may have and how MCDA might be used to help identify a compromise solution between these different groups of stakeholders.

16.3 Health Impact Assessments of Urban Pollution

There are many types of pollution in the urban environment. For the purposes of this study, only a few are reviewed here, with the focus mainly on the epidemiological analyses and risk assessments.

16.3.1 Urban Noise Pollution

The auditory effects of occupational noise are well established and, accordingly, there are health and safety regulations in many countries limiting noise levels in the work place. Unlike noise in the work place, which is amenable to control, community noise is difficult to manage. There are several sources of noise pollution in the urban environment. These include noise generated from road traffic, industry, neighbours and aircraft. The association of urban noise exposure with ill health is now well established (Stansfeld *et al.*, 2000). Noise exposure has been associated with annoyance, sleep deprivation, stress and arterial hypertension. In addition to aircraft noise, the main source of noise in cities is generated from road traffic.

Several epidemiological studies have been carried to determine the impact of road-traffic noise on health. Health-outcome studies included direct measurements of blood pressure (Belojevic *et al.*, 2008b), hospital admissions (Linares *et al.*, 2006) and self-reported symptoms (Zannin *et al.*, 2003). Measurements of noise exposure were carried out either directly using instrumentation (Belojevic *et al.*, 2008a, 2008b) or by modelling (Seto *et al.*, 2007).

Road-traffic noise has been shown to affect children and adults. A cross-sectional epidemiological study carried on preschool children in Belgrade has shown a statistically significant correlation between noise exposure and children's systolic blood pressure (Belojevic *et al.*, 2008a). Heart rate was also found to be higher by two beats per minute among children residing in noisy environments compared with those in quiet environments. Similar findings were obtained from a time-series epidemiological study performed in Madrid (Linares *et al.*, 2006). This study showed a statistically significant association between emergency hospital admissions of children less than 10 years old and noise levels.

In the case of adults, a cross-sectional epidemiological study in Belgrade has shown that arterial hypertension was positively associated with night-time road traffic noise above a threshold; however, the findings were only statistically significant for men (Belojevic *et al.*, 2008b). In a survey in a Brazilian city, urban noise was also associated with self-reported symptoms, including headaches, irritability, insomnia and ringing in the ears (Zannin *et al.*, 2003). Although these outcomes are subjective, they provide measures of quality of life.

In addition to epidemiological studies, risk models have been used to estimate the health impacts of traffic-induced noise exposure. For example, traffic data in San Francisco were used as an input to a geographical information system-based noise exposure model (Seto *et al.*, 2007). The exposure model was then linked to an exposure-annoyance model (Miedema and Oudshoorn, 2001) to predict and compare the levels of annoyance between different neighbourhoods in San Francisco. The agreement between the real and modelled data was good, enabling future estimates of exposure-annoyance levels and reducing the need for primary (epidemiological) data.

Questions

1. What are the main sources of noise pollution in urban areas?
2. How can noise and noise exposure be measured?
3. What are the main ill-health effects of noise exposure?
4. How can the subjective element of noise perception be dealt with?
5. How could noise pollution in cities be reduced?
6. What are the legal limits for community (non-occupational) noise in your country?
7. How is noise pollution regulated in your country and which government department or body is responsible for dealing with complaints related to noise nuisance? What can they do to ensure that noise is kept within the legal limits?

16.3.2 Urban Air Pollution

The impacts of urban air pollution on human mortality and morbidity have been studied extensively over the past decades (Samet and White, 2004). Epidemiological studies have been carried out to determine the acute and chronic health effects of urban air pollution. Time-series studies were used to determine the short-term (acute) health effects (Prescott *et al.*, 1998; van der Zee *et al.*, 1999) and cohort studies (Sunyer *et al.*, 2006) were used to determine the long-term health effects (of chronic exposure). Time-series studies of urban air pollution associate daily measures of air pollution concentrations with daily counts of deaths, hospital admissions and doctor visits (the latter two are measures of morbidity). Cohort studies, on the other hand, monitor the health and adverse health events, such as deaths among a sample of individuals over a period of time.

Many single-country studies and comparative multi-country studies have been carried out to investigate the association of urban air pollution and respiratory ill health. For example, a 15-year time-series study carried out in Edinburgh, Scotland, suggested a small but nevertheless significant positive association between concentrations of black smoke and respiratory mortality among the old. However, as with many such studies, reliance was placed on measuring exposure at only one point in the city (Prescott *et al.*, 1998).

In relation to children's health, a time-series study carried out in the Netherlands investigated the acute effects of particle concentrations on the health of children with and without chronic respiratory symptoms living in urban areas where there is heavy road traffic (van der Zee *et al.*, 1999). The study period covered three consecutive winters. Daily concentration values of particles (PM_{10} and smaller), black smoke, sulfur dioxide (SO_2), sulfates and nitrogen dioxide (NO_2) were used as measures of exposure. Lung function along with records of medication use and incidence of respiratory-related symptoms were used as measures of health outcomes. This study suggested that children with respiratory symptoms are more affected by particulate air pollution than children without symptoms are. The results also indicated that use of medication for asthma does not prevent the adverse effects of particulate air pollution in children with symptoms.

With regard to the long-term effects of urban air pollution, a cohort study was carried out in 10 European countries to investigate the association between the prevalence and incidence of chronic bronchitis and urban air pollution (Sunyer *et al.*, 2006). A mixture of city-level and individual-level exposure to particulates ($PM_{2.5}$) and NO_2 was used. The study showed that chronic bronchitis symptoms were positively associated with NO_2 concentrations among women. In addition to epidemiological studies, models were also used to assess the risks on respiratory health of urban air pollution.

In another study, cardiopulmonary mortality and morbidity from air particulates in Beijing were assessed using exposure–response functions (Zhang *et al.*, 2007). The study found that elevated levels of urban air pollution not only cause cardiopulmonary problems, but can also increase cancer risk. The latter is because some of the compounds, such as polycyclic aromatic hydrocarbons (PAHs) and benzene, released due to incomplete combustion of motor-vehicle fuels, are carcinogenic (Armstrong *et al.*, 2004).

A related study of lifetime leukaemia risk from benzene exposure in Naples, Italy, considered both outdoor and indoor sources of benzene exposure and found that sources other than vehicle combustion can also contribute significantly to poor health. For example, males had higher exposure to benzene due to smoking and less from indoor sources, which was more significant for females.

A study carried out in Bangkok, Thailand, considered potential cancer risks in school children due to PAHs by investigating the damage to the DNA (Ruchirawat *et al.*, 2007). The study suggested a higher cancer risk in children living in Bangkok compared with those living in less-PAH-polluted areas.

Questions

1. What are the main sources of air pollution in cities and how can urban air pollution be reduced? Discuss both technological and legislative/regulation options.
2. What are the main ill-health effects of air pollution? How do they differ for different air pollutants and which sections of society are most vulnerable?
3. What is the difference between time series and cohort epidemiological studies?
4. What are the measures of morbidity that have been used in air pollution studies?

16.3.3 Urban Soil Pollution

In the urban environment, there are several pathways by which humans can ingest soil contaminated with pollutants, particularly heavy metals. These include consumption of home-produced vegetables and inhalation of dust particles. There are several risk assessment models which can help to assess health risks of exposure to heavy metals in contaminated soils; two of these are described below.

The first model was developed to estimate the health risks of consuming home-grown vegetables in an urban area in the West Midlands, England (Hough *et al.*, 2004). The overall model combined several sub-models:

- a model of heavy metal (Cd, Cu, Ni and Zn) uptake by vegetables;
- a model of dust inhalation;
- a model of soil-ingestion; and
- a dose–response relationship for each metal defined in terms of a 'hazard quotient'.

The hazard quotient represents the ratio of average daily dose of the metal divided by the 'reference dose'. The reference dose is defined as the maximum tolerable value of that metal which does not cause ill-health effects.

The hazard quotients are summed over all metals to give an overall health impact estimate (Hough *et al.*, 2004). If the total hazard quotient is greater than unity, then the affected population group is deemed at risk. The study concluded that although vegetables grown in 92% of the urban area studied do not pose health risks to individuals, highly exposed individuals are, however, vulnerable.

The second risk assessment model used a data-based statistical approach to predict the monthly average fluctuations of lead (Pb) levels in the blood of children living in urban areas (Laidlaw *et al.*, 2005). The variables used in the analysis were monthly average values of soil moisture, PM_{10}, wind speed and temperature. The analysis assumed that the resuspension of Pb-contaminated soil in the air is controlled by several environmental factors, including soil moisture, and that this mechanism may explain the monthly variation in the blood Pb level in children due to inhalation and ingestion of lead particles.

Questions

1. What are the main exposure pathways of ingestion of soil?
2. How do you interpret a hazard quotient lower than unity?
3. What other pollutants, in addition to heavy metals, can be found in urban soils? What are the sources of these pollutants and what health effects do they cause?
4. What measures could be used for preventing or reducing soil contamination in urban areas?

16.3.4 Multiple Sources of Urban Pollution

It is often not possible to attribute ill-health effects in urban areas to a single source of urban pollution. For example, a cross-sectional study carried out in Mexico City identified several environmental risk factors for high blood Pb levels in children (Romieu *et al.*, 1995). These included Pb content in the material (glazed ceramics), used for preparing children's food (highest risk factor), Pb content in the dirt on children's hands and Pb in the air from motor vehicles.

Another cross-sectional study carried out in Mexico City also confirmed the Pb content in glazed-ceramics material used in food preparation as one of the determinants of blood Pb levels in teenagers (Farias *et al.*, 1998). In addition, this study identified that the Pb in bones (which is accumulated over a longer time than that in blood) also influences the levels of Pb in the blood. The bone Pb levels were in turn associated with high traffic density, mother's smoking history and time spent outdoors.

Questions

1. Why is it difficult to attribute ill-health effects to a single source or pollutant in an urban environment?
2. Describe some important routes of Pb exposure for children; consider which are the most important in a town in which you live/have lived.

16.4 Case Study: Health Impact Assessment of Schiphol Airport

The previous sections reviewed the HIA models and illustrated how they can be used to estimate health risks in the urban environment. In this section, we present a case study related to the ill-health effects of living near an airport, to illustrate further how some of the HIA tools can be used. The case study is related to the real case of Schiphol airport in Amsterdam. Other sustainability aspects of airports and aviation are discussed in Chapter 15.

16.4.1 Health Effects of Airports

Several ill-health effects have been associated with people living in the proximity of city airports. The evidence for this comes from various sources:

- the reporting of symptoms such as headaches, upset stomach, tiredness, insomnia, annoyance and stress (Black *et al.*, 2007; Franssen *et al.*, 2002, 2004);
- the excess use of prescribed medication for insomnia, stress, blood pressure and cardiovascular disease (Franssen *et al.*, 2002, 2004);
- direct measurements of blood pressure (Black *et al.*, 2007; Jarup *et al.*, 2005, 2008) and stress hormones (Jarup *et al.*, 2005, 2008); and
- epidemiological studies, such as one suggesting an excess risk of haematological malignancies (Visser *et al.*, 2005).

Some studies have been carried out to determine the health impacts of urban pollution generated by air traffic on populations living in the proximity of airports (Tunnicliffe *et al.*, 1999; Meister and Donatelle, 2000; Franssen *et al.*, 2002, 2004; Jarup *et al.*, 2005, 2008; Visser *et al.*, 2005; Black *et al.*, 2007; Lin *et al.*, 2008). These studies were conducted on airports in Europe (Jarup *et al.*, 2005, 2008), USA (Meister and Donatelle, 2000; Lin *et al.*, 2008) and Australia (Black *et al.*, 2007). Schiphol airport in Amsterdam, Netherlands, stands out in terms of the number of HIAs carried out (Passchier *et al.*, 2000; Franssen *et al.*, 2002, 2004; Visser *et al.*, 2005). Some of the findings of these studies are discussed below.

16.4.2 Health Impact Assessment of Schiphol Airport, Amsterdam

The impact assessment study of Schiphol airport considers the area of $55 \times 55\,\text{km}^2$ around the airport and the population of 2 million living within this area. Noise, odour, air pollution and radio-frequency radiation from the radar have been identified as the relevant exposures (Franssen *et al.*, 2002, 2004). Here, we consider noise exposure only.

A mathematical model was used to calculate the annual noise exposure and discrete exposures levels were then mapped to the population distribution in the study area. Two ill-health effects were considered: annoyance (psychological) and hypertension (clinical).

The Kosten (Ke) unit was used to quantify noise exposure. The Ke integrates maximum noise level (decibels) with the total number of flights weighted by the time of the flights, with evening flights having higher weighting than day flights (Franssen *et al.*, 2002, 2004). Exposure–response relationships from literature were used to associate noise exposure with the health outcomes. In the case of annoyance, exposure–response relationships were derived from published surveys on annoyance carried out on the adult population living in the vicinity of Schiphol airport. For hypertension, exposure–response relationships were based on published epidemiological data on the prevalence of hypertension in the vicinity of Schiphol airport.

Figure 16.3 shows the estimated health impact due to annoyance related to the exposure–response data. The top figure shows the percentage of people being severely annoyed rising with the noise index (in Ke). By applying this relationship to the

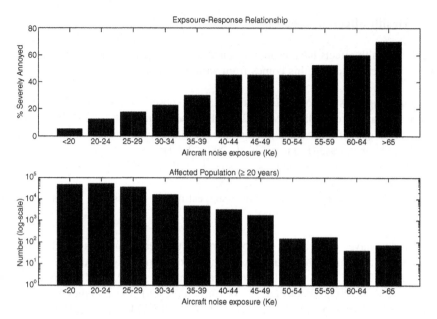

Figure 16.3 *Annoyance due to noise exposure. The top figure shows the exposure–response relationship associating noise and reporting of severe annoyance. The bottom figure is the number of adults who are estimated to be severely annoyed by noise (log-scale). (The figures are based on tabulated data from Franssen et al. (2002))*

distribution of the population, the expected number of people who are severely annoyed by the noise can be estimated; this is shown in the bottom figure. This calculation uses an absolute risk rather than a relative risk model, so that the outcome is annoyance to aircraft noise, not annoyance in general, and thus the background annoyance rate away from airports is zero.

Figure 16.4 shows the health impact in relation to hypertension. The upper figure gives the exposure–response relationship and the lower figure gives the estimated excess number of adults who become hypertensive due to the aircraft noise exposure. The relative risk is presented relative to the lowest category (<30 Ke). There may also be some variation of risk within people exposed to <30 Ke, but, because hypertension is not so common, the data have been aggregated into broader bands of exposure.

Using this HIA method, the total number of severely annoyed adults is estimated to be 160 000 and the total number of additional cases of hypertension attributed to the aircraft noise is 1500.

This illustrative example was limited to two ill-health effects associated with one exposure – the impact will be greater if more exposures and their associated health effects are considered.

Health is only one component for assessing the impact of an airport on the local community. There are trade-offs in terms of perceived benefits to the economy (local and wider) on the one hand and against the potential risks to health of the local population and the wider environment on the other hand. If a new city airport is to be built, or an existing airport is to be expanded, MCDA can be used to support decisions related to the construction or expansion of the airport.

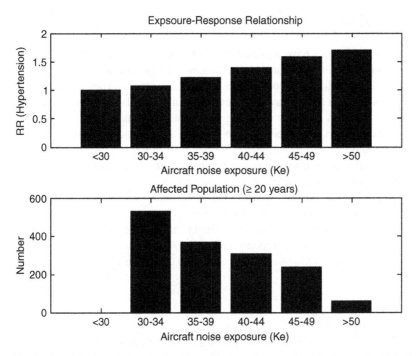

Figure 16.4 *Hypertension due to noise exposure. The top figure shows the relationship between noise exposure and the relative risk of hypertension. The bottom figure is the excess number of adults estimated to become hypertensive because of the airport noise. (The figures are based on tabulated data from Franssen et al. (2002))*

Questions

1. What are the main local pollution exposures generated by air traffic and airports?
2. How would you adapt the methodology outlined in Section 16.2.2 to carry out the risk assessment of Schiphol airport?
3. What are the main measures of health outcomes used in epidemiological studies investigating the health impacts of populations living in the proximity of airports?
4. In addition to health, what other sustainability issues are associated with airports and aviation? Discuss environmental, economic and social aspects. Consult Chapter 15 for clues.
5. Use the sustainability issues identified in the previous question to discuss how MCDA could be used in the case of a proposal for an airport expansion? Discuss what criteria would need to be considered and what would different stakeholders (developers, government and citizens) be interested in.
6. Airports provide mobility and serve a large number of people; however, they affect negatively a small number of people living nearby. Discuss the tensions and ethical dilemmas associated with this issue – should the well-being of the minority be sacrificed for the 'greater good'? Why?
7. Examine the case of Schiphol in more detail by reading Franssen *et al.* (2002), Franssen *et al.* (2004). What other health effects were considered and what was found? What, if anything, can be concluded in general about the impacts of city airports on human health?

16.5 Conclusions

Epidemiological studies have demonstrated a range of adverse health effects associated with urban environments. Polluted air, contaminated land, and air and road transport have all been implicated. However, epidemiological data are scant and health impacts often have to be estimated using the best available evidence and models. This chapter has described some of the methods used for assessing the health impacts of urban pollution. A case study of Schiphol airport has been used to illustrate for a real-case example the application of these methods.

The case study illustrates the types of health impact often found in cities. It also raises some difficult questions and ethical dilemmas: airports provide mobility and serve a large number of people, but they also affect negatively, often significantly, a small number of people living nearby. Similar tensions between the 'greater good' and 'pain of the minority' are found in many other areas where satisfying the needs of society at large may be in conflict with the needs of smaller sections of society. Like the other case studies in this book, this one, too, serves to illustrate the scope and the challenge of sustainable development.

Acknowledgements

Part of the work presented in this chapter has been funded by the UK Engineering and Physical Sciences Research Council (EPSRC) within the project 'Pollutants in the Urban Environment (PUrE)' (grant no. EP/C532 651/2). This funding is gratefully acknowledged.

References and Further Reading

Armstrong, B., Hutchinson, E., Unwin, J. and Fletcher, T. (2004) Lung cancer risk after exposure to polycyclic aromatic hydrocarbons: a review and meta-analysis. *Environmental Health Perspectives*, **112**, 970–978.

Belojevic, G., Jakovljevic, B., Stojanov, V. *et al.* (2008a) Urban-road traffic noise and blood pressure and heart rate in preschool children. *Environment International*, **34**, 226–231.

Belojevic, G.A., Jakovljevic, B.D., Stojanov, V.J. *et al.* (2008b) Nighttime road-traffic noise and arterial hypertension in an urban population. *Hypertension Research*, **31**, 775–781.

Belton, V. and Stewart, T. (2002) *Multiple Criteria Decision Analysis: An Integrated Approach*, Kluwer Academic Publishers, Dordrecht.

Black, D.A., Black, J.A., Issarayangyun, T. and Samuels, S.E. (2007) Aircraft noise exposure and resident's stress and hypertension: a public health perspective for airport environmental management. *Journal of Air Transport Management*, **13**, 264–276.

Farias, P., Hu, H., Rubenstein, E. *et al.* (1998) Determinants of bone and blood lead levels among teenagers living in urban areas with high lead exposure. *Environmental Health Perspectives*, **106**, 733–737.

Figueira, J., Greco, S. and Ehrqott, N. (2005) *Multiple Criteria Decision Analysis: State of the Art Surveys*, Springer, New York.

Franssen, E.A.M., Staatsen, B.A.M. and Lebret, E. (2002) Assessing health consequences in an environmental impact assessment. The case of Amsterdam Airport Schiphol. *Environmental Impact Assessment*, **22**, 633–653.

Franssen, E.A.M., van Wiechen, C.M.A.G., Nagelkerke, N.J.D. and Lebret, E. (2004) Aircraft noise around a large international airport and its impact on general health and medication use. *Occupational and Environmental Medicine*, **61**, 405–413.

Hough, R.L., Breward, N., Young, S.D. *et al.* (2004) Assessing potential risk of heavy metal exposure from consumption of home-produced vegetables by urban populations. *Environmental Health Perspectives*, **112**, 215–221.

Jarup, L., Dudley, M.-L., Babisch, W. *et al.* (2005) Hypertension and expsoure to noise near airports (HYENA): study design and noise exposure assessment. *Environmental Health Perspectives*, **113** 1473–1478.

Jarup, L., Babisch, W., Houthuijs, D. *et al.* (2008) Hypertension and exposure to noise near airports: the HYENA study. *Environmental Health Perspectives*, **116**, 329–333.

Kollamthodi, S. (2005) Technical and non-technical options to reduce emissions of air pollutants from road transport. Final report to the Department for Environment, Food and Rural Affairs, AEA Technology Environment, Didcot, Oxfordshire.

Laidlaw, M.A.S., Mielke, H.W., Filippelli, G.M. *et al.* (2005) Seasonality and children's blood lead levels: developing a predictive model using climatic variables and blood lead data from Indianapolis, Indiana, Syracuse, New York, New Orleans, Louisiana (USA). *Environmental Health Perspectives*, **113**, 793–800.

Lin, S., Munsie, J.P., Herdt-Losavio, M. *et al.* (2008) Residential proximity to large airports and potential health impacts in New York State. *International Archives of Occupational and Environmental Health*, **81**, 797–804.

Linares, C., Diaz, J., Tobias, A. *et al.* (2006) Impact of urban air pollutants and noise levels over daily hospital admissions. *International Archives of Occupational and Environmental Health*, **79**, 143–152.

Meister, E.A. and Donatelle, R.J. (2000) The impact of commercial-aircraft noise on human health: a neighborhood study in metropolitan Minnesota. *Environmental Health*, November, 63 (4), pp. 9–15.

Miedema, H.M.E. and Oudshoorn, G.M. (2001) Annoyance from transportation noise: relationships with exposure metrics DNL and DENL and their confidence intervals. *Environmental Health Perspectives*, **109**, 409–416.

Passchier, W., Knottnerus, A., Albering, H. and Walda, I. (2000) Public health impacts of large airports. *Reviews on Environmental Health*, **15**, 83–96.

Phillips, L. and Stock, A. (2003) Use of multi-criteria analysis in air quality policy. A report prepared for the Department for Environment, Food and Rural Affairs. Defra, London.

Prescott, G.J., Cohen, J.R., Elton, R.A. *et al.* (1998) Urban air pollution and cardiopulmonary ill health: a 14.5 time series study. *Occupational and Environmental Medicine*, **55**, 697–704.

Romieu, I., Carreon, T., Lopez, L. *et al.* (1995) Environmental urban lead exposure and blood lead levels in children of Mexico City. *Environmental Health Perspectives*, **103**, 1036–1040.

Ruchirawat, M., Settachan, D., Navasumrit, P. *et al.* (2007) Assessment of potential cancer risk in children exposed to air pollution in Bangkok, Thailand. *Toxicology Letters*, **168**, 200–209.

Saaty, T. (2000) *The Fundamentals of Decision Making and Priority Theory with the Analytic Hierarchy Process*, RWS, Pittsburgh.

Samet, J.M. and White, R.H. (2004) Urban air pollution, health, and equity. *Journal of Epidemiology and Community Health*, **58**, 3–5.

Seto, E.Y.W., Holt, A., Rivard, T. and Bhatia, R. (2007) Spatial distribution of traffic induced noise exposures in a US city: an analytic tool for assessing the health impacts of urban planning decisions. *International Journal of Health Geographics*, **6**, 24.

Stansfeld, S., Haines, M. and Brown, B. (2000) Noise and health in the urban environment. *Reviews on Environmental Health*, **15**, 43–82.

Steele, K., Carmel, Y., Cross, J. and Wilcox, C. (2009) Uses and misuses of multicriteria decision analysis (MCDA) in environmental decision making. *Risk Analysis*, **29**, 26–33.

Sunyer, J., Jarvis, D., Gotschi, T. *et al.* (2006) Chronic bronchitis and urban air pollution in an international study. *Occupational and Environmental Medicine*, **63**, 836–853.

Tunnicliffe, W.S., O'Hickey, S.P., Fletcher, T.J. *et al.* (1999) Pulmonary function and respiratory symptoms in a population of airport workers. *Occupational and Environmental Medicine*, **56**, 118–123.

Van der Zee, S., Hoek, G., Boezen, H.M. *et al.* (1999) Acute effects of urban air pollution on respiratory health of children with and without chronic respiratory symptoms. *Occupational and Environmental Medicine*, **56**, 802–812.

Visser, O., van Wijnen, J.H. and van Leeuwen, F.E. (2005) Incidence of cancer in the area around Amsterdam airport Schiphol in 1988–2003: a population-based ecological study. *BMC Public Health*, **5**, 127.

Zannin, P.H.T., Calixto, A., Diniz, F.B. and Ferreira, J.A.C. (2003) A survey of urban noise annoyance in a large Brazilian city: the importance of a subjective analysis in conjunction with an objective analysis. *Environmental Impact Assessment Review*, **23**, 245–255.

Zhang, M., Song, Y. and Cai, X. (2007) A health-based assessment of particulate air pollution in urban areas of Beijing in 2000–2004. *Science of the Total Environment*, **376**, 100–108.

17

Social and Ethical Dimensions of Sustainable Development: Mining in Kakadu National Park

Slobodan Perdan

This case study examines a controversy concerning the proposal to open a uranium mine in Kakadu National Park in Australia involving several stakeholders with diverse and conflicting views. Sustainability issues raised by the proposal are complex: there are varied cultural, ethical and social concerns, entangled with economic and environmental issues, as happens in so many development projects. The aim of the case study is to highlight a wide range and complexity of sustainability concerns that emerge from such and similar controversies, and to illustrate how different cultures, value systems and worldviews influence one's perception of appropriate development.

Throughout the case study the reader is invited to reflect on the issues raised, and to deploy critical and reflective thinking about different stakeholders, their interests and values. The case study is not designed to offer a decisive calculus to assists us in deciding whether the mining should proceed, but rather to pose some important questions about our fundamental values and priorities. In this respect, the case study is less concerned with scientific or engineering aspects of sustainability than with its social and ethical sides. There is at least one important benefit of viewing the challenge of sustainability through this perspective: it brings it into the domain of dialogue, discussion and participation. Rather than being a 'technical' or 'management' problem that technology, experts or the government can solve for us, when seen as an ethical or social issue, sustainability becomes the concern for all of us.

Sustainable Development in Practice: Case Studies for Engineers and Scientists, Second Edition
Edited by Adisa Azapagic and Slobodan Perdan
© 2011 John Wiley & Sons, Ltd.

17.1 Introduction

Mining, as an important economic activity, has a significant role to play in achieving sustainable development. In the context of the mining and mineral sector, the goal of sustainable development should be to maximize the contribution to the well-being of the current generation in a way that ensures an equitable distribution of its costs and benefits, without reducing the potential for future generations to meet their own needs (IIED and WBCSD, 2002). Yet, as our case study will demonstrate, on its road to sustainable development, the mining industry faces a range of challenges. The following section gives a brief overview of these challenges.

17.2 Mining and Sustainable Development

Mining, defined simply as 'the extraction of minerals from the Earth', is of fundamental importance in the economy of a number of countries, both developed and developing. It is estimated that 30 million people are involved in large-scale mining, representing 1% of the world's workforce, with a further 13 million involved in small-scale mining (IIED and WBCSD, 2002). It is likely, therefore, that, including dependants, 250–300 million people rely on mining. Many other people are also directly or indirectly employed in the rest of the minerals supply chain.

Mining, together with oil and gas extraction, creates most of the energy and resources needed to meet society's needs. Minerals are essential to everyday life, making up numerous products we all use. They are also vital raw materials in a large number of industries, including ceramics, construction, cosmetics, detergents, drugs, electronics, glass, metal, paint, paper and plastics (Azapagic, 2003). The mining industry generates wealth in direct and indirect ways, and creates many opportunities, including jobs and the development of local infrastructure and services.

Mining activities, however, also result in serious consequences for the environment and society – locally and globally. Mining has had adverse impacts on local communities and cultures, destroyed natural habitats, polluted the air, soil and water, and produced enormous amounts of waste that can have environmental impacts for decades after mine closure. Problems have resulted from land clearance, particularly in the case of strip mining, processing of ore and from the 'tailings' or waste products that many mines produce (WWF, 2002). Mining, therefore, carries a range of present and future environmental and social costs, both direct and indirect, which need to be balanced against the benefits it brings.

Until relatively recently, mining companies did not give great importance to these environmental and social impacts. In many ways the picture today is already more positive than it was a decade ago, and environmental and social concerns are now increasingly integrated in the planning and operation of mines. However, many operations, particularly in developing countries, still need to be upgraded in order to meet current expectations of sustainable practice. Concerns about the social and environmental effects of minerals development and disparities in the distribution of costs and benefits are still very real (IIED and WBCSD, 2002). In short, there remains much to be done in improving the sector's contribution to all aspects of sustainable development.

Following a widely accepted categorization of sustainability concerns, the key sustainability issues for the mining and minerals sector can be classified into three major categories: economic, environmental and social (Azapagic, 2003). These issues are discussed briefly below (for further details, see Chapter 4).

17.2.1 Economic Issues

Economic viability and competitiveness of the mining and minerals sector is important for sustainable development, as the industry brings various economic benefits to society, including provision of employment and generation of wealth. To provide economic benefits to society, a minerals company must, like any other business, perform well at the micro-economic level by minimizing costs and maximizing profits and shareholder returns. This may lead to macro-economic benefits through various investments and injection of 'hard' currency (particularly in poorer countries), contribution to gross domestic product (GDP) and tax, royalty and other payments to the public sector. However, a number of factors can influence the ultimate returns to society from minerals developments (see Chapter 4).

One of these factors is management and distribution of mineral wealth and revenues. The micro-economic issues have traditionally dominated business decision-making with a focus on short-term returns, which is in the mining and minerals industry often based on production volumes rather than on valued-added products and services. This, combined with price volatility of some minerals, has in some cases led to a profligate use of mineral resources and a faster depletion of minerals reserves, therefore causing greater environmental damage and returning little economic benefit to society.

One of the ways to partly offset this unsustainable resource depletion is to increase the added value of minerals by further processing the raw materials closer to the front end of the supply chain (Azapagic, 2003). This would not only maximize financial returns to the industry, but would also enable producer countries to derive more benefits from their resources. However, one of the great obstacles in adding more value to minerals at source is the tariffs imposed by industrial countries on imports of processed goods. For example, exporting copper wire or aluminium tubes into the EU, USA, Japan, Canada and Australia is, on average, 3.2% and 5.3% more expensive respectively than exporting unprocessed copper and aluminium ores is (IIED and WBCSD, 2002).

A further challenge is distribution of revenues from minerals among private sector, central government and local communities (Azapagic, 2003). This is a contentious issue, which has often created tension, political controversy and sometimes even armed conflicts. The common practice has been to split the earnings between the company and the central government, thus bringing little benefit to the local communities. Governments often use corporate taxation and royalty payments to gain an adequate share of revenues from a mineral development. Developing countries as a whole derive 80% of their mineral revenues from taxes on corporate profits (Cawood, 2001).

However, this approach can deprive these economies of valuable income in the case of non-profitable mineral developments. Royalty payments and other taxes (e.g. added value, stamp duty and fuel) are also used to further increase a government's gains from minerals resources. However, high taxes can also deter investors, thus depriving a country of perhaps a vitally important income. To encourage investments, some countries introduce subsidies; this approach has often been criticized for underpricing mineral resources and stimulating unsustainable levels of production, thus leading to a faster depletion of mineral reserves.

Although many countries are now trying to address this issue, few have been able to institute policy and regulatory frameworks which enable more equitable sharing of the wealth generated from minerals. Yet, equitable distribution of wealth is one of the prerequisites for more sustainable societies, making this not only an important economic issue, but also a social issue.

17.2.2 Environmental Issues

Given the scale of mining activities, it is not surprising that they have a wide range of environmental impacts at every stage of operation. Depletion of nonrenewable resources and environmental impacts as a result of air emissions, discharges of liquid effluents and generation of large volumes of solid waste are the most important environmental issues for the mining and minerals industry (Azapagic, 2003). Energy consumption and contribution to global warming are also considered to be significant. Some estimates show that the mining and minerals industry consumes 4–7% of the energy used globally (IIED and WBCSD, 2002).

Mining activities, such as extraction, have a visual impact on the landscape and lead to destruction or disturbance of natural habitats, sometimes resulting in a loss of biodiversity. Mining of some types of mineral (e.g. some metals) is also associated with an acid drainage problem, which can cause a long-term acidification of waterways and can affect biodiversity. Furthermore, some effluents generated by the metals mining industry can also contain large quantities of toxic substances, such as cyanides and heavy metals, which can pose significant human health and ecological risks. This was demonstrated by the two recent incidences of the tailings dams failures, at the Baia Mare goldmine in Romania and at the Aznalcollar zinc, lead and copper mine in Spain. In general, the environmental impacts of metals mining are likely to be greater than for other minerals, because of the toxic chemicals that are often used in minerals separation (Azapagic, 2003).

A number of environmental issues can also arise in the rest of the life cycle of mineral products, including the use and disposal stages. For instance, the use of some minerals can have toxic effects on humans and the environment. The most drastic examples here are asbestos, lead and uranium. Other issues include generation of solid waste and loss of valuable resources at the end of a product's useful life. Some minerals can be recovered and recycled to increase minerals eco-efficiency.

At the end of their useful life, the mine and production facilities can also pose several environmental problems, including water contamination due to acid mine drainage and other toxic leachates, irreversible loss of biodiversity, loss of land and visual impact. A number of abandoned mine sites and unrestored quarries are a testimony to the unsatisfactory environmental performance of the industry in the past (EC, 2000). This practice is set to change, as modern development projects increasingly include plans for decommissioning and rehabilitation. However, a few years ago, a PriceWaterCoopers survey revealed that, although 88% of surveyed companies have environmental post-closure mitigation plans, only 45% have detailed socio-economic plans that are regularly reviewed and have updated cost estimates (PWC, 2001).

17.2.3 Social Issues

In addition to more conventional socio-economic concerns related to employees (wages, benefits, occupational health and safety, education and skills development, equal opportunities, etc.), mining companies have to deal increasingly with a set of wider social issues. Many mining companies see the emergence of those wider social issues as by far the most difficult part of the sustainability agenda. They particularly point with some anxiety to the complexity of relations with communities, indigenous people, and with nongovernmental organizations (NGOs) at both the local and international levels.

Employment opportunities in the local area, capacity building, involvement in decision making and distribution of wealth and revenue between company and local community are some of the issues that can arise in relations of the mining companies with the local communities in which they operate.

Employment in the mining sector is generally falling in most parts of the world. However, employment opportunities provided by the mining industry can be substantial, and in some cases a mining company is the main employer in the area. This can bring wealth and prosperity to communities, but can also cause considerable disruption in the social life and structure. An increasing trend in the industry is contracting out or outsourcing, which means that local communities are less likely to benefit from new jobs and business opportunities (Azapagic, 2003). A typical example of this is the 'fly-in, fly-out' operations which bring the workforce from different parts of the world to exploration sites. Lack of a locally available skilled workforce is often quoted as a reason for outsourcing. Yet, capacity building through education, training and skills development of the local labour force could help overcome the skills shortage problems and, at the same time, contribute towards more sustainable communities, even after mine closure.

In addition to jobs and training, mining companies frequently build schools and hospitals or health facilities for workers and their families. Their investments and activities usually produce significant economic and social benefits. Yet, many mineral-rich areas have traditionally been inhabited or used by indigenous peoples. If mining takes place in such an area, contacts with the exogenous mining personnel and a foreign culture have sometimes unintentional consequences for the local community, such as the influx of diseases against which indigenous groups do not have natural immunity (sexually transmitted diseases being only a minor component of the problem), and the devaluing or even disappearance of indigenous traditions and cultures. It is of critical importance for the mining industry, therefore, that, in its relationship with indigenous people, it is guided by the principle of respect for their cultural values and ways of life.

The challenge for the mining companies at the community level, as elsewhere, is to maximize the benefits and to avoid or mitigate any negative impacts of mining. Determining the best way of doing this should be through participatory processes, involving all relevant actors, including members of the affected community, and in accord with the local context. This requires appropriate processes for participation and dialogue, involving all relevant stakeholders. Particular attention should be paid to including potentially disadvantaged groups, such as the already mentioned indigenous peoples, but also women and minorities.

Protection of human rights is another relevant social concern that should be addressed when considering sustainability of the mining and minerals sector. There have been accusations that some mining companies abuse human rights, in actions taken either independently or in collusion with governments (IIED and WBCSD, 2002). This includes paying unfairly low wages, denying the right to employees to organize in trade unions, the use of child labour, abuse of women, forced and compulsory labour, violation of indigenous rights and use of force to gain control over land. These are all serious sustainability issues which require a concerted action of the industry and national and international community.

This is also true for corruption, which is one of the main obstacles in equitable distribution of wealth from minerals (Azapagic, 2003). Some companies in the sector have been involved in bribing officials, for example to secure or speed up the permitting process. Although in many cases these payments are done in the interests of business efficiency, bribery and corruption are damaging for the economy and human development as they divert revenue away from the government priorities and bring little benefit to local communities. A corruption survey by Transparency International found out that, out of 32 leading countries with minerals deposits, 23 appear to have some kind of corruption problem (Hodess *et al.*, 2001). This, like the human rights abuse, is a large-scale problem which cannot be addressed by the mining companies alone, but in collaboration and partnership with all relevant stakeholders.

To sum up, the mining and minerals sector is facing a range of sustainability challenges, and if the mining industry is to contribute positively to sustainable development, it needs to demonstrate continuous improvement of its economic, environmental and social performance.

Most of the sustainability challenges mentioned above are reflected in the case study discussed below. The case study is concerned with the issue of mining in Kakadu National Park in Australia's Northern Territory. Kakadu is a place of immense ecological and cultural significance, which also happens to be very rich in minerals. The proposal by Energy Resources of Australia, Rio Tinto's listed uranium subsidiary, to explore the Jabiluka uranium deposit, considered to be one of the largest undeveloped uranium ore bodies in the world, has caused a great controversy, which is the main focus of the case study. Before we explore the Jabiluka mining proposal in more detail, to understand better why the project has caused such a controversy, let us first see why Kakadu is so ecologically important and such a culturally sensitive place.

17.3 Case Study: Mining in Kakadu National Park

17.3.1 The Background

Kakadu National Park is a unique archaeological, ethnological and ecological reserve, located in the tropics at the northern end of Australia's Northern Territory, 120 km east of Darwin, covering a total area of $19\,804\,km^2$. Kakadu has been inhabited continuously for more than 40 000 years. The cave paintings, rock carvings and archaeological sites present a record of the skills and the ways of life of the region's inhabitants, from the hunters and gatherers of prehistoric times to the Aboriginal people still living there. It is a unique example of a complex of ecosystems, including those of tidal flats, floodplains, lowlands and plateaus, providing habitat for a wide range of rare or endemic species of plants and animals.

Kakadu has a monsoonal climate, and during the wet season, rivers and creeks flood and spread out over the broad floodplains to form vast wetlands. These extensive wetlands, which include floodplains, billabongs, rivers, and coastal and estuarine areas, are recognized internationally as being significant for migratory birds, and are listed under the Convention on Wetlands of International Importance (the Ramsar Convention).

Kakadu is rich in mineral resources such as uranium which have been exploited. The photograph shows the existing Ranger uranium mine. Photograph by S. Perdan.

Kakadu protects the entire catchment of a large tropical river, the South Alligator, and examples of most of Australia's Top End habitats. From this range of habitats stems a remarkable abundance and variety of plants and animals. Many are rare or not found anywhere else, such as the black wallaroo, chestnut-quilled rock pigeon and the white-throated grass wren.

The Alligator Rivers region, which encompasses the park, is considered to be the most floristically diverse area of monsoonal northern Australia. More than 1600 plant species have been recorded from the park, reflecting the variety of major landform types and associated plant habitats in the region. Of particular importance is the diverse flora of the sandstone formations of the western Arnhem land escarpment, where many species are endemic. Based on recent surveys and records of the Northern Territory, some 58 plant species occurring in the park are considered to be of major conservation significance.

Kakadu is also one of the few places in Australia where there have been limited, if any, extinctions of plants or animals over the last 200 years. New species continue to be discovered in Kakadu, and the area remains a stronghold for some globally threatened species, such as ghost vampire bat, estuarine crocodile, loggerhead turtle and hooded parrot. Kakadu also contains an extremely rich bird fauna of 274 species.

This biological diversity makes Kakadu a place of immense ecological significance.

Kakadu is also extremely important to Aboriginal people, who regard it as a place of special spiritual significance. There are several places in Kakadu which are regarded as 'sacred and dangerous' by Aborigines (see Box 17.1).

Kakadu has some very significant Aboriginal archaeological sites, and one of the finest and most extensive collections of rock art in the world, a tangible reminder of

Kakadu's wetlands provide habitats for a wide range of rare or endemic species of plants and animals, and are recognised internationally as being significant for migratory birds. Photograph by S. Perdan.

Aboriginal people's long and continuing association with the area. The art sites, concentrated along the Arnhem Land escarpment and its outliers, display a range of art styles, including naturalistic paintings of animals. The most significant art sites are those associated with 'Bula', a Creation Time being who created a number of sacred and potent sites that, even today, are considered by Aborigines to be dangerous. The art also includes more recent 'contact' images of European items and people. The numerous Aboriginal art sites not only represent a unique artistic achievement, but also provide an outstanding record of human interaction with the environment over tens of thousands of years.

The art sites of Kakadu are recognized as a major international cultural resource and are part of the reason that Kakadu is inscribed on the United Nations List of World Heritage properties. Sites nominated for World Heritage listing are inscribed on the list only after carefully assessing whether they represent the best examples of the world's cultural and natural heritage.

Kakadu National Park was inscribed on the World Heritage List in three stages, in 1981, 1987 and 1992. It is one of the few sites included on the list for both outstanding cultural and natural universal values (EA, 2003):

- Natural:
  - as an outstanding example representing significant ongoing ecological and biological processes;

Box 17.1   Sacred and dangerous sites (AAPA, 2003)

'What is a Sacred Site?

Aboriginal people believe that the entire world, including the seas, continent, living things, and human beings, originates in the deeds of Ancestral Spirits. These Spirit Ancestors were active in the past, in the time often referred to as 'the Dreamtime', but are also present in the landscape today. They continue to influence all aspects of the natural and social worlds. The rules governing human life are grounded in the deeds and continuing presence of these Ancestors.

Features in the landscape mark episodes in the deeds associated with these Ancestors. Some Ancestors became transformed into physical features, such as mountains, rocks or celestial objects. Others became species of plants and animals. While the Ancestors travelled across the whole landscape, the strongest concentration of their powers can be found in places where they created a landform, left an object behind, or remain in the ground. These are sacred sites. Sometimes these are obvious features, but in other places they may not be spectacular or interesting to non-Aboriginal eyes.

Aboriginal people know that sacred sites are dangerous places. They are concerned to protect ignorant people, including non-Aboriginals, from hurtful contacts with such places. Some activities, such as lopping a sacred tree or digging into sacred ground, may disturb the Spirit Ancestors, with grave consequences both for the person causing the disturbance and for the Aboriginal people who are custodians for that place. In some cases, custodians believe that, if they allow a site to be damaged, other Aboriginal people will hold them responsible and will invoke powerful supernatural punishments.'

by Aboriginal Areas Protection Authority, Northern Territory Government

---

- as an example of superlative natural phenomena; and
- containing important and significant habitats for in situ conservation of biological diversity.
• Cultural:
  - representing a unique artistic achievement; and
  - being directly associated with living traditions of outstanding universal significance.

Kakadu's outstanding scenery, numerous recreational opportunities, significant archaeological sites and Aboriginal rock art attract over 200 000 visitors every year, making it a significant tourist attraction and an important contributor to the Australian tourist industry.

Kakadu is also rich in mineral resources, such as gold, platinum, palladium and uranium, which some think should be mined. Mining already goes on in the Kakadu area and there is pressure to allow more. The most recent mining proposal concerns the Jabiluka uranium deposit. An economics study commissioned by the company that owns the deposit, Energy Resource of Australia (ERA), indicates that Jabiluka will contribute A\$6.2 billion to Australia's GDP over 28 years. According to ERA, all Australians will benefit directly from the royalties and taxes flowing from Jabiluka. ERA also estimates that the Jabiluka mine will provide jobs and benefits for the local community, and will generate \$210 million in royalties for the Northern Territory Aboriginal community (ERA, 1998, 2002).

The local Aborigines, supported by various environmental and social justice groups, are strongly opposed to the mine. They are concerned over threats to the natural and cultural values of Kakadu National Park. Concerns over the effects of the mine on the cultural values include the concerns about over 200 sacred sites within the lease area, including burial sites, creation sites, living areas and art sites. Concerns over the potential impact of the mine on the natural values of the park include the possibility of escape of radioactive materials into Kakadu's ecosystems, the lack of information on whether the mine will affect any rare or endangered species and the necessity of building an access road for the mine.

Before we consider the latest mining proposal in more detail, let us pause here for a moment to reflect first on some general questions.

Questions

1. Should more mining be allowed in Kakadu? Could mining in such ecologically and culturally important place as Kakadu be regarded as an appropriate or sustainable economic activity? How do we compare the benefits of protecting Kakadu with the economic benefits of the mine which might improve the lives of a number of people, including the lives of the local Aboriginal people? How exactly might we reach answers to these questions?
2. If you are concerned about environmental and/or cultural and/or other impacts of the mine, and think that protecting Kakadu is more important than the potential economic benefits of the mine, explain the reasons behind your concerns? What influences your views?
3. If you think that the benefits of mining outweigh environmental or other concerns in this case, explain why you hold such position? What influences your views?

In answering the above questions, you might have felt that you needed more 'facts' to reach an appropriate decision. It is indeed essential to acquire knowledge and understanding about potential social and environmental impacts of the project as well as about economic and wider social benefits from the mining. This, however, may, in itself, be a difficult task. As we shall see later in the chapter, technical data and information concerning the Jabiluka mining proposal and its environmental and cultural impacts are voluminous and complex. Different stakeholders hold different and often conflicting views on the potential impacts of the mining proposal. This should not be surprising, since the knowledge surrounding many development projects is contested and open to diverse interpretations.

For example, the opponents of the mining proposal may claim that it is likely that the mine will pollute the waters of Kakadu, greatly disturb the ecosystems, endanger some species and generally have adverse impacts on the cultural and natural values of Kakadu. The opposition to mining will, therefore, rely on empirical claims: that is, claims about what will in fact happen. The proponents may dispute these claims, for instance, by pointing out that only a small piece of land will be affected. Some may think that, even if the opposition claims are true, it is better to go ahead with the development of the mine, because benefits from the project outweigh the costs. It is important, therefore, to bear in mind that even if the facts are settled, the issue will not necessarily be resolved. In this case we shall have to pay attention not only to factual evidence, but also to different value systems and cultural contexts which influence stakeholders' perceptions of the benefits and costs involved in this project. The controversy of mining in Kakadu is an example of situations in which 'facts are uncertain, values in dispute, stakes high and decisions urgent' (Funtowitcz and Ravetz, 1992).

The key question, therefore, will be: how do we reconcile different and conflicting value judgments and worldviews? We shall return to this question at the end of our case study. Let us now turn out attention to the Jabiluka mining proposal and examine the controversy in more detail.

17.3.2 The Jabiluka Uranium Deposit

The Jabiluka uranium deposit is situated inside the World Heritage listed Kakadu National Park, about 230 km east of Darwin and 20 km north of the existing Ranger uranium mine.

The Jabiluka uranium deposit is considered to be one of the largest undeveloped ore bodies of its type in the world, with 19.5×10^6 t of ore and the potential to yield more than 90 400 t of uranium oxide over 28 years. Uranium oxide production is expected to peak at 4600 t per annum.

As already mentioned, the mining company ERA, which is majority owned by London-based mining multinational Rio Tinto, holds the Jabiluka mineral lease. Although within the outer boundaries of Kakadu National Park, the lease is not legally part of the park and, therefore, not subject to the legal prohibition on mining within Kakadu.

The Jabiluka uranium deposit was discovered in 1971. The proposal to mine the deposit was first submitted in 1979 by the initial leaseholder Pan Continental Ltd, and the Australian Government approvals were granted by 1982. The original Jabiluka Mining Project, however, did not go ahead. Between 1983 and March 1996 a 'three mines policy' was in operation in Australia with respect to uranium mining. This policy limited the number of operational uranium mines in Australia to three (including the Ranger mine located within, but excised from, the Kakadu National Park) and, therefore, effectively excluded the possibility of uranium ore extraction in the Jabiluka mineral lease. With a March 1996 change in policy, this limitation on the construction of new uranium mines in Australia came to an end.

In 1991 ERA bought the lease from Pan Continental Ltd for A\$125 million. After the change in the mining policy in 1996, ERA lodged its new application to mine Jabiluka and the Government approvals were granted in 1997.

The Jabiluka uranium mine had originally been proposed as an open cut mine by Pan Continental Mining Ltd, which had potential for serious environmental management problems. ERA has proposed an underground mine with two options for progressing the Jabiluka mine. Under the Ranger Mill Alternative (RMA) (the company's preferable option), Jabiluka ore is to be transported to the existing Ranger mine (20 km south of Jabiluka) for milling and processing, and tailings are to be disposed of in surface pits, and covered on the mine's closure. This project option, however, requires the traditional owner consent under the 1992 Deed of Transfer of the Jabiluka lease. The second option, known as The Jabiluka Mill Alternative (JMA), involves constructing and operating a mill on site at Jabiluka and disposing of tailings via a combination of surface pits and underground storage.

According to ERA, it is estimated that the operation of the Jabiluka mine will increase Australia's national economic welfare by $3.8 billion over its 28-year life. This amount represents the economic benefit of the mine, but excludes any environmental costs associated with mine development or operation. The operation of the mine is also estimated to increase economic activity in Australia by a $6.2 billion increase in real GDP over the mine's 28-year life.

However, there is a very strong opposition to the Jabiluka mining proposal. The Mirrar Aboriginal people, Australian and international environmental NGOs, and individuals and groups speaking on behalf of the Aboriginal people have opposed the mining proposal because they believe that the Jabiluka mine threatens the people, culture and environment of Kakadu. They think that 'one of Australia's most beautiful places is in danger of being sacrificed to Australia's ugliest industry'. Mining at Jabiluka, according to the opponents, will have an irreversible impact on the integrity of the World Heritage cultural and natural values of Kakadu National Park and the Mirrar community. Under Australian law, the Mirrar people are recognized as the traditional owners of the land, and their senior member has responsibility for the care of the land and the people. The traditional lands of the Mirrar people cover the Ranger and Jabiluka mineral leases, the Jabiru township and other surrounding areas within the World Heritage property.

Environmental and other NGOs worked with the Mirrar people to blockade the mine site in 1998. This initiative gained significant media coverage and placed the issue of Jabiluka firmly on the public agenda.

In 1998 the UN World Heritage Committee sent a special mission to Kakadu to investigate claims by traditional owners and environmental groups that Kakadu was 'in danger' from the impact of the Jabiluka mine, and to assess 'ascertained and potential threats to the World Heritage values of Kakadu National Park posed by the Jabiluka mining proposal' (UNESCO, 1998).

The mission delivered its report in November 1998, finding that Jabiluka posed serious threats to the cultural and natural values of Kakadu and made 16 recommendations, including 'that the proposal to mine and mill uranium at Jabiluka should not proceed' (UNESCO, 1998). However, after a successful lobbying by the Australian Government (the opponents of the mine called it 'political bullying'), the World Heritage Committee ruled against placing Kakadu on its 'In danger' list, which means that the uranium mining option has remained open.

Construction work at the Jabiluka mine began in June 1998, and it had been expected that the first uranium oxide would be recovered in 2001. ERA completed the core sampling drilling work and construction of the tunnel into the Jabiluka ore body in September 1999. The Jabiluka mine was then placed on standby and environmental monitoring mode, meaning that no construction activity is occurring until the issue concerning where to mill the uranium and store the tailings could be resolved.

In October 1999 ERA formally sought approval for the Ranger milling alternative from the Northern Land Council. The Northern Land Council, operating on behalf of the Mirrar traditional owners and acting on their instruction, vetoed further discussions of the RMA for a period of 5 years (because of the Mirrar's fundamental opposition to mining). This means that if ERA are to pursue the development of Jabiluka then their only project option is the JMA, which would probably greatly increase the project's environmental and cultural impacts. Following the moratorium on consideration of the RMA for 5 years, ERA undertook a strategic review and evaluation of the Jabiluka mine, focusing on progressing the JMA. In order to progress the JMA in stages and have a mill operating at commercial levels, ERA needed to conduct further site assessment work to develop specifications and tender for supply of mill equipment. Construction of the mill would then progress in stages, in accord with the Australian Government's regulations. Building and commissioning the new mill could take up to 3–4 years and it involves planning and associated above-ground and below-ground works. ERA expected that full-scale commercial mining at Jabiluka would be reached by about 2009.

Throughout this period, protest actions against the project and the companies involved continued in both Australia and overseas, and Jabiluka remains one of Australia's most controversial industrial developments.

The two following sections provide some insight into the conflicting views of the key stakeholders. Section 17.3.3 ('The proponent's position') outlines ERA's views. Section 17.3.4 ('The opponents' view') summarizes the opposition's standpoint.

Questions

1. Draw up a comprehensive list of the interest groups (stakeholders) involved in the Jabiluka case.
2. Specify what are, in your opinion, the major concerns of each group.
3. Identify potential conflicts of interest and analyse what may cause them.

17.3.3 The Proponent's Position

17.3.3.1 The Company's Profile

ERA is a uranium enterprise selling uranium oxide from the Ranger mine in the Northern Territory and uranium concentrates sources outside Australia to nuclear energy utilities in Japan, South Korea, Europe and North America. The company is currently producing ore from its Ranger 3 open pit and is proceeding with the development of the new Jabiluka mine. The company is intent on maximizing profitable sales with a secure portfolio of medium- and long-term sales contracts and, as the third-largest uranium mining company in the world, has maintained a good reputation within the marketplace. ERA is a 68.4% owned subsidiary of Rio Tinto and has strong shareholder–customer links with electric utilities in Japan, France and Sweden. The following pages, based on the documents produced by ERA (1998, 2002), offer the company's perspective on the Jabiluka uranium mine proposal.

17.3.3.2 ERA's Proposal to Mine Uranium at Jabiluka

ERA claims that:

- the proposal offers a balanced approach to resource development;
- the Jabiluka uranium lease is outside the World Heritage listed Kakadu National Park;
- strict international safeguards have been put in place to prevent the use of the uranium from Jabiluka for military purposes;

- the use of existing infrastructure at Ranger allows a considerable reduction in the scale, complexity and environmental impact of the Jabiluka mine;
- the mine operation will be designed in such a way as to protect ecosystems in the area and will have minimal visual or physical impact on the surrounding environment;
- the World Heritage values of Kakadu National Park will not be adversely affected;
- Jabiluka will not be a health risk;
- it will provide additional benefits, such as jobs, training opportunities, new housing and so on, to the local Aboriginal community over and above the $210 million in royalties the Jabiluka mine is expected to generate for the Northern Territory Aboriginal community;
- the Jabiluka project will provide significant benefits for the local and regional population, as well as the nation; and
- the Jabiluka proposal provides significantly more benefits to the local community than the 'no project' option.

These key points are expanded below.

17.3.3.2.1 A Balanced Approach to Resource Development

The Jabiluka development has been planned to minimize impact on the environment while providing major economic benefits for traditional Aboriginal owners and all Australians. Jabiluka's Mineral Lease Number 1 was granted in August 1982 and covers an area of 7275 ha. The original proposal to mine the Jabiluka deposit has changed dramatically in response to concerns of local traditional owners and the environmental movement. ERA's preferred option involves 75.5 ha, less than 1% of the lease and less than 10% of the previously approved Pan Continental proposal.

17.3.3.2.2 Jabiluka is Outside Kakadu

The Ranger and Jabiluka uranium leases are outside the World Heritage listed Kakadu National Park. Kakadu was created progressively, after the leases were granted. The Jabiluka operation will be an underground mine. It will be built on the opposite side of the hill from tourist viewpoints and the Magela Wetlands and the intended mine site is tiny – smaller than the area covered by Parliament House in Canberra.

17.3.3.2.3 Strict International Safeguards

Uranium from Australia is sold only to make electricity. ERA will export uranium to electricity utilities in Europe, the United States and Asia. Strict international safeguards have been put in place to prevent the use of ERA's uranium for military purposes. The safeguards take the form of legally binding agreements between Australia and countries to which it exports the mineral. No uranium has ever been diverted from a genuine civil reactor to weapons.

17.3.3.2.4 Two Alternatives for Milling

The Ranger Mill Alternative

Under ERA's preferred milling option there will be minimal surface facilities because the ore will be milled at nearby Ranger. The use of existing infrastructure at Ranger allows a considerable reduction in the scale, complexity and environmental impact of the Jabiluka mine. This option is called the RMA. Under the RMA, Jabiluka will produce about 90 400 t of uranium oxide over 28 years. There is enough energy contained in that tonnage to generate electricity equal to 20 times Australia's current annual needs. Ore will be mined at a rate of 100 000 t per year, increasing to 900 000 t a year midway through the mine's life. A stockpile pad for the placement and handling of ore and waste rock, a retention pond to collect runoff water from the stockpiles and mine operations area, a small administration and amenities block and a mine portal entrance will be built at Jabiluka. A 22.5 km haul road will also be built to transport ore from Jabiluka to Ranger and back-haul low-grade uneconomic ore from the Ranger stockpiles to be used underground as cemented fill. Once at Ranger, the Jabiluka ore will be blended with material from Ranger 3 and processed through the Ranger mill, which is currently designed to produce over 5000 t of U_3O_8 a year, but with Jabiluka ore will be capable of producing over 6000 t of U_3O_8 a year. Approximately 17 ha of land will be required for the Jabiluka mine site, plus 54 ha for the haul road between Jabiluka and Ranger. This is 1% of the Jabiluka mineral lease. Tailings – the dewatered slurry left at the end of the milling process – will be permanently stored in the mined-out (closed for operation) Ranger Pit 1 and later in the mined-out Ranger 3 pit. The pits will be specially treated to ensure there is no leakage into the environment.

The Jabiluka Mill Alternative

A second proposal for Jabiluka – the JMA – has been put forward by ERA for consideration in recognition of opposition by some traditional Aboriginal owners to the company's preferred option of transporting Jabiluka ore to the existing Ranger operation for treatment and milling. The JMA is a small-scale, stand-alone mine and mill which will incorporate the latest technology in water and waste management. This alternative would require an area of 135 ha. As with the RMA, the JMA will not be visible from tourist viewpoints or the Magela Wetlands. If the JMA is adopted, then the ore production rate will increase and reduce the mine life to 26 years. Production would commence at a rate of 450 000 t of ore a year, corresponding to annual output of about 2500 t of uranium until 2008 and then to a maximum of 900 000 t of ore a year, corresponding to annual output of about 4000 t of uranium. As with the RMA, tailings will be buried deep underground in pits designed to prevent leakage into the environment. ERA is committed to a programme of 'zero release' of any mine water at the Jabiluka mine, mill and tailings facility.

The JMA would require the establishment of a new milling and processing plant instead of using the Ranger facilities. However, the improved stand-alone option offers a feasible alternative development strategy that delivers real benefits to the local and national economies.

ERA also has the option to provide a further environmental assessment to the Government on 'cemented past fill technology' which could be adopted for the disposal of mill tailings. Tailings would be dewatered and treated with cement to form a paste and used as backfill, first in the underground development and then in the below-ground storage area. Two disposal pits would be built to accommodate tailings not disposed of underground.

Negotiations with traditional owners will be undertaken to decide where the processing will take place. ERA would prefer to process the ore at Ranger.

17.3.3.2.5 Minimum Impact on the Environment

The JMA was the subject of detailed technical studies in the environmental impact assessment (EIA) and a Public Environment Report (PER). These are the key findings of the EAI and PER:

- Jabiluka will have no detrimental impact on Kakadu. The World Heritage values of Kakadu National Park will not be adversely affected. In addition, the mine's facilities and operations will not be visible from tourist routes.
- Jabiluka will not disturb areas of cultural or biological importance. No items of significant cultural value or areas of notable biological value will be disturbed.
- Jabiluka will not be a health risk. Predicted radiation levels from the mine will be well within international guidelines, with no health risk to the general public or employees.

The proposed Jabiluka mine will operate according to strict internationally recognized requirements that protect the environment. The mine operation will be designed in such a way as to protect ecosystems in the area and will have minimal visual or physical impact on the surrounding environment. Jabiluka will be subject to stringent environmental requirements and will be strictly monitored by two independent authorities, the Commonwealth Supervising Scientist Group and the Northern Territory Department of Mines.

ERA has a long-standing commitment to high environmental values with an 18-year record of responsibility, accountability and environmental sensitivity at the Ranger mine. Ranger is one of the most highly regulated mines in the world and is governed by more than 50 Commonwealth and Northern Territory pieces of legislation. The environmental practice, standards and compliance established by ERA coupled with government regulation of Ranger are world class. Similarly, Jabiluka will set a very high environmental benchmark. ERA has made guarantees about the operation of the Ranger mine to ensure that the fragile and pristine ecosystems within the park are not disturbed; these guarantees will continue. No mining, or activities associated with mining, will be carried out in the park. ERA has shown at Ranger that it is committed to excellent environmental management. Stringent safeguards will be put in place at Jabiluka to protect the water quality and constant monitoring and measuring will take place to detect any adverse effects downstream. In the unlikely event of environmental problems, immediate remedial action will be taken. ERA is committed to a 'zero-release' mine water management programme from the Jabiluka mine. This means only clean water will be released and all stormwater runoff within the 'total containment zone' will be contained in a 9 ha retention pond and treated. The pond will be lined with a synthetic membrane which will prevent seepage to groundwater. The pond is designed to withstand a 1 in 10 000 year rainfall event. When mining is completed at Jabiluka, the site will be rehabilitated. Over time, it will be difficult to detect evidence of mining activity.

17.3.3.2.6 Health and Safety

The Jabiluka mine will set a new standard in health and safety practices. Stringent international requirements will not just be met, but built upon. ERA will put in place safeguards and work practices which ensure radiation exposure for employees is less than 20 mSv (millisieverts) per annum. This is below the level set by the International Commission on Radiological Protection (ICRP), where there is minimal health risk to workers or the general public. The ICRP recommendation allows for an exposure of 100 mSv to be averaged over 5 years and that the exposure in any one year must not exceed 50 mSv. With multi-skilling, management and control of the ventilation system and a number of special design features and practices, the Jabiluka mine will be safe for workers and the general public. With the use of appropriate equipment, the annual exposure for the most exposed workers (that is, those working underground) will be approximately 12 mSv a year – well below the internationally recommended levels of 20 mSv a year. All other workers will have even lower exposure. ERA has an excellent record in mine radiation safety. In its 18 years of operation at Ranger, no worker has been exposed to excess radiation. Stringent international workplace health and safety standards will be implemented at Jabiluka to ensure this proud record is repeated at Jabiluka.

17.3.3.2.7 Aboriginal Owners

A key concern of ERA is the possible impact of mining on traditional Aboriginal owners in the region. To ensure these issues are fully addressed, a comprehensive social and cultural impact study of the region was undertaken by a group of Aboriginal people within the Kakadu region and a group of stakeholder representatives. ERA contributed half the funding for the Kakadu Region Social Impact Study (KRSIS). The study was an independent assessment of the impact of mining on Aboriginal groups and tourism in the region and provides a community action plan to deal with the regional impacts on the Aboriginal community. ERA has already implemented a number of initiatives recommended in the KRSIS report. ERA acknowledges that concern about the impact of mining on the social and cultural fabric of the Aboriginal community has been expressed by a senior traditional Aboriginal owner of the Jabiluka and Ranger sites. The company wants to address the concerns of Aboriginal owners and is working with the community to help it to achieve social and economic independence. Following consultations with the Northern Land Council, the company has agreed to provide additional benefits to the local Aboriginal community over and above the $210 million in royalties the Jabiluka mine is expected to generate for the Northern Territory Aboriginal community.

These benefits include:

- employment and training opportunities for local Aboriginal people with approximately 20% of people working on the Jabiluka project to be Aboriginal;
- provision of new housing for approximately 65 Aboriginal families;
- assistance for Aboriginal businesses;
- funding of a women's resource centre;
- funding for a bridging education unit for local Aboriginal children;
- traineeships for Aboriginal students.

The company, with the support of the Gunbang Action Group, which represents 18 community groups, has also stopped takeaway alcohol sales from the Jabiru Sports and Social Club. This reduced alcohol intake in Jabiru by 30% in the first 6 months. To support this initiative ERA also funded the appointment of an alcohol counsellor for the Jabiru region.

17.3.3.2.8 Employment, Training and Education

The Jabiluka project will provide significant benefits for the local and regional population, as well as the nation. Targeted employment, training, education and investment opportunities, as well as increased income for the local people, will assist in helping to eliminate some of the social disadvantages experienced by members of the Aboriginal community. The social impact assessment in the EIS found the impacts of the Jabiluka mine were likely to be relatively limited. Although the Aboriginal community in Jabiru currently experiences some social disadvantages, it is not anticipated that these conditions will be exacerbated by the small population change associated with the mine development. The assessment found that Jabiru provided a full range of community facilities and services that would normally be expected of a much larger town. Furthermore, the assessment found that the principal social impact of the development may occur in the medium to longer term, as the benefits from investment of the substantial compensation payments made to the Aboriginal community associations were realized. If the Jabiluka project did not go ahead, the life of the Ranger operation would be significantly shortened and would adversely impact the long-term viability of the township of Jabiru. Mining is the single largest employer in the area, accounting for 37% of the employed labour force. It is likely that most people employed by ERA would leave the area when mining ceased. This would place considerable strain on the viability of community services, such as health and education, and the local and regional economy. This reduced level of service and amenity would impact on the quality of life of those living in the region.

17.3.3.2.9 Economic Benefits

Mining continues to be one of Australia's most important export industries and, as such, is fundamental to national prosperity. Jabiluka and Ranger will generate more than $12 billion in revenue during the next 28 years. At least 87% of this revenue will be distributed within Australia. Access Economics estimates Jabiluka will increase economic activity in Australia by a $6.2 billion in real GDP. Throughout the staged development of Jabiluka, ERA will employ a total of 380 people, of which 110 will be at Jabiluka itself, 230 at Ranger, 20 in Darwin and 20 in Sydney. Under the JMA, a workforce of up to 170 people will be required at Jabiluka. All Australians will benefit directly from the royalties and taxes that will flow from Jabiluka. In fact, the money ERA will pay to the Commonwealth and Northern Territory Governments is estimated to be the equivalent of 1500 jobs per year. As well as jobs, the traditional Aboriginal owners will receive royalties and rent from ERA. Total royalties from the Jabiluka development are expected to be approximately $210 million plus $9 million in benefits.

17.3.3.2.10 'No Project' Option

While it could be argued that the 'no project' option could lead to a strengthening of traditional Aboriginal community values and culture, this option would also result in the cessation of royalty payments to Aboriginal communities. This would mean approximately $63 million in financial benefits from Jabiluka would not be paid to the local Aboriginal owners. This amount is on top of more than $37 million already paid to the Aboriginal community in royalties from Ranger. Royalties have provided wide-ranging community services, facilities and businesses, such as the Cooinda Lodge and Crocodile Hotel, the establishment of an endowment fund for children, and health, food and other support services for outstations. The social impact assessment concluded that the Jabiluka proposal provides significantly more benefits to the local community than the 'no project' option.

Questions

1. What are the main social and environmental concerns related to uranium mining in general? What are specific concerns raised by the Jabiluka mining proposal? How does the company propose to address those concerns? In your opinion, does the company cover all important sustainability aspects in its proposal?
2. What is your view on the company's proposal? To what extent does the Jabiluka mining project correspond to or differ from your vision of 'appropriate' development?
3. Is mining, and particularly uranium mining and milling, in such close proximity, and upstream from a World Heritage property, compatible with the protection of its natural and cultural values? Should World Heritage properties be recognized as 'no-go' areas?
4. Australia has no nuclear power plants, so that uranium from Jabiluka will be exported to nuclear utilities in Europe, the USA and Asia, and used to generate electricity. Australia has only one nuclear reactor (at Lucas Heights in southern Sydney), which is used mostly to generate isotopes for X-ray machinery, sterilization equipment and smoke alarms. In your opinion, should Australia be exporting uranium to other countries to use in their nuclear facilities while refusing to have nuclear plants itself?
5. What is your position on nuclear power? What are the advantages and disadvantages of nuclear power? Why is nuclear power so controversial? Is this controversy justified or simply the result of some people's ignorance of the technology involved? Should nuclear power be actively promoted as a clean source of energy?
6. The company promises to deliver various mine-derived benefits to the local community, including housing and education for the Aborigines. That could be seen as an example of corporate social responsibility in practice. Yet, the critics would say that the company should not assume the role and responsibilities of government. If you were an ERA manager, how would you answer the following question: 'How many communities in Sydney or Melbourne (or, for that matter, in any other city in the world) would accept a situation where their children only received education if they agreed to their local park being excavated for a uranium mine and the funding for the school being controlled by the mining companies?'
7. Take the position of an ERA's engineer/shareholder. What do you think their benefit/cost assessment criteria would be? Where do your criteria fit in relation to their position? What criteria do you think are relevant for assessing the costs and benefits associated with the Jabiluka mine? Compare your criteria with those of your colleagues.
8. Put yourself in the position of an ERA manager. What challenges would you face in trying to explain the project to local people?

17.3.4 The Opponents' View

There is a very strong opposition to the Jabiluka uranium mining proposal. Environmental and other NGOs and the Mirrar Aboriginal people, traditional owners of the Jabiluka Mineral Lease, have opposed the mining proposal because they believe that mining activity within the external boundaries of Kakadu National Park poses a direct threat to the natural and cultural values of the Kakadu World Heritage area, and has been responsible for significant adverse environmental and social impacts.

The opposition to mining argues that the original Jabiluka mining agreement was unfair and unjust. They claim that the agreement, signed in 1982 by the Northern Land Council, representing the Mirrar people, and Pan Continental Ltd, the first mining company to own the mining lease, emerged from the 'bad old days' of Aboriginal mining agreements in which alcohol, duress, complex legal concepts, the exploitation of language difficulties, unconscionable conduct and outright lies were used to gain the 'consent' of Aboriginal land owners.

The opposition to mining has also expressed many specific concerns raised by the proposal to mine uranium at Jabiluka. The Australian Conservation Foundation, one of the most active conservationist groups in the campaign to stop mining at Jabiluka, claims that there are very solid arguments as to why Jabiluka should not be mined, including (ACF, 2000):

- There have been serious procedural irregularities with the Government approval of JMA – including that this was done without an EIA despite a written assurance from the supervising scientist to the contrary.
- The project design that received approval was not that which was presented in the Jabiluka Mining Alternative Public Environment Report or received any public examination. Rather, it was developed during dialogue between the Government and the project proponent.
- A number of sacred sites will be disturbed by any exploration and mining in the Jabiluka area and damage would be done to the areas with World Heritage listed cultural values.
- The social and economic problems facing the Aboriginal community in the Kakadu region are complex and ongoing. Industry research prepared as part of the Kakadu Regional Social Impact Study has shown there has been no net economic benefit for Aboriginal people in the region from uranium mining operations.
- The Jabiluka mine would have a significant and long-term impact on the cultural and natural World Heritage values of Kakadu National Park. The Ranger/Jabiluka project areas would be a uranium development province within Kakadu for an additional quarter of a century.
- Mining operations at Jabiluka would result in the creation of an additional 20 million tonnes of radioactive tailings. Over time these will seep and erode into Kakadu and contaminate the natural resources of the region. These tailings retain almost all their radioactivity for hundreds of thousands of years.
- The nearby Ranger mine has been plagued with significant water management problems since the mine began and regularly releases contaminated water into Kakadu against the wishes of Aboriginal people. This happened again in early 2000 – mining operations at Jabiluka would add to this pressure.

- The Jabiluka ore-body is a health and safety hazard for workers because of its high radioactivity and the special problems of underground uranium mining. Proposals by ERA to address this are not international best practice and are insufficient to guarantee worker health and safety.

Other NGOs, such as Friends of the Earth, the Wilderness Society and so on, share these views. They all express serious concerns about potential damaging social and environmental impacts of the Jabiluka mine, including the concerns about potential leaks of radioactive materials into the thriving Kakadu ecosystem, radioactive waste and associated environmental and health hazards, and adverse social impacts on the local Aboriginal community. In their report to the World Heritage Committee of UNESCO, Australian environmental NGOs argued that mining operations at Jabiluka pose 'both ascertained and potential dangers' to the World Heritage values and properties of Kakadu National Park. These dangers include (ACF, 2000):

- disregard for traditional owners and their cultural values;
- inadequate, piecemeal and inconsistent approvals process for the mine;
- inadequate regulatory framework for mining in the region; and
- limited detail and public disclosure about the project – for instance, important details regarding tailings disposal remain unavailable to the public.

The Mirrar people, Aboriginal traditional owners of the area, are unequivocally opposed to the project. The most pressing concern of the Aboriginal traditional owners is the destruction of their living tradition which will result from continued mining on their land (GAC, 1999). The Mirrar believe that mining and its associated impacts (such as the establishment of the mining town of Jabiru) are destroying their culture and society, and that the development of another uranium mine will have a continuing 'genocidal impact on Aboriginal people in the region' (Mirrar, 2003). Specific concerns have been expressed about sacred sites. The Mirrar believe that the Jabiluka uranium mine will directly interfere with sacred sites, which 'will result in cataclysmic consequences for people and country'. An additional mine, the Mirrar argue, will push their culture 'past the point of cultural exhaustion to genocidal decay' (Mirrar, 2003).

In a joint letter of concern the Mirrar Gundjehmi, Mirrar Erre, Bunitj and Manilakarr clan leaders have stated:

> A new mine will make our future worthless and destroy more of our country. We oppose any further mining development in our country . . . We have no desire to see any more country ripped up and further negative intrusions on our lives . . . If the project is completed, the total loss of cultural value will be inevitable. The loss of cultural value encompasses both the destruction of cultural sites of significance by specific mining activity and a structural decline in the Mirrar living tradition resulting from imposed industrial development manifested as an attack on the rights of Mirrar.

Through the Mirrar and NGOs' concerns and action the Jabiluka mine is currently stalled.

Kakadu has some very significant Aboriginal archaeological sites, and one of the finest and most extensive collection of rock art in the world. Photograph by S. Perdan.

Questions

1. What are the opponents' main concerns about the proposed development? In your opinion, are their concerns justified? What evidence do they present to support their claims that the Jabiluka mine threatens 'the people, culture and environment of Kakadu'? You may wish to visit their respective websites to find more information on this.
2. If Jabiluka is not part of Kakadu National Park, how can the mine project affect the World Heritage Area?
3. Suggest an economically viable alternative to the mining in Kakadu. Is it more sustainable than the proposed development? If you think so, explain why?
4. Some Mirrar people are fundamentally fearful of the possible destructive impact of the Jabiluka uranium mine on the 'sacred and dangerous' sites. Should their beliefs be allowed to stand in the way of modern development that might improve the lives of many people?
5. What is, in your opinion, the role that NGOs play in this controversy? Has their contribution been helpful or has their involvement made the agreement less likely? Do NGOs have a legitimate role to play in projects like the mining at Jabiluka?
6. The NGOs involved in the Jabiluka controversy are actively campaigning to stop uranium mining and Australia's involvement in the nuclear industry. They reject nuclear power as unsafe and argue that there is still no long-term, totally satisfactory method of disposing of radioactive wastes. If you were an anti-nuclear campaigner, how would you dispute the following claims:
   - 'Nuclear power is the safest form of large-scale commercial power generation, much safer (in terms of human lives lost) than fossil fuel-burning power plants.'
   - 'Nuclear power is cleaner and less damaging to the environment than other sources of energy – it does not produce harmful, carbon-based greenhouse gases such as carbon dioxide, nor does it emit particulates, sulfur dioxide, and similar harmful substances into the environment.'

17.4 Role-Play Exercise

Share and compare your views on this proposed development at Jabiluka with those of your colleagues, classmates or friends. Carry out the following tasks:

1. Indicate in the matrix below which position you hold.

I believe that ...	There should be no mining at Jabiluka.	There should be no mining unless maintenance of critical ecological and social values can be guaranteed.	The mining should proceed with responsible management.	The mining should proceed.
Your position				

2. Take one of the following roles:
   a. an ERA engineer;
   b. an ERA shareholder;
   c. the Mirrar traditional owner;
   d. an environmental activist;
   e. an independent scientist/environmental consultant;
   f. an Australian Federal government official from the Department of Industry, Tourism and Resources;
   g. an official from the Northern Territory Government's Department on Infrastructure, Planning and Environment; and
   h. a UNESCO–World Heritage commissioner.
3. Get into a group with seven others, preferably with those of whom have supported a different position to yours, and discuss the case. Before the group discussion, identify what would influence your views in your new role and analyse your strong and weak points. Represent your position forcefully and with as much detail as you can summon. If it is not possible to reconcile your views with the views of those who oppose them, question their premises and assumptions. At the same time, try to understand the views of other parties involved. Make, as a group, a list of issues on which you agree and on which you do not. Suggest a way to overcome the identified differences and disagreements.
4. When you have finished the above group discussion, indicate in the matrix above your current position. Have you changed the viewpoint you had held before discussion? If so, explain how and why?
5. Based on all that has been presented in this chapter and the discussions you have had with your colleagues, write a short essay answering the following questions:
   a. What are, in your opinion, the main sustainability issues raised by the Jabiluka mine proposal?
   b. What are the contentious issues? How deep are the differences expressed?
   c. Is it possible to reach a win–win solution? If not, what are the trade-offs involved?
   d. If you agree that the main conflict is between the different values and worldviews, can you suggest a way of reconciling those conflicting views?
   e. What 'sustainability' lessons can we learn from the Jabiluka mining controversy?

17.5 Conclusions

We live in a highly differentiated, pluralistic society which involves different cultures with not only different but also conflicting values and interests. Indigenous peoples and their cultures are part of the fabric of modern society. As the Johannesburg Declaration on Sustainable Development has reaffirmed, they play 'the vital role in sustainable development'. We recognize that, for thousands of years, many indigenous groups worldwide have been living in harmony with their natural environment, and we have been starting to re-evaluate the significance of their cultures and traditions and incorporate their knowledge and expertise into our own. We increasingly support the rights of indigenous people to self-identification and their rights to preserve their collective identity and living culture.

Yet, what should we do in a situation where at stake is a huge economic benefit from a mine that happens to be on the land owned by an indigenous group and they happen to be opposed to the development? How are we to reconcile their rights to preserve their collective identity and living culture with legitimate economic interests of the mining industry? Moreover, should certain areas be beyond reach for any human activity that will disturb them, including mining, because they contain critical natural and cultural values? In which circumstances, if any, should cultural, environmental, or other factors override access to valuable minerals?

These are difficult questions. They are not just about the decision on whether or not to explore and mine minerals in a certain area. These questions go to the heart of sustainable development and concern our fundamental values and priorities. They remind us that on our path toward sustainable development we will have to make many complex decisions. In some cases we will have to decide whether it is acceptable to suffer minor environmental damage in exchange for major social and economic gain, or whether it is worth sacrificing economic and social benefits for a significant environmental goal. There may be a conflict between global, national and local priorities, or between long-term sustainability objectives and short-term imperatives. In many cases, a majority perhaps, reaching a consensus will not be possible and we will have to resort to compromises. Our decisions will have to involve trade-offs: between different stakeholders' interests, between different objectives and dimensions. And in some cases we will have to make decisions not to proceed with a certain project because it may go past some widely accepted limits, such as transgressing fundamental human rights or destroying biological diversity.

How we deal with these questions is critical for sustainable development. The aim of sustainable development is to improve the quality of life for all people in ways which simultaneously protect and enhance the environment. It is an ethical vision, confronting us with the question of our responsibilities towards nature, to the world's poor and to future generations. Realizing this ethical vision will be difficult without a set of values which promote social equity, respect for cultural and biological diversity, and a culture of cooperation and shared responsibility in achieving sustainability.

As we have pointed out at the beginning of this book in Chapter 1, one of the core principles of sustainable development is greater equity in access to opportunities and in the distribution of costs and benefits. The importance of equity considerations in assessing 'sustainability' of a mining project has been clearly demonstrated in our case study. Who will benefit from it and how the costs and benefits (not only economic, but also environmental and social) should be distributed are the questions that have polarized the parties involved.

The Jabiluka mining controversy has also raised the issue of biological and cultural diversity and its relation to sustainable development. It should be said that, in many ways, biological and cultural diversity are essential for achieving sustainable development. Various forms of cultures and institutions in human society – political, religious, social or economic – have been built upon services provided by natural resources arising from biological diversity. Innumerable cultural practices depend upon specific elements of biodiversity for their continued existence and expression. At the same time, significant groups of biological diversity are developed, maintained and managed by cultural groups. The biologically diverse landscapes created and maintained by Aboriginal Australians through their astute use of fire is but one well-documented example.

There is, therefore, a mutual dependency between biological diversity and human culture, and the Aboriginal culture in Kakadu is a good example of that dependency.

Over the course of their history, Aboriginal people have developed the lifestyle and culture which are intricately tied to nature. Their value and belief systems have evolved to enable them to respect and live in harmony with nature, conserving the diversity of life upon which they depend. The species-diverse environment in which Aboriginal people live has shaped their productive activities and spiritual values. This relationship is expressed in Aboriginal art, music, song, dance, ceremonial body painting, craft and story-telling.

The way of life of indigenous people depends on biological diversity, and the way of life of Aboriginal Australians is not an exception to this. Their cultural and religious beliefs and traditional spiritual values have often served to prevent overexploitation of resources and sustain the systems in which their communities live for their own benefit and that of future generations. The concept of the sustainable use of biological diversity, one of the objectives of sustainable development, is inherent in the value systems of indigenous and traditional societies.

Unfortunately, both biological and cultural diversity are now in imminent danger owing to present-day human activities. Not only biological species, but also many ethnic groups around the world are now faced with extinction. The causes and consequences of this loss lie in the increasingly unsustainable exploitation of the Earth's natural resources and the growing marginalization and dispossession of indigenous and minority groups. The causes of loss of biodiversity are also major causes of depletion of the foundations of peoples' lives and their distinct cultures.

This aspect of sustainability appears particularly important for the mining industry, since mining often takes place in biologically diverse areas inhabited or used by indigenous people. The activity of mining almost inevitably involves altering the landscape and disturbing the flora and fauna, and has significant impacts on the indigenous communities. Concerns about these environmental and social impacts feature prominently in the case of mining in Kakadu. We have seen that the major concern of the Mirrar people is the threat the mine poses to their culture and way of life. Their concerns have been expressed very strongly – they even talk about possible 'exhaustion' and 'decay' of their culture. Additionally, the environmental groups involved have been warning us about adverse impacts the mining will have on Kakadu's biodiversity and unique ecosystems.

These concerns over biological and cultural diversity present a huge challenge to the mining company involved. Here, as in many other mining projects, the challenge for the industry is to find a way of contributing positively to 'sustainability imperatives': the economic imperative to raise the standard of living and quality of life, the environmental imperative to protect the natural environment and respect biodiversity, and the social and ethical imperative to maintain harmonious relationships and respect cultural diversity and human rights. And, as our case study confirms, these are not easy tasks at all. Yet, as already mentioned, it is of critical importance for the mining industry that, in its relationship with indigenous people, and when operating in biologically important places such as Kakadu, it is guided by the principle of respect for the cultural and biological diversity.

Indeed, there are no simple solutions to the problems raised by the Jabiluka mining proposal. There is, however, at least one important lesson to be learned. A well-thought framework for consultation, benefit sharing and dispute resolution, and involvement of local communities and the key stakeholders in decision making at the earliest possible stages of a mining project appear to be critical to success. This early involvement of the people and communities most directly affected is also an appropriate way for the mining sector to deal with the complexity of social and cultural issues raised by their activities. Bringing the decision-making process as close as possible to the people and communities most affected and making decisions in cooperation with them secure the rights of people to be informed about issues and conditions that influence their lives and ensure recognition of diverse values. Public participation in decision-making processes is also consistent with equity, because it provides every individual an equal and fair chance to defend their personal interests and values, and to contribute to the definition of the collective goal of sustainable development (Perdan and Azapagic, 2000). In its deepest form, cooperation and public participation should involve local community in all steps of planning, implementation and evaluation of projects, in order to enlist people's support and commitment, and increase their awareness of shared responsibility in delivering sustainable development.

As we have seen, the Jabiluka mining proposal raises many important and fundamental questions. There is no decisive calculus available to assists us in answering these questions. There are many different sets of values in play, which makes finding the right decision more complicated. But, as Andrew Brennan put it 'life is complicated, and we will not make progress in tackling the grave difficulties we face unless we learn to avoid shallow thinking and simple solutions' (Brennan, 2002).

Finally, however difficult it is to decide whether or not to explore and mine uranium at Jabiluka, the ultimate decision must be based on an integrated assessment of economic, environmental, cultural and social impacts and, thus, be governed by the principles of sustainable development.

17.6 Post Scriptum

In February 2005, ERA, the Mirarr Gundjeihmi Aboriginal people and the Northern Land Council signed the *Jabiluka Long-Term Care and Maintenance Agreement*. While the Jabiluka mineral lease and the 1982 Jabiluka mining agreement remain in force, the *Jabiluka Long-Term Care and Maintenance Agreement* obliges ERA (and its successors) to secure Mirarr consent prior to any future mining development of uranium deposits at Jabiluka. The agreement also waives some of ERA's financial obligations flowing from construction of the mine's decline in 1998. The signing of the agreement followed nearly 3 years of negotiation over the future management of the lease.

The *Agreement* gives the traditional owners veto rights over future development of Jabiluka. However, in 2007, Rio Tinto suggested that the mine could reopen one day (PM, 2007).

At the time of writing, however, there have been no further developments regarding Jabiluka. In January 2010, ERA chief executive Rob Atkinson stated that there had been 'no change there at all' in relation to Jabiluka, and that ERA 'fully respect the agreement . . . and we fully abide by that' (The Sydney Morning Herald, 2010).

The Mirrar's opposition to developing Jabiluka remains unchanged.

References and Further Reading

AAPA (2003) Aboriginal sacred sites. Aboriginal Areas Protection Authority. http://www.nt.gov.au/aapa/text/sites1.htm.

ACF (Australian Conservation Foundation), Environment Centre of the NT, and Friends of the Earth Australia (2000) Kakadu: World Heritage under threat. Report to the World Heritage Committee of UNESCO by Australian environment NGOs, ACF, Victoria.

Azapagic, A. (2003) Developing a framework for sustainable development indicators for the mining and minerals industry. *Journal of Cleaner Production*, **12** (6), 639–662.

Brennan, A. (2002) Moral Pluralism and the Environment. In D. Schmidtz and E.Willott (eds.) *Environmental Ethics*, Oxford: Blackwell, 2001, pp. 146–160.

EA (2003) Kakadu – World Heritage site, Environment Australia. http://www.ea.gov.au/heritage/awh/worldheritage/sites/kakadu/index.html March, 2003.

EC (2000) Communication from the Commission on Promoting Sustainable Development in the EU Non-energy Extractive Industry. The European Commission, Brussels, 3.5.2000, COM(2000) 265 final.

ERA (1998) The Jabiluka report. Energy Resources of Australia, Sydney.

ERA (2002) Jabiluka overview, Energy Resources of Australia. http://www.energyres.com.au/jabiluka/overview.shtml January 2002.

Funtowitcz, S.O. and Ravetz, J.R. (1992) Environmental problems, post-normal science, and extended peer communities. Read to the Environment Department, The World Bank, Washington, DC, 26 October 1992.

GAC (1999) Mirrar fighting for country: information kit. Gundjehmi Aboriginal Corporation, 1999.

Hodess, R., Banfield, J.and Wolfe, T. (eds) (2001) Global corruption report 2001. Transparency International, Berlin.

IIED and WBCSD (2002) Breaking new ground: mining, minerals and sustainable development. Final report on the Mining, Minerals and Sustainable Development Project (MMSD). International Institute for Environment and Development and World Business Council for Sustainable Development. www.iied.org/mmsd (30 October 2002).

Mirrar (2003) The Mirrar oppose the Jabiluka uranium mine. http://www.mirrar.net/jabiluka.html March 2003.

Perdan, S. and Azapagic, A. (2000) Sustainable development and industry: ethical indicators. *Environmental Protection Bulletin*, Issue 066, May 2000, IChemE.

PM (2007) Rio's Jabiluka talk causes anger, A transcript from PM programme broadcast around Australia on Radio National and on ABC Local Radio. http://www.abc.net.au/pm/content/2007/s1931353.htm.

PWC (2001) Mining and sustainability: survey of the mining industry. PricewaterhouseCoopers/MMSD, London.

The Sydney Morning Herald (2010) Ranger finally powers ERA, The Sydney Morning Herald, 30 January 2010.

UNESCO (1998) Bureau of the World Heritage Committee. Report on the mission to Kakadu National Park Australia, 26 October to 1 November 1998.

WWF (2002) To dig or not to dig: criteria for determining the suitability or acceptability of mineral exploration, extraction and transport from ecological and social perspectives. WWF International and WWF-UK, Gland.

Index

9 780470 718728